THE
REALEAT
ENCYCLOPEDIA
OF VEGETARIAN
LIVING

PETER COX

BLOOMSBURY

Also published by Bloomsbury:
The New Why You Don't Need Meat, Peter Cox
Linda McCartney's Home Cooking, Linda McCartney and Peter Cox

Peter Cox publishes 'The Superliving! Letter' which regularly updates and advances many of the topics covered in this book. If you would like a free copy and subscription details, please send two first-class stamps to: 'The Superliving! Letter', PO Box 1612, London NW3 1TD. Peter would also like to hear from you with any comments about this book, or suggestions for future editions.

First published in 1994 by
Bloomsbury Publishing Ltd
2 Soho Square
London W1V 5DE

Copyright © by Peter Cox 1994

The moral right of the author has been asserted

A copy of the CIP entry for this book is available from the British Library

ISBN 0 7475 1806 8

10 9 8 7 6 5 4 3 2 1

Typeset by Hewer Text Composition Services, Edinburgh
Printed and bound in Great Britain by
Butler & Tanner Ltd, Frome and London
The paper used in this book is derived from sustainable sources and is acid free

CONTENTS

PART SIX: **THE WORLD'S BEST VEGETARIAN RECIPES**

INTRODUCTION

It is with very great pleasure that I introduce you to the Realeat Company, sponsors of the world's first *Encyclopedia of Vegetarian Living.*

There could be no finer sponsor. Realeat have done more than any other organization I can think of to help millions of people take their first practical steps towards meat-free living. Through their popular and ever-growing range of vegetarian and vegan products, Realeat have made it easier than ever before to lead a healthier and kinder lifestyle.

With great perception, British author George Orwell once wrote that 'changes of diet are more important than changes of dynasty or even of religion'. He could easily have been describing the remarkable vegetarian revolution which is taking place at the moment. It's a peaceful revolution, and one which is progressively changing the world for the better. The front line of this revolution is to be found in all the supermarkets and healthfood shops right across the nation, and it's there that you'll encounter Realeat products.

Realeat are the inventors of the VegeBurger.[1] This mighty little burger has totally revolutionized vegetarian food by making it firmly accessible to everyone. Gone is the rather 'freaky' image of the past – since the advent of the VegeBurger, vegetarian food has suddenly become a mass-market phenomenon. Quicker than meat, easier than meat, cheaper than meat, healthier than meat . . . Who could resist?

But that's not all. The Realeat Company also commissions an independent polling organization to produce the world's most detailed survey into the growth of vegetarianism. Many companies would keep this sort of market intelligence strictly secret, but Realeat have always made these findings freely available to all. Without the authoritative Realeat survey, we simply wouldn't know how many vegetarians there are, who they are, and what their reasons are for going meat-free. Believe me, many charities, campaigning organizations (and probably some competitors, too!) have been very grateful for this vital year-on-year information.

Today, Realeat remain at the forefront of the food revolution. For example, they are the only healthfood manufacturer to win BS5750 accreditation (an independently-controlled British Standards award denoting total quality and service). And, of course, they continue to pioneer exciting new products. The VegeBurger is the undisputed king of the market sector which Realeat created, and it's available in an ever-wider range of flavours and servings. The Vege-Banger duplicates this success in the sausage market. Most recently, we have VegeMince, a clever new product which offers all the taste and texture of conventional beef mince, but without the meat! With characteristic creativity, VegeMince is pre-cooked and can be used straight from the freezer.

In my talks and travels nationwide, I'm continually made aware of the fact that products such as these really have changed peoples' lives. For example, cooking for a 'mixed' vegetarian/meat-eating family often used to be a nightmare. But no longer, thanks to the Realeat product range, which is equally suitable for everyone.

I'm delighted by Realeat's success in the marketplace – it's good to see wholesome vegetarian food getting the recognition it deserves; and I'm very pleased to have their support for this encyclopedia. The research task was, as you can imagine, monumental and could not have been accomplished without them. I should add that all the opinions in this book are mine and mine alone; at no stage have Realeat sought to influence the editorial content.

Peter Cox

Footnotes

1 VegeBurger, VegeBanger and VegeMince are all trademarks owned by The Realeat Company Ltd

PART ONE:

IN THE BEGINNING

This is where you start . . .

Welcome to the very first *Encyclopedia of Vegetarian Living*! Far wider in scope than an ordinary cookbook, this unique encyclopedia has been designed to be your companion and guide as you explore the world's healthiest, kindest and most environmentally-sound lifestyle.

If you are interested in eating a vegetarian diet but don't know where to begin, then you'll find clear and simple advice here. If you are already vegetarian and are thinking about going vegan, then you'll find all the help you need in these pages. Even if you are a long-standing, experienced vegetarian or vegan, you'll still find this book to be a valuable one-stop source of hard-to-find information, facts, figures, answers and advice.

What The Words Mean

Here are the words used to describe the different sorts of diets generally associated with or included within the term 'vegetarian':

- **Vegetarian**: One who does not eat fish, flesh or fowl.
- **Lacto-vegetarian**: One who does not eat fish, flesh or fowl, but who consumes dairy produce. Usually only encountered in scientific or pedantic use.
- **Ovo-lacto-vegetarian**: One who does not eat fish, flesh or fowl, but who consumes dairy produce and eggs. Again, not a term used in everyday speech. For most practical purposes, 'vegetarian', lacto-vegetarian' and 'ovo-lacto-vegetarian' all mean the same thing.
- **Vegan**: One who doesn't consume or use any animal products. This means excluding fish, flesh and fowl, eggs and dairy, and the use of animal

products such as leather, silk and wool. Sometimes called 'strict vegetarian', which is unnecessarily severe – the words 'pure vegetarian' are better.

Inevitably, with the huge upsurge of interest in vegetarian living, various other terms have been used, sometimes inaccurately. For example, it is incorrect to call someone who refrains from red meat, but who still eats chicken and fish, a vegetarian. Other terms, such as 'semi-vegetarian' or 'demi-vegetarian' are occasionally encountered, although they have very little practical meaning. The essence of vegetarianism is the absolute refusal to eat another creature; and that is not something which is amenable to compromise. Calling oneself 'partially vegetarian' is as irrational as claiming to be 'partially pregnant'.

How do you decide whether to eat a vegetarian or vegan diet? Some factors to consider are:

VEGETARIAN	VEGAN
Easy to find a wide choice of food in supermarkets and restaurants.	Less choice, but availability improving. Wholefood and healthfood shops stock many vegan products.
Less need to check labels and recipes for 'forbidden ingredients'.	Hidden ingredients in many products are not vegan – need to read labels carefully.
Healthier than meat-eating, but the inclusion of dairy produce can make this a high-fat option.	Inevitably lower in fat, especially low in harmful saturated fat (which mainly comes from animal products).

VEGETARIAN – contd	VEGAN – contd
Little need to worry about nutritional inadequacies if eating a broad range of foods.	Need to develop awareness of best sources of certain nutrients.
Provides indirect financial support to the meat industry – dairy cows and battery chickens can lead miserable lives.	Provides no support to the meat industry, doesn't exploit animals at all.
Culturally easy for family/partners to adapt to.	A significantly different diet to the one most meat-eaters are used to.

Many people adopt a vegetarian diet, and then find that they gradually progress towards the vegan alternative. This is quite natural. You can make moves in this direction by substituting free-range eggs for battery produced ones, and vegetarian cheeses for ones made with animal rennet. The most important thing is to eat a healthy, satisfying diet which you feel comfortable with.

Why Vegetarian?

People go meat-free for many reasons. One important consideration is simply the high cost of meat (which would be much higher in many countries were it not for substantial government aid to this much-favoured industry). Meat is inevitably more costly than plant foods (unless the price is artificially distorted by subsidies). It has been calculated that one acre of land planted with soya beans can produce 584lbs of edible protein every year. If that same acre is instead devoted to beef production, the amount of edible protein produced shrinks to an insignificant 58lbs – just 10 per cent of the soya bean yield.[1] Also, the costs of raising and slaughtering beef cattle are far higher than the costs involved in soya bean production, so that cattle farming produces considerably less food, at a far higher cost. Meat is therefore a more expensive commodity for consumers to buy.

For many people, however, the lower weekly food bill is simply a pleasant side-effect of the meat-free way of living. In general, the major arguments in favour of vegetarianism fall into three broad headings:

RESPECT FOR OTHER CREATURES

Vegetarians and vegans are sometimes accused by their opponents of being 'animal lovers', 'preferring animals to people', 'being sentimental about animals' and so forth. This is an unpleasant distortion of the very sincere belief held by many people that all creatures are worthy of consideration. If you believe that humans, non-humans, and indeed the environment itself is worthy of respectful treatment, then you will logically stop eating animal flesh.

Treating others with respect involves showing consideration and compassion. It also involves a degree of empathy, which is where another criticism is sometimes levelled against vegetarians – the accusation of being 'sentimental' about animals. Precisely why this should be such a heinous crime is never made clear. As writer Brigid Brophy points out: 'Whenever people say "we mustn't be sentimental", you can take it they are about to do something cruel. And if they add "we must be realistic", they mean they are going to make money out of it. These slogans have a long history. After being used to justify slave traders, ruthless industrialists, and contractors who had found that the most economically "realistic" method of cleaning a chimney was to force a small child to climb it, they have now been passed on, like an heirloom, to the factory farmers. "We mustn't be sentimental" tries to persuade us that factory farming isn't, in fact, cruel. It implies that the whole problem had been invented by our sloppy imaginations.'[2]

When you stop eating meat, you are not only refusing to participate in a system which ruthlessly exploits other creatures. By buying meat replacement and substitute products, you are also actively encouraging the development of a remarkable new sector within the food industry – one which will eventually make animal exploitation and slaughter as obsolete as sending children up chimneys.

RESPECT FOR YOUR HEALTH

As you will see in Part Four, the meat-free way of living has many substantial health benefits, among them a reduced risk of cancers, coronary heart disease, and a host of other common scourges. Scientists and doctors increasingly accept that the meat-free diet contains a multitude of nutritional factors which can help to prevent many of today's most prevalent afflictions.

Additionally, there are solid grounds for suspecting that meat itself may be the cause of a significant number of diseases. The recent payment of $1.3 million by a hamburger company to settle a lawsuit brought by the parents of a two-year-old boy who died after eating one of their products again focused public attention on meat's close involvement with food poisoning.[3] The US Centers for Disease Control (CDC) estimate that 20,000 cases of similar infection with a particularly dangerous strain of E. coli occur each year, most of which are caused by undercooked hamburgers.[4]

In Britain, the meat industry claims that 'meat itself doesn't cause disease or ill-health – it is only unprofessional or unhygienic handling and preparation which can bring about a problem.'[5] This is a very questionable assertion. More than 1500 types of salmonella have now been identified, usually isolated from the intestinal tract of humans and animals. Salmonella organisms are responsible for a variety of human diseases, ranging from typhoid fever to food poisoning, but it is salmonella typhimurium which has accounted for most cases of food infection. It is difficult to estimate with certainty how many animal carcasses are contaminated with salmonella, although, in the case of chicken, estimates have ranged from 25 per cent to 80 per cent.[6] When you learn that cases of salmonella poisoning in the United Kingdom rose by 25 per cent in 1992 compared to 1991, it does suggest that we are living in the midst of an epidemic.[7] In America, there are approximately 2.5 million cases of salmonella poisoning a year, 500,000 hospitalizations, and 9,000 deaths.[8] There are now moves to allow poultry processors to irradiate chickens with gamma rays in an attempt to destroy disease-causing bacteria, but it remains to be seen whether consumers will accept meat processed in this drastic way.[9]

The use of pharmaceutical drugs on food animals is also open to considerable criticism. According to scientists from the CDC, the practice of putting antibiotics in animal feed to promote livestock growth may be creating antibiotic-resistant strains of salmonella bacteria.[10] A 1987 CDC investigation noted a marked increase in salmonella strains that are now resistant to various antibiotics, and pinpointed antibiotics in animal feed as one possible reason. In 1994, it is apparent that many common bacteria are indeed evolving into forms untreatable by all known medicines. In the post-antibiotic world, warns Alexander Tomasz of Rockefeller University, the simplest infections could quickly escalate into fatal illnesses.[11]

Beyond even these serious issues of food poisoning and antibiotic resistance is the alarming situation of entirely new diseases which are emerging as a result of current meat production practices. Bovine spongiform encephalopathy (or 'mad cow disease') was first identified in November 1986 by the British Central Veterinary Laboratory.[12] Despite persistent official assurances that the disease cannot be transmitted to humans, some scientists express very real fears. Scientists have shown that the 'infective agent' (neither a virus nor a bacterium) can indeed infect other primates.[13] The recent discovery of bovine leukaemia virus, which causes cancer of the lymph tissue in cows, and bovine immunodeficiency-like virus (BIV) which is genetically and biologically similar to HIV, can only make us more cautious about taking the absolute safety of animal-derived products for granted.[14] Many of us tend to forget that the process of human-animal disease transmission is constantly unfolding. Every year millions of people throughout the world become ill, and sometimes die, because they catch a disease from another species. The scientific term for a disease which originates in animals and can be transmitted to humans is a 'zoonosis'. Many of them – such as anthrax, rabies, leptospirosis, listeriosis, toxoplasmosis, brucellosis, tuberculosis and trichinosis – are serious, often fatal, diseases. Unfortunately, the extremely unnatural conditions often encountered in modern livestock production systems often seem to facilitate the development of new and alarming zoonoses.

For all these reasons, more and more people are deciding that the vegetarian option is a healthier and superior lifestyle.

RESPECT FOR OUR WORLD

Today's meat production industry is a vast consumer of the world's natural resources. For those of us who try to 'tread lightly on the earth', meat-eating is one of the most important, and easiest, activities to eliminate. Alan B. Durning of the Worldwatch Institute believes that the unpaid ecological price of meat-eating is so ruinous that we could end up eating ourselves 'out of planetary house and home.'[15] Here are some of the hidden costs of the Western highly-intensive system of meat production:

- livestock grazing is the world's number one cause of soil degradation[16]

- livestock are major depleters of precious water resources
- organic waste from livestock is a major source of pollution
- intensive animal agriculture devours fossil fuel reserves
- livestock production is a significant source of greenhouse gases – carbon dioxide, nitrous oxide, and methane
- livestock grazing is a major cause of plant species extinction[17]

Many of us have heard of 'hamburgerization', the process of turning a tropical forest into hamburgers, using cows as an intermediary. Alan Durning explains: 'Costa Rica, for example, was once almost completely cloaked in tropical forest, holding within its small confines perhaps 5 per cent of all plant and animal species on earth. By 1983, after two decades of explosive growth in the cattle industry, just 17 per cent of the original forest remained. Throughout the period, Costa Rica was exporting between one-third and two-thirds of its beef, mostly to the US, and it continues to export smaller quantities today. Producing a single Costa Rican hamburger involves the destruction of 55 square feet of rain forest – an area about the size of a small kitchen. Such a swath typically contains one tree, fifty saplings and seedlings of twenty to thirty species, thousands of insects comprising hundreds of species . . . Clearing that single patch of wet, lowland Costa Rican forest would also release as much as 165 pounds of the carbon it naturally stores into the atmosphere in the form of the greenhouse gas carbon dioxide . . . as much carbon as the typical American car releases in a twenty-day period.'[18]

All these severe problems would be considerably mitigated if we were all prepared to eat lower on the food chain.

Wheat-Eaters, Not Meat-Eaters

Some people still mistakenly believe that humans are born to be meat-eaters. An objective comparison between the characteristics of naturally vegetarian animals and naturally carnivorous ones, as outlined in the chart below, reveals the fallacy of that supposition:

WHY HUMANS ARE NATURAL VEGETARIANS

VEGETARIAN	FLESH-EATER	HUMAN
Hands/hoofs as appendages	Claws as appendages	Hands as appendages
Teeth flat	Teeth sharp	Teeth flat
Long intestines to digest fully nutrients in plant foods	Short intestines, to allow rapid excretion	Long intestines to digest fully nutrients in plant foods; flesh foods cause constipation
Sweats to cool body	Pants to cool body	Sweats to cool body
Sips water	Laps water	Sips water
Vitamin C obtained solely from diet	Vitamin C manufactured internally	Vitamin C obtained solely from diet
Exists largely on a fruit and nut diet	Consumes flesh exclusively	Diet depends on environment, highly adaptable
Grasping hands capable of using tools or weapons	No manual dexterity	Grasping hands capable of using tools or weapons
Inoffensive excrement	Putrid excrement	Offensiveness of excrement depends on diet
Snack feeder	Large meals infrequently taken	Combines habits of vegetarians and flesh-eaters
Predominantly sweet-toothed	Preference for salty/fatty food	Likes both sweet and salty/fatty food
Likes to savour food, experiment with variety, combine flavours	Bolts food down	Likes to savour food, experiment with variety, combine flavours
Large brains, able to rationalize	Small brains, less capable of adaptive behaviour	Large brains, able to rational-ize (at least in laboratory studies)

It is sometimes suggested that the existence of canine teeth in humans proves that we are adapted to eat meat. In fact, this is not the case. In primates, canines function as both defence weapons and visual threat devices. Most significantly, the primates with the largest canines – gorillas and gelada baboons – both have strictly vegetarian diets.

What part, then, did meat-eating play in our evolution? Scientific evidence suggests that our ancestors probably originated in the East African Rift Valley, which is a dry and desolate place today, but would have been very different 2–4 million years ago. At that time, the habitat was very lush. There were large, shallow freshwater lakes, with rich, open grassland on the flood plains and dense woodland beside the rivers. Fossil evidence shows that foodstuffs such as *Leguminosae* (peas and beans) and *Anacardiaceae* (cashew nuts) were readily available, as were *Palmae* (sago, dates, and coconuts). Evidence gained from the analysis of tooth markings indicates that our ancestors' diet was much the same as the Guinea Baboon's is today – hard seeds, stems, some roots, plant fibre – a typically tough diet requiring stripping, chopping and chewing actions.

Our ancestors also had very large molars, with small incisors, unsuited to meat consumption but ideal for consuming large quantities of vegetable matter. By 2.5 million years BC, however, evidence shows that the land began to dry out, forcing *Australopithecus* (the name of one of our early ancestors) to desert this idyllic 'Garden of Eden' and to try and survive on the savannahs, where they were poorly prepared for the evolutionary struggle that was to come.

Before this crucial point, there is little doubt that our ancestors had largely followed a vegetarian diet, typical of modern-day primates. Recent studies of minute scratches on the dental enamel of *Australopithecus* suggest that their diet consisted largely of hard, chewy seeds and berries, although a few eggs and small animals may have been consumed too. Most scientists consider it unlikely that *Australopithecus* was a systematic hunter, or 'killer ape', as this species has sometimes been depicted.[19] After this point, however, the amount of meat in our diet increased.

As our old habitat receded, we found ourselves competing with other creatures for a dwindling food supply. Scientists speculate that this is the point at which organized hunting first emerged. In his book *The Naked Ape*, the zoologist Desmond Morris made an interesting observation about this period when he wrote: 'We were driven to become flesh eaters only by environmental circumstances, and now that we have the environment under control, with elaborately cultivated crops at our disposal, we might be expected to return to our ancient primate feeding patterns.'[20]

So here we have a picture of a species which was originally vegetarian, which then due to force of circumstances adapted to become omnivorous. It is clear from recent analyses of human remains that even during this period of our development, plant food was still by far the most important source of food. The level of strontium present in bones is an accurate guide to the amount of plant food consumed, and scientists at the University of Pisa, Italy, who have analyzed the bones of early Europeans, have found that they were eating an 'almost exclusively vegetarian diet' right up to the time agriculture was developed.[21]

Further, the sort of hunting that our ancestors practised was never a good enough way of providing food for everyone. Careful studies of societies who lead similar lifestyles to those of our ancestors, such as the Bush People of the Kalahari, reveal that the probability of obtaining meat on any one hunting day was about one in four.[22] By contrast, the women always returned from their gathering expeditions with food – a 100 per cent success rate. From this it is obvious that in societies such as these, hunting is only possible 'on the back' of an effective, dependable and reliable source of plant food. Once the tribe is certain of its staple foods, then those men who want to (about a third of the Kalahari males never hunted) can go off and gamble on a kill – nothing is jeopardised if they come home empty-handed.

The truth is that most traditional accounts of human evolution greatly exaggerate the importance of hunting. Explains Adrienne Zihlman, professor of anthropology at the University of California at Los Angeles: 'The most popular reconstruction of early human social behaviour is summarized in the phrase 'man the hunter'. In this hypothesis, meat eating initiated man's separation from the apes. Males provided the meat, presumed to be the main item in early hominid diet, by inventing stone tools and weapons for hunting. Thus males played the major economic role, were protectors of females and young, and controlled the mating process. In this view of things, females fade into a strictly reproductive and passive role – a pattern of behaviour inconsistent with that of other primates or of modern gathering and hunting peoples. In fact, the obsession with hunting has long prevented anthropologists from taking a good look at the role of women in shaping the human adaptation.'[23]

There are two main reasons for this serious bias towards hunting in traditional anthropological accounts of human evolution – and their neglect of the far more significant benefits of gathering plant foods. First, the historical record itself colours our judgement. The garbage that is generated as a result of eating meat is more enduring than the remains of plant-based meals – bones last longer in the ground than husks or seeds. Consequently, anthropologists have traditionally focused their attention on the tools and artefacts of hunting, rather than the easily-overlooked remnants of horticulture. And this can produce some very misleading results indeed. For example, with only their rubbish-tips to go on, archaeologists studying the Bush people of the Kalahari would conclude that they were an almost exclusively meat-eating tribe – the very opposite of the truth. Adrienne Zihlman explains the other reason:

'Our notion of women's and men's role in prehistory,' she says, 'derives in part from currently perceived differences in status of the sexes. Popular pictures drawn of the past are too often little more than backward projections of cultural sex stereotypes onto humans who lived more than a million years ago. Themes of male aggression, dominance, and hunting have long pervaded reconstructions of early human social life; and this had led to a belief that present-day inequality of the sexes has its roots in an ancient life-style and in inherent biological differences between the sexes . . . Beginning with Darwin's discussion of human evolution, the theme of male dominance and female passivity and the use of tools as weapons has run through thinking about evolution. The emphasis on hunting, as with male dominance, is an outcome of male bias, however unconscious it may be, and this bias pervades even studies of primate behaviour. In Darwin's case, given the values of Western society, especially Victorian England, and the nature of available evidence, his emphasis on males is not surprising.'[24]

It is indeed rather shocking that the contribution of women, and horticulture, to human evolution has been so badly neglected for so long. Horticulture could arguably be said to be the single most important developmental step in our evolution. For horticulture represents a quantum leap in the amount of food that can be amassed for a given amount of effort. Instead of wandering and gathering, it was now possible to stay in a single spot and work continuously at harvesting grain.

Modern experiments have shown that it is possible to manually harvest about 5lbs of grain an hour. If four people worked continuously for the three weeks that wild wheat was ripe, they could produce about 1 ton of grain – enough to feed themselves for an entire year!

Vegetarianism Today – And Tomorrow

Today, the vegetarian revolution is growing apace. There are encouraging signs everywhere you look. The estimated number of vegetarians in the United States is 8 million to 9 million, according to the North American Vegetarian Society.[25] Airlines report that demand for vegetarian meals has doubled in the space of twelve months. Supermarket shelves are groaning under the weight of newly-launched vegetarian products. A lifestyle which was once perceived as being dangerously radical is now commonplace.

Without any doubt, the most exciting developments right now are occurring in the United Kingdom. Here – in the birthplace of modern Western vegetarianism – the meat-free revolution has really ignited. We know this because, uniquely among Western nations, we have been able to follow the results of an ongoing, professionally-conducted opinion poll – the Realeat Survey.

Originally commissioned in 1984, the Realeat Survey has always been conducted by Gallup, one of the world's leading polling organizations. The sample size is very large – over 4000 people are interviewed at more than 200 sampling points, which is considerably more than most political opinion polls. We can, therefore, assume that the results have a high degree of accuracy. Here are the most recent findings about Britain:

- A record 4.3 per cent of the adult population (2.5 million adults) are vegetarian
- For the last three years, 2000 people have gone vegetarian every week
- Over 6 million people (11 per cent of adults) are either vegetarian, vegan or don't eat red meat. This is the population group which is leading the vanguard of change.
- Four out of every ten adults (40 per cent) are cutting back on their meat consumption. These people are 'next year's vegetarians'.

- Over 13 per cent of young women aged sixteen to twenty-four are now entirely vegetarian.
- Realeat predict that current rates of growth suggest there will be 5 million vegetarians by the turn of the century, and 50 per cent of the population will be actively eating less meat.

Hard facts such as these give us well-grounded hope for the future. The irresistible logic of a kinder, saner way of living has already touched the lives of millions of people; in the next century, it will inspire many millions more.

Today, we are at a crossroads in the development of our species. We must choose either to return to our ancestral plant-based feeding habits, or be content to blaze a precarious path into the unknown. Plant-eaters, or flesh eaters? It is our decision. I have faith that we will choose wisely.

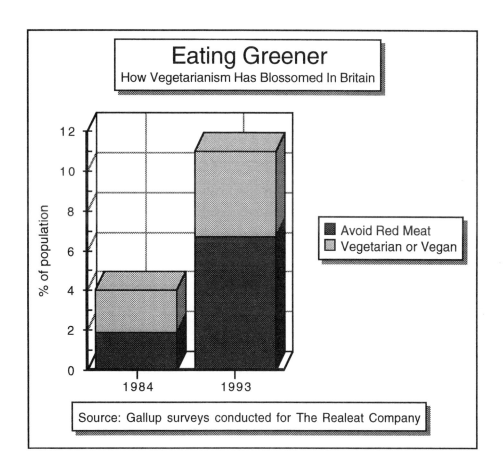

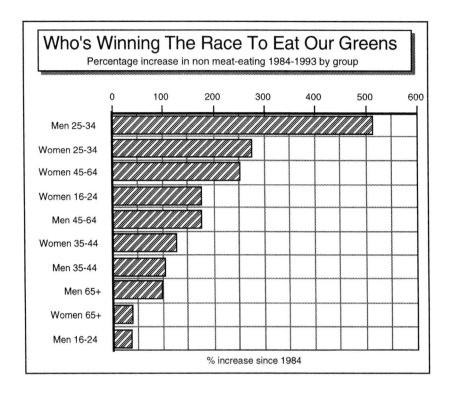

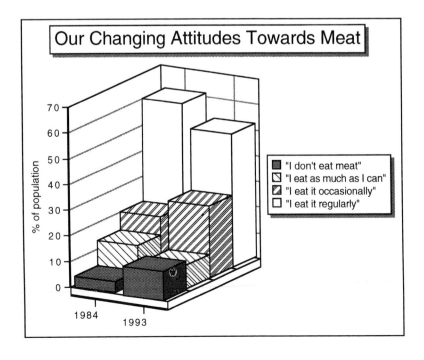

Footnotes

1 Calculated from United States Department of Agriculture data

2 B. Brophy, *Unlived Life – a manifesto against factory farming*, quoted in J. Wynne-Tyson (ed); *The Extended Circle* (Centaur Press, 1985)

3 Reuters, 18 February 1994

4 Associated Press, 5 May 1993

5 *Meat Messenger*, issue no12 (Meat and Livestock Commission, 1992)

6 'Give salmonella the elbow', *New Scientist*, 17 Sep 1987; J. Erlichman, *Gluttons for Punishment*, (Penguin Books, 1986)

7 *The Independent*, 31 July 1992

8 'The Top 10 Most Censored Stories of 1989', Project Censored, Sonoma State University

9 Associated Press, 18 September 1992

10 UPI, 18 September 1987

11 Associated Press, 19 February 1994

12 'Agriculture Committee Fifth Report 89–90 : Bovine Spongiform Encephalopathy (BSE) Report and Proceedings of the Committee', HCP 449, 1989–1990

13 P. Cox, *The New Why You Don't Need Meat* (Bloomsbury Publishing Ltd, 1992)

14 M. A. Gonda, M. J. Carter, T. A. Kost, J. W. Bess, L. O. Arthur, M. J. Van der Maaten, 'Characterization and molecular cloning of a bovine lentivirus related to human immunodeficiency virus', *Nature*, Nov 26–Dec 2 1987, 330 (6146), pp388–91

15 *World Watch* magazine, July 1992, Worldwatch Institute, Washington DC

16 L. R. Oldeman, V. W. P. van Engelen, J. H. M. Pulles, 'The extent of human-induced soil degradation', in Annex 5 of *World map of the status of human-induced soil degradation: an explanatory note*, International Soil Reference and Information Centre, Netherlands 1990

17 'The Price is Wrong' Wuerthner G. *Sierra* September/October 1990, pp40–41

18 *World Watch, op. cit.*

19 *Academic American Encyclopedia*, 1992

20 D. Morris, *The Naked Ape* (Jonathan Cape, 19??)

21 G. Fornaciari and F. Mallegin, 'Palaeonutritional studies on skeletal remains of ancient populations from the Mediterranean area: an attempt to interpretation', *Anthropol Anz*, Dec 1987, 45 (4) pp361–70

22 Truswell and Hanson, 'Medical Research amongst the !Kung', in Lee, DeVore (eds), *Kalahari hunter-gatherers*, (Harvard University Press, 1976)

23 A. Zihlmanin in F. Dahlberg (ed), *Woman the Gatherer* (Yale University Press, 1981)

24 *ibid.*

25 *Christian Science Monitor*, 18 April 1990

PART TWO:

EVERYTHING YOU WANTED TO KNOW, BUT DIDN'T KNOW WHERE TO ASK

*Questions, questions, questions –
When you're making the transition to meat-
free feeding, everything can suddenly seem
pretty perplexing.
Well, here are the answers.*

Your First Steps – Help!

Eating a vegetarian or vegan diet is not like taking holy orders, running for sainthood or canvassing for the presidency. In fact, perfectly ordinary people do it all the time. The very phrase 'becoming a vegetarian' can be off-putting, because it carries overtones of withdrawing from the world, and even of moral smugness. So let's remind ourselves that the only common ground that all vegetarians and vegans have is the fact that we don't do something – in this case, eat animal flesh. If that's all you want it to be, fine. It's your decision.

Labels carry baggage with them. I know people who lead vegan lifestyles, but who refuse to identify themselves as 'vegans' – and I can sympathize with them. When someone meets me for the first time, I want him or her to relate to me as a person, not as a dietary habit.

So do whatever you feel comfortable with. There's one thing, however, that you must never do. And that's apologize. Saying, 'I'm sorry, I don't eat meat' is demeaning to you, to other vegetarians and vegans, and to a healthy and deeply principled way of living. Subconsciously, it reinforces the prejudice which a few still have towards vegetarianism. It implies that vegetarianism is so freaky that its 'followers' have to apologize for it.

Words carry multitudes of meanings. When you say, 'Don't cook any meat for me,' you're often putting yourself into a minority. But turn it around, and say, 'If you're going to eat animal flesh today, count me out,' then you're making people think about what they're really putting into their mouths. And they often squirm.

It's all a matter of perception. Here's something else that's a question of perception – the question that frequently baffles many would-be vegetarians and vegans: Just *how* do you do it? When you live in a society which – for the time being – views the eating of dead animals as the norm, how do you make the break?

This can puzzle many people. If you're used to thinking of a meal as 'meat and two veg', and you take away the meat . . . what are you left with? Just how long can you live on boiled potato and cabbage?

There's one group of people who this question doesn't puzzle, however. And that's existing vegetarians and vegans. Now I have to tell you that – useful as I hope this book is – the very best source of help and advice about the flesh-free way of living is other vegetarians and vegans. They can, and will, help you – in the same way as you will help others, I hope, in the months and years ahead. However, I've noticed one strange circumstance in which existing vegetarians and vegans don't seem able to offer much in the way of assistance – and that's in the transition to vegetarianism. Here's why. Meat-eaters find it difficult to imagine what vegetarians live on; but vegetarians find it equally difficult to imagine why that should be so. For many vegetarians and vegans, their lifestyles are so easy, and so natural, that they simply can't conceive of it ever appearing to be the least bit difficult or intimidating. I've frequently seen vegetarians look genuinely perplexed when asked, by an enquiring meat-eater, 'What do you eat?'

That's a very tough question for any vegetarian to answer. To understand why it should be so, try thinking about it like this. Meat-eaters mainly ingest just two types of animals – pigs and cows. But as you'll see in Part Five, there are well over 100 different types of commonly-available vegetarian foods (not counting dairy produce) for us to choose from. Where do you begin?

So be patient with your vegetarian friends and acquaintances if you ask them, 'What's the best way to start?' and they respond by giving you an amazed look. Not long ago, that question probably bothered them, too. But now, they genuinely can't see what the problem is. Pretty soon, you won't either.

MAKING THE BREAK

So what happens? Do you come home at six o'clock one Friday evening and have a nut cutlet instead of a lamb cutlet? Do you have to sign a pledge that meat will never pass your lips again? Or do you just do it in private, with consenting adults? Here are some ideas for making the break that I know have worked very well for other people. But do remember that fundamentally it's *your* decision – you're trying to find what genuinely suits you. So you should take everything that follows as suggestions, not as firm rules.

Cut back . . .

This method is a gradual transition from meat-eating to vegetarianism. Aim to reduce your meat intake by about 50 per cent per week. For example, if you used to eat meat at two meals a day, cut this back during the first week to just one meal a day. Then, for the second week, cut it back again to one meal every other day. The third week you probably won't eat more than a couple of meat meals in total. And the fourth week you'll be free. This gradual process of cutting back gives you the chance to spread the transition over several weeks, and so allows you to experiment with lots of new meat-free recipes. It also creates some thinking space in your life – something which is in very short supply for most of us these days. When you're eating meat, just think about what you're *really* eating – where it came from, what it really tastes like.

Other cultures are fundamentally different to us in the way they encourage an awareness of – and respect for – food. In many Western countries, fast food is king. We don't judge food by its qualities and subtleties – for us, the fastest food is the best. We barely have time to bite the food as we shovel it down, before we bulldoze the next mouthful in.

Once you start to become aware of what sort of food you're really putting inside your body, you may be rather shocked. For example, try chewing your food rather longer, and leave it in your mouth a few more seconds to experience the full range of tastes it offers. You'll find that a mouthful of dead flesh is really rather repugnant to hold there for more than a second or so. And you'll find that much of the processed food now sold to us tastes truly awful after the first 'hit' – chemicals in the food give you an initial sensation of flavour, which produces maximum salivation, thus deceiving your senses into thinking that the food is appetizing, which is then followed by a bitter, synthetic disintegration of unwholesome tastes. When you allow your mind and body to guide you in your food choices, then you will, quite naturally, stop eating meat.

Cut out . . .

Here's another technique which many have used as a successful transition to vegetarianism. It creates a clearly-defined moment in your life when you take charge of your food intake; it represents a kind of personal watershed.

What you do is to eat a completely raw diet for seven to ten days. Nothing – absolutely nothing – that has been cooked, processed or preserved is allowed down! Meat, of course, is automatically excluded. Similarly, bread, biscuits, jams, butter, tea, coffee, alcohol, and tinned food are all absolutely out. However, the diet *must* contain lots of fresh fruit and vegetables – there is no limit to the quantity, eat as much as you can take. Aim to buy only organic vegetables. Don't overlook nuts and seeds, and try making salad dressings using only cold-pressed oils and lemon juice.

You'll find it very difficult to overeat on raw food. Although you'll be taking in lots of vitamins from all this fresh food, it might be a good idea to supplement your diet with a good multivitamin and mineral pill as well. During this period all sorts of things may start to happen. You may feel wonderfully elated or (very rarely) rather depressed. Your body may start to feel lighter and younger. On the other hand, you may very well have some kind of 'deferred reaction' – you may get spots and pimples, and a bad headache is quite common as your body detoxifies. After seven to ten days, you can start to add some cooked food. In this short but intense period, your tastes will have changed for good. You will have developed an appreciation for fresh food, and a lasting desire to eat something fresh at least once a day. And then you won't look back! You will have made the break, given your body a thorough detoxification, and started to set the pattern for a better, healthier life.

. . . And replace!

Without doubt, this is the easiest method of all. A few years ago, it wasn't possible to find meat replacement or meat substitute products anywhere. Then a host of products such as Vegeburger, Vegemince, Sosmix, Protoveg and the Vegebanger came along, and times changed for good. Today, the easiest way of going meat-free is simply to replace meat with any one of these convenience products (they're nutritionally superior to animal flesh, too). You can find them in all health food stores (as dry mixes and also fresh in the frozen foods section) and increasingly, supermar-kets sell them too. Products such as these are real life-savers in many circumstances. Many of them were featured in *Linda McCartney's Home Cooking* (of which I was co-author), and the response from readers was overwhelming – it was clear that for many people, the availability of meat replacement products like these had quite literally changed their lives. If there's just one vegetarian in the family (a younger son or daughter for example) then this may be the way to go. It seems what frequently happens is that the rest of the family come to the conclusion that the vegetarian option is actually much better than meat (and cheaper), and very often they'll go vegetarian too.

A few brief words of advice: if you or your family like a 'meaty' taste and texture, remember that TVP (textured vegetable protein) can be bought in all health food shops. Remember also that, contrary to most people's expectations, ordinary gravy mixture is often totally vegan (check the label). Please don't just replace meat with mountains of hard-type cheese – it's far too high in fat. Also, consider expanding your 'culinary repertoire'. Many of the world's finest cuisines don't use meat or dairy products; it's only in the West that our diet has become so unhealthily meat-dominated. You'll find some stimulating ideas in Part Five and Part Six. Now – start enjoying it! As the instruction booklets which accompany all those dazzling Japanese high-tech gadgets always begin by saying: 'Congratulations! You've made the right decision!'

Surviving And Thriving With Your Family – The Secrets Of Peaceful Coexistence

It's not difficult to stop eating meat, people do it all the time! But sometimes, the hardest part is coping with the unpredictable – and occasionally hostile – reactions of friends or family. In my own case, it was quite easy. In common with many other children, I refused point blank to swallow dead animals from the age of two. After all, animals were my friends and, as George Bernard Shaw put it, 'I don't eat my friends!'. I even persuaded my parents to go vegetarian a few years later. This, by the way, isn't unusual: I've met many children who've done the same thing.

Sadly, some people seem to have more opposition than I had. The lone vegetarian in a large family can be teased to the point of persecution; and when one partner in a relationship decides to stop eating meat, but the other one insists on continuing, then the strain can sometimes be considerable. Although there is no simple answer to cover every possible situation, the combined experiences of many vegetarians and vegans do suggest that there are techniques and approaches you can use which usually work successfully. Here, in their own words, a variety of vegetarians describe how they've coped, and what's worked for them:

THE HARD WAY

David Hobbs[1], a senior sociology major in New York, has been vegetarian for two years, and he's the first to admit they've been two difficult years. 'I've been subject to plenty of criticism,' he says. 'Being the only one in my family, it took them a long time to accept my decision, and I had to really stand by my position before they gave up trying to make me eat meat. My father still continues to tell me there's no room in this world for my ideas about animal rights . . . my maternal grandmother says I should be more flexible in my diet since when I go out to eat with friends they might want to eat at a restaurant that only serves meat. But why should I be expected to eat something that makes me nauseous and is bad for me? This is terribly unfair to my sense of ethics.

'The event that originally compelled me to abandon eating dead animals was in a biology lab, when I had to dissect the brain of a pig foetus! This sounds insane and it is – even the lab instructor told us he'd rather use computer models if the school had the funds. Anyway, after this depraved lab activity, I went to the delicatessen for lunch where I bought my usual turkey sandwich on a hard roll. The colour and texture of the meat reminded me exactly of the pig's brain and I vowed to myself I'd never eat another animal for the rest of my life. I was literally about to vomit while eating it!

'The only time I've eaten meat since then was on one Father's Day when my maternal grandparents insisted on going to a restaurant where the only entrées were fish. When I looked at the menu before we were seated and realized this, my father sarcastically asked me if I intended to order ten portions of the carrot soufflé (a side dish). I ultimately reluctantly ordered a piece of dead salmon but I hated every bit of it. My grandmother was satisfied that I was flexible enough to compromise my ideals. My whole family, including my younger sister who claims to love animals, was paranoid that I would humiliate them and "make a scene" as my mother would put it. I truly resented them for making me do something that contradicted my entire set of values. They all think I am too opinionated and, as my mother would say, if I don't watch what I say, "Someone might take out a knife!"

'Eventually, my parents caught on and reluctantly gave in to my refusal to eat dead beings. I've also discovered a local group of vegetarians where I can meet like-minded people and hopefully develop close friendships.

'It took my family a long time to accept my "radical" decision to go veggie, but eventually my mother started buying me prepared dinners. I wish I could figure out a way to convince them to kick the meat habit for their own benefit, without being told not to give them a "lecture", as my mother and sister would say. I want to enjoy family get-togethers without being seen as a "kook". As far as other people who want to become vegetarians, I advise them to stand up for what they believe in no matter what may stand in the way. People who want to stop eating animals should not be afraid to openly defy the *status quo*. What makes any country great is the ability and desire of its people to stand up for what they believe in. It is better not to conform to accepted standards if you see an injustice being committed as a consequence of that norm.'

ENLIGHTENMENT BY DEGREES

Happily, the transition to a flesh-free way of living doesn't always have to be as painful or as fraught with conflict. Jo Ann Davis, a library assistant in Pennsylvania, was much luckier with her family and, in the process, converted most of them to vegetarianism. 'My transition to vegetarianism was quite easily accomplished,' she says, 'because of the ethical position my parents always have taken regarding animal life and kindness. Eighteen years ago, I decided to become a vegetarian 'temporarily' because of the deer hunting season in Pennsylvania. Being opposed to hunting, I found it difficult to refute the hunters' statements about my consumption of meat. So that year, I became a vegetarian for a few weeks, just so I could say that I didn't eat any meat. My parents supported me because they too believed as I did. At the end of hunting season, I had found it was so easy being a vegetarian, that I decided to stay meatless for a while longer. I prepared my own meals, separate from my parents, so there was no conflict in that respect. After about a year, my mother saw that I didn't wither up and die, so she decided to try vegetarianism herself. Her hardest struggle was in social situations – she felt that it wasn't polite to refuse the meat passed to her when visiting friends, so she still sometimes ate meat. Since my parents are both excellent cooks, my father would make his own meat, my mother would usually make the rest of the meal.

'Several years later, my brother and sister-in-law, also for ethical and moral reasons, became vegetarians. Whenever my father eats at their house, he eats vegetarian along with the rest of us – and has no problem with it. Although he sometimes mulls over the idea of joining our side, he can't quite give up meat. After seventy-four years of eating it, it is a hard habit to break. I occasionally try to coax him to turn veggie, but he can't make the commitment. That's okay, though, because we all are happy with our chosen diets and don't feel the need to nag him. At least there are four out of five of us that animals aren't dying for.

'I think the main opposition most parents have to vegetarianism is their fear of the "unknown" – they have been raised in a system that taught them that "meat is might", and without meat, a person will wither away to nothing. A visit to the local library should offer sources of support, too. I work in an academic library, and we have a number of books on meatless diets, ethics of vegetarianism and recipes for veggies. I suppose the main thing is enlightenment. The more that the family/parents are educated, the better the chance of their acceptance of the dietary change. I'm an avid canoeist, and when people ask if I'm weak because of being a veggie, I just point to my solo canoe and tell them the tales of my wilderness adventures!'

Jane Evans, currently a university student, is another who sees her chosen lifestyle gradually having its effect on those around her. 'I was fifteen when I decided to become a vegetarian,' she says. 'My motivation to become a vegetarian was pretty simple. I wasn't able to rationalize the reason that human beings think they are given the power to end another living creature's life. I believe that every living creature is given one thing – life – and no one is allowed to take that from them. That's where my family and I differ the

most; they can understand the health aspect of vegetarianism, but they have always had the mentality that animals were put on this earth for our use. Even if they were, I still can't rationalize how they deserve to be tortured and made miserable during their keep before slaughtering!

'My parents and family were very much against this way of life. My family believed that meat was an essential part of everyone's diet. So I made an agreement with my mother: I told her I would do it for a summer and if I showed any signs of being unhealthy I would stop. So I did my research and was on a mission to prove to everyone that my choice was a good one. It was, and since then I have remained a vegan: I also don't use any animal products, or wear leather. The criticism from my family was pretty minimal once they understood that this was a major decision on my part. It is something that I truly believe in and they have grown to respect it. As for peers and new acquaintances, I still get the meat waved in my face, the comments asking if I want a big fat juicy burger and so on. I have been able to conclude that these rude comments are not directed to me out of dislike, but rather, they are ways in which people are unconsciously defending their meat-eating habits. Some individuals are put into an uncomfortable position around me and are trying to deal with their own insecurities about their own ways of life.

'Today, my immediate family has taken my new lifestyle to "heart" and they rarely consume red meat. It's a step for them. I am living proof that a teenager can grow and develop without consuming meat!'

For Sarah LaPorte, a computer programmer in Cupertino, California, the process was also one of gradual change. 'I became vegetarian in college,' she says, 'so when I went home for Thanksgiving vacation, I was the only vegetarian. Initially I was not successful in coping with it. My mother was concerned about my nutrition, and had made a tuna fish casserole, with the tuna shredded into microscopic pieces. I didn't have the heart to turn it down, and I regretfully ate it.

'I must say that she was correct in assuming that I hadn't learned enough about nutrition. However, I was correct in my gut feeling that my diet was already terrible, even though I was eating meat. You know the come-back you get when you tell a family member you're a new vegetarian – "But how can you get a balanced diet?" As if meat is the answer!

'The truth is that my mother didn't know too much about nutrition either! The next time I went home, in

February, I had learned a bit more. They were dubious, but could not get me to eat meat, so we had a truce.

'Now I am married. I have learned a lot more in the last sixteen years. Through his own reading, and my influence, my husband has become convinced to eat vegetarian at home, and to raise the children vegetarian.'

PERSISTENCE PAYS!

Student Steve Keen was seventeen years old when he decided to become a vegetarian. 'At first,' he says, 'my mother kept saying that "that's nice". But when she started realizing that I wasn't going to eat any kind of animal flesh, she got upset. She thought that I couldn't grow up healthy without eating meat. She would say things like, "You're still going to eat turkey and fish, right?" When I convinced her that I could get all the protein and vitamins even without meat, she tried a different approach. She started to tell me that I couldn't be a vegetarian because it was too much trouble for her. So I said that I would take care of all my cooking. Well, I started cooking for myself and was pleased with what I was coming up with. She would occasionally try some of the things I made, such as Tofu Loaf and Tofu Chilli, and she began to realize that it is possible to be healthy and happy while being a vegetarian. After the first three months, she stopped pestering me about eating meat and finally accepted it. Now she fully understands and accepts my lifestyle and is much less ignorant. I am still the only vegetarian in my family, but the rest of them are a bit more aware now of the great joys of being a vegetarian.'

A CHANGE OF HEART

An experience common to many vegetarians is a 'paradigm shift' of awareness after regular meat-eating has ceased. For a time, new vegetarians are often content to tolerate the habits of their meat-eating friends or family – even, sometimes to prepare meat for them. Then, things change. This was the experience of Ann Mason, another student. When she first went vegetarian, it didn't bother her to see others eating meat. 'In fact,' she says, 'I even prepared meat at a café I worked in. Things have changed a lot over the last year. I just cannot bear watching people consume a dead animal. It sometimes brings tears to my eyes. I've had problems with my mom over this, because she thinks that I've become too radical. She wants me to

come to family gatherings, but I refuse if I know there is going to be a carcass present. I spent Thanksgiving with vegan friends rather than going home to my family. I think my mom understands that the way I feel is not going to change, so she avoids eating meat when I am at home. She's close to being vegetarian herself, but does not seem to want to completely disclaim her "God-given right" to eat meat. Problems only arise when other people are involved in the situation – my mom will do without for me, but my other relatives won't. I think the best way to get loved ones to do without meat when you are with them is to let them know exactly how it makes you feel – the pain, disgust, whatever. If someone really loves you, they will not do something that brings you pain.'

STEP BY STEP

Jane Green, an administrative assistant, went vegetarian together with her husband in gradual stages, as part of a conscious programme to improve the quality of their diets. 'When I married my husband,' she says, 'he was very health conscious, but I was a meat and junk food consumer. As we began our life together, we both agreed to eliminate red meat and endeavour to have a healthy food programme. I, being a compulsive overeater, ate good healthy food at mealtimes, but continued to sneak my atrocious snacks on the sly.

'Gradually, we eliminated more and more animal flesh, enjoying vegetarian meals several times a week. I made the decision to become an ovo-lacto [a vegetarian who eats eggs and dairy produce] vegetarian about three years ago. My husband continued eating chicken and fish – I cooked vegetarian meals, but very occasionally I would make tuna sandwiches for my spouse or cook him some fish or chicken. Eventually that stopped – he didn't want it as much – and felt concerned asking me to do that for him as well. He did often have chicken at restaurants. For the past year or so, he has wanted fowl or fish less and less, now he can't recall the last time he ate it. He also considers himself ovo-lacto vegetarian. I, now, am on the verge of making a commitment to veganism.'

This was very much the strategy of Helen Littlewood, a systems analyst, who initially faced some resistance from her spouse. 'He thought it was a passing stage,' she recalls. 'He initially supported the idea, then became a little exasperated when it became obvious how much of an impact it was going to have on the life we were living. He believed that we had a good life and did not really want to see it disturbed. There were all the standard problems with going out to friends. Even when I made no criticism of the restaurants chosen, it would upset him that I didn't eat (sometimes there was nothing I could eat) but I would go for the community only. However, occasions like that did convince him that I wasn't undertaking a fad.

'There were a few harsh conversations about what I perceived as his inability to accept change, and in the end, his eyes were opened. It's interesting. While he continues along his own way, it is he that constructs the better arguments in favour of vegetarianism when it comes up in conversations with others. He has told me that although it is not for him at this stage, he admires people who have consciously chosen vegetarianism in the kinds of societies most of us find ourselves living in. I suppose if I had more of a tendency to preach and press the issues, I might have converted him by now, but I guess I'd rather that he came to vegetarianism not out of pressure from me, but by his own free will.'

TOLERANCE TRIUMPHS

Stephanie Stevens, a management consultant, went vegetarian in her student days seven years ago, mainly because she simply couldn't afford to eat meat. 'After quitting meat,' she says, 'I noticed that I lost 15lbs without even trying, and I felt great! I was a college athlete (volleyball, basketball) and I also felt that quitting meat helped me have more endurance and better performance. Now that I've thought more about my family's heart disease, high cholesterol, high blood pressure and arteriosclerosis, I would never change my dietary habits, even though I can afford to eat meat if I want to.

'I'd say that I'm one of the lucky ones when it comes to veggie-compatible significant others! I don't get grossed out if other people in my life want to eat meat. I see vegetarianism as a healthy, sane alternative to the average American diet. I met my husband-to-be at a vegetarian restaurant, so at least I could see that he was open-minded enough to be there! As I got to know him, I discovered that he was not a vegetarian, but wasn't opposed to trying the foods I would make and exploring foods he hadn't tried before. He had noticed problems with his digestive/excretory health before, and when we started living together he didn't drop meat altogether, but he said (without me asking) that he felt more energetic and his digestive discomforts

disappeared almost completely when he cut down on the amount of meat he ate. He still eats meat every so often (probably about once a month), but he'll go out and get a hamburger, or make it when I'm not home and then he'll confess when I come home from work. So – we've reached a sort of compromise, that when we eat together we eat vegetarian-style, but he doesn't get any negative feedback from me when he occasionally decides to eat meat. I figure that it's healthier than eating meat all of the time. The best part is that we've agreed to bring up our children as vegetarians, and we're hoping to promote the idea that meat is an *alternative* to being vegetarian, the way people now think of vegetarianism as being alternative to meat.'

TELL THEM THE TRUTH

Women who are responsible for feeding a family can have a particularly difficult time. Often feeling under an obligation to cook the sort of food their family demands to eat, the woman can also find herself at odds with her own conscience – ultimately, an impossible situation. Sometimes, the problem can be simply overcome by resolving to have a frank discussion with all family members about the ugly truth of meat production.

'If my family can avoid animal products in small-town Kansas', says Serita Bricklin, a secretary, 'anyone can!' Serita succeeded in converting her family to the meat-free way of living, motivated in part by the staunch refusal of her eight-year-old son to eat animal flesh since birth. 'He really helped put me on the right track,' she says, 'since I had to find something for the kid to eat!' To begin with, Serita continued to cook meat for her husband, but then she refused. 'At first my husband complained,' she says. 'I quietly told him how much healthier he would be and he began losing weight. Now he prides himself on the fact that he no longer eats meat. My daughter was easy. She's only five so I just explained to her that hamburger came from cows, bacon from pigs, and so on. She grossed out and doesn't complain at all now. She says all animals are her friends.'

Sometimes it's not possible to eliminate meat from a family's diet at a single step. But even then, there is still plenty you can do. Robbie Dennis, a senior banker, is married with a seventeen-year-old daughter, and is the only vegetarian in the household. 'I respect the rights of people to make these choices for themselves,' she says. 'However, because I am the only cook at home, I have established boundaries for myself. I don't cook meat and I only buy it for the family members if we go out to eat and I am buying. I expect that my husband and daughter will purchase and cook meat for themselves if they choose to eat it. I like to cook, so I serve a lot of delicious food that everyone likes. They seldom bother going out of their way to eat meat.

'My family have actually moved more and more towards a vegetarian lifestyle. I suspect that someday they will go all the way. We are all animal lovers. When we hear stories of animals being mistreated so humans can eat them, it gives my family more of a resolve to continue in the direction of complete vegetarianism.

'I think you win converts by showing people the positive benefits of the desired action, not by shaming, preaching or moralizing! Share great vegetarian foods with those who you would like to convert, give them little facts to think about, and give them lots of good suggestions for making the change – after all, changing can be very difficult for some people. The best way to convert a person is to find recipes and restaurants that offer delicious alternatives. Cheer like hell when people try new things and respect their choices otherwise. Also, if you can't get support from the family, find it elsewhere! I started a vegetarian group at work. It really helps.'

Marcia Singer, a marketing manager, adopts a similar 'wean-them-off-it' approach, with the difference that she is prepared to serve some meat to her family. This is how she explains it: 'I go to my local grocery store which sells pesticide- and hormone-free meat products, and buy chicken breasts in bulk. I wrap them separately in freeze-lock bags and put them in the freezer. When I make dinner I typically serve rice, beans and lots of vegetables and fruit, and I'll quick-fry slices of tofu for myself in soy and top with shredded ginger and daikon; the same with the chicken breasts for my husband and daughter.

'I began by cooking one completely vegetarian meal a week for everyone, and serving chicken or fish the other six days. I am now cooking four completely vegetarian meals a week and serving chicken or fish on three. My family hardly notices because I have gradually gained more expertise in cooking vegetarian dishes – with the help of a lot of wonderful vegetarian cookbooks that I bought at my local bookstore! My college daughter thinks it's really cool that her mom is a vegetarian; last weekend she brought a new boyfriend home (he is also a vegetarian), but she called ahead to discuss the menu with me; requesting several of her favourite vegetarian dishes! Next year at this time, I hope to have everyone off meat altogether!'

AIMING FOR EXCELLENCE

Although women still unfairly bear the brunt of food preparation in our society – and therefore most often face the moral dilemma of whether they should cook to please their families or to salve their own consciences – times are slowly changing. When Daniel Sharon, an engineer, met his partner, he was vegetarian (more lately, vegan) – but she wasn't. This is how he resolved the situation: 'When my current spouse and I met, she was an omnivore, but not a big meat eater (although a very serious cheese user). Her son was a complete omnivore (he would eat anything that doesn't move, and even some things that do!).

'Upon our very first "encounter", I made it clear to this girl that she was getting into a different experience: we didn't meet at a restaurant or on any such "neutral" ground, but rather, I invited them over to my place for dinner. I went all out and made an excellent gourmet dinner (broccoli salad, pad thai, fresh bread, vegetable stir-fry, black forest chocolate cake with coffee/butter icing, Spanish coffee . . .). This trend has kept up. I must state (in a humble manner) that I am a very good cook, and I have used an approach of making excellent food in order to convince and "convert" people.

'We dated, and eventually got engaged, and bought a house together last year. Right from the start, I made it well known that there was no way any meat products would get cooked in the house. This was a "condition" which was stated initially, and has held (and is non-negotiable). I let the kids eat whatever they want (the more you try to prevent them, the more they will – and I'd rather have them understand the health and ecological issues, and do as they will with them). However, they can*not* cook meat in the house.

'When we have a meal together, I cook it and we all eat the same vegan food. I make it good in order to "convince" everyone. Occasionally, the three kids get together and cook a gourmet vegan dinner for us (with a little bit of my help and many of my recipes). My spouse cannot stand even the sight or smell of meat anymore. She still uses cheese, but at a much lower rate. She simply loves the food we cook together, and I would claim that she is now fully converted. Her conversion, however, is her own choice – she liked what she ate, she switched slowly, and now claims she couldn't go back. So in a nutshell, omnivores can be "converted" by following these three major guidelines:

— Use positive reinforcement to do it – good vegan food is a lot more convincing than an entire book full of facts.

— Lay down the ground rules right from the start – I don't think I could get meat out of the house today if I'd ever allowed it in.

— Disperse a little bit of information at a time – too much and you sound like an activist, too little and you're not making your point. I do want my kids and my wife to understand why, not just how good it can taste.'

THE BREAK POINT

Not every case is such a gradual transition from meat-eating to vegetarianism. Janet Benson, a publisher, found that there came a crucial moment in her relationship when she found she could no longer prepare her partner's meat-based meals. This is how she successfully handled it: 'After a lifetime of meat-eating I decided to become a vegetarian about six months ago. I didn't feel I had the right to insist that my partner make the same decision, because him being a vegetarian was not a "requirement" before we were married. I didn't feel that it was fair to "change the rules" after already making a lifetime commitment. In our relationship, I am almost always home earlier than he, and I love to cook, while he detests it. So I do all the cooking, and he always cleans up the kitchen (which I hate!) As I was making my adjustment early on, I would prepare vegetarian meals, but then cook a small portion of meat for him, such as grilling a chicken breast. With time, I became more and more uncomfortable with this, and actually became more grossed out by it! My diet was also evolving more and more towards veganism, until the only dairy or eggs that I ever ate were in baked goods that were purchased outside our home. I finally told him that what he chooses to eat is his decision, but I will not have any part of preparing meat for him anymore. If he wants to eat it in our home, he will have to purchase it, prepare it, and clean it up himself. Since I do most of the grocery shopping also, this has proved to be more trouble for him than it's worth, so he joins me in eating vegan meals at home. However, he still eats meat when we eat out, and will occasionally stop at fast-food places for some of their horrible concoctions.

'The important thing, I think, is that in all of the discussions we have had about eating, I have made a

very strong effort to be non-judgmental and respectful of him and his right to make his own decisions. At first, I pulled the "righteous indignation" trip when he would eat a hamburger, but this only served to irritate him and make him defensive, especially since I had joined him in eating the same thing only weeks before. So we had a long talk, and I promised to be more supportive, even though I don't agree with what he eats sometimes. The result of all of this is that he has been much more receptive to my veganism, has shown more of an interest in my cooking (our running joke is that I'm making tofu-lentil surprise), and has significantly cut down on his meat consumption. He may never become a vegetarian himself, but he does realize (even if he does only grudgingly admit) that my diet is healthier, and he is open to eating the vegetarian things I prepare.

'We are still young (twenty-four and twenty-six), and don't have any kids yet. I will insist that our children be raised vegetarian or vegan, and will hold my ground on that one, because the health evidence is very convincing to me. I suspect that all of this would have been much more difficult if we had been married a long time, or already had kids, but I think it is important in marriage (or any lifetime commitment) to respect both your partner's right to change, and their right to make their own decisions.'

In summary – the golden rules of vegetarian family life

- Make sure your family and friends clearly understand the reasons why you've adopted the meat-free way of living. Be assertive if necessary, but not aggressive. You are entitled to have your views respected by everyone, even if they don't agree with you.
- Aim to be an expert cook yourself, even if your repertoire consists of just a handful of dishes, prepared excellently. Good food changes minds.
- If you don't normally get involved in the kitchen, now is the time to pull your weight! Don't expect someone else to have to learn a new way of cooking just to please you.
- If you normally prepare the food for your family, and there is initial resistance to your desire to go meat-free, plan to achieve a three-stage transition:
  1 Explain that buying and preparing animal flesh is a task which you find increasingly unpleasant, and ask those who wish to eat meat to cook it for themselves.

2 After a time, all the additional inconvenience involved in meat preparation will almost certainly mean that it is only eaten outside the home. Consolidate this and make it known that you would rather meat were not brought into the house.
3 Once in a while, take a few moments to educate the rest of your family about the truth of meat production, and about the many advantages of the meat-free way of living.

- If you have little or no support from within your family, find it elsewhere from like-minded people. There are lots of us around!

From Gourmet Cuisine To Grandma's Cooking – How To Survive When You're Eating Out

Sharing a meal with your friends or family is one of the great pleasures of living – a pleasure which, until recently, has all too often been a trial of endurance for vegetarians. I used to work in the advertising business, which is renowned for its lavish entertaining of clients and would-be clients. On one particularly orgiastic day I vividly remember eating three lunches in rapid succession, with three different clients, and rounding it all off with a lavish dinner party with a prospective client. It was shortly after this rather disgusting episode that I decided to stop being a professional lunch-eater, and I left the advertising business. Eating at hundreds of different restaurants had taught me, however, that vegetarians were generally very badly catered for. What most infuriated me was the lame but often repeated excuse for poor food: 'Why didn't you phone us before you came?'

The idea that vegetarians should be obliged to warn restaurateurs of their dietary preferences in advance of arriving, like some culinary leper, was highly offensive to me. Luckily, vegetarianism is now so widespread, especially in Britain where the vegetarian movement originated in the Western world, that it has been some years since I have heard that particular excuse. It has been my invariable experience that a good restaurant (by which I do not mean an expensive restaurant) will always go to considerable lengths to ensure that their customer is satisfied and well catered for – vegetarian or not. A bad restaurant, on the other hand, is not the

slightest bit interested in making its customers happy, and views its customers' special requests as nothing short of an unmitigated nuisance.

Gone, too, are the days of cheese salads and omelettes. Once the traditional standby of restauranteurs who wished to boast that they 'catered for vegetarians', these bland, boring, and unhealthy dishes are the terrible twin skeletons in vegetarianism's closet. Boycott all restaurants offering these dishes!

So where should vegetarians go to eat? Clearly, in choosing a restaurant, you will need to take into account your own personal food preferences, the company you will be with, the price range you have in mind, and the availability of different types of cuisine in the area. Although various societies and publishers produce listings and booklets containing reviews of restaurants from a vegetarian perspective, it is now so unusual to find a restaurant which does not cater for vegetarians that these publications are, to a large extent, unnecessary. Worse, they can sometimes foster a kind of vegetarian 'apartheid' that encourages consumers, and indeed restaurateurs, to perceive the vegetarian market as a small and exclusive one. I do not believe this is a forward step; rather than catering for the tastes of an exclusive minority, I would prefer to see many more vegetarian options seamlessly integrated into the main menus of many more restaurants. After all, you do not have to be vegetarian to eat vegetarian food. So let us now consider the many types of restaurants to be commonly found in most cities, and assess their general suitability for vegetarians.

INDIAN RESTAURANTS

The typical 'Indian' restaurant is usually not genuinely Indian at all. The food you are eating is more often than not a strange hybrid of various Asian and Western cuisines, and it is all too frequently unhealthy by virtue of its high fat content. This is very unfortunate, because real Indian food is perfect for vegetarians.

The Indian sub-continent offers an awe-inspiring range of culinary styles, focusing around the four major cities of Delhi, Madras, Bombay and Calcutta. In the north, where wheat is of greater importance than rice, breads form much more of a staple food (generally being cooked in a tandoori oven). South Indian food is far less meat-based and, although it tends to be spicier than the north, makes liberal use of the coconut, which has the miraculous power of being able to extinguish even the most fiery of dishes. The west, again, has differing culinary techniques and ingredients; Gujerati food is almost entirely vegetarian. With such a wide choice available, it is a great pity that more Indian restaurants do not offer a far wider range of dishes on their menus.

Even so, vegetarians and vegans can comfortably survive in almost any Indian restaurant. The overriding culinary sin of many Indian restaurants is to overcook their food in prodigious quantities of fat. In the worst restaurants, limp and lifeless vegetables are frequently served swimming in a sea of grease. It is not surprising that the lighting seems to be particularly dim in these places! Luckily, spotting a good Indian restaurant is quite easy. It is almost always family run, and this is something you can usually discern the moment you enter. Family restaurants have a particular atmosphere – a pride in appearance is evident, small touches such as flowers on the table may be in evidence, and children or younger members of the family may be around (Indian restaurants are often particularly welcoming to families who themselves have young children). A family-run restaurant is almost always better value than a chain of Indian restaurants, and the food will unquestionably be better. It is well worth getting to know the owner and his family, if you intend to use the restaurant regularly, because they will certainly be in a position to cook dishes for you which do not appear on the menu. If they happen to originate from the south or west of India, then it is a fair bet that they, too, will be vegetarian.

One of the best choices when you are eating at an Indian restaurant for the first time is a vegetarian thali (pronounced 'tarly'); this consists of a huge silver platter upon which up to a dozen small 'samples' of the range of dishes available will be presented. In the middle, there will be rice and/or some kind of bread, perhaps chapati, or puri (fried bread) or nan (made in the tandoori oven). A thali is a particularly good choice by which to test a restaurant's capability, and it is also an extremely impressive dish to order when you are entertaining. A note about eating the food: turn all of the little containers upside down so that their contents fall out on to the large platter, then tear a small strip from your chapati and use this to pick up the food between your fingers and eat. The combination of flavours you will achieve like this is phenomenal, and you may soon forget that there is any other method of eating.

If you do not wish to eat a sumptuous thali each time you visit an Indian restaurant, consider alternating this with more basic fare – a wonderfully nutritious and economical meal can be obtained by simply eating rice and dhal, together with one or perhaps two vegetable dishes. Again, you will enjoy your meal far more if you eat it the way most Indians eat, and place your vegetable dish on top of the rice, pouring the dhal on top.

Vegans usually eat very well in Indian restaurants. Eggs are hardly ever used in Indian cooking, and although dairy products feature prominently in most Indian desserts, relatively few main course dishes use them. The major exception to this would be ghee, or clarified butter, which is an indispensable part of most classical Indian cooking. These days, most Indian restaurants use vegetable ghee, rather than the more expensive dairy kind, so this is usually not a problem. If in doubt, ask.

A particularly welcome development in recent years is the emergence of the south Indian vegetarian restaurant in major cities. These are totally different in character and cuisine from the typical, old-fashioned Indian restaurant. They are usually far more restrained in their use of oils and fats, and therefore produce healthier food. But the main difference, which you will notice immediately, is the fantastically different menu. Gone are the overspiced range of anonymous 'meat' curries. In their place, you will find a mouthwatering range of delicacies – all vegetarian; and the majority vegan, too. The south Indian vegetarian restaurant is a vegetarian's paradise; it will take you many visits before you have tried everything on the menu, and many more before you have become tired of them. Actually, it is difficult to find anything bad to say about this new breed of Indian restaurant. Your first meal at a south Indian vegetarian restaurant will not be your last.

CHINESE RESTAURANTS

Traditionally, Chinese cuisine has not used dairy products, which is good news for vegans. Unfortunately, animal fat is quite widely used, notably pork fat, and this must be carefully discussed with your waiter before you order. The best Chinese restaurants, just like Indian ones, are family run. In these establishments, if you become a regular customer, you will almost certainly be offered dishes that are not on the menu (although almost certainly consumed by the family themselves). The Chinese are generally well aware of the requirements of vegetarians – there is, in fact, a traditional school of Buddhist Chinese cookery, named Zhai, which has for several centuries specialized in replicating meat and fish dishes using only wheat and soy products.

Most large cities will have one or two Chinese restaurants which are exclusively vegetarian, and these are well worth seeking out, since the range of food on offer will undoubtedly include many dishes rarely experienced by Westerners. But even the most basic Chinese restaurant should be well able to cope with vegetarian and vegan requirements – if they are not, it is a reflection upon the quality of the restaurant concerned, rather than a comment on Chinese cuisine. Many of the better Chinese restaurants today either have vegetarian menus or incorporate plenty of vegetarian choices on their main menu. For those who don't, an extremely good meal can be easily put together; rice, several kinds of stir-fried vegetables, and bean curd (tofu) comprise a tasty and nutritious meal.

The use of monosodium glutamate, although of no ethical concern, is still undesirable. It seems to be almost endemic in some restaurants, and even though you might request that it is not added to your food, it probably will be, anyway. Newer Chinese restaurants may have a policy of not using MSG at all, preferring to bring out the flavour of their food through the excellence of their cuisine. Such restaurants are also very likely to cater extremely well for vegetarians, now that vegetarianism is generally perceived as a fashionable lifestyle.

ITALIAN RESTAURANTS

The cooking of northern Italy is far more meat-orientated than that of the south, and, as a result, the health of northern Italians is worse than their southern compatriots. Additionally, the types of food used in northern-style Italian cooking – veal, for example – tend to be particularly repugnant to vegetarians. Nevertheless, no vegetarian will ever starve when there is an Italian restaurant nearby; the Italians are, of course, world masters of pasta dishes, most of which are eminently suitable for vegetarians and vegans.

The simplest pasta dish is made with a light olive oil dressing and perhaps a hint of garlic. Although some restaurants may turn their noses up at cooking such a simple dish, it can be revealing – poorly cooked pasta is unappetizing, and sits heavily on the stomach. A restaurant which is capable of cooking inspiring simple pasta can be trusted to produce more complicated food. Another universal standby for vegetarians eating their first meal at a new Italian restaurant is pesto. Originating from Genoa, it consists of a sublime combination of basil, garlic, pine nuts, olive oil and parmesan cheese (a vegan version is available in many health food shops). Every Italian restaurant in the world will be able to produce an acceptable pasta with pesto sauce; though not all of them will manage to reach the sublime heights which this simple yet exquisite food is capable of achieving.

The ubiquitous pizza is, of course, not much of a problem for vegetarians – although more so for vegans. However, it need not be so, as the cheeseless pizza is well established in Italian cooking and indeed an altogether finer, purer, and more intense gastronomic sensation. By no means all pizza restaurants will even be aware that there is such a thing; however, try ordering a pizza marinara (this generally includes olives, garlic, a fine tomato sauce and basil) but specify that you do not want anchovies or other sea creatures. One day, hopefully soon, today's trend in Italian cooking will reverse itself and the food of southern Italy will once again become more popular; at which point, it will become even more of a delight for vegetarians. In the meantime, it is worth noting that many of the best dishes, ingredients, and techniques of southern Italian cooking have been quietly usurped by the new wave of Californian food.

MIDDLE EASTERN RESTAURANTS

The countries bordering the north-eastern, eastern and southern Mediterranean share many common ingredients and dishes in their culinary repertoire – many of which are wonderfully suitable for vegetarians or vegans. Very often the widespread prevalence of a particular dish will reflect ancient population migrations, sometimes many thousands of years old. Consequently, it is impossible to tell with any certainty where many dishes first originated – hummus, for example, is considered to be a national dish in Greece, Turkey, Israel, Egypt, and many other countries. Many Middle Eastern restaurants, too, will reflect the cuisine of more than one country on their menu.

In the restaurants which specialize in the cuisine of the eastern Mediterranean, the best choice for vegetarians and vegans is undoubtedly a mezze, which consists of a huge assortment of *hors d'oeuvres*. Expect vine leaves stuffed with rice, hummus, falafel (made with chickpea flour), tabblouleh (a Lebanese speciality made from bulghur wheat mixed with tomatoes, mint and lemon juice), baba ghannoush (a delicious dip made from roasted aubergines) and a host of other goodies. As your table groans under the weight of these and other classical ingredients of mezzes, just relax and feel royally pampered!

Another classical dish for vegetarians is couscous, a traditional north African speciality made from very fine grain, lightly steamed. The couscous is made either with meat, fish, or vegetables – obviously vegetarians will choose the latter. Couscous is prepared in a couscoussier, a split level pan which consists of a lower part in which the vegetables are cooked, and an upper part through which steam from the vegetables percolates and so gently cooks the grain. Couscous is one of the simplest of all dishes – perhaps deceptively simple, being virtually impossible for the untrained chef to cook to perfection.

OTHER RESTAURANTS

The Western world has become so obsessed with the consumption of animal flesh that sometimes, we forget that the majority of the earth's peoples consume diets which, for the most part, are based upon vegetable foodstuffs. Consequently, almost all types of ethnic styles of cooking contain a wide variety of foods which are suitable for vegetarians and vegans. Unfortunately, in their adaptation to Western tastes, many of the more unusual styles of food have sacrificed their plant-based dishes in favour of meat or fish foods. With a little persistent questioning, most of these restaurants will be delighted to discuss and cater for your off-menu requirements: cuisines falling under this category would include Caribbean, Indonesian, Mexican, Ethiopian, Thai, and many other besides. Additionally, most Japanese restaurants are also happy hunting grounds for vegans, although it may sometimes be necessary to make some minor modifications to the menus on offer. Macrobiotic restaurants, too, reflect a style of cooking that is essentially Japanese, excluding dairy foods, but occasionally including fish.

VEGETARIAN AND WHOLEFOOD RESTAURANTS

Obviously, vegetarians can be assured of finding acceptable food at these establishments. Vegans, how-

ever, are not necessarily so lucky; astonishingly, a surprising number of vegetarian restaurants have little or nothing in the way of vegan food available. The question of whether vegetarians should deliberately go out of their way to patronize vegetarian restaurants is a difficult one. It is rarely possible to feel underdressed in a vegetarian restaurant, particularly one whose pedigree reaches far back to the heady, hippy days of the 1960s. All too often, the proprietor makes it abundantly clear that he or she believes that vegetarians have a moral obligation to support vegetarian restaurants in preference to others, even when the value is poor or the service is sloppy. Thankfully, there are marvellous exceptions to this.

Increasingly, the question must be asked, 'Are vegetarian restaurants really necessary?' Now that most 'normal' restaurants offer many acceptable vegetarian dishes, is it right for vegetarians to segregate themselves in this way? It is not an easy question. A few decades ago, when vegetarian food was genuinely difficult to find in most restaurants, there were very good reasons for vegetarian restaurants to become established. Today, the case is less clear. In the final analysis, you should judge a vegetarian restaurant by the same criteria as any other: if it provides the type of food you like to eat, offers good service and value for money, then support it. Otherwise, your money can be equally well spent educating other restaurants about the needs of their vegetarian customers. In the final analysis, the acid test of a vegetarian restaurant is this: would you be happy to take your meat-eating friends there? If it would impress them, and perhaps even inspire them, then it is undoubtedly a good restaurant. If, on the other hand, it would reinforce all their worst prejudices about vegetarian food, then perhaps it is not worth supporting.

FAST FOOD RESTAURANTS

Forty years ago the citizens of Hamburg, West Germany, hadn't even heard of 'hamburgers'. Now, the hamburger religion has spread throughout the world. Once shunned by vegetarians – some burger companies seemed actively hostile to us – you can now buy a vegetarian burger in many, but not all, burger bars. Most operators have at last realized that it pays to offer a vegetarian burger, and to have a well-stocked salad bar available. If you choose to eat a vegetarian burger at one of these establishments, check that they are cooked separately from the meat burgers. The prime virtue of fast food outlets is, of course, that they do indeed serve food to you quickly. Whether this should be a key factor in determining our food choices is questionable. However, the fact remains that, for many people, they are a convenient source of quick food, and a vegetarian option on the menu probably encourages more and more people to effortlessly try the meat-free way of living.

AIRLINE FOOD

All airlines will cater for vegetarians and vegans on long haul flights, and most will provide vegetarian and vegan fare on medium distance trips. For shorter flights, where the provision of food is less of a meal and more of a snack, it is unlikely that the airline will bother to provide a choice of food, nor will they usually accept special dietary requests in advance. There is absolutely no doubt that vegetarians and vegans eat far better airline food than meat eaters. This is how one airline pilot explains it:

'Airline meals will never be restaurant meals. A restaurant, at most, may cook for several hundred dinner patrons. An airline's flight kitchen cooks for tens of thousands of dinner patrons, and the food has to be refrigerated and then warmed up in a warming oven. There is an alternative. When you enter a flight kitchen you'll see a food assembly plant that practically rivals a car factory. Conveyors of chops are continually dumped into vast meat bins, where hairnetted women slap them quickly into tray compartments. It's a little unappetizing. But in the back of that kitchen, perhaps off to the side somewhere, past the utensil wrapping gadget and the slicers and the napkin folders, you'll see a small operation that's about the size of a restaurant kitchen in which trays are being assembled, individually, on serving dollies. This is your place – it's where they make the 'special diet menus'. All the meals here are prepared individually whether kosher or salt-free or vegetarian or diabetic, they are handled in an atmosphere that rivals at least a pretty decent restaurant operation. My advice to the traveller is to order from these special menus.'[2]

To ensure that you receive good quality vegetarian or vegan food on your next flight, follow these rules. First, make sure that the airline knows, either at the time of buying your ticket or when you reconfirm your flight, and certainly no less than five days before your departure date, of your dietary requirements. Whether you buy your ticket direct from the airline, or whether you buy it through an agent, you should always telephone the airline directly about two days before your flight just to confirm that they have your details logged in the computer. So far so good. Unfortunately, problems often occur at the time the meal is actually served on the flight. The flight attendants rarely seem to know where their vegetarian or vegan customers are sitting, and it is common for meals to go astray.

Sometimes, the flight attendants will ask for those wishing for vegetarian meals to put their hands up, and it is surprising to see how many meat eaters suddenly decide they wish to experiment with the vegetarian diet! To ensure that you receive the meal you requested, it is important that you grab the nearest flight attendant immediately before they start serving, and explain that you have already ordered a vegetarian or vegan dish. This will ensure that you are almost always served first, and should eliminate the possibility of your meal going missing. If you are travelling business or first class, such precautions should not be necessary. With a few glorious exceptions, airline food is rarely memorable, and sometimes proves to be downright dangerous. Meals often cover many thousands of miles before they are eventually served, and if handling, preparation or hygiene precautions are inadequate, then food poisoning inevitably results. You can eliminate this possibility, and ensure that the food is to your taste, by taking your own packed meal with you.

SOCIAL OCCASIONS

Socially, there are one or two considerations of which vegetarians should be aware. On occasions such as weddings, birthday parties and other functions when the catering arrangements are planned in advance, it is well worth having a word with the organizer to ensure that a wide range of vegetarian food will be on offer. You could point out that meat eaters can – and frequently do – consume large quantities of vegetarian food. Therefore, a social occasion which provides the majority, or even the entirety, of its food in the vegetarian style is certain to be acceptable to just about everyone. This is particularly true of children's parties, where parents who wouldn't otherwise dream of feeding their children junk food frequently surrender and cater to what they erroneously perceive to be the tastes of the younger generation. Be firm! If you serve junk food at your children's party, you are only increasing its desirability amongst children, who are thus encouraged to view it as a treat.

A problem less frequently encountered today than a few years ago is what to do with a 'meat bore'. It is important to make a distinction between this type of person, who only wishes to offend, and others who express a genuine interest in learning about vegetarianism. It is remarkable how often conversations are struck up over dinner, when someone notices that you are eating flesh-free foodstuffs. The meat bore however, is in an entirely different category. This is the person who will sit as close to you as possible, and loudly order the most bleeding steak they can obtain, or toy interminably with a piece of dead baby cow (veal) just to see what reaction they can get out of you. All I can say is, don't sit there and take it! When confronted by blind ignorance and aggression, the best advice I can give to you is to speak straight from the heart. Such words can sometimes penetrate even the thickest of skulls. Although it may take several years, minds can and do change.

Finally, do not be shy of making your presence known in any restaurant. It is often necessary to educate restaurateurs about the less obvious aspects of vegetarianism. This doesn't have to be done in a combative or imperious way; kind words are usually much more effective in producing positive results. If the menu you are initially shown has little or nothing for you to choose from, ask to see the manager and ask what s/he can suggest for you. This is really the acid test for any restaurant: if the management genuinely cares about satisfying their customers, they will be more than willing to take a little extra care and produce a dish to suit you. In my own experience, such 'special' dishes are usually greeted with envy by the non-vegetarians in the party, simply because the chef and management have tried extra-hard to please. There's every chance that such 'pioneer' dishes will subsequently be incorporated into the restaurant's main menu, so you will also have performed a useful service for future vegetarian diners at that restaurant.

If the manager or waiter asks you, 'what would you like?' it is best, unless you have a clear idea in mind, to simply bounce the question back to them – what do they suggest? They are, after all, the experts. Don't settle for an insipid salad if you really want something more exciting. If the discussion comes to an impasse, politely suggest that the chef pops out from the kitchen to contribute his or her thoughts, too.

Just occasionally, the management may simply shrug their shoulders when asked to suggest an acceptable meat-free dish. There's only one course of action in these circumstances: leave. No restaurateur has an automatic right to our custom, although a few still behave as if they do. Again, there's no need to be melodramatic about it, but neither should you slink away so quietly that the management doesn't realise you've gone. Some restaurateurs erroneously believe that since vegetarians are still a minority, catering for them doesn't matter. When such people see parties of four, six or more people quit their establishments because the vegetarians are not well served, they will begin to see the error of their ways. And don't hesitate to spread the word about bad establishments to your friends and associates: it has been estimated that one unhappy customer will, on average, tell 25 people about their unpleasant experience – a powerful consumer weapon indeed.

Restaurateurs must also be made to understand that it is absolutely unacceptable for a vegetarian to have his food prepared with or cooked in the same utensils which were used seconds before for a meat dish. Neither is it remotely hygienic. Meat has a nasty habit of exuding liquid which is particularly prone to cause food poisoning. So, for example, if meat is stored on the top shelves of a refrigerator, and salad vegetables on the lower shelves, it is more than likely that there will be some cross-contamination. Knives, too, are another potent source of meat-related food poisoning. Ideally, all restaurants should have separate areas in their kitchens, together with their own utensils, for the exclusive preparation of non-meat food. Owners and chefs must be made aware that for most vegetarians, this is a very important matter of hygiene, aesthetics and ethics.

Similarly, the question of 'hidden' food ingredients must also be raised. Gelatine is a particularly ubiquitous food ingredient, made from the boiled bones, skins and tendons of slaughtered animals. It is used for making jellies, numerous cold or iced desserts, and also as a setting and firming agent in many savoury dishes. Several alternatives to this rather gruesome product are readily available, although not particularly well known in the catering business. They include agar, made from seaweed, and kuzu (arrow root). Guar gum and carrageenan are other plant-based thickening agents, and some Jewish kosher gelatine products are also not made from animals.

In soups, cooks of the old school still blithely combine bones and other reject material from animal carcasses into even the most innocuous vegetable soups. It is quite easy to taste their presence, and they should be immediately objected to (and it should be pointed out that the menu description of the product itself is misleading). Similarly, unenlightened chefs are sometimes tempted to douse everything in the cooking juices of meat products, and fried foods, such as roast potatoes, are sometimes cooked using meat fat. None of this is necessary, and your polite insistence that you do not want your food prepared using animal-derived substances such as these will ensure that more and more chefs become better educated about changing consumer tastes.

Never be afraid to compliment a chef in person when you have eaten a particularly good meal; chefs are a hard-working breed who rarely receive all the compliments they should. A gesture on your behalf to praise a particularly good vegetarian meal will be appreciated and remembered for a long time.

How To Eat Your Way Through A Healthy, Happy Pregnancy

Pregnancy is a natural, healthy condition which most women experience at some point in their lives. It is not a disease, a disorder or in any sense an illness or state of handicap. In fact, many women describe feeling at their healthiest during pregnancy; certainly it can be a time when you are naturally inclined, even driven, to adjust your diet and lifestyle to create a condition of optimum health in which to grow a baby. If you can remember this simple, obvious fact: that your 'job' during pregnancy is to grow a whole and healthy baby, then you will inevitably steer yourself along the course of healthy eating – not just for your baby, but for yourself as well.

A woman who is eating, or considering, a meat-free diet at this time can establish a pattern of eating which will promote good health in both the immediate future and long term, both for herself and her child. She can reduce her exposure to animal-related causes of disease, while increasing her intake of the many proven health-promoting factors present in the animal-free diet.

A woman embracing a plant-based diet for herself and her child must simply and efficiently become aware of what she and her baby need to eat in order to stay well. It is no longer enough to accept the dietary advice and traditions which have been passed on because, by and large, they are founded on an animal-based diet. Rather, the opportunity is now present for generations of medical, scientific and practical everyday knowledge and experience of the meat-free way of living to be put to use. It is not enough to eat bread and jam without the butter, or to eat potatoes, gravy and two veg without the meat. This pattern of eating keeps you firmly locked into the meat-eating tradition with all the illness and distortion of health and spirit which that can bring. Instead, a fresh and enthusiastic look at food – what it means, what it provides, how best to prepare it – will reward you with good health and an exuberance about your diet that you may then pass on to your child.

Pregnancy is the time when you first begin to pass on your dietary choices, and their effects, to your children. A diet free of animal products can provide an ideal start for your baby. Note that requirements for key nutrients will increase during this time in order that you may provide all that is necessary for yourself and your developing baby. These key increases are approximately as follows.

ENERGY (CALORIES)

Increase your calorie intake by about 300 calories per day in the second and third trimesters. This increase is certainly easy to achieve; it is more a question of achieving it to best effect. A can of soft drink and a Danish pastry will certainly make the numbers but remember you are doing rather special work with those calories and they are best derived from more wholesome food that will nourish you in other ways as well. Calories are most easily obtained from carbohydrates and fats. The body readily converts these to energy in a way that is not stressful to your body, especially if the carbohydrates are complex – from unrefined wholefoods.

Do not be worried by carbohydrates and fats: they are essential foods and promote good health if they are carefully selected. Unfortunately, for women who are used to dieting, both have strong associations with 'bad foods'. It is helpful to view them as units of energy: the carbohydrates for immediate and short-term use, the fats for storage of energy. We all need both and, especially in pregnancy, women must ensure that their body has appropriate amounts so that they may deal with the demands of a body that is changing and a baby that is growing. In addition to their calorific value, complex carbohydrates and fats are rich in other vitamins and minerals which improve the nutritional value of your diet. Complex carbohydrates are also high in fibre which helps to maintain your health in other ways. Useful snack ideas to help you meet your additional calorie requirement healthily are:

- ripe bananas sliced into plain soya yogurt
- a cupful of mixed nuts and dried fruit
- a serving of avocado vinaigrette
- a soya milkshake with ground almonds and banana (see p184)
- muesli with soya milk
- a bowl of fresh fruit salad
- tempeh burger with salad topping
- a bowl of pea soup (see p265)
- oat and dried fruit flapjacks or fruit cake (see p300)
- a bowlful of dried bananas, figs, dates and apricots
- a serving of wholewheat pasta with pesto sauce.

Each of these examples is wholesome yet provides calories as well as other nutrients essential to health. In other words, not the empty calories of a sugary drink or highly refined pastry.

PROTEIN

Increase your protein intake throughout pregnancy and lactation. Protein is classically known as the building block of life: the collection of amino acids which comprise proteins do the work of building and repairing cells throughout the body. So it makes sense that, if you are growing a new baby, you are going to need a bit extra. Just one word of caution: don't overload on protein-rich foods to the exclusion of carbohydrates and fats. If you do this, your body will have to convert the protein into calories just to get enough energy – this is very stressful for the body and can create health problems. Aim, instead, for a diet high in complex carbohydrates, adequate in fats, and with just enough protein to do the job of growing your baby and making essential, motherly changes to your body. You can eat enough protein for you and your growing baby almost without trying. Grains, legumes, nuts and seeds are all protein-rich foods which you can combine easily in meal form or use to 'top you up' in snack form. Some excellent, easily digested, sources of extra protein are:

- tofu (see Scrambled Tofu, p291) or sliced into a sandwich or salad
- tempeh (see Marinated Tempeh, p293) or sautéed and put in a bun
- soya products such as yogurt, cheese, milk or TVP
- steamed aduki beans with brown rice and greens
- baked beans on toast
- hummus (see p203) with pitta bread
- peanut butter and banana sandwich on wholewheat bread
- Frijoles with Tortillas and Salsa (see p325).

VITAMINS AND MINERALS

. . . nourish the cells of your body through their individual actions but also in combination with each other. These relationships are often complex and understanding them can sometimes take a bit of time. Be assured, however, that you don't have to do this alone: nature is doing it already. So if you eat natural foods (whole and unrefined) you can enjoy their nourishment immediately and take your time learning about the more subtle actions taking place.

Fresh vegetable juices are an excellent source of vitamin- and mineral-rich wholefoods that give you their nutrients immediately and with all of these natural relationships in place. They are ideal during pregnancy as they are packed with nutrients yet are easy to digest (and easy to 'hold down' if you are suffering from sickness). Fresh vegetable juices tend to have a very healthful effect on the kidneys and in general on the elimination processes. A juicer may be purchased as a single piece of equipment or as part of a food processor and is an excellent family investment. You will use it for yourself, throughout your pregnancy, but also for your baby as he or she grows into childhood.

If possible, buy organically grown vegetables for juicing, scrub them well and then simply push them, raw, through the juicer. In this way, you will find it easy to consume large quantities of fresh vegetables without having to chew your way through the same amount piled high on a plate. Of especial value for the pregnant woman are vegetable cocktails made by combining – to suit your taste – carrot, celery, cabbage and cucumber juices with sensitive additions of beetroot, turnip leaves, parsley and spinach. 570ml (1 pint) or more of vegetable juice each day will greatly increase your intake of minerals such as calcium, iron, phosphorus, potassium, sulfur, zinc, magnesium and manganese, iodine and trace minerals such as selenium and copper. If of a leafy nature, the vegetables will dramatically increase your intake of chlorophyll and folic acid; most vegetables will also augment your intake of vitamins A, B and C.

CALCIUM

Increase your calcium intake by about 400mg per day to a total of about 1200mg per day; try to meet this increase using calcium-rich foods rather than supplements so that your intake will be spread throughout the day. Calcium is necessary for the proper development of your baby's bones and teeth and for the maintenance of your own teeth and bones during this time. It is best absorbed when you have adequate vitamin D in your body (see below) and when plenty of boron, a trace mineral, is also present in the diet. Boron is available in apples and other fresh fruits and vegetables. Thus, an apple a day during pregnancy may well have more to do than keep you regular! (See also calcium, p77, Part Three and osteoporosis, p155, Part Four.)

This new calcium requirement is easily met with additional servings of green, leafy vegetables, calcium-enriched soya products such as milk and tofu, nut and seed butters such as almond spread, cashew butter and tahini, and all sorts of legumes and grains. Some ideas for calcium-rich meals include:
- fresh vegetable juices, as above
- hummus (see p203)
- dhals (see pp344)
- Buttery Lentil Paté (see p234)
- tahini and miso sandwiches
- Broccoli and Almond Casserole (see p170)
- sauerkraut
- soya milk shakes (see p184).

VITAMIN D

Made when a substance (dehydrocholesterol) in the skin reacts with sunlight; it is essential in order to maintain appropriate levels of calcium in the bloodstream and should be gained by regular exposure to sunlight. Some margarines, breakfast cereals and soya milks are fortified with vitamin D for those who wish to supplement this vitamin, but a daily walk or sitting in the sunlight for at least 15 minutes with face, hands and arms exposed is usually considered sufficient to manufacture this vitamin. (See Vitamin D, Part Three, p74).

IRON

Increase your iron intake during pregnancy. Iron is necessary for the formation of new blood cells for you and your baby so it is reasonable that you should require more during pregnancy. Women vary greatly in their ability to absorb iron from the diet, so recommendations for how much you need vary greatly. Vitamin C helps your body absorb iron, especially if it is present in the same food as the iron. The fresh vegetable juices mentioned above are therefore ideal to boost your intake of this essential combination. Cooking your food in iron pots will also increase the presense of iron in your food. Iron-rich foods you may include in your diet are:
- dried fruits such as apricots, figs, prunes and currants
- aduki beans served with brown rice and steamed broccoli
- fresh or roasted nuts and seeds (see Pumpkin, p279)
- whole grains such as oats (see Creamy Porridge, p247), breads (see Pumpernickel, p355) and cornmeal (see Cornbread, p331)
- blackstrap molasses, spread on toast or stirred into a milkshake.

VITAMIN C

Increase your intake of this vitamin on a daily basis to assist your body's absorption of iron, and to help protect you against infection. Vitamin C is essential for the development of your new baby and seems to play a part in how almost every other vitamin and mineral affect the body. It is available in fruits and green vegetables as well as, to a lesser extent, potatoes and tomatoes. Increase your intake easily with these foods:
- fresh vegetable juices
- fresh fruit juices
- salads and crudités
- fruit snacks.

FOLIC ACID

This vitamin is crucial to the development of your baby's nervous system. Try to double your intake of folic acid by greatly increasing your consumption of green, leafy vegetables (folic has the same linguistic root as foliage, meaning leaf). Some folate-rich foods

to enjoy:
- spinach salad
- green leaf sandwiches
- a handful of fresh or dried dates
- wholemeal toast with yeast extract (ie Vegemite, Marmite)
- a handful of mixed nuts
- fresh vegetable juices.

VITAMIN B12

This vitamin is essential to the development of normal blood cells and to healthy nerve function. You may ensure additional intake of vitamin B12 by including a fortified food product in your diet two or three times per week. Some examples include:
- fortified cereals
- fortified soya products such as milk and TVP
- some brands of nutritional yeast flakes.

ZINC

This mineral is necessary for your baby's normal growth and development. Recommendations vary but you should aim to increase your intake of zinc during pregnancy; only about half of the zinc you consume will be absorbed, depending on the level of other nutrients in your body as well as the form in which zinc is taken. The best option is, as always, to consume fresh wholefoods when possible (rather than supplements) to ensure that this mineral is adequately absorbed. Foods especially rich in zinc include:
- roasted pumpkin seeds (see p280)
- wholewheat toast with yeast extract
- porridge made with soya milk (see Creamy Porridge, p247)
- tahini and miso sandwiches (wholewheat bread, please)
- 2 tablespoons alfalfa sprouts
- Simple Rice and Peas (see p335)
- roasted or steamed parsnips
- Marinated Tofu (see p339)
- Pea Soup (see p265).

Of course, these are only some of the nutrients which your body requires. Others, which are required in minute doses for instance, are not listed here but are still essential for good health and the healthy development of your baby. To eat an excellent diet throughout your pregnancy follow these guidelines:

- eat whole, unrefined foods whenever possible
- eat them raw or with minimal cooking to preserve nutrients
- buy fresh, organically grown fruit, nuts, grains and vegetables whenever possible
- eat as great a variety of plant foods as possible
- choose your food as though it were medicine, prepare it with pleasure, eat it with exuberance
- as much as possible, gain your nutrients from food rather than supplements.

Nature gives you a handy three-month period at the beginning of your pregnancy in which to make changes that will improve your and your baby's diet and health. During this time you may suffer the fatigue, nausea and sickness which can occur during the early weeks of pregnancy. These must be endured, of course, but this time can also be used as an opportunity to 'clean' the body. In fact, some attempts to explain the phenomenon of morning sickness include the possibility that the body is trying to detoxify. If this is so, then you can help it along by using this time to eliminate unhealthy foods gradually from your diet, replacing them with foods that will keep you well while you grow your baby.

In the first three months of pregnancy your baby's organs, cardiovascular system, skeleton, brain and nervous system form; in fact, the baby is complete but very immature and unspecialized by the end of the first trimester. Your job, during this time, is to provide the basic ingredients for your baby's development. It is useful to realize this as early in your pregnancy as possible and if you do nothing else during this time (leave buying cots until later), do your best to establish a good diet and a deep understanding of good nutrition. To do so now will set you up for the rest of your pregnancy and for the years ahead.

Here are some further ways in which what you eat can affect your health during pregnancy.
- To counter feelings of nausea, pour boiling water over one teaspoon of freshly grated root ginger in a cup and drop in a slice of lemon. Drink one to three cupsful each day, sweetened with one teaspoon barley malt syrup if you feel you need a sweet drink.
- Eating small amounts of plain food at frequent intervals during the day will also help to allay the discomfort of nausea, as this is always worse on an empty stomach. Plain rice cakes, oatcakes, rye crisp, cream crackers or dry toast are useful to have at hand. These are sustaining without being fattening (the oatcakes are the most calorie-dense).

- Clear fluids, fruit juices and freshly juiced vegetables are preferrable to coffee or tea. Tea, coffee, cocoa and other caffeinated drinks, such as some soft drinks, are not health-enhancing, no matter how much you enjoy them, and as the caffeine will pass through the placenta, you can expect that your developing baby will be receiving a dose of this powerful substance. Although no study of the effect of caffeine on the developing baby is, as yet, conclusive in its recommendations to curb caffeine consumption, there is a general move by nutritionists and some governments (ie the US Food and Drug Administration) to discourage consumption of this drug during pregnancy. Also, it may be well to drop caffeine from your diet if you want to conceive; it is certainly wise to avoid it if you are lactating.
- It is important to avoid constipation (see Part Four, p130) during pregnancy; retention of faeces is toxic to the body and straining to expel it is increasingly hard on the muscles and veins around the anus and perineum, especially if there are problems with haemorrhoids. If you had relied on your morning cup of coffee to begin a bowel movement, but have since given up coffee (well done!), you will need other triggers to help you. A large glass of filtered water drunk first thing in the morning, every morning, will get things going and keep you regular.
- Finally, take especial note of the benefits of fresh vegetable juice, mentioned above, and drink approximately 570ml (1 pint) daily from the moment you realize you are pregnant, to ensure a diet rich in vitamins and minerals right from the start – when your baby most needs these nutrients.

Nourishing the New Mother

The hours you spent planning and preparing during your pregnancy will suddenly seem like times of relaxed luxury somewhere in ancient history. For here you are with your baby: you've done it and now there is the rest of your life ahead of you. Well, at least there's the rest of today for that seems to be as far ahead as you can think at the moment! There are two essential jobs to be started immediately, however, and you don't have much time for planning. The first, though not necessarily in this order, is to

build yourself up again after the birth. The second is to make certain that the milk you are providing is first class and that there is plenty of it.

Let's look at you first. You still need to eat all of the extra nutrients so essential during your pregnancy and a few more besides! In fact, requirements for calories, protein and vitamin B12 are all higher during lactation than they were during pregnancy. Your diet during lactation should therefore be similar to the diet you enjoyed while pregnant but with an extra snack or two during the day to boost your calorie and protein intake and with especial consideration given to finding B12-fortified products. Here are a few simple meals that can help you to meet your special needs deliciously.

- A sandwich made of wholewheat bread: spread tahini on one slice, B12-fortified yeast extract on the other slice. Fill with sliced tofu, 2 tbsp alfalfa sprouts, lettuce or spinach leaf and sliced tomato.
- A milkshake made with 285ml (1/2 pint) calcium and B12-fortified soya milk, 50g (2oz) ground almonds, 2 tsp blackstrap molasses and 1 ripe banana or 1/2 ripe avocado.
- A slice of homemade flapjack (made from wholewheat flour, oats, sunflower seeds, oil, molasses) served with a tub of soya yogurt.
- A serving of brown rice and dhal (see p344), sautéed tempeh or marinated tofu (p339) served with a sprinkling of nutritional yeast flakes.
- A bowl of pea soup (see p265) sprinkled with nutritional yeast flakes.

You may have thought that you were eating for two during pregnancy, but now you really notice it, and the weight might still drop off of you! Please, for your sake and your baby's, for the first four to six months of breast feeding do not reduce your calorie intake or the quality of your diet.

BOOSTING IRON

If you lost a lot of blood during the birth, you may need to boost your intake of iron. This is entirely possible with diet alone but you have to commit yourself to a few days of intensive iron-snacking (see also Anaemia, Part Four, p105). Also, remember that vitamin C helps you absorb more iron from your diet, so increase your consumption of that a little, too. Here are some ideas for iron-snacking foods.

- Measure 100g (4oz) each of dried figs, apricots, dates and prunes into a mixing bowl and cover with water in which 1 tbsp of blackstrap molasses has been dissolved. Leave to stand overnight then serve for breakfast, or in small portions throughout the day with its juice and topped with 1tbsp crushed pistachios. This may provide as much as 20mg of iron.

- Juice 1kg (2lbs) organic carrots with 225g (8oz) parsley, stalks and all. This is a strong flavour so you may wish to juice this amount in two or three batches during the day. Also, you might try blending it with soya milk and a little apple juice to make it more sweet. This drink can provide up to 20mg of iron. Other iron-rich juicing vegetables are beet greens and, to a lesser extent, broccoli. These juices contain vitamin C as well.
- An iron-rich granola can be made by mixing 25g (1oz) each of sesame seeds and sunflower seeds and 50g (2oz) each of pistachios, pumpkin seeds and rolled oats. Stir in 1 tbsp of blackstrap molasses and enough fruit juice to cover and leave to soak. Serve with fresh fruit to taste and eat for breakfast or in small portions throughout the day. This provides about 25mg of iron.
- Sauté 450g (1lb) of fresh spinach in with some onion and garlic then serve over brown rice. It is easy to eat this amount of spinach and, with the rice, this dish can provide up to 20mg of iron.

ADDING VITAMIN C

To boost your vitamin C intake, concentrate on eating citrus fruits several times during the day. These are easy to eat when you are on the go. Here are some useful ideas.

- Make a citrus salad with 1 orange, 1 grapefruit and 1 lemon, each of them peeled and divided into segments. Mix in a pretty bowl and drizzle a little lemon juice over. Keep covered until you are ready to eat it – all at once or in small nibbles.
- To enhance the flavour, texture and vitamin C content of the above, slice in a ripe mango and a whole green pepper. This salad can provide up to 300mg of vitamin C.

MORE FROM THE B GROUP

You might well need additional vitamins from the B group during the weeks just after baby is born. This group of vitamins help the body deal with stress and there is certainly plenty of that in the early days! As the B vitamins are water-soluble, you will need to make certain that you get plenty in your diet each day. Main sources are whole grains, nuts and seeds, yeast extract, legumes and vegetables. Here are favourite B-group snacks which you might appreciate.

- A sandwich made from wholewheat bread – spread one slice with tahini, the other slice with yeast extract or miso and fill with 2 tbsp of alfalfa sprouts. Add sliced tofu if you want a more substantial sandwich.
- Steamed brown rice served with a stir-fry of mushrooms, peas, broccoli, tofu and cashew nuts.
- A bowlful of Creamy Porridge (p247) served with a spoonful of barley malt syrup.

GUARANTEE VITAMIN D

To lift your spirits and ensure a good supply of vitamin D for yourself and your baby, promise yourself a 30 minute walk each day, no matter what the weather is like. Or set your favourite chair in the most sunny corner of your home and snuggle up with your baby while the sun bathes you for as long as you both enjoy it. Aim to give your baby about two hours of sunlight each week – especially during the summer – on head and hands to ensure sufficient vitamin D is manufactured. (See Vitamin D, Part Three, p74)

MAKING BREAST THE VERY BEST

When you are eating a diet with sufficient calories and rich in nutrients, you are almost certain to produce ample, nutrient-rich milk for your baby. For the first six months of your baby's life, this is all he or she needs and your baby may well be happy with just breast milk, or little else, for a few months longer. Here are some foods that really help to produce lots of good milk. (I know these are good because I asked my wife what she ate to make our son so plump and happy!)

- Eat at least 450g (1lb) of cooked brown rice each day.
- Try a daily serving of Creamy Porridge (see p247), topped with flaked almonds or ground hazelnuts if desired.
- Tahini Dip (see p347) seems to work miracles when baby gets frustrated at about seven months. Suddenly your milk is rich and abundant again, and you'll love it!

• Make up a serving of Hummus (see p203) once or twice a week to set you up for serious milk production. This is especially useful if you breast-feed for longer than 6–8 months as you may need an extra bit of building-up around this time. Remember, hummus is made from chickpeas and tahini, both of which are good sources of protein, iron, calcium, folic acid and vitamin B6. So a good serving of hummus will give you an concentrated but easily digested package of nutrients to help maintain your health and your milk supply.

Feeding Your Vegetarian Child

When your baby is somewhere between six and eight months old, one of you will get the idea that something other than breast milk might be a good idea. This is natural and healthy but does not mean that you are going to suddenly stop nursing or that you will be confined to the kitchen for the next fifteen years. Simply, at about this time your baby will enjoy some contact with solid (in fact, it's generally semi-solid) food. Some babies display signs of hunger which make them interested in solid food, others seem only to want a good chew, something most mothers are reluctant to allow while breastfeeding! Whatever the reason for this sudden interest, there is no need to rush into a transition from a breast milk-only to a solids-only diet. For some children, this transition takes two to three years!

Solid foods should be gently introduced, one at a time, one per week or fortnight, when the child shows an eagerness to try them. If you are breastfeeding at this time, do not suddenly stop, but let the breastfeeding provide the child with the nourishment he or she needs. Breastfeeding at this time should serve to reassure you, as well, that your child is not being deprived of nourishment while he or she explores a variety of solid foods. Gradually, solid foods will become the main source of nourishment and your milk will become the optional extra, supplying plenty of love and security on a daily basis as well as essential nutrients for those times when your child is ill or overwrought.

There is no single, correct sequence in which to introduce solids into your child's diet. What follows is one possible sequence which you or your child may well put into reverse! What matters is that you are gentle, gradual and attentive to the possibility of single food items causing upset or allergy. A few things to remember as you go:

• Breast milk is naturally sweet, so your child will enjoy a sweet taste in the solids you begin to introduce. This is naturally present in sweet potatoes, parsnips and fruit, for instance, and should not be achieved by the use of sugar or syrups of any sort. If you can, avoid introducing your child to the regular inclusion of sweet fruit juices in their diet. Filtered or mineral water is the healthiest drink available and, if you can encourage your child to get used to this on a regular basis, fruit juice can then become an occasional treat.

• A tendency to have allergies often runs in families. If any of your family has eczema, asthma, rashes or other signs of allergy, you may expect your child to have the same tendencies. For this reason, postpone introducing certain foods until your child is much older and their digestive and immune systems more mature. Such foods include wheat, citrus, peanuts, cow's milk, soya, eggs, strawberries and brewer's yeast.

• Breastfeeding should continue for as long as possible into and through a child's toddlerdom. A fashion for paring down the 'necessary' length of time to breastfeed a child (sometimes to as little as six weeks) is, thankfully, being reversed and it is now more widely recognized that long-term breastfeeding benefits the child, the mother and the family. Introduction of solids does not mean that you must cease breastfeeding, only that it takes a different place in your child's diet. Long-term breastfeeding can help ensure optimum health and nutrition while your child's digestive and immune systems mature (they are not mature when he or she is born) and can prevent the development of food allergy.

INTRODUCING SOLIDS

• **From three months:** offer filtered water on demand and one teaspoon of fruit or vegetable juice (ie melon, apple, carrot, celery) diluted if a greater quantity is desired.

• **From six months:** offer mashed banana, unsweetened applesauce, puréed peaches or mangoes. Mashed avocado may be appropriate for some children of this age.

• **From eight months:** present baby with small

amounts of raw fruit and vegetable juices, diluted with water if necessary. As you know, these will provide a rich source of vitamins and minerals without the fibre and bulk of the whole food. Begin offering cooked rice and/or oat porridges, stirring in the juices, if you like, to further enhance these foods.

- **From 10 months:** steamed organic vegetables such as sweet potato, carrot, parsnip and squash may be offered, mashed or puréed so that the child can begin self-feeding. Most soft fruits and avocados can be offered and some children are, by this age, well into chewing peeled apples, whole bananas, dried apricots and the like. Let them do it if they won't let you postpone it another month or two, but stay near and keep an eye on them – choking is a very real danger at this age.

- **From twelve months:** offer the occasional rice cake, oatcake or piece of dry toast. A broader range of vegetables may be offered such as peas, asparagus, broccoli and potatoes. Nut milks, made from hazelnuts, almonds or cashews (see p170), are delicious treats which may be introduced at this time. Well-cooked beans may be mashed into a fruit or vegetable 'gravy' and soya yogurt can become a regular feature in a lunch or snack.

- **From fourteen months:** your child's diet begins to more closely resemble your own and he or she may be happy to have a plate of whatever you are eating. You may need to adjust the texture somewhat, by mashing, puréeing or finely chopping, and you may need to separate the individual foods from one another (many children do not like casseroles and other mixed foods). Pasta shapes usually become popular around this time as do other cooked grains such as millet, rice and barley. Introduce tofu, tempeh, sandwiches, soups and dhals, almond or cashew nut butters (keep away from peanut butter for another year, if possible) and gradually present your child with raw vegetable sticks and fruit chunks. Tahini and hummus are excellent foods for children from this age onwards, as is Guacamole (see p181) and soya milkshakes of all descriptions (see Banana Milkshake, p184). Dried fruits are excellent sources of minerals and calories and children love their sweetness. Limit their consumption of these to avoid too much sugar and stay in the room with them while they are eating these as they are easy to choke on.

Let your child have a real say in what he or she eats, but guide them in a subtle way by offering healthy food that is visually appealing, has an interesting texture, an attractive colour and, of course, a wonderful flavour. As your child matures, he or she will want to participate in the preparation of their food: welcome and encourage this – no matter how much patience it requires – as a first stage in developing an enthusiasm for preparing healthy food. I feel certain that if a child develops a close association with and interest in food preparation at an early age, they are more likely to place value on food throughout their lives and to discriminate in a positive way when selecting the food that nourishes them as they grow.

Growing Up on Good Food

From early childhood through to adolesence, the diet you offer your child must provide the energy, protein, vitamins and minerals essential to steady growth and the maintenance of good health. There are two obvious ways you can do this: one is to fret and worry and occasionally panic, the other is to set a determined, well-plotted course and do your best. What follows is a guide to plotting your course with a few words that might help you in your determination.

VARIETY IS YOUR INSURANCE

To help you provide a complete and sufficient profile of nutrients, you may divide food into five groups, each of which offers a specific range or type of nutrient.

- Whole grains: including pasta, breads, porridge, oatcakes, rice and rice cakes, millet, buckwheat, noodles, cereals.
- Nuts and seeds: including walnuts, almonds, brazil nuts, cashews, peanuts, hazelnuts, pumpkin seeds, sunflower seeds, sesame seeds, pistachios, and the nut and seed butters made from these, such as tahini and peanut butter.
- Legumes: including all beans and peas and the products made from them such as bean sprouts, soya milk, tofu, tempeh, soya cheese and TVP.
- Fruit: including avocados and all the familiar fruits.
- Vegetables: divided in terms of green or yellow vegetables.

When you prepare meals for your children, aim to

provide something from each of these groups – ideally within each meal, but more realistically within each day. Of course, you should eat from these groups as well – it's just that when considering what to feed your child, it is useful to have a mental map to help you determine whether you are including all the essentials. You won't accomplish this ideal every mealtime, or even every day, however. This is what you aim for. To help fill the gaps, have plenty of food available in a ready-to-eat form so that when your child is hungry he or she may help themselves to something healthy, rather than a convenient packet of junk food. Some ideas for handy foods are:

- a bowlful of fresh crudités, including cucumber, carrots, cauliflower florets, tomato wedges, turnips and green pepper (keep this in the fridge or in a covered carton)
- a bowlful of pitted olives or gherkins
- homemade sugar-free or low-sugar flapjacks
- washed fruit (apples, pears, grapes, plums, peaches etc)
- marinated tofu cut into cubes
- oat or rice cakes made into sandwiches with nut butter or tahini and miso filling
- a carton full of mixed dried fruits
- a tub of mixed nuts, seeds and dried fruits
- plenty of bread, crackers, spreads and nut butters for those children who are old enough to do a bit themselves
- fresh popcorn
- dips such as Guacamole (p181), Hummus (p203), Tahini Dip (p347) and Rupiza (p324) served with toast or crackers
- vegetable and tofu kebabs
- tempeh or bean burgers (see Akara Kosai, p316)
- pancakes (see Buckwheat Pancakes, p327)
- tea breads such as banana bread and coconut bread
- milkshakes – make them fun, fancy, colourful and (secretly) nutritious
- fresh fruit or vegetable juices – with special glasses and straws or anything to increase their appeal.

THE TICTAC FORMULA

No matter how healthy and well planned your child's diet is, they have to want to eat it. To help you present them with irresistible meals, I have devised the TICTAC formula.

- **T**aste: make it aromatic with strong, not bland flavours.

- **I**nterest: present a pleasing array of foods on the plate.
- **C**olour: make sure colours complement one another.
- **T**exture: make it the texture they like (chopped, puréed).
- **A**tmosphere: ensure a calm, happy eating place.
- **C**ontentment: give plenty or more than plenty and always include a 'treat' to keep them well in the comfort zone!

DON'T PANIC

Most children go through periods (sometimes it seems like eras!) of being 'fussy' and eating only one or two types of food. This can throw even the most stable parent into the panic zone and is precisely the time you need to stay your course. The most you can do is to keep offering the good stuff and wait until it is accepted again. In times such as these, try to:

- Ensure your child is taking in sufficient calories – if they get enough calories, they will keep growing. Do your best to make sure they are eating calorie-dense sandwiches, dried fruits or other snack foods which they enjoy. Do not create an atmosphere of tension and worry around food, even if that is what you are feeling. It may help to temporarily reduce the amount of fibre in their diet so they don't feel full; richer foods can then take the place of high-fibre foods.
- Be sneaky. Encourage and incorporate foods high in healthy fats, such as nut and seed butters, olives and olive spreads, or fatty foods such as avocados, Hummus (p203) or Tahini Dip (p347). Such foods are high in calories but also contain vitamins and minerals essential to good health. Subtle additions of tahini to milkshakes, cereals and puddings add valuable nutrients, as does molasses added to flapjacks, nutritional yeast added to dips, sandwiches and milkshakes, or all of these mixed into your homemade bread.

The idea of hidden extras might induce you to keep a store of foods that naturally supplement the diet. These include nutritional yeast flakes, molasses, seaweed powder (such as kelp), vitamin B12 liquid supplement or tablets (which you can crush) or any food which is fortified with essential nutrients (such as soya milk fortified with calcium or B12), all of which can be used sparingly but regularly to supplement the diet.

- Introduce completely new foods or dishes – not just

to your child, but to the whole family. This can be as simple as changing from straight spaghetti to little pasta bows or tricolore pasta; or it might involve serving burgers and nut roasts when you have never made them before. Declare your boredom with what you have been eating and see what ideas your child comes up with.

- Involve your child further in food preparation. It may start with spreading apple butter on toast but it can result in a young person who is entirely competent in the kitchen. Ask them to set the table or lay a cloth for a picnic on the sitting room floor; another fun way of getting them interested in eating again is to have a 'backwards meal' with the pudding first and the starter last. Whatever you do, try to keep the happiness in food and eating.

- Finally, let them be. When all else fails, leave them alone. When they are really hungry, they will eat. The most you can do is your very best!

Vexatious Veggy-Mites – How To Get Children To Eat Their Greens

Here's a paradox: most young children won't willingly eat meat (especially when they know what it comes from). On the other hand, most children aren't particularly keen to eat their vegetables, either.

Every parent knows how important it is to instil good eating habits in their children; and most parents know just how difficult that can be. Patterns set in childhood usually stay with us for life: a fact well recognized by all the sweet manufacturers in their advertising. So how do you go about getting your children to eat their greens, and junk the junk food? The answer is one word: psychology. Here, parents who have struggled with this problem reveal the techniques that worked successfully for them – and they'll work for you, too.

PUT YOUR FOOT DOWN!

'We have a phrase around our house,' says Abigail, a mother of two spirited girls. ' "*I am not a short-order cook!*" From the time the children were little, I have always served healthy meals which included plenty of greens and grains. I do *not* buy junk food, nor even keep it in the house. The rule is, you eat what is being

served or you are on your own. Perhaps I was just lucky, but both of my daughters now eat their vegetables. My advice is, start 'em young, with their first solid food. They will stray occasionally, but I think they will eventually stick to the healthy path.'

That's the rule in writer Gillian's household, too. 'At my house,' she says, 'if they want junk food, they have to want it badly enough to buy it with their own money! And that goes for visiting mothers-in-law, too!'

REWARDS FOR HEALTH

'This is what happens in my house,' says Mary, a part-time computer programmer from London. 'My children, aged six and nine, were diagnosed (first by me) with food allergies this past year. Straight away, I put them on a vegan and additive-free diet, and that's helped a lot. Neither of them now wants to eat junk food again, because it made them feel so bad. However, my nine-year-old has had a certain amount of trouble, because other children are always trying to give her food to be 'nice'. Also, food is constantly used in school as rewards or a part of celebrations. To counter this, I have stocked her teacher's cupboard with acceptable treats and snacks. She has been extremely successful academically and I am constantly trying to reinforce the idea that her mind works well because her body works well; if you use good petrol, your engine works better.

'One of the rewards that they have seen is that they almost never get sick – remarkable for kids who used to have chronic ear and respiratory infections. When I realized that children sometimes like to get ill to stay home for special attention with mum or dad, I started to give them an incentive to stay well. A healthy month – without any sickness – means a trip to Toys R'Us or a special movie – it's their choice. The only way they can stay healthy is to eat properly, and they know it.

'They eat their greens because they are there. I cook them and they eat them – this started right from the beginning. They always had to eat *at least* one bite. Fortunately or unfortunately for my kids, their parents are very stubborn! They love vegetables now, and there are very few they won't eat. But I do feel that you need constantly to provide good food choices – they are free to eat almost anything they want at any time at home largely because we rarely have a "bad choice" available. When we eat out it must be at a place with plentiful vegetables, not a place that only serves fried matter in a basket. We *never* go to fast food restaurants at all and they don't bother to ask me to go.'

TIMING IS EVERYTHING

'We have two daughters, one a teenager, one in first year university,' says Martin, a veterinary surgeon. 'They both eat healthy diets, especially compared to their peers. I credit that to the early pre-school years when we restricted junk food "treats" to special occasions and outings. The real key we have found is to insist on a wholesome breakfast – a lot of problems arise if a child heads off to school without breakfast because throughout the day they are hungry and then more interested in the junk food that is available because it's quick and easy to satisfy hunger cravings with a bite of a chocolate bar. We never "banned" any junk food, rather we talked about it, and pointed out why too much was unhealthy.

'Another thing we've found (and other parents agree) is that there appears to be an age period from eight or nine to about fifteen or sixteen when it is *impossible* to introduce any new foods. New foods at that time are viewed with suspicion. So we recommend introducing a wide range of food early before that time period. I've heard it said that it is biologically based – independence is growing, and it is the body's way of being cautious because the individual is moving out beyond the parent's ability to supervise everything that is eaten.

'We never forced them to eat their greens directly, but sometimes we had to resort to some creative solutions. For example, we'd give them a little less of a vegetable than we knew they could easily eat, and when they showed signs of balking we would say, "You must be really enjoying that broccoli because you're taking so long to eat it, I've got a whole bunch more on the stove, wait a minute I'll go get some more for you." Guaranteed, the broccoli was gone almost immediately, and over eighteen years we never had to actually carry out the implied threat of adding more!'

MAKE YOUR HOME A JUNK-FREE ZONE

'Here are a few strategies that worked for me,' says Joan, a college professor. 'We home-educate our children, which automatically circumvents a lot of the negative peer pressure that most children have to deal with. Also, the most important factor we've found is to instil a love of animals right from the start.

This can be supplemented by appropriate reading and colouring books, visits to the zoo, nature walks, and so on. Another thing – if my children don't want to eat what I've prepared, I won't force them to; but I won't provide an alternative, either. They'll just have to wait until the next mealtime. And if you don't keep any junk in the house, it's pretty hard for the kids to eat it instead of the good stuff (this principle works well for the adults, too!). Another tip: when introducing solids, you should start with vegetables, not fruits, so that they acquire a taste for vegetables.'

SET A SHINING EXAMPLE

Says Paul, a lawyer, 'I've watched my step-sons (my wife's children from a previous marriage) make fairly drastic changes in their eating habits with no overt pressure to do so from us. I think this has happened because of two things Carol (my wife) and I do: first, we set an example by following a low-fat vegetarian eating style ourselves and secondly, at every opportunity, we debunk inaccurate and misleading advertising. For example, if a fast food restaurant has a spot on TV about their "healthy" chicken sandwich, Carol and/or I will laugh and say something like, "Yeah, and I bet they've got some Florida swampland for sale, too." We've educated ourselves about nutrition and we've managed to share what we've learned with Adam and Ross in low-pressure, non-coercive kinds of ways. They both still eat a small amount of chicken and fish, but Adam now eats lots more vegetables than he did a year ago. Once you know the truth that the advertising ignores or tries to hide (that a chicken sandwich with a high fat sauce really isn't healthy, or how much fat there is in ordinary cheese, for example), the advertising becomes much easier to resist.'

The importance of setting a good example is confirmed by Diane, a musician. 'I always try to make nutritious meals at home,' she says, 'and I won't keep junk food in the house. I had a firm rule when they were little: "Mom never ever buys sugary cereal, so don't even ask." Also, I *never* told a child he or she *had* to eat something. They grew up seeing adults eating salads, vegetable dishes and ethnic foods and enjoying them, and they never questioned that they were good to eat. When they wanted snacks, the choices were usually pretty nutritious. End result: three kids who are teenagers now (nineteen, seventeen, fourteen) and decided for themselves to become vegetarians (out of animal welfare/environmental concerns, led by the oldest, who did it herself at about age thirteen). They are all adventurous eaters as well – they'll try new things, willingly, and enjoy what they eat. All three kids now say they appreciate the fact that we didn't make an issue of their eating vegetables when they were younger, but simply served a good and interesting diet.'

A GIFT FOR LIFE – NURTURE GOOD JUDGEMENT

'For me,' says Colin, an artist, 'it's really a question of fostering good judgement in your child. It has to do with striking a balance. This has applications in other areas besides diet but diet is a good example. In the first place, we don't watch much TV. We have one small set which is not on display as the living room family altar. It's actually in my son's room, and he uses it mostly on Saturday mornings to watch cartoons. Of course, he gets a massive infusion of advertising at that time and I can tell you from experience, he is as attached to the ads as to the cartoons.

'My strategy in dealing with this and with all issues has been educational – we talk about it, and rationalize. Also, on a practical level, I think children can tolerate more fat than adults. Their little metabolisms seem to be whizzing along at twice the speed of light! So I let my son eat whole grain crisps, but I don't eat them. When he offers to share, I take the opportunity to expound. I tell him about heart disease and pimples and how he might have to change his eating habits at some point.

'It is sad to reveal that my son's diet used to be much better than it now is. For example, he won't touch broccoli anymore. However, he still loves salads and loves to make his own. Occasionally he will binge on raw carrots or celery and he likes fruits in moderation. He loves artichokes. On the whole, I try to give him as much freedom as I can in selecting his diet while limiting severely things like sweets, and explaining the reasons. I have found that putting forth an explanation is very important. It bypasses the power issue on a very important topic, and leaves the possibility of future experimentation open. And you know, this can actually happen! Last night he was seen nibbling at the raw broccoli that came with his Burger King salad (just between you and me!).'

The importance of developing an awareness in the child for good and bad foods is echoed by Kenneth, a designer. 'Assume the child is intelligent,' he says. 'Then educate her, specifically about television adver-tising, and the manipulation of consumers. This will help put the mass media in some perspective. The television set does have an off button, and it usually works. Also, remove temptation. If junk food simply isn't available in the house, that helps a great deal. Next avoid self-righteousness. Don't make a religion out of it. Then, when the child rejects its parents' values (and most of them do, at some stage) they won't give up on good eating practices as well. Try enlisting the child's help, too. Our daughter became extremely aware of the effect sugar had on her behaviour, and quickly became adept at reading labels to uncover hidden ingredients. Oh yes, finally – don't worry about it. Relax!'

Feeding Young Adults

We are about to come full circle: three chapters ago you were growing a baby. Now you are growing an adult who, you hope, will be healthy well into adulthood and perhaps one day healthy enough to grow a baby themselves. This aspect of nutrition is often overlooked. It often seems that once we get our children through weaning we place little importance on nourishing them through the remainder of their lives with us. Yet these years are crucial for laying the foundations for life-long health and patterns of illness. Certainly your child's needs and preferences will change over the years, but your commitment to their eating habits must not diminish yet. The guidance you give now can set them on a life-long path of healthy eating, can provide them with basic and robust good health, can sustain them in times of stress and debility, can help them to grow into fertile, healthy adults.

Young people in adolescence are usually very interested in food, an interest which you may help to focus by helping them acquire new skills and an awareness of the broader issues surrounding what they eat. Teenagers have special nutritional needs which you can very easily meet with a plant-based diet.

● This is a time of growth and physical and mental development, so your child needs calories. This is suddenly a difficult issue: on the one hand obesity amongst children and young people is on the increase but, on the other hand, more and more young people, especially girls, are becoming chronic dieters in a bid to fit in with glossy fashion images. If you haven't done so already, sit down and have a long chat with your son or daughter and make these points:

¶ Adolescence is a time of change and so their bodies will alter drastically during this time. This is essential to their development and should not be curbed or in any way minimized. If, in a year or two, they are unhappy with how they look they can then begin a fitness programme to help adjust their body shape. In the meantime, there is plenty that you can do to improve their self-image by helping them plan wardrobe and make-up.

Include plenty of calorie-dense foods in your child's diet and reassure them that, provided they eat a variety of whole, plant foods they will not become obese. In fact, they may naturally have the clear skin, shining eyes and glossy hair which their peers are so keen to accomplish.

- Protein is necessary for the growth and development your adolescent is going through. Later, in adulthood, protein intake may be reduced to a level which will maintain an adult body. Right now, your child is growing and needs regular servings of high-protein food.

- Vitamin and mineral-rich foods are crucial during this time as well. Think of all those bones, sometimes growing inches in a year! That is not to mention the development of extra nerve, muscle and skin tissue. And for young women, the level of calcium they include in their diet now will have an impact on the health of their bones and teeth during future pregnancies as well as in their post-menopausal years (see Osteoporosis, Part Four, p155). Teach your son or daughter how to juice their own favourite combination of vegetables so that they can 'dose up' with vitamins and minerals even when they don't feel like eating.

- Daughters beginning their monthly cycle will benefit from a basic understanding of how what they eat can affect how they feel during this time. Encourage them to prevent premenstrual stress by eating foods high in complex carbohydrates during the days prior to their periods, with the possible addition of an evening primrose supplement. Give her the recipes for iron-snacking (see Nourishing the New Mother, p30) to help her avoid the fatigue which can sometimes set in during or just after a period.

- Both sons and daughters will be intermittent victims of the hormones raging through their bodies. A good, plant-based diet along the lines you have established can help them through this time because the vegetarian and vegan diets tend to have a normalizing effect on the way the body functions.

This is not to say the hormones won't rage, just that your child will be nutritionally better equipped to deal with them.

- Sons in particular may be deeply engrossed in sporting activities at this age. The vegetarian or vegan diet in no way impairs their performance or the likelihood of them achieving excellence or fame in their chosen sport. In fact, many very accomplished and well known sports people eat vegetarian or vegan diets and most of them attribute their stamina to the wholesome quality of their diets.

Keep passing on the skills you have acquired during the years you have followed a plant-based diet so that your son or daughter can continue eating well when you are not with them. If you haven't done so already, teach them basic cooking techniques as well as how to purchase and prepare raw foods. Buy them a juicer when they move out and give cookbooks and chopping boards for birthday presents. Above all, make sure your child has understood that what they eat becomes who they are.

Self-Defence For Vegetarians – Nifty Answers To Those Niggling Questions

Don't ask me why, but there's a range of topics which reliably crop up time and again whenever non-vegetarians get into conversation with vegetarians and vegans. Here are some of the most frequent ones, together with the answers I usually supply. Hopefully, they'll furnish you with enough information to construct your own responses. Of course, if you ever get fed up answering questions (and believe me, vegetarianism is endlessly interesting to those who aren't) then you could offer to lend this book instead!

'Hitler was a vegetarian, therefore vegetarians aren't really compassionate at all!'

Usually more of a triumphant debating-point than a genuine question, the subject of Hitler crops up with surprising regularity. Here's how a certain Robert Milch put it, in a testy letter to the *New York Times*: 'Adolf Hitler was a vegetarian all his life and wrote extensively on the subject. If vegetarians choose not to eat meat, they ought to acknowledge that it is a personal quirk and not preach at the rest of us so self-righteously.'[3]

Sometimes, the spectre of Hitler is evoked in other ways. Most vegetarians are also opposed to vivisection, and vivisectors have on occasion found it useful to exhume the old Nazi to use as a weapon against those who oppose their cruel trade. In a recent British television programme, one of those trendy, jean-wearing scientists who the media find so irresistible put forward an argument which vegetarians everywhere will find deeply offensive.[4] According to the vivisector, vegetarian Hitler banned animal experiments because he preferred to use Jews, Gypsies and other 'defectives' instead. This, apparently, is supposed to prove that vegetarians and others opposed to vivisection are racist Nazis.

In the anti-Nazi magazine *Searchlight*, writer Colin Meider took him severely to task for such abhorrent and incoherent reasoning: 'It is not only profoundly unscientific, it is especially rich coming from a man whose own profession devised and carried out the programme of human mutilation and slaughter. It was scientists and doctors who executed the Nazi programme of Racial Hygiene whereby all "inferior" humans were at first sterilized and then exterminated . . . In 1932 the German Medical Association was already discussing eugenics in the service of the state. No other profession supported it on such as scale.'[5]

But was Hitler a vegetarian? And in any case, does it matter? It certainly seems to matter to our critics, who seem to believe that the entire vegetarian ethos can be demolished on the basis of it. 'The bigger the lie, the easier it is to deceive people,' said Hitler's head of propaganda Josef Goebbels. He might well have been talking about the modern-day myth of Hitler's vegetarianism. Historian and author of *Judaism and Vegetarianism* Richard H. Schwartz makes this reply 'Because Hitler suffered from excessive flatulence he occasionally went on a vegetarian diet. But his primary diet included meat. In *The Life and Death of Adolf Hitler*, Robert Payne mentions Hitler's fondness for Bavarian sausages. Other biographers, including Albert Speer, point out that he also ate ham, liver and game. Hitler banned vegetarian organizations in Germany and the occupied countries, though vegetarian diets would have helped solve Germany's World War II food shortage.'[6]

This hardly sounds like a card-carrying member of the Vegetarian Society. Adds Jewish historian Ralph Meyer, writing in *The Jewish Vegetarian*: 'How can someone be a strict vegetarian and take injections of pulverized bull testicles, as Hitler did? How can someone be a strict vegetarian who ordered his enemies "hung up like carcasses of meat", who urged the Hitler youth to become "like beasts of prey", who said "it is not by the principles of humanity that man lives, but by brute force . . . close your eyes to pity . . . act brutally". Surely a person who worshipped brutality and literally shrieked for blood is the antithesis of a vegetarian.'[7]

Ultimately, I don't believe we have to brawl over the amount of sausage that Hitler ate, nor his prodigious appetite for stuffed squab (baby pigeon), which was, according to chef Dione Lucas 'a great favourite with Mr. Hitler' (and she should know – she cooked it for him).[8] Let us remind ourselves of the fundamental philosophy of Nazism, in these chilling words spawned by Oswald Spengler: '*The beast of prey is the highest form of active life. It represents a mode of living which requires the extreme degree of the necessity of fighting, conquering, annihilating, self-assertion. The human race ranks highly because it belongs to the class of beasts of prey. Therefore we find in man the tactics of life proper to a bold, cunning beast of prey. He lives engaged in aggression, killing, annihilation. He wants to be master in as much as he exists.*'[9]

Can you think of more appalling words? Words which speak of life without love, without compassion, without joy. Words which will serve to excuse any atrocity, any barbarism. Now, can you think of anything more fundamentally opposed to the vegetarian philosophy of respect, compassion and love? I rest my case.

'How can vegetarianism be justified philosophically?'

All right, you asked, so I'll tell you. Ethical theory can be divided into two main schools of thought – one called consequentialist, the other nonconsequentialist. These wordy labels disguise (as is often the case with philosophy) ideas which are basically extremely simple. Consequentialist ethics are based on the idea that an action's 'rightness' or 'wrongness' depends on the consequences of the action. For example, if you steal your friend's watch, thus causing him to miss an important meeting, then the act of stealing would be wrong, because the consequences of your action were detrimental to your friend. However, if your friend never missed his watch, then it might be argued that what you did was not wrong, because no negative consequences ensued; indeed the outcome was positive for you.

Nonconsequentialist theories take a different point of view. They hold that, irrespective of consequences, an action may be either morally right or morally wrong in itself. Stealing, for example, would generally be considered to be a bad thing according to many nonconsequentialist schools of thought, even if there was no harm as a result. Now, what is most interesting is this: within both major ethical theories, there are highly-developed arguments in favour of vegetarianism – it is not the exclusive property of one or other major (and mutually antagonistic) school. Let me summarize for you.

Within consequentialist ethics, we find the doctrine known as utilitarianism, which had its origins among the British philosophers of the 17th and 18th centuries. Again, it is a straightforward enough idea, simply expressed in the words of 18th-century philosopher Jeremy Bentham, who believed that an individual should seek 'the greatest happiness of the greatest number'. Utilitarian philosophers therefore judge an action's rightness or wrongness by its overall impact on the balance-sheet of happiness – if it creates more happiness than suffering, the action is good, but if it creates more pain than pleasure, then it is wrong. Consequently, utilitarians advocate vegetarianism for the very good reason that the trivial amount of pleasure created by eating meat is more than offset by the huge amount of suffering inflicted on the animal population. Within the utilitarian school, Peter Singer (who wrote the classic book *Animal Liberation*) is one of its chief modern advocates. Note that utilitarians rarely talk in terms of absolute 'animal rights' or even 'human rights'. Singer, for example, could foresee certain very restricted circumstances in which even vivisection would be right. As he says, 'If one or even a dozen animals had to suffer experiments in order to save thousands, I would think it right and in accordance with equal consideration of interests that they should do so. This, at any rate, is the answer a utilitarian must give.'[10] The attraction of utilitarianism lies in its coherent and flexible basis; it sees morality as a human creation with the aim of increasing the amount of happiness in the world.

Nonconsequentialist ethics, on the other hand, include those philosophers who argue in favour of animal (and human) rights. For nonconsequentialists, rights are absolute things – they are not subject to a cost–benefit analysis. For example, according to some people, dropping the atomic bomb on Hiroshima shortened the duration of World War II, and therefore saved lives on both sides. Some utilitarians might argue that this was on balance a good thing, but those philosophers representing the rights viewpoint would disagree, saying that killing is always wrong, whatever the circumstances or putative benefits. Those nonconsequentialist philosophers who advocate vegetarianism (such as Tom Regan, who wrote *The Case For Animal Rights*) do so on the principle that the basic moral right possessed by all beings is the right to *respectful treatment*. They also hold that animals, like humans, have inherent value in themselves – they have the potential to lead fulfilling lives, and should be allowed to do so. Where the inherent value of an animal is debased – as, for example, in the case of the degrading conditions in which battery chickens are kept – then their rights have also been violated. Similarly, if an animal can be either treated fairly or unfairly, their basic right to justice dictates that we must treat them fairly. The attraction of the philosophy of animal rights is that it provides clear and unambiguous guidelines about the way we should treat animals; and anyone who accepts the philosophy of human rights must, logically, also accept the validity of animal rights. If they do not, then they are acting as a speciesist, blood relation to the racist and the sexist.

Plainly, these are powerful ideas. The flux line where these two major systems of ethics engage each other has provided some of the most intense and thought-provoking discussions – and produced some of the most original work – in the field of ethical theory in the past few decades. This is not the place to develop these ideas any further, but whenever I have been to talk and debate at the invitation of philosophy departments of universities and colleges, I have been forcibly struck by the excitement of new ideas in gestation; ideas which will, perhaps, determine the emerging morality of the 21st century. Sometimes, people remark that 'humans come before animals', and imply that time spent considering issues such as these is wasted, since they are of academic interest only. This line of reasoning is completely fatuous. What is needed by humankind, now more desperately than ever before, is a new kind of ethic; a universally-appropriate morality which, in the words of Albert Einstein, will 'widen our circle of compassion to embrace all living creatures and the whole of nature'. A century before Einstein, Abraham Lincoln had predicted the fundamental importance of

wouldn't be tempted to include them in every meal? It is important to remember, however, that beans can either look like beans or they can be transformed into one of the many delicious and nutritious bean products which supply the food value but not the same beany experience. Among these are soya milk, tofu, TVP, tempeh, soya yoghurt and ice cream, marinated tofu and soya cheeses of every description.

Second. It is true, beans can be a musical fruit if you don't follow the three golden rules of cooking them:

- Let them soak overnight. Do it last thing before turning in, ands you'll be able to use them any time in the next day or so. Isn't this a terrible hassle? Not really, it's the very small price we pay for what is practically the ultimate in convenience foods – what other foodstuff would be perfectly happy to wait around your kitchen for months on end, and still be in great nutritional shape when you eventually decide to use it? Certainly not meat!
- Don't cook them in the soaking water, and never cook them without rinsing them.
- People often under-cook beans (help-yourself salad bars are particularly bad). Here's the secret: do the tongue-test. Put one bean in your mouth, and try to squash it against the roof of your mouth using normal pressure from your tongue. If you can't squash it, it isn't well-cooked. Anything less may create gas and digestive discomfort.

Third. Cooking beans in an open pot can indeed take hours, which is why I'd suggest you should use a pressure cooker. You can cook most beans in a pressure cooker in less than thirty minutes. Buy a stainless steel one.

And while we're on the subject of pressure cookers, here are some other utensils I find very useful:

- cast-iron pans (or enamel, but not aluminium or copper)
- wok (for really fast stir-frying of vegetables using minimal oil, or with care can even be used without any oil if you watch over it and sprinkle water on when necessary)
- garlic press (releases the flavour better than chopping)
- a food processor (allows you to make delicious raw salads in a flash, including tasty vegetables such as beetroot, turnip, swede, carrot, etc.)
- steamer (never boil the nutrients in vegetables away again!)
- mortar and pestle (for grinding spices).

'But vegetarian food is more expensive, isn't it?'

No, it's cheaper! In order to understand why this should be so, you have to grasp the underlying economics of the meat industry. A meat animal is treated as nothing more or less than a machine – a machine that the industry uses to convert vegetable protein into animal protein. As a machine, it is deplorably inefficient. For every kilo of meat protein that is produced as a steak, twenty kilos of vegetable protein have to be put into it (twenty kilos that could have gone to feed human mouths). It is a disgraceful, obscene waste of food. The chart on page 44 shows you just what inefficient machines food animals are.[15]

As you can see, beef animals are extraordinarily wasteful converters of vegetable protein, only managing to convert a miserly 6 per cent of it into meat protein. This is the reason behind the desperate use of chemicals (and genetic engineering techniques) in animal rearing – it's an attempt by the farmer to improve on a process that is notoriously inefficient.

So when someone buys a steak, they're actually paying not just for the meat, but also for a vast amount of wasted vegetable food that the cow has consumed and excreted. Which means that consumers are actually paying to create all the pollution problems associated with that excreta, too. For example, here's just one problem that most people don't know about: the global cattle population emits 100 million tonnes of methane gas each year.[16] Concentrations of methane in the air have been rising at 1 per cent per year since 1950, four times the rate of increase of carbon dioxide. Scientists fear that soon, methane may be the prime greenhouse gas responsible for global warming.

But let's return to the faulty economics of meat production, because this is where the story gets very intriguing. Although the meat industry constantly stresses the 'naturalness' of meat, they go to great pains to conceal the fact that they themselves are violating one of the most fundamental laws of nature – the law that explains why large, fierce animals are rare, and why smaller, vegetable-feeding ones are much more numerous.

In the wild, food chains exist whereby one level of the chain consumes something on a lower level of the chain. Close to the bottom of the chain, there are lots and lots of animals feeding on a profusion of plant foods (for example, rabbits feeding on grass). At the top of the chain, there are just a few carnivorous

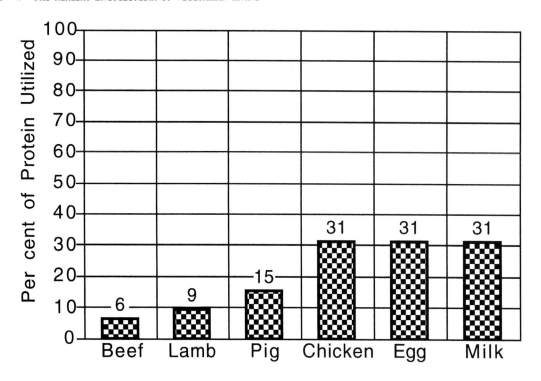

HOW MUCH VEGETABLE PROTEIN ANIMALS CONVERT TO MEAT PROTEIN

animals who feed on the lower levels (foxes feeding on rabbits). Thus, the foxes are indirectly eating the lowest level of the chain – grass. If things get out of balance, and the fox population suddenly expands, there won't be enough rabbits to go round. So the foxes starve until things get back into balance again.

Therefore, if humans were designed to be predominantly carnivores, there would be relatively few of us, and we would live at a considerable distance from each other. That way, there would be enough flesh to go round. Now, does that sound like the way most of us live today?

Of course it doesn't. But that's just where the meat industry tries to buck nature. The more meat they sell us, the more cattle they have to breed, feed and bleed. There are now 1.3 billion cattle on the face of our planet, consuming its food resources at a truly incredible rate.[17] As biologist Dr David Hamilton Wright of Emory University in Atlanta, Georgia observes, 'An alien ecologist observing Earth might conclude that cattle is the dominant animal species in our biosphere.' As long as we continue to eat at such a perilously high position in the food chain, there will be more and

more cattle, creating bigger and bigger problems for our ravaged planet.

'In all of the ongoing public debates around the global environmental crisis,' says President of the Greenhouse Crisis Foundation Jeremy Rifkin, 'a curious silence surrounds the issue of cattle, one of the most destructive environmental threats of the modern era. Cattle grazing is a primary cause of the spreading desertification process that is now enveloping whole continents. Cattle ranching is responsible for the destruction of much of the earth's remaining tropical rainforests. Cattle raising is indirectly responsible for the rapid depletion of fresh water on the planet, with some reservoirs and aquifers now at their lowest levels since the end of the last Ice Age. Cattle are a chief source of organic pollution; cow dung is poisoning the freshwater lakes, rivers, and the streams of the world. Growing herds of cattle are exerting unprecedented pressure on the carrying capacity of natural ecosystems, edging entire species of wildlife to the brink of extinction. Cattle are a growing source of global warming, and their increasing numbers now threaten the very chemical dynamics of the biosphere. Most Americans and

Europeans are simply unaware of the devastation wrought by the world's cattle. Now numbering over a billion, these ancient ungulates roam the countryside, trampling the soil, stripping the vegetation bare, laying waste to large tracts of the earth's biomass.'[18]

Unfortunately, most of us don't realize that the meat industry is playing this grotesque game with nature. But it is, and consumers are paying for it. I hope you can now see that the original question raises some extremely profound yet little-known issues.

And now, to answer that question directly: the cheapest way to eat vegetarian food is to buy in season fruits and vegetables and use them, with a few grains and pulses, to design your menu. This approach can allow you to provide truly hearty meals for two to four persons every day of the week for something like £1 per meal. Of course, they're nothing fancy nor are they five courses, but such meals are wholesome, tasty, nutritious and, of course, cheap.

Next cheapest is to buy the same fruit and veg but to add a few special things from the supermarket (tofu, soya milk, pastas, nuts, VegeBurger mix, etc.) and the 'ethnic' grocers (Asian, Chinese, Jamaican) to liven up your cooking repertoire. A revolution has been taking place over the past few years that has meant foods such as herbs, spices, soya and meat-replacement products are stocked in most of the major supermarket chains, and at reasonable prices.

'Plants scream when you dig them up – that's just as cruel as eating meat.'

This crackpot idea is trotted out by meat-eaters with guilty consciences. Unlike animals, plants don't have a central nervous system, and they can't feel pain. As far as I can discover, the myth of the screaming carrot first arose when founder of Scientology, L. Ron Hubbard, came to England.

'It was not long before television and Fleet Street reporters were beating a path to Saint Hill Manor [his chosen home near East Grinstead, Sussex] demanding to interview Hubbard about his novel theories,' writes Russell Miller in his biography of Hubbard.[19] 'Always pleased to help the gentlemen of the press, he was memorably photographed looking compassionately at a tomato jabbed by probes attached to an E-meter – a picture that eventually found its way into *Newsweek* magazine, causing a good deal of harmless merriment at his expense. Alan Whicker, a well-known British television interviewer, did his best to make Hubbard look like a crank, but Hubbard contrived to come

across as a rather likeable and confident personality. When Whicker moved in for the kill, sarcastically inquiring if rose pruning should be stopped lest it cause pain and anxiety, Hubbard neatly side-stepped the question and drew a parallel with an essential life-preserving medical operation on a human being. He might have wacky ideas, Whicker discovered, but he was certainly no fool.'

All the scientific evidence is against Mr Hubbard. 'Plants simply have no evolutionary need to feel pain,' notes psychologist Dr Ted Altar. 'Animals, being mobile, would benefit from the ability to sense pain; plants would not. Nature does not create gratuitously such complex capacities as that of feeling pain unless there should be some benefit for the organism's survival.'[20] But let us suppose, for a moment, that Mr Hubbard is right, and that even without having the biological equipment needed to experience pain (the central nervous system) plants somehow can do so. In that case, we would have a duty to cause the least amount of suffering possible. As you have already seen, meat-eaters indirectly consume *far more plants* than vegetarians, because the animals which they eat themselves consume vast amounts of plant food (most of which is wasted). Meat-eaters therefore would cause more suffering than vegetarians. Either way, therefore, vegetarianism comes out on top.

'Is it OK to wear leather?'

Only if you think it's OK to eat meat. Bear in mind that 25–50 per cent of slaughterhouse profits come from the leather industry.[21] Leather alternatives are increasingly available in the shops, and the more you ask for them, the more there will be.

Non-leather shoes can be made from plastic compounds, and are entirely indistinguishable from the animal-hide varieties (although you can quickly find them in shops and stores, because they are always far cheaper to buy). Alternatively, canvas or nylon can be used to produce sports shoes and trainers – many of the big brand names in this sector use no leather. Leather alternatives are increasingly available in department stores and national chains of shoe shops, although you may have to be persistent in your questioning of sales people – many of them don't seem to be very familiar with the stock they carry, and at first may tell you that they don't sell non-leather shoes when in fact they do. If you encounter this problem, try phrasing your request slightly differently: 'man-made uppers and man-made soles' may elicit a more positive response. In the UK the national chain Freeman Hardy Willis usually has a good selection; in North America, non-leather shoes can often be found at Payless Shoe Source, Fayva, Kinney, K-Mart, Sears, J.C. Penny, Pic 'N Pay, Woolworth, Thom McAnn, Wal-Mart, Marshalls, and other inexpensive chains.

Are non-leather shoes harmful to the environment, because they use plastics which are derived from petrochemicals? While this may be true to some extent, it should be remembered that the production of leather is immensely more destructive. Livestock production is responsible for many severe environmental problems, as outlined on page 44. Comments vegetarian ecologist Keith Akers: 'Hardly a single environmental problem in the world today is unrelated to meat consumption. Water pollution, soil erosion, energy shortages, the destruction of forests – all of these problems and others are part of the environmental cost of meat in our diet.'[22] Akers points out that Western agriculture is very fuel-inefficient, using more fossil fuel energy than it produces in food energy. 'The energy input to the food system now account for 16.5 per cent of the total energy budget', he calculates. Plant food agriculture is, of course, far less energy-intensive than livestock agriculture. Adds Jeremy Rifkin, founder of the 'Beyond Beef' campaign: 'It now takes the equivalent of a gallon of gasoline to produce a pound of grain-fed beef in the United States. To sustain the yearly beef requirements of an average family of four requires the use of more than 260 gallons of fossil fuel.'[23] One of the most surprising, but hidden, costs of livestock farming is its extravagant use of water. '80 per cent of the total water requirements for the average daily food intake in the United States goes for animal products', says Akers. 'A pound of wheat contains more calories than a pound of beef; but the beef requires from 40 to 50 times more water'.

All these hidden factors begin to make a humble pair of plastic shoes look like the ultimate in environmentally-friendly footwear. But we haven't finished adding up the hidden costs of a pair of shoes. 'Turning animal hides into leather is an energy intensive and polluting practice', says vegetarian researcher Sally Clinton.[24] 'It involves soaking (beamhouse), tanning, dyeing, drying, and finishing. Most leather produced in the United States is chrome tanned [also true in the EC]. The effluent that must be treated is primarily related to the beamhouse and tanning operations. The most difficult to treat is effluent from the tanning process. All wastes containing chromium are considered hazardous by the U.S. Environmental Protection Agency [this is not the case in the EC]. Many other substances involved in the processing of leather are associated with environmental and health risks. In terms of disposal, one would think that leather products would be biodegradable, but the primary function for a tanning agent is to stabilise the collagen or protein fibres so that they are no longer biodegradable.'

The conclusion? It is wrong to automatically assume – as many people do – that 'plastic is bad, leather is good'. And when you take the ethical dimension into account, there really is no doubt about it; after all, leather was once someone else's skin – just as fur once was. Of all leather-made products, shoes are probably the most troublesome item for ethical vegetarians and vegans to replace: other items, such as belts, handbags, underwear, jackets and briefcases are widely available in non-leather varieties. Here are some of the main mail order and catalogue sources of non-leather goods; national vegetarian and vegan organizations (see following section) usually maintain current lists of smaller suppliers, and their magazines generally keep members up to date with new product news.

Wild Things
7 Upper Goat Lane
Norwich
NR2 1EW
UK
Tel. 0603-765595

The Green Catalogue
Freepost SN 20091
Chippenham
Wilts
SN13 6QZ
UK
Tel. 0934-732469

Vegetarian Shoes
12 Gardner St
Brighton
BN1 1UP
UK

Heartland Products Ltd.
Box 218
Dakota City
IA 50529
USA
Tel (515) 332-3087

Aesop Unlimited
P.O. Box 315, N.
Cambridge
MA 02140
USA
Tel (617) 628-8030

In addition, 'The Compassionate Shopper' regularly lists companies that sell non-leather shoes. Contact:

Beauty Without Cruelty
175 W. 12th St., #16G
New York
NY 10011-8275
USA

'Should I Buy Vegetarian Cheeses?'

Many cheeses contain rennet, an enzyme taken from the stomachs of slaughtered calves, a small amount of which helps to coagulate milk into cheese. Not all cheese includes animal rennet but if you want to be sure, buy a specially-marked cheese from a healthfood shop, or a growing number of supermarkets. Vegetable rennet is sometimes called rennin to distinguish it from the animal-derived type. In my view, the rennet controversy tends to be exaggerated by some vegetarians. If you're buying dairy produce, you indirectly support the meat industry in any case. There's a growing range of completely animal-free cheeses on the market (try your local healthfood shop) which I would urge you to investigate. Personally, I ate a vegetarian diet for many years before I went vegan, and I found that dairy produce simply became less and less important in my diet, until one day I realized that I'd made the transition.

'Can My Cat Or Dog Go Vegetarian?'

Yes, both animals can be fed a vegetarian diet. Cats need food fortified with an amino acid called taurine, found in the muscles of animals. Synthetic taurine has been developed, and vegetarian cats should be fed it as a supplement. For information on these products, contact:

Happidog Petfoods (dog food)
Bridgend
Brownhill Lane
Preston
PR4 4SJ

Wafcol (dog food)
The Nutrition Bakery
Haigh Avenue
Stockport
SK4 1NU

The Watermill (dog food)
Little Salkeld
Penrith
CA10 1NN

Katz Go Vegan (cat food)
P.O. Box 161
7 Battle Road
St. Leonards-on-Sea
East Sussex
TN37 7AA
('Vegekit' for kittens; 'Vegecat' for cats over 10 months old)

Wow-Bow Distributors (cat and dog food)
309 Burr Rd
East Northport
NY 11731
USA
Tel. (516) 449 8572

Natural Life Pet Products, Inc (dog food)
Frontenac
Kansas 66762
USA

'Speaking of dogs, what are hot dogs made from?'

Many people are rather nauseated when they find out what goes into burgers, but hot dogs have, so far, escaped much scrutiny. That is about to change! A good friend of mine had the opportunity to tour a factory where these especially loathsome comestibles were made, and in the process somehow seemed to acquire a copy of the recipe. It passed to me in due course, and I reprint it here, with no further comment, since nothing I could say could be more revolting than the ingredients themselves: fish; chicken feet; chicken carcasses; chicken heads; lungs and trachea; udder; liver; fresh blood; wheat flour; salt; PP530; water; phosphate; carageenan.

'If everyone went vegetarian, what would happen to all the farm animals?'

The simple answer is this: if everyone was vegetarian, fewer and fewer food animals would be born.

Eventually, we would have just a few cows, a few pigs, and so on – all valued as beautiful creatures in their own right, rather than as lumps of flesh to be consumed. More rare breeds would flourish, instead of the few sickly species bred at present. Another aspect which is rarely considered is the negative environmental impact of meat-rearing. In Britain, fewer farm animals would mean more green and pleasant land – and more trees. In America, it would mean more diversity of species. 'Most of the public lands in the West, and especially the Southwest, are what you might call "cow burnt," says conservationist and author Edward Abbey. 'Almost anywhere and everywhere you go in the American West you find hordes of cows. They are a pest and a plague. They pollute our springs and streams and rivers. They infest our canyons, valleys, meadows, and forests. They graze off the native bluestems and grama and bunch grasses, leaving behind jungles of prickly pear. They trample down the native shrubs and cacti. Even when the cattle are not physically present, you see the dung and the flies and the mud and the dust and the general destruction. If you don't see it, you'll smell it. The whole American West stinks of cattle.'[25]

'My doctor's told me I should eat meat – what should I do?'

Give him (it *is* a man, isn't it?) this book.

Vegetarian and Vegan Groups Around The World

The following national groups and organizations will be able to provide you with a range of resources and information about the meat-free way of living. Many of them organize regular meetings and other events to which you will be welcome, and many of them can suggest good restaurants for you to try when travelling to a foreign city or country. Only national organizations have been included in this listing – there will almost certainly be smaller regional groups or societies which can offer the traveller useful tips and advice – ask the national societies to help you make contact with them. Most of these groups are voluntary organizations, so please make a donation, or consider joining them, when using their facilities. Please note that addresses and phone numbers can change quite quickly.

AUSTRALIA

Vegan Society of Australia
PO Box 85
Seaford
VIC 3198
Tel. (03) 786-6192

Australian Vegetarian Society
PO Box 65
Paddington
NSW 2021
Tel. (02) 698-4339

BELGIUM

International Society Of French Speaking Vegetarians
25 Avenue Chazal
B 1030
Brussels

Vegans International – Belgium
Fr Rooseveltlaan 223
9000 Ghent

Vegetariersbond Vzw
Koewacht 16a
9190 Stekene
Oost-Vlaanderen

BRAZIL

Sociedade Vegetariana Do Brasil (Brazilian Vegetarian Society)
Rua: Riachuelo No 220 apt. 406
Centro
Rio de Janeiro
Cep 20230

CANADA

Toronto Vegetarian Association
736 Bathurst Street
Toronto
Ontario
M5S 2R4

Vancouver Island Vegetarian Association
9675 Fifth Street
Sidney
British Columbia
V8L 2W9

Vegetarian Lifestyle International
1500–1176 West Georgia Street
Vancouver
British Columbia
V6E 4A2

CZECH REPUBLIC

Vegetarian And World
03601 Martin
Fucikova 11

ESTONIA

Estonian Vegetarian Society
Kauba T.
30 a
Tallin
200013

FRANCE

Alliance Vegetarienne
Alvignac
46500
Gramat
Tel. 33 85 33 63 33

French Vegan Society
c/o Godiwalla
75 rue Mouffetard
75005 Paris
Tel. 1 43 31 82 41

Societé Veganiste De France
12 Allee Jacques Becker
Aubervilliers 93300
Tel. 33 1 48 33 63 41

GERMANY

Vegetarier-Bund Deutschlands E V
Blumenenstrasse 3
D-3000
Hannover
Tel. 49 511 42 46 47

HONG KONG

Environmental Protection Vegetarian & Vegan (HK)
Society
GPO Box 11634
Hong Kong
Tel. 852 775 2798
Fax. 852 775 2756

Hong Kong Vegetarian Society
c/o 34 Belcher's Street
4/F Block 11
Kennedy Town

Vegetarians And Vegans In Hong Kong
Flat 1 11/F
3 Ede Road
Kowloon Tong
Tel. 852 338 8902

INDIA

Indian Vegetarian Congress
2nd Floor 17 Damodaran Street
Gopalapuram
Madras 600 086
Tel 91 44 473648

ITALY

Associazione Culturale Vegetariana
Via Aristolele 67
(MM Precotto)
20128 Milano

Associazione Vegetariana Italiana
Via XXV Aprile 41
20026
Novate Milanese

JAMAICA

Vegetarian Society Of Jamaica Ltd
c/o 36 Calypso Crescent
Caribbean Terrace
Kingston 17

JAPAN

Japanese Midori Vegetarian Society
6-34-24 Higashioizumi
Nerima-ku
Tokyo
Tel. 81 3 3922 0724
Fax. 81 3 3922 7400

Japanese Vegetarian Union
c/o Japan Medical Centre of Health Care
718 Dalsen
410-21 Nirayama
Tel. 81 5597 8 5849

LATVIA

Vegetarian Society Of Latvia
Stabu Street 18 dz 14
Riga
226001

LITHUANIA

Vegetarian And Vegan Society Of Lithuania
Antakalnio 67-17
Vilnus
232040

MAURITIUS

Vegetarian Society Of Mauritius
c/o Hare Krishna Land
Pont Fer Pheonix PO Box 108
Quatre-Bornes
Tel. 222 6965804

NETHERLANDS

De Nederlandse Vegetariersbond
Larensweg 26
1221 CM
Hilversum
Tel. 31 35 834796

European Vegetarian Union
Larensweg 26
1221 CM
Hilversum
Tel. 31 35 834796

Veganisten Organistatie Vereniging (Dutch
Vegan Society)
Postbus 1087
6801 BB Arnhem
Tel. 31 85 420746

NEW ZEALAND

New Zealand Vegetarian Society
PO Box 77034
Auckland 3

NIGERIA

Nigerian Vegetarian Education Network
PO Box 489
Orlu
Imo State

Nigerian Vegetarian Society
PO Box 3893
Oshodi
Lagos

PORTUGAL

Vegetarian Club Of Lisbon
Sakoni Centro Comercial Mouraria
Loja 230.A.236 largo Martim Moniz
1100 Lisbon
Tel. 351 1 875652

REPUBLIC OF IRELAND

Vegetarian Guide To Ireland
East Clare Community Co-op
Main Street
Scariff
County Clare

Vegetarian Society Of Ireland
PO Box 3010
Dublin 4

RUSSIA

St Petersburg Vegetarian Society
Post Box 161
193315
St Petersburg
Tel. 7 0812 266 1449

Tolstoyan Moscow Society
Molostovykh Street Building 11
Korpus 2 Appartment 160
111555
Moscow

Vegetarian Society Of Russia
39-3-23 Volsky Bulvar
109462
Moscow

SOUTH AFRICA

Vegans In South Africa
Box 36242
Glosderry
7702
South Africa

SWEDEN

Svenska Vegetariska Foreningen
Radmansgatan 88
11329
Stockholm
Tel. 46 8 32 49 29

Swedish Vegan And Vegetarian Society
Klovervagen 6
S-64700
Mariefred
Tel. 46 159 12467

Swedish Vegan Society
c/o Troeng
Klovervagen 6
S-150 30
Mariefred

TANZANIA

Vegetarian Association
PO Box 71439
Dar es Salaam

UNITED KINGDOM

The Vegetarian Society of the United Kingdom
Parkdale
Dunham Road
Altringham
Cheshire WA14 4QG
Tel. (061) 928-0793

The Vegan Society
7 Battle Road,
St Leonards-on-Sea
East Sussex TN37 7AA
Tel. (0424) 427393

Jewish Vegetarian Society
855 Finchley Rd
London NW11 8LX
Tel. (081) 458 2441 or (081) 455 0692

UNITED STATES

American Vegan Society (AVS)
PO Box H
Malaga
NJ 08328
Tel. (609) 694 2887

North American Vegetarian Society (NAVS)
PO Box 72
Dolgeville
NY 13329
Tel. (518) 568 7970

Vegetarian Resource Group (VRG)
PO Box 1463
Baltimore
MD 21203
Tel. (301) 366 VEGE

Vegetarian Awareness Network
Tel. 1-800-USA-VEGE. or
(615) 558-VEGE in Nashville, TN.

EarthSave
706 Frederick Street
Santa Cruz
CA 96062
Tel. (408) 423 4069

Vegan Action
PO Box 2701
Madison
WI 53701

Vegetarian Education Network (VE*Net)
PO Box 3347
West Chester
PA 19381
Tel. (717) 529 8638

Vegetarian Life
Special Interest Group of MENSA
PO Box 3425
Shell Beach
CA 93448

Vegetarian Society, Inc.
PO Box 34427
Los Angeles
CA 90034
Tel. (619) 492 8803/(714) 647 5590

Afro-American Vegetarian Society
PO Box 46
Colonial Park Station
New York
NY 10039

Friends Vegetarian Society of North America
PO Box 6956
Louisville
KY 40206

Jewish Vegetarians of North America
PO Box 1463
Baltimore
MD 21203
or
6938 Reliance Road
Federalsburg
MD 21632
Tel. (410) 754 5550

Physicians Committee for Responsible Medicine
PO Box 6322
Washington
DC 20015
Tel. (202) 686 2210
Fax. (202) 686 2216

Association of Vegetarian Dieticians &
Nutrition Educators
(VEGEDINE)
3674 Cronk Road
Montour Falls
NY 14865
Tel. (607) 535 6089

Making Yourself Understood – How To Say 'No' to Meat In 21 Languages

ARABIC

Ana Nabatee
(I am vegetarian [male])
Ana Nabateeya
(I am vegetarian [female])
Mish Akool Lahma walla Ferekh khalis!
(I don't eat meat or chicken at all)

CHINESE

Most foreigners experience insurmountable problems in speaking transliterated Chinese. I therefore show below Chinese text which can be presented to non-English speaking cooks and chefs. Extremely thorough descriptions of the vegetarian and vegan diets are given to avoid any confusion or misinterpretation.

1. I am a vegetarian. This means because of my conviction I don't eat anything obtained from a killed animal. So I don't eat: meat (including minced meat, all kinds of sausages etc), fish, shrimps, mussels, poultry (including chicken), or other meat products. But I do eat: vegetables, potatoes, tomatoes, nuts, mushrooms, rice, fruit, butter, milk, cheese, eggs, corn and corn products. Soups and sauces may be made with vegetable stock, but not with meat or chicken extracts. Frying or baking may only be done in vegetable oil, vegetable margarine or butter, but not in any other animal fat.

我是相对素食主义者（可以吃乳制品、蛋类和蜜）。

这就是说，根据我的原则，我不吃杀死动物由动物身上所得的食品。我不吃肉、鱼、虾、贻贝、鸟类（禽类），也不吃别的肉食；如肉块、香肠等。

我吃蔬菜、土豆、西红柿、核桃、蘑菇、大米、水果、黄油、奶子、乳酪、蛋类、坚类和谷物制品等。

汤类、调味汁均不得加肉或禽肉一类的东西，只可加蔬菜类。烧烤食品只可用植物油或人造奶油（或奶油），可就是不能用动物油。

2. I am vegan. This means because of my conviction I don't eat anything of animal origin. So I don't eat: meat (including minced meat, all kinds of sausages etc), fish, shrimps, mussels, poultry (including chicken), or other animal products such as milk, cheese, eggs or any dairy produce. But I do eat: vegetables, potatoes, tomatoes, nuts, mushrooms, rice, fruit, corn and corn products. Soups and sauces may be made with vegetable stock, but not with meat or chicken extracts. Frying or baking may only be done in vegetable oil or vegetable margarine, but not in any other animal fat.

我是绝对素食主义者。

这就是说，根据我的原则，我不吃任何来源于动物的食品。

我不吃肉、鱼、虾、贻贝、鸟类（禽类）或其他肉类，如肉块、香肠等，甚至连奶子、乳酪、蛋类或其他乳制品也不吃。

我吃蔬菜、土豆、西红柿、核桃、蘑菇、大米、水果、谷类和谷物制品等。

汤类、调味汁均不得加肉或禽肉一类的东西。烧烤食品只可用植物油或人造奶油，但不得用奶油或动物油。

DANISH

Jeg spiser ikke kött
(I don't eat meat)

DUTCH

Ik ben een vegetarier
(I am a vegetarian)
Ik eet geen vlees, vis of gevogelte
(I don't eat meat, fish or poultry)
Ik houd niet van vlees
(I don't like meat)
Ik eet geen eieren en melk
(I don't eat milk and eggs)
Heeft u ook vegetarische gerechten?
(Do you have vegetarian dishes also?)

FINNISH

Olen kasvisyöjä
(I am a vegetarian.)
En syö eläimiä
(I don't eat animals)
En syö lihaa
(I don't eat meat)
En syö edes kanamunaa
(I don't eat eggs either)
Ei edes maitotuotteita
(Not even milk products)

FRENCH

Male:
Je suis un vegetarien. Je ne mange pas de la viande, porc ou du poulet
(I am a vegetarian. I do not eat meat, pork or chicken)
Je mange (ne mange pas) des oeufs, du lait et du fromage
(I do (do not) eat eggs, milk and cheese)

Female:
Je suis une vegetarienne. Je ne mange pas de la viande, de porc ou de poulet
(I am a vegetarian. I do not eat meat, pork or chicken)
Je mange des oeufs, du lait et du fromage
(I eat eggs, milk and cheese)
Je ne mange pas des oeufs, du lait ou du fromage
(I do not eat eggs, milk or cheese)

The French word for 'vegan' is 'vegetalien(ne)'

GERMAN

Ich bin Vegetarier(in)
(I am a vegetarian)
Ich esse kein Fleisch, auch kein Huhn (und keinen Fisch)
(I do not eat meat, chicken (or fish))
Ich esse (ich esse keine) Eier, Milch oder Käse
(I do (do not) eat eggs, milk or cheese)
Welches dieser Gerichte kann ich essen?
(Which of these dishes could I eat?)
(Dairy products = Milchprodukte, poultry = Geflügel)

GREEK

Phonetically:
EE-may hor-to-FAH-gos. Then tro KRAY-ahs ee ko-TO-poo-lo
[Eimai hortofagos. Den troo kreas i kotopoulo]
(I am a vegetarian. I do not eat meat, pork or chicken)
(Then) tro ahv-GA, GA-la, keh (ee) tee-REE
[(Den) troo avga, gala, kai (i) tiri]
(I do (do not) eat eggs, milk or cheese)

INDONESIAN

(This will also be understood in Malaysia)
Saya tidak makan daging
(I don't eat meat)
Saya tidak bisa makan daging
(I can't eat meat – sometimes more useful than the above)
Janganlah pakai daging
(Please don't use meat)

ITALIAN

Sono vegetariano. Non mangio karne, pesce, polli.
(I am a vegetarian. I do not eat meat, fish, or chicken.)
Sono un vegetariano rigoroso. Non mangio nulla di derivazione animale. Nessun tipo di formaggio, uova o altri latticini come il burro.
(I am a vegan. I do not eat anything made from animals. Not even cheese, eggs, or dairy produce.)

NEPALI

Malai maasu nakhanne
(I don't eat meat)
Malai maasu monpardaina
(I don't like meat)
Malai dudh ra phul nakhanne
(I don't eat milk and eggs)

NORWEGIAN

Jeg er vegetarianer
(I am a vegetarian)
Jeg er veganer
(I am a vegan)
Jeg spiser ikke kjøtt, egg eller meieriprodukter
(I don't eat meat, eggs nor dairy products)
Jeg spiser verken kjøtt, kylling eller fisk
(I eat neither meat, chicken nor fish)
Jeg liker ikke kjøtt.
(I don't like meat)
Har du noen vegetarretter
(Do you have any vegetarian dishes?)

POLISH

Phonetically:
yestem vegetarianinem/vegetariankauw
[Jestem wegetarianinem (male)/wegetarianka (female)]
(I am a vegetarian)
nyea yem miowsa, drobewe, rip, yayek, serah
[Nie jem miesa, drobiu, ryb, jajek, sera]
(I do not eat meat, poultry, fish, eggs, cheese)
nyea piaow mleka
[Nie pije mleka]
(I don't drink milk)
tCHey soww danya vegetarianski/yaraskia
[Czy sa dania wegetarianskie/jarskie?]
(Do you have vegetarian dishes?)

PORTUGUESE

Phonetically:
Es-toe veg-et-air-ee-ahn-oh
[Estou vegetariano]
(I am a vegetarian)
Now coe-may kar-nay, pay-shay oh ahv-ays doe-mes-chi-cas
[Nao come carne, peixe ou aves domesticas]
(I don't eat meat, fish or poultry)
Now coe-may lay-chee oh oh-vohs ou kay-joe
[Nao come leite ou ovos ou quejo]
(I don't eat milk or eggs or cheese)
Now coe-may kwal-kair coy-za pre-par-ah-doe cone gra-sha ani-mal (toy-seen-yo oh lar-doe)
[Nao come qualguer coisa preparado com graxa animal (toicinho ou lardo)]
(I do not eat anything cooked with animal fat (bacon or lard)

ROMANIAN

Sint vegetarian (I am a vegetarian)
Nu maninc carne
(I do not eat meat . . .)
Oua (eggs)
Peste (fish)
Lactate (dairy)
Nu maninc nimic gatit in grasime animala (slanina sau
untura)
(I do not eat anything cooked in animal fat (bacon or
lard))
There is no word for vegan in Romanian.

SLOVENIAN

Ne jem mesa
(I don't eat meat)
Ne maram mesa
(I don't like meat)
Ne jem mleka in jajc
(I don't eat milk and eggs)

SPANISH

Yo soy vegetariano/a
(I am a vegetarian [male/female])
Yo no como carne, puerca, o pollo
(I do not eat meat, pork or chicken)
Yo como (no como) huevos, leche, o queso
(I do (do not) eat eggs, milk or cheese)
No, no quiero ningun pescado
(No, I don't want any fish)

SWEDISH

Jag äter inte kött
(I do not eat meat)
Jag är vegetarian
(I am a vegetarian)

TAMIL

*Capital letters are elongated vowels eg nAn rhymes with
'pawn':*
nAn saivam

(I am vegetarian)
nAn saiva sAppAdu-thAn sAppiduven
(I eat only vegetarian food)
nAn asaivam sAppiduvathu illai
(I don't eat non-vegetarian food)
nAn mAmisam sAppiduvathu illai
(I don't eat meat)
nAn meen sAppiduvathu illai
(I don't eat fish)
nAn kozhi sAppiduvathu illai
(I don't eat poultry)
nAn muttai sAppiduvathu illai
(I don't eat eggs)
nAn pAl sAppiduvathu illai *or*
nAn pAl kudippathu illai
(I don't eat (drink) milk)

THAI

Phom kin phak
Phom kin jeh
Phom mang-sa-wirat
(All three mean I am a vegetarian)
Phom mai kin plaa
(I don't eat fish)

TURKISH

Phonetically:
(heech et yee-yeh-mem)
[Hic et yiyemem]
(I can't eat any meat)
[Et suyu bile yiyemem]
(I can't even eat meat juices)
. . . yiyemem
(I can't eat . . .)
Et yiyemem
(I can't eat meat)
tah-vook [Tavuk] (chicken)
pee-leech [Pilik] (chicken)
yoo-moor-tah [Yumurta] (egg)
bah-luck [Balk] (fish)
Et-seez yeh-mek var muh?)
[Etsiz yemek var mi?]
(Do you have any dishes without meat?)

Footnotes

1 The names of interviewees in this chapter have been changed to purely fictional ones, any similarity to the names of living people is pure coincidence. The case histories are, however, entirely real and are told by the interviewees concerned in their own words.

2 Captain X and Reynolds Dodson, *Unfriendly Skies* (Sphere Books, 1990)

3 *New York Times*, 2 September 1991

4 *Open Space – Flying Fur*, BBC2 Television, 1991

5 *Searchlight*, June, 1991. See also: R. Proctor, *Racial Hygiene: Medicine Under the Nazis* (Harvard, 1988)

6 *New York Times*, 21 September 1991

7 *The Jewish Vegetarian*, December 1989

8 *New York Times*, 21 September 1991, citing *The Gourmet Cooking School Cookbook* (1964)

9 O. Spengler, *Der Mensch Und Die Technike* (Munich, 1931)

10 P. Singer, *Practical Ethics* (Cambridge University Press, 1979)

11 P. L. Pick (ed), *Tree of Life* (A.S. Barnes & Co, 1977)

12 A. Linzey, *Christianity and the Rights of Animals* (Crossroads Publishing Company, New York, 1987)

13 *The Independent*, 7 July 1990

14 Personal correspondence, January 1988

15 From data in P.N. Wilson, 'Biological Ceilings and Economic Efficiencies for the Production of Animal Protein AD 2000', *Chemistry & Industry*, 6 July 1968

16 F. Pearce, 'Methane, the hidden greenhouse gas', *New Scientist*, issue 1663, 6 May 1989

17 Foundation on Economic Trends, Washington DC, 1992

18 Beyond Beef Campaign, Washington DC, 1992

19 R. Miller, *Bare-Faced Messiah* (Michael Joseph, 1987)

20 Personal communication, 1994

21 L. Howlett, *Cruelty-free shopper* (Bloomsbury, 1989)

22 K. Akers, *A Vegetarian Sourcebook* (Vegetarian Press, 1983)

23 J. Rifkin, Beyond Beef Campaign. Washington, D.C 1992

24 S. Clinton, *A shopper's guide to leather alternatives*. The Vegetarian Resource Group, P.O. Box 1463, Baltimore, MD 21203 USA

25 Speech before cattlemen at the University of Montana in 1985

PART THREE:
THE ENCYCLOPEDIA OF VEGETARIAN NUTRITION

*Just about everything you need to know
(and some things that you don't)
about the art and science of
flesh-free feeding*

'Is it difficult to be a well-nourished vegetarian or vegan?'

No. Millions of people eat balanced vegetarian or vegan meals every day, without so much as a second thought.

'So why do we need to read about it?'

That's a very good question. In the best of all possible worlds, you wouldn't need to. Just by following your instincts, as other animals do, you'd probably be pretty well nourished. The problem is, we don't live in that sort of world. Our diets have gone seriously haywire over the past century. Fat intake has soared, fresh food consumption has plummeted, and the unhealthy rule of King Junk Food shows no sign of ending. People have weird and distorted perceptions, too, of the so-called 'risks' involved in the meat-free ways of living; while being utterly blind to the host of health and environmental benefits. Recently, I expressed this view in the British Medical Association's *News Review* like this:

'For a profession whose exacting admission requirements exclude all but the most intellectually astute, you are remarkably easy to sucker. Perversely ignoring decades of published epidemiology which unmistakably attests to the overwhelmingly beneficial effects of the meat-free way of living, you all too willingly succumb to the blandishments and deceptions of the meat industry's vast propaganda machine – an unambiguous example, in my view, of unscientific and unprofessional conduct. A news report in *The Times* perfectly captures this deeply irrational point of view. Headlined 'Vegetarians face risk of deficiency', it reported the words of a learned professor, speaking at a 'London conference' (actually a meat trade seminar – a fact omitted from the report).[1] 'Those who ate no meat might be at risk of deficiency,' opined the good Professor; although his speech advanced not one jot of evidence to support this alarming assertion.[2]

Tucked away at the foot of the article was fleeting mention of a real piece of research from the University of Surrey, which revealed that vegetarians were hospitalized *five times less frequently* than meat-eaters. This kind of research – and it is now so plentiful that I have more than filled a book with it – is routinely ignored by most of your profession, whose quasi-Pavlovian response to the word 'vegetarian' is invariably 'deficiency' . . . There is compelling evidence that the totality of the healthy meat-free diet (as opposed to one unique factor) can significantly reduce the incidence of heart disease, cancers, hypertension, diabetes, osteoporosis, and many other afflictions.[3] Yet it is truly shocking that this hard-won knowledge should be so consistently ignored. Isn't it time that your profession cast its prejudices aside, refused to listen to the siren voices of the beef barons, looked at the evidence – and got angry?'[4]

So vegetarians and vegans not only need to know something about nutrition for their own health, they also need to be able to defend themselves too – and hopefully, spread a little enlightenment in places where it will do some good.

Don't feel you have to read this section from beginning to end in order to 'win' your qualifications to be vegan or vegetarian. For starters, just examine the chart which follows. It shows you – in a very simple way – just what you should eat if you want to be an extremely well-nourished vegetarian. I hope your mouth waters just looking at it! Devised by Dr Michael Klaper, one of America's foremost experts on achieving optimum health through pure vegetarian nutrition, this table shows you how easy it is to eat well on a vegetarian diet.[5] Actually, if you look closely, you'll see that it includes *no animal produce whatever* – it's a 'pure vegetarian' or vegan diet. Personally, I prefer a vegan diet, but it took me some years to realize that. If you want to consume some dairy produce in addition to the below, that is, of course, your decision – it will increase still further the already high level of nutrition you'll be getting from your diet, although you should be careful to keep your saturated fat consumption as low as possible, preferably by only using skimmed milk products. From the ethical point of view, too, veganism is certainly superior.

In A Nutshell – Everything You Need To Know About Meat-Free Eating

FOOD GROUP	WHAT IT PROVIDES	SOME EXAMPLES	HOW OFTEN TO EAT
whole grains and potatoes	energy, protein, oils, vitamins, fibre	brown rice, corn, millet, barley, bulghur, buckwheat, oats, muesli, bread, pasta, flour	2–4 servings daily
legumes	protein, oils	green peas, lentils, chickpeas, kidney beans, baked beans, soya products including soy milk, tofu, tempeh, TVP	1–2 servings daily
green and yellow vegetables	vitamins, minerals, protein	broccoli, brussels sprouts, spinach, cabbage, carrots, marrow, sweet potatoes, pumpkins, parsnips	1–3 servings daily
nuts & seeds	energy, protein, oils, calcium, trace minerals	almonds, pumpkin seeds, walnuts, peanuts, sesame seeds, nut butters, tahini, sunflower seeds	1–3 servings daily
fruit	energy, vitamins, minerals	all kinds	3–6 pieces daily
vitamin and mineral foods	trace minerals & vitamin B12	(a) sea vegetables (b) B12-fortified foods such as soy milk, TVP, breakfast cereals, soy 'meat' products	1 serving of (a) and (b) 3 times a week

Let me disclose my hand here – I want you to be the healthiest vegetarian or vegan in the world! So healthy, that people will say, 'Wow! If you can look that good without meat, maybe I should give it a go!'. The truth is that, to some extent, vegetarians are on public display

– if we catch a cold, someone will blame it on our diet. So let's not give them the chance!

In the pages that follow, you'll find most of the major nutrients described, together with their fifty best sources. If you scan these specially compiled tables, you will find the same foodstuffs cropping up time and again as extremely good sources of high-quality nutrition. I hope this serves to suggest ideas to you about the ways in which you can begin to construct a healthy diet around a few key foods of your own preference. The nutrient amounts in the tables that follow have been calculated as average values from several different analyses. Do remember that the nutrient composition of a food can vary very substantially between samples, depending on many factors, such as its degree of freshness, the time of year, the cooking process, method of analysis used, etc. So use all nutrient analyses as approximate guides, not as rigid rules.

The final point I'd like to make concerns nutrient supplementation. Vegetarians and vegans become very macho when it comes to taking vitamin and mineral supplements – it's as though if we admit to doing it, it may be considered a sign that our diets are somehow inadequate. Personally, I used to think that too. But now, I don't have to prove that the meat-free way of living is superior – the scientists have done it for me. What increasingly concerns me is the very grave threat posed to our well-being by previously unparalleled environmental stress (including an all-out assault from a vast spectrum of pollutants, our increasingly unnatural lifestyles, and our rapidly deteriorating habitat). This has nothing to do with whether or not we consume meat. One example: vegetarians naturally consume much more vitamin C than meat-eaters. Even so, there is increasing evidence to suggest that all of us – vegetarians, vegans and most definitely meat-eaters – could appreciably benefit from a far greater intake. Vitamin C is a very effective antioxidant and free radical quencher. Antioxidants are compounds that inhibit chemical reactions with oxygen. In the environment, rust and decay are byproducts of oxidation. In the human body, the equivalent of 'rust and decay' is the damage done by free oxygen radicals, now implicated in the development of many serious disease states such as cancer, heart disease, immune-deficiency diseases, and aging. Antioxidants such as vitamin C can actively prevent free radical damage. You can see this process at work for yourself – cut an apple in half, and put one half aside. Pour lemon juice, which is high in vitamin C, on

the other half. The half without the lemon juice will go brown through oxidation much faster than the half which is protected by the antioxidant vitamin C. In a recent study conducted at the University of California at Berkeley, scientists isolated plasma from human blood, incubated it at body temperature and added a chemical that is known to produce free radicals as it decomposes. When vitamin C was added it neutralized 100 per cent of the free radicals generated.[6]

As for many nutrients, the official recommended daily allowance of vitamin C is calculated on the basis of the vitamin's ability to prevent symptoms of deficiency (such as scurvy), and *not* on its antioxidant powers. Various researchers have suggested an optimal intake of between 250 and 5000mg daily. Twice Nobel prizewinner and distinguished scientist, Linus Pauling, a long-time advocate of vitamin C, goes further, and has proposed 6g (6000mg) and up to 18g (18,000mg) orally every day for most adults.[7] Not even the most enthusiastic vegetarian will get this kind of nutrition from foods alone. In my opinion, the judicious use of vitamin and mineral supplements is a good idea for everyone.

VITAMIN A

Vitamin A or retinol, was the first fat-soluble vitamin to be detected, and is only found in certain animal tissues. Retinol can be quite toxic if taken excessively. There is evidence that it is teratogenic, in other words, it can cause foetal malformations if high doses are taken both before and during pregnancy.

Since retinol is only found in animal foods, you may wonder where vegetarians obtain their supply from. The answer is that the plant kingdom is an abundant source of substances which are converted inside the human body to form vitamin A. These substances are sometimes called provitamin A, or carotenoids. Sounds like 'carrot'? That's right – carrots are a lavish source of carotenoids.

Of the several hundred naturally-occurring carotenoids, the most widespread and most active form is beta-carotene. Unlike retinol, foods which contain beta-carotene can be consumed in plentiful amounts without fear of toxicity. Also, beta-carotene is not teratogenic[8]. Furthermore, the latest exciting research suggests that vegetarians' greater intake of beta-carotene is one reason why they suffer considerably less from heart disease, cancers, and a host of other modern afflictions.

Importance and function

- Essential for good eyesight
- Enables tissue growth and bone development to take place
- Helps maintain integrity of mucous membranes, thus building a barrier against infection
- Enables proper growth and functioning of the reproductive system

Signs of deficiency

- Dry, scaly and rough skin ('goose flesh')
- Dryness of membranes lining eyelids
- Night blindness eventually leading to total blindness
- Breakdown in the integrity of mucous membranes, which predisposes to all kinds of infections, particularly of the lungs, alimentary canal and urinary tract

Best vegetarian sources

A varied vegetarian diet will provide a multitude of excellent sources of beta-carotene. The following table has been compiled from an extensive analysis of several thousand vegetarian foodstuffs, and shows many of the most concentrated sources of this vitamin. A note about the way vitamin A is measured: originally, it was analysed in terms of International Units (IU) and some older textbooks still reflect this. Today, however, it is more common to find it expressed as Retinol Equivalents (RE). This is a more useful measure of the total vitamin A activity of a food or diet, because it takes account of the different biological activity of the various forms of vitamin A and provitamin A found in nature.

1 RE = 1 mcg retinol
or 6 mcg beta-carotene
or 12 mcg of other provitamin A carotenoids
or 3.33 IU vitamin A activity from retinol
or 10 IU vitamin A activity from beta-carotene.[9]

Food	Measure	Retinol Equivalents
carrots canned	1 can:454g	5979
sweet potatoes cooked	1 cup mashed:328g	5592
pumpkin canned	1 cup:245g	5404

carrot juice canned	1 glass:184g	4738
peas and carrots frozen	1 pack:284g	2698
broccoli raw	1 spear:151g	2416
margarine soft, corn	1 pack 227g	2254
carrots raw	1 carrot:72g	2025
carrots cooked	1 serving:78g	1914
vegetables mixed, canned	1 cup:163g	1898
spinach canned	1 cup:214g	1878
apricots dehydrated	1 cup:119g	1507
kale boiled	1 cup:130g	962
peppers hot chili, green	1 pepper:73g	867
melons cantaloupe, raw	1/2 fruit:267g	859
butter	1 stick:113.4g	855
mangos raw	1 fruit:207g	805
chicory greens, raw	1 cup:180g	720
passion-fruit juice	1 glass:247g	595
pizza, with cheese	1 pizza:503g	588
chard Swiss, cooked	1 cup chopped: 175g	549
broccoli raw	1 spear:151g	453
cabbage Chinese (bok-choi), cooked	1 cup:170g	436
peppers sweet, red, raw	1 pepper:74g	421
paprika	1 tbsp:6.9g	418
amaranth cooked	1 cup:132g	365
persimmons raw	1 fruit:168g	364
peaches dried	1 cup halves:160g	345
tomato puree canned	1 cup:250g	340
prunes dried	1 cup:161g	320
apricots raw	3 fruits:106g	276
peas green, canned	1 can:313g	241
cheese brie	1 pkg:128g	232

asparagus canned	1 can:411g	193
spinach raw	1/2 cup:28g	188
watermelon raw	1/16 fruit:482g	178
lettuce iceberg, raw	1 head:539g	177
tomatoes red, ripe, cooked	1 serving:240g	177
parsley raw	1/2 cup:30g	156
tomatoes red, ripe, canned	1 cup:261g	151
vegetable juice cocktail canned	1/2 cup:121g	141
soup tomato, condensed	1 cup:251g	140
avocados raw	1 cup purée:230g	140
guavas raw	1 cup:165g	130
cabbage savoy, cooked	1 cup shredded:145g	129
cheese cream	1oz:28g	122
tempeh	1 cup:166g	114
eggs chicken, fried	1 egg:46g	114

Is getting enough vitamin A likely to be a problem for vegetarians?

Not at all. Lack of beta-carotene is, however, a real problem for meat-eaters. For example, it has been calculated that a diet which was richer in beta-carotene could save the lives of more than a third of the 400,000 Americans who die of cancer every year. Comments a US federal researcher, studying the protective impact of vitamin A: 'Most of the studies that the present trials are based on are epidemiological ones that have shown that people who eat foods high in these nutrients – vitamin A, beta-carotene, vitamin E – have lower rates of cancer, with the inference that the nutrients lower the risk for cancer.'[10]

RECOMMENDED INTAKES
Vitamin A (mcg) RE

	Age	US RDA	Can RNI	UK RNI
Infants	up to 6 months	375	400	350
	six months-1 year	375	400	350
	1–3	400	400	400
Children	4–6	500	500	500
	7–10	700	700	500
Males	11–14	1000	900	600
	15–18	1000	1000	700
	19–24	1000	1000	700
	25–50	1000	1000	700
	51 +	1000	1000	700
Females	11–14	800	800	600
	15–18	800	800	600
	19–24	800	800	600
	25-50	800	800	600
	51 +	800	800	600
Pregnant		800	+ 100	+ 100
Lactating	first 6 months	1300	+ 400	+ 350
	second 6 months	1200	+ 400	+ 350

Note:
US RDA = United States Recommended Dietary Allowance
Can RNI = Canadian Recommended Nutrient Intake
UK RNI = United Kingdom Reference Nutrient Intake
The '+' sign in front of values for pregnancy and lactation indicates that the value should be added to the suggested intake for the relevant age group.

THIAMIN

Also called thiamine or vitamin B1, thiamin was discovered to be the nutritional factor responsible for preventing the disease beriberi (Singhalese for 'I cannot', meaning that the sufferer is too ill to do anything). Epidemics of beriberi were produced in Asia by eating a diet of white polished rice, where all the nutritional content of the outer layers of rice is discarded during processing. Although beriberi is primarily a disease of tropical countries, nutritional deficiencies of thiamin are also seen in the West.

Importance and function
- Plays an essential role in converting carbohydrate into energy for muscles and nervous system
- Helps keep mucous membranes healthy
- Helps maintain positive mental state and may assist learning capacity

Signs of deficiency
- Loss of appetite
- Anorexia
- Indigestion

- Constipation
- Fatigue
- Nausea and vomiting
- Depression and other mental problems, eg memory loss, personality changes
- Tender muscles
- Pins and needles, numbness in legs
- Gross deficiency manifests in symptoms of beriberi

Best vegetarian sources

The thiamin content of foods will be adversely affected by prolonged cooking, as it leaches out in to the cooking water which is then discarded. Cooking in chlorinated water also has an adverse effect. The following vegetarian foodstuffs are good sources of this vitamin:

Food	Measure	Mg of thiamin
brewers yeast	1 oz:28g	4.37
sunflower seeds dried	1 cup:144g	3.30
spirulina dried	1 pack:100g	2.38
brazilnuts dried	1 cup:140g	1.40
oats	1 cup:156g	1.19
barley	1 cup:184g	1.19
sesame seeds whole, dried	1 cup:144g	1.14
pistachio nuts dried	1 cup:128g	1.05
chicory raw	1 head:513g	1.03
peanuts raw	1 cup:146g	0.93
pecans dried	1 cup:108g	0.92
sausage meatless	1 patty:38g	0.89
millet raw	1 cup:200g	0.84
wheat durum	1 cup:192g	0.80
rice brown, medium-grain, raw	1 cup:190g	0.78
peas green, frozen	1 pack:284g	0.73
cabbage cooked	1 head:1262g	0.72
soy flour defatted	1 cup:100g	0.70
bakers yeast dry	1 oz:28g	0.65
spaghetti in tomato sauce w/cheese, canned	1 can:432g	0.60
sausage meatless	1 sausage:25g	0.59
hazelnuts dried	1 cup:115g	0.58
peas and carrots frozen	1 pack:284g	0.54
pumpkin and squash seeds roasted	1 cup:227g	0.48
peas green, cooked	1 cup:160g	0.41
soy milk fluid	1 cup:240g	0.39
split peas cooked	1 cup:196g	0.37
toast white bread	1 slice:22g	0.37
breakfast cereals e.g. corn flakes	1 serving:36.9g	0.37
tahini	1 tbsp:28.4g	0.36
molasses third extraction or blackstrap	1 cup:328g	0.36
hummus	1 cup:246g	0.36
pine nuts dried	1 oz:28.4g	0.35
peanut butter	1 cup:258g	0.35
chestnuts roasted	1 cup:143g	0.35
vegetables mixed, frozen	1 pack:284g	0.35
quinoa	1 cup:170g	0.34
lentils cooked	1 serving:198g	0.33
pinto beans cooked	1 serving:171g	0.32
couscous dry	1 cup:184g	0.30
brussels sprouts frozen	1 pack:284g	0.30
bean sprouts mung	1 pack:340g	0.29
kidney beans cooked	1 serving:177g	0.28
natto	1 serving:175g	0.28
spaghetti whole-wheat, dry	1 serving:57g	0.28
miso	1 cup:275g	0.27
soya beans cooked	1 serving:172g	0.27
adzuki beans cooked	1 serving:230g	0.26
tempeh	1 serving:166g	0.22
potatoes baked	1 potato:202g	0.22

Is getting enough thiamin likely to be a problem for vegetarians?

No, since all plants contain thiamin. Note that several foodstuffs contain thiamin-inhibiting factors, notably tea and raw fish. Alcohol similarly prevents this vitamin from being utilised; in fact, alcohol-related thiamin deficiency is a common cause of dementia in developed nations.[11] Since thiamin requirements are linked to energy metabolism, certain population groups may need more of this vitamin, particulary children and teenagers, the elderly, those under stress, and alcoholics. As with many vitamins, the human body retains some ancient capacity to synthesize this vitamin internally, but the amount thus produced is not thought to be significant in relation to our overall requirements.

RECOMMENDED INTAKES
Thiamin (mg)

	Age	US RDA	Can RNI	UK RNI
Infants	up to six months	0.3	0.3	0.2
	6 months– 1 year	0.4	0.4	0.3
	1–3	0.7	0.6	0.5
Children	4–6	0.9	0.7	0.7
	7–10	1.0	0.9	0.7
Males	11–14	1.3	1.1	0.9
	15–18	1.5	1.3	1.1
	19–24	1.5	1.2	1.0
	25–50	1.5	1.1	1.0
	51 +	1.2	0.9	0.9
Females	11–14	1.1	0.9	0.7
	15-18	1.1	0.8	0.8
	19–24	1.1	0.8	0.8
	25–50	1.1	0.8	0.8
	51 +	1.0	0.8	0.8
Pregnant		1.5	+ 0.1	+ 0.1
Lactating	first 6 months	1.6	+ 0.2	+ 0.2
	second 6 months	1.6	+ 0.2	+ 0.2

RIBOFLAVIN

Also known as vitamin B2, riboflavin was first observed in 1879 as a greenish fluorescent pigment present in milk, but its function was not fully understood until 1932. It is often found in combination with other B-group vitamins, and since it is not stored in the human body for any period of time, it is important to include a regular dietary source of this vitamin.

Importance and function

- Functions with other vitamins and enzymes in utilisation of energy from food
- Helps keep mucous membranes healthy
- Essential for normal tissue respiration

Signs of deficiency

- Cracks in skin at corner of mouth
- Soreness of lips, mouth and tongue
- Scaling of skin around nose, mouth, scrotum, forehead, ears, scalp
- Sometimes heightened sensitivity to light, watering of eyes, conjunctivitis
- Anaemia

Best plant sources

Riboflavin is not significantly destroyed by cooking, but will disappear if exposed to light (especially ultraviolet) and an alkaline environment. For this reason, do not add bicarbonate of soda to beans or peas when cooking them. The top fifty non-animal sources of riboflavin are:

Food	Measure	Mg of riboflavin
almond paste	1 cup:227g	1.66
pizza with cheese topping	1 pizza:520g	1.61
yeast bakers	1 oz:28g	1.51
milk condensed	1 cup:306g	1.27
yeast brewers	1 oz:28g	1.19
almonds dried	1 cup kernels:142g	1.11
cheese feta	1 pkg, 7 oz: 198g	0.84
cheese edam	1 pkg, 7 oz: 198g	0.76
buckwheat	1 cup:170g	0.73

cabbage cooked	1 head:1262g	0.69
bacon meatless	1 cup:144g	0.69
miso	1 cup:275g	0.68
quinoa	1 cup:170g	0.67
molasses cane, barbados	1 cup:328g	0.65
millet raw	1 cup:200g	0.58
spinach raw	10 oz pkg:284g	0.53
welsh rarebit	1 serving:232g	0.53
barley	1 cup:184g	0.52
milkshake vanilla	10 fl oz:283g	0.51
wheat germ crude	1 cup:113g	0.49
breakfast cereals e.g. corn flakes	1 serving:39g	0.49
soya beans cooked	1 cup:172g	0.49
egg scrambled	2 eggs:94g	0.48
yogurt plain, lowfat	8 oz:227g	0.48
carob flour	1 cup:103g	0.47
lambsquarters cooked	1 cup chopped:180g	0.46
sesame seed kernels toasted	4oz:100g	0.46
cocoa powder	4 oz:100g	0.46
dried mixed fruit	11 oz pkg:293g	0.46
kidney beans sprouted	1 cup:184g	0.46
sweet potatoes cooked	1 cup mashed:328g	0.46
pumpkin and squash seed kernels dried	1 cup:138g	0.44
macaroni and cheese canned	1 can, 15oz:430g	0.43
spinach cooked	1 cup:180g	0.42
bean sprouts mung, raw	12 oz pkg:340g	0.42
wild rice raw	1 cup:160g	0.4
cheese cottage, 2% fat	1 cup:226g	0.4
beet greens cooked	1 cup:144g	0.41

hummus	1 cup:246g	0.41
molasses cane, second extraction or medium	1 cup:328g	0.39
asparagus canned	1 can:411g	0.37
sunflower seed kernels dried	1 cup:144g	0.36
peas green, canned	1 Can:482g	0.35
egg substitute powder	1 tbsp:19.8g	0.35
peaches dried, uncooked	1 cup halves:160g	0.34
natto	1 cup:175g	0.33
passion-fruit juice	1 cup:247g	0.33
tomato paste canned	6 oz can:170g	0.32
raisins golden seedless	1 cup:165g	0.31

Is getting enough riboflavin likely to be a problem for vegetarians?

Not for vegetarians – dairy products contain considerable quantities of riboflavin (for example, a cup [10 fl oz/285ml] of milk contains 0.4mg, about a third of the suggested daily intake). Vegans should be mindful of the need to choose foods which provide dietary riboflavin – see the table above. It is worth noting that breakfast cereal products are supplemented with riboflavin (one 30g serving provides a quarter of the suggested daily intake).

RECOMMENDED INTAKES
Riboflavin (mg)

	Age	US RDA	Can RNI	UK RNI
Infants	up to 6 months	0.4	0.3	0.4
	6 months–1 year	0.5	0.5	0.4
	1–3	0.8	0.7	0.6
Children	4–6	1.1	0.9	0.8
	7–10	1.2	1.1	1.0
Males	11–14	1.5	1.4	1.2
	15–18	1.8	1.6	1.3

	19–24	1.7	1.5	1.3
	25–50	1.7	1.4	1.3
	51 +	1.4	1.3	1.3
Females	11–14	1.3	1.1	1.1
	15–18	1.3	1.1	1.1
	19–24	1.3	1.1	1.1
	25–50	1.3	1.0	1.1
	51 +	1.2	1.0	1.1
Pregnant		1.6	+0.3	+0.3
Lactating	first 6 months	1.8	+0.4	+0.5
	second 6 months	1.7	+0.4	+0.5

NIACIN

Niacin, also called vitamin B3, is the collective name for nicotinamide (niacinamide) and nicotinic acid. Its importance was realised in 1937 when it was discovered that the disease pellagra was caused by niacin deficiency. The amino acid tryptophan can also be converted to niacin in the body, which means that scientific analyses can sometimes underestimate the effective niacin yield of foodstuffs by simply measuring the niacin content alone.

Importance and function

- Essential to the release of energy from carbohydrates, fats and proteins
- Assists in DNA synthesis
- Maintains function of skin, nerves and digestive system

Signs of deficiency

- Fatigue and muscle weakness
- Loss of appetite
- Indigestion
- Skin lesions and eruptions
- Mental imbalance
- Gross deficiency leads to pellagra

Best vegetarian sources

In addition to the foods listed below, it should be remembered that tryptophan-rich foods (present in soya products) can also supply the body with a good source of convertible niacin. The niacin present in

seeds (grains, corn) is available for use by the body when the seeds are immature; later, it becomes bound to the seed's carbohydrate and is not so available. Cooking the seed in an alkaline environment (for example, using bicarbonate of soda as a leavening agent) will release this niacin for use by the body. Niacin is resistant to destruction by exposure to heat, light, air, and acid and alkaline environments. The following are good sources of this vitamin:

Food	measure	Mg of niacin
bakers yeast compressed	1 oz:28g	40.32
peanut butter	1 cup:258g	35.32
peanuts oil-roasted	1 cup:144g	20.56
peanuts raw	1 cup:146g	17.62
peanut flour defatted	1 cup:60g	16.20
wheat durum	1 cup:192g	12.94
buckwheat	1 cup:170g	11.93
spaghetti whole-wheat, dry	8 oz:227g	11.65
bacon meatless	1 cup:144g	10.89
brewers yeast	1 oz:28g	10.61
bakers yeast dry	1 oz:28g	10.28
potatoes dehydrated granules	1 cup:200g	9.53
rice bran crude	1/3 cup:28g	9.52
millet raw	1 cup:200g	9.44
rice brown, long-grain, raw	1 cup:185g	9.42
barley pearled, raw	1 cup:200g	9.21
sunflower seed kernels dry roasted	1 cup:128g	9.01
brown rice medium-grain, raw	1 cup:190g	8.19
spaghetti in tomato sauce w/cheese, canned	15 oz can:432g	7.78
tempeh	1 cup:166g	7.69
wheat flour whole-grain	1 cup:120g	7.64

mixed nuts with peanuts, oil roasted	1 cup:142g	7.19
bulgar dry	1 cup:140g	7.16
sesame seed kernels	1 cup:150g	7.02
peaches dried	1 c halves:160g	7.00
wheat germ crude	1 cup:	6.81
rice white, short-grain, cooked	1 cup:205g	6.79
molasses cane, third extraction or blackstrap	1 cup:328g	6.56
couscous dry	1 cup:184g	6.42
dried mixed fruit	11 oz pkg:293g	5.65
ginkgo nuts canned	1 cup:155g	5.62
passion-fruit juice	1 cup:247g	5.53
macaroni whole-wheat, dry	1 cup:105g	5.39
wild rice raw	1/2 cup:80g	5.39
kidney beans sprouted, raw	1 cup:184g	5.37
breakfast cereals eg corn flakes	1 serving:36.9g	5.02
peas green, canned	1 lb :454g	4.99
quinoa	1 cup:170g	4.98
sweetcorn frozen, kernels	10 oz pkg:284g	4.90
peas green, frozen	10 oz pkg:284g	4.85
almonds dried,	1 c whole kernels:142g	4.77
sweetcorn canned	1 can:482g	4.53
spaghetti in tomato sauce w/cheese, canned	1 cup:250g	4.50
avocados raw	1 c puree:230g	4.42
peanut butter	2 tbsp:32g	4.38
tomato puree canned	1 cup:250g	4.29
apricots dehydrated	1 cup:119g	4.26
sausage meatless	1 patty:38g	4.25

prunes dehydrated	1 cup:132g	3.95
dates	1 cup chopped:178g	3.92

Is getting enough niacin likely to be a problem for vegetarians?

No. Scientific studies show that vegetarians and vegans both consume satisfactory amounts of niacin from their diets.[12,13,14]

RECOMMENDED INTAKES
Niacin (mg) (Niacin equivalents)

	Age	US RDA	Can RNI	UK RNI
Infants	up to 6 months	5	4	3
	6 months– 1 year	6	7	5
	1–3	9	9	8
Children	4–6	12	13	11
	7–10	13	16	12
Males	11–14	17	20	15
	15–18	20	23	18
	19–24	19	22	17
	25–50	19	19	17
	51 +	15	16	16
Females	11–14	15	16	12
	15–18	15	15	14
	19–24	15	15	13
	25–50	15	14	13
	51 +	13	14	12
Pregnant		17	+ 0.2	no increment
Lactating	first 6 months	20	+ 0.3	+ 0.2
	second 6 months	20	+ 0.3	+ 0.2

VITAMIN B6

Vitamin B6, also known as pyridoxine, is the name used to identify a group of closely related chemical compounds. Like other B-group vitamins, it is soluble in water. Some vitamin B6 may be stored in body muscle, but this capacity is limited in humans and a daily dietary intake is needed.

Importance and function

- Helps the body manufacture and convert amino acids and metabolize protein
- Necessary for the production of haemoglobin
- Assists in conversion of tryptophan to niacin
- Facilitates release of glycogen for energy from liver and muscles
- Helps body process the essential fatty acid linoleic acid
- Helps build and maintain integrity of nervous system and brain

Signs of deficiency

- Broad range of possible non-specific symptoms, including weakness, mental confusion or depression, low glucose tolerance, loss of hair, water retention, skin lesions, hyperactivity, anaemia, numbness and cramps, discolouration of tongue, twitching, kidney stones

Best vegetarian sources

Vitamin B6 is destroyed by exposure to light. When cooking, it is best preserved in acidic dishes and recipes. About half of a food's vitamin B6 content is destroyed by freezing. The highest-quality food sources are yeast, wheatgerm and cereals. The vitamin B6 available in potatoes, spinach, beans and other legumes is present in a beta-glucoside form which is not so easily absorbed by the body. The following are good sources of vitamin B6:

Food	measure	Mg of Vitamin B6
avocados raw	1 fruit:304g	1.76
wheat germ crude	1 cup:113g	1.30
sweet potatoes canned, mashed	1 can:496g	1.17
rice flour brown	1 cup:158g	1.16
peanut butter	1 cup:258g	1.16
rice bran crude	1/3 cup:28g	1.14
sesame seeds whole, dried	1 cup:144g	1.14
chickpeas canned	1 cup:240g	1.14
sunflower seed kernels dried	1 cup:144g	1.11

prunes dehydrated	1 cup:132g	0.98
brown rice medium-grain, raw	1 cup:190g	0.97
cabbage raw	1 head:908g	0.86
cabbage cooked	1 head:1262g	0.81
wheat durum	1 cup:192g	0.80
baked potato topped w/ sour cream and chives	1 potato:302g	0.79
millet raw	1 cup:200g	0.77
chestnuts roasted	1 cup:143g	0.71
filberts or hazelnuts dried	1 cup chopped kernels:115g	0.70
baked potato flesh and skin	1 potato:202g	0.70
watermelon raw	1/16 fruit:482g	0.69
bacon meatless	1 cup:144g	0.69
walnuts dried	1 cup:120g	0.67
breakfast cereals eg corn flakes	1 serving:36g	0.65
tomato paste canned	6 oz can:170g	0.65
wild rice raw	1 cup:160g	0.63
potatoes canned	1 can:454g	0.62
apricots dehydrated	1 cup:119g	0.62
miso	1 cup:275g	0.59
barley	1 cup:184g	0.59
soy flour defatted	1 cup:100g	0.57
prune juice	1 cup:256g	0.56
spinach raw	10 oz:284g	0.55
raisins seedless	1 cup:165g	0.53
barley pearled, raw	1 cup:200g	0.52
corn yellow	1/2 cup:83g	0.52
carrots canned	1 can:454g	0.51
peanuts raw	1 cup:146g	0.51
spaghetti whole-wheat, dry	8 oz:227g	0.51
sweetcorn frozen, kernels cut off cob	10 oz pkg:284g	0.51
tempeh	1 cup:166g	0.50

bulghur dry	1 cup:140g	0.48
dried mixed fruit	11 oz pkg:293g	0.47
brussels sprouts cooked	1 cup:155g	0.45
figs dried	1 cup:199g	0.45
spinach cooked	1 cup:180g	0.44
vegetable soup canned, ready-to-serve	1 can:539g	0.43
prunes dried	1 cup:161g	0.43
asparagus canned	1 can:411g	0.40
soya beans cooked	1 cup:172g	0.40
quinoa	1 cup:170g	0.38

Is getting enough Vitamin B6 likely to be a problem for vegetarians?

No. Vegetarians and vegans can easily obtain all the vitamin B6 they need from their diets. A survey of the vitamin B6 intake of vegans compared to meat-eaters revealed that vegans averaged an intake of 1.9mg compared to 1.5mg for meat-eaters.[15] Obtaining sufficient vitamin B6 may, however, be a problem for some people: women taking oral contraceptives are likely to have an increased requirement for it, and many other medications interfere with vitamin B6 metabolism. Alcoholics or other drug-abusers may become deficient. Since the body's requirement for vitamin B6 increases with protein consumption, meat-eaters consuming large quantities of protein have a greater need for this vitamin than non-meat eaters.

RECOMMENDED INTAKES
Vitamin B6 (mg)

	Age	US RDA	Can RNI	UK RNI
Infants	up to 6 months	0.3	–	0.2
	6 months–1 year	0.6	–	0.4
	1–3	1.0	–	0.7
Children	4–6	1.1	–	0.9
	7-10	1.4	–	1.0
Males	11–14	1.7	–	1.2
	15–18	2.0	–	1.5
	19–24	2.0	–	1.4
	25–50	2.0	–	1.4
	51 +	2.0	–	1.4
Females	11–14	1.4	–	1.0
	15–18	1.5	–	1.2
	19–24	1.6	–	1.2
	25–50	1.6	–	1.2
	51 +	1.6	–	1.2
Pregnant		2.2	–	no increment
Lactating	first 6 months	2.1	–	no increment
	second 6 months	2.1	–	no increment

FOLATE

Folate and folacin (sometimes called vitamin B9) are the names used to describe a group of substances which are chemically similar to folic acid. Its importance to growth and the prevention of anaemia was established in 1946. The word 'folate' comes from the Latin word *folium*, meaning a leaf, which should tell us something about the best sources of this vitamin.

Importance and function

- Plays an essential role in the formation of DNA and RNA
- Functions together with vitamin B12 in amino acid synthesis
- Essential for the formation of red and white blood cells
- Contributes to the formation of haem, the iron constituent of haemoglobin

Signs of deficiency

- Disruption of DNA metabolism manifesting as changes in red and white blood cells (various anaemias), and abnormalities of linings of stomach, intestines, vagina and cervix
- Poor growth
- Irritability
- Sore red tongue
- Mental confusion

Best vegetarian sources

Folate is easily destroyed by exposure to air, so raw,

fresh foods will provide the highest-quality sources. The following are good sources of folate:

Food	measure	Mg of folate
spinach raw	10 oz pkg:284g	552.09
cabbage raw	1 head:908g	514.84
pizza with cheese	1 pizza:503g	467.79
okra frozen	10 oz pkg:284g	419.18
wheat germ toasted	1 cup:113g	397.76
asparagus boiled	10 oz pkg:293g	394.67
spinach soufflé	1 average:813g	369.91
asparagus canned	1 can:411g	350.58
peanuts raw	1 cup:146g	350.11
sunflower seed kernels dried	1 cup:144g	327.46
mung beans boiled	1 cup:202g	320.78
soy flour defatted	1 cup:100g	305.4
lettuce iceberg	1 head:539g	301.84
pinto beans boiled	1 cup:171g	294.12
chickpeas cooked	1 cup:164g	282.08
wheat germ crude	1 cup:113g	281
adzuki beans cooked	1 cup:230g	278.53
lima beans cooked	1 cup:182g	272.82
spinach cooked	1 cup:180g	262.44
cabbage cooked	1 head:1262g	256.19
black beans cooked	1 cup:172g	255.94
navy beans cooked	1 cup:182g	254.61
peanut butter	1 cup:258g	237.36
asparagus canned	1 can:248g	237.08
kidney beans cooked	1 cup:177g	229.39
peanuts dry-roasted	1 cup:146g	212.14
collards frozen	10 oz pkg:284g	207.61
bean sprouts mung, raw	12 oz pkg:340g	206.72
chicory greens, raw	1 cup chopped:180g	197.1
seaweed wakame, raw	100g	195.5
hummus	1 cup:246g	190.90
sweetcorn canned	1 can:482g	183.65
lentils cooked,	1/2 cup:99g	178.99
broad beans cooked	1 cup:170g	176.97
turnip greens cooked	1 cup chopped:144g	170.5
almond butter	1 cup:250g	163
avocados raw	1 cup purée:230g	150.65
rice white, short-grain, cooked	1 cup:205g	147.6
burrito w/beans, cheese, and chili peppers	2 burritos:336g	144.48
sesame seeds dried	1 cup:150g	144
peas canned	1 can:313g	138.66
spinach cooked	1/2 cup:90g	131.22
spaghetti whole-wheat, dry	8 oz:227g	129.39
split peas cooked	1 cup:196g	127.21
avocados raw	1 fruit:201g	124.42
baked beans	1 cup:253g	122.46
mixed nuts with peanuts, oil roasted	1 cup:142g	117.86
papayas	1 fruit:304g	115.52
broccoli raw	1 spear:151g	107.21

Is getting enough folate likely to be a problem for vegetarians?

Absolutely not. Since most meats are a poor source of folate, and the best sources are common items in the meat-free diet, studies show that vegetarians and vegans consistently have a better intake of this important vitamin than meat-eaters.[16,17] Some studies show that only vegetarians and vegans achieve the recommended intake of this vitamin.[18]

RECOMMENDED INTAKES
Folate (mcg)

	Age	US RDA	Can RNI	UK RNI
Infants	up to 6 months	25	50	50
	6 months–1 year	35	50	50
	1–3	50	80	70
Children	4–6	75	90	100
	7–10	100	125	150
Males	11–14	150	150	200
	15–18	200	185	200
	19–24	200	210	200
	25–50	200	220	200
	51 +	200	220	200
Females	11–14	150	145	200
	15–18	150	160	200
	19–24	150	175	200
	25–50	150	175	200
	51 +	150	190	200
Pregnant		400	+ 300	+ 100
Lactating	first 6 months	250	+ 100	+ 60
	second 6 months	250	+ 100	+ 60

VITAMIN B12

Also called cobalamin, this vitamin is the most controversial nutrient in the field of non-meat nutrition. It is often wrongly claimed that meat is the only source of this vitamin. This is incorrect. Vitamin B12 is manufactured by microorganisms such as yeasts, bacteria, moulds and some algae. The human body can store this vitamin for long periods (five or six years) so a daily dietary source is therefore not necessary. In addition, the healthy body recycles this vitamin very effectively, recovering it from bile and other intestinal secretions, which is why the dietary requirement is so low (being measured in millionths of a gram).

Importance and function

- Essential for the normal metabolic function of all cells

- Works with folate to prevent anaemia
- Assists in the process of DNA synthesis
- Promotes growth and normal functioning of nervous system

Signs of deficiency

- Eventual depletion of body stores will produce megaloblastic anaemia and neuro-psychiatric abnormalities

Best vegetarian sources

Unfortunately, this is not known with absolute certainty at the moment. It was initially thought that fermented foods such as tempeh and sea vegetables provided considerable resources of this vitamin. This was reflected in numerous tables of food composition, some of which continue to show these and other similar foods as significant sources. Later scientific work suggested that B12 was not present in the amounts previously thought since substances analogous to B12 were present instead. It is also thought that some of these B12 analogues may actually interfere with the body's metabolism of B12.

However, at least one piece of recent research now indicates that true B12 may indeed be present in some fermented food.[19] The confused situation is primarily caused by the nature of the vitamin. It is manufactured by microorganisms and it is impossible to say with certainty which foodstuffs may or may not be rich with these B12-producing microflora. It could, for example, change dramatically from one batch to the next.

All this is perhaps rather irrelevant to the normal everyday concerns of non-meat eaters, because there are plenty of foods which are known with certainty to be good sources of B12. They are: 1) for vegetarians, dairy products, and 2) for vegans, many fortified foods, such as soya milk, yeast extract, textured vegetable protein foods (such as the 'Protoveg' range[20]) and most breakfast cereals. Check the product's label for information on its B12 content. The typical B12 composition of these foods is such that one average serving will provide about a quarter to a half of the suggested daily requirement of this vitamin.

Is getting enough Vitamin B12 likely to be a problem for vegetarians?

Vegetarians easily obtain all the vitamin B12 they require from dairy sources (note: vegetarians who boil their milk will destroy a high proportion of its B12). Since many of the most common foods in the vegan diet are fortified with B12, it is not likely to be a problem for vegans either. Women who are pregnant or breastfeeding should take care to ensure that they receive an adequate amount of this and other nutrients; the easiest way to do this is to take a well-formulated vitamin and mineral supplement. Since some studies suggest that vegan and macrobiotic infants and children may be at greater risk of B12 deficiency, a wise parent will ensure that such children receive regular allowances of suitably fortified food.

It is important to note that the British government's Committee on Medical Aspects of Food Policy Panel on Dietary Reference Values states that the most common cause of vitamin B12 deficiency in humans is failure to properly absorb the vitamin – not inadequate dietary intake.[21] To be properly assimilated, B12 must combine with a mucoprotein enzyme called 'the intrinsic factor' (or Castle's intrinsic factor) which is normally present in gastric secretions. This allows the vitamin to be absorbed by a receptor in the membranes of the ileum (lower small intestine) from where it is transported to the cells. If the intrinsic factor is absent or impaired, B12 will not be received by the body, no matter how much is present in the diet. The scientific deliberations about the food presence and activity of this vitamin will no doubt continue for many years. In the meantime, all vegans need to do is to periodically consume B12-fortified foods as an 'insurance policy'. Far from being one of the most difficult vitamins to obtain, it is actually one of the easiest: the growing range of B12-supplemented foods has effectively seen to that.

RECOMMENDED INTAKES
Vitamin B12 (mcg)

	Age	US RDA	Can RNI	UK RNI
Infants	up to 6 months	0.3	0.3	0.3
	6 months–1 year	0.5	0.3	0.4
	1–3	0.7	0.4	0.5
Children	4–6	1.0	0.5	0.8
	7–10	1.4	0.8	1.0
Males	11–14	2.0	1.5	1.2
	15–18	2.0	1.9	1.5
	19–24	2.0	2.0	1.5
	25–50	2.0	2.0	1.5
	51+	2.0	2.0	1.5
Females	11–14	2.0	1.5	1.2
	15–18	2.0	1.9	1.5
	19–24	2.0	2.0	1.5
	25–50	2.0	2.0	1.5
	51+	2.0	2.0	1.5
Pregnant		2.2	+1.0	no increment
Lactating	first 6 months	2.6	+0.5	+0.5
	second 6 months	2.6	+0.5	+0.5

PANTOTHENIC ACID

Part of the B-group vitamins, pantothenic acid (also known as vitamin B5) is widely distributed in nature (it occurs in all living cells, both animals and plants – hence its name, meaning 'widespread'). It can also be produced by the bacterial-flora of the human intestines.

Importance and function

- Essential to cell metabolism
- Involved in the metabolism of carbohydrates, proteins and fatty acids
- Contributes to the synthesis of cholesterol, hormones and haemoglobin

Signs of deficiency

- So widely distributed in foods that symptoms of deficiency are not observed.

Best vegetarian sources

A diet which provides a good nutritional intake of the other B-group vitamins will necessarily be adequate in pantothenic acid.

Is getting enough pantothenic acid likely to be a problem for vegetarians?

Not in the least.

BIOTIN

Another water-soluble B-group vitamin, biotin (occasionally called vitamin H) is an essential nutrient which appears in all animal and plant tissue to a greater or lesser extent. The human body also produces considerable amounts by synthesis of intestinal bacteria. It was isolated in 1936, as the cure for 'egg white injury', a human disease which is caused by the overconsumption of egg whites (a protein in egg whites binds to biotin and prevents its use by the body).

Importance and function

- Assists in the synthesis and oxidation of fatty acids
- Aids in the utilization of protein
- Functions to effectively utilize other B-group vitamins

Signs of deficiency

- Only likely in people who consume large amounts of egg white, or who have been receiving intravenous feeding for several years
- Dry scaly dermatitis
- Nausea and vomiting
- Anorexia

Best vegetarian sources

Good non-meat sources include mushrooms, bananas, grapefruit, watermelon, strawberries, peanuts, and yeast.

Is getting enough biotin likely to be a problem for vegetarians?

Not at all. Both meat and milk are poor sources of biotin, so the theoretical risk of deficiency applies more to meat-eaters than vegetarians or vegans.

VITAMIN C

Vitamin C, or ascorbic acid, is perhaps one of the most important vitamins known to science. Long derided as only relevant to the prevention of scurvy, there is now increasing evidence that a first-class intake of vitamin C can help to prevent a wide range of human diseases. Humans are one of the few species unable to synthesize vitamin C internally, and therefore we need to be certain of a regular intake. In this respect, the evidence shows that vegetarians and vegans are much better placed than meat-eaters.

Importance and function

- Assists in the production of collagen, a protein which is the body's building block for all connective tissue, cartilage, bones, teeth, skin and tendons
- Helps wounds, fractures, bruises and haemorrhages

heal
- Maintains function of immune system
- Greatly facilitates the absorption of iron from the diet
- Assists haemoglobin and red blood cell production
- An essential cofactor for metabolism of many other nutrients
- Helps the body cope with physiological and psychological stress
- Lowers risk of various serious diseases

Signs of deficiency

- Wounds fail to heal
- Previous scar tissue breaks down
- Increased liability to infection
- Swollen and inflamed gums
- Loosening of teeth
- Dryness of mouth and eyes
- Loss of hair
- Severe deficiency manifests as scurvy

Best vegetarian sources

Meat and dairy products contain little or no vitamin C, and even this negligible amount will be further diminished by food processing (vitamin C is easily destroyed by exposure to air, heat or an alkaline environment). Non-animal sources are, therefore, the only significant food sources of this vitamin. An extensive analysis of several thousand vegetarian foodstuffs reveals that the following are good sources of this vitamin:

Food	measure	Mg of vitamin C
papayas	1 fruit:304g	187.87
guavas	1 fruit:90g	165.15
chicory raw	1 head:513g	160.06
broccoli raw	1 spear:151g	140.73
orange juice	1 cup:248g	124
oranges raw	1 fruit:159g	112.89
melons cantaloupe	1/2 fruit:267g	112.67
lemon juice	1 cup:244g	112.24
kale	10 oz pkg:284g	111.61
peppers hot chili, green	1 pepper:45g	109.13

currants	1/2 cup:56g	101.36
peppers sweet, red	1/2 cup chopped:50g	95
grapefruit juice	1 cup:247g	93.86
kiwifruit	1 fruit:91g	89.18
kohlrabi cooked	1 cup slices:165g	89.1
tomato purée, canned	1 cup:250g	88.25
peas edible-podded, raw	1 cup:145g	87
strawberries	1 cup:149g	84.48
lime juice	1 cup:246g	72.08
kale boiled	1 cup chopped:130g	68.64
asparagus canned	1 can:411g	67.4
sweet potatoes canned	1 cup mashed:255g	67.32
cranberry juice cocktail	6 fl oz:190g	67.26
lambsquarters boiled	1 cup chopped:180g	66.6
peppers green	1 pepper:74g	66.08
breadfruit	1 cup:220g	63.8
tangerines	1 cup:195g	60.06
mangos	1 fruit:207g	57.34
tomatoes cooked	1 cup:240g	54.72
amaranth cooked	1 cup:132g	54.25
vegetable juice canned	6 fl oz:182g	50.41
potato baked and topped w/ cheese sauce and broccoli	1 potato:339g	48.48
brussels sprouts boiled	1/2 cup:78g	48.36
salad vegetable	1–1/2 cup:207g	48.02
watermelon	1/16 fruit:482g	46.27
grapefruit	1/2 fruit:123g	45.51
passion-fruit juice	1 cup:247g	44.95
bean sprouts mung	12 oz pkg:340g	44.88
collards boiled	1 cup chopped:170g	44.88

lemons whole	1 fruit:84g	44.52
cabbage chinese (bok-choi) boiled	1 cup shredded:170g	44.2
gooseberries	1 cup:150g	41.55
broccoli raw	1/2 cup chopped:44g	41.01
cauliflower raw	3 florets:56g	40.04
cabbage red, raw	1 cup shredded:70g	39.9
swede raw	1 cup cubes:140g	35
sauerkraut canned	1 cup:236g	34.69
pizza with cheese topping	1 pizza:567g	34.02
sweetcorn canned	1 can:482g	32.29
melons honeydew	1/10 fruit:129g	31.99

Is getting enough vitamin C likely to be a problem for vegetarians?

Not at all. The better health of vegetarians and vegans compared to meat-eaters is probably due, in part, to their increased consumption of this vitamin. Study after study reveals that non-meat eaters consume far greater quantities of vitamin C than meat-eaters. It has been calculated from an average of several studies that the mean vitamin C intake of vegans is 162mg a day, compared to 112mg for meat-eaters.[22] Vegans on average therefore consume nearly 50 per cent more vitamin C.

RECOMMENDED INTAKES
Vitamin C (mg)

	Age	US RDA	Can RNI	UK RNI
Infants	up to 6 months	30	20	25
	6 months– 1 year	35	20	25
	1–3	40	20	30
Children	4–6	45	25	30
	7–10	45	25	30
Males	11–14	50	30	35
	15–18	60	40	40
	19–24	60	40	40

	25–50	60	40	40
	51 +	60	40	40
Females	11–14	50	30	35
	15–18	60	30	40
	19–24	60	30	40
	25–50	60	30	40
	51 +	60	30	40
Pregnant		70	+ 10	+ 10
Lactating	first 6 months	95	+ 25	+ 30
	second 6 months	90	+ 25	+ 30

VITAMIN D

Also called calciferol, this fat-soluble vitamin can be obtained either through the diet or by exposure to sunlight. Its only role in the body is to provide the raw material from which two more biologically-active forms of the vitamin are manufactured; these substances function as hormones which regulate growth and repair of bones. Vitamin D can be obtained:

- **From the diet**
  A precursor substance to vitamin D, called 7-dehydrocholesterol, is found in animal tissue. When ultraviolet light (supplied by sunlight) strikes the animal's skin, it is converted to the 'provitamin' D_3 (cholecalciferol). When the animal's flesh is eaten by a human, the D_3 is converted by the liver into a biologically-active metabolite (25-OHD_3), and further converted by the kidneys into an even more biologically-active form ($1,25$-$(OH)_2D_3$, or calcitriol). These two substances are the most important final products of vitamin D. On the one hand, they act on the intestine to increase calcium and phosphate absorption; and on the other, they act on the bones to increase calcium and phosphate resorption.

- **From sunlight**
  Humans, just like other animals, manufacture vitamin D_3 from the action of sunlight on the skin. The D_3 thus manufactured is then converted by the liver and kidneys into the two substances mentioned above.

The process of vitamin D production from sunlight is so effective that 'no dietary intake is necessary for individuals living a normal lifestyle', according to the British government's Committee on Medical Aspects of Food Policy Panel on Dietary Reference Values.[23] It should be noted that Britain is situated at a more northerly latitude than the United States, and receives far less intense sunlight than countries further to the south.

Importance and function

- Regulates bone formation, hardening and repair
- Prevents rickets

Signs of deficiency

- Rickets, a childhood disease: malformed bones, bowed legs, late tooth development, listlessness
- Osteomalacia, adult rickets: brittle bones, muscle weakness, pain in ribs and lower limbs

Best vegetarian sources

- Sunlight
- Some vegan products are fortifed with vitamin D_2, which is made by exposing ergosterol (found in plant tissues) to ultraviolet light

Is getting enough vitamin D likely to be a problem for vegetarians?

No. It has been calculated that exposure of the hands and face to summer sunlight for as little as ten to fifteen minutes a day will provide sufficient Vitamin D to prevent rickets.[24] Very little vitamin D occurs in meat and cow's milk, the main dietary sources being fatty fish such as herring and mackerel, eggs, and fortified foods such as margarine and breakfast cereals (the latter two being acceptable to vegans). In Britain, levels of vitamin D rise and fall according to the time of year. From November to the end of March there is no ultraviolet light of the correct wavelength to produce vitamin D, which means that we are dependent on exposure during the summer months to build up our vitamin D levels. Even so, supplemental dietary vitamin D is unnecessary except for the following special categories:

- The increased pigmentation of dark-skinned people can prevent ultraviolet light from reaching the deeper layers of the skin where vitamin D is synthesized. This is sometimes a problem for people of Asian origin living in northerly countries such as Britain, and there have been cases of rickets developing in such communities. The British Department of Health recommends that Asian women and children in the UK should take supplementary vitamin D (which is, as mentioned above, available from plant sources).

- The elderly are unlikely to expose sufficient skin to sunlight in Britain, and the Department of Health therefore recommends a supplement of 10mcg (microgrammes) of vitamin D daily.
- Pregnant women in the north of Britain have lower vitamin D levels, and a supplement of 10mcg of vitamin D daily is also recommended. This amount is also recommended for breast-feeding mothers.
- Infants and children between six months and three years are most vulnerable to vitamin D depletion because of the rate at which calcium is being used to form bones, and because many children do not gain sufficient exposure to sunlight. The Department of Health regards it as prudent for children up to at least the age of two to receive a supplement of 7mcg of vitamin D daily.

Note: Vitamin D is often included in multivitamin and mineral preparations, making it unnecessary to seek out and purchase specific vitamin D supplements. Vitamin D is sometimes measured in International Units (IU). The conversion is as follows:

1 International Unit (IU) = 0.025mcg vitamin D*

* Vitamins D_2 and D_3 have equal biological activity and are usually both described in terms of vitamin D_3. Where a vitamin preparation contains vitamin D and is described as being 'suitable for vegetarians and vegans' then the source of vitamin D will be from plants (ergosterol transformed by ultraviolet light to ercalcitriol).

Toxicity

Vitamin D is one of the most toxic of vitamins in overdose. Consumption of as little as 45mcg a day has been found to be excessive in young children. Symptoms of overdose are:

- Headache
- Weakness
- Nausea and vomiting
- Constipation
- Excessive thirst and urination
- Excessive calcification of bones
- Formation of kidney stones
- Calcium deposits in soft tissue (eg lungs)

Vitamin D is, and will remain, a controversial nutrient. Some scientists dispute that vitamin D should even be designated as a vitamin. In 1992, Professor Jim Moon wrote in the Journal Of The American College Of Nutrition: 'in as much as vitamin D is not an essential dietary component for the vast majority of people, and relatively small excesses may be toxic in the long term, we concur with the recommendation . . . that [its] reclassification as a potent, carefully controlled hormone should be seriously considered. We similarly agree with recommendation . . . that fortification of foods with vitamin D should be curtailed, preferably abolished, that excessive fortification of animal foods be reduced to the level required, and that the use of dietary supplements be restricted. We further recommend that, to avoid confusion that might lead to excessive self-administration, the more correct hormone name, 'calciferol', rather than the common name, 'vitamin D', be used for labelling purposes. Calciferol should be available, on the advice of a physician, for those infants or others at risk of a deficiency, but should not be administered to the general, calciferol-sufficient population.'[25] Professor Moon, and others, have advanced evidence to suggest that synthetic and dietary forms of vitamin D may be implicated in the development of many diseases, including atherosclerosis and osteoporosis. The safety of vitamin D which is naturally produced by the action of sunlight on the skin is not, however, disputed; and this should therefore be your major source of this substance.

RECOMMENDED INTAKES
Vitamin D (mcg)

	Age	US RDA	Can RNI	UK RNI
Infants	up to 6 months	7.5	10	8.5
	6 months–1 year	10	10	7
	1–3	10	5	7
Children	4–6	10	5	–
	7–10	10	2.5	–
Males	11–14	10	5	–
	15-18	10	5	–
	19–24	10	2.5	–
	25-50	5	2.5	–

	51+	5	5	10 after age 65
Females	11–14	10	5	–
	15–18	10	2.5	–
	19-24	10	2.5	–
	25-50	5	2.5	–
	51+	5	5	10 after age 65
Pregnant		10	+ 2.5	10
Lactating	first 6 months	10	+ 2.5	10
	second 6 months	10	+ 2.5	10

VITAMIN E

First discovered in 1922, the importance of fat-soluble vitamin E (also known as tocopherol) was realized when it was observed that vegetable oils (a rich source of vitamin E) could prevent reproductive abnormalities. The name 'tocopherol' comes from the Greek, literally meaning 'substance which brings forth childbirth'. Vitamin E is comprised of two sets of compounds: the tocopherols (alpha, beta, gamma and delta) and the less potent tocotrienols. The most active form of vitamin E is alpha-tocopherol.

Importance and function

- An important antioxidant which protects polyunsaturated fatty acids
- Enhances vitamin A activity by preventing it from being oxidized
- Protects cells from damage by scavenging free radicals
- Acts as anti-blood clotting agent
- Promotes normal red blood cell formation
- Despite mounting evidence, most authorities do not yet accept that vitamin E can prevent cancers or circulatory diseases

Signs of deficiency

- Fragility of blood cells resulting in their rupture
- Muscular wasting or abnormal fat deposits in muscles
- Impaired haemoglobin formation
- Faulty absorption and metabolism of fats
- Peripheral neuropathy; tension and pain in legs

while walking

Best vegetarian sources

Vitamin E is available in many foods, but is liable to be destroyed by exposure to the following:

- Alkaline environment
- Light
- Air
- Rancid fats
- Lead
- Iron
- Freezing
- Deep frying

It is not significantly destroyed by heat or acids. The richest sources of vitamin E come from the plant kingdom – meat is a poor source. The major vegetarian food sources are as follows:

Food	Measure	Mg of vitamin E
wheat germ oil	1 cup:218g	555.03
soya bean oil salad or cooking (hydr)	1 cup:218g	224.54
corn oil salad or cooking	1 cup:218g	181.38
margarine soft, soybean (hydr&reg)	1 cup:227g	170.25
sunflower oil linoleic (less than 60%)	1 cup:218g	138.65
grapeseed oil	1 cup:218g	134.72
apricot kernel oil	1 cup:218g	110.09
sunflower oil linoleic (60% & over)	1 cup:218g	104.20
hazelnut oil	1 cup:218g	102.90
margarine regular, hard, sunflower & soybean (hydr)	4oz:113.4g	100.93
poppyseed oil	1 cup:218g	95.48
almond oil	1 cup:218g	87.42
rice bran oil	1 cup:218g	84.58
safflower oil salad or cooking, linoleic (over 70%)	1 cup:218g	83.06

walnut oil	1 cup:218g	69.98
sesame oil salad or cooking	1 cup:218g	63.44
peanut oil salad or cooking	1 cup:216g	54.00
wheat germ oil	1 tbsp:13.6g	34.63
olive oil salad or cooking	1 cup:216g	27.22
margarine regular, hard, soybean (hydr&reg)	4oz:113.4g	17.58
soybean oil salad or cooking	1 tbsp:13.6g	12.74
butter	4 oz:113.4g	1.81
coconut meat raw	1 cup shredded or grated:80g	0.01

Is getting enough vitamin E likely to be a problem for vegetarians?

No. Vegetarians and vegans eating a good wholefood diet will naturally consume more of this important vitamin than meat-eaters. You should note, however, that the body's requirement for vitamin E depends upon the amount of polyunsaturated fatty acids consumed. The popularity of polyunsaturated fats as a 'health' food means that people using these fats must also take care to increase their intake of vitamin-E-containing foods. There are no definitive guidelines for this, so it would make sense to only use oils which are naturally high in vitamin E, as shown above.

Note: Because several different compounds contribute towards the total vitamin E content of foodstuffs, vitamin E is usually measured in terms of the equivalent amount of its most active form, alpha-tocopherol. Alpha-TEs (alpha-tocopheral equivalents) are measured in milligrams. One milligram of alpha-TE equals 1.49 IU (International Units, still sometimes used).

RECOMMENDED INTAKES
Vitamin E (mg) (alpha)-tocopherol equivalents

	Age	US RDA	Can RNI	U.K. RNI
Infants	up to 6 months	3	3	–
	6 months–1 year	4	3	–
Children	1–3	6	4	–
	4–6	7	5	–
	7–10	7	7	–
Males	11–14	10	9	–
	15–18	10	10	–
	19–24	10	10	–
	25–50	10	9	–
	51 +	10	7	–
Females	11–14	8	7	–
	15–18	8	7	–
	19–24	8	7	–
	25–50	8	6	–
	51 +	8	6	–
Pregnant		10	+ 2	–
Lactating	first 6 months	12	+ 3	–
	second 6 months	11	+ 3	–

CALCIUM

Calcium is the most plentiful mineral in the human body, amounting to 1kg or so of the average adult's weight. 99 per cent is deposited in the bones and teeth, with the remainder fulfilling essential regulatory functions in the blood and cellular fluids. The body stores its skeletal calcium in two ways: in the nonexchangeable pool (calcium which is on 'long-term deposit' in the bones) and in the exchangeable pool, which can act as a short-term buffer to smooth over the peaks and troughs in the day-to-day dietary calcium intakes. If dietary intake is consistently too low then the exchangeable pool of calcium will become so depleted that the calcium on 'long-term deposit' in the bones will be put to use, thus inducing bone degeneration.

Although calcium is often thought of as the 'bone mineral', the 1 per cent of serum calcium in the human body (calcium held outside the skeletal structure) is responsible for a vital and complex range of tasks. Calcium is clearly a critical nutrient, and we all need to ensure that we have a sufficient intake. Many people erroneously believe that the consumption of heroic quantities of dairy produce is the only way to prevent bone-depleting afflictions such as osteoporosis. In this context, it is often surprising for the consumers of meat and dairy products to learn that as a group, they are significantly more at risk of bone loss than non-meat eaters.[26]

Importance and function

- Helps build and maintain bones and teeth
- Helps control transport of chemicals across cell membranes
- Facilitates release of neurotransmitters at synapses
- Influences function of protein hormones and enzymes
- Helps regulate heartbeat and muscle tone
- Initiates clotting of blood

Signs of deficiency

- Muscle spasms, such as leg cramps
- High blood pressure
- Bone deformities, demineralization and fragility

Best vegetarian sources

Meat is virtually devoid of calcium content: both meat-eaters and dairy-consuming vegetarians alike, therefore, rely on much the same range of foods to achieve their daily calcium requirements. Vegans generally obtain their calcium from rather different sources.

Milk and milk products are widely believed by both the general public and many doctors and nutritionists to be an excellent source of calcium – if not the only source. This is in part due to a highly-visible publicity campaign by the milk industry, and partly because milk does indeed contain calcium in a water-soluble form, which makes it easily absorbed. The full picture, however, is not so well known.

Milk and milk products do contain considerable amounts of bioavailable calcium. But ingesting large quantities of calcium does not, in itself, seem to eliminate bone loss:

- A 1990 Mayo Clinic study which examined dietary calcium intake and actual rates of bone loss in women, and determined that 'these data do not support the hypothesis that insufficient dietary calcium is a major cause of bone loss in women'.[27]
- Many populations with high intakes of calcium also have high rates of osteoporosis.[28]

The Inuit, for example, consume twice the amount of calcium found in the average Western diet (about 2000mg daily). This does not prevent them from suffering from high rates of osteoporosis, and it has been estimated that compared to US Caucasians, the Inuit have an average of 10 to 15 per cent less bone mass. This is almost certainly due to the Inuit's considerable intake of protein (250g to 400g daily) from fish, whale and walrus.[29]

On the other hand, Bantus living in Africa on low-calcium (400mg daily) and low-protein vegetable diets (47g daily) are essentially free of osteoporosis.[30]

The British government's own nutritional advisory panel confirms this paradox: 'Several populations of the world consume calcium at levels lower than the current RDA for the UK yet show no evidence of adverse effects.'[31] Celebrated dietary expert Nathan Pritikin comments on this paradox on page 156, where the question of osteoporosis is further discussed.

It is important to note that careful scientific studies whose objective has been to reveal the true absorption of calcium (using radioactive labelling techniques) have shown that only 18 to 36 per cent of the calcium in milk is assimilated.[32] This is taken into account by the authorities responsible for setting recommended nutrient intakes, who generally assume that something in the range of 20 to 40 per cent of the diet's calcium content is actually absorbed, and therefore have to build a 'safety factor' for this into their figures. Dark green leafy vegetables (such as kale, collards, turnip greens and broccoli) are good plant sources: one study shows that 27 per cent of the calcium in watercress was absorbed. Another study has demonstrated that calcium absorbability is actually higher for kale than for milk, and concludes: 'greens such as kale can be considered to be at least as good as milk in terms of their calcium absorbability.'[33]

Certain plants, such as rhubarb, spinach and chard contain chemicals (eg oxalic acid) which bind with the calcium to render it relatively insoluble in the gut: it has been estimated that no more than 5 per cent of the calcium in spinach can be absorbed.[34] This and other factors are alleged to be significant obstacles to calcium absorption in the plant-based diet, and nutrition textbooks regularly echo this warning – perhaps without always checking to see if the effect is more theoretical than real. The American Dietetic Association comments on this question: 'Calcium absorption appears to be inhibited by such plant constituents as phytic acid, oxalic acid, and fibre, but this effect may not be significant. Calcium deficiency in vegetarians is rare, and there is little evidence to show that low intakes of calcium give rise to major health problems among the vegetarian population. One recent study has shown that vegetarians absorb and retain more calcium from foods than do non-vegetarians.[35] Other studies[36] cite lower rates of osteoporosis in vegetarians than in non-vegetarians.'[37]

The wisest course when planning a vegan diet, therefore, is to obtain dietary calcium (as with all nutrients) from a wide range of sources. The following are good sources of calcium:

Food	Measure	Mg of calcium
molasses cane, third extraction or blackstrap	1 cup:328g	2243
cheese gruyere	1 pkg:170g	1718
cheese edam	1 pkg:198g	1447
sesame seeds whole, dried	1 cup:144g	1404
pizza with cheese topping	1 pizza:520g	1149
tofu fried, prepared w/calcium sulfate	100g	961
molasses cane, second extraction or medium	1 cup:328g	951
endive raw	1 head:513g	928
tofu raw, firm, prepared w/calcium sulphate	1/2 cup:126g	860
cornbread	1 loaf:703g	843
molasses cane, barbados	1 cup:328g	803
cheese blue	1 cup:135g	712
cake plain or cupcake	1 cake:1109g	709
potatoes au gratin, dry mix, prepared with water, whole milk and butter	5-1/2 oz pkg:822g	682
almond butter	1 cup:250g	675
pancake and waffle mix dry	1 cup:147g	661
cake devil's food, w/ eggs	1 cake:1107g	653
baking powder	1 tbsp:13.5g	650
cheese cheshire	100g	643
seaweed agar, dried	100g	625
rhubarb pie baked	1 pie:945g	605
welsh rarebit	1 cup:232g	582
collards chopped	10 oz pkg:284g	571
tofu raw, firm, prepared w/calcium sulphate	1/4 block:81g	553
molasses cane, first extraction or light	1 cup:328g	541
lambsquarters cooked	1 cup chopped:180g	464
pumpkin pie baked	1 pie:910g	464
milk shake vanilla	1 glass:313g	457
yogurt plain, skim milk	1 tub:227g	452
soup cream of celery, canned	1 can:602g	452
tofu raw, regular, prepared w/calcium sulphate	1/2 cup:124g	434
soup cream of mushroom, canned	1 can:602g	433
cabbage raw	1 head:908g	427
tostada with guacamole	2 tostadas:261g	423
wheat flour white, self-raising, enriched	1 cup:125g	423
potatoes o'brien	1 dish:1162g	418
tofu raw, regular, prepared w/calcium sulphate	1/4 block:116g	406
kale raw	10oz pkg:284g	386
soup tomato, canned	1 can:602g	385
cheese parmesan	1 oz:28g	385
natto	1 cup:175g	380
almonds dried	1 cup kernels:142g	377
macaroni and cheese	1 cup:200g	362
carob flour	1 cup:103g	358
collards cooked	1 cup chopped:170g	357

rhubarb cooked	1 cup:240g	348
turnip greens	10 oz pkg:284g	335
eggs yolk only	1 cup:243g	333
spinach frozen	10 oz pkg:284g	315
seaweed dulse, raw	100g	296

Is getting enough calcium likely to be a problem for vegetarians?

No. Amongst vegetarians, vegans and meat-eaters, meat-eaters are perhaps worst off in respect of the overall calcium intake/utilization picture. Research certainly demonstrates that they suffer more from bone loss than do vegetarians.[38] Vegetarians, while consuming dairy produce, also consume a good range of calcium-containing plant food. It is very likely that meat-eaters do not have the benefit of these additional sources of calcium within the scope of their meat-based diets. However, certain populations groups (whether vegetarian or meat-eating) need to pay particular attention to their calcium intakes – see below.

Vegans do not consume milk, and might therefore be supposed by some to be at risk of calcium deficiency. Interestingly, the evidence does not support this, and suggests that, although vegans do indeed consume less calcium in their food, their bodies process and conserve it far more efficiently than meat-eaters.

How much calcium do vegans actually take in from their diets?

Several surveys have examined this question. Early studies conducted amongst British vegans in the 1950s and 1960s found levels of intake ranging between 500mg and 1000mg daily.[39] A 1985 study showed an average intake of around 500mg[40], a 1986 study suggested 554mg[41] and a 1987 study found 585mg daily, with the lowest individual intake being 157mg.[42] A study amongst Swedish vegans found an average intake of 626mg.[43] Among children aged 12 to 55 months, a 1981 study found an average intake of about 300mg, which is half the officially recommended figure.[44] Significantly, none of the children studied showed signs of calcium deficiency and all were in good health. An American study of children at The Farm vegan community in Tennessee also found that they were receiving about half of the recommended 800mg a day intake, but again, all children studied were well and thriving.

What should we conclude from this scientific work?

Says Dr Gill Langley, an expert on vegan nutrition: 'The dietary calcium intake of adult vegans is adequate according to British RDAs, although the intake of some vegan children may be well below the recommended amounts. Vegan parents should take care to ensure that the diets of their children include calcium-rich foods such as tofu, mashed beans, nut and seed "butters" or spreads using almonds or sesame seeds (tahini), home-made dried fruit spreads and molasses instead of sugar.'[45]

How effectively do vegans manage calcium in their bodies?

Several studies have examined this, and their results suggest that the vegan body has adapted well to handling this mineral with considerable efficiency. A 1987 study found that, despite having a lower dietary intake of calcium, the blood-levels of this mineral were the same in near-vegan women as in meat-eating women, because of an adaptation to increase calcium absorption from the intestine.[46]

Dr Neal Barnard, president of the Physicians Committee for Responsible Medicine, summarizes the evidence thus: 'The amount of calcium in your bones is very carefully regulated by hormones. Increasing your calcium intake does not fool those hormones into building more bone, any more than delivering an extra load of bricks will make a construction crew build a larger building . . . For the vast majority of people, the answer is not boosting your calcium intake, but rather, limiting calcium loss.'[47]

The wisdom of these words contrasts with the prevailing recommendations of other authorities. Currently, the adult recommended daily intake for calcium is about 700mg a day. Yet at a recent conference on osteoporosis in Virginia, USA, experts put the recommended level as high as 1500mg per day for women,[48] and a British symposium on osteoporosis has proposed the following intakes for women:

Age	Intake requirement (mg)
Normal adult	800
Adolescent growth	1100
Pregnancy	1000
Lactation	1200
Elderly with HRT	1000
Elderly without HRT	1500

At the upper level, an intake of 1500 mg of calcium a day would have to be supplied by nearly half a pound of hard cheese, 4 cups of yogurt or 5 cups of milk! Most people would find it difficult to include these amounts of dairy food in their diet, and in any case, there are most undesirable health implications in eating such quantities of these foods:

- Dairy foods tend to be very high in fat, especially saturated fat, and cholesterol. A regular consumption of such large amounts would increase the risk of obesity, cardiovascular disease, and stroke. If you wish to eat dairy foods to this extent, make sure you at least choose those with reduced fat content.
- Consuming large amounts of animal protein is associated with increasing bone loss – the very problem it is intended to solve. A diet high in animal-based proteins increases the amount of acid in the body. This triggers a buffering mechanism, which releases stored calcium from the bones. The body would normally reabsorb the calcium released, but the animal protein inhibits the parathyroid function that orders this reabsorption. The body then excretes the calcium, causing bone loss. One researcher who put this theory to the test concluded: 'This study suggests that a diet higher in vegetable protein might actually be somewhat protective against osteoporosis'[49].

What should you do to get enough calcium?

The British government's own panel on nutrition admits that the whole question of calcium requirement, intake and absorption is indeed complex. After reviewing all the available evidence, they concluded: 'The panel considered that much further research was necessary to give data on which to base future recommendations'.[50] In the meantime, a prudent course of action would seem to be as follows:

- If you are vegetarian, do not rely for your calcium intake exclusively upon dairy products. Including the best plant food sources of calcium in your diet as regularly as possible will give you a good and varied supply of this mineral.
- If you are vegan, develop an awareness of the full range of good calcium sources, and make a point of including them regularly in your diet.

Of equal importance is the need to reduce calcium loss from your body. Here are some points to remember:

- Reduce caffeine consumption. A study of women aged thirty-six to forty-five found that those who drank two cups of coffee a day suffered a net calcium loss of 22m daily. Reducing this to one cup daily reduced the loss to just 6m daily.[51]
- Reduce alcohol consumption. Alcohol speeds bone loss because it interferes with the way your body absorbs calcium.
- Get some sun. Sunlight reacts with dehydrocholesterol in your skin to produce vitamin D, which is essential to the proper absorption of calcium and a deficiency will cause you to lose bone mass.
- Eat more plants. Magnesium works with other vitamins and minerals, including calcium, to promote bone growth and the healthy functioning of nerves and muscle tissue. A deficiency of magnesium can affect the manufacture of vitamin D, so it is important in preventing osteoporosis. Magnesium is a constituent of chlorophyll and so is abundant in green vegetables. Other excellent sources are whole grains, wheat germ, molasses, seeds and nuts, apples and figs.
- Eat even more plants! The trace mineral boron helps to prevent calcium loss, and is thought to help in the manufacture of vitamin D in the body. Boron can double the most active form of oestrogen (estradiol 17B) in the blood.[52] Foods rich in boron are easily obtained and include apples, grapes, pears, prunes, dates, raisins, almonds, peanuts and hazelnuts.
- Get some exercise. Weight-bearing exercise (walking, running, dancing etc – but not swimming) is also important in building and maintaining strong, healthy bones.

Special cases

Sometimes it may be necessary to increase calcium intake beyond that which would normally be provided by dietary means. Dr Michael Klaper, a vegan himself and an expert on vegan nutrition, gives the following advice:

If 'calcium insurance' is required, to assure meeting the 1200mg of the US recommended daily allowance, a supplement of an additional 500mg of calcium, preferably in the 'ascorbate' form – that means the calcium is coupled with vitamin C – should be employed. A liquid or powder preparation, mixed in juice and sipped throughout the day, would be the gentlest and most efficient way to ingest the calcium. Tablets are less well absorbed than liquid. For proper mineral balance, the 500mg of calcium should also be combined with 200 to 300mg of magnesium – read the label on the supplement package to see how much magnesium is present. Such a mineral supplement is prudent for most pregnant women, and thus is recommended. If calcium supplements are used be sure that they are not made from bone meal, dolomite or oyster shell. These substances are often contaminated with arsenic lead or mercury that accumulates in the bones and shells of these animals.'[53]

Note: A very high intake of calcium and the presence of a high intake of vitamin D may cause hypercalcaemia, a condition which causes excess calcium deposition in the bones and soft tissues. Knowledgeable professional advice should be obtained before the long-term use of calcium supplements.

RECOMMENDED INTAKES
Calcium (mg)

	Age	US RDA	Can RNI	UK RNI
Infants	up to 6 months	400	250	525
	6 months–1 year	600	400	525
	1–3	800	550	350
Children	4–6	800	600	450
	7–10	800	700	550
Males	11–14	1200	1100	1000
	15–18	1200	900	1000
	19–24	1200	800	700
	25–50	800	800	700
	51 +	800	800	700
Females	11–14	1200	1000	800
	15–18	1200	700	800
	19–24	1200	700	700
	25–50	800	700	700
	51 +	800	800	700
Pregnant		1200	+ 500	no increment
Lactating	first 6 months	1200	+ 500	+ 550
	second 6 months	1200	+ 500	+ 550

IRON

Like protein, iron is traditionally thought of as one of those nutrients which you can't get too much of. There is an element of truth in this – but only an element – because iron deficiency is the most common of all deficiency diseases in both developing and developed countries. Scientists vary in their estimate of what precisely constitutes a state of 'iron depletion', and the general cut-off point is variously calculated to be between 12 and 25mcg of ferritin (one of the chief iron storage forms) per litre of plasma. In Britain, a recent survey showed that 34 per cent of all women had a ferritin level which was under 25mcg/l, and 16 per cent had less than 13mcg/l. Amongst men, only 6 per cent had a value of less than 25mcg/l, and 3 per cent less than 13mcg/l.

These figures reflect the fact that iron is well conserved by the body (90 per cent of the 3 to 5g in our bodies is continually recycled). The major cause of iron depletion is loss of blood itself – as in menstruation, which on average causes about 0.5mg of iron to be lost for every day of the period. However, this can vary very widely (losses as high as 1.4mg a day have been reported) so the official recommended daily allowances (RDA – (see table below)) for women attempt to take this into account by building in a generous safety margin. For example, an iron intake of 10.8mg a day appears to meet the needs of 86 per cent of all menstruating women,[54] yet the official American RDA has been set at 15mg a day in an attempt to meet the needs of the remaining 14 per cent. This is an uneasy compromise because even at this level of iron consumption, 5 per cent of women who have very heavy periods will not have an adequate intake to replace losses. At this point, US officials suggest that women with higher blood losses appear to compensate with an increased rate of iron absorption from their diets. The British suggest that 'the most practical way of meeting their high iron requirements would be to take iron supplements'. This well illustrates the dilemma facing officials whose task it is to set uniform nutritional intakes for a population whose individual needs naturally vary very widely indeed.

Although iron depletion is a problem for many women, it is not a problem which is specific to vegetarians or vegans. Research shows that both diets are well capable of supplying the iron needs of women. For people with particularly high requirements – for example, teenage girls, pregnant women or women with heavy periods – all health foods shops sell vegan iron supplements made from natural ingredients. Supplementation should, however, only be undertaken with the help of a sympathetic and knowledgable health professional. Various blood tests are undertaken to establish iron status, including checking the haemoglobin level (the oxygen-carrying, iron-containing molecule in red blood cells) and haematocrit (the volume percentage of red blood cells in the blood). Additionally, vegan nutrition expert Dr Neal Barnard suggests that the following tests should also be conducted:

- Serum ferritin (normal values are 12–200mcg per litre of serum)
- Serum iron
- Total iron binding capacity (TIBC)

Says Dr Barnard: 'Doctors divide the serum iron value by the TIBC. The result should be 16 to 50 per cent for women and 16 to 62 per cent for men. Results below these norms indicate iron deficiency. Results above these norms indicate excess iron. A further test sometimes used to check for iron deficiency is the red cell protoporphyrin test. A result higher than 70mcg/dl (microgrammes per decilitre) of red blood cells is considered abnormal. If two of these three values (serum ferritin, serum iron/TIBC and red cell protoporphyrin) are normal, iron-deficiency anaemia is not likely. Serum iron and total iron binding capacity should be done after fasting overnight.'[55]

Importance and function

- Iron is involved in the transport of oxygen from lungs to tissue
- Transports and stores oxygen in muscles
- A co-factor in several essential enzymes
- Involved in function of immune system and intellect

Signs of deficiency

- Abnormal test results (as above)
- Pale appearance
- Listlessness, fatigue, irritability
- Cravings for unusual food, especially ice
- Increased susceptibility to infection
- Heart palpitations on exertion
- Iron-deficiency anaemia (hypochromic microcytic anaemia)

Best vegetarian sources

Iron is available in the diet in two forms: haem and non-haem. Haem iron is only found in animal flesh, and being in a form most similar to the body's own iron, is absorbed more effectively than non-haem (although absorption crucially depends upon several other factors, see below). The presence of haem iron in animal flesh such as liver has led countless doctors and dieticians over the years to recommend its consumption by people suffering from iron depletion, irrespective of all other considerations.

Non-haem iron is, in fact, the form in which the majority of meat's iron is held, and it is also the form in which all the plant sources of iron supply this nutrient. Even for meat-eaters, therefore, non-haem iron is a potentially important source of this mineral. The rate of absorption of iron from the diet can be significantly affected, for better or worse, by several factors. It is important for all of us to know what they are, so that we can take steps to ensure that we receive a regular and sufficient source of iron:

- In the first place, the rate of iron absorption is controlled by the degree to which iron is needed by the body. Normally, only 5 to 15 per cent of the iron in food is actually absorbed; this can rise to 50 per cent in cases of iron deficiency.
- Vitamin C taken at the same time as iron-containing food will considerably increase absorption. Iron must be delivered in a soluble form to the small intestine if it is to be absorbed, and vitamin C can make sure that non-haem iron remains soluble in the acidic environment normally found there. Other organic acids found in fruit and vegetables, such as malic acid and citric acid, are also thought to possess this iron-enhancing attribute. This effect is substantial: adding 60mg of vitamin C to a meal of rice has been shown to more than triple the absorption of iron; adding the same amount to a meal of corn enhances absorption fivefold.[56] Vegetarians and vegans are fortunate inasmuch as many excellent sources of iron are also naturally good sources of vitamin C.
- Several factors can significantly reduce the absorption of iron, among them tea (the tannin forms insoluble iron compounds) and the food preservative EDTA. Both of these can reduce assimilation by as much as 50 per cent.
- Other plant food factors – phytates, oxalates and

phosphates – can reduce iron take-up. Research with vegans, who consume foods containing these substances, suggest that the problem is likely to be more theoretical than real – probably because vegans generally consume considerable amounts of iron, and because their diets are also naturally rich in vitamin C.[57,58,59] It has also been suggested that a high fibre intake may reduce iron absorption, but experimental evidence has contradicted this.[60]

• Milk and milk products are practically devoid of iron. Worse, milk may reduce the absorption of iron from other foods, thereby compounding iron-deficiency problems.[61,62] One study has shown that 44 out of 100 infants receiving whole cow's milk had blood in their faeces. This would also contribute to an iron deficiency problem.[63] Egg yolks do contain iron, but this is poorly absorbed due to the presence of an inhibitor, phosvitin.

An extensive analysis of several thousand vegetarian foodstuffs reveals that the following are good sources of this nutrient:

Food	Measure	Mg of iron
molasses cane, third extraction or blackstrap	1 cup:328g	52.8
pumpkin & squash seed kernels roasted	1 cup:227g	33.91
potato flour	1 cup:179g	30.78
spirulina dried	100g	28.5
breakfast cereals eg corn flakes (fortified)	1 cup:33g	20.95
sesame seeds whole, dried	1 cup:144g	20.95
molasses cane, second extraction or medium	1 cup:328g	19.68
quinoa	1 cup:170g	15.73
natto	1 cup:175g	15.05
molasses cane, first extraction or light	1 cup:328g	14.1
tofu raw, firm, prepared w/calcium sulphate	1/2 cup:126g	13.19

Food	Measure	Mg of iron
pizza with cheese topping	1 pizza, 12-in diam:482g	11.56
broadbeans (fava beans) raw	1 cup:150g	10.05
sunflower seed kernels dried	1 cup:144g	9.75
soy flour	1 cup stirred:100g	9.24
cocoa dry powder, plain	1 cup:86g	9.2
soya beans cooked	1 cup:172g	8.84
endive raw	1 head:513g	8.72
pistachio nuts dried	1 cup:128g	8.68
tofu raw, firm, prepared w/calcium sulphate	1/4 block:81g	8.48
hummus	1 cup:246g	8.41
dried mixed fruit	11 oz pkg:293g	7.94
quinoa	1/2 cup:85g	7.86
tomato paste canned	7 oz can:170g	7.7
miso	1 cup:275g	7.535
apricots dehydrated	1 cup:119g	7.5
oats	1 cup:156g	7.36
lima beans canned	1 can:454g	7.21
wheat durum	1 cup:192g	6.75
peanuts raw	1 cup:146g	6.68
barley	1 cup:184g	6.62
molasses cane, third extraction or blackstrap	1 fl oz:41g	6.6
lentils cooked	1 cup:198g	6.59
peaches dried	1 cup halves:160g	6.49
spinach cooked	1 cup:180g	6.43
wheat germ crude	1 cup: 100g	6.26
apricots dried	1 cup halves:130g	6.11

potatoes cooked in skin	1 potato:136g	5.94
peas green, canned	1 lb:454g	5.902
ginger root crystallized, candied	1 oz:28g	5.88
sesame butter paste	1 oz:28.4g	5.45
beets canned, drained solids	1 can:294g	5.35
peas green, canned	1 can:482g	5.35
cashew nuts oil roasted	1 cup wholes & halves:130g	5.33
thyme ground	1 tbsp:4.3g	5.31
kidney beans cooked	1 cup:177g	5.28
almonds dried, blanched	1 c whole kernels:145g	5.27
cabbage raw	1 head:908g	5.08
baked beans	1 cup:253g	5
peanut butter	1 cup:258g	4.9

Is getting enough iron likely to be a problem for vegetarians?

Anyone can be iron deficient – vegetarian, vegan or meat-eater. But iron deficiency is not a problem which should overly concern vegetarians and vegans who make a point of eating a varied diet which includes several good plant-food sources. For times when extra iron is required above and beyond that which can be supplied by dietary means, animal-free supplements can easily be taken (for some practical suggestions to boost iron intake see 'Nourishing The New Mother' on page 30). On the other hand, the disadvantages of excess iron in the body may be considerable (see 'Annulling Anaemia' on page 105). And although too little bodily iron can increase the risk of infections, so too can too much, because invading microorganisms require iron in order to proliferate. Normally, two iron-binding proteins, transferrin and lactoferrin, appear to be able to protect against infection by 'locking up' iron and thus preventing it from being used by infectious organisms. In the presence of excess iron, however, this function can be compromised, and immunity will suffer.

To summarize: plant-based diets are superior to meat-based ones, because they can furnish us with all the iron normally necessary, whilst naturally protecting us from the health hazards which some experts believe are associated with iron overload.

RECOMMENDED INTAKES
Iron (mg)

	Age	US RDA	Can RNI	UK RNI
Infants	up to 6 months	6	0.3	4.3
	6 months–1 year	10	7	7.8
	1–3	10	6	6.9
Children	4–6	10	8	6.1
	7–10	10	8	8.7
Males	11–14	12	10	11.3
	15–18	12	10	11.3
	19–24	10	9	8.7
	25–50	10	9	8.7
	51 +	10	9	8.7
Females	11–14	15	13	14.8
	15–18	15	12	14.8
	19–24	15	13	14.8
	25–50	15	13	14.8
	51 +	10	8	8.7
Pregnant		30	+10	no increment
Lactating	first 6 months	15	no increment	no increment
	second 6 months	15	no increment	no increment

MAGNESIUM

The adult human body contains about 28g of this essential mineral, which is largely deposited in the bone, with lesser amounts found in the muscles, soft tissue and body fluids. It works in a similar but opposite way to its partner calcium – for example, calcium helps muscles to contract and magnesium helps them to relax. Diarrhoea and vomiting cause lower body levels of magnesium, and high intakes of calcium, protein, vitamin D and alcohol all increase the body's need for it (as does physical or psychological stress). It is widely distributed in foods, although meat and milk are poor sources because they are not bioavailable.

Importance and function

- Helps bones develop
- Helps nerves and muscles to function
- Required for the functioning of some enzymes
- Assists in metabolism of proteins and nucleic acids
- Works in the cell with calcium, sodium and potassium
- May help to reduce clogging of arteries and prevent heart disease and kidney stones

Signs of deficiency

- Loss of appetite and failure to grow
- Muscle weakness, irritability, mental confusion
- Gross symptoms of deficiency are rare

Best vegetarian sources

Magnesium is an essential constituent of chlorophyll, so vegetarians and vegans are naturally inclined to consume this mineral in all green produce. Meat and animal produce also contain magnesium, but 'the simultaneous intake of calcium, phosphate and protein from these sources reduces its bioavailability', according to the British government's panel on nutrition.[64] The best sources of magnesium in the diet are cereals and green vegetables, of which there is no shortage in the meat-free way of living!

Is getting enough magnesium likely to be a problem for vegetarians?

No. On the contrary, diets high in meat, refined foods and dairy products are inferior providers of magnesium.

RECOMMENDED INTAKES
Magnesium (mg)

	Age	US RDA	Can RNI	UK RNI
Infants	up to 6 months	40	20	60
	6 months–1 year	60	32	80
	1–3	80	50	85
Children	4–6	120	65	120
	7–10	170	100	200
Males	11–14	270	185	280
	15–18	400	230	300
	19–24	350	240	300
	25–50	350	250	300
	51 +	350	250	300
Females	11–14	280	180	280
	15–18	300	200	300
	19–24	280	200	270
	25–50	280	200	270
	51 +	280	210	270
Pregnant		320	+ 45	no increment
Lactating	first 6 months	355	+ 65	+ 50
	second 6 months	340	+ 65	+ 50

PHOSPHORUS

The second most abundant mineral in the body after calcium, phosphorus is present in bones and teeth, combining with calcium to form calcium phosphate, the substance which gives the skeleton rigidity and structure. It is also present in every single cell of the body, and in the extracellular fluid too, fulfilling a host of important functions.

Importance and function

- Helps build strong teeth and bones
- Essential component of nucleic acids and cell membranes
- Essential in the utilization of energy from food
- Crucial to many aspects of metabolic control

Signs of deficiency

- Very widespread in foods, dietary deficiency unknown except for those being fed intravenously, and alcoholics with liver disease

Best vegetarian sources

Nuts, legumes, cereals, grain, dairy produce.

Is getting enough phosphorus likely to be a problem for vegetarians?

No.

RECOMMENDED INTAKES
Phosphorus (mg)

	Age	US RDA	Can RNI	UK RNI
Infants	up to 6 months	300	150	400
	6 months–1 year	500	200	400
	1–3	800	350	270
Children	4–6	800	400	350
	7–10	800	500	450
Males	11–14	1200	900	775
	15–18	1200	1000	775
	19–24	1200	1000	550
	25–50	800	1000	550
	51 +	800	1000	550
Females	11–14	1200	850	625
	15–18	1200	850	625
	19–24	1200	850	550
	25–50	800	850	550
	51 +	800	850	550
Pregnant		1200	+ 200	no increment
Lactating	first 6 months	1200	+ 200	+ 440
	second 6 months	1200	+ 200	+ 440

ZINC

Much touted by the meat industry as one of those nutrients, together with protein and the B-group vitamins, of which meat is an unparalleled source: the truth of the matter is that plant foods also supply more than ample amounts of zinc, too. In fact, the importance of zinc in human nutrition has only been recognized in recent decades (the first reports appeared in 1963). The mere 2g of zinc in the human body are distributed in all tissues, although in varying concentrations. It is still the subject of much research with regard to its function and dietary requirement.

Importance and function

• Essential component of many enzymes which work with red blood cells to transport carbon dioxide from tissues to lungs
• Needed for wound healing
• Factor in many vital processes, such as immune function and expression of genetic information

Signs of deficiency

• Diminution of taste and smell
• Prolonged wound healing
• Reduced growth in children
• Falling hair, rashes, skin problems
• Night blindness
• Inflammation of tongue, mouth, eyelids
• Reduced sperm count
• Severe depletion results in dwarfism, small testicles, enlarged spleen/liver

Best vegetarian sources

There are many good sources of zinc in the meat-free diet. Unrefined cereals and unleavened bread also contain other factors (principally phytic acid) which, it was suggested, combine with zinc in the intestine and thus interfere with absorption. However, more recent work reveals that phytic acid only exerts its inhibitory effect on zinc in the presence of large quantities of calcium in the diet. And the British government's panel on nutrition comments: 'Unrefined cereals contain zinc in sufficient amounts to offset the limited bioavailability of the metal.'[65] An extensive analysis of several thousand vegetarian foodstuffs reveals that the following are good sources of this nutrient:

Food	Measure	Mg of zinc
pumpkin and squash seed kernels roasted	1 cup:227g	16.89
wheat germ crude	1 cup:	12.29
sesame seeds whole, dried	1 cup:144g	11.16
peanuts all types, roasted	1 cup:144g	9.55
wild rice raw	1 cup:160g	9.54
miso	1 cup:275g	9.13
wheat durum	1 cup:192g	7.99
cheese gouda	1 pkg:198g	7.72
almonds roasted	1 cup:157g	7.69

cashew nuts roasted	1 cup:137g	7.67
almond butter	1 cup:250g	7.63
cheese edam	1 pkg:198g	7.43
mixed nuts with peanuts, roasted	1 cup:142g	7.21
peanut butter	1 cup:258g	7.17
sunflower seed kernels roasted	1 cup:135g	7.03
cheese gruyere	1 pkg:170g	6.63
pizza with cheese	1 pizza:503g	6.49
brazilnuts dried	1 cup:140g	6.43
oats	1 cup:156g	6.19
pecans roasted	1 cup:110g	6.05
chicory raw	1 head:513g	5.95
quinoa	1 cup:170g	5.61
natto	1 cup:175g	5.30
barley	1 cup:184g	5.10
peanuts all types, raw	1 cup:146g	4.77
wild rice raw	1/2 cup:80g	4.77
broadbeans (fava beans) raw	1 cup:150g	4.71
milk cow, dry	1 cup:128g	4.28
barley pearled, raw	1 cup:200g	4.26
buckwheat	1 cup:170g	4.08
adzuki beans cooked	1 cup:230g	4.07
hummus	1 cup:246g	3.69
baked beans canned	1 cup:254g	3.56
millet raw	1 cup:200g	3.36
walnuts dried	1 cup:120g	3.28
tempeh	1 cup:166g	3.00
tahini	1 oz:28.4g	2.97
milk condensed	1 cup:306g	2.88
cheese cheshire	100g	2.79
bulgar dry	1 cup:140g	2.70
natto	1/2 cup:88g	2.67

chickpeas canned	1 cup:240g	2.54
lentils cooked	1 cup:198g	2.51
chickpeas cooked	1 cup:164g	2.51
peas cooked,	1 pkg:253g	2.38
broadbeans (fava beans) raw	1/2 cup:75g	2.36
soya beans sprouted, stir-fried	100g	2.10
potato baked and topped w/cheese sauce and broccoli	1 potato:339g	2.03
sesame seeds whole, roasted and toasted	1 oz:28.4g	2.03
tofu raw, firm	1/2 cup:126g	1.98

Is getting enough zinc likely to be a problem for vegetarians?

No. Studies reveal that vegetarians and vegans generally consume as much zinc – sometimes more – as meat-eaters.[66]

RECOMMENDED INTAKES
Zinc (mg)

	Age	US RDA	Can RNI	UK RNI
Infants	up to 6 months	5	2	4
	6 months– 1 year	5	3	5
	1–3	10	4	5
Children	4–6	10	5	6.5
	7–10	10	7	7
Males	11–14	15	12	9
	15–18	15	12	9.5
	19–24	15	12	9.5
	25–50	15	12	9.5
	51 +	15	12	9.5
Females	11-14	12	9	9
	15–18	12	9	7
	19–24	12	9	7
	25–50	12	9	7
	51 +	12	9	7

Pregnant		15	+6	no incre-ment
Lactating	first 6 months	19	+6	+6
	second 6 months	16	+6	+6

SELENIUM

Selenium is an integral part of the enzyme glutathione peroxidase, a powerful scavenger of free radicals, whose importance was discovered as recently as 1973. It is a trace element in nutrition, the amounts needed for health being measured in microgrammes (millionths of a gram). It is toxic in excess. The selenium content in foods is closely related to the selenium content of the soil in which it is grown, which makes generalizations about the selenium content of foods difficult. Some areas of the world are known to be deficient in selenium; they include China, Finland, New Zealand, and the northeast Pacific, southwest, and extreme southeast areas of the United States, as well as north central and eastern Canada. In such areas, taking supplemental selenium may be an effective nutritional 'insurance policy'.

Importance and function

- Works in association with vitamin E to protect cells from the ravages of oxidation by free radicals
- Helps synthesize antibodies and co-enzyme Q
- Helps transport ions across cell membranes

Signs of deficiency

- Gross deficiency results in damage to the heart (Keshan Disease) or osteoarthritis (Kashin-Beck disease)
- Subtle deficiency may increase risk of free-radical associated afflictions, eg cancers, heart disease, ageing, etc

Best vegetarian sources

Selenium content of foods vary as explained above, but the best vegetarian sources appear to be:
- Brazil nuts
- Wheatgerm
- Molasses
- Sunflower seeds
- Wholewheat bread
- Dairy produce

Is getting enough selenium likely to be a problem for vegetarians?

Not because of the exclusion of meat from the diet. People living in selenium-deficient areas should consider supplements.

RECOMMENDED INTAKES
Selenium (mcg)

	Age	US.RDA	Can RNI	UK RNI
Infants	up to 6 months	10	–	13
	6 months – 1 year	15	–	10
	1–3	20	–	15
Children	4–6	20	–	20
	7–10	30	–	30
Males	11–14	40	–	45
	15–18	50	–	70
	19–24	70	–	75
	25–50	70	–	75
	51 +	70	–	75
Females	11–14	45	–	45
	15–18	50	–	60
	19–24	55	–	60
	25–50	55	–	60
	51 +	55	–	60
Pregnant		65	–	no incre-ment
Lactating	first 6 months	75	–	+15
	second 6 months	75	–	+15

IODINE

The only role for iodine in the body is as an essential component of the hormones produced by the thyroid gland, and this is where the majority of this element is stored. Milk is a major source of iodine in the Western diet, partly because cattle feed contains iodine, and partly because substances such as lactation promoters and teat-sterilizing chemicals contain it. On the non-animal side seaweed is a very rich source.

Importance and Function

- Helps form hormones which control metabolic rate, cellular metabolism and integrity of connective tissue
- Keeps skin, hair and nails healthy
- Protects thyroid gland after radiation exposure

Signs of deficiency

- Listlessness (low thyroid hormone level)
- Goitre, an enlargement of the thyroid gland, afflicting 200 million people worldwide
- Severe deficiency leads to cretinism in newborn

Best vegetarian sources

Pre-eminently, the best vegan and vegetarian sources of iodine are sea vegetables. The amount of iodine in vegetables and grains depends on the amount present in the soil. In some areas of the world, iodine supply is extremely restricted, and here the most reliable source is iodized table salt.

Is getting enough iodine likely to be a problem for vegetarians?

No. The increasing popularity of cooking with sea vegetables, following Chinese and Japanese styles of cuisine, makes the meat-free diet a good supplier of iodine. Certain natural substances, known as goitregens, can block absorption or utilization of iodine. They are found in cabbage, turnips, peanuts and soya beans, but happily are inactivated by cooking.

RECOMMENDED INTAKES
Iodine (mcg)

	Age	US RDA	Can RNI	UK RNI
Infants	up to 6 months	40	30	60
	6 months–1 year	50	40	60
	1–3	70	65	70
Children	4–6	90	85	100
	7–10	120	110	110
Males	11–14	150	160	130
	15–18	150	160	140
	19–24	150	160	140
	25–50	150	160	140
	51 +	150	160	140
Females	11–14	150	160	130
	15-18	150	160	140
	19–24	150	160	140
	25–50	150	160	140
	51 +	150	160	140
Pregnant		175	25	no increment
Lactating	first 6 months	200	50	no increment
	second 6 months	200	50	no increment

PROTEIN

It is an astonishing fact that the 'sacred cow' of protein is still a major concern for an extraordinary number of lay people and even health professionals when they consider the meat-free way of living. In many conversations with doctors and dieticians, I have been made painfully aware that their first reaction to the word 'vegetarian' is 'protein – how do you get enough of it?' When one considers all the positive, health-promoting qualities of the meat-free diet, it is sad to see health professionals reacting in such an uninformed way.

The 'question' of protein intake has been raised so many times with vegetarians and vegans that it has become a depressingly boring subject. There is no protein 'problem': studies consistently show that vegetarians and vegans have a satisfactory protein intake. How has this myth of deficiency arisen? In two main ways. Firstly, early research (circa 1914) into protein consisted of experiments on rats. These unfortunate laboratory animals were found not to grow as quickly when fed plant protein as when given animal protein. The plant protein was, however, sufficient for growth if supplemented with certain lacking amino acids. Hence the idea arose that plant protein was second class, and animal protein superior. The snag with this line of reasoning is summarized by expert on vegan nutrition, Dr. Gill Langley: 'The weanling rat grows, relatively, at a much faster rate than the human infant and therefore requires a much more concentrated source of nutrients, including protein. A comparison with human (breast) milk makes the difference quite clear: protein comprises only 7 per cent of the calorie content of breast milk, while rat milk contains 20 per cent protein. If weanling rats were fed solely human milk, they would not thrive. Using the same logic as was applied in the early experiments, it could be argued from this that breast milk is also inadequate for human infants!'[67]

In other words, people are not rats. The second 'protein myth' arose from an unexpected quarter, a book written in the late 1960s which exposed the terrible wastes inherent in a meat-centred diet. *Diet for a Small Planet*[68] sold over 3 million copies, and popularized the idea of 'protein complementarity'. Written with the best of intentions, its effect was to make plant sources of protein again seem second class, unless carefully combined with each other, and to make the whole subject of protein nutrition seem vastly complex and fraught with danger. Commented nutritional reformer Nathan Pritikin: 'Unfortunately, the book is one of the most misleading documents in the last few years because everybody now thinks food balancing is essential. [The book] gives the impression that vegetable proteins don't have sufficient percentages of amino acids.'[69]

In subsequent editions of the book, this mistake was corrected. But still, the myth lives on, no doubt due in part to the zealous promotional efforts of the meat industry. For example, in one currently-used nutritional textbook, the following advice is given to trainee dieticians about vegetarians: 'Deficiencies of some essential amino acids in vegetable proteins require the use of careful planning to provide the complementarity necessary for adequate protein synthesis'.

This is an utterly misleading statement, but as long as textbooks repeat it, dieticians will continue to believe it. Here, then, are the basic facts which vegetarians need to know in order to educate their health professionals:

Importance and function

- Provide amino acids needed to build and maintain body tissues
- Capable of yielding some dietary energy (4kcal/g)
- Help form enzymes, hormones, antibodies
- Help transport fats, vitamins, minerals
- Help control body's self-regulating systems (homeostasis)

Signs of deficiency

- Susceptibility to infection
- Weakness, loss of vitality
- Skin degradation
- Wasting of tissues with oedema

- Fatty liver
- Mostly seen as protein-energy malnutrition (PEM) in those living in extreme poverty: conditions such as narasmus and kwashiorkor develop

Best vegetarian sources

An extensive analysis of several thousand vegetarian foodstuffs reveals that the following are good sources of protein:

Food	Measure	Grams of protein
pumpkin and squash seed kernels, roasted	1 cup:227g	74.84
peanut butter	1 cup:258g	63.44
pizza with cheese topping	1 pizza, 13-3/4in dia: 520g	62.4
cheese fontina	1 pkg:227g	58.11
spirulina dried	100g	57.47
cheese gruyere	1 pkg:170g	50.68
soy flour	1 cup:100g	47.01
sesame seed kernels, dried	1 cup:150g	39.57
broadbeans (fava beans) raw	1 cup:150g	39.18
peanuts raw	1 cup:146g	37.67
spaghetti whole-wheat, dry	8 oz:227g	33.21
sunflower seed kernels, dried	1 cup:144g	32.8
hummus	1 cup:246g	32.74
endive raw	1 head:513g	32.63
miso	1 cup:275g	32.48
tempeh	1 cup:166g	31.46
natto	1 cup:175g	31.01
almonds blanched	1 cup:145g	29.61
soya beans cooked	1 cup:172g	28.62
oats	1 cup:156g	26.35
pistachio nuts dried	1 cup:128g	26.34
wheat durum	1 cup:192g	26.27

rice white, short-grain, cooked	1 cup:205g	25.99
mixed nuts with peanuts, dry roasted	1 cup:137g	23.7
wild rice raw	1 cup:160g	23.57
couscous dry	1 cup:184g	23.48
wheat germ crude	1 cup:113g	23.15
barley	1 cup:184g	22.96
buckwheat	1 cup:170g	22.53
quinoa	1 cup:170g	22.27
millet raw	1 cup:200g	22.04
lima beans canned	1 can:454g	20.66
tofu raw, firm, prepared w/calcium sulphate	1/2 cup:126g	19.88
Welsh rarebit	1 cup:232g	18.79
lentils cooked	1 cup:198g	17.86
white beans cooked	1 cup:179g	17.42
adzuki beans cooked	1 cup:230g	17.3
walnuts dried	1 cup:120g	7.15
kidney beans cooked	1 cup:177g	16.8
macaroni and cheese	1 can:430g	16.77
wheat flour whole-grain	1 cup:120g	16.44
split peas cooked	1 cup:196g	16.35
bacon meatless	1 cup:144g	15.38
soup cream of asparagus	1 can:602g	15.35
soup tomato	1 can:602g	14.81
rice brown, long-grain, raw	1 cup:185g	14.69
chickpeas cooked	1 cup:164g	14.53
gazpacho	1 can:369g	13.14
egg scrambled	2 eggs:94g	13.01
baked beans	1 cup:254g	12.17

Is getting enough protein likely to be a problem for vegetarians?

Only because they're nagged about it. There are two issues to be addressed here: first, the total amount of protein ingested, and secondly, the quality (ie amino acid composition) of the protein.

How can you get enough protein?

Some simple calculations can prove just how easy it is to get enough protein without eating meat, or indeed, consuming dairy produce. Let's consider three types of people: adult male, adult female and teenager. Each one of them has rather different energy and protein requirements, as outlined below:

Person	estimated average requirement for energy (in kcalories) per day[70]	Protein requirement per day (g)
Adult male	2550	55.5
Adult female	1940	45
Teenager	2220	42.1

Now we know the two values given above, we can calculate what percentage of the day's calorie intake must be supplied by protein. 1g gram of protein yields approximately 4 calories, so an intake of 55.5g of protein (adult male) will yield 222 calories. An intake of 45g (adult female) yields 180 calories, and 42.1g of protein (teenager) yields 168.4 calories.

Now we can express the calories supplied by protein as a percentage of the day's total calorie intake, as below:

Person	% of calories needed as protein
Adult male	9
Adult female	9
Teenager	8

At last we've arrived at a simple figure which will help us to compare the protein content of foods with our own protein requirement. Let's take the case of an adult female. Assuming she eats foods which supply her average requirement of 1940 calories a day, just 9 per cent of those calories need to come from protein in order to satisfy her protein intake.

How easy is this? Well, if she eats foods which on average contain more than 9 per cent of their calories as protein, she'll consume more protein than the suggested requirement. If she eats foods which supply less than 9 per cent protein as calories, she'll consume less.

Now let's analyze some foods, and see how many foods are over the 9 per cent threshold, and how many under:

Food	% Calories As Protein
cottage cheese 1% fat	68%
asparagus raw	56%
alfalfa sprouted, raw	55%
spinach, boiled	52%
tofu raw, firm	44%
broccoli boiled	43%
yogurt skim milk	41%
bean sprout mung, raw	41%
milk, skimmed	39%
soya beans cooked	38%
tempeh	38%
grated parmesan	36%
broadbeans boiled	34%
mushrooms raw	33%
natto	33%
egg poached	33%
soy milk	33%
cauliflower raw	33%
oat bran cooked	32%
salad vegetable	31%
lentils cooked	31%
lettuce iceberg, raw	31%
kidney beans canned	31%

Food	% Calories As Protein
wheatgerm toasted	30%
swiss cheese	30%
kidney beans cooked	29%
sausage meatless	29%
peas canned	29%
kale boiled	27%
2% lowfat milk	27%
egg scrambled	27%
parsley raw	27%
cheddar cheese	25%
miso	23%
baked beans	19%
welsh rarebit	18%
sesame seeds dried	18%
chickpea cooked	17%
pumpkin seeds roasted	17%
peanut butter chunky	16%
tomato puree	16%
falafel	16%
sunflower seeds dried	16%
quinoa	14%
almonds toasted	14%
couscous cooked	14%
cornflakes	8%
rice brown, cooked	8%
peaches canned	3%

Seeing our daily foods presented in this new way is little short of a revelation. Suddenly, you can see that far from being deprived of protein sources, they literally surround us. In fact, the only food group which falls short of the 9 per cent calories-from-protein-benchmark is fruit. Providing you eat a good mixed diet, and don't starve yourself of energy (calories), you will naturally obtain enough protein. For those whose protein requirements may be higher than normal (for example, during pregnancy or illness) the meat-free way of living has its own high-protein star performers. Soya products are always abundant sources of protein – textured vegetable protein (eg Protoveg) being one of the best and cheapest available.

But what about protein quality?

Is meat protein the same as vegetable protein? The answer is no. Protein (more properly, proteins) are large molecules which exist in a diversity of structures. All proteins are made from about twenty amino acids, linked together in a variety of ways. When we eat protein in food, it is digested and broken down into its amino acids, which are then used by the body for a variety of life-support functions, including building our own body protein. Plants synthesize all the amino acids required for building all the necessary proteins; animals, however, cannot synthesize eight essential amino acids (sometimes one or two more) and therefore depend on food to obtain them. All eight are available from vegetarian and vegan diets. So although vegetable proteins are not the same as meat – their amino acid composition varies from one plant source to another – they are *not* second class.

The 'Big Eight' amino acids are termed 'Indispensible Amino Acids' by scientists (abbreviated to IAA) meaning that they must be present in our diets. If one IAA is in short supply, the body's process of protein synthesis will be impaired.

Different foods naturally have different amino acid patterns. For example, cereals, nuts and seeds are high in an IAA known as methionine (pronounced 'meth-EYE-oh-neen') but low in lysine. Pulses are rich in lysine but lower in methionine. Put them together, and their IAA patterns complement each other very well. Which is where is the idea of 'protein complementarity' came in.

The book *Diet for a Small Planet* popularized protein combining – using the amino acid strengths of one protein source to complement the weaknesses of another one. Unfortunately, it also made the whole concept seem very intimidating. The fact is, however, that our normal way of eating combines foods which naturally complement each other, without having to worry about it. This is made clear by two major nutritional authorities, one British, one American:

'The panel took the view,' reads the 1991 Report of

the Panel on Dietary Reference Values for the British government, 'that it is unlikely that there were any groups in the UK who are consuming food which supplies sufficient protein and energy to satisfy overall requirements who would be deficient in IAA.'[71]

The 1993 position paper of the authoritative and respected American Dietetic Association summarized its views even more strongly:

> Plant sources of protein alone can provide adequate amounts of the essential and nonessential amino adds, assuming that dietary protein sources from plants are reasonably varied and that caloric intake is sufficient to meet energy needs. Whole grains, legumes, vegetables, seeds, and nuts all contain essential and nonessential amino adds. Conscious combining of these foods within a given meal, as the complementary protein dictum suggests, is unnecessary. Additionally, soya protein has been shown to be nutritionally equivalent in protein value to proteins of animal origin and, thus, can serve as the sole source of protein intake if desired. Although most vegetarian diets meet or exceed the Recommended Dietary Allowances for protein, they often provide less protein than nonvegetarian diets. This lower protein intake may be associated with better calcium retention in vegetarians and improved kidney function in individuals with prior kidney damage. Further, lower protein intakes may result in a lower fat intake with its inherent advantages, because foods high in protein are frequently high in fat also.[72]

With impressive support such as this, there really should no longer be any question at all that the meat-free way of living provides satisfactory – and probably superior – sources of protein for healthy human nutrition.

RECOMMENDED INTAKES
Protein (g)

	Age	US RDA	Can RNI	UK RNI
Infants	up to 6 months	13	12	12.7
	6 month–1 year	14	12	14.9
	1–3	16	22	14.5
Children	4–6	24	26	19.7
	7–10	28	30	28.3

Males	11–14	45	50	42.1
	15–18	59	55	55.2
	19–24	58	58	55.5
	25–50	63	61	55.5
	51 +	63	60	53.3
Females	11-14	46	42	41.2
	15–18	44	43	45
	19–24	46	43	45
	25–50	50	44	45
	51 +	50	47	46.5
Pregnant		60	+ 24	+ 6
Lactating	first 6 months	65	+ 20	+ 11
	second 6 months	62	+ 20	+ 11

AND LASTLY. . . A WORD ABOUT OILS AND FATS

Many people are confused about the type and quantity of oils and fats they should be eating. Is margarine better than butter? Or should we all be eating olive oil instead? We seem to get one message one week, and the opposite the next. This makes it very difficult for anyone to understand what to do any more. So let's start with some basics . . .

What is fat?

Fats are solid at room temperature, oils are liquid. But scientists now use the term 'fat' to include all oils and fats, whether or not they're solid or liquid. So we will, too.

Chemically, fats are made up of three molecules of fatty acids and one of an alcohol called glycerol. What's a fatty acid? We'll come to that in a moment. You'll also hear the word 'triglycerides' used to describe fat – it means three fatty acid molecules ('tri') plus glycerol. . . triglyceride.

What's a fatty acid?

Fatty acids are – not surprisingly – acids that are found in fats. There are four major fatty acids: palmitic, stearic, oleic and linoleic. Remember, each molecule of fat contains three of these four fatty acids. Now it's the *combination* of these acids in the fat molecule that determines whether the fat is saturated, unsaturated, or polyunsaturated – words we've all heard a great deal in

the past few years. So let's explain them.

All fats consist of long chains of carbon and hydrogen atoms. When all the available sites on the carbon atoms are filled with hydrogen atoms, the fat is saturated. If there are unfilled spaces, the fat is unsaturated. The more empty spaces, the more unsaturated the fat is.

Saturated

Palmitic fatty acid has sixteen carbon atoms and no unsaturated carbon bonds. So it's called 'saturated'.

Stearic fatty acid has eighteen carbon atoms and no unsaturated carbon bonds. So it's also called 'saturated'.

Saturated fat is known to raise the level of cholesterol in your blood. The more you eat, the higher your cholesterol level, and the greater your chances of suffering a stroke or heart attack. As a guide, saturated fat is usually sold at room temperature and is therefore solid. Animal fat such as lard, meat and butter contains lots of saturated fat. A few plant fats also contain significant amounts – principally coconut and palm oil.

Monounsaturated fat

Oleic fatty acid has eighteen carbon atoms and one unsaturated carbon bond. So it's called 'monounsaturated'.

Ongoing research suggests that monounsaturated fat is much healthier that saturated fat. A major source is olive oil. Experiments on humans show that switching to monounsaturated fat from the saturated kind can not only decrease the risk of heart disease, but it may also be able to lower your blood pressure. It is also less prone to go rancid than other types of fat, and rancidity is believed by some scientists to promote cancer.

Polyunsaturated fat

Linoleic fatty acid has eighteen carbon atoms and two unsaturated carbon bonds. So its called 'polyunsaturated'.

Early research indicated that polyunsaturated fats lowered total and LDL cholesterol (low density lipoprotein – the 'bad' form of cholesterol) more than did monounsaturated fats. The latest research, however, finds no difference in their cholesterol-lowering ability. However, the more polyunsaturated an oil is, the more it can be damaged by excess heat, air and light. Most polyunsaturated oils should only be used raw, because once damaged, they form free radicals. Good sources of polyunsaturated fats include sunflower and corn oil. We all need a little linoleic acid in our diets every day, because, of the four major fatty acids, this is the only one we can't synthesize for ourselves internally.

You can see from the following diagram just how the ratio of monounsaturated, polyunsaturated and saturated fats vary between some common types of fats:

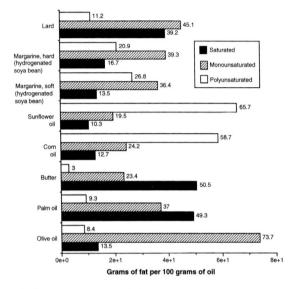

Black = saturated, shaded = monounsaturated, grey = polyunsaturated.
Units are grams of fat per 100g of oil
margarine, soft = soybean (hydrogenated)
margarine, hard = soybean (hydrogenated)

Butter or margarine?

For a long time, heart specialists have been calling for people to reduce consumption of saturated fats contained in red meat, full cream milk and butter. Instead they should turn to vegetable margarines, wholemeal foods and more vegetables. Fierce advertising wars have tried to persuade us over the years that one or other is healthier. In fact, some margarines can contain as much total fat as butter, although their saturated fat content would be less. Advertising has also tried to persuade us to increase the amount of polyunsaturated margarine we eat, which, if we didn't reduce our other fat consumption, would simply result in us eating more fat than ever. So what should you do?

In reality, there is probably little practical difference between butter and most of the mass-market margarines. Butter will certainly be higher in saturated fat, but

many margarines contain hydrogenated oils, which may be equally bad for health. The process of hydrogenation fills some unsaturated bonds of the fat molecule with hydrogen atoms, making it more similar to a saturated fat. For example, soybean oil in its natural state is only 15 per cent saturated, but when it's partially hydrogenated it's closer to 25 per cent saturated, similar to vegetable shortenings. Manufacturers do this to margarine to increase its shelf life, but it also has the effect of increasing its saturated fat content. Hydrogenation also produces 'transformed unsaturated fats', usually called 'trans fatty acids', which may be just as bad for your heart as saturated fats are. So avoid hydrogenated fats where you can.

A third alternative is the range of margarines usually only sold in health food shops. These may be somewhat more expensive, but are not usually hydrogenated and often contain high-quality oils such as cold-pressed sunflower oil and olive oil. These are almost always the healthiest and best choice.

Choosing oils

Also, consider whether you really need to eat quite so much margarine or butter. If you want something to put on your toast in the morning, why not try lightly brushing a little olive oil on to it? Similarly, when cooking, replace butter with olive oil. The way oils are produced is important, too. There are three methods of extraction:

• Cold pressing. This is the traditional hydraulic pressing process where the temperature is kept low throughout and which therefore preserves temperature-sensitive vitamins. The end product is expensive, mainly because there is a high percentage of waste in the discarded pulp, but the oil is nutritious and tastes and smells good. To compensate for the higher price of cold-pressed oils, try to consume less.
• Screw or expeller. This process involves high pressure pressing which generates high temperatures. Vitamins are destroyed during this process and although it enables more oil to be extracted it is dark, strong-smelling and needs further refining and deodorizing.
• Solvent extraction. This is the most common process because it produces the highest yields. The grains or seeds are ground, steamed and then mixed with solvents. The solvents used are either the petroleum-based benzene, hexane or heptane.

The mixture is then heated to remove the solvents and then washed with caustic soda, which has the effect of destroying its valuable lecithin content. After this it is bleached and filtered, which removes precious minerals as well as any coloured substances. Finally, it is heated to a high temperature to deodorize it. Vegetable oils produced by solvent extraction have also lost their vitamin E content. This vitamin helps stop the oil from going rancid. Rancid oils are dangerous because they provide the raw material for producing free radicals in our bodies. Sometimes chemical retardants are added to stop the oil from turning rancid, but it would seem to be much more sensible to stick with the cold-pressed oils which can keep well, if properly stored, for up to six months.

Essential fatty acids

The two classes of essential fatty acids (EFAs) are named omega-6 and omega-3. They are both necessary for good health because they provide the catalysts for various metabolic functions (eg they can activate prostaglandins, or cell regulators). Through a complicated transformation process, essential fatty acids become biologically active and therefore become useful links in many metabolic systems. They are called 'essential' because the body cannot make them, and they must be obtained from food sources. Most vegetable oils provide the EFAs to a greater or lesser extent, but they are not significantly present in meat.

- Omega-6 fatty acids (eg linoleic acid) are found in vegetable seeds and the oils produced from them. Good sources include oils made from safflower, sunflower, corn, soya, evening primrose, pumpkin, walnut, and wheat germ.
- Omega-3 fatty acids (eg alpha linolenic acid) are found in deep-water fish oils and are alleged to have near-miraculous properties (see 'A fishy business' below), hence the popularity of fish oil supplements. They are also, however, found in linseed, rapeseed (canola) and soya bean oil, so vegetarians need not consume fish if they wish to increase their omega-3s. The food supplement spirulina also contains both linoleic and linolenic acids.

A fishy business

Contrary to popular opinion, fish is not the only source of omega-3 acids. Flaxseed (linseed) oil actu-

ally contains about twice as much omega-3 essential fatty acids as is found in fish oil. According to nutritionist Ann Louise Gittleman, co-author of *Beyond Pritikin*, flaxseed oil's greatest attribute is its ranking as the vegetable source highest in omega-3 fatty acids. 'Fish is the best-known source of the omega-3's,' she says, 'but flaxseed oil contains 55 to 60 per cent omega-3 – about twice as much as is found in fish oil.'[73] Flaxseed is also rich in omega-6 fatty acids.

Although fish oil has been touted as the ultimate cure for heart disease, the evidence is by no means as clear-cut as the publicity suggests. Some studies have indeed shown that large doses of fish oil can lower triglycerides (blood fats). But when continued over a longer period of time – six months or so – the initial triglyceride-lowering effect of fish oil in patients with high levels almost disappears.[74] The 'fish oil myth' is pretty shaky on other grounds, too:

- A further study casts doubt on the benefits of fish oil for heart patients who have had angioplasty, a medical treatment for narrowed arteries. Because fish oil makes your blood thinner, it was thought that it could help keep clogged arteries open. And three small studies first hinted that it could. However, a larger study from Harvard Medical School and Beth Israel Hospital shows that people taking fish oil actually had a higher rate of recurrent narrowing of the arteries and more heart attacks than people taking olive oil![75]
- It has now passed into folklore that Eskimos have much less heart disease than other Westerners, and that this reduction in heart disease is due to the fish oil they consume. Actually, if you study almost any native population, you'll find they have much less heart disease than we do. In March 1990, the *American Journal of Public Health* published a review of previous scientific work on this subject. The author of the review wrote: 'Several studies have reported that Arctic populations, which typically consume large amounts of fatty fish, have a low rate of atherosclerosis and cardiovascular disease. But a thorough examination of the methods used in these projects reveals that the evidence may not have been reliable. Two studies that reported causes of death used data from a modest number of autopsies that were performed without standard procedures by inadequately trained personnel.'[76]

In fact, there have been persistent questions asked in

scientific journals about the accuracy of the 'Eskimo' evidence. One medical critic has already pointed out the original study was seriously flawed, because far fewer deaths from cardiovascular disease were recorded than actually took place.[77]

- The same research that was supposed to demonstrate that fish oil could reduce deaths from heart disease also revealed that Eskimos were dying in greater numbers from cerebrovascular haemorrhages. Since fish oil is known to thin the blood, this is a perfectly possible consequence. But this finding has received very little publicity.
- A recent study conducted to assess the benefits of fish oil on young people with raised levels of fats in their blood ended up proving just how dramatic this blood-thinning effect can be. Of eleven patients, eight of them had nosebleeds while taking the oil. 'It is concluded,' wrote the scientists, 'that the dose of fish oil necessary to reduce blood lipid levels may be associated with an extremely high risk of bleeding problems in adolescents.'[78]
- Can fish oil help in arthritis? Again, the evidence is far less conclusive than the publicity indicates. A 1985 study found that people who took one specific omega-3 (known as EPA) reported less morning stiffness when compared to another group of people who didn't take the oil[79]. But there were no improvements in other areas, such as grip strength, exercise ability, fatigue or swelling. Note – the people on fish oil didn't actually get any better, it was just that the people not taking fish oil got worse.
- As far as cholesterol is concerned, the results are very mixed indeed. Some studies have shown that large doses of fish oil can lower cholesterol levels dramatically. But other studies have shown just the opposite – that it can, in fact, raise them, and in particular raise the level of 'bad' LDL cholesterol.

Finally, to summarize: Fats should supply no more than 30 per cent of our total calorie intake. Today, the average is more like 40 per cent and in some cases even higher. And even that 30 per cent figure is too high for those who wish to take active steps to combat modern scourges such as coronary heart disease. Meat and meat products contribute at least a quarter of the total fat content of the average diet, the majority of which is in the form of saturated fat – the unhealthiest of all. Cut out meat and meat products, and you will automatically be eating a better diet!

Footnotes

1 *The Times*, 14 March 1986

2 Paper presented at the Meatex 86 seminar

3 P. Cox, *The New Why You Don't Need Meat.* (Bloomsbury Publishing, 1993)

4 BMA *News Review*, May 1993

5 From M. Klaper, *Pregnancy, Children and the Vegan Diet* (Gentle World, 1987)

6 *Proc Nat Acad Sci*, (vol 86, 1989)

7 L. Pauling, *How to Live Longer and Feel Better* (Avon Books, New York, 1987)

8 *Beta Carotene*, (American Hospital Formulary Service, February 1987, American Society of Hospital Pharmacists, Inc.)

9 L. K. Mahan and M. T. Arlin, *Krause's Food, Nutrition and Diet Therapy*, 8th edition (W.B. Saunders Company, 1992)

10 *UPI*, 19 March, 1988

11 L. K. Mahan and M. T. Arlin, *op. cit.*

12 S. K. Roma and T. A. Sanders, 'Taurine concentrations in the diet, plasma, urine and breast milk of vegans compared with omnivores' *Br J Nutr*, Jul 1986, 56 (1) p17–27

13 T. A. Sanders and M. T. Arlin, 'Blood pressure, plasma renin activity and aldosterone concentrations in vegans and omnivore controls' *Hum Nutr Appl Nutr* Jun 1987, 41 (3) p204–11

14 A. H. Lockie, E. Carlson, M. Kipps, J. J. Thomson, 'Comparison of four types of diet using clinical, laboratory and psychological studies' *R Coll Gen Pract*, Jul 1985, 35 (276) p333–6

15 S. K. Rana and T. A. Sanders, *op. cit.*

16 *Ibid.*

17 T. A. Sanders and T. J. Key, *op. cit.*

18 A. H. Lockie, E. Carlson, M. Kipps, J. J. Thomson, *op. cit.*

19 S. Areeku., S. Pattanamatum, C. Cheeramakara, K. Churdchue, S. Nitayapabskoon, M. Changanguan, 'The source and content of vitamin B12 in the tempehs', *J Med Assoc Thai*, Mar 1990, 73 (3) p152–6

20 Protoveg is available in all health food shops, and is a proprietary trademark

21 *Dietary Reference Values for Food Energy and Nutrients for the United Kingdom* (Department of Health, 1991)

22 G. Langley, *Vegan Nutrition, A Survey of Research* (Vegan Society, 1988)

23 Department of Health, *op. cit.*

24 H. DeLuca, 'Vitamin D and its metabolites' *Modern Nutrition in Health and Disease* 7th edition, eds. M. E. Shils and V. R. Young (Lea and Febiger, 1988)

25 J. Moon *et al*, 'Etiology of atherosclerosis and osteoporosis: are imbalances in the calciferol endocrine system implicated?' *J Am Coll Nutr*, 1992, 11(5), pp567–583.

26 A. G. Marsh, T. V. Sanchez, O. Michelsen, F. L. Chaffee, S. M. Fagal, 'Vegetarian lifestyle and bone mineral density' *Am J Clin Nutr*, Sep 1988, 48 (3 Suppl), pp837–41

27 B. L. Riggs, H. W. Wahmer, L. J. Melton 3rd, L. S. Richelson, H. L. Judd, W. M. O'Fallon, 'Dietary calcium intake and rates of bone loss in women' *J Clin Invest*, Oct 1987, 80 (4) pp979-82

28 D. M. Hegsted, 'Calcium and Osteoporosis', *J Nutr*, 1986;116 2316–19

29 J. B. Kim, 'Fractured truths', *Bestways* 1990, vol 18, no 2, p26(7)

30 *ibid*

31 Department of Health, *op. cit.*

32 Department of Health, *op. cit.*.

33 R. P. Heaney, C. M. Weaver, 'Calcium absorbability from kale' *Am J Clin Nutr*, 1990; 51, pp656–7

34 R. P. Heaney, C. M. Weaver, R. R. Recker, 'Calcium absorbability from spinach' *Am J Clin Nutr*, 1988, 47, p707

35 N. Nnakwe, C. Kies, 'Calcium and phosphorus utilization by omnivores and lactoovovegetarians fed laboratory controlled lactovegetarian diets' *Nutr Rep Int*, 1985, 31, p1009

36 A. G. Marsh, T. V. Sanchez, O. Michelsen, J. Keiser, G. Mayor 'Cortical bone density of adult lacto-ovovegetarians and omnivorous women', *J Am Diet Assoc*, 1980, 76, p148

37 S. Havala and J. Dwyer, 'Position of the American Dietetic Association: Vegetarian Diets – technical support paper', *J Am Diet Assoc*, 1988, 88:3, pp352-5

38 A. G. Marsh, T. V. Sanchez, O. Michelsen, F. L. Chaffee, S. M. Dagal, *op. cit.*

39 F. R. Ellis, P. Mumford, 'The nutritional status of vegans and vegetarians' *Proc Nutr Soc*, 1967, 26, pp206–212

40 A. H. Lockie, E. Carlson, M. Kipps, J. J. Thomson, *op. cit.*

41 S. K. Rana, T. A. Sanders, *op. cit.*

42 T. A. Sanders, T. J. Key, *op. cit.*

43 M. Abdulla, I. Andersson, N. G. Asp, K. Berthelsen, D. Birkhead, T. Dencker, C. G. Johansson, M. Jagerstad, K. Kolar, B. M. Nair, P. Hilsson-Ehle, A. Norden, S. Rassner, B. Akesson, P. A. Ockerman, 'Nutrient intake and health status of vegans. Chemical analyses of diets using the diplicate portion sampling technique' *J Clin Nutr*, Nov 1981, 34 (11), pp2464–77

44 T. A. Sanders, R. J. Purves, 'An anthropometric and dietary assessment of the nutritional status of vegan preschool children' *Hum Nutr*, Oct 1981, 35 (5), pp349–57

45 G. Langley, *op. cit.*

46 B. L. Specker, R. C. Tsang, M. H., D. Miller, 'Effect of vegetarian diet on serum 1,25-dihydroxyvitamin D concentrations during lactation' *Obstet Gynecol*, Dec 1987, 70 (6), pp870–4

47 N. Barnard, *Food for Life* (Harmony Books, 1993)

48 National Osteoporosis Foundation, National Institutes of Health, American Society of Bone and Mineral Research, 'Research Advances in

osteoporosis' Conference, Arlington, Virginia, USA February 1990

49 N. A. Breslan, L. Brinkley, K. D. Hill, C. Y. Pak, 'Relationship of animal protein-rich diet to kidney stone formation and calcium metabolism' *J Clin Endocrinol Metab*, Jan 1988, 66 (1), pp140–6

50 Department of Health, *op. cit.*

51 R. P. Heaney and R. R. Recker, ' Effects of nitrogen phosphorus, and caffeine on calcium balance in women' *J Lab Clin Med*, Jan 1982, 99 (1), p46–55

52 F. H. Nielsen, C. D. Hunt, L. M. Mullen, J. R. Hunt, 'Effect of dietary boron on mineral, estrogen, and testosterone metabolism in postmenopausal women' *FASEB J*, Nov 1987, 1 (5), pp394–7

53 M. Klaper, *Pregnancy, Children and the Vegan Diet* (Gentle World Inc, 1987)

54 L. K. Mahan and M. T. Arlin, *op. cit.*

55 N. Barnard, *op. cit.*

56 A. Bezkorovainy (ed), D. Narins, cited in *Biochemistry of Nonheme Iron* (Plenum, 1980)

57 A. H. Lockie, E. Carlson, M. Kipps, J. J. Thomson, *op. cit.*

58 T. A. Sanders and T. J. Key, *op. cit.*

59 T. A. Sanders and T. J. Key, *op. cit.*

60 J. L. Kelsay, K. M. Behall, E. S. Prather, 'Effect of fiber from fruits and vegetables on metabol;ic responses of human subjects. II. Calcium, magnesium, iron and silicon balances' *Am J Clin Nutr*, 1979, 32, pp1876–80

61 F. A. Oski, 'Is bovine milk a health hazard?' *Pediatr*, 75, pp182–86

62 'Control of nutritional anemia with special reference to iron deficiency', *WHO Technical Report Series*, 1985, p580

63 C. Anyon 'A cause of iron-deficiency anaemia in infants' *N.Z. Med J*, 74, p24-5

64 Dietary Reference Values for Food Energy and Nutrients for the United Kingdom. Department of Health 1991

65 Department of Health, *op. cit.*

66 G. Langley, *op. cit.*

67 G. Langley, *op. cit.*

68 F. M. Lappé, *Diet for a Small Planet* (Ballantine Books, 1971)

69 *Vegetarian Times*, 43, p22

70 Department of Health, *op. cit.*

71 *ibid.*

72 S. Havala, J. Dwyer, 'Position of the American Dietetic Association: Vegetarian Diets', *J Am Diet Assoc* November 1983, vol 93, no 11

73 *Better Nutrition*, Feb 1990, vol 52, no 2, p24(2)

74 *Nutrition Research Newsletter*, May 1989, vol 8, no 5, p56(1)

75 G. J. Reis, T. M. Boucher, M. E. Sipperley, D. I. Silverman, C. H. McCabe, D. S. Baim, F. M. Sacks, W. Grossman, W. R. C. Pasternak, 'Randomized trial of fish oil for prevention of restenosis after coronary angioplasty', *Lancet*, Jul 22, 1989, 2 (8656), pp177–81

76 John P. Middaugh, 'Cardiovascular deaths among Alaskan natives, 1980–86' *American Journal of Public Health*, March 1990, 80, (3), pp282(4)

77 W. J. Cliff, 'Coronary heart disease: Animal fat on trial' *Pathology*, 1987, 19, pp325–28

78 J. T. R. Clarke, G. Cullen-Dean, E. Regelink, L. Chan, V. Rose, 'Increased incidence of epistaxis in adolescents with familial hypercholesterolemia treated with fish oil' *Journal of Pediatrics*, Jan 1990, 116, (1), pp139(3)

79 *Men's Health*, July 1989, 5, (7), p4(3)

PART FOUR:

TOTAL HEALTH

*How the meat-free lifestyle
can help prevent disease
and promote health*

Trying to figure out just how healthy – or unhealthy – we are is uncommonly difficult. The one basic statistic, widely available and ceaselessly repeated by scientists and politicians, concerns life expectancy. In America, life expectancy has increased from an average of 71.3 years in 1970 to 76.4 years in 1990. In Europe, the figures have risen from 71.5 to 75.3 in the same period.[1] On the face of it, this seems encouraging enough. After all, if we're all living longer, we must all be healthier, mustn't we? In fact, life expectancy has risen worldwide in the same period. A citizen of Planet Earth born in 1970 could expect to live, on average, for 58.5 years; a baby born in 1990 could anticipate living to age 65.5.

But this is only a fragment – and a highly misleading one – of the bigger picture. Let me give you another, rather different, statistic to think about. In the year 1906, a Western man who had lived to the age of 40 could, on average, look forward to another twenty-seven years of life.[2] That's an official statistic, by the way. Now, how long do you think a man who reached forty in the year 1981 could expect to live? The answer may surprise you. He would, on average, have a further thirty-three years to live. This means that, in the first three-quarters of the 20th century, all the might of modern medicine and healthcare could only manage to extend the life expectancy of a forty-year-old by six years. Astonishing, isn't it?

Someone who was fifty in 1906 averaged another twenty years of life. A fifty-year-old in 1981 averaged just twenty-four more years. The gap narrows even more with older people. The sixty-five-year-old in 1906 had eleven more years of living to look forward to. The 1981 sixty-five-year-old could anticipate thirteen more years. So for this group, all the great medical innovations of the 20th century could barely extend their life expectancy by two years. A sobering thought.

Confused? Let me explain how these figures work. The truth is that the biggest statistical gains in life expectancy have been made by reducing infant mortality. Globally, 35,000 children under five years of age currently die every day from preventable diseases.[3] This amounts to some 13 million preventable deaths every year; a shaming indictment of the inhabitants of a planet who it has been said squander close to one billion dollars a day on the arms and military industries[4] – yet who cannot seem to manifest the necessary resources or sense of moral outrage to wipe out childhood malnutrition.

Now, even a minor change to these appalling mortality figures can dramatically affect the figures for life expectancy. For example, UNICEF states that malnutrition is a major contributory cause in approximately one-third of child deaths.[5] Supplying just a few of those children with better diets will result in fewer deaths, and the life expectancy figures will shoot up. The concept we need to grasp here is this: the statistics for life expectancy can *rise*, while the population itself becomes steadily *sicker*. The fact that fewer children die in infancy doesn't necessarily mean that the rest of us are living any longer, nor any better.

Here's another example of the way these statistics paint a different picture to the one we're usually given. In the period from 1970 to 1990, life expectancy rose in England from 68.9 to 73.1 years. Impressive, isn't it? Enough of an increase for us to proudly boast that 'we've never been healthier' – after all, 'we' are living an extra four years.

But wait a moment. Let's look at it in more detail. In the period mentioned, infant mortality declined somewhat (the cause is open to speculation). This fall in infant deaths contributed *over 25 per cent* of the difference in life expectancy figures for the two dates.[6] Hardly ground for claiming that 'we've never been healthier'. Even more disturbing is this: in the same period, *rates of sickness shot sky-high!* Surveys conducted by the Office of Population Censuses and Surveys show that in 1972, 21 per cent of the total population of Britain suffered from some type of long-standing illness. By 1990, the figure had risen to 34 per cent. One-third of the total population now suffer from some kind of long-standing illness![7] Amongst children, the upsurge in sickness is especially startling. In 1972, official records show that 8 per cent of children suffered from some kind of long-standing illness. Eighteen years later, that figure had more than doubled to 19 per cent. Curiously, these disturbing figures rarely seem to get the publicity they so plainly warrant.

These steep declines in child health are happening in the USA, too. A recent report from the American Health Foundation reveals that, just in the last decade, American children have become measurably less physically fit, more prone to diseases, and far more obese at a younger age. AIDS and homicide rates among children have also skyrocketed since 1985. Warns Dr Robert J. Ruben, a childhood disease specialist at Albert Einstein College of Medicine in New York: 'with the state of healthcare today for children, you're sitting on a powder keg.' Ruben blames the worsening health situation on rising poverty, more sedentary lives among children and lack of extensive school-based health programmes.

The truth is often buried away in the official public health records. There, you will find statistics which reveal a silently unfolding health crisis of unprecedented dimensions. The trends in disease are both appalling and consistent across most Western nations. Take a look at the charts that follow. They've been compiled from officially-recorded statistics which are produced by doctors themselves, who for several decades have kept records of the numbers of patients consulting them, and the reason for the consultation. The trend is remorseless – up, up, up. Now, we shouldn't hold the medical profession uniquely responsible for the fact that our society as a whole is getting sicker. But we must realize that we are indeed living in an age of ill-health – and it is up to *us* to take whatever steps necessary to fight for our right to well-being.

One of the most amazing qualities about the human race is our ability to adapt to almost anything – including persistent ill-health. The proportion of Americans who are satisfied with their health and physical condition has fallen from 61 per cent in the 1970s to 55 per cent in the last decade.[8] Surveys report most people experienced less than one serious, acute or disabling illness per year in the 1920s, but that figure more than doubled by the early 1980s, and it's getting worse. Even so, it seems that most of us would rather suffer chronic ill-health than make dramatic changes to the ways we live our lives. Rather than taking responsibility for our own health, we expect our doctors and scientists to provide us with a 'pill for every ill'. It's a conspiracy in which the medical profession, for the most part, seems happy to collude. One reason for this is that doctors have traditionally focused on studying *disease*, rather than promoting *health*. As Dr Joe Collier, a clinical pharmacologist who has studied and written about the drugs industry, puts it: 'Doctors fail patients because they are preoccupied with, even obsessed by, disease. Right from their earliest days at medical school, training concentrates on the recognition and treatment of disease, rather than its prevention . . . Disease is so much a part of a doctor's horizon that it may be difficult for a patient to escape the consulting room without an illness being diagnosed and at least one medicine being prescribed.'[9]

We want them to find a 'cure' for cancer, to eliminate the 'faulty genes' which precipitate asthma, to find a 'magic bullet' to cure AIDS, and so on. Some of this work is valuable. But most of it reinforces the notion that disease and chronic ill-health is the result of factors way beyond our control.

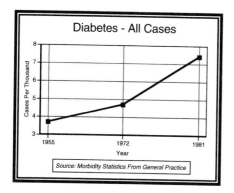

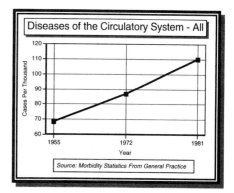

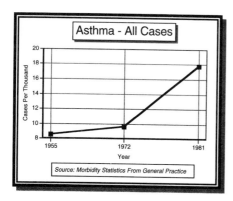

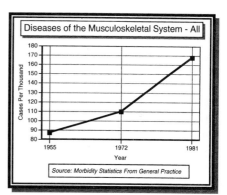

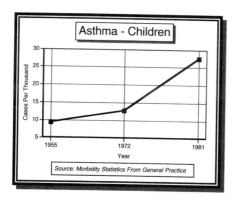

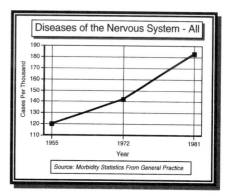

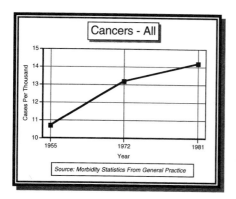

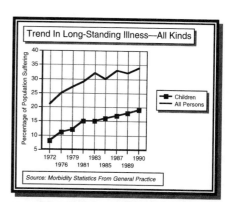

Today, the great white hope of medicine is the all-powerful science of genetics. It is no accident that the rise of the computer in popular consciousness and the upsurge of interest in genetics parallel each other. Genetic engineering seems to offer us the tantalizing possibility of understanding and controlling the ultimate computer program – the code which makes us human. A few tweaks here, and a few tweaks there, and presto! The program is bug-free. Perfect health is assured.

But genetic engineering also raises many troubling questions. 'Every new gene discovery,' points out Dr Patrick Dixon, the author of a book on the new genetic research, 'brings closer the horror of eugenics – designer families for tomorrow's parents with embryos selected for intelligence, hair colour or sexual orientation.'[10] Eugenics was the brainchild of English psychologist Francis Galton (1822–1911) who advocated 'improving' the human race through selective breeding; encouraging 'better' human stock to breed while discouraging the reproduction of 'less desirable' people. His ideas were hugely influential and gave rise to the mental hygiene movements, inspiring racial hygiene legislation in countries ranging from Nazi Germany to America (where, incidentally, laws mandating the sterilization of the mentally disabled remained unrepealed as recently as 1990).[11]

Whether the genetic route is one which we wish to travel is for us all to decide. For many, it is a seductive proposition. Disease and ill-health is almost always the result of an interaction between environment and genes. By concentrating on the genetic 'cause', our attention is distracted from the environmental factors – such as diet. One point which must be clearly understood is this: the recent upsurge in illness which has afflicted us in the space of one generation cannot be put down to 'faulty genes'. It is inconceivable that our species' genetic constitution has changed so rapidly in such a short time to make us so vulnerable to so many diseases. For the cause of this tide of ill-health, we must look elsewhere.

What this means is that protecting our own health is really up to us. It's not something we can, or should, delegate. But to take the right decisions about our health, we need to have access to information. In the past, that has been the preserve of the expert. But today, the role of the expert is changing dramatically. Dr Vernon Coleman, a well-known

medical writer, who says this:

> There are so many medical journals in existence that a new scientific paper is published somewhere in the world every twenty-eight seconds . . . Because they know that they need to publish research papers if they are to have successful careers, doctors have become obsessed with research for its own sake. They have forgotten that the original purpose of research is to help patients . . . Believe it or not, much of the research work that has been done in the last twenty years has never been analyzed. Somewhere, hidden deep in an obscure part of a medical library, there may be a new penicillin. Or a cure for cancer. You don't have to go far to find the evidence proving that many scientific papers go unread: approximately 20 per cent of all research is unintentionally duplicated because researchers haven't had the time to read all the published papers in their own specialized area.'[12]

I believe we are seeing a global change in the way we use and relate to experts, of all kinds. No longer will we have to rely upon a single medical expert for information about a disease and the proposed course of treatment. Increasingly, that information will be accessible to us all – through a variety of media, many of them electronic. Instead, we will seek the skills which experts have developed – such as surgeons, for example – and compare opinions, advice, costs and general expertise until we find an expert who suits our needs. This is, without doubt, a more empowering way of living.

For the moment, however, much of the research into the benefits of the vegetarian diet is effectively useless – simply because it is so routinely ignored. For example, you may be amazed to learn, as I was, that researchers have known for decades that feeding meat to a naturally vegetarian species – such as rabbits – will quickly give them heart disease. And they've also known that in a naturally carnivorous species, such as the dog, it is virtually impossible to produce clogging of the arteries, even when large amounts of cholesterol and saturated fat are fed to them.[13] Now for heaven's sake, doesn't this information tell us something about the sort of diet we humans should be eating? Therefore, since we are clearly not natural carnivores, shouldn't we be eating a more nearly vegetarian diet?

So, what have the doctors and scientists been doing all this time? Why haven't they given us this vital information? What they've been doing is yet more research. Looking in ever closer detail at the mechanisms of disease. Trying to figure out what the 'magic ingredient' of the vegetarian diet is. When studies are published which demonstrate the superiority of the vegetarian diet – in either a preventative or curative capacity – doctors and scientists seem to respond (if they respond at all) by searching for that one elusive factor that makes vegetarians healthier. Is it the reduced animal fat in their diet? Or the larger amounts of antioxidant vitamins A, C and E? Or the trace minerals such as selenium? Or the amino acid pattern in the protein? If they could just put their fingers on it, then the 'problem' would be solved. The problem is, vegetarianism doesn't work like that. Although all of these factors seem to contribute to some extent towards making the vegetarian lifestyle healthier, none of them by itself is the nutritional holy grail which they seek. The truth is that all the components of a healthy vegetarian diet work together to preserve health and combat disease. It's the nearest we have to a totally healthy lifestyle.

ANNULLING ANAEMIA

How can the vegetarian diet prevent anaemia? After all, vegetarians don't eat red meat, do they? You may be surprised to know that, despite all the meat industry propaganda, the facts reveal that a healthy vegetarian diet is an excellent way to get all the iron you need.

WHAT IS ANAEMIA?

Anaemia literally means 'lack of blood'. More precisely, the word is used to refer to a reduction in the oxygen-carrying capacity of the blood – which can be caused in three main ways:

- Loss of blood (i.e. heavy menstrual periods)
- Excessive red blood cell destruction
- Defective red blood cell formation

Oxygen is held within the red blood cell by the pigment haemoglobin, which transports oxygen from the lungs to body cells and returns waste carbon dioxide from the cells to the lungs. About 20 per cent of the total oxygen used each day is used by the human brain. Fatigue and mental dullness occurs when the brain doesn't get enough oxygen – if the haemoglobin level drops, the heart rate will speed up and you will start breathing faster to try to compensate for the lower oxygen delivery. Replacement of haemoglobin requires iron in the diet, as well as vitamin B12 and folic acid. If any of these are inadequately present, or are inadequately absorbed, anaemia will result. There are many kinds of anaemias, but the most common include:

- Iron-deficiency anaemia. Caused by either chronic blood loss or insufficient iron absorption or utilization.
- Pernicious anaemia. More often found in middle-aged and older people. Generally, it is caused by an inability to produce an enzyme (known as the 'intrinsic factor') which is essential for the proper assimilation of vitamin B12.

Iron-deficiency anaemia is thought to be a common nutritional problem, although precise estimates of its incidence range very widely. Some suggest that up to 65 per cent of all women in Western countries may have 'low' iron stores in their bodies; and up to 20 per cent may suffer from iron-deficiency anaemia.[14] In Britain, a survey for the Ministry of Agriculture suggests that young women (ages 15–25) consume, on average, only three-quarters of the recommended daily allowance of iron.[15] Whatever the exact figures, it is clear that this is a widespread health problem, and vegetarians would be wrong to trivialize it. However, the meat industry is equally wrong to imply – as their advertising often seems to – that meat-eaters need not worry about iron-deficiency anaemia. Clearly, such exaggeration is dangerous – with up to one in five women suffering from it, the problem of iron-deficiency anaemia is a real concern for meat-eating women.

HOW THE VEGETARIAN DIET CAN HELP

Since anaemia can result from an inadequate intake of three nutrients – iron, vitamin B12 and folic acid – it is often alleged that vegetarians are risking their health, and are condemned to become anaemic. But is this true? In a word, no! Let's examine each nutrient.

Iron-deficiency anaemia

Iron-deficiency anaemia is uncommon in men, but

more widespread in women. Obviously, iron-deficiency anaemia can simply be caused by not consuming enough iron in the diet, but it can also be produced if the body does not properly absorb the iron in food – for example, chronic diarrhoea or prolonged antacid use may impair absorption.

Iron is a trace element. The adult body contains a total of about 3–5g. About two-thirds of this is bound up in haemoglobin, and about a fifth is held in storage, much of it in the form called ferritin. This remarkable protein allows animals to survive for considerable periods without dietary iron. Most of these ferritin iron stores are found in the liver, bone marrow and spleen. However, minute amounts of ferritin are also found in the blood. One test for iron deficiency will measure the amount of ferritin present in the blood, because that will give a good idea of the quantity of ferritin present at the body's main storage sites. Plasma ferritin of 12mcg per litre or less suggests that iron stores are becoming depleted.[16] Plasma ferritin levels will, however, naturally vary in a normal human. For example, they will tend to be higher in the morning, and lower in the evening. Stress, too, can affect the results of ferritin tests, as can recent infection. But carefully-conducted tests which reveal a consistent picture of steadily declining ferritin levels indicate the beginnings of iron deficiency, which if unchecked, will eventually result in anaemia. Those population groups at particular risk of iron deficiency include:

- infants
- teenage girls
- pregnant women
- women of childbearing years
- the elderly.

Blood loss due to menstruation is the most common cause of iron deficiency among women of childbearing years. It is, therefore, of great importance that people in all these groups should obtain enough dietary iron to replace natural losses.

Since some types of meat (principally liver) provide large amounts of iron, and since some of that iron is in a form (haem) which is more easily assimilated than the iron found in plants (non-haem), conventional wisdom has recommended the consumption of meat as the main source of dietary iron. However, there are several logical objections to this point of view.

- As already mentioned, iron-deficiency anaemia is a problem which affects a large section of the population, who are mostly meat-eaters. Meat consumption, therefore, does not appear to be an effective means of preventing widespread iron deficiency.
- Other primates eat a naturally vegetarian diet (a chimpanzee does not, as a rule, breakfast on fried liver!) and do not suffer from iron-deficiency anaemia.
- A vegetarian or vegan diet is well capable of providing normal dietary iron requirements, generally obtained from dark green leafy vegetables, iron-fortified cereals, and wholegrains.
- Radical new evidence (see following) suggests that the over-consumption of iron-rich foods may in fact be a health hazard.

In addition, scientific fieldwork in this area paints an extremely revealing picture, which flatly contradicts the notion that vegetarians are at particular risk of iron deficiency. For example:

- A study of British vegans concludes that their iron level is 'normal in all the vegans and no subject had a haemoglobin concentration below the lower limit of normality'.[17]
- In their 1988 position paper concerning the vegetarian diet, the American Dietetic Association concluded: 'With both vegetarian and nonvegetarian diets, iron and folate supplements are usually necessary during pregnancy, although vegetarians frequently have greater intakes of those nutrients than do nonvegetarians.'[18]
- Further field studies conducted amongst British vegans report dietary iron intakes of 22.4mg,[19] 31mg[20] and 20.5mg[21] per day. The mean figure of these studies (24.6mg) is more than double the official estimated average requirement (EAR) of 11.4mg a day.
- In Israel, a study compared the iron intakes of meat-eaters and vegetarians, concluding, 'The intake of iron was significantly higher in the vegetarians . . . it is concluded that a long-term ovo-lacto vegetarian diet does not lead to mineral deficiencies.'[22]
- In Holland, another study compared meat-eating and vegetarian pre-school children. While the vegetarian children had a good intake of dietary iron, the meat-eaters 'had intakes of iron below the Dutch RDAs'.[23]

- In Sweden, yet another study compared the diet eaten by vegans to that of meat-eaters, and found that the vegans' iron consumption was 'nearly double' that of the meat-eaters.[24]
- A Canadian study looked at the iron levels of long-term vegetarians (in this case Seventh-Day Adventist women) and concluded: 'The iron and zinc status of these long-term Seventh-Day Adventist vegetarian women appeared adequate despite their low intake of readily absorbed iron and zinc from flesh foods and their high intake of total dietary fiber and phytate.'[25]
- Further – and highly significant – evidence comes from the 'China Study,' the most comprehensive large study ever undertaken of the relationship between diet and the risk of developing disease. The study was truly massive, involving the collection of 367 detailed facts about the diet and lifestyle of 6500 participants across China, from 1983 onwards. It reveals that meat-eating is by no means necessary to prevent iron-deficiency anaemia. The average Chinese adult – who shows no evidence of anaemia – consumes twice the iron an American adult does, but the vast majority of it comes from the iron in plants.
- In a very carefully controlled study of the impact of high and low meat diets on iron levels, scientists from the Grand Forks Human Nutrition Research Center found, to their surprise, that subjects (in this case, postmenopausal women) given a high-meat diet to eat had, after seven weeks, a worse iron level than people eating a low-meat diet! 'The negative effect of meat consumption on iron status was unexpected,' they concluded, 'the results emphasize the need . . . for identifying additional dietary components that influence iron nutriture.'[26] This is a point we'll return to in a moment.

This research, and more besides, disproves the fallacy that a meat-free diet can't provide enough iron. It certainly can – you've just seen some of the evidence.

But what about the other side of the coin? Although the research you've just seen demonstrates that vegetarians can get enough iron, does this mean that they always *do*? Aren't they, after all, more likely to develop anaemia? This is certainly the implication of many medical and nutritional textbooks. Their reasoning is usually as follows:

1) Meat provides haem iron, which is more easily absorbed than non-haem (plant sources),
2) Vegetarians don't eat meat,
3) Therefore vegetarians are likely to be anaemic.

The science of nutrition, just like any other branch of human knowledge, is full of its own folklore. Opinions such as these are often passed down from one generation of practitioners to another; because they sound plausible, and because no-one bothers to check or question the original research in the field. If they did, they'd be in for quite a shock.

A computer search reveals that in the period from 1966 to the begining of 1994, a total of 7,618,328 articles were published in the world's major medical journals.[27] Of these, just sixty-two mentioned the word 'anaemia' in connection with the words 'vegetarians' or 'vegans'. That's just under 0.000814 per cent of the medical literature in twenty-eight years. Not very much, is it?

But when these sixty-two reports are themselves analyzed, the picture becomes even more unequivocal:

- The majority (twenty-two reports) dealt not with iron-deficiency anaemia, but with individual case histories of people on very restricted diets with vitamin B12 deficiency (see below).
- Most of the reports of iron-deficiency anaemia amongst vegetarians (7) dealt with the iron status of impoverished Indians, either in India itself or as immigrants to the West. Is it their vegetarianism causing them to be anaemic – or more likely, their poverty?
- One report described iron-deficiency anaemia amongst macrobiotic subjects. Most vegetarians do not eat a macrobiotic regime (which, by the way, may include flesh).
- Another report described the 'marginal' iron status of a group of elderly Dutch vegetarians, 65–97 years old. Despite the researchers' judgement about their 'marginal' status, their subjects were described as 'apparenty healthy'.
- Another report described the improvement obtained by supplementing the diets of a group of anaemic preschool children not with meat – but with vitamin C. 'The children who received vitamin C supplements showed a significant improvement in haemoglobin level as well as in red cell morphology,' wrote the researchers.[28] Vitamin C is normally well supplied in a vegetarian diet (there

is no vitamin C in meat).

● The rest of the reports consisted of tangential research, summaries or discussions.

The charge that the vegetarian diet causes iron-deficiency anaemia can now be firmly rejected. Nearly thirty years of published research has failed to substantiate it.

Now we come to a particularly interesting aspect of this controversy. Studies comparing the plasma ferritin levels of vegetarians to meat-eaters sometimes show that, although the vegetarians' levels are within the normal range, they are rather lower than meat-eaters, suggesting that meat-eaters store more iron in their bodies than vegetarians. Is this good, or bad? Consider the following warning by a noted researcher on dietary iron: 'Possibly, as discussed in the previous chapters, while decreasing the risk of classical iron-deficiency symptoms, the current RDA [recommended daily allowance] for iron is increasing the risk of infection. In this respect, nutritionists have lowered their RDAs for iron over the past decade – 40 per cent lower in newborn infants and 17 per cent lower in adult females in 1989 as compared to 1980. Certainly, the physiology of these groups has not changed, which leads one to wonder about the accuracy of these values . . . I foresee a continuing downward trend of RDAs for iron and an upward trend for Vitamin C as more hard data becomes available.'[29]

It has been known for some time that very low levels of iron in the human body increase the risk of infection. It is not so well–known, however, that high levels of iron do precisely the same. Invading bacteria require iron to grow – and the more iron made available to them, the faster they'll multiply.

But that's not all. Over the past few years, Dr Randall B. Lauffer has proposed a theory which has been greeted in some quarters as medical heresy. Dr Lauffer is an assistant professor at Harvard Medical School, and an expert on mineral biochemistry and the use of minerals in medical diagnosis and therapy. He is also the director of a research laboratory at Massachusetts General Hospital, and founded a pharmaceutical research company, whose purpose is to find new medical applications of mineral biochemistry. He writes:

Scientific discoveries are coming out every day showing new roles that iron plays in many common diseases. We are coming to recognize that there has perhaps been an overemphasis on iron

deficiency in the past. Worldwide, iron deficiency is a major problem, especially in populations that are malnourished. However, in the well-fed populations of the Western world iron deficiency is increasingly rare, and is mainly observed in certain sub-groups such as pregnant women and children.

Iron is a key component of the free radical theory of disease. This was discovered some time ago, and more and more evidence is being laid down in support of it. Basically, the theory is this: oxygen – which of course is good for you – is used in burning the body's fuel, that is, the foods that we eat. But oxygen also can be converted into toxic by-products. Now, most of these toxic by-products are pretty mild. However, in the presence of iron, and also, in some cases, copper, these mildly toxic forms of oxygen are converted into much more toxic forms. And wherever they are produced, they can damage the tissue that surrounds them. This is true in heart disease. The leading theory of atherosclerosis involves free radical damage to LDL (low density lipoprotein – the 'bad' form of cholesterol). Then certain cells in the artery itself and the artery wall begin sucking up this damaged LDL. And this begins what we call atherosclerotic plaque development. But the most important role for iron is that excess iron in the heart creates more damage when a heart attack actually occurs. The same type of chemical reaction that oxidizes LDL can also damage the heart cells directly. For example, when you have a heart attack, you have diminished oxygen supply to the heart. Then, when you have either coronary bypass surgery, or a procedure, such as angioplasty, where the artery is opened up and blood flow resumes, more oxygen is quickly perfused into the heart, and this generates more damaging oxygen free radicals. And the more iron present, the more damage occurs in the process.

We are now following a major Finnish study which shows that men who have higher iron levels are predisposed to heart attacks. We don't have enormous evidence that excess iron will cause atherosclerosis directly. We do believe, however, that the combination of high cholesterol levels – which are common in Western cultures – and high iron and/or copper levels can contribute to this process. People have wondered for years why men are predisposed to certain diseases from which women seem to be protected. For heart disease, it is not that women are totally protected; they seem to be protected only prior to menopause. The conventional medical view is that it is all hormonal, that in some mysterious way, women's hormones protect them during the childbearing years. Yet there's been no clear mechanism proposed as to how that would actually work. For example, the effects of oestrogen on cholesterol levels are really quite ridiculously small to ever be a mechanism for this. The changes in iron metabolism, however, are dramatic, and appear to be a much more sensible explanation for the difference in incidence of heart disease in men and women. The iron levels match exactly the mortality rates of heart disease in men and women. Men get very high iron levels early in life, say twenty years old, whereas women's iron levels are held down by the natural loss of iron through menstruation. As soon as that ceases, however, their iron levels bound up quickly to that of men, and, at the same time, the incidence of heart disease increases.[30]

Luckily, the same kind of meat-free, dairy-free diet (ie vegan) that lowers cholesterol levels also lowers iron. Says Dr Lauffer: 'It makes sense to look to many of the Asian cultures, where heart attacks are of much lower prevalence, and at the type of diet they eat, and try to mimic that. It's very simple. In fact, the biggest contributor to both high iron and high cholesterol levels is meat consumption. Meat is a one-two punch: it contains a certain form of iron [known as haem] that is very rapidly and easily absorbed. And it contains saturated fat and cholesterol. So every bite of meat is contributing to two problems in the body – both of which lead to heart disease and possibly other chronic diseases that are common in Western meat-eating cultures.'

Dr Lauffer also suggests that iron may play an important role in the causation of cancer: 'We have had evidence for a long time that high iron levels do increase the risk of cancer,' he says, 'and there are two reasons: first of all, iron's role in free radical damage is important in cancer. Cancer arises when the blueprint for the cell, the DNA, is damaged. Second, iron is known to be a key catalyst for this process. The body tries to safely sequester iron away in the cell and keep it away from the DNA. However, free radical damage still occurs. The body repairs the damage as best it can, but it can't sometimes repair every little nick that occurs. And so, the more of these nicks you get,

the greater chance you have of getting cancer. Iron has another role in cancer: iron is a key ingredient for cell division. If the cell doesn't have iron around, it simply does not divide. So if you can restrict the amount of iron to a cancer cell, it actually slows down cancer growth.'

The possible connection between iron levels and heart disease was first proposed in 1981, when Dr Jerome Sullivan, a pathologist at the Veterans Administration Medical Center in Charleston, South Carolina, suggested that menstrual bleeding might protect women from heart disease by reducing the amount of iron in their bodies. Although experts have traditionally blamed hormonal changes for the sudden surge in cardiovascular illness in women after the age of menopause, Sullivan pointed out that women's cholesterol levels change little after menopause, although their iron levels *do* rise sharply. Further evidence to support Sullivan's theory comes from studies which show that surgical removal of the uterus (the site of menstrual bleeding) causes an increase in heart-attack risk – even if the ovaries are left to produce oestrogen.

Then, in 1992, the first major piece of practical research in support of the iron-heart disease connection was published.[31] Researchers at the University of Kuopio in Finland tracked the health of 1931 men from 1984 until 1989, and found that men having higher iron levels in their bodies had twice the risk of heart attack compared to men with lower levels of stored iron. Men with both high iron and high cholesterol were four times as likely to be stricken.

Since then, the debate in medical and scientific circles had been raging. Iron – just like protein before it – has been a sacred cow of conventional nutrition for decades; the idea that it might be a doubled-edged sword is still anathema to many. Nevertheless, the evidence against excessive iron consumption – primarily from flesh foods – is increasing, and cannot be lightly dismissed.

In Summary

- Iron-deficiency anaemia is a widespread problem, particularly for women
- Eating a meat-free diet does not increase the risk of anaemia
- The body naturally regulates its absorption of dietary iron according to its needs
- A healthy meat-free diet will include several good sources of iron (see page 82)

- Eating foods – or supplements – rich in vitamin C will considerably enhance iron bioavailability
- Consuming tea or coffee with meals will greatly reduce iron bioavailability
- Use iron supplements only on medical advice. And keep them away from children – in America, iron pills are the most common cause of childhood poisoning deaths[32]
- Too much iron may be as dangerous as too little. A vegetarian diet which allows our bodies to absorb the right amount of iron from several natural sources is the healthiest option. After all, it works pretty well for our primate relatives!

Other dietary anaemias

Apart from iron deficiency, anaemia will also result if the diet does not contain sufficient vitamin B12, or folic acid (which is sometimes referred to as vitamin B9). Both these vitamins play an essential part in the regular replacement of haemoglobin in the body.

Folic acid deficiency is a widespread problem globally. Unlike vitamin B12, the body does not store appreciable amounts, so it is essential that the diet regularly contains good sources. Apart from eventually resulting in anaemia, it has been shown that pregnant women whose diets are low in this vitamin are more likely to bear children with serious neural tube defects such as hydrocephalus and spina bifida (birth defects in which the spinal column does not form properly). Research shows that the simple precaution of taking folic acid supplements, especially during early pregnancy, can dramatically reduce the incidence of these afflictions. The US Food and Drug Administration is so convinced of the importance of this vitamin in preventing birth defects that it wants it to be added to bread, flour and other enriched grain products.[33]

The good news for vegetarians is that folic acid (the word comes from the Latin for 'leaf') is present in many common green leafy vegetable foods (although note that it can be destroyed by excessive cooking). It is not present in most meat, milk, eggs and root vegetables.

Of far more concern, particularly to vegans, is the question of vitamin B12 deficiency anaemia. Those who are commercially and ideologically opposed to the vegan diet cite the relative lack of vitamin B12 as conclusive proof that veganism is a perverse practice. On the other side, it has been known for ardent vegans to declare that vitamin B12 'simply isn't an issue'. As

with iron deficiency, the truth is far more complex than either of these extremes, and a little basic knowledge about the role of this vitamin in the diet, and its best sources, would calm a debate in which there has frequently been more heat than light.

There is no question that lack of vitamin B12 will eventually cause serious health problems, described here by two medical experts in the field (both, incidentally, practicing vegetarians): 'The pernicious anaemia patient was first described in the medical literature in 1849 as one who appeared pale and sallow with a shiny tongue and complained of weakness and fatigue that progressed gradually to the point of paralysis. Blood tests done on such patients today would reveal low haemoglobin levels and large, pale red blood cells. In the early stages of the illness there are numbness and tingling in the hands and feet with a loss of sensation. Gradually a lack of motor coordination develops. These symptoms are now known to be due to an inability to synthesize myelin, the fatty sheath that insulates nerve fibres. As a result, the nerves to the limbs degenerate. If allowed to proceed unchecked, the deterioration progresses into the spinal cord and ultimately to the brain. Moodiness, poor memory, and confusion give way gradually to delusions, hallucinations, and overt psychosis.'[34]

Clearly, we're dealing with a very serious set of symptoms, which it would be dishonest – and dangeous – to ignore or to trivialise. However, this is only the begining of the story. The fact is that the vast majority of cases of vitamin B12 deficiency occur not in vegans, but in the general meat-eating population. Comments Dr John Lindenbaum, a vitamin B12 researcher and director of the department of medicine at Columbia University: 'We see less than one case a year due to insufficient intake of vitamin B12 alone.'[35] Compare that number to the fifty cases of pernicious anemia that Dr Lindenbaum sees in non-vegetarians in the same period of time.

So if meat-eaters can experience vitamin B12 deficiency – and meat itself contains large amounts of vitamin B12 – what is going wrong? The answer is that although these people consume large amounts of B12 in their diets, they cannot absorb it due to low acidity in the stomach, disease or the absence of an enzyme called the 'intrinsic factor'. In any of these cases, vitamin B12 is blocked from entering the body's normal biochemical pathways, and will therefore never do its work in the body. The fact is that cases of vitamin B12 deficiency are most often due to a defect in absorption, and not to a dietary lack of the vitamin.

Many vegans feel, quite justifiably, persecuted over the matter of vitamin B12. The number of cases on record of vegans exhibiting health problems due to B12 deficiency is very small; certainly when compared to the millions of people who die every year of diseases linked to meat consumption. But there are, indeed, a few clinical cases on record of vegans, and their babies, developing anaemia because of low B12 dietary intake. Such cases are rare, but because the implications are serious – particularly for babies, whose intellectual development may be impaired – they must not be ignored.

Vitamin B12 is itself the subject of much continuing research. The amount needed in the diet – officially put at 1.5mcg a day (a microgram(mcg) is one millionth of a gram) – is absolutely tiny; the smallest of all the suggested daily intakes of vitamins.[36] Measuring the B12 content of foodstuffs is difficult, partly because the quantities are so small, and partly because foods sometimes contain substances which are chemically very similar to B12, but which do not possess the same biological activity (the so-called noncobalamin analogues). Vitamin B12 is almost always manufactured by bacteria (although, even here, the possibility exists that that some peas and beans actually produce their own vitamin B12). The vitamin B12 in meat itself is produced by bacterial action within the gut of the animal in question; it is also likely that bacteria on the surface and around the roots of plants eaten by that animal will also contribute towards the total B12 content of the animal's flesh. The obvious question has been posed that if farm animals can produce vitamin B12 from their internal bacteria, why can't humans, too? In all probability, we can. Bacteria in our gut, in our mouth, around the teeth and gums, in the nasal passages, around the tonsils, in the folds at the base of the tongue and even in the upper bronchial area may all produce vitamin B12. And if we eat foods grown in soils where the bacterial flora is rich, such as organic produce, then we will probably take in a useful dose of B12 from this source, too. All these aspects of vitamin B12 are intriguing, and all are grounds for much additional research work and speculation. But none of these points should be used to obscure the fact that healthy vegans need to make sure they periodically eat foods which they know to contain good sources of B12. Indeed, there are many

(see p70); anyone criticizing the vegan diet on the grounds that 'there are no sources of vitamin B12 in it' is merely demonstrating his or her ignorance.

In summary

- Inadequate folic acid intake is a substantial hazard for many meat-eaters – it is not found in most meats, milk or eggs. Because of their high intake of green leafy vegetables, wheat, beans, lentils and other good dietary sources, vegetarians are well-placed to avoid the health problems associated with folic acid deficiency

- Pernicious anaemia is usually caused by an inability to absorb vitamin B12 – whether or not you eat meat has nothing to do with it.

- Dietary vitamin B12 deficiency is never a problem for vegans who periodically eat food which they know to contain this vitamin (see the guidelines for daily food intake on p71).

ALLIEVIATING ANGINA

WHAT IS ANGINA?

In medical language, angina properly means a spasmodic, choking or suffocating pain; for example, the alarming-sounding complaint *angina acuta* merely signifies a simple sore throat. However, angina is now used almost exclusively to describe *angina pectoris*, a chronic condition of pain in the chest. The word angina comes from the Greek for 'strangling', which sums up both the cause and effect of this serious and threatening condition. It is almost always caused by an insufficient supply of oxygen to the heart muscle, which is itself usually the result of progressive blockage of the coronary arteries. It is closely linked to both coronary heart disease (see page 139) and high blood pressure (see page 150). Angina is most likely to strike during physical exertion or emotion, and will disappear when the excess work load or emotion is relieved.

HOW THE VEGETARIAN DIET CAN HELP

As explained on page 150 in the section relating to heart disease, Dr Dean Ornish's work treating patients with a low-fat vegan diet clearly demonstrates that the plaques which build up and eventually block coronary arteries can be diminished by appropriate diet therapy. This results in increased flow of blood and a corresponding decline in the severity or frequency of angina which has now been verified by several detailed scientific papers.[37] Rather than repeat the evidence here, I will refer readers to the sections relating to heart disease and hypertension, where the science is covered in some detail. It is, however, worth emphasizing that it is the vegan, not the semi-vegetarian, diet which can reverse atherosclerosis. 'Many doctors still recommend "lean meat" diets,' comments Dr Neal Barnard, 'even though such diets do not reverse heart disease for most patients and, in fact, are too weak even to stop the progression of the disease.'[38] Confirms Dr Ornish: 'Our study and now four other studies have shown that, on average, people with heart disease who only make moderate changes – less red meat, more fish and chicken, fewer eggs, and so on – overall they tend to get worse over time. The arteries become more blocked.'

ASSUAGING ARTHRITIS AND RHEUMATISM

WHAT ARE ARTHRITIS AND RHEUMATISM?

Arthritis is a specific term describing inflammation of the joints; rheumatism is used more broadly and describes all aches and pains in the muscles, bones or joints. In this sense, we have all suffered from rheumatism at some time. Rheumatoid arthritis is therefore inflammation and pain of the joints *and* the surrounding tissues. There are, in fact, some 100 different types of arthritis, including:

- Reiter's syndrome, an acute form often accompanied by eye inflammation and more frequently found in young men
- Ankylosing spondylitis, a chronic complaint, affecting the spine, pelvic joints, and sometimes the heart and eyes. It causes pain, fatigue and depression which can last for years.
- Systemic lupus erythematosus, which is much more common in women and is characterized by skin rashes and joint inflammation.

- Gout involves swelling and severe pain, normally in the big toe. It has long been known to be aggravated by diet, especially foods rich in purine, which produces uric acid.

WHY DO PEOPLE GET ARTHRITIS?

Many different causes have been suggested including stress, allergy, food and environmental pollution, malnutrition, hormonal imbalance, and digestive inadequacy. Another is that our body can mistakenly attack itself in trying to fight off foreign bacteria that closely resemble our own tissue. This is called an autoimmune response. Relevant to all of these, there is ever-increasing evidence that diet has a very important role to play in the onset and control of these degenerative disorders.

HOW THE VEGETARIAN DIET CAN HELP

Conventionally, medicine has treated the notion that arthritis might be responsive to the meat-free diet as unsubstantiated folklore. As recently as 1990, for example, the University of California's own health publication advised its readers that 'though scores of clinical studies have been conducted, no dietary regimen or nutritional supplement has been shown to alleviate or prevent arthritis'.[39] Nevertheless, the evidence has steadily accumulated over the years, and at last it seems as if the testimony of countless sufferers is at last being given a sympathetic hearing by many doctors. There is, indeed, a good scientific explanation. Meat and dairy foods contain arachidonic acid, and it has been demonstrated that levels of arachidonic acid in the blood fluctuate according to the consumption of these products, and can indeed promote joint inflammation.[40] Adopting a vegan diet can significantly reduce arachidonic acid, and the subsequent pain of arthritis, as these studies prove.

- In one early study of rheumatoid arthritis, published in 1986, patients were asked to fast for a week, which was then followed by three weeks of a vegan diet. At the end of this time, 60 per cent said they felt better, with 'less pain and increased functional ability'.[41] Studies such as this, however, do not always make the medical headlines, and it was several more years before most specialists began to appreciate just how important the role of diet might be in diminishing the pain of arthritis.

- Some people may be particularly sensitive to dairy products. In this well-constructed experiment, a fifty-two-year-old white woman with eleven years of arthritic suffering was tested to see which food-stuffs – if any – provoked her arthritis the most.[42] Eating her 'normal' diet, she would average about thirty minutes of morning stiffness, with nine tender joints and three swollen joints. After a three-day fast, there was no morning stiffness, just one tender joint, and no swollen joints. However, when she was given milk (the study was 'blinded' – she didn't know what foodstuff she was swallowing) the arthritis returned with a vengeance, with thirty minutes of morning stiffness, fourteen tender joints, and four swollen joints.
- Perhaps the most widely-publicized study appeared in the medical journal *The Lancet* in 1991.[43] Twenty-seven patients were asked to follow a modifed fast for seven to ten days (herbal teas, garlic, vegetable broths and juices), and were then put on a gluten-free vegan diet for three-and-a-half months. The authors of the study had already accepted that 'fasting is an effective treatment for rheumatoid arthritis, but most patients relapse on reintroduction of food'. Their aim, therefore, was to see whether the achievements attained during fast-ing could be maintained. Gradually, the subjects' diet was altered by adding a new food item every other day, eventually arriving at a lactovegetarian diet for the remainder of the study. If the introduc-tion of one food produced symptoms, then it would be eliminated again. A control group ate an ordinary diet throughout the whole study period, for com-parison purposes. After four weeks the vegan diet group showed a significant improvement in number of tender joints, number of swollen joints, pain, duration of morning stiffness, grip strength, white blood cell count, and many other measurements of health. Best of all, wrote the scientists, 'the benefits in the diet group were still present after one year.'

Today, it seems that the dietary treatment of the excruciating pain of arthritis is at last finding wide-spread acceptance by medical specialists. Speaking at the launch of the Arthritis and Rheumatism Council's booklet *Diet and Arthritis*, consultant rheumatologist Dr John Kirwan commented: 'As far as we can tell at present, low-fat diets, cutting out red meat, full-fat milk, butter and confectionery made with butter – together with an increased intake of coldwater fish or

vegetable oil – may enable people to take fewer pain killers and anti-inflammatory drugs'.[44] And that's no bad thing. In an earlier report from 1986, British doctors estimated that non-steroidal anti-inflamma-tory drugs (NSAIDs) used in the treatment of arthritic pain may be causing 200 deaths and 2000 cases of intestinal bleeding each year.[45] Almost all the victims are elderly and most are women.

WHAT ELSE CAN YOU DO?

There are a number of other dietary measures you can consider when making appropriate lifestyle changes to reduce the pain of arthritis:

- Dava Sorbel, a former *New York Times* science writer, and market researcher Arthur Klein sur-veyed over 1000 arthritis sufferers aged ten to ninety in an attempt to find out what the sufferers themselves found to be effective.[46] 47 per cent changed the way they ate because of their arthri-tis. Of these, 20 per cent said the dietary changes helped their condition: in some cases, dramatically. 56 per cent said their doctors had given them no nutritional information, or told them there was no relationship between diet and arthritis. They found that the most avoided foods were red meats (155 patients); sugar (148); fats (135); salt (98); caffeine (56); plants in the nightshade family such as tomatoes, aubergines, etc (48). Most favoured foods were: vegetables (204 patients); fruit (174); fish (89).
- People who alter the bacterial content of their gut often experience relief from rheumatic symptoms.[47] A change of diet combined with a course of colonic irrigation (see p134) and the use of acidophilus supplements could be worth trying.
- A calorie-controlled diet is of benefit to those who suffer rheumatism or arthritis and are overweight. Excess weight only adds to the strain placed on already overstressed joints. A healthy way to lose weight is to eat a vegan diet and, at the same time, cut out all refined sugar. This diet lets you drop the pounds quickly while significantly reducing joint discomfort.
- Fish oils have been shown to have some benefit for arthritis sufferers, probably because of the omega-3 fatty acids they contain. For ethical reasons (and indeed for reasons of health: the North Sea has been described as a gigantic open sewer) you may prefer

to consider instead flaxseed oil supplements, as described on page 97. Also, the linolenic acid in soybean oil (soya lecithin) is believed to be rapidly converted in the body to the same omega-3 fatty acids found in fish oils.

- Vitamin A is necessary for the body to fight infection, a key in many rheumatoid arthritis cases. To make sure you get enough of this vitamin, eat plenty of yellow, orange and green fruits and vegetables such as spinach, carrots, papaya, pumpkin, sweet potato, watercress and parsley.
- If you are taking drugs for a rheumatic disease, it is possible that you are lacking in vitamin B complex. This is found in whole grains and brewer's yeast.
- Vitamin C helps to thin the synovial fluid in your joints, which leads to improved mobility. Arthritics particularly benefit from taking vitamin C because the aspirin they take to reduce pain and inflammation depletes the body of vitamin C. Fresh citrus fruit, blackcurrants, green peppers and cauliflower are all excellent sources.
- Vitamins C and E and the mineral selenium are all antioxidants; oxidation is a process in which nutrients in the body are broken down before the body can use them. Selenium also reduces the production of prostaglandins and leukotrienes, both of which cause inflammation. Whole grains, vegetable oils and nuts are rich in vitamin E. Selenium is a trace mineral available from most plant foods or from supplementation.
- A New England horticulturalist has developed a theory that solanum alkaloids, found in members of the nightshade family of plants, could cause arthritis in some people. The nightshade family includes deadly nightshade, aubergine, red and green pepper, potatoes, tomatoes and tobacco. A group of 3000 sufferers cut this family of foods from their diet and experienced reduced aches, pains and disfigurement.[48]
- People with arthritis sometimes have an enzyme deficiency in their small intestine which means they are unable to absorb gluten, a protein found in wheat flour. In fact, maps of areas where gluten-high cereals are eaten correspond to those areas with the highest incidence of rheumatoid arthritis.[49] And countries where rice or corn is the staple grain show a much lower rate of the rheumatic diseases than those whose staple grain is wheat. Reduce your consumption of gluten by substituting rice cakes and oatmeal or corn bread for wheat bread and cake.

- Yucca is a folk medicine which has been used for more than 1000 years in America. In a study into its effects, 60 per cent of rheumatoid arthritis and osteoarthritis patients experienced an improvement in their symptoms of swelling, pain and stiffness.[50] Yucca is available in supplement form.
- An alfalfa supplement may be of particular help to you. It is rich in protein, minerals and vitamins and contains chlorophyll, an excellent detoxifier of your system, reducing pain and swelling. Consider taking it in tablet or powder form, or as a tea. Also, you may like to add alfalfa sprouts to your salad or sandwich.
- As a last resort (and this is not meant altogether seriously) you might consider getting pregnant. Scientists have long noted that women suffering from rheumatoid arthritis often get better during pregnancy. Why this should be so is open to question, but it is possible that the body's natural defences jump into action against what seems to be a foreign invader – the baby – which somehow relieves the arthritis at the same time.[51]

ACTION AGAINST ASTHMA

WHAT IS ASTHMA?

Asthma literally means 'panting', which rather understates the possible severity of an asthmatic attack. 'Gasping' would perhaps be a better description of this acute condition which is caused by a temporary narrowing of the bronchi (the airways branching from the trachea to the lungs). Asthma attacks can be precipitated by a sensitivity reaction to food, pollens, mould and fungi, but may also be caused by airborne pollution or by infections of the respiratory tract. Most asthma attacks can be controlled by the administration of drug therapy, although this is in no sense a cure. Childhood asthma is very often associated with eczema or similar hypersensitivity reactions, and in many cases it disappears with age.

In the last decade, the death rate from asthma has climbed by 46 per cent, according to the Centers for Disease Control in the USA.[53] The greatest increases were seen among women and black people. 'It's generally thought that asthma is a treatable disease with no fatal outcomes,' commented Dr Jessie Wing of the CDC. 'Unfortunately, we're seeing severe disease with fatal outcomes.' A shocking British television documentary recently found that nearly half of the boys under the age of five in one London borough suffered from asthma.[53]

HOW THE VEGETARIAN DIET CAN HELP

In this case, we're definitely talking about the vegan diet, as opposed to the vegetarian one which may, of course, include dairy products. Food sensitivity was a subject which excited an enormous amount of publicity in the 1980s, and stormy passions were aroused on both sides of the fence. Today, there seems little doubt that food sensitivity can be involved in the development of a range of problems – urticaria, angioedema, anaphylaxis, eczema, asthma, rhinitis, infantile colitis, inflammatory bowel disease, migraine and hyperactivity, to name but a few – although it is by no means certain to what extent diet is a major causative factor. People are, of course, very different creatures, and what provokes a reaction in one person may well not do so in another. It does seem, however, that amongst those whose diet induces asthma, the most likely foods to produce the condition are cow's milk and eggs.[54] Therefore, the vegan diet seems to be a good starting point to test the diet–asthma theory.

This is precisely what some researchers did in 1985.[55] Taking thirty-five patients who had suffered from bronchial asthma for an average of twelve years (all of them on long-term medication, some on cortisone), the scientists prescribed a vegan diet for twelve months – which also excluded chlorinated tap water, coffee, tea, chocolate and sugar. Most fruit, vegetables, beans and pulses were freely allowed, although apples and citrus fruits were not, and grains were restricted or eliminated. The results were quite amazing – in nearly all cases, medication for asthma was either totally withdrawn or drastically reduced. Naturally, there was a significant decrease in asthma symptoms. Twenty-four patients completed the treatment. Of these, 71 per cent reported improvement at four months and 92 per cent after the full year. The scientists concluded: 'Selected patients, with a fear of side-effects of medication, who are interested in alternative health care, might get well and replace conventional medication with this regimen.'

It is important to emphasize the long-term nature of this experiment – some patients needed the full twelve months before achieving maximum effect and freedom from medication. Speculation as to why the vegan diet should have this very profound effect probably centres around the removal of the more likely food allergens (such as eggs and milk), and also the absence of dietary arachidonic acid, found exclusively in animal products. Arachidonic acid is metabolized in the body to produce prostaglandins (which perform a wide range of hormonelike actions in the body) and leukotrienes (which, among other functions, are potent stimulators of bronchial constriction). It has been observed that people with asthma can have an excess of leukotriene activity,[56] and for this reason various experiments have been designed to see whether the consumption of fish oil, which is rich in omega-3 fatty acids, might somehow equalize the production of leukotrienes from arachidonic acid. However, there are conflicting studies about the effect of fish oil on asthma sufferers. Some studies suggest that it may have a useful effect,[57] others do not.[58] One investigation required ten patients with asthma to consume a fish oil enriched diet.[59] After five weeks, it was clear that the patients were doing rather badly – bronchodilator usage was up (thirteen puffs a day using fish oil, compared to seven puffs a day without it). Also, their breathing was less efficient, with the maximum rate of air flow during expiration down by 15 per cent – a significant amount. This hardly amounts to convincing evidence in favour of fish oil consumption and, as already mentioned, whatever beneficial effects fish oil has, they can also be obtained from plant oils such as flaxseed. On the other hand, the vegan study described above does suggest that a diet which eliminates meat products will reduce arachidonic acid and its asthma-provoking metabolites.

WHAT ELSE CAN YOU DO?

Asthma has many possible causes, and it is therefore worth trying a number of different approaches in its treatment. Some which have proven successful for other people are given below.

- Vitamin B6 (pyridoxine) levels have been found to be lower in adult patients with asthma than in non-sufferers.[60] The same study has reported finding a significant decrease in the frequency and severity of wheezing and asthmatic attacks in patients taking B6 supplements.
- 'Reports of the value of vitamin C for the control of

asthma began around 1940' says Linus Pauling, twice Nobel prizewinner and distinguished champion of vitamin C therapy for many modern diseases.[61] 'There is now good evidence that vitamin C has such value as an adjunct to conventional therapy. Some of the older studies gave negative results, perhaps because of the use of too small an amount of the vitamin for too short a time. Most of the recent studies have shown that the vitamin has had an effect.'

Pauling points to several such studies. When six healthy young men were given a drug (methacholine) which simulates the effect of asthma, it restricted their airflow by 40 per cent.[62] Yet when they were given 100mg of vitamin C (about the amount in two oranges) one hour before exposure to the chemical, it only restricted their airways by 9 per cent. A double-blind test (one in which both subject and experimenter don't know who's taking the vitamin C and who's takng the dummy pill) was performed on forty-one asthma patients in Nigeria.[63] In the rainy season, respiratory infections are common – which exacerbates the condition for asthmatics. For fourteen weeks, half the group (twenty-two people) were given 1g (1000mg) of vitamin C a day, the other half given a placebo (dummy pill). When the experiment was over, it was found that those who had been taking the vitamin C had suffered less than a quarter as many asthma attacks during the rainy season as those who hadn't taken the vitamin. Some of those taking vitamin C had no attacks at all for this period – however, the attacks returned after the experiment finished.

A further study looked at the effects of taking vitamin C before exercise. The bane of many asthmatics' lives is the paroxysm they suffer after exertion. 'Characteristically, what happens is that an asthmatic will engage in a sport,' says Dr E Neil Schachter, one of the researchers involved, 'or some kind of exercise, and feel fine throughout the activity. But then three to five minutes after the exercise, he'll feel a tightness in his chest and will start wheezing. The attack tends to get progressively worse over the next thirty minutes.' Patients in this study took just 0.5g (500mg) of vitamin C before exercising and found that the severity of any subsequent attack was significantly reduced.[64]

These and other studies indicate that taking vitamin C, usually in doses far higher than those normally found in food, may be beneficial for some people.

- Other nutritional factors which research suggests plays a part in the reduction of severity of asthma are carotenes (vitamin A), vitamin E and selenium. All these substances have been experimentally shown to decrease leukotriene formation.

- Certain chemicals and food additives may sometimes induce sensitivity reactions in susceptible individuals. The most common include aspirin and other nonsteroidal anti-inflammatory drugs (NSAIDs), sodium benzoate, sulphur dioxide, potassium sorbate and tartrazine.

- The food additive monosodium glutamate (MSG) can provoke asthma in certain people, although the attack itself may not take place for up to twelve hours after MSG-containing food is eaten, which can present a real problem in identifying the cause of the attack for both the sufferer and doctor.[65]

- Babies not fed allergy-triggering foods such as milk and eggs are less likely to suffer from asthma and allergies during the first year of life, according to a British study, conducted on 120 families with histories of allergies.[66] Scientists restricted the diet of both babies and mothers, and found that 'what the mother eats while breastfeeding can be sufficient to sensitize the baby', according to Dr David Hide, of St Mary's Hospital in Newport, Isle of Wight. It seems that proteins from the mother's food transfer into her breast milk and may cause babies to get allergies even if the mother does not suffer from them. The mothers and babies were divided into two groups – one ate 'normally', but the other was excluded from consuming dairy products, eggs, fish, and nuts, wheat and soya. After one year, at least one allergy was detected in 14 per cent of infants in the diet group compared to 40 per cent of babies in the 'normal' group. Over twice as many babies in the 'normal' group showed asthma symptoms compared to those on the special diet. The diet is recommended only for those with a family history of allergies.

- People who develop asthma as a sensitivity reaction to birds' feathers may also become hypersensitive to chickens' eggs, and possibly chicken flesh. One study found that 32 per cent of people who developed bronchial asthma and rhinoconjunctivitis when exposed to bird feathers also developed a sensitivity reaction to egg proteins.[67]

- Relaxation and stress reduction can be important parts of treating the underlying cause of asthma in some people. There is evidence to show that learning yoga, a Hindu discipline that is learned in eight steps, may have a benefical effect – especially that part of yoga which deals with the art of breathing, pranayama.[68] Usually, the best scientific studies are performed on a 'double blind' basis; in which both subject and experimenter are not told whether the treatment is actually being performed. To assess the effect of yogic breathing with a double blind method seems, at first glance, impossible. Yet that is just what some ingenious scientists have done. They achieved this using a device called the Pink City lung exerciser, which is a device used to teach students of pranayama the 1:2 ratio between breathing in and breathing out. The scientists used this machine, and also a look-alike device – which appeared to, but in fact did not, enforce this method of breathing on the students. Both devices were used by eighteen patients with mild asthma, spending a couple of weeks on each machine. Each patient recorded their symptoms, how much medication they had to use, and their best 'deep breaths' both morning and evening. The results were encouraging, suggesting that pranayama exercises may indeed help to control mild asthma.
- We can all press for tighter controls on pollution and acid rain. There is a clear relationship between bronchial disease and air pollution, and children are more vulnerable than any other group to this insidious side-effect of industrialization.

CURBING CANCER

A PREVENTABLE SCOURGE

Did you know:

- Half of all the cases of cancer are suffered by just one-fifth of the world's population – those who live in industrialized countries[69]
- The number of new cases of most major forms of cancer increases, in America and most other developed nations, by about 1 per cent every year[70]
- Cancer is the second most common cause of death for children in Britain (after accidents/violence)[71]
- One in eight American women will get breast cancer, and one in three people will be diagnosed with some form of cancer at some point in their lives.[72]

This is shocking. It means that, far from 'winning the war' against cancer, we're actually losing it. Writers and journalists don't usually make that kind of statement. When you read about cancer, it's always the 'good news' you see. We're supposed to concentrate on the fact that many cancer patients survive longer than they used to a few decades ago, and that the new genetic technologies promise cures undreamt of just a few years ago. Let's hope they do.

But for anyone who's lost a friend or loved one to this ravaging disease, no amount of cheery optimism will convince us that the 'battle' is being won. We've seen the casualties. We know the pain.

Cancer can be prevented. That's not a message which is often heard. But it's true. We already know – and have known for decades – a great deal about the factors responsible for causing cancer. Most of the cancer charities and organizations remain more interested in treating cancer than in preventing it, and so relatively few of us truly understand that many of the factors giving rise to cancer are actually within our control.

For example, it is estimated that 60 per cent or even more of all cancers in the Western world today are related to environmental causes. This is by no means a radically new proposition. As long ago as 1775 the eminent surgeon Sir Percival Pott, one of the great names in the history of medicine, suggested that there might be a link. He was the first to notice how chimney sweeps often developed a particular form of cancer, and put forward the theory that their atrocious working conditions were responsible.

So if we have reason to suspect that our environment might be a factor in the causation of cancer, shouldn't we try to do something to control it, or at least to reduce the risk? After all, we spend huge amounts of money trying to find cures or more effective treatments for cancer. Surely we should be trying to prevent the disease from appearing in the first place?

Of course we should. But that's not what usually happens. In 1991, one of the major British cancer charities spent over £42 million on research – and barely £600,000 on advising the public how they might reduce their risks. The same charity commented in its annual report 'Although circumstantial evidence suggest that diet is linked to the cause of many human cancers, the evidence is extremely controversial.'[74] Commented the director of another major cancer charity: 'the basis for dietary effects on cancer is not understood.'[75] What dismal, discouraging words.

Well, at least one form of preventive medicine is on the agenda. 'Women worried about breast cancer should consider having healthy breasts removed before the disease has a chance to develop', one newspaper recently reported a professor of obstetrics and gynaecology as stating.[76] It's rather like removing 'a redundant gland and pad of fat', he said. Another proposal is to give healthy women Tamoxifen – a powerful anti-cancer drug – before they develop the disease.[77]

But let's get back to reality. In 1981 an epoch-making report was produced by the eminent epidemiologists Richard Doll and Richard Peto.[78] It assembled all the evidence they could find linking the occurrence of human cancers to specific identifiable factors. While the authors of the 1308-page report warn that not all causes of cancer can either be identified or avoided, it does seem from the evidence they collected that some of the causes of cancer they identify are well within our own control. This is what they estimate the main risk factors to be, with their best estimate of the percentage of total cancer-caused deaths that are attributable to them.

FACTOR RESPONSIBLE FOR CANCER	PERCENTAGE OF CANCER-CAUSED DEATHS
Diet	35%
Tobacco	30%
Infection	10%
Reproductive & Sexual Behaviour	7%
Occupation	4%
Alcohol	3%
Geophysical Factors	3%
Pollution	2%
Food Additives	1%
Industrial Products	1%
Medicines & Medical Products	1%

You can see that diet comes right at the top of the list. Diet means what we *choose* to eat, doesn't it? So, by informing ourselves of the evidence, and by taking steps to change our diets accordingly, we ought to be able to significantly reduce our chances of suffering from a diet-related cancer.

Now let's be quite clear. As long as there's been cancer, there have been quacks, charlatans and swindlers who have preyed upon victims and their loved ones, selling them fraudulent 'cures', or exploiting their distress to obtain some kind of unscrupulous advantage. So let's state here that vegetarians aren't immune to cancer. If you were the healthiest-living vegetarian in the world, who just happened to live downwind from Chernobyl, then the odds would be stacked heavily against you irrespective of your diet. There are a host of factors which can predispose us towards this ghastly affliction, and only some of them are controllable. Fundamentally, avoiding cancer is all about reducing your risk, and that's what the evidence you're about to see shows the vegetarian diet can do for you.

WHAT IS CANCER?

Cancer is the word used to describe malignant forms of a larger class of diseases known as neoplasms (literally 'new formation'). It is initiated by exposure to a carcinogen (cancer-causing substance) which can be a chemical, a virus or something physical such as radiation. Certain cancers can also arise as a result of hereditary factors.

A general characteristic of the development of cancer is the time lag between the first exposure to a carcinogen, and the subsequent development of cancer (scientists call this period the tumour induction time). Whether cancer eventually develops, and how quickly, is partly the result of the degree of exposure to a second class of substances called promoting agents. Although tumour promoters do not themselves *initiate* cancer, they can have a very great bearing on its outcome. This two-stage process of initiation followed by promotion is a central characteristic of the cancerous process. And it introduces a wildly uncertain element into the equation, too. It explains, for example, why not everyone who is exposed to a carcinogen will contract cancer. It also offers us a great deal of hope, because the activity of tumour promoters can be greatly affected by a wide variety of factors – including, of course, what we eat.

Cancer begins as a single abnormal cell which starts to multiply uncontrollably. This is the essential feature of cancer – an uncontrolled growth of cells. Malignant groups of such cells form tumours and invade healthy tissue, often spreading to other parts of the body, in a process called metastasis (benign tumours do not metastasize). Because of this fundamental ability to invade and destroy other parts of the body, the Greek doctor Hippocrates called this disorder 'karkinos', literally meaning 'crab' – from which the modern word cancer is derived.

Neoplasms are divided into two fundamental types – benign or malignant. A benign neoplasm does not metastasize – in other words, it only grows at its point of origin – and is usually named by tagging the suffix 'oma' onto the word for the tissue concerned. For example, the Greek for 'fat' is 'lipos', so a benign tumour of fat cells would be called a 'lipoma' (there are, however, several exceptions to this general rule).

Malignant neoplasms (cancers) grow more rapidly than benign forms and invade adjacent, normal tissue. They are described by adding either 'carcinoma' or 'sarcoma' to the word for the site of the cancer (a malignancy of the fat cells would therefore be termed a 'liposarcoma'). These two general classes of malignant neoplasms are defined thus:

- *carcinomas* affect the skin and tissues that cover both the external and internal body, for example, breast cancer, prostate cancer, or cancer of the uterus;
- *sarcomas* affect the body's supportive and connective tissue, such as muscles, blood vessels, bone and fat.

It may take years for a noticeable tumour to develop, and it is undoubtedly true that speed of diagnosis can be a life-saving factor. The American Cancer Society suggests there are seven warning signs which, even if only one is present, should provoke a prompt investigation. They are:

- a change in bowel or bladder function
- a sore that does not heal
- unusual bleeding or discharge
- a thickening or lump in the breast or elsewhere
- indigestion or difficulty in swallowing
- an obvious change in a wart or a mole
- a nagging cough or hoarseness.

The prospects for survival depend, amongst other things, on the site in the body affected, the speed of diagnosis, the treatment given, and, to a considerable extent, on the attitude of the patient towards the disease.

Now, it's been suspected for a very long time – certainly over a century – that a meat-based diet is more likely to produce more cancers in a population than a plant-based one. Consider this extract from *Scientific American* magazine of 1892: 'Inhabitants of cities indulge far too freely in meat, often badly cooked and kept too long; the poor and country population do not often get their meat fresh. Professor Verneuil considers something should be done to remedy this state of things. He points out that Réclus, the French geographer, has proved that cancer is most frequent among those branches of the human race where carnivorous habits prevail.'[79]

Even earlier than this, we find evidence of the vegan diet being used by dietetic reformer Dr William Lambe (1765–1846) to treat patients with cancer. In 1804 John Abernethy, a renowned surgeon of St Bartholomew's Hospital in London (who, incidentally, gave his name to a biscuit flavoured with caraway seeds) wrote the following account of Lambe's diet and its effects. Abernethy's clear-sighted description and interpretation of results would surely put many of our modern-day scientists to shame:

Very recently Dr Lambe has proposed a method of treating cancerous diseases, which is wholly dietetic. He recommends the adoption of a strict vegetable regimen, to avoid the use of fermented liquors, and to substitute water purified by distillation in the place of common water . . . I think it right to observe that, in one case of cancerous ulceration in which it was used, the symptoms of the disease were, in my opinion, rendered more mild, the erysipelatous inflammation surrounding the ulcer was removed, and the life of the patient was, in my judgement, considerably prolonged . . . It seems to me very proper and desirable that the powers of the regimen recommended by Dr Lambe should be fairly tried, for the following reasons:

Because I know some persons who, while confined to such diet, have enjoyed very good health; and further, I have known several persons who did try the effects of such regimen, and declare that it was productive of considerable benefit. They were not, indeed afflicted with cancer, but they were induced to adopt a change of diet to allay a state of nervous irritation and correct disorder of the digestive organs, upon which medicine had but little influence.

Because it appears certain, in general, that the body can be perfectly nourished by vegetables.

Because all great changes of the constitution are more likely to be affected by alterations of diet and modes of life than by medicine.

Because it holds out a source of hope and consolation to the patient in a disease in which medicine is known to be unavailing and in surgery afford no more than a temporary relief.'[80]

Reading those perceptive and open-minded words in our profoundly arrogant late 20th century, one cannot help but be depressed by our lack of progress. Most of Abernethy's comments concerning the impotence of medicine when confronted with cancer are still true. To Abernethy, it made sense to experiment with diet, just to see what might be achieved. Yet the majority of Abernethy's medical successors refused to even contemplate this route, retreating instead to the paraphernalia of the exclusive medical freemasonry – the scalpel, the nostrum, and their ensuing high-tech offspring.

What damns us even more is the hard-won knowledge we now have about diet and health. In Abernethy's day, 200 years ago, there were no epidemiological studies, no vast pools of accumulated data upon which to base decisions. Today, we have that information, but for the most part choose to ignore it. I wonder what Dr John Abernethy would have thought of us.

THE EVIDENCE

As researchers studied facts and figures about mortality from cancer in different countries, they were struck by an odd fact. It seemed that certain countries had a much higher mortality rate than others. What was the factor that made the United States, for

example, so much worse than Japan? The researchers looked for a clue. Then, they tried comparing the amount of animal protein that different nations ate and their cancer mortality.[81] This is what they began to see:

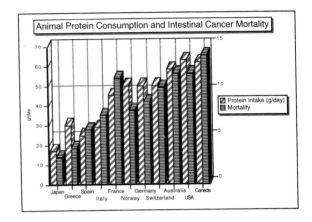

CHART 1: MORE MEAT, MORE CANCER

CHART 1: MORE MEAT MEANS MORE CANCER

There is a clear relationship between the amount of animal protein in the national diet and the incidence of certain types of cancer mortality. But this wasn't the only connection. The same 'straight-line' connection seemed to exist between total fat consumption and cancer, animal fat consumption and cancer, and various other associated factors as well.

But perhaps certain nations were genetically more likely to contract cancers, no matter what they ate? To examine this possibility, studies were undertaken amongst immigrant populations. If the root cause of cancer was genetic rather than environmental, the same races should have the same occurrence of cancers, wherever they lived. The Japanese seemed to be a good subject, because they traditionally had low incidence of most forms of cancer. So three groups of Japanese were chosen, together with a 'control' group of Caucasians.

The first group of Japanese lived in Japan, and followed a largely traditional diet. The second group lived in the United States, but had been born abroad. The third group lived in the States and had been born there. This is what they found:[82]

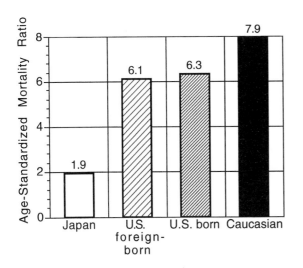

CHART 2: DEATHS FROM COLON CANCER - EAST VERSUS WEST

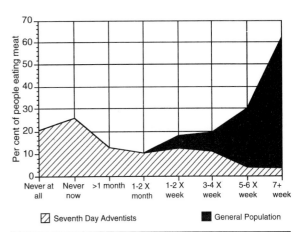

CHART 3: WHY SEVENTH DAY ADVENTISTS ARE IDEAL TO STUDY

The results speak for themselves. A comparison between the extreme left and right columns shows that the Japanese living in Japan (left column) have only one-quarter the risk of contracting cancer of the colon as Caucasian Americans living in the States. But even more significantly, when the Japanese move to the States, their chance of contracting colon cancer increases by three times – almost the same risk as a Caucasian. The place of birth didn't seem to matter. This was good proof that environmental, and not genetic, factors were indeed very significant.

And now the scientific detective work really began. Because if the diet really was so important, then it should be possible to track down which specific factors related most strongly to increasing cancer risk, and, hopefully, try to control them. So the focus began to shift from international comparisons, which had pointed the way, to very specific studies amongst closely similar groups. Similar, that is, except for one or two key factors, which could be isolated, studied, and perhaps even controlled.

A group that was quickly identified as being of particular interest was the American Seventh-Day Adventist population. This group was subject to repeated studies, because the feature that distinguished them from the general American population was their differing diet. One key area of difference is dramatically demonstrated in this chart:[83]

The chart shows that Seventh-Day Adventists eat a completely different diet to the average American one. The vast majority of the general population use meat or poultry products seven or more times each week, but the picture is quite the reverse for the Seventh-Day Adventist group. About half of them don't consume meat or meat products. They do not smoke or drink (although in the survey one-third of the men were previous smokers) and they tend to practise a 'healthy' lifestyle that emphasizes fresh fruits, whole grains, vegetables and nuts. So now the scientists had found a good group of people to study. A seven-year scientific study tabulated the cause of death of 35,460 Adventists. This is what they found:[84]

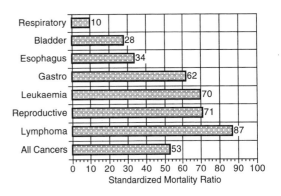

CHART 4: DEATHS FROM CANCER REDUCED IN SEVENTH DAY ADVENTISTS

The death-rate from all cancers among Adventists was amazingly half that of the general population. The bottom bar on the chart shows this – Adventists only having 53 per cent as many deaths from cancer when compared to the norm. Some of this could probably be attributed to their abstinence from smoking – cancer of the respiratory system, for example (the top bar on the chart), is only 10 per cent of the general population's. But other cancers, such as gastrointestinal and reproductive ones, are not causatively related to smoking. The scientists concluded: 'It is quite clear that these results are supportive of the hypothesis that beef, meat, and saturated fat or fat in general are etiologically related to colon cancer.'

Another study set out to check these remarkable findings, this time studying cancers of the large bowel, breast and prostate – the three most common ones that are unrelated to smoking.[85] 20,000 Seventh-Day Adventists were studied, and this time, they were compared to two other population groups. Firstly, they were checked against cancer mortality figures for all US whites, and then they were compared to a special group of 113,000 people who were chosen because their lifestyle closely matched the Adventists – except, that is, for their diet. In other respects, such as place of residence, income and socio-economic status, the third group was very closely matched to the Adventists. This is how the results emerged:

Once again, the picture is pretty dramatic. The Adventists are shown on the chart by the white column, and the general population by the black column. The shaded column represents the special group whose lifestyle closely matched the Adventists – apart from the food they ate. You can see that for all three cancers, deaths among the Adventists were much lower than for the other groups. It is interesting that there does not appear to be a very great reduction in the risk of breast cancer among Adventists – until, that is, you compare the Adventists results with those of the comparable group (shaded in the chart). The comparable group has a higher risk of contracting breast cancer than the national average (probably due to local environmental factors in California, where the study was undertaken). However, the Adventists have succeeded in reducing their own risk back down to below the national average – even though only half of them never consume meat.

A major correlation study analyzed the diets of thirty-seven nations, and then correlated the components of the diets to mortality from cancer of the intestines.[86] Before looking at the results, let me briefly explain what a correlation study is. It's really quite simple. A correlation ends up as a number somewhere in between minus one and plus one. The higher the figure, the closer the connection between the two factors. For example, if someone is paid on a hourly basis, then the more they work, the more money they earn. This is an example of a perfect correlation, and would have a figure of $+1$.

On the other hand, the more money you spend, the less you have in your bank account – this is a perfect negative correlation, since the connection between more expenditure and a decreasing bank balance is an inverse one: in this case, the correlation would be -1. And if any two factors, such as today's temperature and your bank balance, are not related at all, then the correlation would have a figure of zero. So the closer the figure gets to either $+1$ or -1, the stronger the connection, positive or negative. You can see from the following chart that all the meat factors correlate very strongly with cancer. Total calories, total protein, and total fat also correlate strongly, which is not surprising, since meat is heavy in all three. But calories and protein from vegetable sources have a negative correlation – in other words, they confer protection. The study concluded: 'Animal sources of food were clearly associated with the cancer rates.'

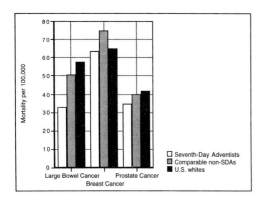

CHART 5: DEATHS FROM CANCER COMPARED

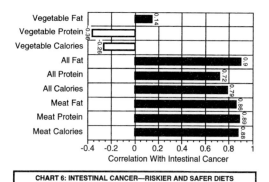

CHART 6: INTESTINAL CANCER—RISKIER AND SAFER DIETS

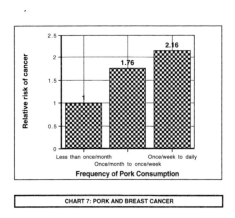

CHART 7: PORK AND BREAST CANCER

Correlation studies like this are very important, because although we may not know precisely why and how meat in the diet contributes to various cancers (this may take many years to finally prove), we can see that there is a clear relationship, and this enables those of us who want to, to take the necessary precautions for our own well-being.

More data, this time from an Israeli study, revealed a connection between both fats from animal sources and fats from plant sources, suggesting that saturated and even unsaturated fats may be connected with increased mortality.[87] The study followed the Jewish population as it grew from 1.17 million in 1949 to 3.5 million in 1975, over which period meat consumption increased by 454 per cent, and the death rate from malignant cancers doubled.

MEAT AND BREAST CANCER

More and more evidence was starting to accumulate. In Alberta, Canada, researchers compared the diets of women with breast cancer to a control group without the disease.[88] Was there any food, or type of foods, which might be linked to the development of breast cancer? Indeed there was. The results were, in the scientists own words, 'consistent with the notion that breast cancer risk is affected by certain dietary patterns, especially those related to the consumption of beef and pork.' In fact, the strongest association of all was with pork consumption – chart 7 illustrates how the relative risk of breast cancer rose with the frequency of pork eating. For beef, anything more than consumption on one day a week was also associated with an increase in relative risk of breast cancer. Yet more disturbing evidence that a meat-dominated diet might indeed be a real health risk.

In Hawaii another study showed the same pattern.[89] The study concentrated on a representative sample of the whole of Hawaii's residents – Caucasians, Japanese, Chinese, Filipinos, and, of course, Hawaiians. The wide variety of ethnic groups was useful, since it included a particularly wide range of food habits. Significant associations were established between:

- breast cancer and all forms of fat and animal protein
- cancer of the uterus and all forms of fat and animal protein
- prostate cancer and fat and animal protein.

The positive correlations between various forms of food and breast cancer are shown in the next chart, and the only negative correlation is between breast cancer and complex carbohydrates – which are, of course, exclusively found in plant food. And almost exactly the same relationship emerged when the same study examined cancer of the uterus.

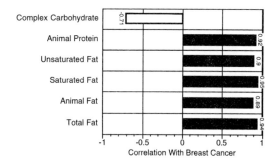

CHART 8: BREAST CANCER AND DIET

More meat equals more risk

In 1981 yet another massive statistical world survey of forty-one countries, including the US and the UK, was completed.[90] The results confirm the connection between eating meat, and risk of certain types of cancer. And yet again, they also show that plant foods seem to confer protection. Here are two charts drawn from data that the survey produced:

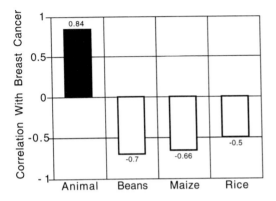

CHART 9: BREAST CANCER—RISKIER AND SAFER DIETS

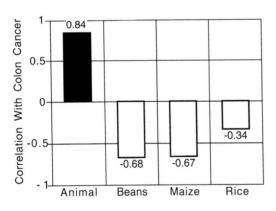

CHART 10: HOW FOODSTUFFS CORRELATE TO COLON CANCER

'Less is better'

One of the largest studies ever undertaken into the effect of meat-eating and cancer was published in 1990.[91] Over 88,000 women aged between thirty-four and fifty-nine were recruited for the study (none of them had a history of cancer or bowel disease). Their health was tracked for six years, and it was found that women who ate beef, pork, or lamb as a main dish every day were two-and-a-half times more likely to

contract colon cancer when compared to those who ate meat less than once a month. What this study clearly demonstrated beyond reasonable doubt was this – meat in itself was a major risk factor. It wasn't that the meat-eaters were deficient in other nutrients – fibre, for example. The more meat they ate, the greater the risk.

The leader of the team of scientists commented: 'Reducing red meat consumption is likely to reduce the risk. There is no cut-off point so, really, less is better.'[92] All by itself, this study well and truly puts paid to the myth that 'meat is part of a healthy diet'.

HOW THE VEGETARIAN DIET CAN HELP

So what actually happens when you start to change your diet? A clue comes from an intriguing study, carried out in Greece, which set out to measure what happened when people increased their consumption of certain types of food – including meat and vegetables.[93] The results show that an increase in consumption of spinach, beets, cabbage or lettuce actually decreases your chance of contracting colo-rectal cancer. But on the other hand, an increase in beef or lamb consumption increases your risk. This is what it looks like graphically:

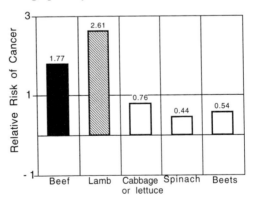

CHART 11: RISK OF COLO-RECTAL CANCER
WITH DOUBLING IN FOOD ITEM CONSUMPTION

The study concludes: 'The results of most of these studies appear to fall into two broad categories: those indicating that animal protein (mainly beef meat) and/or animal fat are conducive to the development of colorectal cancer – and those indicating that vegetables (particularly cruciferous vegetables) or, more generally, fibre-containing foods, protect against the development of this disease.'

Another outstanding demonstration of the impact of the meat-free lifestyle on cancer rates comes from Germany. Scientists from the German Cancer Research Center advertised in *Der Vegetarier*, the German magazine for vegetarians, for participants to study.[94] They knew that nitrate consumption is linked to the development of cancer, and many vegetables contain nitrates. So why don't more vegetarians contract cancer?

One possibility is that the vegetarian diet contains other elements (vitamins A and C, for example) which protect against cancer and so lowers their risk. This was one of the main areas which the researchers were keen to investigate. Eventually, a total of 1904 subjects were recruited. After five years, the results began to emerge. Deaths from all causes were very low indeed – only 37 per cent of the average meat-eating population. All forms of cancer were slashed to 56 per cent the normal rate, and heart disease was down to 20 per cent.

From Japan, and inspired by the insights gained from the American Seventh-Day Adventist studies, comes a study from the National Cancer Center Research Institute in Tokyo.[95] In this investigation, the Japanese decided to track the health of an astonishing 122,261 people, over sixteen years. The logistics alone must have been daunting – each man (they only studied males in this survey) had to be visited at home, by specially-trained public health nurses, and interviewed.

Because of the size of the study, it was possible to divide the participants into various sub-groups according to their dietary and lifestyle preferences. And this is the final conclusion, after much hard work and computing time was expended in analysis: two lifestyles emerged as being very high-risk and very low risk respectively. The high-risk lifestyle included smoking, drinking, meat consumption, and no green vegetables. The low-risk lifestyle was, not surprisingly, precisely the opposite. In Chart 12, you can see how the lifestyles compare. Deaths from all causes were elevated by 1.53 times amongst those who smoked, drank, ate meat and didn't eat green vegetables. The risk of heart disease was 1.88 times higher in this group, and the risk of any kind of cancer was 2.49 times higher.

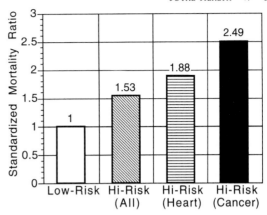

CHART 12: LOW-RISK LIVING, HIGH-RISK DYING

Furthermore, they found that simply adding one factor – meat consumption – to an otherwise healthy lifestyle had a serious effect on mortality. The difference between the lowest-risk group (no smoking, no drinking, no meat eating, and lots of green vegetables) and those people who led a similar lifestyle *except for eating meat* – was that the meat-eaters boosted their risk of dying from heart disease by 30 per cent. Just by adding meat to an otherwise healthy lifestyle!

PIECES FROM THE JIGSAW

We don't know every last detail of the way in which a meat-centred diet predisposes towards cancer. But we do know quite a lot. Consider:

- In just 1kg of charcoal-broiled steak there may be as much benzopyrene (a powerful carcinogen) as in the smoke from 600 cigarettes.[96]
- Scientists at the Lawrence Livermore National Laboratory have been engaged on a five-year project cooking 'thousands of pounds of hamburgers' to see what toxic substances are produced in overcooked meat.[97] They have identified at least eight chemicals which are linked to cancer and chromosome damage. 'You don't get these structures if you cook tofu or cheese,' commented the senior investigator.
- Nitrites may be present in meat products, which can combine with other substances in the human body to form nitrosamines – extremely powerful carcinogens.[98]
- A high-meat diet lowers the age of puberty, and early puberty is associated with an increased risk of breast cancer.[99]

- Certain drugs given to farm animals can cause cancer. One drug given to young pigs for the prevention of respiratory diseases, and used to treat pneumonia in older animals, has been shown to be carcinogenic.[100]
- Vegetarians are known to have a different composition of bile acids when compared to meat eaters, and it is thought that this may profoundly affect the development of cancer.[101]
- The immune system of vegetarians is stronger than that of meat-eaters. One study has shown that, although vegetarians have the same overall number of natural killer cells (the kind that are responsible for nipping cancer in the bud), they are twice as cytotoxic (ie potent) as those of meat-eaters.[102]
- Vegetarians consume fewer environmental pollutants than do meat-eaters. At least one study has indicated that breast milk of vegetarian women is lower in PCBs (polychlorinated biphenyls – widely dispersed industrial compounds which are highly toxic and thought to be carcinogenic) than meat-eaters.[103] Organochlorines, such as DDT and the dioxin family, include some of the most poisonous and environmentally-persistent chemicals known, and a recently-published scientific paper cautions that 80 per cent of the organochlorines absorbed by humans comes from our food.[104] The same paper also states that the main dietary sources of organochlorines are meat, fish, dairy produce and commercial fruit. 'The vegetarian diet including unsprayed fruit minimizes contamination' concludes the report.
- Vegetarians take in a large amount of vitamin A in the form of beta-carotene in plant foods. Beta-carotene is believed to protect people from cancers of the lungs, bladder, larynx and colon.[105]
- Vegetarians also eat diets that are rich in substances which suppress free-radical formation. Molecules of oxygen are turned into free radicals inside your body by the continual process of metabolism. During this process, more molecules are generated which have an electron missing – called 'free radicals'. These free-radical molecules immediately start to scavenge for electrons to kidnap from other molecules, and this sets in motion a continuing chain reaction which produces even more free radicals, in the process damaging cell membranes, proteins, carbohydrates, and deoxyribonucleic acid (DNA). Up to now, some sixty diseases have been associated with free-radical activity,

including Alzheimer's disease, arthritis, multiple sclerosis and, of course, cancer. The vegetarian diet naturally contains substances (such as vitamin A, retinoids and protease inhibitors) which have been shown to be capable of blocking this process and halting the development of cancer.[106]

In addition to these factors, there is another way in which contact with animal flesh might give rise to leukaemia, which is the name used to describe a number of cancerous diseases of the blood-forming organs. The acute and chronic leukaemias, together with the other types of tumours of the blood, bone cells, and lymph tissue, cause about 10 per cent of all cancer deaths and about 50 per cent of all cancer deaths in children and adults less than thirty years old.[107]

Is leukaemia infectious? Such a notion is commonly dismissed as being absurd. When a cancer charity recently released a report about public myths and misconceptions surrounding cancer, they cited a survey showing that 'one in ten teenagers believes that cancer is infectious', presumably with the intention of proving how bizarre our beliefs about cancer can be.

What it really revealed, however, was how out of touch that particular charity was itself. Because there is incontrovertible scientific evidence to show that cancers are, indeed, transmissible – both within species and across them.

It has taken a long time for much of the scientific community to accept that cancers could be caused and transmitted by a virus. In experiments conducted as far back as 1911, it was demonstrated that tumours taken from one chicken and implanted into another would infect the second chicken with a cancerous growth. In 1936, it was demonstrated that breast cancer could be transmitted between mice via a virus present in the milk of lactating mice. More recently, scientists at the University of Glasgow discovered feline leukaemia virus in cats. Today, cancer-causing viruses (oncoviruses) are now scientifically categorized as a part of the retrovirus family. Despite this, the belief still partially persists that cancer somehow 'ought not' to be capable of being virally-induced. One pathologist commented: 'Indefinite statements are often expressed concerning identifying a certain cancer virus in humans by the antibodies produced in an animal. We show no such insecurity with other viruses: why should we do so with cancer viruses? If we find antibodies to smallpox virus or measles virus in an animal we confidently say the animal has had the infection of smallpox or measles. But when a cancer virus stimulates an antibody response in an animal we do not confidently state that the animal was infected by that particular virus. It is as if we are afraid to say that the virus that caused cancer in the cow or dog is the same virus that produces an identical antibody in humans.'[108]

Just like human beings, the animals which we eat suffer from various forms of cancer, sometimes caused by a virus. For example:

- bovine leukaemia virus (BLV) causes cancer of the lymph tissue in cows;
- the avian leucosis viruses (ALV) cause leukaemia in chickens;
- Marek's disease virus (MDV) causes a cancer of the lymph and nervous systems in chickens.

'Virtually all commercial chickens are heavily infected with leucosis virus [ALV],' one American report found. 'Since the tumours induced are not grossly apparent until about twenty weeks of age, this virus is not economically as important as is the Marek's disease virus, which induces tumours by six to eight weeks of age. Bovine leukaemia virus is widespread in commercial dairy herds; more than 20 per cent of dairy cows and 60 per cent of herds surveyed in the USA are infected.'[109]

Now the key question is this: can eating meat, or being exposed to food animals or their produce, result in a greater likelihood of contracting leukaemia or other cancers? To investigate whether these viruses can cross the species barrier and infect humans, a study was established, paid for by the US National Cancer Institute.[110] 'The viruses are widely distributed naturally in their respective hosts,' wrote the scientists conducting the study, 'and are present not only in diseased but also in healthy cattle and chickens destined for human consumption.' Therefore, it seemed logical to examine the health of those people who would have maximum exposure to these animals – slaughtermen.

Accordingly, the health of 13,844 members of a meatcutters union was checked for the period 1949 to 1980. After statistical analysis, it was found that abattoir workers were nearly three times more likely to die from Hodgkin's disease (a cancer of the lymphatic system) than the general population. The

scientists concluded 'The excess risk was observed only in abattoir workers and seems to be associated with the slaughtering of cattle, pigs and sheep ... Thus, the excess risk seems to be in keeping with a postulate of an infectious origin for these cases, as no other occupational exposure could adequately explain this occurrence.'

By itself, this report is very significant. But now, consider the following additional evidence:

- It has been shown in laboratory experiments that bovine leukaemia virus can survive and replicate itself when placed in a human cell culture.[111]
- Scientists have found a close similarity between bovine leukaemia virus and HTLV-1 – the first human retrovirus ever shown to cause cancer.[112]
- A study recently conducted in France has concluded that children of fathers who work in the meat trade are at greater risk of developing childhood cancers.[113] The study examined over 200 cases of leukaemia diagnosed in the Lyons area, and found that a significantly larger number of fathers of children with leukaemia than expected worked as butchers or in slaughterhouses. The scientists suggest that bovine leukaemia virus could be to blame.
- In another experiment, chimpanzees were fed from birth on milk taken from cows known to be infected with bovine leukaemia virus, with the result that two out of six of them died from leukaemia.[114] The idea is often advanced, to defend unpleasant experiments such as these, that they are necessary in order to improve human health. One is forced to wonder, however, whether 'inconvenient' results such as this are acted upon or simply swept aside.
- Statistical analyses of human deaths from leukaemia and other cancers have shown that those people who have close contact with food animals (vets, farmers, butchers) run a significantly higher risk of dying from certain types of cancer than would be expected. For example, in a Nebraskan study, it was shown that men having regular contact with cattle were twice as likely to die from leukaemia.[115]
- In a study from Poland it has been shown that farmers, butchers, and tanners are more likely to develop leukaemia than other people.[116] And a further Polish study concluded: 'It should be inferred that cattle affected with leukaemia may, in favouring circumstances, be a factor disposing man to neoplasms [cancer] especially to the proliferation

of the lymphatic system, either through longer contact with a sick animal or the longer ingestion of milk and milk products from cows with leukaemia. The fact that with a rise in the incidence of leukaemia in cattle there also appears an increase in proliferating diseases of the lymphatic system is particularly worthy of attention.'[117]

- A study conducted in Minnesota amongst leukaemia sufferers showed that a higher than expected number of them were farmers having regular contact with animals.[118] And a similar study conducted in Iowa found a relationship between leukaemia in humans, cattle density, and the presence of bovine leukaemia virus in cows.[119]
- A study of mortality from leukaemia and Hodgkin's disease amongst vets has shown that they run a significantly higher risk of dying from lymphoid cancer than the norm. The vets were in clinical practice, in close contact with food-producing animals, and the authors of the report suggested that a viral cause may be responsible.[120]
- A study conducted in France and Switzerland in 1990 reveals that male sufferers from breast cancer (generally rare in men) were most likely to work as butchers.[121]
- Like the French study previously mentioned, an Italian study conducted by scientists at the University of Turin has confirmed that the children of butchers are more likely to contract cancer.[122]

All this evidence should be considered very seriously, because it has extraordinarily profound implications. 'The Food and Drug Administration states that many unanswered questions remain about BLV,' says Dr Virgil Hulse, a physician who spent fifteen years as a milk inspector for the state of California, 'such as transmission, infectiousness, and whether it's a threat to humans. Some of the questions fuelling the controversy are whether pasteurization, which inhibits infection, destroys the aspect of the virus capable of producing cancer. Also, how great is the risk of pasteurized milk being accidentally contaminated with raw milk? If we wipe out BLV, will we see a reduction of those cancers related to fat consumption? Might it be the viruses and not the fat that are linked to some human cancers?'[123]

But how could an animal cancer virus induce the disease in humans? Unfortunately, there are several possible ways. One theory suggests that a 'helper virus' can form an association with another relatively harmless one, and in the process produce a virus that can induce cancer. An animal virus may not, therefore, directly precipitate the disease in humans, but it may be able to convert otherwise harmless human viruses into killers.

It will certainly be many years before every feature of the complex process of zoonotic carcinogenesis (cancers caused by or transmitted from animals) has been resolved. And there will, no doubt, be many people who will not wish to see these rather dark and disquieting fringes of medical and veterinary knowledge examined too closely. But that, of course, is no reason not to ask questions, nor to take prudent defensive measures.

You can see from all this how difficult it is to isolate just one component of the vegetarian diet, and pin an 'anti-cancer' label on it. Once more, it is the totality of the healthy vegetarian diet – the whole thing – which naturally works to reduce disease. And at long last, the American Heart Association, the American Cancer Society, the National Academy of Sciences, and the American Academy of Paediatrics are just a few of the professional bodies which have now started to publicly urge a shift towards a more nearly vegetarian diet.[124] Other Western countries still lag significantly behind in this respect.

WHAT ELSE CAN YOU DO?

- **Vitamin A.** Beta-carotene is the form of vitamin A available in plant foods, and is strongly suspected of having cancer-preventive properties (several studies are currently underway to validate this).[125] In particular, it is thought to protect people from cancers of the lungs, bladder, larynx and colon.[126] Most researchers believe that beta-carotene is better than retinol for the purpose of protection from cancer. It is unlikely to cause toxicity, is a powerful antioxidant, is taken in and used according to the body's needs and it comes in a 'package' including 'secondary plant constituents' – non-nutritive compounds that seem to inhibit the onset and growth of cancers and which may be vital to beta-carotene's anti-cancer action. To obtain beta-carotene, eat any of the fruits and vegetables with a deep, bright green, yellow or orange colouring. Look for carrots, pumpkin, squash, spinach and broccoli, canteloupe, sweet potatoes and papaya. Eat these foods raw, fresh and organically grown if possible.

- **Vitamin C.** This vitamin helps to minimize the effects of pollutants and carcinogens in your food and environment. In particular, vitamin C seems to block the formation of nitrosamines. Nitrates and nitrites are added to foods to give colour, flavour and to act as preservatives (E249–E252). During digestion these substances are converted by the human body into nitrosamines, which are known to be powerful cancer-causing chemicals (they are particularly associated with cancers of the stomach and esophagus). The good news is that if a vitamin C-rich food is taken at the same time as foods containing nitrates or nitrites, then the production of nitrosamines is greatly reduced.[127] Women with abnormal cervical smear results often have low amounts of vitamin C in their body.[128] This may shed new light on the underlying damage caused by smoking, because it has long been established that women who smoke have higher levels of cervical cancer, and smoking impairs the absorption of vitamin C.
- **Vitamin E.** This vitamin also has antioxidant properties, and can combat the production of free radicals in your body. It is available in cold-pressed vegetable oils, nuts, seeds and soya beans.
- **Selenium.** This trace mineral is essential to health, though only required in minute quantities. In America, the National Research Council has recommended a daily intake of 50–200mcg of selenium for adults (a microgram (1 mcg) is one thousandth of a milligram (mg), so 200mcg equals 0.2mg). However, one authority – Gerhard Schrauzer, PhD, of the University of California – says that 250-300mcg of selenium a day can protect against most cancers, and that most people consume only about 100mcg daily.[129] At higher doses, selenium can be toxic to the human body. Although it is not certain at precisely what level selenium begins to cause adverse effects, it has been found that doses of 900mcg (0.9mg) per day can make hair and nails fall out and can affect the nervous system.[130]

Selenium works best in conjunction with vitamin E, since both are antioxidants and can increase the production of antibodies by up to thirty times,[131] thereby greatly enhancing your immune response. Together they help to detoxify your body and prevent the formation of free radicals. Selenium is naturally present in the soil, and the quantities available in our food relate to soil levels of selenium where the food was grown.

A study undertaken at the University of Tampere, Finland, involved taking blood samples from 21,172 Finnish men. The samples were then frozen. Eleven years after the samples had been taken, 143 men had contracted lung cancer. The researchers found that the men who eventually developed lung cancer had less selenium in their blood than those who did not. Overall, it was found that people with the lowest selenium levels were 3.3 times more likely to develop lung cancer than those with high levels. The researchers said their results were 'in accord with other studies which strongly suggest that poor selenium nutrition is a highly significant risk factor for lung cancer'.[132]

In West Germany, a study conducted at the University of Bonn has shown that selenium can protect against the harmful effects of ultra-violet radiation. Blood selenium levels were examined in 101 patients with malignant melanoma (a lethal form of skin cancer) and compared to a control group of healthy people. The skin cancer patients showed a significantly lower level of selenium, and the researchers concluded that their results 'strongly suggest that sub-optimal selenium nutrition preceded the onset of the disease and may even have contributed to its genesis'.[133]

- **Calcium and Vitamin D.** Calcium may be important in preventing both breast and colon cancer and it has been suggested that it could reduce the risk of colon cancer by two thirds when taken with vitamin D.[134] Vitamin D is necessary for the proper absorption of calcium. Your body manufactures this vitamin when sunlight reacts with dehydrocholesterol, a substance in your skin. Obtain vitamin D either from fortified foods or by ensuring that you have ten minutes of daylight on your face and hands each day. Calcium is available in tofu, dark green leafy vegetables such as spinach, watercress and parsley, seaweeds, nuts and seeds, dairy foods, molasses and dried fruits.
- **Calories.** A high calorie diet may increase your risks of cancer. Cancer seems to be more common in obese people, especially those who are more than 40 per cent over their ideal weight.[135] Do your best to keep your weight within recommended limits.
- **Cabbage.** Cruciferous vegetables include cabbage, broccoli, cauliflower, brussels sprouts and kale. These foods contain what are called 'secondary plant constituents' – non-nutritive compounds that seem to inhibit the onset and growth of cancers.[136]

These compounds, (ie indoles, phenols, flavones) are present in many plant foods but are particularly abundant in cruciferous vegetables. They are not available in supplement form. Eat a serving of cruciferous vegetables at least three times per week.

- Finally – although vegetarians and vegans are renowned for their easy-going ways and pleasant dispositions, it may not pay to be *too* nice! People who are generally viewed as 'nice' – slow to anger, compliant, unassertive and overly co-operative and patient – seem more likely to succumb to cancer. Those who have an aggressive manner or a 'fighting spirit' seem more likely to combat or even conquer it.[137]

CURING CONSTIPATION

WHAT IS CONSTIPATION?

Approximately four people out of every ten in Western countries are constipated. In two out of ten, constipation is so severe that laxatives are used regularly. Here's another startling fact: 77 per cent of the population only excrete between five and seven stools per week. That's over three-quarters of the total population! On top of that, a further 8 per cent of people only pass three to four stools a week. That makes 85 per cent with sluggish bowel movements.[138] Although constipation, and its unwilling products, are jocular subjects to talk or write about, there is a serious side too. As you will see, constipation is a very clear sign that the body is functioning poorly. And when that happens, many serious diseases can follow.

Chronic constipation occurs when you retain your stools in the colon and rectum so that the water they naturally contain is reabsorbed by the body. The stools then harden even more, making defecation more and more difficult. Eventually, your bowel will lose its muscle tone and constipation becomes a way of life. Conventional medicine treats the symptom of constipation and brings about short-term purgative relief through the use of laxatives, most of which fall into these categories:

- Bulk laxatives. These substances increase the size of stools and stimulate bowel motion. They include

ingredients such as bran and methylcellulose. They are generally safe, if somewhat slow to take effect, although internal obstruction may be caused if insufficient water is taken or if excessive amounts of the substances are consumed.

- Irritant laxatives. This group includes such substances as danthron, senna, aloes, rhubarb, and cascara (known as anthraquinone laxatives) and phenolphthalein and castor oil. They are thought to work by stimulating the intestinal smooth muscle, creating contractions and movement which leads to the passing of a motion, but they also may increase the amount of fluid in the intestines. As with all laxatives, over-frequent use can damage natural bowel functions.
- Saline or osmotic laxatives. These substances which include magnesium sulphate, potassium sodium tartrate, sodium sulphate, lactulose and magnesium hydroxide, work by attracting water to the bowel and so increase the bulk of its contents, leading to a watery evacuation.
- Lubricant laxatives. Lubricant laxatives soften and lubricate the stools, making them easier to pass. Liquid paraffin and sodium dioctyl sulphosuccinate are two examples of lubricant laxatives and faecal softeners. Liquid paraffin can dissolve fat-soluble vitamins, and if inhaled it may cause a type of pneumonia.

As you can see, conventional medicine offers us a veritable armory of cathartics with which to goad our sluggish bowels into action. However, you should know that the continuing use/abuse of laxatives can make you dependent on them, thus precipitating further health problems. Although some types of constipation are not diet-related (such as drug-induced constipation), most are. It is, therefore, much better to treat the underlying cause, rather than the eventual symptom.

HOW THE VEGETARIAN DIET CAN HELP

Dr Denis Burkitt – a famous advocate of dietary fibre – performed a classic experiment which revealed just how effective the vegetarian diet can be at preventing constipation.[139] He carefully collected information from various populations concerning the size of their stools, the average time it took food to pass all the way through their bodies, and the type of diet they ate. You can see some of his results in Chart 13:

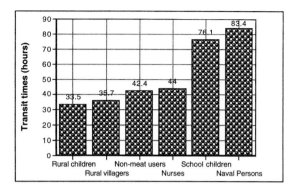

CHART 13: THE WESTERN WAY OF TOILET STRAINING

His findings were extremely revealing. From left to right on the chart, the first group, with the shortest stool transit time, were schoolchildren living in rural Africa, eating an unrefined diet. Their food positively shot through their insides, taking on average less than a day and a half from one end to the other. Next came another group of Africans, this time adults living in villages in Uganda. Once again, their food hardly touched the sides on the way down.

But it is the next group that is so interesting from our point of view. This consisted not of Africans, eating a natural diet, but of ordinary vegetarians living in the United Kingdom. Despite enormous differences in environment and food availability, the Western vegetarians' diet came close to equalling the African results.

The next group on the chart consisted of nurses living and working in southern India. Once again, their diet would tend towards the meat-free, and their transit times were only slightly longer than the UK vegetarians.

But it's after this that the really big jump comes. The next group on the graph – labelled school children – has nearly *twice* as long a transit time as any of the preceding ones. This group was drawn from children at a boarding school in the UK, eating a refined diet typical of institutionalized catering – greasy, meat-dominated, and low in natural fibre. And the next group is even worse – naval ratings and their wives, all shore-based in the UK. This group had a mean transit time of 83.4 hours, and the longest time was 144 hours! That's six whole days for the food to hang around someone's intestines!

This study revealed something else, too. You might suppose that small stools would whiz through the system quickly, but you'd be wrong. For Dr Burkitt found that the larger the stool, the faster it was processed. So, for example, the mean weight of stools passed by naval

ratings was a mere 104g (not even 4oz). On the other hand, the mean weight for rural Ugandan villagers was more than four times as heavy. This is also very significant, because stool weights of below 150g a day denote an increased risk of bowel cancer.[140]

Somewhere in the middle came the UK vegetarians, with a mean weight of 225g (8oz), who compare very favourably with South African schoolchildren (275g, 9oz) and Indian nurses (155g, 5oz).

This information is crucial to our understanding of the importance of a diet high in natural fibre. Further evidence has shown that, without exception, countries which have a refined diet in which meat is predominant face a whole range of diseases that the so-called 'less developed' countries rarely see. Some of these Western plagues are:

- Appendicitis. The commonest abdominal emergency in the West. Over 300,000 appendixes are removed every year in the United States alone. It has now been shown that a low-fibre diet makes the risk of suffering appendicitis much greater.
- Diverticular disease. 30 per cent of all people over forty-five years have symptoms of this.
- Cancer of the large bowel. One of the commonest causes of death from cancer in the West.

All these diseases were all comparatively rare in the West until the beginning of the 20th century. Then the amount of animal fat in the diet began to steadily increase, and the amount of natural fibre began to decrease. Chart 14 shows how the American diet has changed in less than 100 years – the picture in Britain is much the same:

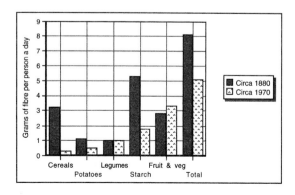

CHART 14: HOW FIBRE FELL FROM FAVOUR

A hundred years ago meat, fat and sugar between them only contributed 15 per cent of the total amount of calories in the diet. Today, the figure is nearer 60 per cent. Perhaps the biggest change in the diet has been the tremendous fall in the quantity of cereal fibre, which has dropped by 90 per cent. Most scientists now accept that there is a definite connection between the increase in modern diseases and the radical change in our eating patterns. I asked Dr Burkitt to explain: 'There are basically two types of fibre,' he told me, 'insoluble fibre and water-soluble fibre. The classic insoluble fibre is wheat fibre, with bran and all the bran products. That is highly effective for combating constipation, increasing stool weight, and preventing things like haemorrhoids and diverticular diseases. It's very good for the guts. But it does almost nothing for what we call the "metabolic diseases" associated with lack of fibre, particularly diabetes, and coronary heart disease.'

'Now soluble fibre, on the other hand, does have an effect on combating constipation, but it also has an effect on lowering raised serum lipid [ie fats in your blood] levels, and also on glucose tolerance, so that it has a profoundly beneficial effect on diabetes. Now, as to how this fibre works in lowering the blood lipids, there are many suggestions. It has effects on bile acids and so on, but the main way in which soluble fibre is beneficial for diabetes is that it enormously slows down the absorption of energy from the gut. So instead of all the energy being absorbed, as it would be in sugar products, if you have a high-fibre product it makes the intestinal content into a sort of a gel, so that the energy is only absorbed into the circulation very slowly, and so you don't have great and sudden demands on insulin, and so on.'

The scope of diseases which Dr Burkitt mentions is quite breathtaking. Suddenly, instead of merely being a useful preventive measure to ward off constipation, it seems as if fibre (in all its many natural forms) lies at the heart of healthy living. Once regarded as revolutionary, Dr Burkitt's views on the importance of fibre are now universally accepted. Actually, it is almost impossible to overstate the huge range of disease to which this drastic change in eating patterns has contributed. Colon cancer, for example, appears to be due to carcinogens created in the colon itself[141] – which can be negatively influenced by consuming a high level of saturated fat in the diet, and positively influenced by a good consumption of dietary fibre. High-fibre diets have also been shown to reduce the incidence of breast, uterine, and ovarian cancer. Experts at the United States Department of Health and Human Services estimate that if Americans ate more fibre and less fat, 20,000 deaths from cancer could be avoided each year.[142]

It is – *just* – possible to be vegetarian and not eat a diet high in natural forms of fibre. But you'd have to work very hard to do so. You'd have to eat a diet composed exclusively of junk food – chocolate, ice cream, sweets and so on – and you'd have to punctiliously avoid contact with anything remotely plant-like. In reality, both vegetarians and vegans can't help but get lashings of dietary fibre in their everyday diets, which accounts for their lack of constipation. By the same token, it is – *just* – possible to be a meat eater and have the same high intake of fibre as a vegetarian. But again, you'd have to work very hard at it. Meat is a dense food and fills you up quickly (scientists term this 'satiety') and so meat-eaters have neither the room nor the appetite to eat significant quantities of food which contains fibre (meat, of course, contains none). In the real world, this is how the various diets compare as far as fibre intake is concerned:

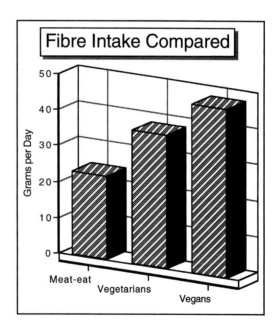

CHART 15: VEGANS GET HIGH ON FIBRE

Studies confirm what common sense suggests. In Britain, scientists measured the actual fibre content of daily food intake for meat-eaters, vegetarians and vegans, and found – not surprisingly – that the meat-eaters did worst of all (a meagre 23g a day), next came the vegetarians (37g) and at the top of the league came the vegans (47g – twice as much as meat-eaters).[143]

Methods of analysing fibre intake vary, and the gram intake of fibre varies from one country to another, depending on the supply of fruit and vegetables, and on the time of year. But significantly, the two-to-one ratio between the different fibre intake of vegetarians and meat-eaters is usually maintained. In America, another study found that meat-eaters were consuming just 12g of dietary fibre per day, compared to 28g for vegetarians.[144] In Sweden, a similar experiment has found that vegans consume three times as much fibre as meat-eaters.[145]

One question which is sometimes asked is: can you consume too much fibre? It has been suggested that fibre may have undesirable nutritional effects – that the phytate it contains, for example, may prevent other nutrients from being absorbed. Although this may be demonstrated in the laboratory, in practice it looks as if this should be the least of our worries. Eating a good nutritious plant-based diet, as described on page 57, provides a naturally high level of both fibre and other nutrients. This is confirmed by a careful analysis of vegetarian's diets performed in Israel.[146] The scientists found that the intake of iron and magnesium was significantly higher in vegetarians compared to meat-eaters, and they concluded that a long-term vegetarian diet does not lead to mineral deficiencies. Another scientific paper examined the benefits of dietary fibre in 1987, and pointed out that 'vegetarians routinely consume 40–50g dietary fiber daily without ill effect'.[147] And finally, a painstaking examination of the effect of dietary fibre confirms these same findings. In this study, the participants were divided into three categories:[148]

- a group of sixty-eight people who regularly supplemented their diet with an average of three tablespoons of bran for a year
- forty-three 'controls' who didn't consume bran supplements
- twenty vegetarians who had a very high fibre consumption for many years.

Then the scientists carefully measured the blood level of nutrients in all three groups, including serum iron, total iron binding capacity, calcium, phosphorus, zinc and magnesium. In their own words: 'We evaluated the hypothesis that a healthy population taking a high-fiber diet may develop deficiencies of various minerals and nutrients . . . There was no correlation between the amount of bran consumed and the blood level of nutrients. The fibre consumption of the vegetarians was very high, more than three times that of the controls. Our study indicates that a moderately or even extremely high consumption of fibre for a long time does not by itself cause mineral or nutrient deficiencies in a western type population.'

These findings have since been confirmed by an American study, which also concluded: 'The higher level of fibre intake did not appear to affect mineral utilization by the vegetarians.'[149] If any group were to be vulnerable to this effect, it would probably be infants. Comments Dr Gill Langley: 'It has been speculated . . . that a vegan diet may not be suitable for infants and small children. In fact it is easy to ensure that infants eat enough suitably-prepared high-energy foods such as beans, grains and nuts.'[150]

WHAT ELSE CAN YOU DO?

Here are a few further suggestions for the natural relief of constipation:

- Beetroot juice – either bottled or freshly juiced – is a very useful short-term natural stool softener and laxative.
- High-Fibre Salad. This salad really has get up and go! Ingredients: tin of kidney beans, carrots, beetroot, cabbage, watercress, broccoli, potatoes, tofu, sunflower seeds, almonds, pumpkin seeds; plus any seasonal vegetables, including winter roots. Choose any six from those ten. There's no need for lettuce but make it a cos if you want it: it's got some flavour and it won't go limp. Next, get a really large bowl. Cube the potatoes and lightly steam them and the broccoli; roast the pumpkin seeds; cube the tofu; grate the raw carrot and beetroot (don't slice); thin-shred the cabbage; fine-chop the watercress; wash and roughly chop the lettuce; don't forget the sunflower seeds and almonds. All this is quick to do, but get a food processor if you want to speed it up even more. Now prepare your favourite dressing. Two suggestions: olive oil, cider vinegar and French mustard (real French mustard if you can get it). Or, for the most unusual dressing you've ever tasted – try this and you'll never try anything else! –

buy some powdered black salt from your local Indian deli. Add 2tsp to oil and cider vinegar, shake thoroughly until dissolved. Finally, place the lettuce in the bottom and round the side of the bowl, if you're using lettuce. Mix the other ingredients together and put them on top. Pour on the dressing. One serving of a salad like this will give you a third of your total daily requirement of protein, almost twice your vitamin A requirement, all your vitamin C, and half your iron and fibre. It's so good you'll want to eat it every day! Tofu and, even nicer, marinated tofu are both available from health food shops.

- Take your time. Set aside half an hour a day to do your business – yes, literally: you can take a phone in there with you if you want, or at least read the paper. Never suppress an urge to go – this is giving your body entirely the wrong message. If you can do some simple exercise just before going – stretching or yoga is good – this will help.

- Colonic irrigation can provide you with an internal spring-clean, and set up your bowels so that you're starting all over again with a nice, clean intestinal passage. Much more natural and pleasant than an enema, colonic irrigation is nothing more complicated or sinister than an internal bath to remove poisons, gases, faecal matter and mucus deposits. Sterilized equipment with an inlet and outlet attachment is used to flush filtered water through the rectum, into the colon and out again, taking the waste products with it. Unlike regular use of laxatives, it is not habit forming!

DEFEATING DIABETES

WHAT IS DIABETES?

Diabetes mellitus is a 'disorder in which the body is unable to control the amount of sugar in the blood, because the mechanism which converts sugar to energy is no longer functioning properly'.[151] It is a disease of the Western world, brought about by both genetic and environmental factors. An estimated 30 million people are thought to suffer it worldwide.

Normally, the food you eat is gradually broken down and converted to glucose (blood sugar), the source of energy for all your body's functions. The conversion of glucose into energy requires insulin, a hormone produced in the pancreas. Insulin is released into your system in order to control the level of glucose in your blood, especially to prevent your blood sugar level from climbing too high. However, in diabetics, there is either a shortage of insulin or the available insulin does not function as it should. The result is that glucose is not converted into energy, but builds up in the blood and eventually spills over into your urine. This is often one of the first signs of diabetes.

Though there is an abundance of glucose in your blood, the body is still deprived of the energy it needs (because the glucose has not been converted to energy) and so the liver begins to produce yet more glucose to meet demands. Soon, your body's stores of fat and protein begin to break down in another attempt to supply more glucose. The resulting weight loss is often a further sign of diabetes. Thus begins a chain of events within your body that can eventually cause severe health problems, even death. In the UK alone, approximately 20,000 people die prematurely each year from diabetes-related problems.[152] There are two main classifications:

- Maturity onset diabetes: non-insulin dependent. 'Overfed, overweight and underactive . . .' – that is a popular summary of many, but not all, adults who develop diabetes in their middle years. Maturity onset diabetics experience the basic symptoms of thirst, fatigue, hunger and frequent urination. However, their health may improve by losing weight, increasing their level of exercise and monitoring their food intake to avoid foods high in calories, fats and sugar. In some people, diabetic symptoms can actually disappear following a strict regime of dietary control and exercise. Others must live the rest of their lives with the precautions, medications and attention to diet which have for so long been associated with the disorder. In maturity-onset diabetes, the adult need not become insulin-dependent.

- Juvenile onset diabetes: insulin dependent. Although any age of person may develop diabetes, those who develop diabetes under the age of forty years are most likely to suffer the more severe, insulin-dependent, form. Children who develop diabetes are almost always insulin-dependent. The insulin-dependent diabetic produces very little or no insulin and so relies on insulin injections. Without a supply of insulin they would not survive. Before the discovery of insulin, diabetes was considered to be invariably fatal, and most patients died within a short time of its diagnosis. Diabetes can be treated effectively today, although it does increase the risk of suffering other serious illnesses, such as cardiovascular disease, eye disorders, gangrene and other circulatory problems, nerve and muscle problems, and an increased susceptibility to ordinary infections.

Diabetes is a serious disorder and unfortunately its incidence is increasing – in Britain an estimated 60,000 new cases are diagnosed each year.[153] Further, the number of children diagnosed as diabetic has doubled in the past twenty years and this appears to be a worldwide trend. In short, this problem is getting worse. But there are simple, effective steps which may prevent the onset of diabetes or minimize its erosion of your health if you already have it.

HOW THE VEGETARIAN DIET CAN HELP

According to a report submitted by Diabetes Epidemiology Research International to the British Medical Journal, between 60 per cent and 95 per cent of cases of insulin-dependent diabetes can be prevented.[154] The DERI group of scientists believes that environmental factors are largely responsible for the increase in diabetes, claiming that genetic factors could not account for such great increases over such a very short period of time. Of the possible environmental causes, diet is perhaps the most significant and certainly one over which we have control.

It also seems that the same dietary measures used in prevention of diabetes can be used with great success in treatment. There have been several clues pointing to this possibility. For instance, Nauru, a remote island in the Pacific, had never had any cases of diabetes until it suddenly became rich and began to import American-style fast food. Now, more than 40 per cent of its population over the age of twenty has diabetes! Similarly, diabetes is noticeably rare in parts of Africa and China where the traditional diet is intact and free of Western influence. So what are the dietary influences which can prevent or treat diabetes?

The American Diabetes Association suggests that diabetics eat a diet in which carbohydrates make up about 60 per cent of total calorie intake; these carbohydrates should be mostly unrefined, complex and high in fibre.[155] Fat intake should total less than 30 per cent of calories consumed, with an emphasis on reducing saturated fats and cholesterol, replacing them with monounsaturated fats such as olive oil. Protein intake should be moderate.

The fact is, diabetes is more common among meat-eating people than non-meat eaters. Meat eating increases consumption of saturated fats which may affect insulin sensitivity. Also, the N-nitroso compounds in meat may actually be a trigger to the development of diabetes.

Some very significant research from the School of Public Health at the University of Minnesota reveals how we can reduce our risk of contracting diabetes.[156] They started a massive study of the subject in 1960, which lasted for twenty-one years and involved 25,698 adult Americans. They belonged to the Seventh-Day Adventist church, a group of people who are often used by scientists investigating the vegetarian diet, because half of them never eat meat.

The results of this investigation showed that people on meat-free diets had a substantially reduced risk (45 per cent) of contracting diabetes when compared to the population as a whole.

They also found that people who consumed meat ran over twice the risk of dying from a diabetes-related cause. The correlation between meat consumption and diabetes was found to be particularly strong in males. The study was carefully designed to eliminate confusion arising from confounding factors, such as over- or under-weight, other dietary habits, or amount of physical activity. The results are summarized in Chart 16:

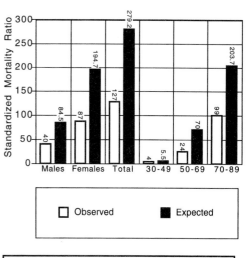

CHART 16: DEATHS FROM DIABETES—WHAT WAS EXPECTED & WHAT ACTUALLY HAPPENED

You can see that there is, of course, a striking difference between the number of people who were expected to die (black bars) and the number of people who actually died (white bars). But the study went even further than this. By analyzing death-certificates over the period under study, it was possible to assess the increased risk of dying from a diabetic illness that those who consumed meat ran. Chart 17 shows how it looks graphically:

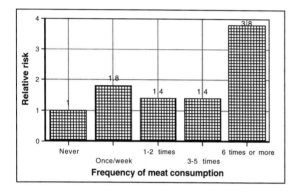

Relative risk

Never | Once/week | 1-2 times | 3-5 times | 6 times or more
Frequency of meat consumption

CHART 17: FREQUENCY OF MEAT EATING AND RISK OF DIABETES MORTALITY

This shows that taking *any* meat in the diet increases the risk, on average, by 1.8 times. For light meat eaters (people who only eat meat once to twice per week) the relative risk compared to a non-meat user is 1.4 times. But for heavy meat-eaters – six or more times a week – the risk rises steeply to 3.8 times.

Why should this be so? One explanation may be that diabetics are particularly vulnerable to high levels of fat in their blood, and meat is a prime source of saturated fat. There may also be an associated problem with excess protein consumption, too. Several clinical studies have now shown that a low-protein diet along with good blood glucose control can help slow the decline in kidney function that can occur in diabetics.[157]

We also know that *existing* diabetics can benefit from a high-fibre vegetarian diet. A study carried out at the Veterans Administration Medical Centre in Lexington compared two diets for the treatment of non-obese diabetic men, all of whom required insulin therapy.[158] The 'control' diet provided 20g per day of plant fibre – an average Western meat-centred diet.

The other diet included over three times as much fibre – 65g a day. The researchers found that the men on high fibre, high carbohydrate diets needed 73 per cent *less* insulin therapy than those on ordinary diets – quite a remarkable reduction.

WHAT ELSE CAN YOU DO?

- It seems that babies who are breastfed early in life may be less prone to developing diabetes, whereas children given cow's milk appear to be more likely to suffer from it in later life.[159] A recent study examined international milk consumption patterns, and found a strong correlation with the incidence of insulin-dependent diabetes. 'The study raises the possibility that when diabetes runs in families, parents may be able to protect their children by eliminating dairy products during the formative first nine months or so after birth,' reported The Associated Press. 'If true, we should be able to do something to prevent diabetes altogether,' comments Dr Hans-Michael Dosch, senior author of the study at the Hospital for Sick Children in Toronto. This study suggests that milk proteins cause an autoimmune reaction in which the body mistakenly attacks its own insulin-producing cells.

- Coffee can raises the concentration of sugar in the blood. As this is the major symptom of diabetes, coffee consumption may have serious implications for diabetics and potential diabetics alike. If you drink large amounts of coffee while pregnant, your children become more susceptible to diabetes.[160]

- Diabetics are commonly lacking in B6 which is vital for insulin production. So give preference to foods in your diet which are rich in vitamin B6 – oatbran and oatgerm, hummus, avocados, bananas, brewer's yeast, yeast extract, brown rice, parsley, spinach and other green leafy vegetables, molasses and whole grains.

- Vitamin C is needed to metabolize insulin and glucose; a deficiency can lead to cell degeneration in the pancreas, where insulin is produced. Eat plenty of citrus fruit, alfalfa sprouts and vegetables such as potato, green pepper and broccoli. As the body cannot store vitamin C, there is no danger of toxicity from supplementation should you wish to take a high dose vitamin C tablet every day.

- Diabetics often have a deficiency of the trace mineral chromium and can benefit from supplementation, with elderly and non-insulin-dependent misinterpretation, evasion, and permission to the beholder to bow down each man to the God of his own stomach?

'Let all who are observant and devout remember that the responsibility is their own; no Jew can use an intermediary, whether in this case it be a Beth Din, a Board of Shechita [ritual slaughter], or just a Kosher butcher with a label on his window. If unaware of the facts, his is a sin of omission; if he is aware and chooses to ignore his personal responsibility, his is a sin of commission; he is eating Trefah [unclean, the opposite of kosher].'[11]

Rev Dr Andrew Linzey explains the Christian argument for vegetarianism like this: 'The Christian argument for vegetarianism is simple: since animals belong to God, have value to God and live for God, then their needless destruction is sinful.'[12] Andrew Brown, religious affairs correspondent for a British newspaper, rather brilliantly describes this 'needless destruction' in the following passage: 'They [factory-farmed animals] are martyred in the cause of mediocrity, confined and tortured to make our diets blander. Not even the weariest and most jaded epicure has ever crowned a lifetime of increasingly decadent sensuality by reaching, as his final perverted thrill, for a handful of chicken McNuggets. This is of course pleasingly moralistic: the fruits of sin turn to fast food in our mouths, as they should.'[13]

Lastly, I would urge Christians to consider thoughtfully what is, for many people, the kernel of Christianity, expressed in Christ's Sermon on the Mount. I won't indulge in selective quotation from it here; read the whole of it (Matthew, Chapter 5) and then think about these words written by scholar Richard Whitehead: 'Let us take two images and place them side by side. The first is of a young preacher, healing the sick, washing his disciples' feet, preaching gentleness and humility and going to the cross without so much as raising a hand against his persecutors. The second is of an industry which systematically and mercilessly slaughters millions of animals which it has compelled to spend their brief lives in cramped, dingy, smelly sheds, and stuffed full of every chemical under the sun in order to produce meat to the maximum economic efficiency, a product which it spends millions of pounds persuading the public to buy. Clearly the two images are not simply incompatible; they are diametrically opposed. Can we really envisage Jesus being anything but a vegetarian if he were to be born into our society?'[14]

'Doesn't it take longer to prepare vegetarian meals?'

Only if you want it to! The example most often given to illustrate the convenience of a meat-based diet goes something like this: 'I can come home from a long, tiring day and take a chop from the fridge and slap it under the grill. It's ready to eat by time the potatoes and peas have cooked – *and* I've slipped into something more comfortable.'

Well, for those who wish to keep this particular schedule, you can prepare exactly the same meal using a vegetable burger or grill instead and nothing else will change. However, you'd be missing a lot of the fun and flavour of eating without meat. In the same period of time, about thirty minutes, you can make:

- Pasta topped with tomato, vegetable or meat-free bolognaise sauce accompanied by a green salad
- Stir-fried vegetables over Basmati rice with a peanut sauce
- A robust Chef's salad followed by onion soup
- Tempeh or vegetable burgers in a sesame bun with the full compliment of garnishes, a side salad and a baked potato
- Scrambled tofu on toast with grilled tomatoes and mushrooms, followed by fresh fruit salad topped with yoghurt.

The list could go on and on. And if you are willing to spend just fifteen minutes longer over your meal you can anticipate home-made pizzas, a variety of vegetable quiches, curries, casseroles and even tantalizing Mexican meals such as tacos or tostadas with bean paste filling and spicy tomato sauce. Of course, most of these can be prepared even more quickly using those handy appliances of the modern kitchen, the pressure cooker, microwave and food processor. And quicker still if some of the meals make partial use of tinned or frozen foods; the choice is yours. Certainly fresh is better if you can manage it, but speed and convenience is often paramount.

Just a few words about beans. Many people suffer from fear of beans on three accounts. First, that a vegetarian diet relies almost entirely on them. Second, that they have drastic and dire effects on the digestive system. And third, that they take hours and hours to cook. Not true on all three counts if you follow a few basic tips.

First. Beans are a marvellous source of protein, fibre, iron, the B vitamins and, when sprouted, vitamin C. With such a healthy nutritional profile, who this emerging ethic, saying, 'I am in favour of animal rights as well as human rights. That is the way of a whole human being.' By exposing ourselves to these revolutionary ideas, and by taking practical steps to incorporate them into our daily lives (and the first step is to become vegetarian), we are actively extending Einstein's 'circle of compassion'. And ultimately, this is the only way in which our world's dire problems will be resolved once and for all. Well, you *did* ask.

'But the Bible says I can eat meat!'

By selectively quoting from the Bible, you can prove almost anything. For example, 19th-century American slave owners frequently justified their odious trade with abundant Biblical quotations. But let's be clear – if we loved animals today in the way humans loved them in the Garden of Eden, we would not eat them. It is only after Adam and Eve were expelled from the Garden of Eden that humans started killing for food.

Other cultures have essentially similar tales of a fall from a once-perfect state of universal kinship. The Cherokee Indians have a tribal myth that says that humans once lived in perfect harmony with all their fellow creatures and plants, and all of them could speak to each other. In China, the Taoist Chuang Tsu wrote in the 4th century BC of a past 'age of virtue' when all humankind lived a common, co-operative life with the birds and the beasts. And in Greece, the philosopher Empedocles wrote of a 'golden age, an age of love' when 'no altar was wet with the shameful slaughter of bulls', and he maintained that the primal sin was man's slaughter of animals. The Old Testament tells us that the world that God creates is, initially, perfect. It is quite clear that in this perfect state, it is not intended for humans to eat the flesh of other creatures: 'Behold I have given you every herb yielding seed, which is upon the face of the earth, and every tree, in which is the fruit of a tree yielding seed; to you it shall be for meat.' Clearly, our task is to strive for that state of perfection once again, and a good starting point is to stop massacring our fellow creatures.

Within Judaism, there is still a very strong vegetarian tradition. An editorial in *The Jewish Vegetarian* magazine eloquently expresses the commands of religious scripture, and the grim reality of our treatment of food animals today:

'The Sabbath day was granted to all, and Rashi [Solomon ben Isaac, 1040–1105, a French rabbi famous for his commentaries] comments that even domestic creatures, at least on that day, must not be enclosed but shall be free to graze and enjoy the work of creation. If now they are incarcerated in darkened containers seven days and seven nights in each week for the entire period of their lives; if they neither see the luminaries of the heavens nor experience the sweet smell and the taste of the pastures, has not the most sacred Sabbath Law been flagrantly violated, and can the flesh of their bodies be Kosher?

'Would the law that states 'Thou shalt not muzzle the ox when he treads the corn' acquiesce in the computerized feeding of chemical fatteners, whilst the poor beast scents the dew and clover in the meadows beyond his darkened cell?

'When it is written 'Thou shalt not yoke an ox with an ass' does it imply that a calf may spend its entire life standing on slats, never to lie down, and effectively chained to the sides by its neck to prevent it doing so? Is this a perversion of the *Torah*? And when the unfortunate victim is slaughtered, can its remains be considered Kosher?

'If the law forbids one to cause distress to a mother bird by removing eggs from the nest in her presence, would it concur that during its lifetime a hen could be shut up in a receptacle of twelve square inches, its beak removed and feathers clipped? And after its throat is cut, would its body be Kosher for food?

'If a cruelly treated animal shall be considered unfit for food, and if the measure of the cruelty is determined by its ability to walk, do the authorities inspect the incarcerated animals in the factory farms, and is there any record as to whether they are able to walk to their own slaughter on their own emaciated legs? And if not is their flesh Kosher?

'If the law forbids the mixing of species, even of plants, and confusion of sexes, would it condone the injection of female hormones into the male beast, even though it is acknowledged to be cancerous in practice? And when this distortion of blood is covered with earth, even as is human blood, is this respect for the Creator who saw that all he created was very good? Or is this confusion, is it defilement, is it sacrilege, and is the flesh still Kosher?

'Shall a certificate of Beth Din [court which deals with matters of Talmudic law] convey that Torah min hashamayim ['the law from heaven'] has been sincerely observed, or shall it become a licence for diabetics responding particularly well. Chromium acts with insulin to transport glucose through cell walls. Highly processed foods always have reduced levels of chromium and years of eating such foods can invite the onset of Type 2, maturity onset diabetes. A diet rich in chromium may prevent this. Eat plenty of wheatgerm, brewer's yeast, whole grains and corn oil.

- Zinc plays a crucial role in the synthesis and storage of insulin in the pancreas. It is a mineral that many of us, not just diabetics, are continually short of. Eat mushrooms, sunflower and pumpkin seeds, brewer's yeast and soya beans to boost your zinc intake.
- Foods rich in magnesium may help to prevent retinopathy, a deterioration of the retina which is a real threat to diabetics. These include nuts, whole grains, dark green vegetables and molasses.
- Although there may be a genetic component in diabetes, obesity is very strongly implicated in its development. In Japan almost all sumo wrestlers become diabetic before they are thirty-five years old, and it is strongly suspected that this is induced by the amazingly high-fat diet they are given.

ECZEMA AND PSORIASIS

WHAT ARE ECZEMA AND PSORIASIS?

Most of us are familiar with the red, scaly, often painful skin which typifies psoriasis and eczema. Both are chronic, non-contagious skin disorders which affect people of all ages. The joints, scalp, back, chest, bottom, hands and legs, and in acute cases virtually the whole body, can all be affected. Both conditions can be brought on by allergy, stress, anxiety, viruses, 'flu, over-tiredness or injury – especially if you have a history of either disorder in the family. Rather than accept the problem as inevitable, however, there are dietary changes which can help to minimize or solve these skin problems.

HOW THE VEGETARIAN DIET CAN HELP

A poorly-functioning digestive system results in the proliferation of various toxins within the gut, some of which may contribute to the development of psoriasis and eczema.[161] Adopting a dairy- and gluten-free diet for at least two to three weeks is certainly worth trying to determine whether your skin problem is aggravated by these food groups. In addition, there are several further dietary steps you may take to improve digestion and therefore prevent or minimize your skin problem.

WHAT ELSE CAN YOU DO?

- Adopt a low-sugar or even a sugar-free diet to prevent an overgrowth of the candida albicans yeast in your gut. This yeast is normally present in a healthy person but, when present to excess, can cause disease or reduced immunity. Psoriasis is particularly responsive to a reduction in your sugar intake and a few days or weeks on a sugar-free diet (sometimes called an anti-fungal diet) may improve your condition.[162] Remember, sugar includes honey, molasses, concentrated fruit juices and syrups.
- In some people, a deficiency in the B-complex of vitamins can hinder the proper metabolism of fats and proteins and problems such as psoriasis and eczema can result. To correct deficiency, you may take a B-complex supplement daily. Simply ensure that your supplement includes the whole range of B vitamins as they work best when taken as a group. The B vitamins are essential to the health of skin, mucous membranes and nerves. In fact, as stress is so often a trigger for eczema and psoriasis, a sufficiency of the B complex may help prevent an attack by reducing the initial effects of stress on your body. Foods especially rich in the B complex are yeasts, such as brewer's or nutritional yeast, and whole grains. Pulses and seeds are also useful sources. Ensure that you have a serving of each of these foods in your diet each day.
- Gamma-linolenic acid is a substance which we produce in our bodies. Some people, however, do not produce enough and are more likely to suffer from eczema as a result. A bowl of porridge each day is a good source of gamma-linolenic acid,[163] as is a supplement in the form of evening primrose oil.[164]
- Omega-3 fatty acids reduce the itching and scaling of eczema and psoriasis in many people.[165] Sources of omega-3 fatty acids include flaxseed and soya oils.
- Selenium and vitamin E are both antioxidants and work together to preserve and promote healthy

metabolic processes. Of particular importance to sufferers of eczema and psoriasis, this combination can delay the oxidation of essential fatty acids which are so crucial to healthy skin. Selenium is a mineral found in whole grains, especially the bran and germ, and vegetables such as onions, celery, cabbage and broccoli. Vitamin E is abundant in the cold-pressed vegetable oils, in soyabeans and in all raw nuts and seeds. Supplements are also available.

- Increase your intake of dietary fibre. Start by altering your diet to include an abundance of fresh fruit and vegetables as well as two to three servings daily of whole, unprocessed grains.

- Boost your intake of folic acid as some psoriasis sufferers have been shown to have low blood levels of folic acid.[166] Folic acid is found in green leafy vegetables and brewer's yeast. Supplements are also available.

- Zinc is essential for the production of hydrochloric acid in your stomach, a shortage of which produces digestive problems which can lead to eczema or psoriasis. Zinc is found in whole grains, pumpkin seeds and brewer's yeast. It may also be taken in supplement form.

- Vitamin A is necessary for the health of all body tissue, especially the skin and mucous membranes. Skin problems such as eczema and psoriasis can be one sign of deficiency and may respond well to increased intakes of vitamin A or carotene, the vegetable substance which your body converts to vitamin A. To boost your intake of vitamin A, eat plenty of carotene-rich foods including dark green leafy vegetables, such as spinach, and vegetables of a dark orange colour such as carrots and pumpkin.

- Some people's eczema or psoriasis is an allergic response. If you suspect this might be true for you, try amending your diet in these ways:
  1 Eat only fresh, organic produce to avoid chemical residues and unnecessary additives.
  2 Eliminate the foods which most commonly cause an allergic response. These include dairy products, eggs, fish, peanuts and soybeans, chicken, citrus, tomato and corn.[167]

- Moderately high alcohol consumption can aggravate psoriasis. A Finnish study concluded that men who consumed five or more units of alcohol per day were likely to suffer a worsening of their condition.[168] Try keeping your alcohol intake to the recommended twenty-one units per week for men, fourteen units per week for women.

GRAPPLING WITH GALLSTONES

WHAT ARE GALLSTONES?

Gallstones are more common amongst women than men – 25 per cent of all women and 10 per cent of all men will develop gallstones before they are sixty years old. This is how gallstones occur: the liver secretes bile, a substance that is high in cholesterol (which literally means 'solid bile' in Greek), and is stored in the gall bladder. Lecithin (found in soya beans and corn) and bile salts together help to keep the cholesterol dissolved in the bile. However, if the level of cholesterol becomes so high that no more can be dissolved, then it begins to precipitate, and gallstones are the result. Stones vary considerably in size. The largest reported stone was almost 17.5cm (7 inches) in diameter, but that is very rare. Most are between 3mm and 18mm ($^1/_8 - ^3/_4$ inch).

When the gallbladder contracts to release bile, a stone may shoot up and plug the opening of the cystic duct. Then, no matter how hard the gallbladder tries to empty itself, bile cannot flow out. The result is intense pain in the upper abdomen which increases until, after several hours, the stone falls back into the gallbladder, ending the attack. About half of all those people with gallstones feel no symptoms. But for those who do, the suffering can be intense. It's like 'being kicked in the guts by a horse – all the time', as one sufferer has described it. Gallstones can also lead to infection, resulting in inflammation of the gall bladder, colic, peritonitis, gangrene of the gall bladder, and jaundice. As an indication of the prevalence of this condition, it is surprising to discover that over 1 million Americans are diagnosed with gallstones every year; and in half of these cases the symptoms are so severe that their gallbladders are surgically removed.[169]

As the Western diet has changed, so has the incidence of gallstones, quadrupling since 1940 in many areas. Significantly, Orientals and rural Africans, who traditionally consume a low-fat, high-fibre diet, suffer very little from them, and only humans and domesticated animals experience them – wild animals do not. All this strongly suggests that the problem is connected with our modern, Western way of eating.

HOW THE VEGETARIAN DIET CAN HELP

In an experiment carried out in Oxford, England, two groups of women were compared to see if their diets might have any influence on the occurrence of gallstones.[170] The first group, consisting of 632 women, were selected at random, and ate meat. The second group consisted of 130 women who did not eat meat, and had a diet naturally higher in fibre. All the women were then given a thorough inspection, using ultrasound detection techniques, looking specifically for gallstones. The experimenters found that the meat-eaters were two-and-a-half times more likely to develop gallstones than the non-meat eaters. The scientists concluded that the low-fat, high-fibre diet of the vegetarian women gave them protection.

Building on this study, the scientists then undertook a further investigation of 121 women suffering from gallstones, who were then age-matched with other women without gallstones (but not vegetarians).[171] The aim was to find out if there was any particular factor in the diets of the women with gallstones which made them more prone to suffer – for example, did they eat more fat? After analysing the diets of both groups, the scientists found out that there was actually very little difference between either group in terms of their nutrient intake. They concluded: 'This may indicate the existence of a threshold effect where virtually all non-vegetarian women in affluent societies have a diet high in saturated fat, animal protein, and simple sugar to the extent that it is not possible to distinguish between cases and controls.' In other words, only vegetarian (and vegan) diets are sufficiently low in saturated fat, and high in fibre, to result in a lower rate of occurrence of gallstones.

WHAT ELSE CAN YOU DO?

- If you are obese you are four times more likely to suffer from gallstones. But a word of warning – rapid weight loss can actually increase your risk of suffering from gallstones. Obese people who lose a lot of weight on very low-calorie diets are quite likely to form stones. Once the weight has been lost, however, and relatively normal eating patterns are restored, the stones may dissolve of their own accord. This, and all other treatments, should naturally be supervised by a doctor.

- Fatty foods are known to stimulate gallbladder contractions, which can cause a painful gallstone attack. So consider trying a reduced fat diet. Also, consuming smaller, more frequent meals may help limit gallbladder contractions and gallstone attacks.

- Research suggests that aspirin can inhibit substances that may cause cholesterol to crystallize into stones.[172] It could therefore prevent gallstones in obese people during weight loss; or halt the recurrence in people who had their stones dissolved with drugs.

- Taking oestrogen or oral contraceptives can increase the amount of cholesterol in your bile fluid and thus the chances of having gallstones.[173] At least three studies have found an increased risk of gall bladder disease among women who use oral contraceptives.

- Recently, there has been speculation that a diet high in soluble fibre might increase the solubility of cholesterol in the bile, and so prevent, and perhaps even reverse, the formation of gallstones. Good sources of soluble fibre include oat bran, pectin, and beans.

- Lastly, a word of warning: the so-called 'olive oil cure', which involves fasting for three days and then drinking a mug of olive oil and lemon juice to make the gallbladder contract and push through extremely small stones, can be dangerous. If larger stones are ejected in this way, they could stick in the bile duct, causing jaundice, infection and a possible medical emergency.

HEALING HEART DISEASE

THE SIZE OF THE PROBLEM

You may be shocked to learn that the first clinical account of someone suffering a heart attack was only recorded as recently as 1912. Until then, it seems as if heart attacks were so rare they just weren't written about or recorded. Today, heart disease is the commonest cause of death in the Western world. Within this century, an ominous change has occurred to our lifestyles – a change which has had the effect of making a once rare and unusual form of death so common that in the United Kingdom, one man out of every fifteen dies from heart disease before the age of 65.[174]

Britain is indeed the 'heart attack capital' of the world. In 1970, both America and Australia had death rates from heart disease which were higher than the UK. Since then, the impact of health-promoting measures in both countries has meant that America's death rate has declined by 55 per cent, and Australia's by 51 per cent. Britain's however, has only fallen by 24 per cent. This means that British males in the most vulnerable age group (35–74) are twice as likely to die from heart disease as Italian men, three times more likely to die than the French, and eight times more likely to die than Japanese males.

But heart disease doesn't just affect men. Although it is responsible for one in three deaths amongst males, it is also the cause of one in four deaths among women. After cancer, heart disease is the leading cause of premature death for women.

On any single day of the year, over 800 people in the United Kingdom will suffer a heart attack. Roughly one third of these attacks are immediately fatal – in other words, 270 people suddenly die from a heart attack each day. Beyond the shocking and tragic reality of sudden death lies the incapacitation of cardiovascular disease, now thought to affect up to two million people in the United Kingdom. These people are often disabled by the pain of angina, the enfeeblement of high blood pressure and its medication, or by the crippling effects of stroke. Undoubtedly, cardiovascular disease alters lives, and not just those who are victim to it – the spouses and families of its victims are also afflicted through the worry, grief and financial hardship that it causes. In the workplace, cardiovascular disease is responsible for eleven per cent of working days lost to illness (in financial terms, a cost of £3296 million).

Cardiovascular disease spreads its net wide and affects us all – personally, socially and economically. And the future looks very bleak: by the ripe old age of ten, almost fifty per cent of children in the United Kingdom have developed eating habits and lifestyle patterns that will predispose them to the development of cardiovascular disease. In their early middle age these children may begin to notice that their contemporaries are dying off. They may lose their parents, often before they have had time to make them grandparents. They may lose their spouse, often just at the point in their lives when they are beginning to feel most mature, most at ease with their family, their work,

and their future prospects. They may die themselves – suddenly, without warning – or they may suffer the often crippling deterioration of health that occurs as cardiovascular disease gradually ruins their lives.

And remember, much of this unfolding tragedy is entirely preventable.

WHAT MAKES YOU TICK?

Every living cell in your body has a specific job to do and in order that each cell may do its job well, it must somehow take essential products *in* and put waste material *out*. To meet this requirement, the cells of your body need a reliable transport system that will perform both deliveries and removals. The circulation of blood is such a system. It is called the cardiovascular system because it is structured around the heart (cardio) and the blood vessels (vascular) and all the functions included in the relationship between them. With almost unbelievable speed and efficiency, your blood is able to maintain the health of every living cell in your body by supplying it with nutrients and oxygen specific to its needs, and then removing waste material and carbon dioxide as the nutrients and oxygen are utilized.

Blood is composed of red cells, white cells and platelets suspended in plasma – if you've ever made a salad dressing from vinegar, oil and a few herbs you'll understand the idea of suspension. When you stir the mixture, it changes in consistency and, temporarily at least, the oil, vinegar and herbs are evenly distributed, making a smooth emulsion. Blood is, in analogy only, a similar mixture. All four components – plasma, platelets, red and white cells – are present in measured and changing proportions to make healthy blood.

● **Plasma.** If any substance on earth could be called primordial soup, it would have to be plasma. To make it, take several litres of water and add microscopic portions of several dozen compounds such as amino acids, hormones, antibodies, 'tissue salts' such as sodium, potassium, calcium and chloride, and proteins such as albumin, globulin and fibrinogen. These nutrients are transferred to your needy cells in exchange for waste material for eventual excretion. Here's how: every cell in your body is surrounded by a plasma-like liquid called tissue fluid. This fluid gets right up next to the cell, every cell, and removes any waste material that the cell generates as it functions. This waste is transferred through the tissue fluid to the plasma and, at this point, is exchanged for whichever of the compounds in the plasma the needy cell requires. These compounds are again transferred: from the plasma, through the tissue fluid to the waiting body cell. The only difference is that this whole cycle happens about 100 times faster than it took you to read about it!

- **Red blood cells.** These cells (also called erythrocytes) are suspended in your plasma. They are red because they contain a red pigment, called haemoglobin, which has a little bit of iron in its centre. However, haemoglobin doesn't only colour your blood red, it is the aspect of each red blood cell that enables that cell to carry oxygen and transfer it, eventually, to your body tissues. In environments where there is a high concentration of oxygen, such as in your lungs, haemoglobin actually combines with oxygen. Then, when that red blood cell moves into the reverse conditions of low concentration of oxygen, such as tissue in your limbs, it releases its oxygen. In other words, the oxygen is transferred from the red blood cell to the needy tissues.

- **White blood cells.** Also called leucocytes, these cells are much larger in size than the red blood cells, but there is only one white cell to every 500 or 600 red, depending on where they are measured in your body. The white blood cells come in three forms, each with its distinct function, but their collective purpose is to destroy or protect you from foreign organisms such as 'germs', viruses, bacteria. So next time you cut your finger, give a special thought to those white blood cells which are rapidly gathering at the site to carry off dead tissue and destroy invading bacteria. And the next cold or bout of 'flu you fall victim to, trust your white blood cells to do battle. It's what they are there for.

- **Platelets.** These are tiny cells that are present to help in the process of clotting. They are necessary in order for fibrinogen (a protein in your plasma) to convert to fibrin. Fibrin forms into fine threads which surround the blood cells and then contract to form them into an ever more solid mass – a blood clot.

The average man has five to six litres of blood in his body at any one time, the average woman has four to five litres. In order for this wonderful liquid to do its work, however, it needs to move around the body, to circulate. Your body achieves circulation of the blood in a fairly mechanical way using a pump, a network of channels or conduits and a variety of valves. Using this equipment, your blood is circulated to all of your organs and to all the tissues of your body. Let's look at each aspect of this circulation.

- **The heart.** Your heart is a small, muscular sac about the size of your clenched fist. It is located in a fairly central position in your body – just behind and slightly to the left of your breastbone – so that its pumping action is performed efficiently. Your heart pumps blood to every part of your body between sixty and ninety times each minute, every day of your life, just by contracting its muscles. We can look inside the heart to see how it is made and precisely what is happening as it pumps. A thick wall divides the inside of your heart into two completely separate halves, left and right. Within each of these halves are two further divisions – the top chambers, called atria, and the bottom chambers, called ventricles. That is four chambers in total: the top chamber on each side communicates with the chamber beneathe it but the left chambers do not communicate with the right chambers.

The top chambers, atria, have thin walls of muscle and these chambers act as 'waiting rooms' for the blood that enters them. Once the blood enters the atrium it cannot leave except by passing through a valve, a sort of one-way door, into the lower chamber. This door only opens when it is forced: the muscular walls of the atrium contract and push the blood against the valve causing it to open and allowing the blood to flow through into the lower chamber.

The lower chamber in each half of your heart is called a ventricle. The ventricles have thick walls of muscle because these chambers have to work harder than the atria. Once blood is pushed out of the atria and into the ventricles it cannot return to the upper chamber (remember, that valve was one way). Instead, it will be pushed out of the ventricle, through another one-way valve, into a narrow conduit. This conduit will channel the blood to a number of destinations in your body – your toes, your fingertips, your lungs, your brain. Wherever it is going, it will need a very strong push to keep it going. The initial push given to that blood occurs when the muscles of each ventricle contract. Now you can see why the muscle walls of these chambers are thicker than those of the atria.

This transfer of blood from the atria to the ventricles takes place in a rhythmic cycle every moment of your life. By and large, one remains unaware of this cycle but, after exertion or by putting a stethoscope or your ear to another person's heart, you may listen to its rhythmic workings. The characteristic 'lubb dupp' sound of the heart beat is caused by the valves closing: the 'lubb' indicates the closing of the valves between the atria and the ventricles, while the 'dupp' indicates the closing of the valves between the ventricles and the conduits, or arteries.

- **The arteries.** Arteries are the conduits that channel blood away from your heart to the limbs and organs. Arteries are round tubes constructed in three layers. The outer layer is tough and fibrous to protect the artery and give it strength. The middle layer is predominantly muscle tissue, with a small number of elastic fibres. This combination gives the artery flexibility as well as the ability to adjust its internal diameter (calibre) to increase or decrease both the amount and the pressure of blood flowing through it. The third and inner layer is in two parts: a lining which is in contact with the circulating blood, and an elastic layer between the lining and the muscular, middle layer of the artery. Arteries vary in size considerably – the aorta and the pulmonary artery are quite large as they leave the heart but gradually branch off into smaller and smaller arteries. Most arteries have specific names which help doctors and other interested persons locate their position in the body. When arteries become very small they are called arterioles. Arterioles link up with the capillaries, the smallest form of conduit, to supply blood to all the body tissues.
- **The capillaries.** Capillaries are tiny channels whose walls are only one cell thick and loosely formed to allow cells to pass through them. Capillaries form a very dense network throughout the body to ensure that all the body tissues are supplied with blood. As the blood passes through the capillary walls, it transfers oxygen and nutrients to the tissue cells and collects waste material and carbon dioxide from them. Because the capillary walls are permeable, this transfer is able to take place instantly without the flow of blood being impaired. The permeable nature of the capillaries also accounts for the speed with which white blood cells accumulate at the site of a wound or infection. Once the blood cells have exchanged oxygen and nutrients for waste products, they must move away from the tissues in order to excrete that waste. The flow of blood continues, but now it is flowing toward the heart. To accomplish this return circulation, the capillaries gradually join up to form venules (small veins) and these in turn join and thicken to become veins.

- **The veins.** Veins are, externally, slightly smaller than arteries but with a larger interior diameter. Their walls are constructed of the same three layers of tissue described for arteries except that each layer is much thinner because the pressure of blood within a vein is much less than the pressure within an artery. Veins are also less elastic than arteries, so there are valves within some veins to prevent the back-flow of blood. These two factors, reduced pressure and reduced elasticity, mean that the veins in your body function at their best when your overall muscle tone is good. Your muscles support the veins and help to prevent collapse of the vein or back-flow of blood, as seen in varicose veins. Veins always carry blood back to the heart. Blood returning to the heart from the lungs enters the left side of the heart through the pulmonary veins. Blood returning from the head and arms enters the right atrium through the superior vena cava; that from the heart through the coronary sinus; that from the middle and lower body through the inferior vena cava. Each of these main veins are the result of many smaller veins and venules merging together.

WHEN THINGS GO WRONG

This beautiful system works with remarkable efficiency and, unlike circulatory systems constructed by humans (for example, your central heating system) is capable of decades of faultless use without any obvious maintenance. The truth is, of course, the human circulatory system is busy repairing itself all the time. Unfortunately, while this repair work is going on, many of us seem determined to inflict as much damage on our precious life-support system as possible. Some of the main ways we choose to self-destruct are:

- smoking
- high blood pressure
- obesity
- high cholesterol
- lack of exercise.

Sometimes, you hear about a genetic factor in heart disease; that people with a history of heart disease in the family are more likely to contract heart disease themselves. Scientific evidence shows that this is true, and doctors have termed this inherited high level of blood cholesterol as 'familial hypercholesterolaemia' or FH for short. However, it would be a great mistake to assume that either you are 'doomed' to suffer from heart disease simply because one member of your family has suffered from it, or, alternatively, that you will miraculously escape it because no close relative has succumbed. Here are some important points to bear in mind.

- Firstly, FH is not a diagnosis you can make for yourself. Just because a relative has died from heart disease doesn't mean that you have FH.
- Secondly, only one in 500 people has FH, whereas one in every five people has an excessively high level of blood cholesterol.
- Thirdly, if you do have a history of heart disease in your family, it is even more important that you take preventive measures.

Arteriosclerosis is the name given to three distinct disease processes which cause a gradual and significant hardening and narrowing of the arteries. In one form, the arteries are hardened by a gradual deposition of calcium in the middle, muscle layer of the artery walls. In a second form, the small arteries, arterioles, become hardened and thick. And in the third most familiar form; the large and medium sized arteries acquire a build-up of cholesterol, fats, blood cells and calcium on their inner layers. This last form is called atherosclerosis.

It is thought that hypertension (high blood pressure) may be one cause or contributing factor in the development of atherosclerosis. Certainly, once either disease is apparent, the other is usually not long in manifesting. Whichever disease comes first, the resulting loss of arterial flexibility increases the likelihood of further damage being done to the lining of the arteries and eventually to the heart itself. Here is the process described.

- When the artery lining is weakened or damaged, muscle tissue from the middle layer of the artery wall multiply and grow into the artery. Then fat molecules already in the blood begin to collect at the site of the damage. Blood normally carries fat molecules so that it may transfer them to body tissues. But when the concentration of fat in the blood is too high or when the artery wall is damaged, these molecules begin to form into plaques which adhere to the artery walls. A build up of fat at specific places along the lining of an already weak and damaged artery increases the stress placed on the artery and it bleeds into the fatty deposits. The white cells in the blood try to fight off bacteria and inflammation while the red cells combine with the platelets in the blood and begin a clotting process. This combination of fatty deposit and clotting blood is called atheroma. No one can *feel* atheroma accumulate. Even when an artery becomes more than half blocked by this fatty, cholesterol-rich sludge, you still may not be aware of any warning signs to tell you that something is badly wrong. In fact, an artery usually has to be more than 75 per cent blocked before blood flow is seriously impeded. But by this stage, time is definitely running out. When a deposit eventually blocks an artery, the blood flow is stopped and, with it, the supply of oxygen to tissue cells. This causes death to the deprived tissues and, if occurring in the heart muscle, a heart attack follows (see below).
- Once the build-up of fat and blood begins, calcium deposits begin to harden the atheroma – especially in people entering late middle age. As the atheroma hardens and becomes brittle, it too can break from the artery wall and float away in the blood where, further along, it may block the artery. This form of blockage is called an embolism. The place in your artery where the brittle atheroma broke away is left raw and bleeding and a blood clot soon forms – called a thrombus. That clot may either block the artery there and then, or it too may break away and block the artery further along.
- In both embolism and thrombosis there is further damage done to the artery and, more importantly, both create an obstruction of the blood flow through the artery. Loss of blood flow means loss of essential oxygen and nutrients, therefore an obstruction such as this usually means subsequent death of the affected tissue. If the obstruction occurs in or near the heart, a heart attack occurs. If in the brain, a stroke occurs. If this obstruction occurs in the eye, a degree of blindness may ensue and if in the extremities, death of tissue may cause gangrene and require amputation of the affected part.

Strokes

There are two basic types of stroke. The first is an aneurysm or haemorrhage. This is the rupture of a blood vessel, such as an arteriole or capillary, that has been weakened by consistently high blood pressure (see p150). The second type is an obstruction of a blood vessel by atheroma (embolism) or by a blood clot (thrombus). Both types of stroke have the result of killing nerve cells in the brain, leaving the area of body controlled by those nerve cells unable to function. Typically a stroke victim may suffer paralysis, impaired speech, loss of memory, confusion, or death. Those who experience a mild stroke have a chance of good recovery through the many therapeutic methods currently employed, such as physiotherapy, speech therapy and correction of diet and lifestyle habits.

Ischemic heart disease

During exercise, stress, or when you are subject to the cold your heart needs to pump harder to maintain a sufficient supply of blood to your tissues. In a healthy person this occurs without any problem, though you may become slightly flushed or breathless. However, when the arteries and arterioles are constricted, as in atherosclerosis, hypertension or through nervous reaction, your heart must work even harder to supply adequate blood to your body tissues. Sometimes it doesn't succeed.

'Ischemic' means an insufficient supply of blood. Therefore ischemic heart disease is an insufficient supply of blood to the myocardium, or heart muscle. There are three forms of this disease, angina pectoris, myocardial infarction and sudden death.

- **Angina pectoris.** In angina pectoris the heart itself becomes deprived of the blood needed to supply its own muscle tissues. This may be due to atheroma which narrows the coronary arteries, or it may occur when the arteries are constricted by nervous reaction from stress or cold. In either case, the result is a strong, distinctive pain in the region of the heart. This pain is often described as 'vice-like, aching, tight, heavy or dull' and is usually felt in the chest. In some angina sufferers, the pain may radiate to the neck, arms (especially the left arm) or even the back. The pain of angina pectoris is usually eased with rest (unlike a heart attack, where the pain is prolonged and does not disappear with rest). Additionally, the underlying cause of angina may be treated in several ways so that the symptoms are minimized or disappear altogether. Drug treatment is an obvious means of affecting the course of angina pectoris, which can disable or cause death if left to progress. However, improving one's level of fitness and finding ways of coping with all forms of stress in everyday life are measures that may be taken immediately to prevent or relieve the threat of angina. Diet and lifestyle are, once again, important factors in both the cause and the prevention of angina pectoris (see page 111).

- **Myocardial infarction.** The myocardium is the muscular wall of the heart and, like all muscle tissue, it is supplied with oxygenated blood which circulates through the arteries. The coronary arteries, those that supply the myocardium, may become obstructed in the same way as other arteries in the body. When obstruction is only partial some blood gets through and the heart only suffers when it is challenged – as with angina pectoris. When the obstruction is total, however, the area of myocardium that is completely deprived of blood dies. This area of dead tissue is called an infarct. The process of obstruction, pain and death of tissue is called a myocardial infarction – or heart attack. Heart attacks may be caused by obstruction of the coronary arteries due to atherosclerosis, embolism or a blood clot (thrombus). In some cases, atheroma and coronary thrombosis are both present and together contribute to the heart attack. The area of myocardium affected by the obstruction stops contracting, or pumping, when it is deprived of blood and that area of tissue dies shortly after, usually within hours. This period of time is very painful for the victim. If the victim survives the heart attack, the myocardium in the region of the obstruction becomes scar tissue – dead tissue which the body cannot replace. If the obstructed artery supplied a small area of myocardium, then the infarct, or scar, will be relatively small also. If, however, a larger coronary artery is obstructed the infarct will be larger. A large infarct is more likely to cause a loss of heart rhythm and, in some people, the sudden loss of heart rhythm due to infarct causes immediate death. In other victims the area of muscle tissue affected is so small that no symptoms are felt – this is called 'silent infarct'. A number of 'silent infarcts' may occur before a major heart attack is experienced.

  During a heart attack the victim suffers from

persistent pains similar to those described for angina. That is, vice-like, tight, crushing pains that radiate to the neck, jaw, arms and sometimes the back. These pains may last for hours or even days and do not disappear with rest or altering position. In addition, the victim may have symptoms such as profuse sweating, vomiting, nausea, feelings of cold and a sense of doom. In the event of any of these symptoms appearing in someone close to you, hospital treatment must be sought immediately to prevent death.

- **Sudden death.** Sadly, this is often the first sign of any cardiovascular disease. Although it may be caused by injury, it is more often due to a combination of atherosclerosis and ischemia which acts swiftly and profoundly on the victim. Such people are often said to die 'instantly'. There is no treatment for this form of heart attack and no way of predicting it. The causes, which are in common with those of all other forms of cardiovascular disease, provide the only insight as to how it may be prevented.

For the majority of heart attack victims, their attack was the first they knew of any cardiovascular problems. Only one in every four or five victims were known to have had symptoms of hypertension or angina prior to their heart attack. Yet, undoubtedly, hypertension and its companion, atherosclerosis, are the basic disorders underlying myocardial infarction. Therefore, it is important that we consider how to prevent or minimize these conditions if we wish to reduce the incidence of stroke, angina pectoris, heart attack, and sudden death. Because make no mistake – this is one epidemic we can prevent.

HOW THE VEGETARIAN DIET CAN HELP

In 1990, the Editor-in-Chief of the *American Journal of Cardiology* wrote these startling words in an editorial:

Although human beings eat meat we are not natural carnivores. We were intended to eat plants, fruits and starches! No matter how much fat carnivores eat, they do not develop atherosclerosis. It's virtually impossible, for example, to produce atherosclerosis in the dog even when 100g of cholesterol and 120g of butter fat are added to its meat ration (this amount of cholesterol is approximately 200 times the average amount that human beings in the USA eat each day!). In contrast, herbivores rapidly develop atherosclerosis if they are fed foods, namely fat and cholesterol,

intended for natural carnivores . . .

Thus, although we think we are one and we act as if we are one, human beings are not natural carnivores. When we kill animals to eat them, they end up killing us because their flesh, which contains cholesterol and saturated fat, was never intended for human beings, who are natural herbivores.[175]

It was an astonishing editorial, because most doctors rarely use such clear and forthright language in support of vegetarianism. After all, drugs, not diet, are the accepted weapons of choice in the war against heart disease. Yet a few doctors – following in the enquiring tradition of Dr John Abernethy, who we encountered earlier (page 119) – have quietly been pursuing their own medical investigations in this area, sometimes with great success. One such is Dr David Ryde, an English family doctor and conventional in every respect, except for the fact that he gained an early reputation for preferring to treat his patients through dietary means rather than pills.

'When I went to medical school', says Dr Ryde, 'we were taught nothing about nutrition. They simply said there were two types of protein – "first class" and "second class". It was only years later that I began to understand that plant protein could be entirely satisfactory for human needs.

'Eventually, I began to become interested in the science of nutritional medicine, and I started to offer my patients nutritional advice. Some patients simply didn't want to know – they'd take the attitude that they didn't want a lecture, they just wanted me to write a prescription for some pills – that's what they regarded as "proper" medicine. But other patients were more willing to try something new, and I started to get some extraordinary results.

'My first was a patient with severe angina. His condition had been deteriorating for about five years, and he'd been into hospital, was taking all the medication, and so on. But his condition was, frankly, almost terminal. It was a really pitiful sight to see him struggle to walk the few yards from the car to the surgery. Now a person in such a desperate state will listen, and they will try anything. So I suggested he try a strict vegetarian diet, actually a vegan one. '

'Just one month later, he could walk one mile. Three months later he could walk four miles, while carrying shopping. "It used to take him a quarter of an hour to climb three flights of steps," his daughter told me. "Now he's up in a few seconds!"

'That was my first success, and it encouraged me to try it with other patients. Another interesting case was a professor of medicine, actually the dean of a medical school. He had been taking anti-ulcer medication for four years, with little success. I suggested he try a vegan diet, and after three days, there was a remarkable improvement in pain reduction. A year later, he had lost about 10lb of weight, and he looked a new man, light-hearted and happy.

'Another interesting case was a woman with severe headaches, and a blood pressure of 185/120. I suggested she try a vegan diet, and the pressure soon came down to 115/75. Now you'd never seen that kind of reduction using medication. And she felt fantastic! Which was another benefit, because anti-hypertensive medication often leaves patients feeling exhausted.

'I've seen results such as these in my patients too often to attribute them to coincidence. Really, this kind of treatment has no side-effects, and the benefits are so worthwhile, that there's no reason not to try it.

'In the early days, my colleagues used to warn me that I wasn't prescribing enough medication. When they charted the prescribing rates of GPs, I would always be right at the bottom, way off the graph. And I think that worried some people. But these days, I'm asked to give talks to colleagues, and to administrators. Obviously, my methods are far less costly to the health service than usual.

'I also feel strongly that we doctors need to examine more closely what actually goes on in the consulting room. You know, the truth is that patients don't usually come and see us because they're ill; they come because they're worried. They're anxious about some aspect of their health. Now, if all we do is simply send them away will a bottle of pills, we have actually reinforced their anxiety, which can make a cure harder. Fundamentally, we must remember that we're not vending machines!'[176]

So there we have two pieces of evidence – one from the Editor-in-Chief of an internationally-respected cardiology publication, another testimony from a general practitioner who has used the vegan diet on the 'front line' – and seen its positive results. By themselves, those two pieces of evidence are surely enough to persuade most intelligent people of the beneficial effects of the meat-free lifestyle. The astounding truth is, though, that there's a great deal more evidence besides.

THE BIG PICTURE

In 1978, a paper appeared in the *American Journal of Clinical Nutrition* authored by Dr Roland L. Phillips, one of America's most respected epidemiologists.[177] He and his team were interested in studying the dietary habits and health of Seventh-Day Adventists, whose church advocates a very different lifestyle from the typical meat-based American one. Dr Phillips' sample size was massive – 25,000 people. Obviously, the more people you study, the less likely it is that a few freak results are going to skew the analysis. In this case, the huge number of people involved makes the study very reliable indeed.

Every year, for six years, Dr Phillips' team would contact each one of those people, just to see if they were still alive. If the person concerned had died, their death certificate was obtained, and the underlying cause of death was determined. Patience and tact are two key qualities for a good epidemiologist! At the end of the six-year period, they had some highly significant results.

All the subjects were living in California. When compared to the average, meat-eating, Californian population, the results showed that the risk of dying from coronary heart disease among Adventists was far, far lower than normal.

For every 100 Californian males who died from heart disease, only twenty-six Adventist males had died – that's about one-quarter the risk. Among females, the risk was one-third. You can see this illustrated in Chart 18:

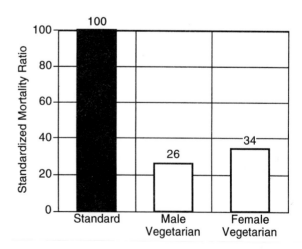

CHART 18:
DEATHS FROM HEART DISEASE: SEVENTH DAY ADVENTISTS
COMPARED TO THE GENERAL POPULATION

This is forceful evidence. It isn't theoretical, or hypothetical, or otherwise concocted. It is straightforward fact. Counting dead bodies is pretty convincing, even for the most hardened sceptics.

Now, the next question is: Why? Well one reason must be the fact that most Seventh-Day Adventists do not smoke. 'But,' say the sceptics, 'it's nothing to do with eating meat, it simply proves that smoking isn't healthy.' But that explanation doesn't hold up as Dr Phillips and his team had considered such possibilities. So they next compared deaths from heart disease amongst Seventh-Day Adventists to deaths from heart disease amongst a representative group of non-smokers, as studied by the American Cancer Society. Clearly, if Adventists were healthier purely because they didn't smoke, then deaths rates in these two groups should be the same.

But they weren't – not by a long chalk. The cold figures showed that Adventists had only half the risk of dying from heart disease, when compared to non-smokers (actually, people identified by the American Cancer Society as 'never having smoked'). So there clearly was something else very special about the Adventist lifestyle. What could it be? A determined opponent could throw up any number of possibilities to explain away these findings.

that about 20 per cent of them ate meat four or more times a week, about 35 per cent ate it between one and three times a week, and the remaining 45 per cent never ate it at all. So he simply compared the health of Adventists who never ate meat to those Adventists who did eat it.

You can see the result in Chart 19. Among Adventist men who ate meat, the death rate from coronary heart disease was 37 per cent of the normal death rate – impressive in itself, and certainly proof that smoking is pretty lethal. But among those Adventists who were vegetarian, the death rate plummeted even further – right down to 12 per cent that of the normal population.

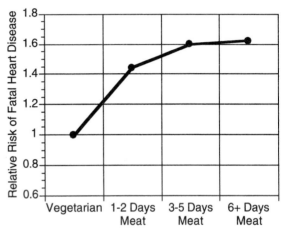

CHART 20: HOW MEAT EATING CORRELATED TO RISK OF FATAL HEART DISEASE (MEN)

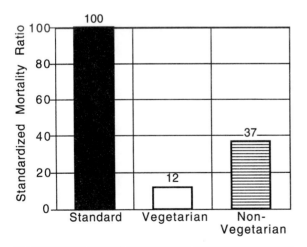

CHART 19: DEATHS FROM HEART DISEASE: SEVENTH DAY ADVENTIST VEGETARIANS COMPARED TO SEVENTH DAY ADVENTIST NON-VEGETARIANS

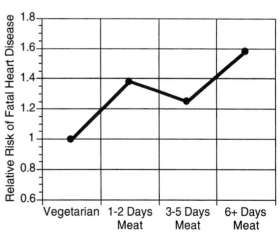

CHART 21: HOW MEAT EATING CORRELATED TO RISK OF FATAL HEART DISEASE (WOMEN)

Dr Phillips realised that, although the Adventist church advocated the vegetarian lifestyle, it wasn't compulsory. Some Adventists still ate meat. So he included that aspect in his research. And he found

One of the great things about large-scale studies such as this is the longer you are prepared to wait, the more interesting and more accurate the results become. Dr Phillips' team waited for twenty long years.

Eventually the final results of this study, which had literally observed people growing old and dying over two decades, were published.[178] This landmark study provided the first ever scientific proof that the more meat you eat, the more at risk you are from heart disease.

Look at Charts 20 and 21 and you'll see a summary of the results. Here, you can see that the relative risk of fatal heart disease closely correlates with the frequency of eating meat.

Those Adventist males who consumed meat on one or two days a week were 44 per cent more likely to die from heart disease. Those who consumed it between three and five times per week were 60 per cent more likely to die. And those who consumed it more than six times a week were 62 per cent more likely to die. For females, the increases are 38, 25 and 58 per cent respectively. The significant finding is that even a small amount of meat – once or twice a week – greatly elevates the risk. And for men in one particular age group – 45 to 54 – the risk is particularly high. For these people, prime candidates for heart disease, the risk when compared to vegetarians is 400 per cent greater!

A study amongst 4671 British vegetarians, which tracked their health (actually, tracked their cause of death) for seven years also found very similar conclusions.[179] The male vegetarians had 50 per cent the death rate from all causes compared to the general population; the females 55 per cent. For heart disease, the male death rate was only 44 per cent of normal, and for female vegetarians 41 per cent.

The study also compared the vegetarians to a similar population group – people who were customers of heathfood shops – and found that the healthfood shoppers were also at less risk from heart disease – 60 per cent of the normal. This probably reflected healthfood shoppers' greater interest in their own health. However, when comparing the two groups, it was obvious that the vegetarians had reduced their risk of heart disease by a further third compared to the healthfood shoppers.

In 'Curbing Cancer' (p117), we examined a major Japanese study which tracked the health of 122,261 people over 16 years.[180] Apart from showing that vegetarians cut their risk of all kinds of cancer by more than one half, this study also provided a large volume of high-quality data on deaths from heart disease. Remem-

ber, the scientists were particularly interested to discover the effects of four lifestyle components on mortality:

- smoking
- drinking alcohol
- eating meat
- eating green and yellow vegetables.

The findings confirmed the previous studies, and are shown graphically in Chart 22. The lowest-risk lifestyle was found to be people who don't smoke, drink alcohol or eat meat, but who do eat green and yellow vegetables.

The next group up the 'ladder of risk' were people who lived the same lifestyle except for smoking. Among this group, the risk of dying from ischemic heart disease was nearly one and half times that of the lowest-risk group. Further up again are people who also drink; for them, the risk is increased 1.7 times. Finally, at greatest risk of all of heart disease are those who smoke, drink, eat meat and don't eat vegetables. Compared to the lowest-risk group, they are nearly twice as likely to die from ischemic heart disease.

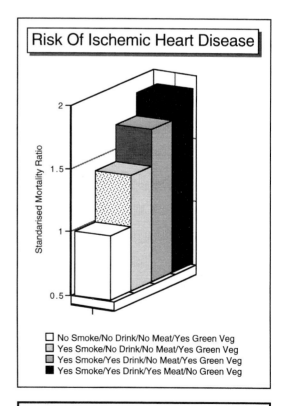

Risk Of Ischemic Heart Disease

Standarised Mortality Ratio

☐ No Smoke/No Drink/No Meat/Yes Green Veg
▨ Yes Smoke/No Drink/No Meat/Yes Green Veg
▩ Yes Smoke/Yes Drink/No Meat/Yes Green Veg
■ Yes Smoke/Yes Drink/Yes Meat/No Green Veg

**CHART 22: HOW THE ODDS ARE STACKED
AGAINST MEAT-EATERS**

Another interesting result of this study was scientists' ability to quantify the extra risk that eating meat confers upon an otherwise low-risk lifestyle. By computer-analysing all the causes of death, it was possible to calculate that the effect of meat consumption on a non-smoking, non-drinking, plenty of green vegetable lifestyle was to increase the risk of dying from heart disease by nearly 30 per cent.

These findings are corroborated by various other studies:

- Again from Britain, scientists recruited over 1000 vegetarians and 1000 meat-eaters and compared their health.[181] The meat-eaters served as the 'control' group, and were chosen from the family and friends of the vegetarians, so that other lifestyle factors would be as close as possible between the two groups. Blood was taken from each person in the study, and analysed. The reseachers found that the meat-eaters had the highest level of cholesterol in their blood, followed by the vegetarians and then the vegans. 'Our data confirm the findings of several other studies,' the scientists wrote, 'that lower concentrations of . . . cholesterol are found in vegetarians than in meat eaters.' By comparing cholesterol levels in the two groups measured, the researchers calculated the relative risks of heart disease, and concluded: 'Our data suggest that in Britain the incidence of coronary heart disease may be 20 per cent lower in lifelong vegetarians and 57 per cent lower in lifelong vegans than in meat-eaters.'

- The German Cancer Research Center investigation cited on page 125 also recorded deaths from heart disease.[182] They found that out of the group of nearly 2000 vegetarians, twenty-five of them would have been expected to die from ischemic heart disease – if they had the same mortality rate as equivalent non-vegetarian Germans. In reality, only five had died – meaning that the vegetarians had reduced their death rate to just 20 per cent that of meat-eaters.

- From Norway, a study was published in 1992 which had tracked the health – and cause of death – of vegetarian Seventh-Day Adventists from 1962 to 1986, an impressive twenty-four years.[183] It confirmed that their lifestyle was protective against heart disease – death rates were significantly lower than the general population: men had only 44 per cent the risk of heart disease, women 52 per cent.

The scientists found that the earlier in life the vegetarian diet was adopted, the lower the subsequent risk became.

The scientific and medical communities have generally responded to these and similar studies by asking the simple question: why? This has, in turn, spurred more research undertaken with the intention of pinpointing the precise reason for the considerably reduced risk of heart disease conferred on vegetarians and vegans. Many possible explanations have been put forward, but none of them are universally accepted or proven beyond doubt. Suggested factors include lower consumption of saturated fat, higher intake of fibre, and greater intake of protective nutritional factors such as beta-carotene, vitamin C and vitamin E.

One really has to question the ethical basis of some of this type of work. If it is established that a certain lifestyle considerably reduces the incidence of the Western world's major cause of death, surely the correct medical response should be to advocate those dietary changes at once, and start saving lives? Undertaking yet more research into every last detail of the process by which the meat-free lifestyle bestows protection is at best perfectionist, and at worst downright immoral. Countless lives could have been saved if our medical masters had not been so reticent to recommend vegetarianism to their patients.

Luckily for some people, a few scientists haven't been quite so reactionary.

THE BEST NEWS OF ALL

In recent years, irrefutable scientific evidence has emerged that a vegan diet can actually heal the damage inflicted on our clogged up arteries. It sounds too good to be true. But here is the proof.

In 1985, a very significant paper was published in the *New England Journal of Medicine*.[184] A team of scientists from the University of Leiden in the Netherlands studied a group of thirty-nine patients, all of whom suffered from angina, and all of whom had at least one blood vessel with 50 per cent blockage, as revealed by coronary arteriography. Then they put the patients on a vegetarian diet.

After two years, the scientists took further measurements. In twenty-one of the thirty-nine patients, the blockages had got worse. However, in eighteen patients things hadn't deteriorated. What was more, it was clear that the coronary lesion growth correlated with total/HDL cholesterol in the blood – the higher the total/HDL cholesterol ratio, the more the disease had progressed. By contrast, in those patients where the ratio was low, there was no progression. This evidence opened up a whole new line of tackling heart disease. First, Dr David Blankenhorn of the University of Southern California and Dr Greg Brown at the University of Washington both performed scientific trials which showed that the build-up of arterial plaque could be reversed – in some people – by a combination of drugs and a low-fat diet.[185]

Then, in 1990, a landmark paper was published in the *Lancet*. For the first time, scientists irrefutably proved that a vegetarian diet – without the assistance of medication or drugs – could be used to regress coronary heart disease.[186] The science was impeccable. The study was both randomized and controlled (meaning that patients were randomly assigned to either the experimental group, or to a control group who were used for comparison). Both groups had their coronary artery lesions carefully measured at the start of the study, and after one year.

The experimental group were asked to eat a low-fat vegetarian diet, consisting of fruits, vegetables, grains, legumes, and soya bean products and they were allowed to eat as much as they wanted to, no calorie counting was required. That's not even dieting by most people's standards!

No animal products were allowed except for egg white and a maximum of one serving per day of low-fat milk or yoghurt. The diet contained 10 per cent of its calories as fat, 15–20 per cent protein, and 70–75 per cent complex carbohydrate. No caffeine, very little alcohol. Relaxation was encouraged, and patients were asked to exercise for a total of three hours a week, even though at the beginning of the study, many participants suffered from such severe chest pain that they could barely walk across a room without resting.

After one year, blockages in the arteries of two-thirds of the control group (the group that hadn't followed the vegetarian diet) had worsened. But for eighteen of the twenty-two in the experimental group, the blockages had reduced in size, resulting in an increased blood flow to the heart. And the more severe blockages showed the most improvement.

Was this regression entirely due to a lowering of cholesterol? Dr Dean Ornish, leader of the team, doesn't think so. 'If lowering cholesterol were the primary factor in causing reversal of heart disease,' he says, 'most of the patients in the studies by Dr

Blankenhorn and Dr Brown who were taking cholesterol-lowering drugs should have shown reversal, since almost all of these patients had substantial decreases in blood-cholesterol levels. Yet only a minority showed reversal.'[187]

Once again, it strongly suggests that it is the totality of the vegan diet which can work this miraculous effect. 'Nutritional factors other than fat and cholesterol play a role in heart disease,' believes Dr Ornish. And one such may be beta-carotene (vitamin A). 'People who consume a low-fat vegetarian diet naturally consume not only beta-carotene', he explains, 'but other anti-oxidants that may play a role in preventing and reversing heart disease.'[188]

This pioneering work has since been confirmed by similar studies published in the *Lancet* and the *American Journal of Cardiology* in 1992.[189,190] If you, or a loved one, might benefit from this research, make sure you bring these studies to your doctor's attention.

HALTING HIGH BLOOD PRESSURE

WHAT IS HIGH BLOOD PRESSURE?

Hypertension is the medical name for high blood pressure, one of the key risk factors in the development of heart and cerebrovascular disease. The United Kingdom government estimate that over 240,000 people die every year as a result of a hypertension-related disease.[191] 33 per cent – one third – of all deaths that occur in people under sixty-five are attributable to hypertensive causes.

Blood pressure is measured by the height in millimetres of a column of mercury that can be raised inside a vacuum. The more pressure there is, the higher the column will rise. Since blood pressure varies with every heartbeat, two measures are taken; one that measures the pressure of the beat itself (called systolic blood pressure) and the other that measures the pressure in between beats, when the heart is resting (this is called diastolic blood pressure, and is the 'background' level). These two figures are written with the systolic figure first followed by the diastolic figure, like this – 120:80.

When we're born, our systolic blood pressure is about forty, then it doubles to about eighty within the first month. Thereafter, the increase is slower, but inexorable, for the rest of our lives. Many people do not realize they suffer from hypertension. There may be no symptoms, and it may only be discovered during a visit to the doctor's surgery for another complaint. In its later stages symptoms may include headache, dizziness, fatigue, and insomnia.

A pressure of 150:90 would be considered above average in a young person, and 160:95 would be abnormally high. In older people, systolic pressure could be 140 at age sixty, and 160 at age eighty years. Comparatively small changes in the pressure of those people who are in the 'at risk' category could have very worthwhile results. This was emphasized by a government report, which stated: 'It has been estimated that a relatively small reduction (2–3mm) in mean blood pressure in the population, if the distribution were to remain similar to the present distribution of blood pressures, would result in a major benefit in terms of mortality, and that a shift of this magnitude would be comparable to the benefit currently achieved by antihypertensive therapy. This estimated benefit seems applicable to mild as well as severe hypertension.'[192]

If a small change in the population's blood pressure could be as beneficial as all the drugs that people are now taking, then what are we waiting for?

HOW THE VEGETARIAN DIET CAN HELP

Scientists have known for a long time that some populations are apparently 'immune' from hypertension, and do not display the rise in blood pressure that is associated in the West with getting older. These populations generally tend to have a high level of physical activity, are not overweight, have a low level of animal fat in their diet, and don't take much salt (sodium) in their food. In other words, hypertension seems to be an illness of our Western way of life.

As long ago as 1926, it was experimentally shown that certain dietary components could be connected to hypertension. In that year, a pioneering Californian study had shown that the blood pressure of non-meat-using people could be raised – by as much as 10 per cent – in just two weeks of eating a diet that centred around meat.[193] Subsequent experiments have confirmed this effect. One was undertaken in Australia, where two groups of people were selected, one of which regularly ate meat in their diets, and the other didn't.[194] The results were extremely significant, summarized in Chart 23:

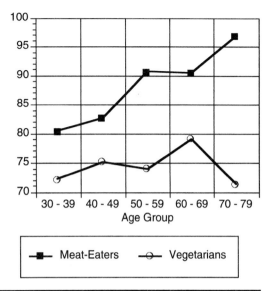

CHART 23: VEGETARIANS' DIASTOLIC BLOOD PRESSURE
COMPARED TO MEAT-EATERS'

The top line charts the blood pressure of the meat-eaters. The bottom line shows the non-meat-eaters, and the bottom axis shows the five age groups that were surveyed. You can see that, at all ages, blood pressure is significantly lower in the non-meat-eaters. Amongst the meat-eaters, there is a steady rise in blood pressure with advancing age. But amongst the non-meat eaters there is very little increase – and, in fact, a surprising drop in blood pressure in the oldest age group. These results were adjusted to exclude other factors such as exercise, tea, coffee or alcohol consumption.

Another study was carried out in Britain, and again compared the blood pressure levels in people who didn't eat meat to those who did.[195] The results showed exactly the same pattern. This was true in men as well as women. Chart 24 shows the mean results that were obtained:

The meat-eaters are shown in black, and non-meat users are shaded. The difference in the 'underlying' blood pressure (diastolic), which is generally thought to be a better guide to the real health of the individual, is considerable. On average, diastolic blood pressure was 15 per cent less in the non-meat-eaters compared to the meat-eaters.

In another study, a group of 115 vegetarians were compared to a similar group of 115 meat-eaters – closely matched to the vegetarians apart from diet.[196] The results demonstrated that systolic blood pressure of the vegetarians was 9.3 per cent lower than the meat-eaters, and diastolic pressure a massive 18.2 per cent lower.

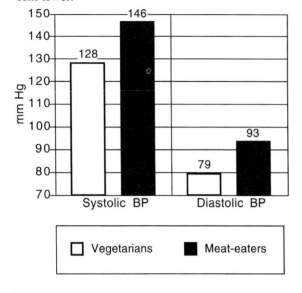

CHART 24: MEAT-EATERS UNDER PRESSURE

In America, a vegetarian diet was devised which included much fibre from whole grain cereals, bran cereals, whole grain breads, vegetables, beans and pulses.[197] Interestingly, the group put on this diet was allowed to use as much salt in their food as they wanted to. This group was then compared to a standard 'control' group, who carried on eating normally. The average blood pressure of the men on the plant fibre diet was 10 per cent lower than the control group.

A recent 'crossover' trial has confirmed the results of the original 1926 study.[198] Fifty-eight patients aged between thirty and sixty-four with mild untreated hypertension were put onto an ovo-lacto-vegetarian diet (including dairy products and eggs). Within a few weeks the average systolic blood pressure dropped by 5mm. When they started to eat meat again, it rose by the same amount – very clear evidence that the meat element of the diet was responsible for the improvement.

We know – from studies such as those mentioned above – that vegetarians generally exhibit lower blood pressure than meat-eaters. But can a vegetarian diet also be used to treat high blood pressure? The evidence clearly shows it can.

Scientists at the Royal Perth Hospital in Australia found that people with high blood pressure could

indeed reduce it, on a vegetarian diet.[199] They wrote: 'If the usual aim of treatment of mild hypertensives is to reduce systolic blood pressure to below 140mmHg then 30 per cent of those eating a meat-free diet achieved this criteria compared with only 8 per cent on their usual diet.' They concluded by suggesting that, if drug therapy was required by a hypertensive, it might also be worthwhile to consider modifying the diet.

Another persuasive case for a vegetarian diet to help hypertensives comes from a year-long study in Sweden, where there is a strong tradition of using dietary means to prevent or cure a number of diseases, including hypertension.[200] All the twenty-six subjects had a history of high blood pressure, on average for eight years. They were all receiving medication, but even so, eight of the group had excessively high readings (more than 165:95). Many of the patients complained of such symptoms as headache, dizziness, tiredness, and chest pains; symptoms which were either due to the disease or the medication they happened to be taking. They were then put on a vegan diet, from which coffee, tea, sugar, salt, chocolate and chlorinated tap water were eliminated. Their fresh fruit and vegetables had to be organic, if possible. When their diets were analyzed, it was found that they were higher in vitamins and minerals than most people on a meat diet.

'With the exception of a few essential medicines (for example, insulin),' wrote the scientists, 'patients were encouraged to give up medicines when they felt that these were no longer needed. Thus, analgesics were dispensed with in the absence of pain, tranquillizers when anxiety was not experienced and sleep was sound, and antihypertensive medication when the blood pressure was normal.'

The results were certainly impressive. First of all, the patients simply felt much healthier. None of them said that the treatment had left them unchanged or made them feel worse, and 15 per cent said they felt 'better'. Over 50 per cent of them said they felt 'much better', and 30 per cent said they felt 'completely recovered'. Reductions in blood pressure ranged from 7–9mm (systolic) and 5–10mm (diastolic). 'When the decrease in blood pressure was considered for the entire group,' the scientists wrote, 'it was found that it occurred at the time when most of the medicines were withdrawn. Of the twenty-six patients, twenty had given up their medication completely after one year while six still took some medicine, although the dose was lower, usually halved.' Several other sorts of benefits were found, as well. Their blood cholesterol levels was found to have dropped an average of 15 per cent. And the health authorities computed that they had saved £1000 per patient over the year, by reducing the costs of drugs and hospitalization.

Many studies have tried to identify the one, single factor which makes the vegetarian diet beneficial for blood pressure, but the evidence so far shows that neither polyunsaturated fat, saturated fat, cholesterol, potassium, magnesium, sodium, or total protein intake are independently responsible for this effect.[201] Again, we are forced to come back to the position that it is the *totality* of the vegetarian diet that is beneficial, and no single component. Hypertension is sometimes prefixed with the word 'essential', which rather confusingly means that the cause is of it is not known. The studies above, and many others, give us convincing proof that a vegetarian diet can offer vital assistance in preventing, and treating, this modern silent killer.

WHAT ELSE YOU CAN DO

A diagnosis of high blood pressure is not a death sentence. There is a lot you can do to bring it down – providing you are willing to try seriously. Much research now clearly shows that many hypertensives can lower their blood pressure by amending their lifestyle and dietary habits.

- Get to understand your own blood pressure. A device which measures blood pressure is called a 'sphygmomanometer', and consists of an inflatable cuff that is wrapped around the arm, connected via a tube to the measuring device. Simple sphygmomanometers are quite cheap, and it could be worth buying one and tracking your blood pressure as it rises and falls over a period of time. Blood pressure fluctuates considerably even in normal individuals – the reading taken at the doctor's surgery won't be the same as the one when you're at home later in the day. Physical activity, excitement, fear, or emotional stress can all send it shooting up. When you understand how your blood pressure changes, you're on the way to controlling it.
- One recent study has found that as many as 20 per cent of patients treated for hypertension could be receiving unnecessary medication, simply because their blood pressure rises in the presence of a doctor. They coined the term 'white coat hypertension' for this phenomenon.[202] With your own sphygmomanometer, you'll be able to rule this out.
- Normalize your weight. Most hypertensives are overweight, yet a 20lb reduction in weight can result in a blood pressure reduction of 20mmHg systolic and 10mmHg diastolic.[203]
- Reduce or avoid alcohol consumption. Most long-term studies have shown that blood pressure can be significantly reduced by cutting out or cutting down on the amount of alcohol consumed. For example, one study shows that among women taking more than two alcoholic drinks per day, one third of all cases of hypertension are caused by alcohol consumption. This suggests that hypertension in these women may be treatable by restriction of alcohol intake.[204]
- Stop smoking. Nicotine stimulates the heart and at the same time constricts the blood vessels – making it difficult for your blood pressure not to rise! If you are a man with high blood pressure and you smoke you are 3.5 times more likely to develop cardiovascular disease than if you were a healthy non-smoker.
- Learn to relax and start to take exercise. Both of these activities help you to feel more in control of your body and your life.
- Consider a drastic change at work. People in demanding jobs with little freedom to make decisions have three times the risk of developing high blood pressure compared to others who have either a less-demanding job or more decision-making latitude.[205]
- Adjust your sodium and potassium intake. Both of these minerals are salts (sodium is table salt) which regulate the balance of fluid in your body. An excess of sodium increases the volume of blood which puts more strain on the circulatory system, causing high blood pressure. Thus sodium has been blamed for many cases of hypertension. However, it is now shown that potassium can protect you from hypertension because it balances the effects of sodium.[206]
- You can reduce your intake of sodium and increase your intake of potassium by limiting the amount of processed foods you eat – these are high in sodium and low in potassium. Instead, eat potassium-rich foods such as avocado, banana, broccoli, brussels sprouts, dates, prunes and raisins. Jacket potatoes and cantaloupes are also good sources.
- Increase your intake of magnesium. This mineral is

lost when you take diuretics – often prescribed for hypertensives. Yet 50 per cent of magnesium-deficient patients have high blood pressure, usually normalizing when this deficiency is rectified. Foods rich in magnesium include green vegetables, nuts, whole grains and yeast extracts.[207]

- Boost your calcium intake. It has been found that people with high blood pressure often have low levels of calcium.[208] In one study, researchers demonstrated a 23 per cent decrease in hypertension risk among women receiving 800mg a day of calcium, compared with women consuming just 400mg a day.[209] Foods rich in calcium include tofu, spinach, figs, molasses, seaweeds, nuts and seeds, watercress and parsley.

- Consider taking a selenium supplement. Although its role is not yet fully known, selenium may act to prevent hypertension caused by cadmium. Cadmium is a heavy metal which raises blood pressure; it comes from some water pipes, pollution, car exhaust and smoking. Dr Raymond Shamberger and Dr Charles E. Willis, of the Cleveland Clinic, Ohio, conducted an epidemiological study which has shown that people living in an area where the soil has a low concentration of selenium are three times more likely to die from hypertension-related diseases than people who live where the selenium level in the soil (and hence in the food they eat) is higher. 'We don't known selenium's precise action concerning high blood pressure,' said Dr Shamberger, 'but our study strongly suggests that it has a beneficial effect on high blood pressure problems in man.'[210]

MUZZLING MULTIPLE SCLEROSIS

WHAT IS MULTIPLE SCLEROSIS?

Multiple sclerosis (MS) is a degenerative disease of the central nervous system. In the course of the disease, myelin (which is a white, fatty substance that acts as an electrical insulator for the nerves) is progressively destroyed, and the formation of hard scar tissue on the protective myelin sheath which surrounds nerves stops the nerve cells from working. This scarring results in permanent loss of nervous control to areas of the body. MS is a crippling disease which attacks every body function; and with time it can be fatal. It affects both men and women, usually first being diagnosed between the ages of twenty and forty.

The cause of multiple sclerosis remains problematic. Literally dozens of explanations have been suggested over the years. A great deal of research has gone into investigating the possibility that MS is caused by a virus, although to date, it has not proved possible to pinpoint precisely which one. Similarly, it has long been suspected that MS is an autoimmune disease, a sort of allergic reaction in which the body responds to an antigen by acting against itself. Again, pinpointing the antigen in question has proved difficult. Yet another theory proposes that giving cow's milk to infants predisposes them to nervous system injury later in life, because cow's milk has only a fifth as much linoleic acid (an essential fatty acid) as human breast milk, and linoleic acid makes up the building blocks for nervous tissues.[211] The list could go on and on. But while waiting for conclusive proof of cause, it is possible to deal with multiple sclerosis so as to minimize its crippling effect and, perhaps, prolong life.

HOW THE VEGETARIAN DIET CAN HELP

Most health professionals have tradtionally dismissed the idea that multiple sclerosis might be linked to diet. However, Dr Roy Swank, former Professor of Neurology at the University of Oregon, was intrigued by some wartime research. During World War II, the consumption of animal fat decreased in western Europe. Meat and dairy products were rationed, and instead, consumption of grains and vegetables increased. It was noticed at this time that patients with MS had two to two-and-a-half times fewer hospitalizations during the war years, when saturated fat consumption was low.[212] Greatly excited by the possible implication of these findings, Dr Swank began treating his own patients with a low fat diet. Over the next 35 years, he treated thousands of MS patients in this way. By any medical standards his results have been remarkable: and many of his success stories were told in a book published in 1977.[213] Patients generally fared better if the condition was detected early, but even long-time MS sufferers experienced a slowing of the disease's progression. The basics of Dr Swank's diet are:

- no more than 10 grams saturated fat per day
- 40–50g of polyunsaturated fat (but *not* margarine or other hydrogenated fats)
- at least 1 tsp cod liver oil daily
- no animal foods (although fish was consumed three times a week).[214]

Protein intake should be kept up with a good supply of mixed vegetable proteins. The long-term results of the Swank diet show that of those who ate less than 20g of fat per day, only 31 per cent have died (close to normal) and the condition of the rest has deteriorated only slightly. Of those who ate more than 20g, 81 percent have died.[215, 216, 217] However, many orthodox medical practitioners are still very wary of accepting such evidence. An editorial in the *Lancet* recently stated, 'There are still no firm answers as to whether a relationship [between MS and dietary fats] does indeed exist and if so, what its mechanism might be . . . more work is needed at the biochemical level . . . Until such studies are undertaken, the role of lipids in MS cannot be said to be proven.'[218] Yet, in the words of another doctor who uses the Swank diet to treat patients: 'I've been very gratified by the results of this dietary treatment, not only because the progress of most of my MS patients' disease has been halted, but also because their overall health has unquestionably improved.'[219]

OBSTRUCTING OSTEOPOROSIS

WHAT IS OSTEOPOROSIS?

The word literally means 'porous bones'. If you are a woman, by the time you are sixty, there is a one in four chance that osteoporosis will have caused you to break a bone.[220] And more than 10 per cent of people who suffer a hip fracture caused by osteoporosis will die.[221] Both men and women *can* suffer from osteoporosis, but it is rarer in men – one estimate is that only one in forty men are ever diagnosed as having it.[222] Oriental and Caucasian women are most at risk due to their tendency to have thinner, lighter bones. Women of African, Mediterranean or Aboriginal extraction are less likely to suffer. You may not even realize that you suffer from it until you suddenly break a bone – by which time, the harm has been done. Other telltale

signs can include severe back pain, loss of height or deformities such as a curvature of the spine. It is estimated that more than 50,000 women fracture their hip each year due to osteoporosis.[223] And the number of deaths from fractured hips is greater than the number of deaths from cancers of the cervix, uterus and breast combined[224] – which makes osteoporosis one of the major killers of our time.

Osteoporosis is caused by a slow loss of bone mass. By the age of thirty-five or so, your bones will be as strong as they're ever likely to be. Hormones in our bodies are responsible for continuously balancing the growth of new bone with the reabsorption of old bone. When levels of these hormones fall significantly, as happens in menopause, this balance is lost and a gradual loss of bone mass occurs. Eventually, the bones can become very brittle and break easily. In some women this process is sufficiently slow to avoid fractures, pain and loss of height. In others, however, the loss is rapid – some women can lose up to half of their bone mass within ten or so years of menopause, leaving them very vulnerable to easy fracture. Since it is clear that oestrogen, the female sex hormone, plays a protective role in the maintainence of bone mass, one current treatment for women suffering from osteoporosis is Hormone Replacement Therapy (HRT). HRT provides your body with a supplement of several hormones, including the female hormone oestrogen. HRT has a number of very worthwhile advantages:

- it slows down the loss of bone mineral content, so decreasing the likelihood of fractures of the spine, hips and wrists
- it prevents loss of height
- it lowers LDL cholesterol in your blood and increases HDL cholesterol, thus prolonging life expectancy by decreasing the risk of heart disease
- it decreases hot flushes, increases sex drive and prevents vaginal dryness
- it decreases the risk of ovarian cancer.[225]

On the other hand, concerns have been expressed about its long-term safety (as they have for the oestrogen-based contraceptive pill). Although many women – and some doctors – are concerned about an increased risk of cancer from HRT, most of the scientific evidence does not confirm these worries. While some studies do indeed show that oestrogen therapy may increase the risk of developing cancer,[226] today's HRT includes other hormones (progestogens) which studies show can actually reduce the cancer risk quite appreciably.[227, 228] This is an area of ongoing research, and it is worth keeping up to date with the latest findings. There are, however, some problems associated with HRT, as with all drugs. These can sometimes include breast soreness, gallstones, weight gain, return of periods, and breakthrough bleeding.

IS MILK THE ANSWER?

Osteoporosis first hit the headlines in 1984, when the US National Institutes of Health issued an advisory paper stating that women should increase their intake of calcium to prevent osteoporosis. The demand for calcium supplements suddenly hit the roof. And the dairy industry wasn't slow to appreciate the potential for increased sales. Since milk contains plenty of calcium (just the right amount for a fast-growing calf, not necessarily so right for humans) they clearly had a hit on their hands. So, with the help of the vast promotional resources of the dairy industry, the public quickly perceived that:

1) osteoporosis is caused by a lack of calcium in the diet;
2) milk contains oodles of calcium;
3) therefore you should gulp gallons of milk to avoid osteoporosis.

On the face of it, it all sounds very plausible. Since osteoporosis is caused by a slow loss of bone mass, a heavy dose of calcium should put things right again, shouldn't it? The answer is no. Although the theory 'has an intuitive appeal', an article in the *British Medical Journal* states, 'the logic is similar to that which might lead doctors to give ground-up brains for dementia.'[229]

Nevertheless, many people now seem to believe that a large intake of dairy produce will safeguard them against this crippling condition. And the myths abound, as plentifully as ever. Take this piece of advice taken from a recent article in a healthfood magazine: 'Vegetarians who do not use dairy products or take supplements are especially at risk in developing osteoporosis, either because they do not get sufficient amounts of nutrients from their diet or do not absorb the nutrients properly.'[230]

Meanwhile, the recommended intakes for calcium continue to skyrocket – up to 3000mg (3g) a day, in some cases.[231] Now to get this amount of calcium from dairy produce, you'd have to drink ten glasses of milk a day, which – even assuming you drank low-fat milk – would also give you a very unhealthy 180mg of cholesterol and 30g of saturated fat.[232] Alternatively, you could munch your way through 1lb of cheddar cheese, which would also give you a whacking 150g of fat, most of it saturated![233]

The fact is, you don't need to drink milk to prevent osteoporosis. For example, most Chinese consume no dairy products at all and instead get all their calcium from vegetables. While the Chinese consume only half the dietary calcium Westerners do, osteoporosis is uncommon in China despite an average life expectancy of seventy years. 'Osteoporosis tends to occur in countries where calcium intake is highest and most of it comes from protein-rich dairy products,' says Dr T. Colin Campbell, a nutritional biochemist from Cornell University and the American authority behind the famous 'China study.' 'The Chinese data indicate that people need less calcium than we think and can get adequate amounts from vegetables.'[234]

At the other end of the scale, the Eskimo population is known to have the highest dietary calcium intake in the world (over 2000mg a day, mainly from fish bones), yet they also have one of the highest rates of osteoporosis in the world.[235]

Clearly, we haven't been given the full picture.

HOW THE VEGETARIAN DIET CAN HELP

Says dietary reformer Nathan Pritikin: 'African Bantu women take in only 350mg of calcium per day. They bear nine children during their lifetime and breast-feed them for two years. They never have calcium deficiency, seldom break a bone, rarely lose a tooth. Their children grow up nice and strong. How can they do that on 350mg of calcium a day when the recommendation is 1200mg? It's very simple. They're on a low-protein diet that doesn't kick the calcium out of the body . . . In our country (America), those who can afford it are eating 20 per cent of their total calories in protein, which guarantees negative mineral balance, not only of calcium, but of magnesium, zinc, and iron. It's all directly related to the amount of protein you eat.'[236]

Now we're getting to the truth of the matter. In fact, the difference in bone loss between vegetarians and meat-eaters can be explained by several factors:

- As Pritikin says, the more protein you consume, the more it 'kicks the calcium out of the body'. Since the 1920s scientists have known that diets that are high in protein cause calcium to be lost through the urine.[237] In one typical study, young men were fed experimental diets whose protein content ranged from 48g a day right up to 141g a day. It was found that the higher level of protein consumption doubled the urinary excretion of calcium.[238] And a diet that is high in animal protein – as opposed to vegetable proteins – particularly increases this effect.[239] Scientists believe that flesh foods cause an acid load in the body, which must be neutralized by a release of calcium stored in bones.[240]
- It has recently been found that boron, a trace mineral, helps to prevent calcium loss and subsequent loss of bone mass. It is also thought to help in the manufacture of vitamin D in the body. The first study to look at the nutritional effects of boron in humans took place in 1987.[241] Twelve post-menopausal women were fed a diet very low in boron for seventeen weeks, after which they were given a daily supplement of 3mg for a further seven weeks. The addition of boron had a dramatic effect – the women lost 40 per cent less calcium and 30 per cent less magnesium through their urine. The study therefore concluded that boron can reduce bodily losses of elements necessary to maintain bone integrity and to prevent osteoporosis. Nutritionist Forrest Nielsen, director of the US Department of Agriculture's Human Nutrition Research Center, called it 'a remarkable effect'.[242]

What was even more extraordinary was the discovery that boron could double the most active form of oestrogen (oestradiol 17B) in the blood of the women – their estradiol levels actually equalled those of women on oestrogen replacement therapy. Curtiss Hunt, of the US Human Nutrition Research Centre, said he 'suspects the body needs boron to synthesise estrogen, vitamin D and other steroid hormones. And it may protect these hormones against rapid breakdown'. He also suggested that boron could be important in treating many other diseases of 'unknown cause including some forms of arthritis'. And where can you get boron from? Why, by eating apples, pears, grapes, nuts, leafy vegetables and legumes – in other words, a healthy vegetarian diet (one medium-sized apple contains approximately 1mg of boron; researchers suggest our boron requirement

is in the region of one or two mg a day).[243]

These two important facts, and probably more yet to be discovered, are reflected in the results of a recent study performed by scientists from Andrews University, Michigan.[244] They used a sophisticated technique called direct photon absorptiometry to compare the bone mass of vegetarians to meat-eaters. After studying a group of 1600 women, they found:

- by the time they reached eighty, women who had eaten a vegetarian diet for at least twenty years had only lost an average of 18 per cent of their bone mineral;
- on the other hand, women who did not eat a vegetarian diet had lost an average of 35 per cent of their bone mineral.

Interestingly, there was no statistical difference in the nutrient intakes between the two groups – in other words, the vegetarian's advantage was *not* due to increased calcium intake.

Just a word to the wise.

WHAT ELSE CAN YOU DO?

- Get enough exercise. Especially important are forms of exercise that are weight-bearing such as walking, dancing, running and many sports. Swimming and chess playing, for instance, are *not* weight-bearing exercises. Proper exercise exerts the muscles around your bones stimulating them to maintain bone density. Leading a sedentary life will increase the likelihood of osteoporosis developing later in your life.
- Avoid smoking, caffeine and excess alcohol – all these can increase your risk of suffering from osteoporosis.[245] A study of women aged thirty-six to forty-five found that those who drank two cups of coffee a day suffered a net calcium loss of 22mg daily. The authors concluded that negative calcium balance of 40mg a day (ie about four cups of coffee) was enough to explain the 1 to 1.5 per cent loss in skeletal mass in post-menopausal women each year.[246]
- Get regular doses of sunlight. Sunlight reacts with a substance in your skin – dehydrocholesterol – to produce vitamin D. This vitamin is essential to the proper absorption of calcium and a deficiency will cause you to lose bone mass. Most people get

enough vitamin D just by being outside for part of the day with their face, hands and arms exposed.[247]

- Several commonly used drugs can induce significant calcium loss, particularly aluminium-containing antacids. If these antacids are used for prolonged periods of time, they may produce bone abnormalities by interfering with calcium and phosphorous metabolism, and so contribute to the development of osteoporosis.[248] So if you must use an antacid, choose one which does not include aluminium in its ingredients.
- Vitamin B complex, vitamin K and magnesium are all believed to play a role in the prevention of osteoporosis. The B group is available in brewer's yeast, whole grains, molasses, nuts and seeds and dark green leafy vegetables. Vitamin K is present in cauliflower, soyabeans, molasses, safflower oil and, again, dark green leafy vegetables. Magnesium is a constituent of chlorophyll and so is abundant in green vegetables. Other excellent sources are whole grains, wheatgerm, molasses, seeds and nuts, apples and figs.
- If you want to take a calcium supplement, consider calcium carbonate, because of its high content of calcium (40 per cent) and low price.

Footnotes

1 UN Population Division calculations

2 *Social Trends 20*, Central Statistical Office (HMSO, 1990)

3 *World Resources*, World Resources Institute (Oxford University Press, 1992)

4 Personal communication, Campaign for Nuclear Disarmament, 1994

5 A. Tomkins and F. Watson, Malnutrition and infection: a review, *Nutrition Policy Discussion Paper No. 5*, United Nations Administrative Committee on Coordination, Subcommittee on Nutrition, 1989

6 Personal communication, Government's Actuary Department, 1994

7 *General Household Survey 1990/91*, Office of Population Censuses and Surveys, Social Survey Division (HMSO, London)

8 *UPI*, 17 February 1988

9 Dr Joe Collier, *The Health Conspiracy* (Century, 1989)

10 *The Associated Press*, 19 July 1993

11 'Your Genome In Their Hands', *New Scientist*, 1990, no1729, p52

12 V. Coleman, *The Health Scandal* (Sidgwick & Jackson, 1988)

13 W. S. Collens, Atherosclerotic disease: an anthropologic theory, *Medical Counterpoint*, Dec 1969, 1, pp53–57

14 N. S. Scrimshaw, 'Iron deficiency', *Scientific American*, Oct 1991, vol265, no4, p46(7)

15 S. A. Barber, N. L. Bull, D. H. Buss, 'Low iron intakes among young women in Britain' *British Medical Journal*, 290, 9 March 1985, pp743–4

16 *Dietary Reference Values for Food Energy and Nutrients for the United Kingdom* (Department of Health, 1991)

17 T. A. Sanders, F. R. Ellis, J. W. Dickerson, 'Haematological studies on vegans', *Br J Nutr*, Jul 1978, 40 (1), pp9–15

18 Suzanne Havala, R.D. and Johanna Dwyer, D.SC., R.D. 'Position of the American Dietetic Association: Vegetarian Diets – technical support paper, *Journal of the American Dietetic Association*, March 1988, vol88, no3, pp352–355.

19 E. Carlson, M. Kipps, A. Lockie, J. J. Thompson, 'A comparative evaluation of vegan, vegetarian and omnivore diets', *Plant Foods*, 6 (1985), pp89–100

20 S. K. Rana and T. A. Sanders, 'Taurine concentrations in the diet, plasma, urine and breast milk of vegans compared with omnivores' *Br J Nutr*, Jul 1986, 56 (1), pp17–27

21 T. A. Sanders and T. J. Key, 'Blood pressure, plasma renin activity and aldosterone concentrations in vegans and omnivore controls', *Hum Nutr Appl Nutr*, Jun 1987, 41 (3), pp204–11

22 N. Levin, J. Rattan, T. Gilat, 'Mineral intake and blood levels in vegetarians', *Isr J Med Sci*, Feb 1986, 22 (2), pp105–8

23 W. A. van Staveron, J. H. Dhuyvetter, A. Bons, M. Zeelen, J. G. Hautvast, 'Food consumption and height/weight status of Dutch preschool children on alternative diets' *J Am Diet Assoc*, Dec 1985, 85 (12), pp1579–84

24 M. Abdulla, I. Andersson, N. G. Asp, K. Berthelsen, D. Birkhead, I. Dencker, C. G. Johansson, M. Jagerstad, K. Kolar, B. M. Nair, P. Nilsson-

Ehle, A. Norden, S. Rassner, B. Akesson, P. A. Ockerman, 'Nutrient intake and health status of vegans. Chemical analyses of diets using the duplicate portion sampling technique', *Am J Clin Nutr*, Nov 1981, 34 (11), pp2464–77

25 B. M. Anderson, R. S. Gibson, J. H. Sabry, 'The iron and zinc status of long-term vegetarian women', *Am J Clin Nutr*, Jun 1981, 34 (6), pp1042–8

26 J. R. Hunt, B. S. Hoverson, L. K. Johnson, 'Low or high meat consumption: effects on triglycerides, HDL cholesterol and indices of iron nutriture in postmenopausal women', *Proc. Am Diet Assn 76th AGM*, 25–28 October, 1993

27 MEDLINE® database produced by the US National Library of Medicine

28 S. Seshardri, A. Shah, S. Bhade, 'Haematologic response of anaemic preschool children to ascorbic acid supplementation', *Hum Nutr Appl Nutr*, Apr 1985, 39 (2), pp151–4

29 Thomas Emery, *Iron And Your Health: Facts And Fallacies* (CRC Press, Boston, 1991)

30 *Good Medicine*, Winter 1993 Physicians Committee for Responsible Medicine, Washington DC

31 J. T. Salonen, K. Nyyssonen, H. Korpela, J. Tuomilehto, R. Seppanen, R. Salonen, 'High stored iron levels are associated with excess risk of myocardial infarction in eastern Finnish men' *Circulation*, Sep 1992, 86 (3), pp803–11

32 *The Associated Press*, 18 February 1993

33 *UPI*, 8 October 1993

34 A. M. Thrash and C. L. Thrash, *Nutrition For Vegetarians* (1982)

35 *Vegetarian Times*, Dec 1992, no 184, pp56(6)

36 *Dietary Reference Values for Food Energy and Nutrients for the United Kingdom*, Department of Health, 1991

37 L. Beilin, 'Strategies and difficulties in dietary intervention in myocardial infarction patients', *Clin Exp Hypertens* [A], 1992, 14 (1-2), pp213–21

38 N. Barnard, *Food for Life* (Harmony Books, 1993)

39 The University of California, *Berkeley Wellness Letter*, May 1990, vol6, no8, p1(2)

40 O. Adam, 'Ernahrung als adjuvante Therapie bei chronischer Polyarthritis', *Z Rheumatol*, Sep–Oct 1993, 52 (5), pp275–80

41 Lars Skoldstam, 'Fasting and Vegan Diet in Rheumatoid Arthritis', *Scand J Rheumatology*, 1986, 15, pp219–223

42 R. S. Panush, R. M. Stroud, E. M. Webster, 'Food-induced (allergic) arthritis. Inflammatory arthritis exacerbated by milk', *Arthritis Rheum*, Feb 1986, 29 (2), pp220–6

43 'Controlled trial of fasting and one-year vegetarian diet in rheumatoid arthritis' *The Lancet*, 12 Oct 1991, 338 (8772), pp899–902

44 *The Independent*, 7 January 1992

45 *The Guardian*, 1 March 1986

46 D. Sorbel and A. Klein, *Arthritis: What Works* (St. Martin's Press)

47 The work of Dr Alan Ebringer, Department of Rheumatology, Middlesex Hospital and Immunologist at King's College, London

48 Norman Childers and G. M. Russo,*The Nightshades and Health* (Horticulture Publications, Somerville, New Jersey, 1973)

49 Raympiid Shatin, M.D., Alfred Hospital, Melbourne, Florida as reported in *Bestways*, September 1989, vol17, no9, p42(2)

50 R. Bingham, R. Bellew, J. G. Bellew, 'Yucca plant saponin in the management of arthritis', *J Applied Nutr*, 1975, 27, pp45–50

51 *The Associated Press*, 12 August 1993

52 *The Associated Press*, 2 October 1992

53 *Panorama*, BBC1, 14 February 1994

54 A. Shabbah, 'L'allergie alimentaire dans l'asthme de l'enfant', *Allerg Immunol*, Oct 1990, 22 (8), pp325–31

55 O. Lindahl, L. Lindwall, A. Spangberg, A. Stenram, P. A. Ockerman, 'Vegan regimen with reduced medication in the treatment of bronchial asthma', *J Asthma*, 1985, 22 (1), pp45–55

56 S. E. Dahlen, G. Hansson. P. Hedqvist *et al.*, 'Allergen challenge of lung tissue from asthmatics elicits bronchial contraction that correlates with the release of leukotrienes C4 D4 E4' *Proc Natl Acad Sci*, 1983:80, pp1712–16

57 J. P. Arm and T. H. Lee, 'The use of fish oil in bronchial asthma', *Allergy Proc*, May-Jun 1989, 10 (3), pp185–7

58 C. M. Kirsch, D. G. Payan, M. Y. Wong, J. G. Dohlman, V. A. Blake, M. A. Petri, J. Offenberger, E. J. Goetzl, W. M. Gold, 'Effect of eicosapentaenoic acid in asthma', *Clin Allergy*, Mar 1988, 18 (2), pp177–87

59 C. Picado, J. A. Castillo, N. Schinca, M. Pujades, A. Ordinas, A. Coronas, A. Agusti-Vidal, 'Effects of a fish oil enriched diet on aspirin intolerant asthmatic patients: a pilot study', *Thorax*, Feb 1988, 43 (2), pp93–7

60 R. D. Reynolds and C. L. Natta, 'Depressed plasma pyridoxal phosphate concentrations in adult asthmatics,' *Am J Clin Nutr*, 1985:41, pp684–8

61 L. Pauling, *How to Live Longer and Feel Better* (Avon Books, New York 1987)

62 C. S. Ogilvy, J. D. Douglas, M. Tabatabai, M. Dubois, 'Ascorbic acid reverses bronchconstriction caused by methacholine aerosol in man', *Physiologist*, 1978:21, p86

63 C. O. Anah, L. N. Jarike, H. A. Baig 'High dose ascorbic acid in Nigerian asthmatics' *Trop Geog Med*, 1980:32, pp132–137

64 M. Bricklin, *Practical Encyclopedia of Natural Healing* (Rodale Press, 1983)

65 D. H. Allen, J. Delohery, G. Baker, 'Monosodium L-glutamate-induced asthma', *J Allergy Clin Immunol*, Oct 1987, 80 (4), pp530–7

66 *The Associated Press*, 19 June 1992

67 B. Bausela, M. Martin Esteban, F. Martinez Alzamora, C. Pascual Marcos, J. A. Ojeda Casas, 'Egg protein sensitization in patients with bird feather allergy', *Allergy*, Nov 1991, 46 (8), pp614–8

68 N. Singh, V. Wisniewski, J. Britton, A. Tattersfield, 'Effect of yoga breathing exercises (pranayama) on airway reactivity in subjects with asthma', *The Lancet*, June 9, 1990, vol335, no8702, pp1381(3)

69 *The Lancet*, 24 August 1990

70 *Facts on File*, June 10, 1988

71 *Childhood Cancer UK* factsheet 15.1, Cancer Research Campaign, 1990

72 National Cancer Institute / The Associated Press, 25 September 1992 and J. Brady (ed.), *1 In 3: Women With Cancer Confront an Epidemic* (Cleis Press, 1992)

73 J. Higson and C. S. Muir, 'Environmental Carcinogenesis', *J Natl Cancer Inst* 1979, 63, pp1291–8, and others.

74 A. Tyler, 'Political Cripples' *New Statesman and Society*, 12 June 1992

75 Letter, *New Statesman and Society*, 26 June 1992

76 *The Independent*, 17 April 1992

77 Personal communication, March 1992

78 R. Doll and R. Peto, *The Causes of Cancer* (Oxford Medical Publications, 1981)

79 *Scientific American*, January 1892

80 J. Abernethy, *Surgical Observations on Tumours* (1804), cited in C. Spencer, *The Heretic's Feast* (Fourth Estate, 1993)

81 O. Gregor, R. Toman, F. Prusova, 'Gastrointestinal Cancer and Nutrition', *Gut*, 10 (12), pp1031–1034

82 E. L. Wynder and Takao Shigematsu, 'Environmental Factors of Cancer of the Colon and Rectum', *Cancer*, 1967, 20:9, p1528

83 R. L. Phillips, 'Role of Life-style and Dietary habits in Risk of Cancer among Seventh-day Adventists', *Cancer Research*, 1975, 35, pp3513–3522

84 *ibid.*

85 R. L. Phillips and D. A. Snowdon, 'Association of Meat and Coffee Use with Cancers of the Large Bowel, Breast and Prostate among Seventh Day Adventists: Preliminary Results', *Cancer Research*, 1983, 43, pp2403–2408

86 M. A. Howell, 'Diet as an Etiological Factor in the Development of Cancers of the Colon and Rectum', *J.Chron.Dis*, 1975, 28, pp67–80

87 A. Palgi, 'Association Between Dietary Changes and Mortality Rates: Israel 1949-1977; a Trend-Free Regression Model', *American Journal of Clinical Nutrition*, 1981, 34, pp1569–1583

88 J. H. Lubin, P. E. Burns, W. J. Blot, R. G. Ziegler, A. W. Lees, J. F. Fraumeni, 'Dietary Factors and Breast Cancer Risk', *Int. J. Cancer*, 1981, 28, pp685–689

89 L. N. Kolonel, J. H. Hankin, J. Lee, S. Y. Chu, A. M. Y. Nomura, M. Ward Hines, 'Nutrient Intakes in Relation to Cancer Incidence in Hawaii', *Br. J. Cancer*, 1981, 44, pp332

90 P. Correa, 'Epidemiological Correlations Between Diet and Cancer Frequency', *Cancer Research*, 41, pp3685–3690

91 W. C. Willett, M. J. Stampfer, G. A. Colditz, B. A. Rosner, F. E. Speizer, 'Relation of meat, fat, and fiber intake to the risk of colon cancer in a prospective study among women', *N Engl J Med*, 13 Dec, 1990, 323 (24), pp1664–72

92 *The Independent*, 14 December 1990

93 O. Manousos, N. E. Day, D. Trichopoulos, F. Gerovassilis. A. Tzonou, 'Diet and Colo-Rectal Cancer: A Case-Control Study in Greece', *Int. J. Cancer*, 1983, 32, pp1–5

94 R. Frentzel-Beyme, J. Claude, V. Eilber, 'Mortality among German vegetarians: first results after five years of follow-up', *Nutr Cancer*, 1988, 11 (2), pp117–26

95 T. Hirayama, 'Mortality in Japanese with life-styles similar to Seventh-Day Adventists: strategy for risk reduction by life-style modification', *Natl Cancer Inst Monogr*, Dec 1985, 69, pp143–53

96 W. Lijinsky and P. Shubik, 'Benzo(a)pyrene and other polynuclear hydrocarbons in charcoal-broiled meat', *Science*, 145, pp53–5

97 *UPI*, 10 May 1986

98 *Accumulation of Nitrate 1972*, Committee on Nitrate Accumulation, National Academy of Sciences

99 Physicians Committee for Responsible Medicine, March 1992

100 'National Pork Producers Council recommends hog farmers suspend use of sulphamethazine', *UPI*, 29 Jan, 1988

101 J. T. Korpela, H. Adlercreutz, M. J. Turunen, 'Fecal free and conjugated bile acids and neutral sterols in vegetarians, omnivores, and patients with colorectal cancer', *Scand J. Gastroenterol*, Apr 1988, 23 (3), pp277–83

102 M. Malter, G. Schriever, U. Eilber, 'Natural killer cells, vitamins, and other blood components of vegetarian and omnivorous men', *Nutr Cancer*, 1989, 12 (3), pp271–8

103 A. H. Kaam, C. Koopman-Esseboom, E. J. Sulkers, P. J. Sauer, C. Govan der Paauw, L. G. Tuinstra, 'Polychloorbifenylen (PCBs) in moedermelk, vetweefsel, plasma en navelstrengbloed; gehalten en correlaties', *Ned Tijdschr Geneeskd*, 3 Aug 1991, 135 (31), pp1399–403

104 R. H. Hall, 'A new threat to public health: organochlorines and food', *Nutr Health*, 1992, 8 (1), pp33–43

105 'Can vitamins help prevent cancer?, *Consumer Reports*, May 1983, vol48, no5, pp243–5

106 W. Troll, 'Prevention of cancer by agents that suppress oxygen radical formation', *Free Radic Res Commun*, 1991, 12–13 part 2, pp751–7

107 *Academic American Encyclopedia* (1992)

108 A. M. Thrash and C. L. Thrash, *The Animal Connection* (Yuchi Pines Institute, 1983)

109 M. B. Gardner, 'Viruses as environmental carcinogens: an agricultural perspective', *Basic Life Sci*, 1982, 21, pp171–88

110 E. S. Johnson, H. R. Fischman, G. M. Matanoski, E. Diamond, 'Cancer mortality among white males in the meat industry', *J Occup Med*, Jan 1986, 28 (1), pp23–32

111 C. A. Diglio and J. F. Ferrer, 'Induction of Syncytia by the Bovine C-type Leukaemia Virus', *Cancer Research*, 36, pp1056–67, cited in *Vet Res Commun*, Dec 1981, 5 (2), pp117–26

112 J. Rifkin, *Beyond Beef* (Dutton, 1992)

113 *New Scientist*, 7 January 1989

114 H. M. McClure, M. E. Keeling, R. P., Custer, R. R. Marshak, D. A. Abt, J. F. Ferrer, 'Erythroleukaemia in two infant chimpanzees fed milk from cows naturally infected with the bovine C-type virus', *Cancer Research*, 34, pp2745–57

115 H. M. Lemon, 'Food-born viruses and malignant hemopoietic diseases', *Bact. Rev.*, 28, pp490–92

116 J. Aleksandrowicz, 'Leukaemia in humans and animals in the light of epidemiological studies with reference to problems of its prevention', *Acta Med. Polona*, 9, pp217–30

117 B. Muszynski, 'Wplyw biaLaczek bydLa na powstawanie chorob nowotworowych u ludzi na podstawie materiaLow zebranych w powiecie zlotowskim', *Przegl Lek*, 25 (9), pp660–1

118 A. Linos, R. A. Kyle, L. R. Elveback, L. T. Kurland, 'Leukaemia in Olmsted County, Minnesota, 1965-1974', *Clin. Proc.*, 53, pp714–18

119 K. J. Donham, J. W. Berg, R. S. Sawin, 'Epidemiologic relationships of the bovine population and human leukaemia in Iowa', *Amer J Epidemiol*, 1980, 112, pp80-92

120 A. Blair and H. M. Hayes, 'Cancer and other causes of death among US veterinarians 1966-1977', *International Journal of Cancer*, 25, pp181–5

121 M. H.Lenfant-Pejovie, M. H. Milka-Cabanne, C. Bouchardy, A. Suquier, 'Risk factors for male breast cancer: a Franco-Swiss case-control study', *Cancer*, Apr 15 1990, 45 (4), pp661–5

122 C. Magnani, G. Pastore, L. Luzzatto, M. Carli, P. Lubvano, B. Terracini, 'Risk factors for soft tissue sarcomas in childhood: a case-control study', *Tumori*, Aug 31 1989, 75 (4), pp396–400

123 *Vibrant Life*, May-June 1992, vol8, no3, p20(3)

124 Beyond Beef Campaign, 1992

125 Physicians' Health Study, begun 1982; Dr Charles Hennekens, Harvard Medical School and Brigham and Women's Hospital Boston National Cancer Institute Cancer Research Laboratory, Bethesda, Maryland, USA; Regina Ziegler, PhD

126 'Can vitamins help prevent cancer?' *Consumer Reports*, May 1983, vol48, no5, pp243–5

127 *Redbook*, April, 1989, vol172, no6, p96(5)

128 'Good diet "curbs cancer risk"', *The Independent*, 3 October 1989

129 Gerhard Schrauzer, PhD, of the University of California cited in *Better Nutrition*, Nov 1989, vol51, no11, p14(2)

130 Redbook, *op. cit.*

131 J. E. Spallholz and J. R. Stewart, 'Advances in the role of minerals in immunobiology', *Biol Trace Elem Res*, Mar 1989, 19 (3), pp129–51

132 Paul Knekt, *et al.*, 'Selenium Deficiency and Increased Risk of Lung Cancer;' abstract of paper read at the Fourth International Symposium on Selenium in Biology and Medicine, Tubingen, West Germany, July 1988

133 U. Reinhold, *et al.*, 'Selenium Deficiency and Lethal Skin cancer'; abstract of paper read at the Fourth International Symposium on Selenium in Biology and Medicine, Tubingen, West Germany, July 1988

134 Cedric Garland, PhD and Frank Gardland PhD, *The Calcium Connection*, (Simon & Schuster, 1989); C. Garland is Director of the Cancer Center Epidemiology Program, University of California, San Diego

135 American Cancer Society, nutritional guidelines; *Health*, June 1984, vol16, p9 (1)

136 'Can vitamins help cancer?', *Consumer Reports*, May 1983, vol48, no5, pp 243-5

137 Various studies including work by Professor Hans Eysenck and Dr Ronald Grossarth-Maticek, Institute of Psychiatry, London; Dr David Spiegel, Stanford University, USA

138 National Advisory Committee on Nutrition Education, *Proposals for nutritional guidelines for health education in Britain*, The Health Education Council, September 1983

139 D. P. Burkitt, A. R. P. Walker, N . S. Painter, 'Effect of dietary fibre on stools and transit times, and its role in the causation of disease', *The Lancet*, 30 December 1972

140 *Dietary Reference Values for Food Energy and Nutrients for the United Kingdom*, Department of Health 1991

141 S. Handler, 'Dietary fiber. Can it prevent certain colonic diseases?' *Postgrad Med*, Feb 1983, 73 (2), pp301–7

142 *Cosmopolitan*, Oct, 1989, vol207, no4, pp98(2)

143 G. J. Davies, M. Crowder, J. W. Dickerson, 'Dietary fibre intakes of individuals with different eating patterns', *Nutr Appl Nutr*, Apr 1985, 39 (2), pp139–48

144 B. R. Goldin, H. Adlercreutz, S. L. Gorbach, J. H. Warram, J. T. Dwyer, L. Swenson, M. N. Wood, 'Estrogen excretion patterns and plasma levels in vegetarian and omnivorous women', *N Engl J Med*, Dec 16 1982, 307 (25), pp1542–7

145 M. Abdulla, K. O. Aly, I. Andersson, H. G. Asp, D. Birkhed, I. Deuker, C. G. Johansson, M. Jagerstad, K. Kolar, B. M. Mair, *et. al.* 'Nutrient intake and health status of lactovegetarians: chemical analyses of diets using the duplicate portion sampling technique', *Am J Clin Nutr*, Aug 1984, 40 (2), pp325–38

146 N. Levin, J. Rattan, T. Gilat, 'Mineral intake and blood levels in vegetarians', *Isr J Med Sci*, Feb 1986, 22 (2), pp105–8

147 J. L. Slavin, 'Dietary fiber: classification, chemical analyses, and food sources', *J Am Diet Assoc*, Sep 1987, 87 (9), pp1164–71

148 J. Rattan, N. Levin, E. Graff, N. Weizer, T. Gilat, 'A high-fiber diet does not cause mineral and nutrient deficiencies', *J Clin Gastroenterol*, Dec 1981, 3 (4), pp389–93

149 J. L. Kelsay, C. W. Frazier, E. S. Prather, J. J. Canary, W. M. Clark, A. S. Powell, 'Impact of variation in carbohydrate intake on mineral utilization by vegetarians', *Am J Clin Nutr*, Sep 1988, 48 (3 Suppl), pp875–9

150 G. Langley, *Vegan Nutrition. A Survey of Research* (Vegan Society, 1988)

151 *Introducing Diabetes*, British Diabetic Association

152 *Diabetes in the United Kingdom, 1988*, British Diabetic Association

153 *ibid.*

154 'Preventing Insulin Dependent Diabetes Mellitus: the environmental challenge', Diabetes Epidemiology Research International, *British Medical Journal (Clinical Research)*, 22 August, 1987, 295(6596), pp479–81

155 'Nutritional Recommendations and Principles for Individuals With Diabetes Mellitus: 1986', American Diabetes Association, *Diabetes Care*, vol10, no1, January-February 1987

156 D. A. Snowdon and R. L. Phillips, 'Does a Vegetarian Diet reduce the Occurrence of Diabetes?' *American Journal of Public Health*, 1985, 75, pp507–12

157 R. Kmeb and C. Beebe, 'Food choices can affect your risks for diabetes complications', *Diabetes in the News*, Sept-Oct 1989, vol6, no5, pp12(4)

158 J. W. Anderson, 'Plant Fiber and Blood Pressure', *Annals of Internal Medicine*, 1983, 98, pp842–6

159 F. W. Scott, 'Cow's milk and insulin-dependent diabetes mellitus: is there a relationship?' *American Journal of Clinical Nutrition*, March, 1990, vol51, no3, pp489(3)

160 J. Tuomilehto *et al.*, 'Coffee consumption as trigger for insulin dependent diabetes mellitus in childhood', Department of Epidemiology, National Public Health Institute, Helsinki, Finland, *British Medical Journal*, 10 March, 1990, 300(6725), pp642–3

161 *Better Nutrition for Today's Living*, June 1990, vol52, no6, pp22–3

162 E. Putzier, 'Haurmykosen und Antipilzdiat' [Dermatomycoses and an antifungal diet] *Wien Med Wochenschr* (Austria), Aug 31 1989, 139 (15-16), pp 379–80

163 Sir James Black, quoted in *The Independent*, 22 October 1988

164 *ibid.*; and John J. Voorhees, MD, reported in *Archives of Dermatology* and *Better Nutrition for Today's Living*, June 1990 vol52, no6, pp22-3

165 Donald O. Rudin, MD, 'The Omega-3 Phenomenon and Better Nutrition for Today's Living', June 1990, vol52, no6, pp22–3

166 L. Fry *et al.*, 'The Mechanism of Folate Deficiency in Psoriasis', *British Journal of Dermatology*, 1971, 84, pp539–44

167 Ranjit Kumar Chandra, Shakuntla Puri, Azza Hamed, 'Influence of maternal diet during lactation and use of formula feeds on development of atopic eczema in high risk infants', *British Medical Journal*, July 22, 1989, vol298, no6693, pp228(3)

168 Dr Kari Poilolainen *et al*, National Public Health Institute, Helsinki as reported in the *British Medical Journal* and *The Independent*, 23 March 1990

169 A. H. Bruckstein, 'Nonsurgical management of cholelithiasis', *Arch Int Med*, May 1990, vol150, no5, pp960(5)

170 F. Pixley, D. Wilson, K. McPherson, J. Mann, 'Effect of Vegetarianism on develoment of gallstones in women', *British Medical Journal*, vol291, 6 July 1985

171 F. Pixley, J. Mann, 'Dietary factors in the aetiology of gall stones: a case control study', *Gut*, Nov 1988, 29 (11), pp1511–5

172 *The Edell Health Letter*, June 1989, vol8, no6, p1(1)

173 *Prevention*, May 1989, vol41, no5, p66(7)

174 UK heart statistics from the British Heart Foundation, 1994

175 W. C. Roberts, 'We think we are one, we act as if we are one, but we are not one', *American Journal of Cardiology*, 1 Oct 1990, 66 (10), pp896

176 Interview with author, 1992

177 R. L. Phillips, F. R. Lemon, W. L. Beeson, J. W. Kuzma, 'Coronary heart disease mortality among Seventh-Day Adventists with differing dietary habits: a preliminary report', *American Journal of Clinical Nutrition*, Oct 1978, 31, ppS191–S198

178 D. A. Snowdon, R. L. Phillips, G. E. Fraser, 'Meat consumption and fatal ischemic heart disease', *Preventive Medicine*, Sep 1984, 13 (5), pp490–500

179 M. L. Burr, and B. K. Butland, ' Heart disease in British vegetarians', *American Journal of Clinical Nutrition*, Sep 1988, 48 (3 Suppl), pp830–2

180 T. Hirayama, *op. cit.*

181 M. Thorogood, R. Carter, L. Benfield, K. McPherson, J. L. Mann, 'Plasma lipids and lipoprotein cholesterol concentrations in people with

different diets in Britain', *British Medical Journal* (Clin Res Ed) 8 Aug 1987, 295 (6594), pp351–3

182 Frentzel-Beyme, Claude, Eilber, *op. cit.*

183 V. Fonnebo, 'Mortality in Norwegian Seventh-Day Adventists 1962-1986', *J Clin Epidemiol*, Feb 1992, 45 (2), pp157–67

184 A. C. Arntzenius, D. Kromhour, J. D. Barth, J. H. Reiber, A. V. Bruschke, B. Buis, C. M. van Gent, N. Kempsen-Voogd, S. Strikwerda, E. A. van der Velder, 'Diet, lipoproteins, and the progression of coronary atherosclerosis. The Leiden Intervention Trial', *New England Journal of Medicine*, Mar 28 1985, 312 (13), pp805–11

185 *Time*, 29 October 1990

186 D. Ornish, S. E. Brown, L. W. Scherwitz, J. H. Billings, W. T. Armstrong, T. A. Ports, S. M. McLanahan, R. L. Kirkeeide, R. J. Brand, K. L. Gould, 'Can lifestyle changes reverse coronary heart disease? The Lifestyle Heart Trial', *Lancet*, Jul 21 1990, 336 (8708), pp129–33

187 *Time*, 29 October 1990

188 *Associated Press*, 13 November 1990

189 G. F. Watts, B. Lewis, J. N. Brunt, E. S. Lewis, D. J. Coltart, L. D. Smith, J. I. Mann, A. V. Swan, ' Effects on coronary artery disease of lipid-lowering diet, or diet plus cholestyramine, in the St Thomas' Atherosclerosis Regression Study (STARS)', *Lancet*, Mar 7 1992, 339 (8793), pp563–9

190 K. L. Gould, D. Ornish, R. Kireeide, S. Brown, Y. Stuart, M. Buchi, J. Billings, W. Armstrong, T. Ports, L. Scherwitz, 'Improved stenosis geometry by quantitative coronary arteriography after vigorous risk factor modification', *American Journal of Cardiology*, Apr 1 1992, 69 (9), pp845–53

191 *Mortality Statistics: Cause (1978)* (HMSO 1980)

192 *Proposals for nutritional guidelines for health education in Britain*, The Health Education Council, National Advisory Committee on Nutrition Education, September 1983

193 A. N. Donaldson, 'The relation of protein foods to hypertension', *Californian and Western Medicine*, 1926, 24, pp328

194 B. Armstrong, A. J. Van Merwyk, H. Coates, 'Blood Pressure in Seventh Day Adventist Vegetarians', *American Journal of Epidemiology*, 1977; 105:5, pp444–9

195 A. P. Hines, R. Chakrabarti, D. Fisher, T. W. Meade, W. R. S. North, Y. Stirling, ' Haemostatic variables in vegetarians and non-vegetarians', *Thrombosis Research*, 1980, 19, pp139–148

196 F. M. Sacks, W. P. Gastelli, A. Donner. E. H. Kass, 'Plasma lipids and lipoproteins in vegetarians and controls', *New England Journal of Medicine*, 1975, 292, pp1148–51

197 J. W. Anderson, 'Plant Fiber and Blood Pressure', *Annals of Internal Medicine*, 1983, 98, pp842–6

198 B. M. Margetts, L. J. Beilin, R. Vandongen, B. K. Armstrong, 'Vegetarian diet in mild hypertension: a randomised controlled trial', *British Medical Journal* (Clin Res Ed), 6 Dec 1986

199 B. M. Margetts, L. J. Beilin, B. K. Armstrong, R. Vandongen, 'A randomized control trial of a vegetarian diet in the treatment of mild hypertension', *Clinical and Experimental Pharmacology and Physiology*, 1985, 12, pp263–6

200 O. Lindahl, L. Lindwall, A. Spangberg, A. Stenram, P. A. Ockermann, 'A vegan regime with reduced medication in the treatment of hypertension', *British Journal of Nutrition*, 1984, 52, pp11–20

201 B. J. Beilin, 'Vegetarian approach to hypertension', *Canadian Journal of Physiology and Pharmacology*, Jun 1986, 64 (6), pp852–5

202 *Los Angeles Times*, 18 July 1989

203 *HeartCorps*, Dec 1989, vol2, no3, pp67(4)

204 J. C. M. Witteman, W. C. Willett, M. J. Stampfer, G. A. Colditz, F. J. Kok, F. M. Sacks, F. E. Speizer, B. Rosner, C. H. Hennekens, 'Relation of moderate alcohol consumption and risk of systemic hypertension in women', *American Journal of Cardiology*, March 1 1990, vol65, no9, pp633(5)

205 *Journal of the American Medical Association*, 11 April 1990

206 Y. K. Seedat, 'Nutritional aspects of hypertension', *South African Medical Journal* (South Africa), Feb 18 1989, 75 (4), pp175–7

207 *Better Nutrition*, July, 1990, vol52, no7, pp14(2)

208 G. Uza and R. Vlaicu, 'Serum calcium and salt restriction in the diet of patients with essential arterial hypertension', Institute of Hygiene and Public Health Medical Clinic no. 1, Cluj-Napoca, Romania, *Med Interne*, Apr-Jun 1989, 27 (2), pp93–7

209 *Medical World News*, Feb 26, 1990, vol31, no4, pp22(2)

210 *Selenium and High Blood Pressure*, The Cleveland Clinic, March, 1976

211 Dr John McDougall, *Vegetarian Times*, June 1989, no142, pp60(3)

212 *American Journal of Medicine* 1950, 220, pp421

213 R. L. Swank, 'Multiple sclerosis: twenty years on low fat diet', *Arch Neurol*, Nov 1970, 23 (5), pp460–74

214 R. L. Swank and M. H. Pullen, *The Multiple Sclerosis Diet Book*, (Doubleday, Garden City NY, 1977)

215 *The Edell Health Letter*, May 1989, vol8, no5, p6(1)

216 Celia Hall, 'Low-fat diet may cut deaths from MS', *The Independent*, 6 July 1990

217 R. L. Swank and B. B. Dugan, 'Effect of low saturated fat diet in early and late cases of multiple sclerosis', *The Lancet*, 7 July 1990, vol336 no8706, p37(3)

218 *Lancet*, 7 July 1990, vol336, no8706, p25(2)

219 Dr John McDougall, *op. cit.*

220 *Newsletter* of the National Osteoporosis Society, no1

221 National Osteoporosis Society leaflet, no2

222 *The Independent*, 23 October 1990

223 *ibid.*

224 John Studd, Consultant Gynaecologist, Kings College and Dulwich Hospitals, Vice-Chairman of the National Osteoporosis Society

225 Edward G. Lufkin, and Steven J. Ory, 'Estrogen replacement therapy for the prevention of osteoporosis', *American Family Physician*, Sept 1989, vol40, no3, pp205(7)

226 T. M. Mack, M. C. Pike, B. E. Henderson *et al.*, 'Estrogens and endometrial cancer in a retirement community', *New England Journal of Medicine*, 1976, 294, pp1262–7

227 M. P. Cust, K. F. Gangar, T. C. Hillard, M. I. Whitehead, 'A risk-benefit assessment of estrogen therapy in postmenopausal women', *Drug Saf*, Sep-Oct 1990, 5 (5), pp345–58

228 B. S. Hulka, 'Hormone-replacement therapy and the risk of breast cancer', *CA*, Sep-Oct 1990, 40 (5), pp289–96

229 Quoted in *Bestways*, Feb 1990, vol18, no2, pp26(7)

230 'Osteoporosis: bone up on the facts', *Better Nutrition*, 1990

231 *ibid.*

232 Data for 2 per cent fat milk from US Department of Agriculture Handbook no8

233 Data for cheddar cheese from US Department of Agriculture Handbook no8

234 *New York Times*, 8 May 1990

235 R. B. Mazess, 'Bone mineral content of North Alaskan Eskimos', *American Journal of Clincial Nutrition*, Sep 1974, 27 (9), pp916–25

236 *Vegetarian Times*, I43, p22

237 M. Hegsted and S. A. Schuette, 'Urinary calcium and calcium balance in young men as affected by level of protein and phosphorus intake', *J Nutr*, 1981, 111, pp553–2

238 N. E. Johnson, E. N. Alcantara, H. Linkswiler, 'Effect of level of protein intake on urinary and fecal calcium and calcium retention of young adult males', *J Nutr*, 1970, 100, pp1425

239 N. A. Breslau, L. Brinkley, K. D. Hill, C. Y. Pak, 'Relationship of animal protein-rich diet to kidney stone formation and calcium metabolism', *J Clin Endocrinol Metab*, Jan 1988, 66 (1), pp140–6

240 J. A. Scharffenberg, *Problems with Meat* (Woodbridge Press Publishing Company, 1979)

241 F. H. Nielsen, C. D. Hunt, L. M. Muillen, J. R. Hunt, 'Effect of dietary boron on mineral, estrogen, and testosterone metabolism in postmenopausal women', *FASEB J*, Nov 1987, 1 (5), pp394–7

242 *UPI*, 4 November 1987

243 *Bestways*, March 1990, vol18, no3, p14(3)

244 A. G. Marsh, T. V. Sanchez, O. Michelsen, S. M. Fagal, 'Vegetarian lifestyle and bone mineral density', *American Journal of Clinical Nutrition*,

Sep 1988, 48 (3 Suppl), pp837-41

245 Lufkin and Ory, *op. cit.*

246 R. P. Heaney, R. R. Recker, 'Effects of nitrogen phosphorus, and caffeine on calcium balance in women', *Journal of Laboratory Clinical Medicine*, Jan 1982, 99 (1), pp46–55

247 *What everyone needs to know about osteoporosis* (The National Osteoporosis Society)

248 J. E. White, 'Osteoporosis Strategies For Prevention', Family Nurse Practitioner Program, University of Pittsburgh School of Nursing, *Nurse Pract*, 1986, 11(9), pp36–46, 50

PART FIVE:
THE WORLD'S BEST VEGETARIAN FOODS

The top 100 foods –
what's in them, how to choose them, and
the best ways to use them

'But what are you going to eat – just vegetables?'

Has this ever happened to you? You've just told your partner/parents/friends about your new lifestyle – and they're aghast. Whatever will you find to eat? How can you survive on just beansprouts? Will you never eat good food again?

You can almost see their minds working. They're imagining a plate of food: steak, French fries, and peas. Take away the steak, and what do you have? Just chips and peas! *And that's what you're going to live on?*

In years gone by, most people were brainwashed – and that's not too strong a word – into believing that a meal was not complete unless it included substantial helpings of meat. 'Where's the beef?', they used to mutter, if the animal tissue was somewhat lacking. Today, most of us know rather better – we know, for example, that eating such meaty meals can be a recipe for health disaster. And yet, there are still plenty of people who *know* that such dietary indulgences are unhealthy, but who don't seem to be able to conceive of any other way of eating.

Well, here's the answer. In this section, you'll find all the most common natural food ingredients – as well as some which aren't quite so widely available yet – together with practical advice on how, when and what

to choose; how to prepare them for maximum enjoyment and nutrition; some of the finest and easiest 'classical' recipes for each foodstuff; and – because many foods have also been used as medicines for centuries – some information about their health-giving properties, too. Additionally, I've sometimes included a few words about their rather surprising history – because in today's modern world, we frequently take our food too much for granted. Food which was revered in ancient times is irrationally ignored, scorned or even despised today. Familiarity certainly breeds contempt – but it also breeds ignorance. Maybe it's time for all of us to take a fresh – and respectful – look at the awesome range and diversity of plant foods which comprise our species' rightful diet.

And while you're doing that, think about this. The vast majority of Western meat-eaters consume only *two species:* cows and pigs. Can you imagine anything more boring – and indeed more unnatural – than eating just *two types* of food all your life? From the plant kingdom, on the other hand, there is a never-ending cornucopia of fine foods for us to dine on. If you don't like one of them, then just pick another – there's an abundance of others to choose from. So much for the assertion sometimes heard that the vegetarian diet lacks variety. Bon appétit!

Ackee Originating in Africa, ackees were taken to the West Indies on the first slave ships (its botanical name *blighia sapida* refers to the infamous Captain Bligh, the first person to bring specimens to England). You can find them in shops which cater for West Indian communities – in Jamaica, they virtually have the status of a national dish. Their taste and appearance is similar to scrambled eggs, and they are delicious when cooked with grated coconut.
See also: Ackee in Pepper Sauce (p334)

NUTRIENT ANALYSIS
1 CUP ACKEES, CANNED (225g)

KCalories	339.75
Total Fat (g)	34.20
Monounsaturated Fat (g)	?
Polyunsaturated Fat (g)	?
Saturated Fat (g)	?
Carbohydrate (g)	1.80
Protein (g)	6.53
Crude Fibre (g)	?
Vitamin A (RE)	?
Ascorbic Acid (mg)	67.50
Thiamin (mg)	0.07
Riboflavin (mg)	0.16
Niacin (mg)	1.35
Pantothenic Acid (mg)	?
Vitamin B6 (mg)	0.13
Folacin (mcg)	92.25
Vitamin B12 (mcg)	0.00
Calcium (mg)	78.75
Iron (mg)	1.58
Zinc (mg)	1.35

Health Note

To be on the safe side, don't buy fresh ackees if you see them in a speciality grocery. The unripe fruit, seeds, and husks all contain a natural toxin, hypoglycin A, which causes vomiting. When the fruit is ripe, levels of this substance are so low in the fruit as to be undetectable.[1] Buy canned ackees from a reputable manufacturer, and you won't have any problem.

Agar This is a seaweed product, also called kanten or agar-agar, which is available in powder form. Agar is a substitute for the animal by-product gelatine which is made from the skin and bones of dead animals. Use agar to make traditional jellies, to help set jams and marmalades, and to make dairy-free mousses and flans. Although agar sets at room temperature, it cannot be combined with vinegar or foods containing oxalic acid such as rhubarb and spinach. It works well with all other fruits and vegetables, however. For a simple fruit jelly, dissolve one packet of agar in 285ml (½ pint) cold water in a saucepan. Place over a medium heat and bring to the boil. Boil for 3–5 minutes then remove from the heat. Add 285ml (½ pint) fruit juice and pour into jelly mould. Leave to set at room temperature then chill until ready to serve. Add chopped fruit etc when the jelly begins to set.
See also: Vegetable Salad Jelly (p333)

Alfalfa One of many types of seeds which can be readily sprouted at home. Any seed is capable of being sprouted, but the most flavoursome are legumes such as peas, beans, fenugreek, alfalfa and clover, and vegetables such as parsley, celery and lettuce. All that is required is air, moisture and a jar – so there is no reason why you should not soon have your own crop of this invigoratingly healthy and versatile food! Here's how to sprout alfalfa, or indeed any seed:

- Use a container with some sort of drainage, such as a colander, strainer, mesh tray, or even a flower pot with a cloth net over the hole. A jar with a piece of cheesecloth or muslin held in place around the top with a rubber band is perhaps the simplest and most effective. The size of the jar depends on how many seeds you are sprouting, but it should hold at least 0.5l (18fl oz).
- Seeds can be bought from health food stores, where they are usually labelled 'organic', and some supermarkets. Do *not* buy seeds from agricultural merchants – they may well be contaminated with seed dressing chemicals which might be fatal if consumed. Use only the clean, whole ones and throw out the rest.
- For every 100ml (4fl oz) the jar holds, use between two and three tablespoons of seeds. First, they must be soaked in four times their own volume of water,

ideally filtered or mineral water, until their bulk is doubled. This normally takes about eight hours, or overnight. After this time, pour off the water. It contains a lot of the seeds' goodness and so should be used in cooking if possible.

- The sprout container should be kept in darkness – just throw a tea-towel over the jar. The seeds must be rinsed two or three times a day through the muslin mesh of the jar. Make sure you drain them thoroughly each time by turning the container upside down, or the sprouts will rot.

- Throw away any seeds that have not sprouted after two days. The rest will be ready to eat after four or five days. On the last day they can be put into the light, but only for a few hours or they will become bitter.

- Most sprouts will need a final rinsing and draining before being put in the fridge in a covered container for storage. Some varieties, however, have loose husks which need to be removed. Place the sprouts in a large bowl of water and agitate until the husks float to the top, then you can skim them off.

Grain or vegetable sprouts do not require cooking, but bean or pea sprouts should be simmered quickly to make them easier to digest, following the times given in the table below:

Mung beans	3 minutes
Lentil beans	10–15 minutes
Peas	5 minutes
Chickpeas	8 minutes
Fenugreek	3 minutes
Soya beans	soak for 2 hours, rinsing frequently and then cook for 10–15 minutes.

Health Note

Alfalfa has been called 'the Father of all foods' in Arabic. Juice from freshly squeezed alfalfa contains the amino acid L-canaverine, which is an anti-bacterial agent and has been shown to possess anti-cancer properties. Colombian natives use the juice as a treatment for sore throats and coughs. Alfalfa can also lower blood cholesterol levels by inhibiting the absorption of cholesterol from the intestinal tract.

Vegetable sprouts are good in salads and sandwiches, or as a garnish for any dish. Grain sprouts can be used in bread – just mix into the dough before baking. Bean sprouts can be steamed with other vegetables or stir fried for a couple of minutes. Sprouted alfafa seeds are a rich source of vitamin C and certain B group vitamins, and can be added as an interesting garnish to salads, or can be used to accompany almost any sandwich filling.

NUTRIENT ANALYSIS
1 CUP ALFALFA, SPROUTED (33g)

KCalories	9.57
Total Fat (g)	0.23
Monounsaturated Fat (g)	0.02
Polyunsaturated Fat (g)	0.13
Saturated Fat (g)	0.02
Carbohydrate (g)	1.25
Protein (g)	1.32
Crude Fibre (g)	0.54
Vitamin A (RE)	5.28
Ascorbic Acid (mg)	2.71
Thiamin (mg)	0.03
Riboflavin (mg)	0.04
Niacin (mg)	0.16
Pantothenic Acid (mg)	0.19
Vitamin B6 (mg)	0.01
Folacin (mcg)	11.88
Vitamin B12 (mcg)	0.00
Calcium (mg)	10.56
Iron (mg)	0.32
Zinc (mg)	0.30

Almonds Eating almonds straight from the shell is perhaps the least interesting thing to do with them. To avoid the dry mouth sensation that almonds can sometimes give, soak shelled almonds overnight in cold water, then simply pop them out of their skins. The nuts in this state will be far more pleasant to eat, and much more digestible. Or try making an almond

nut milk: soak 140g (5 oz) of almonds overnight. In the morning, peel them and add to 570ml (1 pint) of cold, filtered water. Blend in a liquidizer until smooth. Strain the resulting milk through butter muslin. Drink as it is or combine with any number of flavourings (such as banana) to make an appetizing and highly nutritious milkshake which is especially loved by children and those with allergies to soya or cow's milk.
See also: Samsa (p319); Sfihan (p349)

NUTRIENT ANALYSIS
1oz ALMONDS, DRIED (25g)

KCalories	167.28
Total Fat (g)	14.83
Monounsaturated Fat (g)	9.63
Polyunsaturated Fat (g)	3.11
Saturated Fat (g)	1.41
Carbohydrate (g)	5.79
Protein (g)	5.67
Crude Fibre (g)	0.77
Vitamin A (RE)	0.00
Ascorbic Acid (mg)	0.17
Thiamin (mg)	0.06
Riboflavin (mg)	0.22
Niacin (mg)	0.95
Pantothenic Acid (mg)	0.13
Vitamin B6 (mg)	0.03
Folacin (mcg)	16.67
Vitamin B12 (mcg)	0.00
Calcium (mg)	75.54
Iron (mg)	1.04
Zinc (mg)	0.83

Almond and Raisin Phyllo Filling
Serves 4
Preparation time 20 minutes

25g (1oz) walnuts, crushed
100g (4oz) almonds, slivered
100g (4oz) raisins
3 tbsp olive oil
50g (2oz) green olives, sliced

Heat 1 tbsp oil in a frying pan over a medium heat. Add the crushed walnuts and sauté for 3–5 minutes, stirring often. Add the almonds and continue to sauté for a further 7–10 minutes, adding the rest of the oil if needed to prevent sticking. Add the raisins and stir for 2 minutes, then reduce the heat, cover the pan and leave to cook for another 5 minutes. Remove the pan from the heat and stir the sliced olives into the mixture. Use immediately as a filling for a phyllo loaf or pastie, as in the following example: layer three sheets of phyllo pastry and oil in a lightly oiled oven dish. Spread this filling over all and top with another three-sheet layer of phyllo. Brush the surface with oil, bake in a preheated oven 180°C/350°F/Gas Mark 4 for 35–45 minutes, until golden. Slice and serve.
See also: Phyllo Pastry (p348); Sfihan (p348); Spanikopita (p349); Baklava (p349); Almond Semolina Cake (p310)

Avocado and Almond Spread
Serves 4
Preparation time 15 minutes

1 medium avocado, peeled and chopped
75g (3oz) almonds, ground
1 tsp fresh mint, finely chopped
1 tbsp fresh parsley, finely chopped
140ml (¼ pint) plain soya yoghurt
2 tsp fresh chives, chopped
25g (1oz) beansprouts, to garnish

Combine all the ingredients except the beansprouts. Spread on crackers, toast or bread and garnish with beansprouts.

Broccoli in Garlic and Almond Sauce
Serves 4
Preparation time 30 minutes

900g (2lb) broccoli, trimmed and cut into florets
1 tbsp oil
5 cloves garlic, chopped
2 tsp fresh ginger, grated
½–1 tsp freshly ground black pepper
225g (8oz) sliced almonds
1 bunch spring onions, sliced into 2-inch lengths

Steam the broccoli for 5 minutes; leave the pan covered and put to one side, off the heat. Meanwhile, heat the oil in a large saucepan and sauté the garlic for 2 minutes, until just golden. Add the ginger and black pepper and stir for 1 minute. Add the almonds and spring onions and stir for 5 minutes. Add the steamed broccoli to the saute, toss together, cover the pan and leave over a low heat for 7–10 minutes. Serve hot as a side dish or over rice.

Crunchy Almond Muesli

Serves 8
Preparation time 50 minutes

450g (1lb) rolled oats
100g (4oz) sunflower seeds
225g (8oz) sliced or chopped almonds
140ml (¼ pint) barley malt syrup (available in all
   healthfood shops)
140ml (¼ pint) oil
140ml (¼ pint) fruit juice
225g (8oz) raisins
100g (4oz) desiccated coconut

Preheat the oven to 150°C/300°F/Gas Mark 2. Mix oats, sunflower seeds and almonds together in a large bowl. Blend the syrup, oil and juice together in a jug and pour over the oat and almond mixture. Spread this mixture onto a baking tray. Bake for 35 minutes, until lightly browned, stirring every 5–10 minutes. Allow to cool, then stir in raisins and coconut. Store in an airtight container and serve with fruit juice or soya milk.

Health Note

> Research shows that cholesterol levels can be lowered by substituting almonds and almond oil for dietary sources of saturated fats. The monounsaturated fatty acids found in almonds seem to be the factor responsible for this effect.

Apples One of the first fruits ever to be cultivated, it is estimated that there are up to 8,000 named varieties of apple, although unfortunately, only a tiny proportion of these are commercially cultivated – and even fewer eventually arrive on the supermarket shelves. As a general rule, the most flavoursome variety of apple amongst those commonly available is the Cox (the Golden and Red Delicious are reliable as crops but bland in comparison). The Russet is still occasionally available, and certainly worth searching out for its exquisite flavour and unusual texture.

Until very recently, conventional nutritional analysis seemed to reveal that the apple contained no particularly high concentrations of any significant nutrients, other than a modest amount of vitamin C. Now, however, it has been demonstrated that apples, and their seeds, contain small but very important amounts of the trace element boron, which has now been shown to play a crucial role in the hardening and maintenance of bones and may help to prevent osteoporosis. In fact, diets which provide several good natural sources of boron, such as apples, pears, grapes, and nuts, can double the quantity of the most active form of the hormone oestrogen in the female body. Women consuming this kind of diet have been found to have oestrogen levels which equal those of women on oestrogen replacement therapy. The old wisdom that 'an apple a day keeps the doctor away' may well be proving true.

Unfortunately, there have been strong suggestions that apples, in common with other commercially produced fruits, may well provide rather more than a dose of beneficial trace minerals. Of particular concern is the impact of pesticide residue (both from fresh apples and apple juice) on children, who tend to consume more fruit than adults, and who also may well be far more vulnerable to these toxic chemicals. Where it is not possible to buy organically produced apples (or indeed to grow your own) then all apples should first be soaked for at least 20 minutes in water which has had three or four tablespoons of household salt dissolved in it, then scrubbed and rinsed. You will be absolutely amazed by the amount of dirt, and perhaps other less visible pollutants, which this removes.

See also: Apple Pie (p326); Walnut, Date and Apple Strudel (p355

NUTRIENT ANALYSIS
RAW APPLE WITH SKIN (138g)

KCalories	81.42
Total Fat (g)	0.50
Monounsaturated Fat (g)	0.02
Polyunsaturated Fat (g)	0.14
Saturated Fat (g)	0.08
Carbohydrate (g)	21.05
Protein (g)	0.26
Crude Fibre (g)	1.06
Vitamin A (RE)	6.90

Ascorbic Acid (mg)	7.87
Thiamin (mg)	0.02
Riboflavin (mg)	0.02
Niacin (mg)	0.11
Pantothenic Acid (mg)	0.08
Vitamin B6 (mg)	0.07
Folacin (mcg)	3.86
Vitamin B12 (mcg)	0.00
Calcium (mg)	9.66
Iron (mg)	0.25
Zinc (mg)	0.06

Apple Butter

This is a deliciously buttery sauce made by slowly boiling apples until a smooth, thick residue is left. Traditionally made from apples which are substandard or not pretty enough to eat, such as windfalls, apple butter can be used as a healthy spread for use on bread, toast, and home-made scones and pastries. Or serve it as a wholesome dessert, served hot or cold, by itself or with raisins, a sprinkling of ground nuts or a dollop of Soya Creem.

Makes approximately 4 litres (6 pints 14fl oz)
Preparation time 5–6 hours

5kg (11lb) apples, any sort or combination
water
285ml (½ pint) cider vinegar
1.2k (2½ lb) brown sugar
6 tsp ground cinnamon
1½ tsp ground cloves

Wash and quarter the apples, do not peel and do not remove the cores, though you may remove the stalks. Place quartered apples in jam-making pan and cover with water. Place over a medium heat and bring the liquid to a boil. Stir well and reduce the heat just a little. Cook the apples, stirring often, until they are soft. Press cooked apples through a sieve or mouli to make a thick pulp. Discard the pips and peel. Roughly measure the remaining smooth pulp: turn about 7–8 litres back into the cooking pot and stir in the vinegar, sugar, cinnamon, and cloves. Mix well. Cook over a low heat, stirring occasionally, for 3–4 hours or until the mixture is reduced by about half. Test for readiness by placing a spoonful of the butter in a small

bowl, it is ready if it slightly holds its shape with no water around it. Pour the hot butter into sterilized jars and seal.

Apple and Raisin Corn Cake
Serves 4–6
Preparation time 1 hour

2 eating apples, peeled and chopped
100g (4oz) raisins
4 tbsp oil
570ml (1 pint) apple juice or soya milk
340g (12oz) plain flour
340g (12oz) fine cornmeal
50g (2oz) sugar
3 tsp baking powder
1 tsp bicarbonate of soda
1 tsp ground cinnamon
½ tsp ground ginger
½ tsp salt

Preheat your oven to 200°C/400°F/Gas Mark 6 and lightly oil a 23x23cm (9x9 inch) cake tin. Mix the apples and raisins together in a mixing bowl. Blend the oil and apple juice and pour over the fruit; put to one side. Combine the remaining ingredients in a large bowl and stir in the fruit and liquid mixture. Do not over blend. Pour into the cake tin and bake for 35 minutes. Leave to cool in the tin for 15 minutes before slicing. Serve with sweet or savoury sauce or a vegetable accompaniment.

Apple Oat Scones
Makes 12–18
Preparation time 35 minutes

340g (12oz) plain flour
100g (4oz) rolled oats
50g (2oz) sugar
4 tbsp nutritional yeast flakes (optional)
2 tsp baking powder
1 tsp bicarbonate of soda
1 tsp ground cinnamon
½ tsp ground cloves
75g (3oz) margarine
2 eating apples, unpeeled and grated
420ml (¾ pint) apple juice or soya milk

Preheat the oven to 200°C/400°F/Gas Mark 6 and lightly oil a baking tray. Mix the dry ingredients together in a large bowl. Add the margarine and work with a fork to make a crumbly texture. Add grated apple and juice. Stir to form stiff dough then turn out on lightly floured surface. Knead gently to shape into a round ball then roll out flat, to about ½ inch thickness. Cut into scone shapes and place on the baking tray. Bake for 15 minutes, until golden. Serve the same day with jam, apple butter or your favourite spread.

Note: nutritional yeast flakes, see p30.

Apple Chestnut Upside-Down Cake

Makes one 23 × 33cm (9 × 13-inch) cake
Preparation time 1 hour

90ml (3fl oz) oil
1 tbsp tahini
1 tbsp soya flour
285ml (½ pint) chestnut purée (tinned or Chestnut Creme (p352))
570ml (1 pint) apple juice
1 tsp vanilla
500g (1¼ lb) wholewheat flour
2 tsp baking powder
1 tsp bicarbonate of soda
1 tsp ground cinnamon
75g (3oz) brown sugar
2 tbsp margarine
1 sweet apple, peeled, cored and sliced into rounds
8–12 cooked chestnuts, sliced or chopped
juice of 1 lemon

Preheat the oven to 180°C/350°F/Gas Mark 4 and grease a 23x33cm (9x13 inch) cake tin. Blend oil, tahini and soya flour to a smooth cream. Add chestnut purée and blend well. Stir in apple juice and vanilla and beat to a smooth consistency.

In a separate bowl, mix the flour, baking powder, soda and cinnamon. Sprinkle the brown sugar over the bottom of the cake tin and drop dabs of margarine over the sugar. Arrange the apple slices over the margarine and the chestnut pieces over these. Sprinkle the lemon juice over all.

Give the chestnut purée mixture a brisk stir then blend it with the dry ingredients. Stir well and spoon the batter into the cake tin, over the apple and chestnut arrangement. Bake for 35 minutes.

Allow the cake to cool for 5–10 minutes while you prepare a serving dish for it. Place a piece of grease-proof paper over a wire cooling rack or a flat serving platter. When the cake has cooled somewhat, place the rack over the cake tin, turn the whole thing over and allow the cake to slide down onto the greaseproof paper. The apple rings and chestnut pieces will appear in a caramelized sauce on the top of the upturned cake. Leave to cool completely before serving.

Health Note

The reported health benefits of regularly including apples in your diet include a cleansing and blood purifying effect, as well as the treatment of various skin diseases, arthritis, and constipation. The therapeutic effect of apple cider vinegar is legendary, and this very flavoursome vinegar can deliciously replace malt and spirit vinegar for virtually all culinary purposes.

Apricots The name apricot comes from the Roman word *praicocium*, literally meaning precocious, which refers to its tendency to ripen relatively early. Though delicious as a fresh fruit, its main use in the vegetarian diet is as an all-year-round staple dried fruit. Most dried apricots are preserved in a process which uses sulphur dioxide (this usually bleaches the fruit, with the result that artificial colour is sometimes added, and those people sensitive or allergic to this substance should make a special note to only buy naturally sun-dried apricots). In common with many other dried fruits, dried apricots are sometimes packaged with a small amount of mineral oil deposited over their surface. These should be avoided, since mineral oil interferes with the absorption of fat soluble vitamins.

The finest tasting dried apricots (and reputedly the most health-giving) are the Hunza variety, which are said to be responsible for the extreme longevity of these vegetarian people who inhabit the small kingdom of Hunza in northwestern Kashmir.
See also: Khosnal (p310)

NUTRIENT ANALYSIS
1 CUP DRIED APRICOTS (130g)

KCalories	309.40
Total Fat (g)	0.60
Monounsaturated Fat (g)	0.26
Polyunsaturated Fat (g)	0.12
Saturated Fat (g)	0.04
Carbohydrate (g)	80.27

Protein (g)	4.75
Crude Fibre (g)	3.84
Vitamin A (RE)	941.20
Ascorbic Acid (mg)	3.12
Thiamin (mg)	0.01
Riboflavin (mg)	0.20
Niacin (mg)	3.90
Pantothenic Acid (mg)	0.98
Vitamin B6 (mg)	0.20
Folacin (mcg)	13.39
Vitamin B12 (mcg)	0.00
Calcium (mg)	58.50
Iron (mg)	6.11
Zinc (mg)	0.96

Hot and Spicy Fruit Compote

Serves 6
Preparation time 1 hour

225g (8oz) dried apricots, chopped
100g (4oz) dried figs, chopped
100g (4oz) prunes, pitted and chopped
50g (2oz) raisins
570ml–1l (1–2 pints) water
6 plums, pitted
1 sweet apple, peeled and sliced
140ml (¼ pint) blackcurrants, blackberries or
  bilberries
100g (4oz) sugar
juice of 1 lemon
5 whole cloves
1x5cm (2-inch) piece cinnamon
1 orange, using both rind and fruit
140ml (¼ pint) brandy

Measure the apricots, figs, prunes, and raisins into a large pot; add 570ml (1pint) of the water. Bring to the boil over a medium heat, then cover the pan and simmer for about 20 minutes. Add the plums, apple, and blackcurrants or berries, then the sugar, lemon juice and spices. Stir well and add more water if necessary to prevent sticking or burning (this dish should have a very thick, rugged texture when finished).

Cover the pan again and simmer for about 5 minutes while you grate the rind from the orange.

Set the rind aside. Peel the orange and divide into sections, add these to the cooking pot. Stir well and add the brandy. Bring the mixture back to the boil then immediately remove from heat. Stir in the grated orange rind, cover the pan and leave it to stand for at least 15 minutes before serving.

You may wish to fish out the spices before serving, though most people don't object to doing it for themselves; leaving them in only enhances the flavour. This compote is delicious hot or cold but difficult to resist once it is ready. Try it on its own first, then experiment with favourite sauces, syrups and toppings.

Apricot Delight

Makes 450g (1lb)
Preparation time 2 hours, plus soaking overnight, plus cooling 2–4 hours

225g (8oz) dried apricots, finely chopped
filtered or mineral water
500g (1¼ lb) sugar
100g (4oz) chopped almonds
2 tbsp icing sugar

Place the chopped apricots in a bowl and cover with water. Leave to soak at least overnight but preferrably for longer. Press the mixture through a mouli to achieve a fairly chunk-free consistency then turn it into a saucepan with the sugar and cook over a low heat for 1 hour 15 minutes. Stir often to prevent sticking. Pour the mixture into a ceramic flan or oven dish and leave to cool for 2–4 hours. Dip a slightly damp knife into the icing sugar and cut the cooled mixture into squares. Dip each square into the chopped almonds and place on a sheet of greaseproof paper. Sift the remaining icing sugar over all the squares. Keep cool and dry until served.

Health Note

Dried apricots are an extremely rich source of vitamin A and iron; one cup providing all the former and well over half the latter adult daily requirement. Because they are such a good source of iron, they are obviously useful in cases of anaemia due to iron loss, and are reputedly of use in cases of asthma, bronchitis, catarrh and for the detoxification of the skin and whole body system.

Arame Try this exquisite food before you allow prejudices – yours or anyone else's – to interfere with your exploration and enjoyment of marine plants. The fact is, sea vegetables have been eaten for centuries in all maritime regions of the world and that is quite enough time for generations of cooks to devise superb methods of serving this nutritious group of plants. Most seaweeds contain remarkable quantities of the vitamins and minerals which are essential for health, and are rich in a multitude of trace elements which are vitally lacking in today's synthetic diet.

For those who need coaxing to experiment with sea vegetables, arame is probably the best one to start with. Buy it from healthfood, macrobiotic or Japanese grocers where it is sold, dried, in 25–50g (1–2oz) packets. Arame has an attractive, lacey texture which feels good in the mouth and also sets off other foods visually. Cooked arame has a very delicate and subtle flavour (the smell it gives off during cooking can be quite strong, but do not be misled by this). Here's how to prepare arame in a simple but mouth-watering way.

Arame and Vegetable Sauté

Serves 4
Preparation time 1 hour

50g (2oz) dried arame
2 tbsp sesame oil
100g (4oz) mushrooms, sliced
5 spring onions, sliced into 5cm (2inch) lengths
3 medium carrots, cut into fine chunks
1 tbsp soy sauce (see Soya beans, p289)
2 tbsp sesame seeds, roasted
freshly ground black pepper, to taste

First, wash the arame to remove any grit, then soak it in plenty of water, in a bowl, for about 20 minutes. It will swell considerably. Lift the arame into a saucepan and pour most of the soaking water over it (discard the gritty water at the bottom of the bowl or use it to water your houseplants). Place the pan over a medium heat, make sure there is sufficient water to cover the seaweed and bring to a boil. Immediately reduce the heat and simmer for 15 minutes, until the arame becomes very tender. Keep a close eye at this stage as a great deal of froth is created initially and it can easily boil over. Meanwhile, heat the sesame oil in a large pan and sauté the thinly sliced vegetables in it. Drain the tender arame and add to the vegetables (save the cooking water for use in a soup or use it, cooled, to water more houseplants). Stir the arame and vegetables over a medium heat to mix the ingredients well. Season with soy sauce and cook for a few more minutes before serving hot. Serve over rice, sprinkling each serving with a teaspoonful of roasted sesame seeds and a little black pepper.

This is a delicious, low-fat Japanese-style dish which is easy to amend according to whatever vegetables you have to hand. Also, you can make it a delicate little dish, with one or two sautéed vegetables, or a huge and substantial one with half a dozen vegetables in the sauté. Try it very spicy with plenty of garlic and fresh chilli or subtle and sloppy with a little extra broth thickened with kuzu (arrowroot). Over to you!

Arame and Cabbage Winter Salad

Serves 4
Preparation time 1 hour

50g (2oz) dried arame
½ white or red cabbage, finely shredded
3 spring onions, finely chopped
1 eating apple, finely chopped
1 × 285g (10oz) tin sweetcorn kernels, drained (optional)
50g (2oz) pumpkin seeds, roasted (see Pumpkin, p279)
3 tbsp olive oil
1 tbsp cider vinegar
1 tsp black salt
¼ tsp freshly ground black pepper

Wash the arame, and soak for about 20 minutes. Cook the arame in its soaking water over a medium heat, until tender. Drain and leave to cool. Meanwhile, mix the cabbage, onions, apple, sweetcorn and pumpkin seeds in a large bowl. Add the cooled arame and mix well. Measure the remaining ingredients into a jug or jar and stir or shake to make a dressing. Pour over the salad and serve. This salad keeps for one day.

Health Note

Seaweeds such as arame are good sources of many trace minerals, including iodine, which is essential to the proper growth and function of the thyroid gland. Occasionally, however, iodine may aggravate problems for acne-sufferers – in sensitive people, even the smallest amount may be enough to trigger a skin reaction.

Artichokes Two vegetables are referred to as arti-chokes, but only one (the globe) is a true artichoke, the other (Jerusalem, see p225) is an edible tuber which grows underground. Artichokes are the flower bud of *cynara scolymus*, a member of the thistle family and if left to mature become huge, purple blossom instead of the delicious starter or appetizer with which we are familiar. One of their more mysterious char-acteristics is that there is always more of the artichoke after eating it than before! It pays to be particularly fussy when buying artichokes: choose one that is too small and you will find that there is virtually no edible flesh at the base of the leaves, and if it is brown, open or spreading, then it is definitely past its best. Choose a medium- to large-sized artichoke that is firm and evenly green in colour. Once chosen, the artichoke can be rather daunting to prepare. Here is the best way:

- Cut off the stem and remove any tough or damaged outer leaves.
- Make it easy on your dinner guests and remove the choke – the hairy centre of the artichoke which will cause something close to choking if swallowed! Expert artichoke eaters can do this themselves at the table, but most diners will appreciate your efforts. To remove the choke, take some kitchen scissors and snip away the sharp points of the topmost leaves of the artichoke, so that it can be opened up to allow you to work inside it. When you have prised the leaves apart just sufficiently, locate the immature leaves, which usually have a purplish colour, towards the centre and remove them – since they have no fleshy base to them, they are inedible. Once the young leaves have been removed, you will have exposed the choke itself, which should be carefully scooped out with a teaspoon.
- When all the fine hairs have been carefully re-moved, the artichoke should be carefully washed and then placed in boiling water (which may be acidified with vinegar to improve the flavour) and simmered for about half an hour, until the leaves fall effortlessly away when pulled, and the succulent flesh at their base is tender. Drain and cool.
- Serve the artichoke (one shared or one per person) in a shallow bowl. Give each person a small bowl filled with a sharp vinaigrette dressing. Each person then pulls a leaf from the artichoke, dips the tender end in their dressing and scrapes the flesh off the leaf with their front teeth. Used leaves can be tossed into a large empty bowl in the centre of the table.

Tinned artichoke hearts can be purchased at most supermarkets and are useful to add a special touch to salads, sandwiches, sauces or spreads. Keep one or two tins in your larder for convenience but be aware that they are not as nutritious as fresh artichokes.

NUTRIENT ANALYSIS
ARTICHOKE, BOILED (120g)

KCalories	60.00
Total Fat (g)	0.19
Monounsaturated Fat (g)	0.01
Polyunsaturated Fat (g)	0.08
Saturated Fat (g)	0.04
Carbohydrate (g)	13.42
Protein (g)	4.18
Crude Fibre (g)	1.50
Vitamin A (RE)	21.60
Ascorbic Acid (mg)	12.00
Thiamin (mg)	0.08
Riboflavin (mg)	0.08
Niacin (mg)	1.20
Pantothenic Acid (mg)	0.41
Vitamin B6 (mg)	0.13
Folacin (mcg)	61.20
Vitamin B12 (mcg)	0.00
Calcium (mg)	54.00
Iron (mg)	1.55
Zinc (mg)	0.59

Artichoke and Basil Sauce
Serves 4
Preparation time 25 minutes

1 tbsp oil
1 medium onion, finely chopped
½ tsp freshly ground black pepper
¼ tsp ground nutmeg
1 tbsp flour
570ml (1 pint) soya milk
285ml (½ pint) vegetable stock
2 medium tomatoes, chopped

2 tbsp fresh basil, chopped
2 × 400g (14oz) tins artichoke hearts, drained and chopped

Heat the oil in a saucepan and sauté the onion until clear and tender. Add the pepper and stir for 1 minute. Mix the nutmeg into the flour and sprinkle over the saute. Stir to a thick paste (roux). Blend the soya milk and stock together then add, a little at a time, to the roux, stirring well after each addition. Allow the sauce to thicken, stirring often. Add the tomatoes, basil and artichoke hearts. Cook at a low heat for 10 minutes. Serve hot over rice, pasta, baked potatoes or a plate of steamed vegetables.

Artichoke Spread

Serves 4
Preparation time 20 minutes

8 artichoke hearts, fresh if possible, chopped
285g (10oz) plain tofu, mashed
1 tbsp fresh parsley, chopped
1 tbsp chives, chopped
1 tbsp prepared mustard
1 tbsp tahini
juice of 1 lemon
salt and freshly ground black pepper, to taste

Measure all the ingredients into a bowl and blend with a fork to an even, though chunky, consistency. Chill for 1 hour or serve immediately as a sandwich spread or as a filling for tomatoes, baked potatoes or celery sticks.

Health Note

Although the artichoke appears to be a delicate and insubstantial vegetable, it has significant nutritional properties. Very low in calories, an average artichoke provides a quarter of the adult daily requirement of vitamin C, a third of the folic acid requirement, and nearly a fifth of the iron. In years gone by, women were often forbidden to eat artichokes because of their rampant aphrodisiac properties. Today, the juice of their leaves is reported to have powerful diuretic properties, as well as being used to treat bad breath, diarrhoea, and various glandular disorders. It contains a substance – cynarin – which is believed to have significant liver-protecting and regenerating effects.

Asparagus Made fashionable by Louis XIV, the Sun King, who apparently had an insatiable desire for this vegetable, asparagus comes in three varieties, white, purple and green. The fan-shaped root crown of white asparagus is planted about 10 inches below the surface of the soil, and is harvested as soon as the tip of the shoot breaks the surface. The purple variety is allowed to grow to a height of a few inches, and then gathered. Only the green is allowed to grow a little further, and indeed owes its green colouration to the effect of sunlight upon chlorophyll in the plant. The nutritional profile of these varieties is also quite different, the green being far higher in vitamin A and folic acid than the others. To cook asparagus, trim the woody ends of the spears and tie several into a bundle. Then either steam the bundle of spears, plunge it into boiling salted water for about 20 minutes, or make use of a special cylindrical pan which holds the bundle upright as it cooks – the bottom of the stalks remain in water and are boiled, the tips remain out of water and are simply steamed until tender. One of the nicest and easiest ways to eat asparagus is rolled up in thinly sliced brown bread; remove the crusts, lightly coat with olive oil, and roll each slice around an asparagus shoot (trim the ends so they don't protrude). Dainty, decorative and delicious!

NUTRIENT ANALYSIS
1 CUP ASPARAGUS, STEAMED (180g)

KCalories	45.00
Total Fat (g)	0.56
Monounsaturated Fat (g)	0.02
Polyunsaturated Fat (g)	0.25
Saturated Fat (g)	0.13
Carbohydrate (g)	7.92
Protein (g)	4.66
Crude Fibre (g)	1.49
Vitamin A (RE)	149.40
Ascorbic Acid (mg)	48.78
Thiamin (mg)	0.18
Riboflavin (mg)	0.22
Niacin (mg)	1.89
Pantothenic Acid (mg)	0.29

Vitamin B6 (mg)	0.25
Folacin (mcg)	176.58
Vitamin B12 (mcg)	0.00
Calcium (mg)	43.20
Iron (mg)	1.19
Zinc (mg)	0.86

Cavendish Asparagus Salad

Serves 4
Preparation time 45 minutes

450g (1lb) new potatoes, scrubbed and quartered
2 bundles (approximately 24 spears) fresh asparagus
285g (10oz) plain tofu
1 tbsp oil
½ tsp freshly ground black pepper
½ tsp paprika
2 medium carrots, grated
1 small onion, finely chopped
3 tbsp oil
1 tbsp cider vinegar
1 tsp prepared mustard
pinch of salt
crisp lettuce or radiccio

Prepare the potatoes and asparagus and steam them both until tender. Allow to cool. Cube the tofu and preheat a grill. Mix the oil and spices together and gently roll each tofu cube in this mixture. Arrange the tofu on a tray and grill for 3–5 minutes, turn the cubes and grill a further 3 minutes. Leave to cool. Mix the carrots, onion, potatoes and tofu in a salad bowl. Blend the oil, vinegar, mustard and salt to make a dressing and toss into the salad. Place some lettuce or radiccio on each serving plate and arrange the asparagus in a fan shape around it. Fill the lettuce 'bowl' with the salad mixture and serve.

Stuffed Tempeh 'Goose' with Raspberry and Asparagus

Serves 4
Preparation time 1 hour 30 minutes plus overnight marinate

2 x 250g (9oz) blocks tempeh, defrosted (see Tempeh, p292)
285ml (½ pint) raspberry vinegar (see Raspberry Vinegar, p283)
140ml (¼ pint) olive oil

5 cloves garlic, finely chopped
1 medium onion, finely chopped
50g (2oz) fresh parsley, chopped
225g (8oz) mushrooms, thinly sliced
1 tbsp fresh ginger, grated
1 tsp freshly ground black pepper
¼ tsp ground cloves
285ml (½ pint) raspberries
24 asparagus spears

Slice each block of tempeh in half diagonally then slice each half into three triangles – you will end up with twelve slices in total. Mix the vinegar and oil together in a jug and have the remaining ingredients – except the asparagus – ready to hand. In a broad oven dish, arrange a layer of tempeh slices. Now sprinkle the garlic, onion, parsley, mushrooms, ginger, pepper and cloves over the tempeh in the order in which they are given. Arrange the remaining tempeh slices over all. Spread the raspberries over the top layer of tempeh and press them down into any gaps and round the edges. Finally, pour the vinegar and oil mixture over all. Cover the pan and leave to marinate overnight in a cool place or the refrigerator.

Preheat the oven to 180°C/350°F/Gas Mark 4. Gently agitate the oven dish containing the marinaded tempeh and add a little more vinegar and oil if necessary so that you can just see the liquid near the surface. Bake for 50 minutes, covered. Remove the cover and bake for a further 5–10 minutes. Meanwhile, steam the asparagus. When both are cooked, slice through the tempeh 'goose' so that each serving displays a cross-section of layers. Frame the 'goose' with asparagus spears drizzled with the raspberry marinade. Serve with wild rice for a more substantial meal.

Little Italy Asparagus in Tomato Sauce

Serves 4
Preparation time 30 minutes

900g (2lb) asparagus spears
3 tbsp olive oil
1 large onion, thinly sliced
1.5kg (3lb) fresh tomatoes, chopped
½ tsp salt
1 tsp freshly ground black pepper
2 tbsp fresh basil, chopped

Heat the oil and sauté the onion until clear and tender. Add the tomatoes, salt and pepper and simmer until the sauce is reduced and slightly thickened, about 20 minutes. Stir in the fresh basil and leave, covered, over a very low heat. Meanwhile, steam the asparagus until just tender then serve immediately onto a hot plate or asparagus 'trough', or you may prefer to arrange it over millet, rice or pasta. Pour the hot tomato sauce over the asparagus and serve at once.

Health Note

Asparagus is said to have a particularly beneficial effect upon the kidneys. Its juice has been shown to have both antimutagenic and anticarcinogenic properties. Roughly half the population produce odorous urine after eating asparagus; the ability to do so is thought to be a genetically inherited trait in humans.

Aubergine Sometimes referred to as the eggplant, this vegetable is a member of the deadly nightshade family (*solanum*) which also includes tomatoes, potatoes and tobacco. It generally has a glossy purple appearance, but red and white varieties also exist. When first introduced to Europe from the Middle East in the middle ages, it was treated as a purely decorative plant (thought to produce madness if consumed), and, even today, various natural therapists and adherents of the macrobiotic philosophy will scrupulously avoid this vegetable and other members of the deadly nightshade family.

Nutritionally, it contains virtually nothing worth mentioning, and has the added disadvantage of absorbing huge quantities of oil if fried. Furthermore, it should not be consumed raw. The extremely bitter taste of certain larger and older aubergines can be diminished by slicing them and covering with a good coating of household salt for at least half an hour. Bitter liquid will then be seen to seep from the vegetable's exposed surfaces, which should then be thoroughly washed before food preparation is continued.

Aubergine features regularly in Middle and Far Eastern cookery but usually as a venue for other flavours and textures. It is very successful, for instance, when used as an edible container in which to stuff a variety of tasty fillings. When subsequently baked, such dishes have tremendous visual appeal. Aubergine features rather famously in the classical recipes ratatouille and baba ghanoush.

See also: Baba Ganoush (p320); Salatat Aswad (p321); Grilled Aubergine (p338); Spicy Steamed Aubergine (p341); Brinjal Bhaji (p343); Peppered Aubergine (p348); Mussakka (p350)

NUTRIENT ANALYSIS
1 CUP AUBERGINE CUBES, BOILED (96g)

KCalories	26.88
Total Fat (g)	0.22
Monounsaturated Fat (g)	0.02
Polyunsaturated Fat (g)	0.09
Saturated Fat (g)	0.04
Carbohydrate (g)	6.37
Protein (g)	0.80
Crude Fibre (g)	0.93
Vitamin A (RE)	5.76
Ascorbic Acid (mg)	1.25
Thiamin (mg)	0.07
Riboflavin (mg)	0.02
Niacin (mg)	0.58
Pantothenic Acid (mg)	0.07
Vitamin B6 (mg)	0.08
Folacin (mcg)	13.82
Vitamin B12 (mcg)	0.00
Calcium (mg)	5.76
Iron (mg)	0.34
Zinc (mg)	0.14

Ratatouille

Serves 4
Preparation time 4 hours

3 tbsp olive oil
3 medium aubergines, peeled and sliced
1 large onion, sliced
6–8 fresh tomatoes, chopped
2 sweet green peppers
3 medium courgettes, sliced
7 cloves garlic, chopped
1 tbsp fresh basil
1½ tsp dried thyme
1 tsp freshly ground black pepper

½ tsp salt
1 tbsp olive oil

Heat the oil in a large saucepan and sauté the aubergine for 7–10 minutes. Add the onion and continue to sauté until the onion is clear and tender. Add the tomatoes and stir well. Simmer for about 15 minutes, stirring often. Add the remaining ingredients, except the oil, and stir well. Cook for over a low heat for 25 minutes then add the remaining oil and adjust the seasonings to taste. Cook a further 10 minutes, until it has a creamy consistency. Serve immediately or leave to stand and reheat later in the day.

Health Note

Although some people strongly dislike aubergines, others find they are powerfully attracted to them. Perhaps this could be the reason why: aubergines contain nicotine, the addictive substance normally thought of as only being present in tobacco. In fact, nicotine is found in other members of this family of plants, including potatoes and tomatoes. Researchers have calculated that consuming as little as one-third of an ounce of aubergine provides the same intake of nicotine as spending three hours in a faintly smoky room!

Avocado It is extraordinary to think that the avocado was virtually unknown to Western cuisine before the 1970s. Since that time, countries such as Israel and South Africa have done much to establish a mass market for this magnificent fruit. Be thoughtfully choosy when selecting avocados. Very hard ones will probably never ripen satisfactorily, no matter how much time they spend in the airing cupboard (though you might try the tip given on p183, under Banana). The Mexican avocado is generally considered to be the best, and is usually available from January until April. The perfect avocado will slice easily – as if you are drawing a knife through soft butter – has a warm yellow appearance when halved, with only a touch of green visible, and the large stone will slide out easily. Enjoy such perfectly ripe fruits by filling the stone hollow with a vinaigrette and spooning the dressed avocado straight into your mouth!

NUTRIENT ANALYSIS
AVOCADO PEAR (200g)

KCalories	323.61
Total Fat (g)	30.79
Monounsaturated Fat (g)	19.31
Polyunsaturated Fat (g)	3.93
Saturated Fat (g)	4.90
Carbohydrate (g)	14.85
Protein (g)	3.98
Crude Fibre (g)	4.24
Vitamin A (RE)	122.61
Ascorbic Acid (mg)	15.88
Thiamin (mg)	0.22
Riboflavin (mg)	0.25
Niacin (mg)	3.86
Pantothenic Acid (mg)	1.95
Vitamin B6 (mg)	0.56
Folacin (mcg)	124.42
Vitamin B12 (mcg)	0.00
Calcium (mg)	22.11
Iron (mg)	2.05
Zinc (mg)	0.84

Without any question, the finest – and indeed easiest – dish to prepare from avocados is the Mexican dish guacamole. It must be served absolutely fresh (contrary to popular wisdom, guacamole will not keep satisfactorily, even if you add extra lemon juice and put the stone in it) with plenty of hot toast, pitta or corn tortilla chips. Even though guacamole is easy to make, very few restaurants – other than authentic Mexican ones – can prepare it satisfactorily. Watching this being made in Mexico is almost as pleasing as eating it. The ingredients are fresh and aromatic, the surroundings are usually peaceful and homely and the method is definitely low-tech: not a food processor in sight. The cook uses a simple mortar and pestle to achieve the smooth consistency that is so attractive in this dish. A good guacamole should have an edge of sharpness to it, and a hint of spicy hotness. Here is the best recipe I've found in a lifetime of searching:

Guacamole

Serves 4
Preparation time 15 minutes

2 large, ripe avocados
juice of 1 lemon
285ml (½ pint) plain soya yoghurt
¼–½ tsp chilli powder
¼ tsp salt
1 medium, fresh, ripe tomato, very finely chopped

Slice the avocados in half along their length and remove the stones. Scoop out the flesh into a small mixing bowl: it does not matter if the flesh is slightly brown in places, though it should never smell sour. Use a fork to mash the avocado to a fairly smooth consistency with the lemon juice. Now add the yoghurt, chilli and salt; stir well and continue the slight mashing movement. Finally, add the very finely chopped tomato (fresh is much better than canned) and stir well. Serve immediately with toast, corn chips or pitta bread. Of course, this is excellent when served with a salad or crudités but, quite frankly, in our house it always gets eaten well before any such further preparations can take place!

Avocado Milkshake

Serves 4
Preparation time 15 minutes

1l (2 pints) cold soya milk
2 large, ripe avocadoes, peeled and stoned
1 tbsp barley malt syrup
50g (2oz) ground almonds or hazelnuts

Measure all (or half at a time) the ingredients into a blender and purée to a smooth, thick consistency. Pour into chilled glasses and serve immediately with a garnish of ground nuts or a single mint leaf.

Health Note

Conventional nutrition maintains that avocados are 'rogue' plant foods – uncommonly high in fat for fruits, and should be eaten with caution. But new research threatens to overturn this orthodoxy. Australian scientists report that people consuming anything from half to one-and-a-half avocados a day can actually lower their cholesterol levels more than people eating a very low-fat diet! Once again, the avocado's high content of monounsaturates (the same fatty acid present in olive oil) is thought to be responsible.

Baked Beans One of the most widely available of all vegetarian fast foods. Never make the mistake of thinking that baked beans are 'junk' food – they are not! The amino acids found in baked beans and bread (as in beans on toast) complement each other to produce a high protein food perfect for growing children. Furthermore, the combination is almost always low in fat (unless you smother the toast with butter), high in soluble fibre (which can actually reduce cholesterol levels – see Oats, p246), and a useful source of iron, too. A tin of baked beans, served on two slices of toast, provides two-thirds of the adult requirement for fibre, half of the protein, folic acid and thiamine requirements, and a quarter of the calcium, iron and zinc requirements. In short, one of the best fast foods available.

NUTRIENT ANALYSIS
1 CUP BAKED BEANS (254g)

KCalories	236.22
Total Fat (g)	1.14
Monounsaturated Fat (g)	0.10
Polyunsaturated Fat (g)	0.49
Saturated Fat (g)	0.29
Carbohydrate (g)	52.10
Protein (g)	12.17
Crude Fibre (g)	2.90
Vitamin A (RE)	43.18
Ascorbic Acid (mg)	7.87
Thiamin (mg)	0.39
Riboflavin (mg)	0.15
Niacin (mg)	1.09
Pantothenic Acid (mg)	0.24
Vitamin B6 (mg)	0.34
Folacin (mcg)	60.71
Vitamin B12 (mcg)	0.00
Calcium (mg)	127.00
Iron (mg)	0.74
Zinc (mg)	3.56

Home Cooked Baked Beans

Serves 4–6
Preparation time 1 hour 30 minutes, plus overnight soaking

450g (1lb) dried haricot beans, washed and drained
3 bay leaves
2 tbsp oil
5 cloves garlic, chopped
1 large onion, chopped
5 whole cloves or ½ tsp ground cloves
2x5cm (2in) pieces cinnamon stick or 1 tsp ground cinnamon
285g (10oz) tomato purée
140ml (¼ pint) molasses
140ml (¼ pint) prepared mustard
1l (2 pints) vegetable stock or water
2 tbsp cider vinegar
1 tbsp soy sauce

Wash the beans and soak them overnight in plenty of fresh water. Drain, rinse and drain them again before turning into a pressure cooker with the bay leaves. Just cover with fresh water and cook, at pressure, for 20 minutes. Remove from the heat immediately and drain away the cooking water.

Heat the oil in a large stewpot or saucepan over a medium heat and sauté the garlic and onion until clear and tender. Add the cloves and cinnamon and stir for 1 minute. Add the tomato purée, molasses, mustard and stock. Stir well and bring to the boil. Add the beans, bring to the boil again then cover the pan, reduce the heat to low and leave to simmer gently for about 1 hour. Stir once or twice during this time and add more stock if necessary. At the end of this time, stir in the vinegar and soy sauce. Remove the pot from the heat and serve immediately or leave to stand for anything up to 24 hours. The beans should be thick and the sauce richly flavoured.

Health Note

The kind of soluble fibre found in baked beans (and also in oats, prunes, and several other plant foods) breaks down during the digestive process, unlike the insoluble fibre found in grain products. Apart from being able to lower cholesterol levels, soluble fibre also adds bulk and thickness to the contents of the stomach (which may help to control the appetite), and slows the absorption of sugars from the small intestine, which may be of benefit to diabetics.

Bamboo Shoots Several parts of the bamboo plant are eaten in Eastern countries, although the most common in the West is the bamboo shoot, available canned in most supermarkets and all Eastern grocery stores. Bamboo shoots make an interesting and flavoursome ingredient in any stir-fry; they offer a unique texture and are used directly from the tin or sliced into matchstick size strips. Stir-fries are intrinsically healthy meals and need not – indeed *should* not – be made using very much oil. Here are two low-fat best stir-fry techniques for you to experiment with:

- **Lo-Fat Stir-Fry** Use a maximum of 15ml (1 tbsp) of an oil high in linoleic acid, such as sunflower, safflower, corn, soya or olive. Measure it into the pan or wok and heat over a medium to high heat (not smoking or spitting) *before* the ingredients are added. Once added, stir the food constantly, adding other foods as per the recipe. Keep the heat high until the juices from the foods are released into the oil. Then reduce the heat and add any liquid that is required. This method uses a high temperature to seal in the flavour, aroma and goodness of the food, while drastically reducing the fat content.

- **No-Fat Stir-Fry** This radical method uses *no* oil but still achieves the flavour, aroma, texture and nutritional quality desired from a good stir-fry! Like all worthwhile cookery techniques, it will need some practice. Instead of oil, a very small amount (usually 15–30ml/1–2 tbsp) of liquid is heated in the pan until it bubbles furiously. The liquid may be water, stock, tomato juice, vinegar, gravy broth, dilute yeast extract or, indeed, any non-fat liquid you wish to use or that the recipe calls for. Once the liquid is heated, the food is added and stirred constantly over a medium to high heat. As the food is more likely to stick in this method, the sauté time is not so long and the heat is slightly higher than in the lo-fat method.

See also: Quickly Seitan (p340); Tofu Sukiyaki (p351)

NUTRIENT ANALYSIS
1 CUP BAMBOO SHOOTS (131g)

KCalories	24.89
Total Fat (g)	0.52
Monounsaturated Fat (g)	0.01

Polyunsaturated Fat (g)	0.23
Saturated Fat (g)	0.12
Carbohydrate (g)	4.22
Protein (g)	2.25
Crude Fibre (g)	0.88
Vitamin A (RE)	1.31
Ascorbic Acid (mg)	1.44
Thiamin (mg)	0.03
Riboflavin (mg)	0.03
Niacin (mg)	0.18
Pantothenic Acid (mg)	0.12
Vitamin B6 (mg)	0.18
Folacin (mcg)	4.19
Vitamin B12 (mcg)	0.00
Calcium (mg)	10.48
Iron (mg)	0.42
Zinc (mg)	0.85

Bright Moon Stir-Fry

Serves 4
Preparation time 30 minutes

1 tbsp oil
225g (8oz) mushrooms, thinly sliced
1 × 225g (8oz) tin water chestnuts, drained and
  halved
1 × 285g (10oz) tin bamboo shoots, drained and
  sliced
1 large sweet red pepper, deseeded and sliced
5 spring onions, halved and sliced lengthwise
½ tsp chilli powder
140ml (¼ pint) fruit juice
2 tbsp soy sauce
3 tbsp water
2 tsp kuzu (arrowroot)

Prepare all the ingredients before you start cooking
and have them ready to hand. Heat the oil in a large
frying pan or wok over a high heat. Add the mushrooms and stir for 1 minute. Add the water chestnuts
and bamboo shoots and continue stirring for 1 minute.
Add the pepper, spring onions and chilli and stir a
further 1 minute. All the vegetables should by now be
heated. Mix the fruit juice, soy sauce and water

together and dissolve the kuzu in it. Pour this liquid
over the stir-fry. Stir well and reduce the heat. Leave
the stir-fry to cook (you may cover it if you wish) for a
further 5 minutes over a medium heat. Lift the
vegetables out and serve with rice – either on the
rice or in a separate bowl next to it. Add the cooking
juices to each serving according to taste.

Bananas The ubiquitous banana first originated in
India, and is now familiar to consumers in all continents of the world. The governments of entire
countries have risen and in turn been toppled by
the huge economic and political power exercised by
those who trade in this commodity – hence the term
'banana republic'.

Apart from the sweet variety of banana eaten as a
fruit, there is also the plantain, or green banana, a
savoury accompaniment to many West Indian, South
American and African dishes. To cook plantains, boil
them in salted water for approximately 25 minutes, or
until tender, then fry, mash, or use as an ingredient in
soups and stews. (See also Plantain, p271).

Fruit bananas are always picked when green, and
slowly ripened in transit to their destination market.
As they ripen, they give off large quantities of ethylene
gas, which itself causes ripening and development of
colour in other fruits. To help a hard avocado ripen, or
to turn green tomatoes red, simply place them in a
sealed box together with some unripe bananas, and
nature will do the rest! There are, of course, an infinite
number of uses for the banana – they make superb
milkshakes, they are an extremely good baby food, and
any form of cooking will really bring out their full rich
flavour. As a fairly instant way to sample the banana's
delightful flavour and texture, try a banana and peanut
butter (or tahini) sandwich. Nothing could be simpler,
just spread the peanut butter on one slice of bread and
arrange slices of ripe banana over it. Close the
sandwich and go!
See also: Banana Bread (p309); Boija (p336); Orange
Banana Pudding (p336); Banana Rum Bake (p337)

NUTRIENT ANALYSIS
1 BANANA (114g)

KCalories	105.00
Total Fat (g)	0.55
Monounsaturated Fat (g)	0.05

Polyunsaturated Fat (g)	0.10
Saturated Fat (g)	0.21
Carbohydrate (g)	26.71
Protein (g)	1.18
Crude Fibre (g)	1.82
Vitamin A (RE)	9.00
Ascorbic Acid (mg)	10.30
Thiamin (mg)	0.05
Riboflavin (mg)	0.11
Niacin (mg)	0.62
Pantothenic Acid (mg)	0.39
Vitamin B6 (mg)	0.66
Folacin (mcg)	21.80
Vitamin B12 (mcg)	0.00
Calcium (mg)	7.00
Iron (mg)	0.35
Zinc (mg)	0.19

Banana Shake

Serves 4
Preparation time 10 minutes

1l (2 pints) cold soya milk
4 very ripe bananas, peeled
50g (2oz) ground almonds
¼ tsp ground nutmeg

Turn all (or half at a time) of the ingredients into a blender and whisk to a thick, frothy consistency. Pour into chilled glasses and serve immediately with a garnish of flaked almonds or a single banana chip floating on the surface.

Rich Banana Nut Loaf

Makes 1 loaf
Preparation time 1 hour 30 minutes

340g (12oz) plain flour
3 teaspoons baking powder
1 teaspoon bicarbonate of soda
170g (6oz) currants
100g (4oz) walnuts, chopped
50g (2oz) dried peel
3 ripe bananas, peeled

100g (4oz) brown sugar
100g (4oz) margarine
285ml (½ pint) orange or pineapple juice

Preheat oven to 180°C/350°F/Gas Mark 4 and lightly oil a large loaf tin. Mix the first six ingredients together in a large bowl and set aside. Cream the bananas, sugar and margarine then slowly stir in the orange juice. Blend the dry ingredients with the banana mixture, stir briefly then pour the batter into the loaf tin. You may garnish the top of the loaf with chopped nuts and/or a few pieces of dried peel. Bake for 1 hour. Leave to cool in the tin for 10 minutes before turning out onto a wire rack.

Banana Almond Cheesecake

Serves 4–6
Preparation time 2 hours

24 large digestive biscuits, crushed
½ tsp ground nutmeg
3 tbsp margarine, melted
2 × 285g (10oz) blocks plain tofu, drained and mashed
4 ripe bananas, peeled
4 tbsp barley malt syrup
100g (4oz) ground almonds
50g (2oz) slivered almonds

Mix the crushed biscuits and ground nutmeg together in a large bowl. Pour the melted margarine over and stir well. Press this mixture into a large pie dish or ramekin and put to one side. Combine the tofu, bananas and syrup in blender and purée until smooth. Blend the ground almonds into the purée. Pour this mixture into the biscuit crust and spread to the edges. Sprinkle the slivered almonds over the top of the cheesecake and refrigerate until it sets. Serve cold topped with fruit sauce or Soya Creem.

Banana Oat Muffins

Makes approximately 18 muffins
Preparation time 35 minutes

100g (4oz) rolled oats
100g (4oz) currants
570ml (1 pint) soya milk
225g (8oz) wholewheat flour
2 tsp baking powder
1 tsp bicarbonate of soda
1 tsp ground cinnamon
3 bananas, peeled

100g (4oz) brown sugar
140ml (¼ pint) oil

Preheat the oven to 180°C/350°F/Gas Mark 4 and lightly oil or line some muffin tins. Measure the oats and currants into a bowl and cover with the soya milk; leave to one side to soak. Mix the flour, baking powder, soda and cinnamon in a mixing bowl and put to one side. Cream the bananas, sugar and oil together in a blender and add to the soaked oat mixture. Stir well then gradually add the dry mix. Stir briefly then drop a large spoonful of batter into each muffin tin. Bake for 20 minutes.

Health Note

Bananas are a concentrated source of nutrients, one average banana providing about one-fifth of the adult requirement of vitamin C, over a third of the requirement for vitamin B6, and a quarter of the potassium requirement. They are also useful sources of riboflavin, folic acid, and various other minerals. It has been shown that people who regularly consume potassium-rich food such as bananas can lower their risk of suffering a stroke by as much as 40 per cent. It is not certain why this should be so, but one mechanism may be the blood-pressure lowering effect which potassium possesses. Bananas are amongst those foodstuffs least likely to cause allergies or sensitivity reactions; and black, near-rotting bananas have been used to treat a range of gastric and digestive problems, including stomach ulcers, colitis, and diarrhoea.

Beetroot The most dire fate which can befall a beetroot is boiling, a process which yields nothing more than a sickly sweet, tasteless pink globule of starch. Yet, that is precisely what most people do. When cooked, beetroot contains virtually nothing of any nutritive value, but raw (preferably grated into a salad) it contains a useful range of nutrients such as iron, calcium, and vitamins A and C. The leaves of the plant are also edible, and can be cooked and used in a manner akin to spinach. Raw beetroot juice has a powerful taste, and should be combined in a ratio of one measure of beetroot juice to four measures of carrot or other naturally sweet juice in order to make it more palatable. Consumed in this way, it is a powerful

laxative and it has traditionally been used as a purgative and blood purifier. Beetroot is usually dark red in colour, but white and golden varieties are occasionally found, too.

NUTRIENT ANALYSIS
½ CUP RAW BEETROOT (68g)

KCalories	29.92
Total Fat (g)	0.10
Monounsaturated Fat (g)	0.02
Polyunsaturated Fat (g)	0.03
Saturated Fat (g)	0.01
Carbohydrate (g)	6.80
Protein (g)	1.01
Crude Fibre (g)	0.54
Vitamin A (RE)	1.36
Ascorbic Acid (mg)	7.48
Thiamin (mg)	0.03
Riboflavin (mg)	0.01
Niacin (mg)	0.27
Pantothenic Acid (mg)	0.10
Vitamin B6 (mg)	0.03
Folacin (mcg)	62.97
Vitamin B12 (mcg)	0.00
Calcium (mg)	10.88
Iron (mg)	0.62
Zinc (mg)	0.25

Hearty Winter Salad
Serves 4–8
Preparation time 45 minutes

Combine any vegetables, beans or seeds readily and cheaply to hand, such as: tinned or precooked kidney beans, carrots, beetroot, cabbage, watercress, cos lettuce, broccoli, potatoes, tofu, sunflower seeds, almonds, pumpkin seeds; plus any seasonal vegetables, including winter roots.

Get a really large bowl.

Cube the potatoes and lightly steam them and the broccoli; roast the pumpkin seeds; cube the tofu; grate the raw carrot and beetroot (do not slice); thinly shred the cabbage; finely chop the watercress; wash and roughly chop the lettuce; don't forget the sunflower seeds and almonds. All this is quick to do, but a food processor will speed it up even more.

Prepare your favourite dressing. Two suggestions: olive oil, cider vinegar and French mustard. Alternatively, for the most unusual dressing you've ever tasted, try this: visit your local Indian delicatessen and ask for a packet of ground 'black salt' (Kala Namak Powder). Add two teaspoons to oil and cider vinegar, shake thoroughly until dissolved.

Combine all the ingredients and add the dressing.

One serving of a salad such as this will give you a third of your total daily requirement of protein, almost twice your vitamin A requirement, all your vitamin C, and half your iron and fibre. Actually, it's so good you'll want to eat it every day!

Wholesome Borscht

Serves 4
Preparation time 1 hour

1 tbsp oil
5 cloves garlic, chopped
2 medium onions, chopped
2 stalks celery, thinly sliced
1kg (2lb) beetroot, peeled and coarsely grated
3 medium carrots, grated
450g (1lb) potatoes, peeled and diced
1 tsp freshly ground black pepper
½ tsp ground cumin
¼ tsp ground nutmeg
1l (2 pints) vegetable stock
285ml (½ pint) white wine
2 bay leaves
3 tbsp fresh parsley, chopped
1 sprig tarragon, chopped
1 tsp dried thyme
Soya Creem or plain soya yoghurt, to garnish

Heat the oil in a large saucepan and sauté the garlic, onion and celery until clear and tender. Add the beetroot, carrots, potatoes and spices and stir the sauté for 3–5 minutes over a medium heat. Add the remaining ingredients, except the vinegar and Creem, and bring to the boil. Stir well, cover the pan and reduce the heat. Leave to simmer for 45 minutes over a medium to low heat, stirring occasionally. The vegetables must be very tender. Serve the soup as it is if you like a chunky texture, or run it through a mouli to make a thicker, smooth texture, then return it to the heat for a moment before serving. Alternatively, you may strain the soup and serve just the broth. Serve with a garnish of Creem or yoghurt and plenty of fresh, brown bread.

Blackberries Also called brambles, blackberries grow wild throughout the northern hemisphere. The cultivated variety is larger, but far less tasty. Today it is necessary to caution berry pickers against eating any fruit or vegetable which has been grown in a city or near a road, as the pollution levels (lead levels in particular) simply make it too dangerous to do so. In the countryside, you should not eat blackberries taken from hedgerows which divide fields, as it is more than likely that such fruit will have been heavily contaminated by pesticide and other chemical usage. The best areas to find untainted fruit are publicly accessible heaths, common land, scrubland and other areas which have never been cultivated nor are close to intensively farmed areas. Choose the berries right at the tip of the stalk, because they are the sweetest and fattest of all. The berries further up the stalk ripen progressively, although those closest to the centre of the shrub will be small and rather bitter. There are any number of uses for blackberries, including pies, summer puddings, fruit fools, and various drinks, such as steeping them overnight in red wine.

NUTRIENT ANALYSIS
1 CUP RAW BLACKBERRIES (144g)

KCalories	74.88
Total Fat (g)	0.56
Monounsaturated Fat (g)	trace
Polyunsaturated Fat (g)	trace
Saturated Fat (g)	trace
Carbohydrate (g)	18.37
Protein (g)	1.04
Crude Fibre (g)	5.90
Vitamin A (RE)	23.04
Ascorbic Acid (mg)	30.24
Thiamin (mg)	0.04
Riboflavin (mg)	0.06
Niacin (mg)	0.58

Pantothenic Acid (mg)	0.35
Vitamin B6 (mg)	0.08
Folacin (mcg)	48.96
Vitamin B12 (mcg)	0.00
Calcium (mg)	46.08
Iron (mg)	0.82
Zinc (mg)	0.39

Blackberry Jam

Makes approximately 3kg (6lb) jam
Preparation time 2 hours

2k (4½lb) apples, peeled, quartered and cored (Note: this measurement is for the prepared apples. Any apples will do, though cooking apples are best. Go ahead and use windfalls.)
285ml (½ pint) water
juice of 2 lemons
2k (4½lb) blackberries, washed
2k (4½lb) sugar

Prepare the apples and turn them into a large pan. Add the water and place over a medium heat. Bring to the boil and cook for 15–20 minutes, stirring often, until the apples soften. Meanwhile, pour the lemon juice over the blackberries and sugar in a large bowl. Stir well and leave to stand while the apples cook. When the apples have lost their form, add the blackberry and sugar mixture. Stir well and cook for a further 20–25 minutes to ensure a nice, thick jam. Remove from the heat, ladle into sterilized jars, seal and allow to cool.

Health Note

Paradoxically, blackberries and blackberry juice are used to treat both constipation and diarrhoea, and are reported to be helpful in treating cases of catarrh and excessive mucus discharge from the sinuses. Blackberry tea (made from the leaves) is useful in treating a sore throat.

Brazil Nuts The brazil nut tree, *bertholletia excelsa*, grows in the Amazon river valley to a height of 50m (150 feet) and, like most tall jungle trees, has branches only near the top. Its vast seed-pods are about the size of a coconut, have a thick woody shell, and contain up to two dozen seeds which are more familiar to Western consumers as brazil nuts. Buying brazil nuts not only helps to support a fragile local economy, but also helps to ensure the survival of these magnificent jungle trees.

Brazil nuts are widely used as a raw snack or cooked in fruit cakes and biscuits. However, in vegetarian cuisine, there is a special place for them. When I launched the Vegetarian Society's 'cordon vert' cookery courses in 1985, we featured a dish in the press releases called Brazilian Bake. Tactically, this may not have been a particularly sensible move, because the recipe was swiftly analyzed by Britain's meat industry nutritionists, and found to be quite high in fat. This, in turn, was used in the meat industry's publicity to proclaim that the vegetarian diet was certainly no healthier than the flesh-based one.

It is certainly true that brazil nuts are high in fat – just 25g (1oz) provides about 18g of fat in total, or about one-fifth of the adult suggested daily intake. Unusually for a vegetable food, about 20 per cent of its total fat content comes from saturated fat (saturated fat is strongly correlated with heart disease and other major health problems, and is normally supplied in the diet by foodstuffs obtained from animals). However, since then some particularly interesting scientific research has been undertaken, which reveals that, far from being a health hazard, the broad spectrum of nutrition provided by brazil nuts may actually be positively beneficial in the diet.

The first clue comes from studies performed on the Yano Mamo Indians who live in the Amazonian forest. They consume an almost exclusively vegetarian diet, and have an unbelievably low cholesterol level which averages about three millimoles of cholesterol per litre of blood (116 milligrams per decilitre – the average Western level is over twice this). Further direct evidence comes from major scientific studies of vegetarian populations in the West. One such study followed the health of over 31,000 vegetarians.[2] To the researchers' surprise, the vegetarians who ate nuts at least five times a week had only half the risk of suffering a fatal heart attack when compared to those who consumed nuts less than once a week. Next, the scientists put eighteen healthy volunteers on two carefully controlled diets for a couple of months. The first group consumed a standard low cholesterol diet; the diet of the second group was similar except that 20 per cent of the calories came from nuts (in this case, walnuts). On the no-nut diet, cholesterol levels fell by 6 per cent. However, on the nut diet cholesterol levels dropped by an additional 12 per cent.

Although it is too soon to suggest that a relatively high fat diet – where that fat is provided by foods such as brazil nuts – might have the same protective properties as a low fat vegetarian diet, studies such as these are certainly intriguing, and once again suggest that there are many complex nutritional factors at work which respectively make the meat-free diet healthy, and the meat-centred diet unhealthy.

NUTRIENT ANALYSIS
1oz BRAZIL NUTS (28g)

KCalories	186.30
Total Fat (g)	18.81
Monounsaturated Fat (g)	6.54
Polyunsaturated Fat (g)	6.85
Saturated Fat (g)	4.59
Carbohydrate (g)	3.64
Protein (g)	4.07
Crude Fibre (g)	0.65
Vitamin A (RE)	0.00
Ascorbic Acid (mg)	0.20
Thiamin (mg)	0.28
Riboflavin (mg)	0.03
Niacin (mg)	0.46
Pantothenic Acid (mg)	0.07
Vitamin B6 (mg)	0.07
Folacin (mcg)	1.14
Vitamin B12 (mcg)	0.00
Calcium (mg)	49.98
Iron (mg)	0.97
Zinc (mg)	1.30

Savoury Brazil Nut and Olive Roll

Serves 4
Preparation time 45 minutes

1kg (2lb) potatoes, peeled and quartered

170g (6oz) freshly hulled brazil nuts, crushed
100g (4oz) fresh, toasted breadcrumbs
100g (4oz) green olives, finely chopped
3 tbsp soya milk
1 tsp freshly ground black pepper
½ tsp ground allspice

Preheat the oven to 180°C/350°F/Gas Mark 4. Steam the potatoes until tender. Meanwhile, mix the brazil nuts, breadcrumbs and chopped olives together in a mixing bowl. Mash the cooked potatoes with the soya milk, pepper and allspice. Drop spoonfuls of the potato mixture into the brazil nut mixture and roll them to coat them entirely. Place on a baking tray. Alternatively, the potato may be formed into a single log-shape and rolled in the nut mixture. Place on a baking tray. Bake for 15 minutes, to make the nut mixture crisp and golden. Serve hot or cold, as individual balls or in slices of the log-shape.

Health Note

> The protein provided by brazil nuts is high in methionine, the amino acid which is often in shortest supply in the meat-free diet. Additionally, they contain ellagic acid – also present in raspberries, pears and cashews – which researchers believe may prevent carcinogens from inflicting genetic damage on cells. Consequently, using brazil nuts makes sound economic, health and nutritional sense.

Broccoli Broccoli is really one of the most nutrition-ally valuable of all vegetables, and if it is initially not to your taste, it is really worthwhile trying to find a preparation technique or recipe which makes it more palatable to you. As with other members of the cabbage (*Brassica*) family, it has, in recent years, suffered boiling and stewing at the hands of insensitive cooks. It has not always been so: broccoli was well known as a delicacy to the Romans, and highly prized by Catherine d'Medici, who introduced it into France and popularized it. Very tender broccoli can be eaten raw, right down to and including the stem itself, which should be peeled and chopped into thin slices. Alternatively, very light cooking, such as steaming or stir-frying, is the best way to preserve its high nutritional content. It is delicious when served by itself as a side dish; topped with a sharp French dressing (this should be applied immediately after cooking, and left to permeate).

See also: Broccoli and Mushroom Stir-Fry (p341)

NUTRIENT ANALYSIS
1 CUP BOILED BROCCOLI (156g)

KCalories	43.68
Total Fat (g)	0.55
Monounsaturated Fat (g)	0.04
Polyunsaturated Fat (g)	0.26
Saturated Fat (g)	0.08
Carbohydrate (g)	7.89
Protein (g)	4.65
Crude Fibre (g)	1.73
Vitamin A (RE)	216.84
Ascorbic Acid (mg)	116.38
Thiamin (mg)	0.09
Riboflavin (mg)	0.18
Niacin (mg)	0.90
Pantothenic Acid (mg)	0.79
Vitamin B6 (mg)	0.22
Folacin (mcg)	78.00
Vitamin B12 (mcg)	0.00
Calcium (mg)	71.76
Iron (mg)	1.31
Zinc (mg)	0.59

Sweet and Sour Plum and Broccoli Sauce

Serves 4
Preparation time 30 minutes

1 tbsp oil
3 cloves garlic, chopped
1 onion, coarsely chopped
1 tbsp fresh ginger, grated
100g (4oz) mushrooms, quartered
1 bunch spring onions, sliced into 2.5cm (1-inch) lengths
1 large sweet green pepper, coarsely chopped
450g (1lb) broccoli, chopped into florets
140ml (¼ pint) water

450g (1lb) plums, deseeded and quartered or
450g (1lb) tinned pineapple chunks, drained
140ml (¼ pint) cider vinegar
140ml (¼ pint) fruit juice
2 tbsp soy sauce
1 tbsp brown sugar
1 tbsp kuzu (arrowroot)
140ml (¼ pint) water

Heat the oil in a wok or large frying pan over a high heat. Add the garlic and onion and sauté until clear and tender. Add the ginger and mushrooms and stir for 1–2 minutes. Add the spring onions, pepper, broccoli and water and bring the liquid to the boil. Stir over the high heat for 1 minute then cover the pan and reduce the heat to medium. Leave to cook for 3 minutes. Mix the plums, vinegar, fruit juice, soy sauce and sugar in a bowl. Add to the pan and stir well. Cover and cook for 5 minutes. Dissolve the kuzu in the water and pour into the pan, stir well and leave cooking, uncovered, while the sauce thickens. Serve hot over rice.

Three-Colour Salad in Tofu Dressing

Serves 4
Preparation time 30 minutes

450g (1lb) pasta (farfalle, shells or spirals work well)
450g (1lb) broccoli, cut into florets
2 medium carrots, grated
1 sweet red pepper, coarsely chopped
3 spring onions, thinly sliced

For the dressing:
140g (5oz) plain tofu, mashed
2 tbsp soya milk
2 tbsp cider vinegar
1 tbsp olive oil
1 tbsp fresh basil, chopped
2 cloves garlic, crushed (optional)
½ tsp freshly ground black pepper
pinch of salt

Cook pasta, drain and rinse with cold water. Steam the broccoli for 7 minutes. Immediately remove it from the steamer and leave on a platter to cool. Turn the pasta, broccoli, carrots, pepper and onions into a large serving bowl. Combine the dressing ingredients in a mixing bowl and blend well to make a creamy sauce. Pour the dressing over the salad and stir well. Serve at once or chill, covered, for 1 hour.

Health Note

Just one spear of broccoli provides over 10 per cent of the adult daily requirement for calcium. It also provides over two-and-a-half times the vitamin C requirement, half the folic acid requirement, one-quarter that of vitamin A and potassium and a fifth of iron, vitamin B6 and riboflavin requirements. It also contains useful amounts of zinc, niacin, thiamine, and indeed protein. From this, you can see why it is such a nutritionally important vegetable. Additionally, it has been used therapeutically to treat constipation, neuritis and high blood pressure.

Brussels Sprouts Here is another member of the cabbage family, with yet another excellent nutritional profile. Brussels sprouts, sadly, have suffered rather badly from totally unimaginative presentation. Part of the secret of preparing mouthwatering brussels sprouts is knowing which ones to buy; choose only the smallest and firmest, and reject any whose leaves are not tightly packed or are starting to turn yellow. Early brussels sprouts (from September onwards) can be a tasty and healthy ingredient in raw salads; remove the outer leaves and halve or quarter them. Providing they do not overwhelm the salad, they will give a pleasant, sulphurous flavour to it, a tantalizing, crunchy texture and will certainly boost your vitamin C intake at a time of year when it traditionally drops. To cook, remove the outer leaves and cut the sprouts in half before steaming them for a very short time (5 minutes should be adequate). They can then be served as a vegetable accompaniment to almost any style of meal, or included in scrambled tofu or a mixed stir-fry.

NUTRIENT ANALYSIS
1 CUP BOILED BRUSSELS SPROUTS (160g)

KCalories	62.40
Total Fat (g)	0.82
Monounsaturated Fat (g)	0.06
Polyunsaturated Fat (g)	0.42
Saturated Fat (g)	0.17
Carbohydrate (g)	13.87
Protein (g)	4.08
Crude Fibre (g)	2.19
Vitamin A (RE)	115.20
Ascorbic Acid (mg)	99.20
Thiamin (mg)	0.17
Riboflavin (mg)	0.13
Niacin (mg)	0.97
Pantothenic Acid (mg)	0.40
Vitamin B6 (mg)	0.28
Folacin (mcg)	96.00
Vitamin B12 (mcg)	0.00
Calcium (mg)	57.60
Iron (mg)	1.92
Zinc (mg)	0.53

Brussels Sprouts and Arame Sauté
Serves 4
Preparation time 45 minutes

50g (2oz) arame, washed and soaked
450g (1lb) brussels sprouts, trimmed and
  halved
1 tbsp olive oil
1 tsp freshly ground black pepper
5 spring onions, finely chopped
1 tangerine, peeled, quartered and chopped
1 tbsp soy sauce
1 tbsp sesame seeds, roasted

Wash, rinse and soak the arame then cook in plenty of fresh water over a medium heat until tender, about 20 minutes. Drain. Steam the brussels sprouts for 3–5 minutes. In a large frying pan or wok, heat the oil and saute the black pepper for 1 minute. Add the onions and stir for 1 minute over a high heat. Add the brussels sprouts and tangerine and stir well. Add 1–2 tablespoons of water or stock if necessary to prevent sticking. Cover the pan, reduce the heat and cook for 3–5 minutes. Add the drained arame and soy sauce, stir well and cook, uncovered for 2 minutes. Serve hot over rice. Sprinkle a few roasted sesame seeds over each serving.

Health Note

A cupful of boiled brussels sprouts will provide one-and-a-half times the adult requirement for vitamin C, half the folic acid, a fifth of the iron, a quarter of the potassium and over 10 per cent of the thiamine, vitamin B6, vitamin A, and protein needs. They also contain substances identified as flavones and indoles which have been shown to possess anti-cancer properties. The high potassium content of brussels sprouts may also guard against high blood pressure and resulting diseases such as strokes.

Cabbage Another vegetable from the *Brassica* family and one which, like its cousins, has been horribly overcooked, underrated, and generally abused. The cabbage comes in many varieties; red, white, and green; with smooth or crinkled leaves; and in a variety of shapes. One or more varieties of cabbage will be available to you all the year round. Like most vegetables, its nutrients will tend to be destroyed by the preparation process, and cabbage is therefore best eaten raw, preferably soon after purchase and preparation. A food processor is particularly useful to finely chop or shred cabbage, which can then be used as the basis of a salad, or combined with grated carrots, chopped chives, freshly ground black pepper, a handful of raisins and mayonnaise (either vegetarian or vegan) to make a quick, easy and delicious coleslaw.

Another interesting way to prepare cabbage is to produce a sauerkraut: shred the cabbage finely, line the bottom of a container with large cabbage leaves, upon which you should arrange the shredded cabbage in layers, sprinkling each layer with salt. Cover the final layer with a clean cloth and place a plate or other large object on top, and weight it down to produce a firm pressure on the cabbage beneath. The container should be put in a cool place; after about 24 hours, a considerable quantity of water will have been generated, which should cover all of the shredded cabbage, and which may need to be topped up from time to time with pure water over the 3 weeks or so that it takes the sauerkraut to ferment. At no point should the cabbage be allowed to dry out or become uncovered. It is ready when the fermentation has ceased, and no more foam is produced. The microorganism which causes this wonderful fermentation process is the lactobacilli, the same bacteria which are responsible, in large part, for the different flavours and textures of the many varieties of cheese and other cultured milk products.

The health-giving properties of sauerkraut have been known for many centuries – the explorer Captain James Cook carried considerable stores of sauerkraut on board his ship and his crew were required to eat a minimum of 1kg (2lbs) a week; after which there was not one recorded case of scurvy. Since vegans do not, of course, consume fermented dairy products, sauerkraut can provide an important and regular dietary source of these helpful microorganisms.

Reported health benefits of lactobacilli include the ability to produce natural antibiotic substances; preventing or remitting tumours, preventing the formation of carcinogenic substances in the body; reducing the level of cholesterol; producing internally important B-group vitamins and controlling the proliferation of unhealthy yeast products such as *candida albicans*. Through their considerable production of lactic acid they also act generally to enhance the digestibility of foodstuffs.

Yet another way of consuming the goodness of cabbage is to juice it; freshly prepared cabbage juice can be mixed with carrot juice, a dash of beetroot juice and a small amount of fresh root ginger, to produce an excellent and healthy cocktail. Red cabbage, when finely shredded, is particularly good for a hearty winter salad, when combined with raisins, nuts, other winter vegetables to taste, and a sharp vinaigrette dressing made with cider vinegar. Savoy cabbage is particularly suitable for wrapping any number of savoury fillings.

See also: Peppered Cabbage (p332); Pickled Red Cabbage (p354)

NUTRIENT ANALYSIS
1 CUP RAW CABBAGE (70g)

KCalories	16.80
Total Fat (g)	0.13
Monounsaturated Fat (g)	0.01
Polyunsaturated Fat (g)	0.06
Saturated Fat (g)	0.02
Carbohydrate (g)	3.76
Protein (g)	0.85
Crude Fibre (g)	0.56

Vitamin A (RE)	9.10
Ascorbic Acid (mg)	33.11
Thiamin (mg)	0.04
Riboflavin (mg)	0.02
Niacin (mg)	0.21
Pantothenic Acid (mg)	0.10
Vitamin B6 (mg)	0.07
Folacin (mcg)	39.69
Vitamin B12 (mcg)	0.00
Calcium (mg)	32.90
Iron (mg)	0.39
Zinc (mg)	0.13

Hot Red Cabbage Coleslaw

Serves 4
Preparation time 30 minutes

1 tbsp olive oil
5 cloves garlic, chopped
1 large onion, thinly sliced
1 tsp freshly ground black pepper
1 small to medium red cabbage, shredded
140ml (¼ pint) water
2 tbsp tomato puree
juice of 1 lemon
140ml (¼ pint) plain soya yoghurt
2 tbsp soya bacon bits (optional)

Heat the oil in a large saucepan and sauté the garlic and onion over a medium heat until clear and tender. Add the pepper and stir for 1 minute. Add the cabbage, stir well (it may be more effective to lift the cabbage using two wooden spoons, in the way you toss a salad) and cover the pan. After 1 minute, reduce the heat and leave to cook for 5 minutes. Blend the water and tomato purée and pour over the cabbage. Stir again, cover and leave to cook for a further 5 minutes. Add the lemon juice, stir and remove from the heat. Serve as a starter or vegetable side dish with a dollop of yoghurt on each serving and a garnish of soya bacon bits, if desired.

Health Note

One cup of raw shredded cabbage will typically provide over half the adult daily requirement for vitamin C, and about a quarter that of folic acid.

People who regularly eat cruciferous vegetables such as cabbage have a lower risk of contracting certain cancers, and cabbage itself has been shown to reduce the rate at which lung cancer metastases.[3] Research suggests that as little as one weekly serving of cabbage may be enough to reduce the risk of colon cancer by more than half. Further research reveals that it can enhance the functioning of the body's immune system and help to protect against the effects of radiation exposure. Additionally, the common cabbage has been used in natural medicine to cleanse the blood, to treat asthma, gout, constipation, kidney and bladder disorders, and its juice has been used to alleviate stomach ulcers. Half a glass of fresh cabbage juice (preferably organic) every day is one of the best forms of health insurance.

Carob Also called the locust bean or St John's bread, the carob is the aromatic, fleshy bean pod of the carob tree, which grows throughout the Mediterranean area. It has a long history of use as a food for both humans and animals: cattle, pigs and dogs, for instance, all show obvious signs of enjoying this food. Many dogs like to chew the pod itself as a vegetarian 'bone replacement'! You may purchase the pods whole – they are 8–12 inches long and resemble a coarse vanilla pod – or, as is more common, in powder or flour form. Carob thickens food it is added to but is more often used because it has a chocolate-like taste. It can therefore be especially useful for those who wish to avoid chocolate, either for themselves or for their children. Use it to replace chocolate in confections, baked goods or hot drinks. Carob can be obtained from health food shops, and it is highly nutritious, one cup containing half the calcium and potassium, a third of the iron and riboflavin and a fifth of the vitamin B6 daily requirements for the average adult.

NUTRIENT ANALYSIS
1 CUP CAROB FLOUR (103g)

KCalories	185.40
Total Fat (g)	0.67
Monounsaturated Fat (g)	0.20
Polyunsaturated Fat (g)	0.22

Saturated Fat (g)	0.09
Carbohydrate (g)	91.55
Protein (g)	4.76
Crude Fibre (g)	7.41
Vitamin A (RE)	1.03
Ascorbic Acid (mg)	0.21
Thiamin (mg)	0.05
Riboflavin (mg)	0.47
Niacin (mg)	1.95
Pantothenic Acid (mg)	0.05
Vitamin B6 (mg)	0.38
Folacin (mcg)	29.87
Vitamin B12 (mcg)	0.00
Calcium (mg)	358.44
Iron (mg)	3.03
Zinc (mg)	0.95

Carob Walnut Cake

Serves 8
Preparation time 50 minutes

340g (12oz) wholewheat flour
100g (4oz) brown sugar
2 tsp baking powder
1 tsp bicarbonate of soda
100g (4oz) carob chips (or carob bar, grated)
100g (4oz) walnuts, chopped
140ml (¼ pint) oil
285ml (½ pint) water, soya milk or fruit juice
1 tsp vanilla essence

Preheat the oven to 180°C/350°F/Gas Mark 4 and lightly oil a deep, round cake tin. Mix the dry ingredients, carob and walnuts together in a large mixing bowl. Measure the oil, water and vanilla together into a jug. Pour the liquid over the dry ingredients, stir well and turn into the cake tin. Bake for 40 minutes, until a toothpick inserted in the centre of the cake comes out clean. Cool in the tin for 10 minutes, then remove from the tin and cool on a wire rack. Cool completely before serving alone or with Soya Creem or your favourite sauce or topping.

Versatile Carob Sauce

Makes approximately 420ml (¾ pint)
Preparation time 15 minutes

285ml (½ pint) water
225g (8oz) barley malt syrup
100g (4oz) carob flour
1 tsp vanilla essence
1 × 5–7.5cm (2–3 inch) piece vanilla pod (optional)

Measure the ingredients, except the vanilla pod, into a saucepan and stir well. Place over a medium heat and bring to a soft boil. Simmer gently for 10 minutes, stirring often. Serve immediately as a hot sauce over cakes, puddings or soya ice cream. Alternatively, store the sauce in a jar in the refrigerator and use cold. The vanilla pod may be placed in the jar, if you like, to enhance the vanilla flavour and to make the sauce more interesting visually. This sauce may be diluted with water or soya milk to make a refreshing hot or cold drink, or add a little to the blender next time you make a milkshake.

Carrots The carrot possesses both sweet and savoury characteristics, and is therefore one of the most exquisitely adaptable of all vegetables. Originating from Afghanistan, the carrot has been in cultivation in the Mediterranean area since at least 500 BC.

The best carrots are organically grown and of an irregular, or 'interesting' appearance. These may be used unpeeled: simply scrub them and use juiced, sliced into crudités or chopped for cooking lightly. Non-organic carrots, if used, should be scraped to reduce your exposure to pesticide residues. Freshly prepared carrot juice, which can be preserved and enhanced by the addition of some lemon juice, is a tasty and effortless way to absorb much of the carrot's nutrition. Grated carrots are, of course, a wonderful ingredient in any salad, summer or winter, and make a wonderful side salad when combined with redcurrants which have previously been soaked in lemon juice, and then tossed in a tasty vinaigrette dressing.

Boiled carrots are a particularly depressing and uninteresting dish, which should at all costs be avoided for fear of maligning this magnificent food. Instead, consider steaming or thinly slicing them and stir frying them with other vegetables before serving with rice, and a protein food such as tofu or tempeh. Carrots make any number of interesting soups (it is a little-known fact that they are an ingredient in many commercial tomato soups) and can also be made into

carrot cakes, purées, halva, stews and casseroles.
See also: Carrots in Coconut Sauce (p342); Carrot Halva (p346)

NUTRIENT ANALYSIS
1 CUP RAW CARROT (110g)

KCalories	47.30
Total Fat (g)	0.21
Monounsaturated Fat (g)	0.01
Polyunsaturated Fat (g)	0.08
Saturated Fat (g)	0.03
Carbohydrate (g)	11.15
Protein (g)	1.13
Crude Fibre (g)	1.14
Vitamin A (RE)	3094.30
Ascorbic Acid (mg)	10.23
Thiamin (mg)	0.11
Riboflavin (mg)	0.06
Niacin (mg)	1.02
Pantothenic Acid (mg)	0.22
Vitamin B6 (mg)	0.16
Folacin (mcg)	15.40
Vitamin B12 (mcg)	0.00
Calcium (mg)	29.70
Iron (mg)	0.55
Zinc (mg)	0.22

Carrot and Ginger Sauté

Serves 4
Preparation time 30 minutes

1 tbsp oil
3 cloves garlic, chopped
1 medium onion, finely chopped
½ tsp freshly ground black pepper
900g (2lb) organic carrots, sliced diagonally into chunks
1½ tbsp fresh ginger, grated
juice of ½ lemon
1 tbsp fresh parsley, chopped

Heat the oil in a large, deep saucepan and sauté the garlic and onion until clear and tender. Add the pepper and stir for 1 minute. Add the carrot chunks, stir well, cover the pan and leave to cook over a low to medium heat for 20 minutes. The carrots should be just tender and will have released their oils into the sauté. Add the ginger and stir for 1 minute. Add the lemon juice, stir well and cover the pan. Remove from the heat and serve hot with a sprinkling of fresh parsley. This dish really shows off the flavour of organic carrots and is excellent by itself over rice or as a vegetable side dish.

My Own Carrot Cake

What is it about carrot cake? People create huge new mythologies about the flavour, the texture, the impossible wonderfulness of their grandmother's next-door-neighbour's best friend's postman's mother's cake and then go into the kitchen and try to replicate it. I've analyzed this phenomenon as best I can and I've concluded that it is the combination of earthy-sweet carrot taste, the slightly crumbly texture with surprising shreds, and incredibly sweet under-tones-of-cream-cheese icing that does it to people. I'll do my best here with a recipe which I think knocks all those others off the shelf.

Serves 8
Preparation time 1 hour

340g (12oz) wholewheat flour
100g (4oz) slivered almonds
50g (2oz) soya flour
2 tsp baking powder
1 tsp bicarbonate of soda
1 tsp ground cinnamon
1 tsp ground allspice
½ tsp ground cloves
140ml (¼ pint) oil
140ml (¼ pint) soya milk
450g (1lb) barley malt syrup
570ml (1 pint) grated carrot, (approximately 1lb carrots)
100g (4oz) currants
grated rind and juice of 1 lemon

Preheat the oven to 180°C/350°F/Gas Mark 4 and lightly oil a 23x33cm (9x13 inch) cake tin. Measure the flours, almonds, baking powder, soda and spices together in a mixing bowl and stir well. Blend the oil, milk and syrup together in another bowl then stir in the carrot, currants and lemon rind and juice. Turn the carrot mixture into the dry mixture, stir briefly and spoon into the cake tin. Bake for 35-40 minutes, until the toothpick comes out clean. Leave to cool in the tin for 10 minutes, then turn out onto a cake platter. When completely cool, cover with the following icing.

Special Icing

This recipe will make enough to ice a cake made from the recipe given above, but it won't be a thick layer of icing as I find that too sweet. If your taste differs from mine, I suggest you make half again or double the amount listed here. For that hint of cream cheese I mentioned earlier, try this icing with the nutritional yeast flakes listed as an option. You could try other variations as well: a sprinkling of desiccated coconut, a teaspoon of grated orange or lemon rind, even a tablespoon of grated soya cheddar!

Makes approximately 285ml (½ pint)
Preparation time 10 minutes

225g (8oz) icing sugar
4 tbsp margarine
1 tsp vanilla essence
4 tsp soya milk
2 tsp nutritional yeast flakes (optional)

Measure the sugar into a mixing bowl and add the margarine to it. Work gently together with a table knife or fork then add the vanilla essence and stir well. Add the soya milk, one teaspoon at a time, and stir well after each addition. Add the yeast flakes or other extras at this time. Stir well and, when the cake is cool, spread evenly over it.

Health Note

Carrots are particularly rich in beta-carotene, a form of vitamin A, one carrot supplying twice the adult daily recommended allowance. There is substantial evidence to show that consuming vegetables which contain beta-carotene can prevent and fight many forms of cancers. Boron, the trace mineral which has been shown to be important in preventing osteoporosis is also present in carrots (boron may also be effective in promoting efficient brain functioning and in improving alertness). Additionally, there is evidence to show that the nutrients found in carrots can also reduce the risk of heart disease and prevent cataracts. Further reported health benefits include preventing or shortening the duration of colds, relieving peptic ulcers, treating constipation, asthma, bad skin, insomnia, high blood pressure, and kidney and other conditions.

Cashew Nuts Like the brazil nut, the cashew originated from Brazil in South America, from where it was exported by the Portugese to parts of Africa and India. The cashew nut has been cultivated in India for several hundred years, and is frequently found in Indian dishes. It is also often used in Indonesian and Singaporean meals. In the West, it is generally consumed salted and roasted, as a snack.

Like many other nuts, the raw nut can be made into a delicious and nutritious milk by soaking 100g (4oz) of cashews overnight in 570ml (1 pint) water. In the morning, liquidize and strain the blend and serve immediately.

Cashew nuts are a particularly good snack for lunch boxes and for growing children, since most of their energy comes from the healthiest type of fat, mono-unsaturated. Cashew nut butter is now available in many health food shops, and makes a delicious and nutritious alternative to peanut butter.

NUTRIENT ANALYSIS
1oz CASHEWS, DRY ROAST (25g)

KCalories	163.02
Total Fat (g)	13.16
Monounsaturated Fat (g)	7.76
Polyunsaturated Fat (g)	2.23
Saturated Fat (g)	2.60
Carbohydrate (g)	9.28
Protein (g)	4.35
Crude Fibre (g)	0.20
Vitamin A (RE)	0.00
Ascorbic Acid (mg)	0.00
Thiamin (mg)	0.06
Riboflavin (mg)	0.06
Niacin (mg)	0.40
Pantothenic Acid (mg)	0.35
Vitamin B6 (mg)	0.07

Folacin (mcg)	19.65
Vitamin B12 (mcg)	0.00
Calcium (mg)	12.78
Iron (mg)	1.70
Zinc (mg)	1.59

Cashew Nut Paté in Orange Glaze

Serves 4–6
Preparation time 20 minutes, plus time to chill

1 tbsp oil
5 cloves garlic, chopped
2 medium onions, chopped
170g (6oz) roasted cashews
285ml (½ pint) cooked beans, drained (for example: haricot, kidney, chickpeas)
1 tbsp sherry
1 tsp cayenne
½ tsp freshly ground black pepper
salt, to taste

For the glaze:
100g (4oz) sugar
1½ tbsp freshly-squeezed orange juice
grated rind of 1 orange

Heat the oil in frying pan and sauté the garlic and onions over a medium heat until clear and tender. Take your time, allowing 10 minutes for the sauté. Turn the sauté and the remaining ingredients into food processor and blend well to an even consistency. Scrape the paté mixture into a bowl and add a little more sherry if necessary to make a slightly moist paste. In a separate pan, heat the sugar and orange juice until it turns a lovely caramel colour. Pour this into a soufflé dish or ramekin and swirl it round to line most of the inside of the dish. Sprinkle the grated orange rind over the bottom of the dish then immediately spoon the paté mixture into the dish, pressing firmly as you go. Cover the dish and leave to chill for at least 1 hour. Serve with crackers, toast, fresh breads or fruit. This dish begs to be experimented with: try it with different sorts of beans and adjust the spices to suit your sense of adventure.

Health Note

Just 25g (1oz) of cashew nuts will provide one fifth of the adult requirement of iron, and over 10 per cent of that of zinc, folic acid, and protein. They are also a good source of the trace mineral selenium (which today's modern, highly refined diet often lacks) now known to be essential in the prevention of cancer and in the effective functioning of the body's immune system.

Cauliflower Described by American author Mark Twain as 'nothing but cabbage with a college education', cauliflower is yet another member of the great cabbage family. Its attractive texture and mild flavour makes it palatable to those who perhaps dislike cabbage – children, for example. The worst sin you can commit with this vegetable is to overcook it. Why cook it, in any case? It is delicious when consumed raw – a young and fresh cauliflower can be broken up into small, bite-sized florets and combined with other vegetables in a mixed salad, a marinade, or arranged as a plate of crudités with a selection of sauces or dips. Cauliflower is a delicious ingredient in a stir-fry, or – if it is really necessary to cook it – a light steaming is all that is necessary. The green leaves surrounding the head can, if cleaned, be chopped into small pieces and consumed too.

NUTRIENT ANALYSIS
1 CUP RAW CAULIFLOWER (100g)

KCalories	24.00
Total Fat (g)	0.18
Monounsaturated Fat (g)	0.01
Polyunsaturated Fat (g)	0.08
Saturated Fat (g)	0.03
Carbohydrate (g)	4.92
Protein (g)	1.99
Crude Fibre (g)	0.85
Vitamin A (RE)	2.00
Ascorbic Acid (mg)	71.50
Thiamin (mg)	0.08
Riboflavin (mg)	0.06
Niacin (mg)	0.63
Pantothenic Acid (mg)	0.14

Vitamin B6 (mg)	0.23
Folacin (mcg)	66.10
Vitamin B12 (mcg)	0.00
Calcium (mg)	29.00
Iron (mg)	0.58
Zinc (mg)	0.18

SunCauli Salad

Serves 4
Preparation time 15 minutes

225g (8oz) broad beans
1 firm fresh cauliflower, cut into small florets
3 medium tomatoes, chopped
3 spring onions, finely chopped
1 large eating apple, diced
50g (2oz) sunflower seeds, lightly roasted
1 tbsp fresh mint, chopped
1 tbsp soya bacon bits (optional)

For the dressing:
1½ tbsp lemon juice
1½ tsp black salt
4 tbsp good olive oil

Boil the broad beans in salted water for about 7 minutes, until tender and brightly coloured. Drain and leave to cool then combine with the remaining ingredients in a large salad bowl. Blend the dressing ingredients in a small jug, pour over the salad, mix well and serve.

Cauliflower Curry

Serves 4
Preparation time 35 minutes

1 fresh cauliflower, cut into florets
green leaves from the cauliflower, chopped
2 medium sweet peppers,1 red and 1 green, coarsely chopped
juice of 1 lemon
1 tbsp oil
5 cloves garlic, chopped
½ tsp chilli powder
2 tsp fresh ginger, grated
1½ tsp cumin seeds
1 tsp turmeric
2–3 medium tomatoes, chopped
1 fresh chilli, finely chopped (optional)
140ml (¼ pint) fresh coriander, chopped

Prepare the cauliflower and peppers and place in a large bowl. Pour the lemon juice over and stir well. Put to one side. Heat the oil in a large saucepan and sauté the garlic for 2 minutes, until just golden. Add the chilli powder, ginger and cumin and stir for a further 2 minutes. Add the turmeric and stir; immediately add the cauliflower and pepper mixture, including the lemon juice that may have collected at the bottom of the bowl. Stir this mixture in the pan, cover the pan and cook for 5 minutes over a medium heat. Add the tomatoes and fresh chilli, if desired, stir well and cover the pan again. Cook a further 5–7 minutes then stir in the coriander, cover the pan and remove from the heat. Serve hot over rice.

Health Note

> The high sulphur content of cauliflower has been used in natural medicine as a blood purifier, for kidney and bladder problems, and to treat constipation. One cup of raw cauliflower pieces will provide all the adult daily requirement of vitamin C, a third of the folic acid requirement, and a fifth of the potassium requirement.

Celery Every part of the celery plant can be used. Celery root (a variety usually known as celeriac) is served as a cooked vegetable, and is also the source of celery salt, a very subtle and healthful flavouring in many dishes, and excellent for those on salt-free diets. The stalk of the celery plant is, of course, well known as a snack, as a repository for various savoury fillings, and can be used to give flavour and depth to many soups, stews, and stir-fries. The leaves of the celery plant can be used as a garnish for salads and soups, and celery seeds are an extremely useful flavouring and seasoning. Celery juice is particularly delicious, and can be mixed with carrot and/or apple juice to produce a luscious and appetizing drink.
See also: Tofu 'Steak' with Mushrooms and Celery (p340)

NUTRIENT ANALYSIS
1 STALK CELERY (40g)

KCalories	6.40
Total Fat (g)	0.06
Monounsaturated Fat (g)	0.01

Polyunsaturated Fat (g)	0.03
Saturated Fat (g)	0.01
Carbohydrate (g)	1.46
Protein (g)	0.30
Crude Fibre (g)	0.32
Vitamin A (RE)	5.20
Ascorbic Acid (mg)	2.80
Thiamin (mg)	0.02
Riboflavin (mg)	0.02
Niacin (mg)	0.13
Pantothenic Acid (mg)	0.07
Vitamin B6 (mg)	0.03
Folacin (mcg)	11.20
Vitamin B12 (mcg)	0.00
Calcium (mg)	16.00
Iron (mg)	0.16
Zinc (mg)	0.05

Stuffed Celery Sticks

Serves 4
Preparation time 10 minutes

4–6 large stalks celery, scrubbed
4 tbsp tahini
1 tbsp miso
1 tbsp lemon juice (optional)

Cut the celery stalks in half. Mix the remaining ingredients to a smooth paste and press a little of the paste into the hollow of each celery stick. Serve immediately. This snack or starter enjoys your creative input: try spicing it up with a little chilli powder or tabasco for adults or sprinkling sesame seeds over the filling for children.

A completely different filling is made by simply mixing peanut butter and raisins and pressing some into each celery stick.

Braised Celery

Serves 4
Preparation time 45 minutes

8–12 whole celery stalks, scrubbed and trimmed
285g (10oz) plain tofu, mashed
3 spring onions, finely sliced

100g (4oz) firm, cheddar-style soya cheese, grated
3 tbsp fresh parsley, chopped
140ml (¼ pint) vegetable stock
140ml (¼ pint) sherry
2 tbsp tomato purée
1 tsp freshly ground black pepper
2 medium tomatoes, quartered

Preheat the oven to 180°C/350°F/Gas Mark 4. Blanch the celery by lowering into boiling water for 1 minute. Remove and place on a plate. Blend the tofu, onions, cheese and parsley together in a bowl. Press the mixture into the hollows of each celery stalk. Arrange the stuffed celery in a broad, shallow baking dish. Mix the stock, sherry, tomato purée and pepper together in a jug and pour around the celery stalks in the baking dish. Arrange the tomato chunks around the celery also. Bake, covered, for 20 minutes. Uncover the dish and bake a further 5 minutes if you like a slightly dry surface texture. Serve hot as a starter or side dish.

Health Note

In herbal medicine, celery has long been used to treat arthritis and rheumatism, constipation, asthma, high blood pressure, catarrh, diabetes and nervous exhaustion. Recently, some of its reputed health benefits have been confirmed in the laboratory – scientists report that celery contains a substance, 3-n-butyl phthalide, which lowers both blood pressure and blood cholesterol levels. It has been calculated that about four stalks of celery contain enough to produce a blood pressure reduction of approximately 12–14 per cent and a cholesterol decrease of about 7 per cent. Also, depending upon the quality of soil in which it is grown, celery can be a useful source of organic calcium. Celery root (celeriac) additionally contains useful amounts of phosphorus and potassium.

Chard Also called Swiss chard, this is a variety of beet, grown primarily for its spinach-like leaves and thick stalks. The leaves can be prepared in the same way as spinach, and the stems may be steamed or boiled in salted water and served with walnut or sesame oil or any favourite dressing. When very young, the leaves can be chopped and added raw to any salad, although when older it is best to cook the leaves as their taste becomes rather more bitter and the leaves toughen. One cup of boiled chard yields about half the daily requirements for vitamins C, A, iron and potassium.

NUTRIENT ANALYSIS
1 CUP CHARD (36g)

KCalories	6.84
Total Fat (g)	0.07
Monounsaturated Fat (g)	trace
Polyunsaturated Fat (g)	trace
Saturated Fat (g)	trace
Carbohydrate (g)	1.35
Protein (g)	0.65
Crude Fibre (g)	0.29
Vitamin A (RE)	118.80
Ascorbic Acid (mg)	10.80
Thiamin (mg)	0.01
Riboflavin (mg)	0.03
Niacin (mg)	0.14
Pantothenic Acid (mg)	0.06
Vitamin B6 (mg)	0.04
Folacin (mcg)	4.97
Vitamin B12 (mcg)	0.00
Calcium (mg)	18.36
Iron (mg)	0.65
Zinc (mg)	0.13

Chard in Bright Sauce

Serves 4
Preparation time 30 minutes

1 tbsp oil
5 cloves garlic, chopped
1 medium onion, thinly sliced
1 tbsp fresh ginger, grated
½ tsp chilli powder
1kg (2lb) chard, washed and chopped
3 tbsp vegetable stock or water
2 tbsp soy sauce
2 tbsp rice or wine vinegar
2 tsp brown sugar

2 tsp kuzu (arrowroot)
140ml (¼ pint) sherry (optional)

Heat the oil in a wok or large pan over a high heat and sauté the garlic and onion until clear and tender. Add the ginger and chilli and stir for 1 minute. Add the chard, cover the pan and leave to cook for 2 minutes. Stir well, cover the pan and reduce the heat. Blend the remaining ingredients, except the sherry, in a jug and pour over the chard. Stir briefly, cover the pan and cook for 5 minutes over the reduced heat. Pour the sherry over if desired, stir and leave to cook a final 2-3 minutes. The chard should be soft but not soggy. Serve hot with rice and Tofu Steaks (p275) or tempeh.

Health Note

A word of caution – chard tends to be relatively high in oxalic acid which can inhibit calcium absorption. However, since studies show that vegetarians absorb and retain more calcium from foods than meat-eaters, there is probably little real cause for concern. Natural therapists maintain that organic oxalic acid is, in fact, an important element in maintaining the eliminative organs.

Cherries This delightful fruit can be divided into two main categories: sweet and sour. The former are best for eating, the latter best for cooking, as in cherry pie, jams and for various alcohols such as kirsch, cherry brandy and maraschino. One cup of raw cherries provides about a quarter of the daily requirement of vitamins A and C, and significant amounts of potassium, iron and magnesium.

NUTRIENT ANALYSIS
1 CUP CHERRIES (145g)

KCalories	104.40
Total Fat (g)	1.39
Monounsaturated Fat (g)	0.38
Polyunsaturated Fat (g)	0.42
Saturated Fat (g)	0.31
Carbohydrate (g)	24.00
Protein (g)	1.74

Crude Fibre (g)	0.58
Vitamin A (RE)	30.45
Ascorbic Acid (mg)	10.15
Thiamin (mg)	0.07
Riboflavin (mg)	0.09
Niacin (mg)	0.58
Pantothenic Acid (mg)	0.18
Vitamin B6 (mg)	0.05
Folacin (mcg)	6.09
Vitamin B12 (mcg)	0.00
Calcium (mg)	21.75
Iron (mg)	0.57
Zinc (mg)	0.09

Thick Cherry Sauce

Makes approximately 570ml (1 pint)
Preparation time 30 minutes

140ml (¼ pint) barley malt syrup
140ml (¼ pint) water
2 tbsp cornstarch
450g (1lb) pitted sweet cherries, washed and halved
juice of 1 lemon

Combine the syrup, water and cornstarch in a sauce-pan and cook over a medium heat until thickened. Stir constantly. Add the cherries and cook over a low heat for about 15 minutes, until they begin to break down. Add the lemon juice and cook a further 5 minutes over the low heat. Serve hot or cold over desserts or fresh fruits, with a sprinkling of slivered almonds if desired.

Health Note

Cherries have been used in natural medicine to treat catarrh, constipation, cramps, high blood pressure and gout.

Chestnuts Unlike many other nuts, the chestnut is particularly low in fat, whilst being high in many other important nutrients. The chestnut tree is one of the most inspiring of all trees, and there really is no better way to spend a bright autumn day than foraging for these nuts in beautiful woodland (mushrooms and other edible fungi will also be in evidence, well worth scavenging for too,

providing you can confidently recognize them). Most commercially sold chestnuts, however, are imported, usually from France, Spain and Italy. They are obviously a seasonal nut, but dried chestnuts are readily available the year round and should be soaked and cooked in the same way as beans and pulses. Chestnuts should always be eaten *after* cooking, because this reduces their tannic acid content (tannic acid is also found in tea, and is generally regarded as an anti-nutrient because it inhibits the absorption of dietary iron and reduces vitamin A activity in the body. But like many so-called anti-nutrients, it may have a positive role too: recent research suggests that it may be a potent cancer inhibitor).[5] In addition to simply roasting chestnuts by the fireside, they can be added to soups and stews, used to make roasts and stuffings, and they are also delicious when sweetened and used as a purée or sauce for desserts.
See also: Chestnut Creme (p352)

NUTRIENT ANALYSIS
1 CUP ROASTED CHESTNUTS (143g)

KCalories	350.35
Total Fat (g)	3.15
Monounsaturated Fat (g)	1.09
Polyunsaturated Fat (g)	1.24
Saturated Fat (g)	0.59
Carbohydrate (g)	75.73
Protein (g)	4.53
Crude Fibre (g)	2.72
Vitamin A (RE)	2.86
Ascorbic Acid (mg)	37.18
Thiamin (mg)	0.35
Riboflavin (mg)	0.25
Niacin (mg)	1.92
Pantothenic Acid (mg)	0.79
Vitamin B6 (mg)	0.71
Folacin (mcg)	100.10
Vitamin B12 (mcg)	0.00
Calcium (mg)	41.47
Iron (mg)	1.30
Zinc (mg)	0.82

Arame and Chestnut Casserole

Serves 4
Preparation time 1 hour, plus soaking overnight

225g (8oz) dried chestnuts, soaked overnight
25g (1 oz) arame, washed and drained
225g (8oz) short grain brown rice, washed and drained
2 tbsp cider or rice vinegar

Drain the soaked chestnuts. Soak the washed arame in fresh water for about 20 minutes. Drain but save the soaking water. Place the chestnuts in a large saucepan and place the soaked arame over them. Add the rice, pour the arame soaking water over and add enough water to make double the volume of water to solids (rice, arame and chestnuts), about 710ml (1¼ pints). Cover the pan and bring to a boil over a medium heat. Reduce the heat and simmer, covered, for 40 minutes, until the rice is tender and the liquid fully absorbed. Remove from the heat, pour the vinegar over the mixture and leave for 5–10 minutes, covered. Lift the ingredients into a large hot serving dish, gently tossing the mixture as you do so. Serve hot with plenty of soy sauce.

Chilled Fruity Chestnut Soup

Serves 4
Preparation time 30 minutes, plus chilling time

100g (4oz) chestnut purée
420ml (¾ pint) water
1 tbsp soy sauce
½ tsp ground cinnamon
285ml (½ pint) freshly squeezed orange juice
rind of 1 orange, grated
225g (8oz) plain soya yoghurt

Measure the purée and water into a saucepan and stir over a medium heat until the mixture is free of lumps. When the liquid begins to boil, reduce the heat and simmer for 10 minutes, stirring often. Add the soy sauce and cinnamon and continue to simmer for a further 10 minutes. Keep the liquid over a low heat and add the orange juice and grated rind. Remove from the heat and pour into a soup tureen to cool. When the soup is tepid, stir in the yoghurt. Put the soup in the refrigerator or add 6–8 icecubes to it and serve chilled. A nice touch is to add 2–3 icecubes, made of freshly-squeezed orange juice, to each bowl of soup just before serving. A garnish of yoghurt, Soya Creem or a fresh orange slice is also attractive.

Health Note

Nutritionally, three ounces of roasted chestnuts provide less than 2g of fat (in other words, about 2 per cent of the suggested adult maximum intake). Yet they also provide over a third of a adult daily requirement of vitamin C, folic acid, and potassium, as well as significant amounts of vitamin B6 and thiamin. A formidable source of nutrition!

Chickpeas If the soya bean is the king of beans and pulses, the chickpea is unquestionably the queen. With a finer flavour than the soya bean, the chickpea is suitable for eating all by itself immediately after cooking. Also called besan or the garbanzo, the chickpea is an important food in many ancient cultures, both East and West. It is, of course, an essential ingredient in foods such as hummus, pappadams (which are made from chickpea flour, sometimes called gram), falafels and many other Asian and Mediterranean dishes.

Chickpeas should be carefully washed, then soaked in a large volume of water overnight before cooking. Drain away the soaking water, rinse the chickpeas and cook them in fresh water. Cooking times vary: in my experience, the only practical way is to use a pressure cooker. Turn the soaked peas into the cooker and just cover with fresh water; cook at full pressure for approximately 25 minutes. Here's how to check whether your chickpeas are properly cooked – pop a couple into your mouth, and try to squash them against the roof of your mouth using only your tongue. If they do not yield readily, they are not properly cooked, and eating them may cause excessive gas. Unfortunately, many restaurants and cafés fail to cook them sufficiently with the result that some diners can suffer discomfort.

Always cook more chickpeas than you will need for your recipe, the excess can be kept in an airtight container in your refrigerator, and a handful thrown into salads, soups etc over the next day or two, to give them extra flavour and nutritional substance.

See also: Channa Dhal (p345); Couscous (p316); Dafina (p317); Mussakka (p350); Pakoras (p322)

NUTRIENT ANALYSIS
1 CUP CHICKPEAS, COOKED (164g)

KCalories	268.96
Total Fat (g)	4.25
Monounsaturated Fat (g)	0.96
Polyunsaturated Fat (g)	1.90
Saturated Fat (g)	0.44
Carbohydrate (g)	44.95
Protein (g)	14.53
Crude Fibre (g)	4.10
Vitamin A (RE)	4.92
Ascorbic Acid (mg)	2.13
Thiamin (mg)	0.19
Riboflavin (mg)	0.10
Niacin (mg)	0.86
Pantothenic Acid (mg)	0.47
Vitamin B6 (mg)	0.23
Folacin (mcg)	282.08
Vitamin B12 (mcg)	0.00
Calcium (mg)	80.36
Iron (mg)	4.74
Zinc (mg)	2.51

Avocado Chickpea Salad

Serves 4
Preparation time 20 minutes

570ml (1 pint) cooked chickpeas (about 225g/8oz
   when dry)
100g (4oz) pitted green or black olives, sliced
1 small, firm courgette, finely chopped
3 cloves garlic, finely chopped
3 spring onions, finely sliced
1 tbsp fresh parsley, chopped
1 tbsp fresh mint or coriander, chopped
1 tbsp tahini
3 tbsp olive oil
juice of 2 lemons
1 ripe avocado, peeled and chopped

Turn the chickpeas, olives and courgette into a large
salad bowl. Add the garlic, onions, parsley and mint

and stir well. Blend the tahini, oil and lemon juice
together in a jug or jar and whisk. When ready to
serve, add the avocado to the salad, pour on the
dressing and stir well. Serve immediately. This salad
is excellent as a filling for baked potatoes or to stuff
tomatoes.

Spicy Roasted Chickpeas

Serves 4
Preparation time 30 minutes

570ml (1 pint) cooked chickpeas (about 225g/8oz
   when dry)
1 tbsp oil
1 tbsp cornflour
1 tsp salt
1 tsp ground cumin
1 tsp ground coriander
1 tsp cayenne
½ tsp ground allspice

Preheat the oven to 180°C/350°F/Gas Mark 4. Turn
the cooked chickpeas onto a baking tray and drizzle
the oil over them. Stir them to ensure the oil coats the
chickpeas and does not just pool on the tray. Mix the
remaining ingredients together in a small bowl and stir
well. Sprinkle this dry mix over the chickpeas and stir
very well, so that each chickpea has a thin spicy
coating. Shake the baking tray to evenly distribute
the coated chickpeas and bake for 15–20 minutes,
until golden and slightly crisp. You may stir the
chickpeas once or twice while they're cooking, if
you wish. Serve warm or cold as a snack.

Falafel

Serves 4
Preparation time 45 minutes

1l (2 pints) cooked chickpeas (about 450g/(1lb)
   when dry)
3 cloves garlic, finely chopped
2 tbsp tahini
50g (2oz) plain flour
1 tsp ground coriander
1 tsp ground cumin
1 tsp freshly ground black pepper
½ tsp salt
¼–½ tsp chilli powder
oil

Mash the cooked chickpeas in a bowl or blender. Add
the garlic and tahini and mix to a thick paste. Mix the

remaining ingredients, except the oil, together in a small bowl and stir well. Add this mixture to the chickpeas and blend well. Form the mixture into small rounded patties and shallow fry for 3–5 minutes each side, until crisp and golden brown. Serve warm with Tahini Dip (p347), a garnish of chopped fresh coriander and plenty of lemon wedges to squeeze over the falafels. Falafels are excellent stuffed into warm pitta bread as well.

Hummus

Serves 4–6

Preparation time 1 hour 15 minutes, plus soaking over-night

450g (1lb) dried chickpeas, washed and drained
juice of 5 lemons
1 bulb garlic, peeled and finely chopped
450g (1lb) tahini
1 tsp salt, or to taste
140-285ml (¼-½ pint) water
½ tsp paprika

Turn the washed chickpeas into a large bowl and cover them with clean water. Leave to soak overnight or until ready to use. Drain, rinse and drain them then turn into a pressure cooker, just cover with water and cook at pressure for 25 minutes. Meanwhile, squeeze the lemons and prepare the garlic and put to one side. When the chickpeas are cooked, cool the pressure cooker under cold running water, drain the chickpeas and cool under more cold running water. Turn the chickpeas, a little at a time, into a mixing bowl and mash them roughly. Repeat until all the chickpeas have been mashed (if you like, you may reserve a small handful of whole chickpeas for use later, to decorate the hummus). Add the lemon juice, garlic and tahini to the chickpeas and stir well. Add salt to taste and a little water to make a slightly runny mixture.

Ladle the mixture into a hand grinder (eg Mouli) and turn it through a medium blade to make a paste. Add more water if necessary. Turn the hummus into a serving dish, sprinkle with the paprika and decorate with the whole chickpeas if desired. Serve at once with warm, fresh pitta breads and a salad. This will keep 24 hours, though it rarely lasts that long in our house!

Health Note

Chickpeas should be a staple part of everyone's diet – they're cheap, versatile and an extraordinary source of high-quality nutrition. One cup of cooked chickpeas will provide a quarter of the adult protein requirement, one-and-a-half times the folic acid requirement, half of the iron, a fifth of the zinc . . . and yet virtually no fat!

Chicory There is perennial confusion between this vegetable and the endive. In Britain and Germany, chicory is known as a winter vegetable which grows with tightly bunched white leaves, fringed with green. In France and the United States, the same vegetable is called endive. Roasted chicory root is sometimes used as a coffee substitute; otherwise it can be used raw in salads (its natural curvature lends itself well to being a receptacle for any number of fillings) or alternatively, it can be braised and served as an accompanying vegetable to a midwinter feast.

NUTRIENT ANALYSIS
1 CUP RAW CHICORY (50g)

KCalories	74.50
Total Fat (g)	0.25
Monounsaturated Fat (g)	0.01
Polyunsaturated Fat (g)	0.12
Saturated Fat (g)	0.04
Carbohydrate (g)	16.54
Protein (g)	3.18
Crude Fibre (g)	0.75
Vitamin A (RE)	0.00
Ascorbic Acid (mg)	15.60
Thiamin (mg)	0.10
Riboflavin (mg)	0.06
Niacin (mg)	0.35
Pantothenic Acid (mg)	0.30
Vitamin B6 (mg)	0.62
Folacin (mcg)	1.55
Vitamin B12 (mcg)	0.00
Calcium (mg)	90.50
Iron (mg)	0.85
Zinc (mg)	0.58

Chicory Bake

Serves 4
Preparation time 50 minutes

4 heads chicory
1 tbsp oil
5 cloves garlic, finely chopped
100g (4oz) mushrooms, trimmed and finely chopped
1 sprig fresh tarragon, finely chopped
2 tbsp fresh coriander, finely chopped
1 eating apple, peeled, cored and chopped
2–3 medium tomatoes, thinly sliced
1 tsp oil
1 tbsp plain flour
½ tsp freshly ground black pepper
½ tsp ground coriander
570ml (1 pint) soya milk

Preheat the oven to 180°C/350°F/Gas Mark 4. Slice the chicory in half lengthwise and remove the bitter cores. Arrange the halves in an oven dish. Heat the oil in a frying pan and sauté the garlic for 2–3 minutes, until just golden. Add the chopped mushrooms and sauté a further 5 minutes, until they release their juices and begin to reduce. Add the tarragon and coriander and stir for 2 minutes longer. Remove the sauté from the heat and stir in the chopped apple. Spoon this mixture into and over the centres of the chicory halves. Arrange the tomato slices over the top. Heat the oil in a saucepan over a medium heat and sprinkle the flour, pepper and coriander over it. Stir to make a thick paste (roux). Add the milk a little at a time, stirring after each addition, to make a sauce. Pour the sauce over the chicory, apple and tomato and cover the oven dish. Bake for 30 minutes, and remove the cover for the last 5 minutes. Serve hot with steamed greens, sautéd carrots and new potatoes.

Health Note

A cup of raw, chopped chicory will provide a third of the adult daily requirement of folic acid and about 10 per cent that of vitamin A and potassium. The attractively bitter taste of raw chicory is used by natural therapists as an appetite stimulant and to activate the bile and digestive processes.

Coconut A tree of huge economic importance in many areas of the world, virtually all parts of this awe-inspiring palm are put to good use, making our Western, wasteful economies seem scandalously inefficient by comparison. Its root yields medicine; its durable leaves are woven into a wide variety of useful and aesthetically pleasing products, such as baskets, hats and floor coverings. Wood from the tree is good for housebuilding, and the leaves once again provide excellent roofing material. Then, of course, there are the nuts themselves.

Brought to the West by Marco Polo, we have barely begun to scratch the surface of the coconut's usefulness in the 600 years since its arrival here. It is most familiar with us, today, in its most unhealthy and inessential form: sweets, confectioneries, flavourings and garnishes. Like the avocado, the coconut has suffered from bad publicity in recent years as one of the few sources of saturated fat in the plant kingdom. It is certainly true that most of the fat in the raw coconut is in this form (88 per cent of its fat content is saturated), and this means that it should not be consumed too frequently. However, coconuts, like all plant foods, contain no cholesterol, and it has been shown that it is the combination of dietary saturated fat and cholesterol (as found in meat) which is most likely to raise blood levels of cholesterol to unhealthy proportions.

The coconut is an essential element in most African, Asian and South American cuisines but is used in cookery all over the globe. Its earthy-sweet flavour, slightly crunchy texture and creamy white colour all add a subtle depth and interest to the dishes in which it is used. When using coconut cream or milk in a dish, avoid rapid boiling as this may cause the coconut to curdle. Instead, cook at simmering point and sprinkle a tiny bit of cornflour into the pot to help ensure the milk does not curdle. When using creamed coconut, cutting the block into shavings will help you avoid the need for high temperatures which could cause curdling. Coconut cream and milk are often added towards the end of the cooking process to avoid such problems. Desiccated coconut (simply shredded coconut, made fresh or purchased dried) does not present this challenge; its flavour and texture within the dish may be enhanced if you soak the shreds in liquid (milk, water, stock or fruit juice, for example) for a few moments before including it in the dish.

See also: Sweet Potatoes in Orange and Coconut Sauce (p313); Coconut Rice (p313); La Daub (p321); Coconut Bread (p333); Pumpkin Coconut Pudding (p333); Journey Cakes (p334); Boija (p336); Lu Pulu (p338); Coconut Potato Patties (p338); Carrots in Coconut Sauce (p342)

NUTRIENT ANALYSIS
RAW COCONUT 1 PIECE (2″ x 2″ x ½″) (45g)

KCalories	159.30
Total Fat (g)	15.07
Monounsaturated Fat (g)	0.64
Polyunsaturated Fat (g)	0.16
Saturated Fat (g)	13.36
Carbohydrate (g)	6.85
Protein (g)	1.50
Crude Fibre (g)	1.92
Vitamin A (RE)	0.00
Ascorbic Acid (mg)	1.48
Thiamin (mg)	0.03
Riboflavin (mg)	0.01
Niacin (mg)	0.24
Pantothenic Acid (mg)	0.14
Vitamin B6 (mg)	0.02
Folacin (mcg)	11.88
Vitamin B12 (mcg)	0.00
Calcium (mg)	6.30
Iron (mg)	1.09
Zinc (mg)	0.50

Coconut Milk

Makes approximately 420ml (¾ pint)
Preparation time 1 hour, plus 1 hour soaking time

1 ripe coconut
570ml (1 pint) mineral or filtered water

Pierce the eyes at one end of the coconut and pour out the coconut water. You may chill this and drink it or save it and add it to the coconut milk later. Break the coconut in half: a sharp blow with a hammer to its middle will do this easily. Cut the coconut flesh away from the shell and remove any brown skin. Grate the coconut into a mixing bowl and pour the water over it. Alternatively, place small chunks of the coconut in a

blender with the water and blend to a smooth, fine pulp. Leave the coconut and water blend soaking for about 1 hour. Turn this mixture into a square of butter muslin and tie the corners together. Suspend the muslin over a bowl and leave the milk to drip through; squeeze the pulp to extract any further liquid. Stir the coconut water into the milk if desired. Use within 2 days.

Coconut Cream

Makes approximately 140ml (¼ pint)
Preparation time 1 hour, plus 1 hour soaking

1 ripe coconut
200ml (7fl oz) mineral or filtered water

Prepare in the same way as coconut milk. Because there is less water added, the pulp will be thicker and the liquid richer and more concentrated; you may wish to squeeze the blend within the muslin more emphatically. Use within 2 days. (Note: Creamed Coconut, as sold in blocks, is usually concentrated coconut cream, though some brands describe themselves as 'pressed' or 'moulded' coconut.)

Health Note

Frying foods is one of the least healthy ways to cook them (for a good, tasty alternative to frying, see the techniques described under 'Bamboo Shoots', p182). But if you're going to have a fry-up once in a while, a small amount of coconut oil may well be a healthier choice than a polyunsaturated oil such as sunflower. Why should this be? Because polyunsaturated oils decompose at lower temperatures to form free radicals, highly reactive atoms or molecules which are implicated in the development of many of our modern plagues, such as heart disease and cancer. Saturated coconut oil, on the other hand, is destroyed more slowly by light, air and heat. And remember that no fat or oil should ever be used twice; cancer-causing chemicals (such as benzopyrene) will be generated.

Collards Often simply referred to in greengrocers' shops as 'greens', collards have traditionally been used as both human and animal fodder, and have consequently been hugely underrated. In point of fact, they are a very low-cost source of high quality nutrition. A winter vegetable, collards are thought to be ancient relatives of the cabbage, and they certainly retain the same substantial health-giving properties. They can be used as a replacement for cabbage in any recipe. When young and tender, collards can be chopped raw into salads, when older, the leaves should be steamed or stir-fried. As with spinach, collards reduce considerably when cooked.

See also: Mnkhwani (p314); Taushe (p315); Muriwo ne Dovi (p323); Lu Pulu (p338)

NUTRIENT ANALYSIS
1 CUP COLLARDS, BOILED (45g)

KCalories	34.56
Total Fat (g)	0.24
Monounsaturated Fat (g)	trace
Polyunsaturated Fat (g)	trace
Saturated Fat (g)	trace
Carbohydrate (g)	7.85
Protein (g)	1.73
Crude Fibre (g)	0.63
Vitamin A (RE)	349.44
Ascorbic Acid (mg)	15.49
Thiamin (mg)	0.03
Riboflavin (mg)	0.07
Niacin (mg)	0.37
Pantothenic Acid (mg)	0.07
Vitamin B6 (mg)	0.07
Folacin (mcg)	7.68
Vitamin B12 (mcg)	0.00
Calcium (mg)	29.44
Iron (mg)	0.20
Zinc (mg)	0.14

Potato and Collards Curry

Serves 4
Preparation time 30 minutes

1kg (2lb) collards, washed, trimmed and sliced
1 tbsp oil
3–5 cloves garlic, finely chopped

2 tsp cumin seed
1 tsp ground coriander
1 tsp turmeric
½ tsp freshly ground black pepper
½ tsp chilli powder
3 medium potatoes, diced
1 fresh chilli, finely chopped (optional)
3 medium fresh tomatoes, chopped

Prepare the collards, place them in a colander and rinse them briefly under cold water. Put to one side. Heat the oil in a deep saucepan and sauté the garlic for 2–3 minutes, until it is just golden. Add the spices and stir for 2 minutes. Add the diced potato, stir well and cover the pan. Leave the pan over a medium heat for 3 minutes, stir the potato mixture, cover the pan and cook a further 3 minutes. Add the chilli, tomatoes and collards. Stir well, cover the pan and cook for 15–20 minutes. Stir once or twice in that time, adding a little water if necessary to prevent sticking. Serve hot over rice.

Dried Tomatoes with Collards and Garlic

Serves 4
Preparation time 45 minutes, plus marinating overnight

100g (4oz) dried tomatoes, quartered
4 tbsp olive oil
140ml (¼ pint) wine vinegar
1 tbsp soy sauce
1 whole, dried chilli, broken open
1 tbsp oil
7–9 cloves garlic, finely chopped
1 large onion, thinly sliced
1k (2 lb) collards, washed, trimmed and thinly sliced

Turn the chopped tomatoes into a bowl or jug. Blend the oil, vinegar and soy sauce and pour over the tomatoes. Add the broken chilli, stir well and cover the bowl. Leave to marinate overnight. Heat the oil in a deep saucepan and saute the garlic and onion until clear and tender. Add the tomato mixture – both tomatoes and marinade – and stir well (pick out the chilli at this stage). Cook over a medium heat for 5–7 minutes, stirring often. Add the collards, stir well, cover the pan and cook over a medium heat for 5 minutes. Stir again and cook a further 10 minutes, covered, until the collards are tender but still bright green. Serve over rice or pasta.

Health Note

Collards are an extremely good source of vitamins A and C, which may be why they can reduce the spread (metastasis) of cancer. Like other green leafy vegetables, they are a useful source of calcium. Natural therapy uses a collard-rich diet to treat acidosis, constipation and arthritis, and to detoxify the system.

Corn Otherwise known as maize, this cereal grain originated in the Americas and was brought to Europe in the early 16th century by Spanish conquistador Hernando Cortés. One variety of maize is bright yellow and forms a very hard kernel, and this is used predominantly for animal fodder and to grind into the flour from which various grades of cornmeal or polenta is made. Sweetcorn is similar, but larger and less intensely yellow, and when boiled on the cob for about fifteen minutes makes a simple and satisfying first course or snack. Tins of sweetcorn are so cheap and readily available that there is little point in trying to grow sweet corn yourself. Tinned sweetcorn has become a mainstay in many vegetarian larders, since it is so quick and versatile (it can be used in salads, stir-fries, soups etc). Baby sweetcorn is also available fresh and in tins in many supermarkets and/or oriental grocery shops; they are eaten whole and make an exciting and succulent addition to any stir-fry.

Popcorn is made from dried maize kernels: the healthiest way to make it is undoubtedly with a special popcorn machine which 'air pops' the grain without the use of oil. This makes an extremely low-calorie snack. Many other types of maize are starting to reach Western consumers, including an interesting blue variety, which is high in trace minerals, and is now being used to manufacture tortillas for sale in health food shops.
See also: Polenta (p353); Tatali (p312); Polenta Pie (p323); Sadza (p323); Tortillas (p325); Popcorn (p331); Cornbread (p331); Fungi (p335); Sweet Fungi (p336); Boija (p336)

NUTRIENT ANALYSIS
1 CUP CANNED SWEETCORN (256g)

KCalories	156.16
Total Fat (g)	1.15
Monounsaturated Fat (g)	0.33
Polyunsaturated Fat (g)	0.54
Saturated Fat (g)	0.18
Carbohydrate (g)	37.96
Protein (g)	4.97
Crude Fibre (g)	1.25
Vitamin A (RE)	30.72
Ascorbic Acid (mg)	17.15
Thiamin (mg)	0.07
Riboflavin (mg)	0.16
Niacin (mg)	2.40
Pantothenic Acid (mg)	1.34
Vitamin B6 (mg)	0.09
Folacin (mcg)	97.54
Vitamin B12 (mcg)	0.00
Calcium (mg)	10.24
Iron (mg)	0.90
Zinc (mg)	0.92

Sweetcorn and Pepper Chutney
Makes 1.25l (2¼ pints)
Preparation time 30 minutes

420ml (¾ pint) cider vinegar
50g (2oz) sugar
2 tsp grated horseradish
2 tsp prepared mustard
1 tsp celery seed
1 tsp mustard seed
1 tsp turmeric
½ tsp freshly ground black pepper
½ tsp chilli powder
3 sweet peppers (1 each of red, green and yellow), diced
3 stalks celery, finely chopped
1 large onion, finely chopped
1kg (2lb) sweetcorn kernels (fresh, frozen or tinned)
2 tbsp cornflour (optional)

Measure all the ingredients except the sweetcorn and cornflour into a glass or enamel saucepan. Place over a medium heat and bring to the boil. Boil for 5 minutes, stirring often. Add the sweetcorn and stir well. For a thicker chutney, dissolve the cornflour in 4 tbsp cold water and add to the mixture at this point, stir. Bring to the boil once again and boil for 5 minutes. Reduce the heat and simmer for 5 minutes. Ladle into sterilized jars and seal. Serve in sandwiches, with salads and plates of crudités, or as a condiment with a hot meal.

Health Note

Three health tips: Canned sweetcorn is surprisingly nutritious – one tin provides about a fifth of the daily iron requirement for an adult. Eating popcorn for the first 24 hours of a developing cold often shortens its duration. And the soluble fibre found in maize will effectively lower blood cholesterol.

Cucumber Recent archeological evidence suggests that this illustriously ancient member of the gourd family was cultivated by humans as long ago as 10,000 BC, and indicates that it probably originated in Thailand. Many cultures – including the Hebrews, the Romans, the Greeks, and the Pueblo Indians – have revered and celebrated this vegetable in countless culinary forms; it is only recently that its position has been demoted to a rather depressing salad vegetable. All it takes is a little imagination to make those cucumbers shine!

- Gazpacho is a classical and thoroughly mouthwatering Mediterranean cold soup for the summer months (see p356)
- Dill pickles (pickle them yourself or buy them ready made) make an excellent accompaniment to any cold dish and are superb when sliced into sandwiches and salads
- There are any number of unusual cucumber salads from the ethnic cooking of the Mediterranean region (see Cucumber and Yoghurt Salad, p320)
- Cucumbers can be split in two, hollowed out, and packed with a savoury filling (see Stuffed Cucumber Appetizer, p333)
- The cucumber can even be eaten cooked, either baked, sautéed or cooked *au gratin*.

It is certainly an excellent vegetable to juice, and the excessive bitterness of older, larger cucumbers can be reduced by removing a portion of their skin prior to juicing. It combines very well with other vegetable juices, such as carrot, watercress, and even grape juice.
See also: Cool Cucumber Soup (p336)

NUTRIENT ANALYSIS
½ CUP SLICED CUCUMBER (52g)

KCalories	6.76
Total Fat (g)	0.07
Monounsaturated Fat (g)	0.00
Polyunsaturated Fat (g)	0.03
Saturated Fat (g)	0.02
Carbohydrate (g)	1.51
Protein (g)	0.28
Crude Fibre (g)	0.31
Vitamin A (RE)	2.60
Ascorbic Acid (mg)	2.44
Thiamin (mg)	0.02
Riboflavin (mg)	0.01
Niacin (mg)	0.16
Pantothenic Acid (mg)	0.13
Vitamin B6 (mg)	0.03
Folacin (mcg)	7.23
Vitamin B12 (mcg)	0.00
Calcium (mg)	7.28
Iron (mg)	0.15
Zinc (mg)	0.12

Dressed Cucumber and Pepper Salad
Serves 4
Preparation time 1 hour

200ml (7fl oz) rice vinegar
1 tbsp sesame oil or tahini
2 tsp brown sugar
2 tsp soy sauce
2 tsp sesame seeds
¼–½ tsp chilli powder
1 sweet red pepper, sliced lengthwise
1 sweet yellow pepper, sliced lengthwise (it really is worth searching out one of these for the colourful effect)
1 firm cucumber, sliced into very thin rounds
285g (10oz) firm, plain tofu, sliced into thin strips

Blend the vinegar, oil, sugar, soy sauce, sesame seeds and chilli together in a jug. Arrange the peppers, cucumber and tofu slices in an artistic, or at least attractive, way on a shallow platter. (I suggest a ring of alternating red and yellow pepper then the centre taken up with strips of tofu interleaved with cucumber slices. Looks very pretty and the dressing just finishes it off nicely.) Pour the dressing over all and chill the salad for up to 1 hour.

OK Sushi Filling

Serves 4
Preparation time 30 minutes plus 1 hour marinate

1 firm cucumber
1 tsp freshly ground black pepper
1 tsp dill seed
140ml (¼ pint) rice vinegar
4 tbsp fresh coriander, chopped

Slice the cucumber into very thin sticks 3–4 inches long and place in a shallow dish. Sprinkle with the pepper and dill seed then pour the vinegar over all. Leave to sit for one hour, turning once or twice in that time. Prepare the rice and nori for 4 sushi rolls (see p350). Lift the cucumber slices out of the vinegar dressing and arrange across the rice bed. Sprinkle 1 tbsp of chopped coriander over each arrangement and roll as normal. Wrap the sushi firmly and chill until ready for use. Slice into thin rounds and serve.

Health Note

The cucumber is valued in natural therapy for its diuretic properties, and its potassium content makes it useful to treat blood pressure problems. It apparently contains an enzyme which enables the human body to digest proteins more efficiently, and its trace mineral content of silicon and sulphur is believed to promote the growth of hair and strong nails.

Currants Currants, raisins, and sultanas are all slightly different types of dried grapes. Currants are usually the smallest, and originated from Greece (the name is a corruption of Corinth). Raisins (either from a seedless variety or stoned during processing) are somewhat larger, slightly lighter in colour, and sometimes made from the same variety of grapes which are used for wine and table consumption. Sultanas are pale golden in colour – which reflects their origin from

green rather than red grapes – and are not so nutritious as currants. Grapes which naturally possess seeds usually produce the best dried fruit.

Because they are so very concentrated (it takes 1.8kg (4lbs) of grapes to produce 450g (1lb) of currants), they are an extraordinarily good source of nutrients. This, together with the fact that they can be added to a very wide range of dishes means that they should be an essential item in every vegetarian store cupboard. Currants can be eaten alone, mixed with nuts or seeds, and added to salads (especially winter ones using root vegetables), many kinds of rice dishes and pilafs, to couscous and to pastries, cakes and other baked produce.

NUTRIENT ANALYSIS
½ CUP CURRANTS (72g)

KCalories	203.76
Total Fat (g)	0.19
Monounsaturated Fat (g)	0.03
Polyunsaturated Fat (g)	0.13
Saturated Fat (g)	0.02
Carbohydrate (g)	53.34
Protein (g)	2.94
Crude Fibre (g)	1.13
Vitamin A (RE)	5.04
Ascorbic Acid (mg)	3.38
Thiamin (mg)	0.12
Riboflavin (mg)	0.10
Niacin (mg)	1.16
Pantothenic Acid (mg)	0.03
Vitamin B6 (mg)	0.21
Folacin (mcg)	7.34
Vitamin B12 (mcg)	0.00
Calcium (mg)	61.92
Iron (mg)	2.35
Zinc (mg)	0.48

Currant and Apricot Paste

Makes 1 litre (2 pints)
Preparation time 1 hour plus soaking overnight

340g (12oz) dried currants
340g (12oz) dried apricots, finely chopped
570ml (1 pint) apple juice
1 tsp ground cinnamon
½ tsp ground cloves
4 tbsp barley malt syrup
juice and grated rind of 1 lemon
1 tbsp kuzu (arrowroot)
100g (4oz) slivered almonds or pine nuts (optional)

Measure the currants and dried apricots into a bowl and pour the apple juice over. Stir and leave overnight. Turn the mixture through a coarse fitting of a mouli and tip into a glass or enamel saucepan. Add the spices, syrup and lemon juice and place over a medium heat. Bring to the boil and simmer for 10 minutes, stirring often. Add a little more liquid (water or apple juice) if necessary to make a slightly sloppy sauce. Add the kuzu and stir as the sauce thickens to a more paste-like consistency. Continue to simmer for 10 minutes over a low heat then stir in the lemon rind and almonds, if desired. Remove from the heat and turn into sterilized jars. Seal and cool.

This paste is a delicious filling for pies, pastries or cakes or you could spoon some onto a serving of soya ice-cream. A dollop of it on the side of the plate is an excellent condiment for very spicy meals, or add some chilli powder during the cooking process if you know you'd like to use it as a savoury.

Health Note

One cup of currants provides half the recommended daily intake of iron. It also supplies a fifth of the calcium and vitamin B6 requirements – such a good source of nutrition should not be ignored!

Dates The date palm is of massive economic and social significance in many tropical countries, and has been so for thousands of years. It may well be the most ancient plant to have been cultivated by humans; its remains have been discovered during archaeological excavations of Stone-age sites. Date palms are either male or female (which are the only ones to bear fruit) and, by learning how to pollinate the female plants by hand, the Arabs succeeded in increasing the ratio of productive plants to non-productive ones many thousands of years ago. Although the date palm will grow in a variety of climates, the dates will only ripen in areas where the summer temperatures reach at least 40°C.

Apart from being an important export crop, dates are a staple food of many Arab countries. They are ground into flour, juiced to make date honey or fermented to make palm wine. The palm tree itself provides the raw material for baskets, ropes, hats and mats; the tree never stops growing: after about 100 years it becomes so tall that it simply falls over. Palm hearts can be purchased canned in many middle Eastern grocery stores, and make an interesting and unusual appetizer served with a vinaigrette dressing (it makes an interesting topic of conversation at dinner parties when you present your guests with a tree to eat!). However, since the removal of the terminal bud of the palm, which is where the heart is extracted from, causes the death of the tree, this is hardly an ecologically sound foodstuff.

Dried dates are universally available. Avoid those which are coated in syrup or rolled in sugar – the excessive sweetness is quite unnecessary. Fresh dates can also be found in an increasing number of grocery stores, and have a smoother, less intensely sweet flavour – these are the kind that are best for stuffing with almost any sweet or savoury mixture. You will also find packets of chopped dates in most health food shops and some supermarkets; these are usually cheaper than whole dates, and are extremely useful because they allow smaller quantities of dates to be included in a wide range of dishes. Consider adding a handful of chopped dates to a rice salad; they will enhance the rich flavouring of many cakes and puddings, and they make a delicious ingredient in breakfast cereals and mueslis.

See also: Walnut, Date and Apple Strudel (p355) and Hot Mango Chutney (p332)

NUTRIENT ANALYSIS
1 CUP DATES (178g)

KCalories	489.50
Total Fat (g)	0.80
Monounsaturated Fat (g)	trace
Polyunsaturated Fat (g)	trace
Saturated Fat (g)	trace
Carbohydrate (g)	130.85

Protein (g)	3.51
Crude Fibre (g)	3.92
Vitamin A (RE)	8.90
Ascorbic Acid (mg)	0.00
Thiamin (mg)	0.16
Riboflavin (mg)	0.18
Niacin (mg)	3.92
Pantothenic Acid (mg)	1.39
Vitamin B6 (mg)	0.34
Folacin (mcg)	22.43
Vitamin B12 (mcg)	0.00
Calcium (mg)	56.96
Iron (mg)	2.05
Zinc (mg)	0.52

Stuffed Dates

Serves 4–8
Preparation time 20 minutes

450–750g (1–1½lb) fresh dates
285g (10oz) firm tofu
100g (4oz) ground almonds
225g (8oz) Soya Creem
1½ tsp ground coriander
100g (4oz) almond or walnut halves

Slice the dates nearly in half and remove the pits. Leave each date lying open. Mash the tofu in a mixing bowl and blend the ground almonds into it. Add Soya Creem, a little at a time, and stir well after each addition. Stop adding the Creem when you have the consistency you find appealing. Stir in the coriander. Drop teaspoonsful of the filling onto each date and top with an almond or walnut half. Chill before serving if possible. Serve on a plate garnished with fresh mint or coriander leaves.

Date Slices

Serves 4–6
Preparation time 1 hour

1kg (2lb) dried dates, pitted and finely chopped
50g (2oz) margarine
340g (12oz) whole wheat flour
340g (12oz) rolled oats
1 tsp ground cinnamon
1 tsp ground allspice
2 tsp baking powder
1 tsp bicarbonate of soda
225g (8oz) margarine
450g (1lb) barley malt syrup
1 tsp vanilla essence

Preheat the oven to 180°C/350°F/Gas Mark 4 and lightly oil a 23x33cm (9x13 inch) baking tin. Turn the dates into a saucepan and just cover with water. Bring to the boil and stir well. Add the margarine, cover the pan and reduce the heat. Simmer for 10 minutes, stir well and remove from the heat. Mix the dry ingredients together in a large bowl. Add the margarine, syrup and vanilla essence to the dry ingredients. Work to an even consistency and press half of this mixture into the baking tin. Spread the date mixture over this and top with the remaining oat mixture. Press lightly into place and bake for 15–20 minutes, until the crust is golden. Cool in the pan, slice and serve.

Health Note

Nutritionally, ten dates will provide one-quarter of the adult daily requirement of potassium, and are significant sources of niacin, iron, and vitamin B6. Natural therapists have used them in the treatment of stomach ulcers, piles, colitis, and to increase the quality of breast milk.

Dulse This seaweed, also called Irish moss, has a coarse, purple appearance and has for centuries been used as a foodstuff by the traditional maritime populations of the northern hemisphere. In common with many other seaweeds, dulse will thicken soups and stews and is a wonderfully nutritious and tasty addition to stocks and broths which are prepared for later use. It should be chopped into quite small pieces before cooking to allow it to soften, although it always retains a degree of chewiness. Nutritionally, it is a very good source of iodine.

NUTRIENT ANALYSIS
DULSE (100g)

KCalories	0.00
Total Fat (g)	3.20
Monounsaturated Fat (g)	?

Polyunsaturated Fat (g)	?
Saturated Fat (g)	0.00
Carbohydrate (g)	0.00
Protein (g)	0.00
Crude Fibre (g)	1.20
Vitamin A (RE)	?
Ascorbic Acid (mg)	0.00
Thiamin (mg)	0.00
Riboflavin (mg)	0.00
Niacin (mg)	0.00
Pantothenic Acid (mg)	?
Vitamin B6 (mg)	?
Folacin (mcg)	?
Vitamin B12 (mcg)	?
Calcium (mg)	296.00
Iron (mg)	0.00
Zinc (mg)	?

Eggplant see **Aubergine**

Egg Replacers Many people wish, for health or ethical reasons, to avoid eating eggs. This is easy to do once you have a few options for creating the textures, flavours and cookery effects which the egg so readily accomplishes. I have compiled a few useful ideas for replacing eggs in your meals.

Commercial egg replacers are of either the egg- or non-egg-based sort. Egg-based replacers don't, in fact, seem like replacers at all; they are usually pasteurized dried egg, either whole or just the yolk. Non-egg replacers tend to be combinations of lecithin (a soya product) and standard rising agents. These are useful but very expensive unless you buy direct from the manufacturers. The most widely distributed egg re-placer is 'Ener-G', produced by General Design Ltd, PO Box 38E, Worcester Park, Surrey, tel. 081-337 9366. This packet has a number of useful recipes on it. Two more egg replacers (egg white and whole egg) are also made by G.F. Dietary Group of Companies Ltd, 494-496 Honeypot Lane, Stanmore, Middx, HA7 1HJ, tel. 081-204 6968. These are also sold in some health food shops (Boots, for instance) and they also sell mail order (phone them for details).

• For raising purposes, there are three standard substances. The first, cream of tartar, is a natural by-product of wine-making and is usually used in combination with the second substance, bicarbonate of soda, to cause raising in baked goods. The usual ratio called for is 1 part cream of tartar to 2 parts bicarbonate of soda. When replacing eggs, simply add ½ tsp cream of tartar and 1 tsp bicarbonate of soda for every 2 eggs called for in the recipe. The third substance, baking powder, varies in its composition but is often made up of bicarbonate of soda, flour, an emulsifying agent and calcium phosphate, another rising agent. Recipes often call for baking powder as a sole rising agent, though more often a small amount of bicarbonate of soda is also listed. When replacing eggs, use an additional 1 tsp baking powder for every 2 eggs called for in the recipe.

• For binding purposes, two easy options are avail-able. First, replace every egg called for with a scant 1 tbsp tahini, oil or peanut butter. (Other nut or seed butters would do as well.) Or secondly, replace every egg called for with 2 tsp tahini, nut or seed butter or oil, and 2 tsp soya flour. You may whisk the tahini and soya flour with a little water, juice or other liquid in a bowl, if you like, to create the slightly goopy texture of beaten egg.

• To both bind and raise, which is what is often wanted from eggs, I simply combine the above suggestions in one of the following ways: 1 egg = 2 tsp soya flour plus ½ tsp baking powder blended with 2 tsp tahini, oil or peanut butter. 2 eggs = 1 tbsp tahini, oil or peanut butter blended with 1 tsp soya flour plus ½ tsp cream of tartar plus 1 tsp bicarbonate of soda, whisked with 1 tbsp liquid. You may safely devise your own combina-tion, of course.

• To create the fluffiness of egg, as in scrambled eggs, there is nothing better than plain tofu. Mash the tofu in a bowl, add a little soya milk (1–2 tbsp) and whisk with a fork. **See also:** Scrambled Tofu (p291).

• To create the spongy texture found in quiches, blend 285g (10oz) plain tofu with 4 tbsp oil and 140ml (¼ pint) soya milk. Use an electric whisk if possible to add more air to the mixture. Pour over the vegetable ingredients in the quiche and bake as normal.

• To create a golden eggy colour, add 1–2 tsp turmeric to the dish during the cooking process, or dissolve the turmeric in 1 tbsp hot milk before adding to the dish.

- To create the whipped lightness of egg whites try the egg white replacer from the G.F. Dietary Group (listed above). I use a combination of powdered agar and the spongy-texture blend, given above. More precisely, empty one sachet (about 3g) of agar powder into a bowl and pour 140ml (¼ pint) boiling water over it. Stir immediately to dissolve the powder. Add 60ml (2fl oz) cold water to the cup, stir well and leave to cool. Meanwhile, blend 285g (10oz) plain tofu with 4 tbsp oil and 140ml (¼ pint) soya milk. When the agar mixture is beginning to gel, add it to the tofu mixture and whisk the lot together. Use immediately in dishes that require a souffle or mousse-like effect. This combination will not effect the same degree of lightness as whipped egg white, but it gets close. Over to you!

Elderberries Though rarely sold in shops, elderberries are nevertheless plentiful, come September, in most temperate countries of the northern hemisphere. When picking elderberries or elderflowers, bear in mind that those by the roadside or close to agricultural land cannot be trusted to be pollution-free. Elderberries contain small amounts of a poisonous alkalide when raw, and for this reason they should always be cooked before they are eaten. They give an excellent flavour and beautiful colouring to many autumnal dishes, including jams, jellies and this wonderful pickle:

NUTRIENT ANALYSIS
1 CUP ELDERBERRIES (145g)

KCalories	105.85
Total Fat (g)	0.73
Monounsaturated Fat (g)	?
Polyunsaturated Fat (g)	?
Saturated Fat (g)	?
Carbohydrate (g)	26.68
Protein (g)	0.96
Crude Fibre (g)	10.15
Vitamin A (RE)	87.00
Ascorbic Acid (mg)	52.20

Thiamin (mg)	0.10
Riboflavin (mg)	0.09
Niacin (mg)	0.73
Pantothenic Acid (mg)	0.20
Vitamin B6 (mg)	0.33
Folacin (mcg)	?
Vitamin B12 (mcg)	0.00
Calcium (mg)	55.10
Iron (mg)	2.32
Zinc (mg)	?

Elderberry Pickle

Makes approximately 1.8kg (4lb)
Preparation time 1 hour

1kg (2lb) elderberries, washed and destalked
570ml (1 pint) cider vinegar
100g (4oz) sugar or barley malt syrup
3 cloves garlic, finely chopped
1 small onion, finely chopped
1 eating apple, peeled and diced
1 tbsp fresh ginger, grated
1 tsp ground allspice
½ tsp ground cinnamon
¼ tsp ground cloves

Mash the berries and turn into a large enamel saucepan. Add the remaining ingredients, stir well and bring to the boil over a medium heat. Stir again, cover the pan, reduce the heat and cook slowly, stirring occasionally to prevent sticking, for 30–40 minutes, until the pickle begins to thicken. Pour into sterilized jars, seal and cool.

Elderflowers start to blossom in June, and have a most exquisite aroma which lends itself to some truly delicious traditional country cooking. Indeed, it is to the North American Indians that we owe a debt of gratitude for the following creation:

Elderflower Fritters

Serves 4
Preparation time 30 minutes, plus collecting the flowers

Gather a fair number of flower heads including one or two inches of stalk. Choose a hot windless day to collect them so the elderflowers are at their best: fresh and aromatic. Prepare a simple, rather runny batter:

4 tbsp plain flour
1 tbsp tahini
1 tbsp oil
420ml (¾ pint) water

Measure the flour into a bowl and stir the other ingredients gradually into it. Dip the flower heads into the batter, then deep fry until golden brown. An unusual, aromatic and sensuous conclusion to any summer meal.

Elderflower Champagne

Makes 4.5l (1 gallon)
Preparation time 30 minutes, plus 24 hours working, plus 2 weeks

This particularly delightful and refreshing summer drink is also easy to make. Take two fresh flower heads, in the fullness of their blossom, and put them into a large container together with the juice of one lemon and its thinly peeled rind. Add 750g (1½lbs) of white sugar and 2 tsp of white wine vinegar. Then add 4.5l (1 gallon) of filtered (ie unchlorinated) water, cover, and leave for 24 hours. The next day, strain into bottles, cork, and leave for 10 days to 2 weeks. This champagne is hardly alcoholic at all – but please be warned: the explosive force built up inside the bottles may be very great. Use the strongest bottles available, and exercise caution when opening them. Store them somewhere cool, and as an added precaution, cover each bottle with a heavyweight cloth to prevent fragments of flying glass from causing damage.

Endive see Chicory

Figs Since figs do not travel well, they are usually only available as fresh fruit when purchased close to their growing site. For the most part, figs are available either dried or canned. The dried form are by far the tastier, more nutritious, more economical and more versatile. They can be eaten raw as a snack, or stuffed with almonds or walnuts, for instance, to produce a highly nutritious fast food. One of the easiest and tastiest breakfast foods is simply a bowlful of chopped, dried figs combined with other dried fruits (chosen to suit your taste, but perhaps including prunes, pears, apples and apricots), put in a deep bowl the night before and barely covered with fruit juice or cold water. In the morning, you will have a nutritious, cheap, and appetizing breakfast waiting for you (if the sweetness is too intense, combine it with a muesli to dilute the

flavour). Alternatively, the following dried fruit salad can be consumed at any time of the year:

NUTRIENT ANALYSIS
1 CUP DRIED FIGS (199g)

KCalories	507.45
Total Fat (g)	2.33
Monounsaturated Fat (g)	0.51
Polyunsaturated Fat (g)	1.11
Saturated Fat (g)	0.47
Carbohydrate (g)	130.05
Protein (g)	6.07
Crude Fibre (g)	9.55
Vitamin A (RE)	25.87
Ascorbic Acid (mg)	1.59
Thiamin (mg)	0.14
Riboflavin (mg)	0.18
Niacin (mg)	1.38
Pantothenic Acid (mg)	0.87
Vitamin B6 (mg)	0.45
Folacin (mcg)	14.93
Vitamin B12 (mcg)	0.00
Calcium (mg)	286.56
Iron (mg)	4.44
Zinc (mg)	1.01

Persian Fruit Salad

Serves 4
Preparation time 15 minutes, plus 24 hours to soak

450g (1lb) dried fruit, including figs and apricots
100g (4oz) pistachio nuts, broken or crushed
570ml (1 pint) filtered (ie unchlorinated) water
1 tbsp rose water

Wash and chop the fruit and turn it into a deep bowl. Add the pistachios, filtered water and the rose water. Stir well and leave to soak, covered in a cool place, for at least 24 hours. Stir and serve with a dollop of soya yoghurt, or Soya Creem.

Two equally pleasing and substantial fig recipes are Fig

Fingers (based on Fig Newtons, an American biscuit named after the town of Newton in Massachussetts) and the traditional British Figgy Pudding:

Fig Fingers

Serves 4
Preparation time 1 hour

450g (1lb) dried figs, finely chopped
140ml (¼ pint) apple juice
3 tbsp barley malt syrup
170g (6oz) whole wheat flour
170g (6oz) rolled oats
2 tsp baking powder
1 tsp bicarbonate of soda
140ml (¼ pint) oil
140ml (¼ pint) barley malt syrup

Preheat the oven to 180°C/350°F/Gas Mark 4 and lightly oil a 20x20cm (8x8 inch) baking tin. Turn the figs into a saucepan and add the apple juice. Bring to the boil and stir well. Simmer for 10 minutes, add the syrup, stir well and remove from the heat. Mix the dry ingredients together in a large bowl. Blend the oil and syrup and add to the dry ingredients. Work to an even consistency and press half of this mixture into the baking tin. Spread the fig mixture over this and top with the remaining oat mixture. Press into place and bake for 15–20 minutes, until the crust is golden. Cool in the pan, slice into 2.5x5cm (1x2 inch) fingers and serve.

Figgy Pudding

Serves 4–6
Preparation time 4 hours

250g (9oz) shredded vegetable suet
225g (8oz) wholewheat flour
100g (4oz) brown sugar
50g (2oz) rolled oats
50g (2oz) breadcrumbs
½ tsp ground nutmeg
1 tbsp tahini
1 tsp vanilla essence
420ml (¾ pint) soya milk
340g (12oz) dried figs, finely chopped

Mix the suet, flour, sugar, oats, breadcrumbs and nutmeg together in a mixing bowl. Beat the tahini, vanilla essence and milk together in a small bowl. Stir the chopped figs into the dry mix and immediately add the milk mixture. Stir well then spoon into a greased pudding basin. Steam for 2–3 hours. Serve with a favourite sweet sauce or a generous pouring of Soya Creem.

Health Note

> A cup of dried, cooked figs provides most of the adult daily recommended amounts of fibre, and about a quarter of that for vitamin C, riboflavin, vitamin B6, calcium and iron. Figs are well known to have a gently laxative effect, and have also been used in natural medicine to treat asthma, catarrh, gout, rheumatism and skin diseases.

Garlic More than any other foodstuff, garlic most clearly reveals the shortcomings of conventional nutritional analysis. Standard authorities of food composition suggest that garlic is nutritionally worthless – even consuming ten cloves a day would provide nothing more than 15 per cent of the adult daily requirement of vitamin C, and virtually no other major vitamin or mineral. But natural therapists, and indeed the age-old folk medicine of many cultures, know otherwise.

For centuries, garlic has been one of the most important of all medicinal plants. An Egyptian medical papyrus from the 16th century BC lists twenty-two remedies employing garlic for everything from heart disease and worms, to tumours, headaches and bites. Cloves of preserved garlic were found in the tomb of King Tutankhamen. Ancient Olympic athletes chewed it to heighten stamina. Aristotle, Hippocrates and Pliny touted garlic for its healing value. East Indians use garlic for skin ulcers and cleaning wounds. For centuries, the Chinese have drunk onion tea (onion is a cousin of garlic) to relieve fevers, cholera and dysentery. Even Louis Pasteur described the antibacterial properties of garlic. And Albert Schweitzer, deep in the jungle and lacking conventional drugs, found that garlic could effectively treat amoebic dysentery.[6]

In recent years conventional science has at last begun to recognize the extraordinary healing qualities associated with this much-overlooked member of the lily family. Garlic has been found to contain at least 400 constituent compounds, of which more than thirty are known to influence body function: minerals such as selenium and germanium; amino acids such as glutathione, methionine and cysteine; amino alkyl sulfoxides, allin; disulphide oxides, allicin; deoxidised sulphide, disulphide and sulfhydryl-bearing compounds such as diallyldisulphide, S-allyl cysteine and the oxide of trithia-dodecatriene, ajoene. Substances such as these have been shown to be effective in a wide variety of therapeutic applications:

- to reduce the impact of cancer-causing substances and to retard or prevent tumour formation;
- to prevent sticky red blood platelets from clumping together and therefore lessen the risk of stroke and heart attack;
- to improve the function of the body's immune system and help people with AIDS to fight opportunistic infections;
- to retard the ageing process;
- to help the body to detoxify itself of heavy metals and other harmful chemicals;
- to lower blood cholesterol levels and reduce high blood pressure;
- to open the airways and alleviate asthma.

Garlic is thought to be a particularly valuable tool for bolstering the human immune system because it is one of the richest sources of organic selenium and germanium. In one study, ten AIDS patients were given garlic extracts as a food supplement for twelve weeks. A 5g dose of the extract was taken daily during the first six weeks, and a 10g dose was taken each day for the second six weeks. During the experimental period, three patients experienced gastrointestinal and neurological problems and were unable to take the supplement, and sadly, later died. But the seven patients who were fit enough to take the supplement showed signs of a strengthening immune system, and reported fewer bouts of diarrhoea, genital herpes, candidiasis and fever.[7]

The main active principle in garlic is allicin, which has been shown to be effective against twenty-three kinds of bacteria, and sixty types of fungi and yeasts. There is considerable variation in the reported effective dose of garlic – some studies suggest that as little as 1.8g a day can improve the functioning of the immune system, whereas other studies suggest that between seven and twenty-eight cloves daily are necessary to achieve significant drops in cholesterol and blood pressure. Garlic's antibacterial and anti-carcinogenic properties are most effective in its raw state. Boiling garlic creates sulphur compounds which can dilate the bronchial passages of asthmatic indivi-

duals, and act as a decongestant, cough medicine and mucus regulator.

Selecting good quality garlic is quite easy. Very small bulbs should be avoided, because they may be immature and will certainly be difficult to peel. Extremely large bulbs, sometimes called 'elephant garlic' should also be avoided, because they are not true garlic. Reject anything that does not feel firm to the touch, or is obviously broken-skinned or shrivelled. Garlic which has begun to sprout is not necessarily bad, as some of the more active ingredients are actually found in the sprout itself.

In a proper environment, garlic heads can last six months. Keep them dry, cool and exposed to the air – do not refrigerate or store them in tightly wrapped plastic bags. Garlic powder is occasionally useful as a substitute, although the taste is rather different, and the health benefits are not comparable.

Garlic can be used in a number of ways to enhance the flavouring of many dishes. Simply rubbing half a fresh clove round a salad bowl will provide a hint of pungency, without being in any way overpowering. Beyond this, garlic afficionados will obviously find good use for it in most salad dressings, marinades, stir-fries, breads and other baked goods. Garlic soup is surprisingly mild, especially when you consider the quantity of garlic involved.

NUTRIENT ANALYSIS
3 CLOVES GARLIC (10g)

KCalories	12
Total Fat (g)	0.06
Monounsaturated Fat (g)	0
Polyunsaturated Fat (g)	0.02
Saturated Fat (g)	0.01
Carbohydrate (g)	2.97
Protein (g)	0.57
Crude Fibre (g)	?
Vitamin A (RE)	0.00
Ascorbic Acid (mg)	2.70
Thiamin (mg)	0.02
Riboflavin (mg)	0.01
Niacin (mg)	0.06
Pantothenic Acid (mg)	?

Vitamin B6 (mg)	?
Folacin (mcg)	0.30
Vitamin B12 (mcg)	0.00
Calcium (mg)	15.00
Iron (mg)	0.15
Zinc (mg)	?

Good-Hearted Garlic Soup

Makes 1l (2 pints)
Preparation time 50 minutes

12–15 cloves of garlic, coarsely chopped – including
   their skins
1 medium potato, cubed
1l (2 pints) boiling water
1 tbsp fresh ginger, grated (optional)

Place the garlic and potato in a saucepan with the
boiling water. Cover the pan, reduce the heat and
simmer gently for 40 minutes. Add freshly grated
ginger, if desired. Drink one cupful, hot or cold,
every two hours if you feel the early symptoms of a
cold.

Garlic and Ginger Pickle

Makes approximately 285ml (½ pint)
Preparation time 20 minutes

3 bulbs garlic, peeled and finely chopped
3 tbsp fresh ginger, grated
140ml (¼ pint) plus 2 tbsp cider vinegar
1 tbsp brown sugar

Prepare the garlic and ginger and have to hand. Boil
the vinegar and brown sugar together in an enamel
saucepan and add the garlic and ginger. Bring back to
the boil then remove from the heat and spoon into a
sterilized jar. Serve in small doses as a condiment to a
cooked meal or thinly spread in a salad sandwich.

Wonderful Garlic Bread

Serves 4
Preparation time 25 minutes

1 large French loaf (baguette)
75g (3oz) margarine
6 tbsp olive oil
7 cloves garlic, very finely chopped
2 tbsp fresh parsley, chopped
1 tsp salt

Preheat the oven to 180°C/350°F/Gas Mark 4.
Prepare the loaf by slicing it into 2.5cm (1 inch)
thick slices but do not slice all the way through the
loaf. Leave just the bottom crust intact, so that you
may easily 'open' the slices. Place the loaf on a baking
tray. Depending on the size of the loaf, you may have
to cut it in half so that it fits in the oven. In a small
mixing bowl, blend the margarine and oil to a light,
whipped consistency. Now add the garlic, parsley and
salt and stir well. Spread some of this mixture
(liberally would be authentic) onto each slice of
bread. If you have some left over, either spread it
on the other sides of the slices or dab a little over the
top of the loaf. Bake the loaf in the hot oven for 10
minutes. Serve hot, slicing through the bottom crust
as necessary.

Health Note

A word of caution – large amounts of garlic
(more than 20g of garlic a day – approximately
one bulb) can make red blood cells fragile,
increasing the risk of anaemia. Because it
contains irritants, people with hernias and
stomach disorders should not consume large
amounts of raw garlic.

Gooseberries The popularity of the gooseberry has
declined considerably in recent years, partly because it
requires a certain degree of skill to prepare, and partly
for the reason that the gooseberry bush is susceptible
to blister rust, a blight that can be transmitted to
varieties of trees which are grown for commercial
purposes. The gooseberry is virtually unknown in
southern Europe, hardly present in north America,
but in Britain the gooseberry has a long and distinguished history. There are two essential types; the
dessert gooseberry, which is sweet and suitable for
eating raw, and cooking gooseberries which are tart
but are excellent in a variety of cooked dishes. The
Chinese gooseberry is unrelated, being another name
for the kiwi fruit. The gooseberry is usually green in
colour, but occasionally may be amber or even red. As
the basis for desserts, sauces and other condiments,
the gooseberry has a wide range of uses, including:
jam, wine, pie, fruit salads, purée, ice cream, jelly and
syrup. One of the most delightful uses to which the
gooseberry can be put is . . .

NUTRIENT ANALYSIS
1 CUP GOOSEBERRIES (150g)

KCalories	66.00
Total Fat (g)	0.87
Monounsaturated Fat (g)	0.08
Polyunsaturated Fat (g)	0.48
Saturated Fat (g)	0.06
Carbohydrate (g)	15.27
Protein (g)	1.32
Crude Fibre (g)	2.85
Vitamin A (RE)	43.50
Ascorbic Acid (mg)	41.55
Thiamin (mg)	0.06
Riboflavin (mg)	0.05
Niacin (mg)	0.45
Pantothenic Acid (mg)	0.43
Vitamin B6 (mg)	0.12
Folacin (mcg)	?
Vitamin B12 (mcg)	0.00
Calcium (mg)	37.50
Iron (mg)	0.47
Zinc (mg)	0.18

Spicy Gooseberry Pear Butter

Makes approximately 3l (6 pints)
Preparation time 2 hours 30 minutes

2l (4 pints) gooseberries
3 medium pears, peeled, quartered and cored
1 tsp ground cinnamon
1 tsp ground cloves
1 tsp ground ginger
½ tsp ground nutmeg
570ml (1 pint) cider vinegar
1kg (2lb) brown sugar

Measure the fruit into an enamel saucepan and sprinkle the spices over it. Stir well. Add the vinegar and sugar, stir again and place the pan over a medium heat. Bring to the boil then reduce the heat and simmer gently for 2 hours, stirring often to prevent it sticking. Mash the berries somewhat as you stir to help break them down. Ladle the hot butter into sterilized jars and seal. Allow to cool before using.

Health Note

Nutritionally, a cup of gooseberries will provide over two-thirds of the adult daily requirements for vitamin C. In natural medicine, they have been used to treat constipation, liver and gallbladder ailments, poor complexion, catarrh, arthritis, and digestive problems.

Grapefruit The grapefruit is a relatively new fruit, only being commercially grown since 1885. Most of the world's grapefruit crop is grown in the United States, mainly in Florida, Arizona, California and Texas. There are two main varieties, the Duncan, which has many seeds but possesses a robust flavour, and the Marsh, which is seedless but does not compare in terms of taste. Pink varieties of both are available, and have a sweeter, less harsh flavour.

The fruit is ideal for juicing, being sharp but extremely luscious, and is a popular ingredient in many fresh fruit dishes. When cooked, grilled or barbequed, the grapefruit takes on an altogether milder and more sensual flavour, and can provide a clean, crisp counterpoint to richer and denser foods (for example tempeh, tofu, textured vegetable protein chunks, etc). Consider, for example, a kebab made up of slices of grapefruit, chunks of marinated tofu, and wedges of onions.

Grapefruit Washingtons can be made by halving the grapefruit, using a special grapefruit knife to cut round the edges and to loosen the segments, then each half sprinkling with brown sugar and placing under the grill until the sugar is caramelized. Served with a red cherry in the middle, this makes an extremely easy and tasty appetizer or dessert.

A relative of the grapefruit is the ugli fruit, a hybrid produced by crossing the grapefruit with the mandarin. Often available in West Indian grocery stores, the ugli has a scraggy, lumpy appearance, but is every bit as juicy as the grapefruit and has a less acerbic taste. Grapefruit juice can be used as a solidifying agent in the production of tofu (see under Soya Beans, p289) which yields a tangy, fruity flavour suitable for use in desserts.

NUTRIENT ANALYSIS
½ FRESH GRAPEFRUIT (120g)

KCalories	38.40
Total Fat (g)	0.12
Monounsaturated Fat (g)	0.02

Polyunsaturated Fat (g)	0.03
Saturated Fat (g)	0.02
Carbohydrate (g)	9.70
Protein (g)	0.76
Crude Fibre (g)	0.24
Vitamin A (RE)	14.40
Ascorbic Acid (mg)	41.28
Thiamin (mg)	0.04
Riboflavin (mg)	0.02
Niacin (mg)	0.30
Pantothenic Acid (mg)	0.34
Vitamin B6 (mg)	0.05
Folacin (mcg)	12.24
Vitamin B12 (mcg)	0.00
Calcium (mg)	14.40
Iron (mg)	0.11
Zinc (mg)	0.08

Fruit and Tofu Salad

Serves 4
Preparation time 15 minutes

2 avocados, peeled and sliced
2 grapefruit, peeled, divided into sections and
   chopped
1–2 bananas, peeled and sliced
285g (10oz) plain tofu, cubed
50g (2oz) sunflower seeds, lightly roasted
140ml (¼ pint) raspberry or cider vinegar
2 tbsp olive oil
1 tbsp fresh mint, chopped
1 tbsp fresh coriander, chopped

Toss the prepared avocados, grapefruit, bananas, tofu
and sunflower seeds together in a large salad bowl.
Combine the vinegar and oil in a jar or jug and shake
or stir to make a dressing. Stir in the herbs then pour
the dressing over the salad, toss gently and serve on a
bed of lettuce or in chilled bowls with a garnish of a
single, whole spring onion.

Grapefruit and Beetroot Coleslaw

Serves 4
Preparation time 20 minutes

¼ head white cabbage, shredded

1 medium, raw beetroot, grated
1 grapefruit, peeled, divided into segments and sliced
3 spring onions, finely chopped
3 tbsp fresh coriander, chopped
140g (5oz) plain tofu
3 tbsp soya milk
1 tbsp oil
1 tsp prepared mustard
juice of 1 lemon

Toss the cabbage, beetroot, grapefruit, onions and
coriander together in a large salad bowl. Blend the
tofu, soya milk, oil and mustard to a smooth creamy
consistency, add the lemon juice and stir well. Pour
this dressing over the salad and toss together. Serve
immediately or chill for 30 minutes before serving.

Health Note

Half a fresh grapefruit provides over two-thirds
of the adult daily requirement for vitamin C. The
grapefruit has been used to treat arthritis, liver
and gallstone disorders, to dissolve catarrh, to
restore digestion and elimination, and to
improve skin complexion. A glass of grapefruit
juice taken before bedtime can promote sleep.
The seeds of the grapefruit have been used to
produce an extract which is used to curb the
growth of undesirable yeasts, such as candida,
and also certain parasites, including giardia.

Grapes There are said to be over 8000 varieties of
grape, although only a dozen or so of these are
important as table grapes. Of the white varieties, the
most common are Perlette (seedless, generally from
Israel or Cyprus, small in size with a slightly bitter
taste), the Thompson (seedless, from South Africa,
Australia, Israel, Chile and America, medium-sized,
sweet and juicy), and the Italia (seeded, from Italy,
large and greenish yellow in appearance, with a musky
flavour). Common black varieties include Napoleon
(seeded, small and sweet, from Spain) and Flame
(seedless, medium-sized and very sweet, from
Chile). The most certain way to buy finest quality
grapes is simply to try one before you buy, something
which greengrocers are generally quite happy to let
you do, supermarkets less so. As a guide, seeded
varieties tend to have more depth of flavour beyond
the bland sweetness of seedless grapes, and muscatel
varieties (both white and black) possess a delicacy of

flavour and bouquet which many find most appealing.

Since the grape is probably the most widely cultivated fruit in the world, it is, inevitably, also the most highly chemically treated. The United Farm Workers Union has asked consumers to boycott table grapes for years, claiming that, 'Growers cannot be trusted when it comes to the use of poisonous pesticides. They will do what is profitable for them without concern for the safety of farm workers and consumers.'[8] The Union believes that 300,000 American farm workers are poisoned each year by pesticides, and that miscarriages and child cancer rates are abnormally high in areas where grapes are under intensive cultivation.

The whole question of pesticide residue, and its impact upon the health of adults and children who may consume small amounts in food, is highly contentious. It is most unlikely that a scientific study could ever be designed to measure the effect of ingesting minute quantities of residue over a person's lifetime, and even if it could, the results would be immediately open to challenge. It makes sense, therefore, to be prudent when selecting grapes and other produce which may have been chemically treated: where an organic or minimal chemical use alternative is available, choose that; make your concerns known to both the shop or supermarket you frequent and to central government; and ensure that all produce is extremely well washed before consumption. This will not affect the presence of systemically absorbed substances, but it will appreciably reduce the risk of ingesting undesirable substances which may be present on the surface of the fruit.

Soak the grapes for 20 minutes or so in cold water to which 2 tbsp vinegar has been added, follow by a further soak in water in which several tablespoons of salt have been dissolved, and then rinse; this simple procedure will wash away a surprising amount of dirt.

Grapes have no end of uses in the kitchen, ranging from an essential component of a fresh fruit salad, through to jams, juices, sauces, and lunch box snacks. The young leaves of grape vines are used to make most excellent dolmades, grape seeds themselves yield a distinctive oil which is high in essential fatty acids.

It is preferable to make your own grape juice, rather than buying it ready made, since the commercial variety often tastes excessively sweetened. If you have an electric juicer, this becomes a very quick and easy morning routine. An extremely healthy and tasty cocktail can be made by combining various proportions of the following to taste: grape juice, lemon juice and pineapple juice.

NUTRIENT ANALYSIS
1 CUP GRAPES (160g)

KCalories	113.60
Total Fat (g)	0.93
Monounsaturated Fat (g)	0.04
Polyunsaturated Fat (g)	0.27
Saturated Fat (g)	0.30
Carbohydrate (g)	28.43
Protein (g)	1.06
Crude Fibre (g)	0.72
Vitamin A (RE)	11.20
Ascorbic Acid (mg)	17.28
Thiamin (mg)	0.15
Riboflavin (mg)	0.09
Niacin (mg)	0.48
Pantothenic Acid (mg)	0.04
Vitamin B6 (mg)	0.18
Folacin (mcg)	6.24
Vitamin B12 (mcg)	0.00
Calcium (mg)	17.60
Iron (mg)	0.42
Zinc (mg)	0.08

Pretty Party Jelly

Serves 8–12
Preparation time 4 hours

570ml (1 pint) filtered (ie unchlorinated) water
2 × 3g packets agar powder
570ml (1 pint) grape juice, red or white
450g (1lb) red or white grapes, sliced in half and
    deseeded
2 ripe bananas, peeled and sliced

Measure the water into a saucepan and stir in the agar powder. Place the pan over a medium heat and bring to the boil, stirring constantly. Immediately remove from the heat and add the grape juice. Stir well and put to one side to cool. Arrange some of the grape halves and banana slices in a jelly mould (or moulds). Stir the remaining fruit into the cooled jelly and pour or ladle gently into the jelly mould.

Chill the jelly in the refrigerator for 2-4 hours, until set. Serve chilled.

Health Note

Grapes have a very special position in natural therapy. For centuries, they have been revered as 'the queen of fruits' because of their ability to cleanse and purify the body of many toxins. Being eliminative in nature, 'grape cures' have most successfully been used to treat disorders such as constipation, gout, rheumatism, skin, and liver and kidney disorders. Recently, science has identified a substance in the skin of black grapes – resveratrol – which possesses considerable antifungal and antioxidant properties. Resveratrol can neutralize free radicals, and can also lower blood cholesterol levels. It is speculated that the presence of resveratrol in the French diet allows them to consume high-fat foodstuffs whilst having a rate of heart disease which is significantly lower than many other countries.

Guava Because guavas ripen and spoil very quickly, it is unusual to find fresh ones on sale at any distance from the tropical regions in which they are grown. Should you happen to find any fresh ones, they may well be unripe, and therefore not yet particularly edible. However, unripe guavas can be used to make guava jelly. Take approximately 2kg of fresh guavas, wash them and slice into a large pan. Add water to cover, and a couple of cardomom seeds (optional), and bring to the boil for 15 minutes. Turn the pulp into a fine muslin jelly bag and leave to drain, carefully collecting the juice in a bowl. For each 570ml (1 pint) of resulting juice, add 450g (1lb) of sugar, and boil together for about 15 minutes until the jelly is ready to set. Pour into sterilized jars, seal and allow to cool.

Alternatively, guava 'cheese' can be made by pushing the cooked guavas through a seive and boiling the pulp until it is reduced to the consistency of jelly. Pour this pulp into a dish. When cool, it is firm enough to be sliced, and is considered a delicacy in Brazil.

In Western countries, guavas are most usually encountered canned. Their use is therefore restricted to fruit salads and garnishes.

NUTRIENT ANALYSIS
1 CUP GUAVAS (165g)

KCalories	84.15
Total Fat (g)	0.99
Monounsaturated Fat (g)	0.09
Polyunsaturated Fat (g)	0.42
Saturated Fat (g)	0.28
Carbohydrate (g)	19.60
Protein (g)	1.35
Crude Fibre (g)	9.24
Vitamin A (RE)	130.35
Ascorbic Acid (mg)	302.78
Thiamin (mg)	0.08
Riboflavin (mg)	0.08
Niacin (mg)	1.98
Pantothenic Acid (mg)	0.25
Vitamin B6 (mg)	0.24
Folacin (mcg)	?
Vitamin B12 (mcg)	0.00
Calcium (mg)	33.00
Iron (mg)	0.51
Zinc (mg)	0.38

Health Note

Guavas are extraordinarily high in vitamin C – one raw guava contains over eight times the adult daily requirement, and about a fifth of the requirements for niacin, vitamin B6, vitamin A and potassium. In natural medicine they have been used to treat diarrhoea, prolonged menstruation, high blood pressure, asthma and catarrh.

Hazelnuts Several similar varieties of this useful and pleasant-tasting nut are available, including the cobnut which grows wild in northern Europe and can be eaten fresh or dried, and the filbert, more common in southern Europe. Hazelnut oil is a particularly delicate oil suitable only for the finest cold uses (such as salad dressings); it should not be heated. Like most nuts, they should not be purchased ready shelled, since the shell provides an excellent protection against rancidity, and without this the oils will slowly oxidize and the nut lose its health-giving and flavourful properties. Hazelnuts can be used whole or chopped in a wide variety of foods, including mueslis, cakes and biscuits, salads, and, of course, as a snack by themselves or with dried fruit.

A variation on the Spanish horchata yields a nutritious and appetizing soft drink as follows: mix 100g (4oz) of finely ground hazelnuts and 1 tsp freshly grated ginger together in a blender and purée with 570ml (1 pint) cold water. Strain this mixture through a fine seive and add soya milk to make 570ml (1 pint) of liquid. Stir in one tablespoon of barley malt syrup. Chill, then serve in a chilled glass with a twist or slice of orange. You may stir in a little chilled wine if desired. **See also:** Shoo-Fly Pie (p327)

NUTRIENT ANALYSIS
½ CUP HAZELNUTS (60g)

KCalories	395.00
Total Fat (g)	39.15
Monounsaturated Fat (g)	30.68
Polyunsaturated Fat (g)	3.75
Saturated Fat (g)	2.88
Carbohydrate (g)	9.56
Protein (g)	8.15
Crude Fibre (g)	2.38
Vitamin A (RE)	4.38
Ascorbic Acid (mg)	0.63
Thiamin (mg)	0.31
Riboflavin (mg)	0.07
Niacin (mg)	0.71
Pantothenic Acid (mg)	0.72
Vitamin B6 (mg)	0.38
Folacin (mcg)	44.88
Vitamin B12 (mcg)	0.00
Calcium (mg)	117.50
Iron (mg)	2.04
Zinc (mg)	1.50

Health Note

Hazelnuts are one of the best natural sources of the trace mineral boron, consumption of which has been shown to be essential in the prevention of osteoporosis. Just one gram of hazelnuts provides approximately 16mg of boron, enough to satisfy most individuals daily requirements.

Honey Honey occupies a highly equivocal place in vegetarian/wholefood cooking. On the one hand, its proponents ascribe health-giving properties to it which verge on the magical. On the other hand, those opposed to all forms of animal cruelty and exploitation, notably vegans, oppose honey on the grounds that its production may involve unacceptable suffering and even death to the insects who manufacture it.

Chemically, honey is a mixture of glucose, fructose and water. The bee gathers plant nectar, a kind of sweet sap secreted by flowers, for eventual use as a food for larvae. During this process, of course, the bee also serves the valuable function of pollinating the plant. When the bee's honey sac is full, it returns to the hive and disgorges it into the cells of the honeycomb. Natural evaporation concentrates the sweetness of the plant nectar, and the bee adds two enzymes, one to create different types of sugar, and another to prevent bacterial infection. Bees are also used to produce a range of other health food products, including bee pollen, royal jelly (a substance secreted by worker bees and fed to future queen bees, for which extravagant health claims have been made), and propolis (a waxy, resinous substance collected by bees from the buds of various conifers, and used to repair cracks and openings in the hive).

Leaving aside the more extreme promotional avowals made by the vendors of bee products, there is indeed some truth in their assertion that honey possesses health-giving properties. It is known, for example, that honey has been used for wound dressing for over 4000 years. Indeed, both honey and sugar can prevent or hinder bacterial growth on wounds by the process of osmotic action. The enzymes in honey, however, can also produce hydrogen peroxide, a powerful antimicrobial agent, and there is evidence that some types of honey may also contain antibacterial substances produced by the flowers that the bees have visited.

The average hive contains about 60,000 bees, and produces about 36.5l (8 gallons) of honey every year.

The sheer effort involved in this is quite astonishing; to produce 450g (1lb) of honey, bees have to gather about 1.8kg (4lb) of nectar – which means visiting two million flowers! Furthermore, each worker bee has an average productive life span of only three to six weeks – just long enough to collect, on average, about a teaspoon of nectar. Connoisseurs of honey claim that it is possible to detect a difference in taste between the various types of flowers visited by the bees; the more popular varieties being acacia, alfafa, buckwheat, clover, heather, lavender, lime and orange blossom, and eucalyptus. In practice, it would be unusual for bees to collect nectar from one exclusive species of plant, and the varieties are likely to be to a greater or lesser extent combined.

Commercial honey production is a very large scale enterprise, and, accordingly, the techniques of mass production are used. Honey bees live in artificial hives, designed to facilitate the easy removal of the combs. When these are removed, or returned to the hive after inspection, it is inevitable that – even with the utmost care – bees will be crushed and killed. Bees are regularly transported all round the world, where they will face new diseases, enemies and alien environmental conditions. This, once again, is profoundly unnatural and is bound to cause stress and casualties. Where it is necessary to destroy a hive, either because of disease or simply because it is too expensive to keep the colonies going in the harsh winters of the more northerly countries, this is done by pouring petrol over the hive – the fumes from which kill most of the bees – and then setting it alight.

The queen bee is obviously of paramount importance, both to the hive and the beekeeper, and through selective breeding characteristics such as hardiness, non-aggression and a reluctance to swarm (when the entire colony deserts the artificial hive and looks for a new home) are encouraged. One way swarming can be prevented is to simply remove the queen's wings – if she subsequently emerges from the hive in an attempt to swarm, she will obviously fall to the ground and perish. Although the queen would naturally live for about five years in the wild, in commercial production she will be killed off as her fertility declines, usually at the age of two or soon thereafter. Not content with the bee's natural techniques of procreation, large scale beekeeping now increasingly resorts to the techniques of artificial insemination, a process which necessarily involves close physical handling and resulting discomfort.

After all this, it is just as well to remember that the bee itself is an extremely intelligent creature with a sophisticated language and complex forms of communication which are one of the most advanced of any animal species. It has a brain, and several smaller ganglia (sub-brains), running through its body, and its capacity to experience pain and distress is beyond dispute.[9]

Another sobering reality, which somewhat detracts from the more mythological aspects of honey, is the possibility of contamination with agrochemicals. If the bees are kept on or near agriculturally active land, the possibility of such contamination cannot be excluded. In the final analysis, it is up to each individual to decide whether they wish to consume honey or not, but its production inevitably involves some suffering and exploitation which, notwithstanding honey's modest but proven health benefits, is hard to justify.

NUTRIENT ANALYSIS
1 CUP HONEY (339g)

KCalories	1030.56
Total Fat (g)	0.00
Monounsaturated Fat (g)	?
Polyunsaturated Fat (g)	?
Saturated Fat (g)	0.00
Carbohydrate (g)	279.00
Protein (g)	1.02
Crude Fibre (g)	0.00
Vitamin A (RE)	?
Ascorbic Acid (mg)	3.39
Thiamin (mg)	0.02
Riboflavin (mg)	0.14
Niacin (mg)	1.02
Pantothenic Acid (mg)	?
Vitamin B6 (mg)	?
Folacin (mcg)	?
Vitamin B12 (mcg)	?
Calcium (mg)	16.95
Iron (mg)	1.70
Zinc (mg)	?

Health Note

There are many substitutes for honey; including molasses, maple syrup, golden syrup, corn syrup, and barley malt syrup. Of these, molasses is the healthiest (see p241) and all are available at healthfood shops and/or supermarkets.

Horseradish An extremely pungent member of the mustard family, the horseradish has been cultivated in eastern and northern Europe for many centuries as the basis for producing one of the strongest sauces you are likely to encounter. Sparingly used, it makes an excellent accompaniment to very strongly flavoured dishes, and can cut through food which would otherwise taste too fatty or greasy. Use fresh horseradish root where possible, in the following two recipes – if that is unobtainable, then dried or preserved horseradish would make an acceptable substitute, although the quantities may have to be adjusted.

To prepare raw horseradish, first wash the root, then remove the skin with a potato peeler or sharp paring knife, to reveal the pure white flesh, which should then be grated. The fumes produced by this process can be quite acrid, so it is best done out of doors, or under running water. Horseradish will lose much of its potency unless it is used fairly quickly. Unsurprisingly, the horseradish has been used to stimulate the appetite and produce digestive secretions, and it can clear stuffy noses and blocked sinuses very effectively.

NUTRIENT ANALYSIS
1 tbsp PREPARED HORSERADISH (15g)

KCalories	5.70
Total Fat (g)	0.03
Monounsaturated Fat (g)	?
Polyunsaturated Fat (g)	?
Saturated Fat (g)	0.00
Carbohydrate (g)	1.44
Protein (g)	0.20
Crude Fibre (g)	0.14
Vitamin A (RE)	?
Ascorbic Acid (mg)	0.00
Thiamin (mg)	0.00
Riboflavin (mg)	0.00
Niacin (mg)	0.00
Pantothenic Acid (mg)	?
Vitamin B6 (mg)	?
Folacin (mcg)	?
Vitamin B12 (mcg)	?
Calcium (mg)	9.15
Iron (mg)	0.14
Zinc (mg)	?

Horseradish Sauce
Makes 285ml (½ pint)
Preparation time 15 minutes

1 tbsp margarine
1 tbsp plain flour
285ml (½ pint) soya milk
25g (1oz) grated horseradish
1 tsp sugar
¼ tsp cayenne pepper
pinch of salt
1 tsp wine vinegar

Melt the margarine in a saucepan then sprinkle the flour over it and stir to make a thick paste (roux). Keep stirring over a medium heat, as you gradually add the soya milk. Stir well after each addition to ensure a smooth, creamy sauce. Now add all but the vinegar and cook for 5 minutes, stirring often. Finally, add the vinegar, stir over the heat for 1 minute then serve. Excellent over steamed vegetables, vol-au-vents, baked potatoes, nut roasts, etc.

Horseradish Relish
Makes 140ml (¼ pint)
Preparation time 10 minutes

50g (2oz) firm tofu
1 tbsp prepared mustard
2 tbsp cider or wine vinegar
1 tsp sugar, preferably brown
¼ tsp salt
25g (1oz) grated horseradish

Mash the tofu in a small mixing bowl. Add the remaining ingredients, in the order in which they are listed, blending well after each addition. Serve immediately as a condiment to your meal or cover and keep chilled for 2–3 days.

Jerusalem Artichokes Though the name implies otherwise, this plant has nothing to do with either Jerusalem or the (globe) artichoke (see p176). It is, in fact, the edible tuber of a plant which, above ground, most resembles the sunflower. It comes originally from North America but has found its way over the centuries to Europe and Asia, where it is well established in both the botanical and culinary senses. The Jerusalem artichoke is slightly more sweet and watery than the potato but is often used and cooked in ways similar to the potato. As it is usually rather distorted in shape, it can be difficult to peel; the peel is edible, however, and a good scrub will make it ready for use. Trim the artichoke into evenly sized pieces and cook: it may be baked, steamed, roasted, sautéed or mashed.

Jerusalem Soup
Serves 4
Preparation time 45 minutes

1.5kg (3lbs) artichokes, roughly peeled and cut into
  chunks
3 tbsp margarine
1 large onion, chopped
1 tsp freshly ground black pepper
1 tbsp plain flour
1l (2 pints) vegetable stock
570ml (1 pint) soya milk
2 tsp fresh tarragon, chopped
½ tsp ground cinnamon

Place the artichoke pieces in a steamer and steam until just tender, about 15 minutes. Remove from the heat. In a large saucepan, melt the margarine over a medium heat and sauté the onion until clear and tender. Add the black pepper and stir for 1 minute. Sprinkle the flour over the sauté and stir to make a thick paste (roux). Combine the stock and milk in a jug and add to the roux, a little at a time, stirring well after each addition to make a slightly thick broth. Remove the broth from the heat and work the steamed artichokes and the broth, together, through a mouli to produce a thick, evenly textured soup. Return the soup to the saucepan and place over a medium heat once again. Add a little more stock or soya milk if a less thick soup is desired. Add the tarragon and cook until the soup returns to simmering point. Serve hot with a sprink-

ling of ground cinnamon over each serving. A garnish of Soya Creem is both attractive and tasty.

Kale This member of the cabbage family is a robust winter cabbage which is recently descended from the wild cabbage. It is sometimes called borecole or curly kale, after its tightly curled leaf formation. Kale is often considered a coarse food, but I ask you to reconsider any prejudices you might hold towards it. Certainly, it has a strong colour, texture and flavour and, yes, it is definitely earthy. All it needs is a little considerate cooking to become a delicacy. Although kale can be eaten raw in salads, it is excellent cooked in the following way:
See also: Mnkhwani (p314); Taushe (p315); Muriwo ne Dovi (p323)

Delicious Curly Kale
Serves 4
Preparation time 45 minutes

1kg (2lb) curly kale
1 tbsp oil
5 cloves garlic, chopped
1 large onion, thinly sliced
1 tsp freshly ground black pepper
½ tsp ground nutmeg
1 sweet red pepper, deseeded and thinly sliced

Trim the kale and immerse it in cold, salty water for 5 minutes. Rinse each leaf under cold running water, slice into narrow pieces and place in a colander. Heat the oil in a large saucepan over a medium heat. Sauté the garlic and onion until clear and tender. Add the pepper and nutmeg and stir the sauté for 1 minute. Add the sliced kale and immediately cover the pan. Leave it cooking over a medium heat for 5 minutes. Stir the kale so that the onion sauté is distributed through the greens. Cover the pan, reduce the heat to low and leave to cook for 10 minutes. Stir the contents again, add the pepper and cover the pan. Leave to cook over the low heat for a final 10 minutes. Stir well and serve immediately with rice, tempeh and sautéed carrots or baked pumpkin.

Kidney Beans The red kidney bean is one of the most useful of all pulses, being economical, tasty, very nutritious and highly adaptable. They can be bought either dried or canned, the former for cheapness, the latter for convenience. As with most other beans and pulses, dried red kidney beans should always be soaked overnight and given a very thorough cooking. Improperly cooked kidney beans contain substances known as lectins, which can cause gastroenteritis. For this reason, they should not be given to very young children. Unfortunately, many canned varieties of kidney beans are not sufficiently cooked (if you can't easily squash one against the roof of your mouth with your tongue, then it isn't cooked) and should not be used without further boiling, thus greatly diminishing their supposed convenience.

The need to soak dried beans and pulses, such as red kidney beans, for several hours is sometimes used by critics to suggest that vegetarianism is an impractical lifestyle in today's fast-food world. Such critics have clearly never visited a fine restaurant, where good food often takes some time to prepare, but is certainly worth waiting for. It would be entirely wrong to categorize vegetarian cuisine as being more time-consuming. A plate of pasta, for example, can easily be produced in about 10 minutes – which surely is fast enough for all but those hell-bent on developing a world class ulcer! Soaking dried pulses overnight inevitably implies a certain amount of forward thinking; but what meal does not? Thirty seconds is all it takes to wash dried pulses and put them to soak – and there is a certain satisfaction to be gained from knowing that, overnight and for part of the next day, the ingredients for your next main meal are naturally bringing themselves to a state of readiness. Kidney beans need to be pressure-cooked for about 25 minutes (individual pressure cookers vary, check your own instructions) which means the total active preparation time is less than half an hour. When cooked and cooled, they make a first class ingredient in any number of cold dishes, particularly salads.

See also: Irio (p313); Frijoles (p325); Chilli Without Carne (p325); Simple Rice and Peas (p335)

NUTRIENT ANALYSIS
1 CUP COOKED KIDNEY BEANS (177g)

KCalories	224.79
Total Fat (g)	0.89
Monounsaturated Fat (g)	0.07
Polyunsaturated Fat (g)	0.49
Saturated Fat (g)	0.13
Carbohydrate (g)	40.37

Protein (g)	15.35
Crude Fibre (g)	4.97
Vitamin A (RE)	0.00
Ascorbic Acid (mg)	2.12
Thiamin (mg)	0.28
Riboflavin (mg)	0.10
Niacin (mg)	1.02
Pantothenic Acid (mg)	0.39
Vitamin B6 (mg)	0.21
Folacin (mcg)	229.39
Vitamin B12 (mcg)	0.00
Calcium (mg)	49.56
Iron (mg)	5.20
Zinc (mg)	1.89

Kidney Beans à la bourguignonne
Serves 4
Preparation time 2 hours, plus soaking overnight

225g (8oz) dried kidney beans, washed
3 tbsp margarine
1 tbsp olive oil
5 cloves garlic, coarsely chopped
2 large onions, coarsely chopped
450g (1lb) mushrooms, cleaned and quartered
1 tsp freshly ground black pepper
570ml (1 pint) red wine
1 x 7.5cm (3 inch) piece cinnamon

Cover the washed beans in water and soak overnight. Drain them, rinse and turn into a pressure cooker. Cover with fresh water and cover the pan. Cook at full pressure for 25 minutes; cool the cooker immediately and drain the beans of all but the thickest cooking juices. Meanwhile, heat the margarine and olive oil together in a large saucepan and sauté first the garlic then the onion until tender and slightly golden. Add the mushrooms and continue the sauté, stirring often. When the mushrooms begin to release their juices, sprinkle the pepper over all and cover the pan. Reduce the heat and cook for 5 minutes. Stir well then add the beans and their juices, the red wine and the cinnamon stick. Stir, cover the pan and leave to cook over a low heat for at least 1 hour.

Stir occasionally, adding a little stock or water if

necessary to prevent sticking.

This dish may be allowed to cool and then reheated later if you prefer. Serve hot, alone or with rice, roast potatoes or steamed pumpkin.

Health Note

Kidney beans are a superb food. Just one cup provides over a quarter of the adult daily recommended intake of protein, iron, potassium and thiamin; all of the adult folic acid requirements, and virtually no fat. There is, however, one aspect of kidney (and other) beans which is sometimes less than welcome: their ability to generate intestinal gas. They contain complex carbohydrates called oligosaccharides which are relatively resistant to the digestive processes in the stomach and upper parts of the intestine, and therefore pass undigested into the lower intestine. There they are acted upon by the bacteria which are normally resident in the colon, with gas as the end result. This only affects certain people; a genetic factor is thought to affect whether we can or cannot effectively process oligosaccharides. If you can't, and if it's causing a real problem, do this: wash the beans thoroughly – several times – at each stage of cooking. The more times you rinse them, the more oligosaccharides will be washed away. Don't cook beans in their soaking water, and pour away the cooking water. Of course, this will jettison some of their nutrients, but the trade-off in comfort might be worth it.

Kiwi Fruit Also known as the Chinese gooseberry, this luscious green fruit originated in China but was massively popularized by the growers of New Zealand. It is an attractive ingredient in fruit salads, or as a garnish for any number of sweet or savoury dishes. The rise of nouvelle cuisine seemed, for some chefs at any rate, to be largely a vehicle for the promotion of the kiwi fruit, with the result that it has suffered from 'faded trendiness' and may, to some, seem rather passé and even somewhat vulgar. Since its popularity waned, its price has become rather more reasonable and there are often bargains to be had in the kiwi fruit department of many produce markets. Kiwi has a generally mild flavour, and makes an attractive juice either by

itself or in combination with other tropical fruit, such as guava, mango, papaya or pineapple. Nutritionally, it contains heroic amounts of vitamin C, a single fruit more than meeting the adult daily recommended intake.

NUTRIENT ANALYSIS
1 RAW KIWI FRUIT (76g)

KCalories	46.36
Total Fat (g)	0.33
Monounsaturated Fat (g)	?
Polyunsaturated Fat (g)	?
Saturated Fat (g)	?
Carbohydrate (g)	11.31
Protein (g)	0.75
Crude Fibre (g)	0.84
Vitamin A (RE)	13.68
Ascorbic Acid (mg)	74.48
Thiamin (mg)	0.02
Riboflavin (mg)	0.04
Niacin (mg)	0.38
Pantothenic Acid (mg)	?
Vitamin B6 (mg)	?
Folacin (mcg)	?
Vitamin B12 (mcg)	0.00
Calcium (mg)	19.76
Iron (mg)	0.31
Zinc (mg)	?

Kiwi Fruit Flan
Makes one 30x30cm (12x12) inch flan
Preparation time 2 hours

For the crust:
170g (6oz) plain flour
¼ tsp salt
100g (4oz) shredded vegetable suet
1–2 tbsp cold water

For the filling:
140ml (¼ pint) cold water
1 × 3g packet agar powder

420ml (¾ pint) apple juice
6–8 ripe kiwi fruits, peeled and sliced
1 ripe banana, peeled and sliced
4 glace cherries, halved

Preheat the oven to 180°C/350°F/Gas Mark 4. Mix the flour, salt and suet together in a mixing bowl. Add the water and work to an even consistency with a fork or your fingers. Turn into a 30.5cm (12 inch) flan dish and press into place, ensuring that the pastry reaches all the way up the sides of the dish as well. Bake for 15 minutes, until golden. Remove from the oven and leave to cool.

Measure the cold water into a small saucepan and dissolve the agar in it. Bring to the boil over a medium heat then immediately remove from the heat and stir in the apple juice. Put to one side. Arrange the kiwi and banana slices in the bottom of the flan case and place the cherries over these. (Note: you may consider both the banana and the cherries optional.) When you are happy with the look of the arrangement, pour the apple juice and agar mixture over all and leave the flan to cool. Chill it in the refrigerator for at least 1 hour. Serve chilled with a little Soya Creem.

Kohlrabi Literally meaning 'cabbage turnip' in the German, kohlrabi is a variety of cabbage, available in the autumn and used in a broadly similar way to turnips, or celeriac. Buy them small and young, preferably organically grown so that the skin need not be removed, for this is where most of the delicate and sweet flavour lies. Its leaves can be lightly steamed, like collards, as can the root, which may also be diced and sautéed in oil and garlic. Alternatively, it can be shredded and added to a winter salad.

NUTRIENT ANALYSIS
1 CUP BOILED KOHLRABI (165g)

KCalories	47.85
Total Fat (g)	0.18
Monounsaturated Fat (g)	0.01
Polyunsaturated Fat (g)	0.09
Saturated Fat (g)	0.02
Carbohydrate (g)	11.04
Protein (g)	2.97
Crude Fibre (g)	1.82

Vitamin A (RE)	6.60
Ascorbic Acid (mg)	89.10
Thiamin (mg)	0.07
Riboflavin (mg)	0.03
Niacin (mg)	0.64
Pantothenic Acid (mg)	0.26
Vitamin B6 (mg)	0.25
Folacin (mcg)	19.97
Vitamin B12 (mcg)	0.00
Calcium (mg)	41.25
Iron (mg)	0.66
Zinc (mg)	0.51

Kohlrabi Bake
Serves 4–6
Preparation time 1 hour 15 minutes

1kg (2lb) kohlrabi, scrubbed and peeled if necessary
1 tbsp oil
7 cloves garlic, finely chopped
2 medium onions, chopped
50g (2oz) margarine
1–2 tsp freshly ground black pepper
50g (2oz) breadcrumbs

Preheat the oven to 180°C/350°F/Gas Mark 4 and lightly oil a deep baking dish. Halve or quarter the cleaned kohlrabi and slice each piece as thinly as possible – a food processor would do this wonderfully quickly and easily. Place the slices in a deep bowl, cover in cold water and quickly swirl the water through the slices. Drain the slices and quickly dry them with a clean tea towel. Heat the oil in a frying pan and sauté the garlic and onion over a medium heat for just 3 minutes. Remove from the heat. Place a layer of kohlrabi slices in the bottom of the oven dish and spread with a thin layer of the garlic and onion sauté. Cut tiny dabs of margarine and arrange them over the saute and then sprinkle a little of the black pepper over all. Repeat these layers – kohlrabi, sauté, margarine, pepper – until the kohlrabi is used up. Top the dish with breadcrumbs and any remaining margarine and black pepper. Bake, uncovered, for 30–40 minutes, until very tender and aromatic. Serve hot with vegetable sausages or tempeh, and greens.

Health Note

The anti-cancer properties of cruciferous vegetables such as kohlrabi have been established beyond doubt. Scientific evidence reveals that populations who consume significant amounts of these vegetables suffer far less from various common cancers, particularly those of the gastrointestinal and respiratory tracts. In natural medicine, kohlrabi has been used to cleanse the blood and improve the complexion of the skin, and it is used to treat kidney and bladder irritation. Kohlrabi is very rich in vitamin C – one cup of raw shredded kohlrabi will supply one-and-a-half times of the adult daily recommended daily intake.

Kombu This seaweed deserves to have a permanent place in your larder. It serves three extremely useful functions. First, the addition of a 15cm (6 inch) strip of kombu to sautées, soups, stews, simmering rice or cooking beans will help the foods to soften evenly and quickly. Second, the kombu will add flavour similar in all but intensity and detrimental effect to that of monosodium glutimate (MSG). And third, kombu adds important nutrients to whatever you cook it with. Among these are calcium, iron and iodine – in which, like most seaweeds, it is especially rich. If you actually eat the kombu – not necessary, but certainly tasty, though chewy – you can gain other trace minerals as well. Rinse dried kombu before you drop it in the pot but don't worry about a fine white deposit you might detect, as this is a natural salty residue. Keep kombu in a dry and airtight container until you are ready to use it.

Kumquats An interesting citrus fruit which originated in China but is now grown in many warm countries, the kumquat is unusual in that its rind is usually sweeter than its flesh. Consequently, they should not be peeled, but carefully washed before serving fresh. Some can taste very sour indeed, and for this reason are perhaps best stewed whole in sugar syrup, or turned into a preserve. Alternatively, they can be thinly sliced and deseeded, and used as an ingredient in fruit salads. Kumquat has been used in natural medicine to treat high blood pressure, catarrh, fevers and pneumonia. Its prime nutritional constitu-

ent is vitamin C, three fruits yielding about one third of the adult daily requirement.

NUTRIENT ANALYSIS
1 KUMQUAT (19g)

KCalories	11.97
Total Fat (g)	0.02
Monounsaturated Fat (g)	?
Polyunsaturated Fat (g)	?
Saturated Fat (g)	?
Carbohydrate (g)	3.12
Protein (g)	0.17
Crude Fibre (g)	0.70
Vitamin A (RE)	5.70
Ascorbic Acid (mg)	7.11
Thiamin (mg)	0.02
Riboflavin (mg)	0.02
Niacin (mg)	0.10
Pantothenic Acid (mg)	?
Vitamin B6 (mg)	?
Folacin (mcg)	?
Vitamin B12 (mcg)	0.00
Calcium (mg)	8.36
Iron (mg)	0.07
Zinc (mg)	0.02

Ladies' Fingers see Okra

Lambs' Lettuce A welcome winter alternative to hot house lettuces, lambs' lettuce (also called corn salad) is generally available in the months from September to March, and gives a very good, robust flavour to a winter salad. It has a particularly attractive, deep green appearance, indicating its wealth of vitamin A, and makes a spectactular ingredient in a side salad suitable for dinner parties.

Laver see Nori

Leeks This vegetable was mentioned in the Bible as one of the foodstuffs – together with cucumbers, melons, onions and garlic – which the Israelites most missed in their sojourn in the wilderness.[10] When peeled of its green and tough outer layers, the leek can be sliced into small circles, which can then be further subdivided and judiciously included as a fresh vegetable in a raw winter salad. Alternatively, the leek can be lightly steamed, which will dispel all of its strong odour, leaving a delicate and enticing vegetable which is quite delicious when served with a vinaigrette dressing (the dressing can be applied while the leeks are still warm, and allowed to penetrate, see Leeks Vinaigrette, p352). Other quick and easy leek recipes are listed below. The Roman Emperor Nero consumed leek soup every day, believing that it would help him to develop a clear and magisterial voice for speech making.

NUTRIENT ANALYSIS
1 LEEK, BOILED (124g)

KCalories	38.44
Total Fat (g)	0.25
Monounsaturated Fat (g)	0.00
Polyunsaturated Fat (g)	0.14
Saturated Fat (g)	0.03
Carbohydrate (g)	9.45
Protein (g)	1.00
Crude Fibre (g)	1.02
Vitamin A (RE)	6.20
Ascorbic Acid (mg)	5.21
Thiamin (mg)	0.03
Riboflavin (mg)	0.02
Niacin (mg)	0.25
Pantothenic Acid (mg)	0.09
Vitamin B6 (mg)	0.14
Folacin (mcg)	30.13
Vitamin B12 (mcg)	0.00
Calcium (mg)	37.20
Iron (mg)	1.36
Zinc (mg)	0.07

Chilled Leek Salad

Serves 4
Preparation time 1 hour 15 minutes, plus cooling time

1kg (2lbs) leeks
90ml (3 fl oz) olive oil
2 small carrots, peeled, quartered and diced
50g (2oz) uncooked brown rice
2 teaspoons sugar
salt to taste
juice of ½ lemon
420ml (¾ pint) water
wedges of lemon, to garnish

Trim the leeks and remove a few of the outer layers. Slice into thick rounds and wash these in plenty of salty water. Drain, rinse under running water and drain again. Heat the oil in a large saucepan and place over a low heat. Add the leeks and carrots, cover the pan and cook over the low heat for 30 minutes, shaking the pan occasionally. Stir in the rice, sugar, salt, lemon juice and water. Cover the pan and simmer for 30 minutes over a low heat. During cooking, add a tiny amount of hot water if necessary: the salad should be moist but not watery. Remove from the heat and allow to cool; chill in the refrigerator if possible. Serve cold garnished with lemon wedges so that each person may sprinkle their serving with lemon juice to taste.

Leek and Potato Soup

Serves 4–6
Preparation time 1 hour

2 tbsp oil
3 cloves garlic, chopped
1 tsp freshly ground black pepper
1½ tsp caraway or fennel seed, slightly crushed
1k (2lb) leeks, trimmed, sliced, washed, rinsed and drained
1k (2lb) potatoes, scrubbed and cut into chunks
2l (4 pints) vegetable stock
1x6-inch strip kombu (optional)
1 tbsp miso or yeast extract (optional)

Heat the oil in a large stewpot or saucepan and sauté the garlic until just golden. Add the pepper and caraway and stir for 1 minute. Add the leeks and potatoes, stir well and cover the pan. Cook over a medium heat for 5 minutes, stir quickly then cook a further 5 minutes. Add the vegetable stock and the kombu, if desired, and bring to the boil. Stir again, cover the pan and reduce the heat. Let the soup simmer gently for 30–45 minutes. Remove from the heat and serve immediately or stir in the miso before serving. Alternatively, you may reheat the soup later as the flavours will blend and mellow somewhat.

Cream of Leek Soup

Serves 4–6
Preparation time 1 hour

2 tbsp oil
3 cloves garlic, chopped
1 small onion, chopped
3–5 stalks celery, chopped
½ tsp freshly ground black pepper
½ tsp cayenne
½ tsp ground allspice
1½ tbsp plain flour
850ml (1½ pints) vegetable stock
850ml (1½ pints) soya milk
3 medium leeks, trimmed, sliced, washed, rinsed and drained
4–6 tbsp fresh coriander, chopped

Heat the oil in a large stewpot or saucepan and sauté the garlic and onion for 3 minutes. Add the celery and spices and continue the sauté until the celery is clear and tender, about 15 minutes. Do not rush this stage and keep the heat rather lower than medium. Sprinkle the flour over the sauté and stir to make a smooth paste (roux). Add a little more flour if necessary and increase the heat slightly. Combine the vegetable stock and soya milk in a jug and add to the roux, a little at a time, stirring after each addition. When the broth is well mixed and beginning to thicken, add the prepared leeks and bring the soup to a low boil. Stir well, cover the pan and cook over a low heat for 15 minutes. Stir in the chopped coriander or, if you prefer, use it as a garnish for each serving. Serve the soup hot.

Lemons Originating in tropical Asia, and brought to Europe in the 12th century by the Arabs, the lemon now occupies a central position in Western cuisine. Although there are relatively few dishes which use lemons as their centrepiece, lemon juice, pith, rind and zest contribute enormously to an innumerable number of popular dishes. The high vitamin C content in lemon juice gives it powerful anti-oxidant properties, which can be used to prevent the browning of other fruit and vegetables (apples and avocado pears,

for example) when exposed to air. Lemons are available all year round, partly because lemon trees bloom and ripen fruit every month of the year, and partly because the fruit is generally picked unripe, and put in storage for up to 4 months to 'cure'. They are then gradually released on to the market. When buying lemons, look for a deep yellow colour, indicating ripeness, and a weight that is heavy for their size, indicating juiciness. Avoid lemons that are bruised, have green patches, or areas which feel soft – these are all indications of a substandard or damaged fruit, and decay may already be present. Most lemons will have been chemically treated (waxed or treated with fungicide) and while this may not effect the internal juice, you should never use the zest or rind of lemons which have been anything other than organically grown. Increasingly, supermarkets are stocking organic fruits and vegetables, and lemons are usually amongst them.

A judicious quantity of lemon juice can really bring out the flavour of many other foods: add just enough to soups, stews, desserts and marinades to give them a slightly sharp edge, but not so much as to overwhelm them completely. Lemon juice makes a very good substitute for vinegar in salad dressings, especially vinaigrette dressing. The zest of the lemon (the aromatic oil contained in small cysts in its skin) can be obtained by grating or by rubbing the rind hard with a sugar lump, and is used as a flavouring in many sweets and desserts, as is candied lemon peel. Here is a small selection of the easiest and most successful recipes featuring the ubiquitous lemon; there are, of course, thousands more.

NUTRIENT ANALYSIS
1 CUP LEMON JUICE (244g)

KCalories	61.00
Total Fat (g)	0.00
Monounsaturated Fat (g)	trace
Polyunsaturated Fat (g)	trace
Saturated Fat (g)	trace
Carbohydrate (g)	21.06
Protein (g)	0.93
Crude Fibre (g)	0.00
Vitamin A (RE)	4.88
Ascorbic Acid (mg)	112.24

Thiamin (mg)	0.07
Riboflavin (mg)	0.02
Niacin (mg)	0.24
Pantothenic Acid (mg)	0.25
Vitamin B6 (mg)	0.12
Folacin (mcg)	31.48
Vitamin B12 (mcg)	0.00
Calcium (mg)	17.08
Iron (mg)	0.07
Zinc (mg)	0.12

Easy Lemon Syrup

Makes approximately 1 pint
Preparation time 20 minutes

570ml (1 pint) water
285g (10oz) sugar
140ml (¼ pint) lemon juice

Place the water and sugar in a saucepan and place over a medium heat. Stir constantly until the sugar is dissolved, then bring the liquid to the boil. Boil for about 10 minutes, until the liquid reduces and thickens. Remove the pan from heat and stir in the lemon juice. Leave the syrup to cool then pour into a sterilized bottle. This syrup can be spooned over puddings, ice creams and desserts, or may be diluted with bubbly mineral water or herb tea.

A variation: add the peel of 1–2 organic lemons to the syrup as it boils. Boil for 10 minutes then strain the syrup, add the lemon juice and bottle in the usual way. The peel may be discarded or used immediately in baking.

Ahh! Lemonade

Serves 4
Preparation time 2 hours

6–8 organically grown lemons
570ml (1 pint) boiling water
50g (2oz) sugar
285ml (½ pint) cold, filtered or mineral water
at least 285ml (½ pint) lemon juice (the juice of those same 6–8 lemons)
4 sprigs fresh mint

Wash the lemons and carefully remove the peel, avoiding the bitter pith. Slice the lemons in half and squeeze them. Place the peelings in a large bowl and pour the boiling water over them. Add the sugar, stir well and leave to cool. When tepid, strain the liquid into a large jug and add the cold water (you may add this quantity of water as ice cubes if you prefer) and the lemon juice. Stir well and chill in the refrigerator or serve immediately over ice cubes and a sprig of fresh mint placed in each glass. A twist of lemon or a half slice of orange is also attractive as a garnish.

Lemon Barley Water

Makes approximately 570ml (1 pint)
Preparation time 1 hour

100g (4oz) barley
850ml (1½ pint) water
peel of 1 organically grown lemon
1 tbsp sugar

Measure the barley into a saucepan and wash well in cold water. Drain and cover with 850ml of fresh water. Place the pan over a medium heat and bring to a rapid boil. Boil for 55 minutes, until the barley softens and the liquid reduces. Remove the pan from the heat. Place the lemon peel and the sugar in a large, heat-proof bowl or jug. Strain the barley from the boiling liquid and pour the liquid over the lemon in the jug. Stir well to dissolve the sugar then leave to cool. Pour into a sterilized bottle and cork. Use diluted as you would a squash.

Fresh Herb and Lemon Dressing

Makes approximately 285ml (½ pint)
Preparation time 15 minutes

3 tbsp olive oil
grated rind of 1 lemon
140ml (¼ pint) fresh lemon juice (2–3 lemons)
3 spring onions, finely chopped
2 cloves garlic, finely chopped
1 tbsp fresh rosemary or tarragon, chopped
¼ tsp freshly ground black pepper, or to taste

Measure all the ingredients into a jar and blend well. Serve immediately. Both rosemary and tarragon are potent herbs which enhance strongly flavoured or oily foods. Try this sauce over a beany salad or use to dress sautéed tempeh or seitan.

Lemon Tofu Marinade

Serves 4
Preparation time 30 minutes, plus marinating overnight

2 × 285g (10oz) blocks tofu, drained and cubed
200ml (7fl oz) fresh lemon juice
60ml (2fl oz) soy sauce
60ml (2fl oz) tomato purée
1 tbsp water
1 tbsp barley malt syrup
1 tbsp fresh ginger, grated
5 cloves garlic, chopped
1 tbsp oil
1 bunch spring onions, finely sliced
1 × 285g (10oz) tin bamboo shoots, drained and
  thinly sliced
1 sweet green pepper, deseeded and thinly sliced
1 sweet red pepper, deseeded and thinly sliced
50g (2oz) fresh beansprouts, rinsed and drained

Place the tofu cubes in a bowl or oven dish. Blend the lemon juice, soy sauce, tomato purée, water, syrup, ginger and garlic together in a jug. Pour the marinade over the tofu and stir gently. Cover the dish and leave the tofu to marinate all day or overnight. Heat the oil in a wok or frying pan over a medium heat. Add the onions and bamboo shoots and stir for 3–5 minutes. Add the peppers and stir for 2 minutes. Now add the tofu and the marinade. Bring the liquid to a boil, stir gently and sprinkle the beansprouts over the stir-fry, cover the pan, lower the heat and cook for a further 3–5 minutes. Serve hot over rice.

Preserved Lemons

Preparation time 30 minutes, plus 2 months

Find a very large jar and buy enough organic lemons to fill it. Wash the lemons very carefully, then insert about 12 cloves into each lemon, pressing in the cloves right up to their crown. Pack the lemons into the jar, and fill with very good quality olive oil (organic extra virgin is best). Seal the jar and leave it in a cool, dark place for at least two months before opening. This will be difficult: the lemons look beautiful in the oil and you will be tempted to put them on the windowsill where everyone can see them! At the end of the two months you may begin to use the lemons and the oil. Always use a very clean wooden or plastic spoon to lift out the lemons and a wooden or enamel ladle to remove the olive oil, then simply close up the jar again and the lemons and oil will keep well. Use the lemons sliced, as a garnish or an unusual ingredient in fruit salads or stir-fries; the olive oil will acquire a delicious and rare quality which will provide a unique flavour for salad dres-

sings. You might even enjoy a teaspoon of this oil drizzled onto hot toast.

Health Note

Lemons are a prime source of vitamin C – one raw lemon contains one-and-a-half times the adult daily requirement. Surprisingly, it also contains about 10 per cent of the daily requirements of calcium, iron and potassium. Lemons have a considerable use in natural medicine. Their naturally antiseptic properties have been used for a variety of skin problems, including acne, blackheads and eczema, and also on the scalp to treat dandruff. After the lemon juice has been worked into the scalp the hair should be shampooed in the normal way, and then rinsed. Finally, the juice of one lemon and a glass of water should be applied. This will help to remove any traces of shampoo and provide a lustrous shine to the hair.
Natural therapists caution that the powerfully detoxifying effect of lemon juice should be used with caution; if the organs of elimination are not working effectively, then toxins will be released by the body which cannot be eliminated, causing further health problems.
An old and well trusted 'flu remedy is as follows: Take a lemon and bake it for 20 minutes, then squeeze half of it into a glass of hot water: a sip of this mixture should be consumed every half hour as long as the fever persists.

Lentils The lentil has been cultivated for thousands of years and is highly prized by many societies, especially as it is one of the staples of the vegetarian diet. Lentils are believed to have originated in south-west Asia, were later cultivated in Egypt and Greece, then imported in bulk to Rome. Today, India is by far the largest producer. Lentils are an important member of the legume family of plants (*leguminosae*), a group which includes beans, peas, clover and alfafa. They are amongst the most environmentally-friendly food crops of all, because they have the extraordinary ability to transform nitrogen in the air into a form that can be utilized by the plant itself. This is achieved by nitrogen-fixing bacteria which exist on their no-dule-bearing roots. They thus replenish the soil and reduce the need for expensive, polluting and un-healthy nitrogen fertilizers.

The two main types of lentil are the Egyptian, which are small and orange and usually sold split; and the French type, which can be grey, green, or brown, and are also known as continental lentils. The former are usually called red or orange lentils, and are the only types that may be cooked without prior soaking. Because lentils are dried, they are available all year round, and should always be very economical to buy. They are frequently quite dusty, and should therefore be given several good rinses before use, and particular attention should be given to the presence of any small stones. Whole lentils usually only need to be soaked for 2–4 hours, although in most cases it is just as easy to soak them overnight. If you have to delay using them, they should stay fresh for up to 48 hours, although the soaking water should be changed every 8–12 hours. All varieties, apart from split lentils, can be sprouted following instructions on pages 168–9.

See also: Red Lentil Dhal (p344); Lentil Soup (p319)

NUTRIENT ANALYSIS
1 CUP LENTILS, COOKED (198g)

KCalories	229.68
Total Fat (g)	0.75
Monounsaturated Fat (g)	0.13
Polyunsaturated Fat (g)	0.35
Saturated Fat (g)	0.10
Carbohydrate (g)	39.88
Protein (g)	17.86
Crude Fibre (g)	5.46
Vitamin A (RE)	1.98
Ascorbic Acid (mg)	2.97
Thiamin (mg)	0.33
Riboflavin (mg)	0.14
Niacin (mg)	2.10
Pantothenic Acid (mg)	1.26
Vitamin B6 (mg)	0.35
Folacin (mcg)	357.98
Vitamin B12 (mcg)	0.00

Calcium (mg)	37.62
Iron (mg)	6.59
Zinc (mg)	2.51

Buttery Lentil Pate

Makes approximately 1l (2 pints)
Preparation time 1 hour, plus time to cool

225g (8oz) red lentils, washed and drained
570ml (1 pint) water
1 tbsp soy sauce
1 tbsp oil
5 cloves garlic, finely chopped
1 tbsp fresh ginger, grated
1 tsp freshly ground black pepper
1 tsp turmeric
100g (4oz) porridge oats or 50g (2oz) each of oats and rice flakes

Turn the washed lentils into an enamel saucepan with the fresh water and place over a medium heat. Cover the pan, watch carefully, and bring to the boil. Stir well, reduce the heat and leave to simmer, covered, for 20–25 minutes. Stir occasionally during this time. When the lentils have lost their form completely, stir in the soy sauce. Heat the oil in a small frying pan over a medium to low heat and sauté the garlic and ginger for about 3 minutes. Add the pepper and stir for 1 minute. Finally, add the turmeric, stir well and remove the sauté from the heat. Stir the sauté into the cooked lentils and remove them from the heat also. Add the oats, or oats and flaked rice, to the lentil mixture and stir very well. Turn the whole mixture into a lightly oiled ramekin or jelly mould and press firmly into place. Leave the paté to cool and then chill it in the refrigerator. Serve on crackers or bread, or with a salad to accompany.

Continental Lentil Burgers

Makes 12 burgers
Preparation time 2 hours

100g (4oz) continental lentils, washed
450g (1lb) potatoes, peeled and quartered
60ml (2fl oz) water
2 tsp yeast extract
1 small onion, finely chopped
1 tsp freshly ground black pepper
1 tsp ground coriander
½ tsp chilli powder, or to taste
50g (2oz) rice flakes

Turn the lentils into a mixing bowl and cover with warm water. Leave for 5 minutes, then rub the lentils vigorously in a scrubbing movement to loosen their skins. Skim the skins off the surface of the water and repeat this procedure, with fresh water, twice more (you do not need to leave them to soak again, however). When you have discarded most of the skins, rinse the lentils under running water then cover them with fresh water and leave to soak for about 1 hour. Alternatively, you may pour boiling water over them and leave them for 15 minutes. At the end of their soaking time, discard the water, rinse them once again and turn them into a deep saucepan. Just cover them with fresh water and place over a medium to high heat. Bring to the boil, stir well and cover the pan. Reduce the heat and simmer for about 30 minutes, until the lentils lose their form.

Meanwhile, place the potatoes in a steamer and steam for 20 minutes, until tender. Leave to one side. Blend the water and yeast extract in a cup, pour into a saucepan and place over a medium heat. When the liquid is bubbling, add the onion, pepper, coriander and chilli. Leave to sauté for 3–5 minutes over a medium heat, stirring often. Remove from the heat and add the steamed potatoes to this mixture. Mash the potatoes into the sauté and stir to an even consistency. When the lentils are cooked (they should be very soft and the water should have been absorbed), mix them with the mashed potatoes and the rice flakes to make a firm paste. Leave to stand for 10 minutes. Shape the mixture into patties. Heat some oil in a frying pan and fry the burgers for 5 minutes on each side. Serve hot or cold, in a bun or on a plate, with plenty of your favourite sauce and garnish.

Health Note

Lentils are extremely low in fat yet high in protein and complex carbohydrates. They are used in natural medicine as a nourishing, body-building food – recommended in cases of emaciation and lack of appetite. They are very unlikely to provoke allergy, and have a mild taste which is universally acceptable. Their limiting amino acid is methionine and so, for maximum protein yield, should be consumed with methionine-rich foodstuffs, such as yeast extract, or wheat or corn products. One cup of cooked lentils will provide one third of the adult daily requirement for protein, nearly twice the folic acid requirement, two-thirds the iron requirement, and a fifth of the thiamin, vitamin B6, and zinc requirement. Another high-value food!

Lettuce The lettuce has been cultivated for thousands of years, and was believed by the Assyrians, Greeks and Egyptians to possess considerable aphrodisiac properties. The name itself derives from the Latin *lactuca*, meaning milk, because it exudes a milky juice when cut. During the middle ages, lettuce was frequently consumed as a hot dish, braised in much the same way as fennel is, and it can still be eaten that way today. For the Romans, however, and for most of the contemporary Western world, the lettuce is essentially a salad vegetable. A firm lettuce can be shredded and incorporated into most types of salads, or used as a garnish to any number of dishes, sandwiches, burgers, etc.

However, a much more stylish way of eating lettuce, favoured by many European countries, is simply to serve it with a light vinaigrette dressing as a first course for any meal. It is probably the cheapest starter you can make, but certainly one of the best. Indeed, so great is its power to excite and stimulate the appetite that one French nobleman, the Chevalier d'Albignac, made his fortune in England in the late 18th century as an itinerant salad dresser, carrying with him the ingredients to make a first class dressing and visiting all the fashionable dining houses of his day. There are several varieties of lettuce commonly available: make sure you choose one which does not disappoint. If in doubt, the Cos lettuce is always a safe choice.

- Butterhead. The most common of all lettuces, the cheapest, and usually the least attractive gastronomically. Unless you happen to pick the lettuce yourself, many of its leaves will be limp by the time you get it home, and the remaining heart will have a taste which approaches, at best, a wet flannel. Best avoided.
- Cos. The best type of lettuce to use in a salad. A few diced vegetables, together with some roughly torn leaves of cos lettuce, with a simple vinaigrette dressing make an excellent and rapid snack or accompaniment to almost any meal. The cos lettuce is far superior to most other kinds because it is both firm and flavoursome, and will stay fresh once picked for several days. For an interesting side

salad, take one whole cos lettuce and finely chop it, sprinkle with the juice of two oranges, a pinch of salt and freshly ground black pepper to taste.

- Iceberg. Crisp and round, with a firm heart, this is preferable to the Butterhead for most purposes, although it generally lacks any taste but the most transitory bitter one. It makes a good shredding lettuce for burgers and garnishes, where the main purpose of the lettuce is not to provide gustatory enjoyment, but rather visual appeal.
- Radiccio. Not really a lettuce, more of an endive, it can nevertheless be used in place of lettuce in many salads, and its firm and attractive red leaves provide good taste and excellent appearance.
- Endive. The curly-leaved variety has both green and red parts to its extremely spiked leaves, and it makes another excellent alternative to the overused butterhead.
- Feuille de chêne. Also called oak leaf lettuce, this is a limp-leaved plant, with an almost seaweed green appearance, and an attractively bitter flavour. Best used arranged on the plate where its unique appearance can be fully appreciated, rather than being tossed in a salad.
- Rocket. Its hot, often spicy flavour prevents it from being a real alternative to lettuce in tossed salads (as does its price) but a few young leaves, which should be smooth and hairless, make an extremely attractive and flavoursome ingredient in a mixed leaf salad.

NUTRIENT ANALYSIS
½ CUP LETTUCE, SHREDDED (28g)

KCalories	4.48
Total Fat (g)	0.06
Monounsaturated Fat (g)	0.00
Polyunsaturated Fat (g)	0.03
Saturated Fat (g)	0.01
Carbohydrate (g)	0.66
Protein (g)	0.45
Crude Fibre (g)	0.20
Vitamin A (RE)	72.80
Ascorbic Acid (mg)	6.72
Thiamin (mg)	0.03
Riboflavin (mg)	0.03

Niacin (mg)	0.14
Pantothenic Acid (mg)	0.05
Vitamin B6 (mg)	0.01
Folacin (mcg)	38.00
Vitamin B12 (mcg)	0.00
Calcium (mg)	10.08
Iron (mg)	0.31
Zinc (mg)	0.07

Health Note

The nutritional content of lettuces varies from species to species, also according to the time of year and freshness of the plant, but most forms of lettuce are relatively high in folic acid: one cup of shredded cos lettuce will yield about a third of the adult daily requirement. It also contains about a fifth of the requirement for vitamin C. Lettuce has been used by natural therapists to treat insomnia, catarrh, gout, to stimulate a jaded palate, and for constipation. The cos lettuce is very valuable as a detoxicant. Roughly chop a whole lettuce and put it to simmer slowly with 2 pints of water for several hours. A brownish liquor will be produced which is wonderfully purifying; particularly useful as a hangover cure or for other detoxification processes.

Limes The lime is closely related to the lemon, although it usually has a green skin and is about half the size. Where flavouring, and not simply sharpness, is required it is preferable. Because it has a distinct flavour of its own, you may need to use rather less lime juice than the equivalent amount of lemon juice; for example, in salad dressings lime juice by itself produces a far too fruity flavour, and should be used to accompany, rather than replace, lemon juice or cider vinegar.

NUTRIENT ANALYSIS
1 CUP LIME JUICE (246g)

KCalories	66.42
Total Fat (g)	0.25
Monounsaturated Fat (g)	0.02

Polyunsaturated Fat (g)	0.07
Saturated Fat (g)	0.03
Carbohydrate (g)	22.16
Protein (g)	1.08
Crude Fibre (g)	0.00
Vitamin A (RE)	2.46
Ascorbic Acid (mg)	72.08
Thiamin (mg)	0.05
Riboflavin (mg)	0.02
Niacin (mg)	0.25
Pantothenic Acid (mg)	0.34
Vitamin B6 (mg)	0.11
Folacin (mcg)	20.17
Vitamin B12 (mcg)	0.00
Calcium (mg)	22.14
Iron (mg)	0.07
Zinc (mg)	0.15

Lime and Coriander Relish

Makes approximately 570ml (1 pint)
Preparation time 1 hour

140ml (¼ pint) olive oil
juice of 4–6 limes
3 tbsp cider vinegar
5 cloves garlic, crushed
1 fresh chilli, finely chopped (optional but recommended!)
25g (1oz) pickled pimento, finely chopped
2 small gherkins, finely chopped
1 small onion, very finely chopped
1 bunch coriander, chopped

Blend the oil, lime juice and vinegar together in a mixing bowl and add the remaining ingredients one at a time, stirring well after each addition. Cover the bowl and leave to stand for 30–40 minutes. Serve with salads, burgers, rice dishes, curries, cold soups or sandwiches.

Health Note

One lime contains about a third of the adult daily requirement for vitamin C. Lime juice is said by natural therapists to have a beneficial effect upon people suffering from anger, hatred or other brain disturbances.

Lychees Principally known in the West for being one of the few fruits on offer in most Indian and Chinese restaurants; lychees (also known as litchis) are almost invariably tinned, and do not benefit from being preserved in an oversweet syrup. Tinned lychees are available in oriental grocery shops, and increasingly at major Western supermarkets, and can be used for making jellies or sorbets. Fresh lychees are available from some grocers mainly from November to January; they have an attractively dimpled appearance with a hard, dusky red skin which is easy to peel. Inside you will find luscious, moonstone-coloured flesh surrounding an inedible nut. Piled high on the dinner table, or incorporated into table dressings and decorations, the lychee makes a feature in its own right. Fresh lychees have an exquisite, sweetly perfumed aroma reminiscent of elderflowers. The rambutan, a close cousin of the lychee, has a similar, although rather more acidic, flavour and is distinguished from the lychee by its extraordinarily hairy appearance.

NUTRIENT ANALYSIS
1 LYCHEE, RAW (10g)

KCalories	6.00
Total Fat (g)	0.04
Monounsaturated Fat (g)	trace
Polyunsaturated Fat (g)	trace
Saturated Fat (g)	trace
Carbohydrate (g)	1.59
Protein (g)	0.08
Crude Fibre (g)	?
Vitamin A (RE)	0.00
Ascorbic Acid (mg)	6.90
Thiamin (mg)	0.00
Riboflavin (mg)	0.01
Niacin (mg)	0.06
Pantothenic Acid (mg)	?
Vitamin B6 (mg)	?

Folacin (mcg)	?
Vitamin B12 (mcg)	0.00
Calcium (mg)	0.00
Iron (mg)	0.03
Zinc (mg)	0.01

Macadamia Nuts Expensive and not always readily available, the macadamia nut is found most often served as a cocktail *hors d'oeuvre*. It has a flavour about halfway between a hazelnut and a coconut, and makes an interesting addition to a tropical-style mixed salad, or – grated – can be sprinkled on desserts or other dishes. Macadamias are quite fatty: 25g (1oz) provides about one-fifth of the total recommended fat intake for adults.

NUTRIENT ANALYSIS
1 oz MACADAMIA NUTS, DRIED (25g)

KCalories	199.37
Total Fat (g)	20.94
Monounsaturated Fat (g)	16.52
Polyunsaturated Fat (g)	0.36
Saturated Fat (g)	3.13
Carbohydrate (g)	3.90
Protein (g)	2.36
Crude Fibre (g)	1.50
Vitamin A (RE)	0.00
Ascorbic Acid (mg)	0.00
Thiamin (mg)	0.10
Riboflavin (mg)	0.03
Niacin (mg)	0.61
Pantothenic Acid (mg)	0.12
Vitamin B6 (mg)	0.06
Folacin (mcg)	4.46
Vitamin B12 (mcg)	0.00
Calcium (mg)	19.88
Iron (mg)	0.68
Zinc (mg)	0.49

Maize see Corn

Mangoes An exotic fruit with a unique flavour which some (including myself) believe to be – at its best – as close to a taste of paradise as humans may ever achieve on this earth. Originating in India, which is still the world's largest producer, mangoes are now also imported from Malaysia, the East Indies, the Philippines, Florida, Mexico and Hawaii, which means that mangoes of one origin or another are available most of the year round. Skin colour is not by itself a good guide to the fruit's ripeness; hundreds of varieties of mango are grown, some with yellow skins, some with orange, others with greenish-yellow through to a rich red. A ripe mango will feel soft all over, harder ones should be allowed to ripen at room temperature for a few days. But even unripe mangoes can be eaten – in the Philippines they are consumed with salt or soy sauce, and mango chutney is a delicious home-made condiment which utilizes underripe fruit. Because they are such voluptuous fruits, they are probably best eaten raw as a dessert or snack. Very ripe mangoes can be cut in two, the stone removed, and their flesh scooped out with a spoon. Mangoes of slightly lower quality are not so easy to divide (the woody seed often conquers the sharpest steel). Some authorities recommend peeling the mango then paring away at it with a knife, although the shavings thus produced do scant justice to such an exuberant fruit. A classic dinner presentation is to slice the ripe mango in half, remove the seed, then carefully score – in a criss-cross pattern – the flesh, stopping short of slicing through the skin. Then simply turn each mango half inside out so that the scored fruit becomes an umbrella of bite-sized chunks of mango just waiting to be eaten. Serve immediately on a plate with spoon, knife and fork, leaving the diner to decide how best to proceed from there! I am of the opinion that a mango is best peeled then served whole to your guests to deal with as they please, fingers and all other necessary devices permitted. Those offended by a summary lack of table manners would probably not appreciate the fruit in any case.

See also: Hot Mango Chutney (p313)

NUTRIENT ANALYSIS
1 MANGO, FRESH (207g)

KCalories	134.55
Total Fat (g)	0.56
Monounsaturated Fat (g)	0.21
Polyunsaturated Fat (g)	0.11

Saturated Fat (g)	0.14
Carbohydrate (g)	35.19
Protein (g)	1.06
Crude Fibre (g)	1.74
Vitamin A (RE)	805.23
Ascorbic Acid (mg)	57.34
Thiamin (mg)	0.12
Riboflavin (mg)	0.12
Niacin (mg)	1.21
Pantothenic Acid (mg)	0.33
Vitamin B6 (mg)	0.28
Folacin (mcg)	?
Vitamin B12 (mcg)	0.00
Calcium (mg)	20.70
Iron (mg)	0.27
Zinc (mg)	0.08

Mango and Avocado Salad

Serves 4
Preparation time 20 minutes

2 ripe avocados, peeled and sliced
2 ripe mangoes, peeled and sliced
50g (2oz) slivered almonds
285g (10oz) plain tofu, cut into tiny cubes
radiccio leaves, washed and drained
¼ tsp salt
¼ tsp freshly ground black pepper
pinch of nutmeg (optional)
50g (2oz) alfalfa sprouts, rinsed and drained

Gently mix the avocados, mangoes, almonds and tofu in a large salad bowl. Arrange the radiccio leaves on each plate or bowl and spoon the avocado mixture over them. Sprinkle a little of each of the salt, pepper and nutmeg over each serving then garnish with some of the alfalfa sprouts. Serve at once. This salad is excellent without a dressing, but you may, of course, wish to add one of your choice.

Spicy Fruit Salad

Serves 4
Preparation time 20 minutes

2 ripe mangoes, peeled and diced

½ ripe honeydew or canteloupe melon, cubed or scooped out into balls
3 ripe kiwi fruit, peeled and quartered lengthwise
1 ripe banana, peeled and sliced
1 sweet red pepper, finely chopped
50g (2oz) pine nuts
2 tbsp fresh coriander, chopped
140ml (¼ pint) wine vinegar
½ teaspoon paprika

Mix the mangoes, melon, kiwi, banana, pepper, pine nuts and coriander together in a large salad bowl. Stir the vinegar and paprika together in a small jug and pour over the fruit. Stir gently and serve immediately or chill for 1 hour before serving in pretty bowls with a dollop of plain soya yoghurt if desired.

Health Note

> Nutritionally, one cup of mango slices yields about three quarters of the adult daily requirement for vitamins A and C, and significant amounts of vitamin B6, potassium and thiamin.

Melons Members of the cucumber family, melons are amongst the world's most promiscuous fruit: given half a chance, they freely hybridize with other varieties, and with other gourds, too. Not surprisingly, there are countless varieties of melons in the world today. Only a few, however, regularly appear on the greengrocer's shelves. They are:

- Honeydew. A winter melon, and a delicious breakfast fruit when eaten with powdered ginger, or even salt and pepper. Only ripe when yielding to the touch. Recognize it by its smooth yellow skin and pale green flesh.
- Gallia. Also called Mosque Melon, Gallia is round like a small football, and has a ribbed, mustard coloured, net-like skin. This melon has a pleasantly aromatic smell when ripe, and is ideal for making melon balls. It is commonly served by scooping out the flesh and combining with other fruits before returning the mixture to the melon skin together with an accompanying liqueur. It may also be sliced and combined creatively with a variety of savoury food for an enticing dinner party starter.
- Canteloupe. Including the Ogen (bright yellow) and

the Charentais (sweet, orange flesh), these are the gourmet's choice of melons, either for eating on their own or for combining with other fine fruits into a fresh fruit salad.

See also: Malangwa Stew (p342)

NUTRIENT ANALYSIS
½ CANTELOUPE MELON (267g)

KCalories	93.45
Total Fat (g)	0.75
Monounsaturated Fat (g)	trace
Polyunsaturated Fat (g)	trace
Saturated Fat (g)	trace
Carbohydrate (g)	22.32
Protein (g)	2.35
Crude Fibre (g)	0.96
Vitamin A (RE)	859.74
Ascorbic Acid (mg)	112.67
Thiamin (mg)	0.10
Riboflavin (mg)	0.06
Niacin (mg)	1.53
Pantothenic Acid (mg)	0.34
Vitamin B6 (mg)	0.31
Folacin (mcg)	45.39
Vitamin B12 (mcg)	0.00
Calcium (mg)	29.37
Iron (mg)	0.56
Zinc (mg)	0.43

Port Melon with Almond and Rosemary

Serves 4
Preparation time 30 minutes

1 honeydew melon, halved
1 canteloupe melon, halved
50g (2oz) ground almonds
1 tsp ground coriander
¼ tsp ground nutmeg
285ml (½ pint) port
4 tiny sprigs fresh rosemary

Remove the seed pulp from the melon halves and discard. Use a melon scoop to scrape the flesh out into melon balls. Put the balls into two separate bowls, one for each type of melon, and save any juice that accumulates. Place each of the melon halves into its own serving bowl; slice a tiny bit off the bottom of each, if necessary, to allow them to stand firmly. Mix the ground almonds, coriander and nutmeg together in a small bowl and sprinkle a little of the mixture into each of the melon shells; use no more than half of the almond mixture at this stage. Return the melon balls to the melon shells, mixing the two types of melon as you do so to give a blend of colours. Pour any extra melon juice over the melon balls then pour one quarter of the port over each serving. Sprinkle the remaining almond mixture over each serving and garnish with a sprig of rosemary. Serve immediately or, better still, chill for 1–2 hours in the refrigerator. Encourage your guests to chew on one or two of the tiny rosemary leaves as they eat this dish.

Health Note

Bitter melon, which looks like a lumpy cucumber, is used throughout Asia as a food and also as a traditional medicine: to remedy cold sores, insect bites, asthma, and also to lower diabetics' blood-sugar levels. Now, reports suggest that it may be effective against HIV (the AIDS virus). Bitter melon contains a protein, called MAP-30, which posesses anti-tumour and anti-viral properties. Patients of New York acupuncturist Qing Cai Zhang who have taken bitter melon have had encouraging results; some have seen their CD4 cell count rise appreciably (CD4 cells are immune cells which are targeted by HIV). Opportunistic infections have decreased, while patients' energy and stamina have increased. Wider-scale trials are currently planned.

Millet A cereal grain frequently used in Africa and Asia as an important source of dietary protein and iron, millet is sadly overlooked in the West, where it is most often encountered as animal fodder. The antiquity of this ancient grain can be appreciated by the following quotation from the Old Testament: 'Take thou also unto thee wheat, and barley, and beans, and lentils, and millet, and fitches, and put them in one vessel, and make thee bread thereof'.[10] Perhaps one of the earliest recipes ever recorded! ('Fitches' are similar to broad beans.) There are many varieties of millet, some of which are available in health food shops primarily in the form of grains, flakes and flour.

Once a staple food crop for the poor of many Western feudal economies, millet fell from grace partly because of its peasant food associations, and partly because the grain contains no gluten, and is therefore not suitable for turning into leavened bread. Ironically, this very quality now makes it a popular food for those who are allergic to gluten. It is an adaptable grain, and is well worth including as a nutritious and healthy supplement in your diet every few days. It is very easy to prepare: simply cook it for about 20 minutes in twice its volume of boiling water. A nuttier flavour can be obtained by toasting the millet, prior to boiling, in a saucepan (with no oil) over a moderate flame for three minutes or so, until some of the grains begin to pop. Simply prepared like this, it makes an excellent base for a variety of accompanying vegetables. Millet flakes can be quickly cooked to produce a creamy, and highly nutritious breakfast porridge – especially when combined with sunflower seeds, dried fruits etc. One variety of millet which is increasingly available in health food shops is the Ethopian grain Teff (see recipes: Steamed Teff, p311; Njera, p311).

See also: Taushe (p315); Funkaso (p315)

NUTRIENT ANALYSIS
1 CUP MILLET, COOKED (70g)

KCalories	285.60
Total Fat (g)	2.40
Monounsaturated Fat (g)	0.44
Polyunsaturated Fat (g)	1.22
Saturated Fat (g)	0.41
Carbohydrate (g)	56.81
Protein (g)	8.42
Crude Fibre (g)	0.86
Vitamin A (RE)	0.00
Ascorbic Acid (mg)	0.00
Thiamin (mg)	0.25
Riboflavin (mg)	0.20
Niacin (mg)	3.19
Pantothenic Acid (mg)	0.41
Vitamin B6 (mg)	0.26
Folacin (mcg)	45.60
Vitamin B12 (mcg)	0.00
Calcium (mg)	7.20
Iron (mg)	1.51
Zinc (mg)	2.18

Mini Millet Cakes

Makes 12 cakes
Preparation time 35 minutes

170g (6oz) millet flour
170g (6oz) plain flour
75g (3oz) sugar
50g (2oz) roasted millet
2 tsp baking powder
6 tbsp margarine
1 tbsp tahini
140ml (¼ pint) soya milk

Preheat the oven to 200°C/400°F/Gas Mark 6 and lightly oil a baking tray. Mix the flours, sugar, millet and baking powder in a large bowl. Add the margarine and use a fork or your fingers to work to an even, rather granular, consistency. Stir the tahini and soya milk together in a small bowl or jug and add to the dough. Stir until just mixed, then sprinkle a little flour on a board and roll the dough to 6mm (¼ inch) thick. Cut into scone-sized cakes and arrange on the baking sheet. Bake for 10–12 minutes, until the cakes are just golden. Lift onto a wire cooling rack, cool for 10–15 minutes and serve warm with plenty of jam, fruit butter or sauce.

Health Note

> Just one cup of cooked millet will provide about a fifth of the adult daily requirement for the following nutrients: protein, thiamin, riboflavin, niacin, vitamin B6, iron, and zinc.

Miso see **Soya Beans**

Molasses A by-product of the sugar industry, molasses is the most nutritionally valuable part of the entire refining process. It is ironic that sugar – the least nutritious part – is used for human consumption, while molasses is generally consigned to unproductive purposes such as animal feed manufacture. After it's harvested, the raw sugar cane is crushed, shredded, and juiced. This is then boiled, and the liquid spun in a centrifuge, where the sugar crystals are separated from the residue – which is the molasses. Several types of molasses are available, depending upon the stage at which they are extracted. The most nutritionally important is the 'third extraction' or blackstrap molasses; which is the final residue from the whole process, and therefore lowest in sugar, and highest in concentrated minerals.

The best molasses comes from the West Indies, where the soil is mineral-rich. Molasses is an important health food: it can be added to most baked foods to increase their nutritional content, and can be used as a sugar, jam or honey replacement. It adds a wonderfully rich flavour to biscuits and cookies; and adds a new taste dimension to homemade baked beans (see page 182).

Recently, a new product called nutritional yeast has become available in health food shops – it is a special kind of yeast (*saccharomyces cerevisiae*) which is actually grown on molasses, and therefore has many of its nutritional properties. It has a pleasant-tasting, cheesy flavour and can be used directly on foods as a condiment, and is also a good source of vitamin B12. **See also:** Shoo-Fly Pie (p327); Pumpernickel Bread (p355)

NUTRIENT ANALYSIS
½ CUP BLACKSTRAP MOLASSES (164g)

KCalories	349.32
Total Fat (g)	0.00
Monounsaturated Fat (g)	0.00
Polyunsaturated Fat (g)	0.00
Saturated Fat (g)	0.00
Carbohydrate (g)	90.20
Protein (g)	0.00
Crude Fibre (g)	0.00
Vitamin A (RE)	0.00
Ascorbic Acid (mg)	0.00
Thiamin (mg)	0.18

Riboflavin (mg)	0.31
iacin (mg)	3.28
Pantothenic Acid (mg)	?
Vitamin B6 (mg)	?
Folacin (mcg)	?
Vitamin B12 (mcg)	?
Calcium (mg)	1121.76
Iron (mg)	26.40
Zinc (mg)	?

Health Note

Molasses is famed for its health-giving properties, having been used to treat arthritis, ulcers, dermatitis, hair damage, angina, constipation and anaemia. Gram for gram, molasses contains six times as much calcium as cow's milk, and twice as much iron as liver! Molasses is also rich in a host of trace elements, amongst which is chromium – said to be deficient in 90 per cent of Western diets – a mineral which may have therapeutic effects for acne sufferers. A tablespoon dissolved in a glass of water and consumed daily provides an easy and pleasant way to take advantage of all the goodness molasses contains.

Mushrooms Usually considered to be a fungus, the mushroom is, more precisely, its fruit. The fungus itself remains underground (consisting of a mass of thin roots called mycelium) from whence it sends up the mushroom stem and the cap. Fungi are themselves simple plants, which neither flower nor possess chlorophyll, the green colouring matter in plants which is essential to the process of photosynthesis. Although mushrooms are not a key nutritional feature of a vegetarian diet, they are nevertheless an important and stimulating part of its gastronomic repertoire. Potentially, there are several dozen edible varieties available (it is estimated that there are over 2000 palatable varieties of mushroom in the world, unfortunately only a very small percentage are harvested). Leaving aside the pleasures to be had gathering your own wild mushrooms (the safest course is to be personally taught this by an expert) there is an increasing range of mushrooms being commercially marketed:

- Common Mushroom. The most widely available mushrooms of all are varieties of the *agaricus* family. Button mushrooms are the smallest generally sold and have not yet opened their gills. They are delicious raw, served whole in sauces, or marinated. Slightly older mushrooms will have opened to reveal their gills, and are more appropriate for cooking rather than raw use; when sliced they make an excellent ingredient in a stir-fry. Large open mushrooms are mainly used for stuffing. *Champignons de Paris* and *champignons marron* are similar, but rather more flavoursome, varieties.
- Oyster Mushroom. Increasingly cultivated, but still quite expensive, it has a slightly fishy flavour, a toughish texture, and is therefore usually used in stews, soups and casseroles. When sprinkled with lemon juice, dipped in batter, rolled in breadcrumbs and fried until golden it is said to be indistinguishable from fried oysters.
- Ceps. Highly rated and often highly expensive, the cep has a stumpy appearance and lacks the usual gills under its hamburger-bun-like cap. It is delicious simply sautéed in olive oil and garlic. *Funghi porcine* are Italian dried ceps, with a concentrated flavour which lends itself to many uses.
- Chanterelle. Also known as Girolle, this is a gourmet mushroom whose slightly peppery, apricot aroma should not be overwhelmed by stronger flavours. With a fairly tough texture, it should be stewed in soya milk for ten minutes or so before being served, or alternatively it makes an excellent and exotic refinement to Scrambled Tofu (p291)
- Morel. Another gourmet mushroom which looks nothing like other fungi, having a honeycomb-like cap. Good fried, or added to casseroles, sauces and soups. Experts caution against eating it raw, and against taking alcohol at the same time as the morel is consumed, since this seems to produce stomach upset.
- Truffle. An edible fungus which grows underground, the ultimate in gourmet fungi, although thought by some to be overrated and certainly overpriced. Black truffles are generally sautéed in champagne, white ones are sliced extremely thinly and sprinkled over rice dishes.
- Shiitake. Generally available dried from oriental grocery shops, the shiitake mushroom is both delicately flavoured and affordable; an increasingly popular ingredient in stir-fries, and many Japanese and Chinese dishes. It also has a formidable reputation in the East as a health food.
- Chinese Straw Mushroom. Increasingly available in supermarkets as well as Chinese foodstores, these delicate mushrooms are invariably bottled or tinned, and familiar to patrons of Chinese restaurants as an important and delicious ingredient in such dishes as fried mixed vegetables.
- Woodear Mushroom. Another Chinese favourite, available dried, and when reconstituted (use the soaking water for stock) gives a thick, glutinous texture to any dish.

Despite the traditional advice given in most cookery books, it is not wrong to wash most mushrooms briefly and then blot them dry – indeed, with varieties such as the morel and anything gathered from the wild, this is most advisable. When in doubt peel off the top layer of skin also.

See also: Mushrooms in Garlic and Fresh Tarragon (p352); Tofu 'Steak' with Mushrooms and Celery (p340); Quick Sweet and Sour Mushrooms (p341); Broccoli and Mushroom Stir-Fry (p341)

NUTRIENT ANALYSIS
1 CUP MUSHROOMS, FRESH (70g)

KCalories	17.50
Total Fat (g)	0.29
Monounsaturated Fat (g)	0.00
Polyunsaturated Fat (g)	0.12
Saturated Fat (g)	0.04
Carbohydrate (g)	3.26
Protein (g)	1.46
Crude Fibre (g)	0.52
Vitamin A (RE)	0.00
Ascorbic Acid (mg)	2.45
Thiamin (mg)	0.07
Riboflavin (mg)	0.31
Niacin (mg)	2.88
Pantothenic Acid (mg)	1.54
Vitamin B6 (mg)	0.07

Folacin (mcg)	14.77
Vitamin B12 (mcg)	0.00
Calcium (mg)	3.50
Iron (mg)	0.87
Zinc (mg)	0.51

Hazelnut and Mushroom Paté

Makes approximately 850ml (1½ pints)
Preparation time 25 minutes plus chilling time

2 tbsp margarine
450g (1lb) mushrooms, cleaned and chopped
½ tsp ground coriander
½ tsp ground cumin
½ tsp ground allspice
¼ tsp chilli powder
¼ tsp freshly ground black pepper
285g (10oz) plain, firm tofu
50g (2oz) rice flakes or breadcrumbs
1 tbsp soy sauce
2 tbsp dry sherry or dry white wine
100g (4oz) ground hazelnuts

Melt the margarine in a frying pan and sauté the mushrooms for 7–10 minutes over a medium heat, stirring often. The mushrooms should darken and become soft. Sprinkle the spices over the mushrooms and stir for a further 1 minute. Turn the sauté into a bowl and mash the tofu and rice flakes into it. Add the soy sauce, sherry and hazelnuts and stir well. Press the paté into a jelly mould or ramekin and chill in the refrigerator. Garnish with whole peppercorns and a sage leaf. Serve with crackers, fresh bread or as an accompaniment to salad.

Tomatoes Stuffed with Mushroom and Pine Nut Sauté

Serves 4
Preparation time 45 minutes

2 tbsp oil
3 cloves garlic, finely chopped
1 medium onion, thinly sliced
½ tsp freshly ground black pepper
450g (1lb) mushrooms, trimmed and chopped
50g (2oz) pine nuts
4 tbsp fresh parsley, finely chopped
1 tbsp cider or wine vinegar
4 beef tomatoes

Heat the oil in a large frying pan and sauté the garlic and onion until clear and tender. Add the pepper and stir for 1 minute. Add the mushrooms, stir well and cover the pan. Leave to cook over a medium heat for 5 minutes. Stir again and add the pine nuts. Leave the pan uncovered and cook for 3-5 minutes, until the mushrooms are soft and reduced. Add the parsley and vinegar, stir well and remove the sauté from the heat. Slice the tops off the tomatoes, scoop out the seed pulp and discard. Spoon the mushroom mixture into the tomato shells. Serve immediately or allow to cool. These look nice set onto a bed of lettuce or chicory.

Garlic Mushrooms in White Sauce

Serves 4
Preparation time 40 minutes

1 tbsp olive oil
9 cloves garlic, finely chopped
1 small onion, finely chopped
900g (2lbs) mushrooms, cleaned, trimmed and chopped or thinly sliced
1 tbsp oil
1 tbsp plain flour
1 tsp turmeric (optional)
½ tsp freshly ground black pepper
½ tsp ground allspice
285ml (½ pint) soya milk
285ml (½ pint) vegetable stock
1 tbsp soy sauce
3 tbsp nutritional yeast flakes (optional)
3 tbsp fresh parsley (optional)

Heat the oil in a large frying pan and sauté the garlic and onion until clear and tender. Add the mushrooms and sauté over a medium to low heat for 5 minutes, until the mushrooms just begin to release their juices. Remove from the heat. In a saucepan, heat the second measure of oil and sprinkle with a mixture of the flour, turmeric, pepper and allspice. Stir to make a thick paste (roux). Mix the milk and stock together and add to the roux, a little at a time, stirring after each addition to make a sauce. Cook over a low to medium heat, adding the soy sauce and the yeast flakes and/or parsley if desired. Add the mushroom sauté to the white sauce, stir well and bring to a simmer. Serve immediately over pasta, toasted French loaves or to fill vol-au-vents.

Mushrooms with 'Sausage' Stuffing

Serves 4
Preparation time 1 hour

1 pkt Realeat VegeBanger dry mix
1 medium carrot, grated
4 tbsp fresh parsley, chopped
1 tsp dried thyme
1 tsp dried oregano
¼ tsp freshly ground black pepper
1 small onion, finely chopped
1 tbsp soy sauce
16 large mushrooms, stems removed

Preheat the oven to 180°C/350°F/Gas Mark 4 and lightly oil a large baking tray. Prepare the VegeBanger mix as per the eggless instructions and stir in the remaining ingredients, except the mushrooms. Leave the mixture to stand for 10 minutes. Stuff each mushroom cap with some of the 'sausage' mixture and arrange the mushrooms on the baking tray. Bake for 20–25 minutes or until tender. Serve hot with wild rice, stewed tomatoes and steamed greens.

Tomato Mushroom Sauce

Serves 4
Preparation time 1 hour

140ml (¼ pint) red wine
7 cloves garlic, finely chopped
1 medium onion, sliced
1 tsp dried marjoram
2 tbsp fresh basil, chopped
450g (1lb) mushrooms, cleaned and sliced
6–7 medium tomatoes, chopped
1 tsp freshly ground black pepper

Measure all the ingredients, except the tomatoes and black pepper, into a large saucepan and bring to a low boil. Reduce the heat, cover the pan and let the sauce simmer gently for 10–15 minutes. Stir well, add the tomatoes and pepper and leave to simmer for 30 minutes. Use immediately or leave until later and reheat. This sauce is excellent over pasta, in lasagne, on pizza or just spooned over a piece of toast.

Health Note

A word to the wise: mushrooms are particularly vulnerable to absorbing radioactive fallout (especially caesium) and it would therefore be extremely prudent to avoid buying mushrooms from areas which have recently suffered from nuclear contamination.

Natto see **Soya Beans**

Nectarines This is a mysterious fruit: no-one knows with certainty where it comes from! It was certainly known in Britain several hundred years ago, because it inspired John Milton to write in Book Four of *Paradise Lost*, 'To their supper-fruits they fell, nectarine fruits which the compliant boughs yielded them'.

Certainly, many consider the nectarine to be a finer fruit than the peach. Different varieties of nectarine produce flesh of varying colours, including red, yellow and white. It is a late summer fruit, and should be bought only when ripe and ready for eating. Underripe fruit, which are often small in size, will not ripen on their own; a ripe nectarine has a good colour all the way round (not just on one side) and is decidedly soft to the touch. They are best eaten at their peak of ripeness, by themselves as a superb dessert. They can be used in other dishes, such as preserves, jams, ice cream, stewed or baked, to replace or accompany peaches.

NUTRIENT ANALYSIS
1 NECTARINE (136g)

KCalories	66.64
Total Fat (g)	0.63
Monounsaturated Fat (g)	trace
Polyunsaturated Fat (g)	trace
Saturated Fat (g)	trace
Carbohydrate (g)	16.02
Protein (g)	1.28
Crude Fibre (g)	0.54
Vitamin A (RE)	100.64
Ascorbic Acid (mg)	7.34
Thiamin (mg)	0.02
Riboflavin (mg)	0.06
Niacin (mg)	1.35
Pantothenic Acid (mg)	0.21
Vitamin B6 (mg)	0.03
Folacin (mcg)	5.03
Vitamin B12 (mcg)	0.00
Calcium (mg)	6.80
Iron (mg)	0.20
Zinc (mg)	0.12

Avocado Nectarine Delight

Serves 4
Preparation time 20 minutes

4 ripe avocados, peeled
4 ripe nectarines
50g (2oz) crushed walnuts
juice of ½ lemon
1 tbsp walnut oil
freshly ground black pepper, to taste
140ml (¼ pint) plain soya yoghurt (optional)

Slice the avocados and nectarines and arrange in circles on each plate. Sprinkle a little crushed walnut over each serving. Mix the lemon juice and walnut oil together and drizzle a little over each serving. Finally, sprinkle a pinch of black pepper over all and serve immediately. This is exquisite all by itself and does not require beds of lettuce or other accessories. However, some people enjoy a dollop of plain yoghurt placed in the centre of the plate and used as a compliment to the subtle flavours of the salad. This dish serves as a starter, salad or light dessert.

Health Note

The 'nectarine diet' has been used in natural medicine to reduce high blood pressure, and treat asthma, rheumatism and bladder ailments.

Nori This seaweed is usually sold in paper-thin flat sheets or those same sheets already cut into lacy shreds. It is, in fact, dried laver – that of laver bread and other foods traditionally Celtic or British. Of late, nori has become popular in the West because it is used to wrap the rice and fillings of sushi (see page 350). Buy nori that is purple-black if you can, rather than green-black, and roast it gently over an open flame to make it crisp and aromatic. Use it then to wrap sushi or rice balls, or cut it into shreds and use as a garnish to salads and stir-fries.

Rice Balls

Serves 4
Preparation time 2 hours

450g (1lb) short grain brown rice, washed
8 umeboshi pickled plums, (see p273)
8 sheets nori, roasted

Place the washed rice in a deep saucepan with twice its volume of fresh water and place over a medium heat.

Bring to the boil, stir once, cover the pan and reduce the heat. Simmer the rice for 40 minutes, until tender and all the liquid is absorbed. The rice at the bottom of the pan should start to stick to the pan slightly. Remove the pan from the heat and leave it, uncovered for 5 minutes then turn the rice out onto a platter or into a large bowl and let it cool. Fluff the rice once or twice to allow more heat to escape. When the rice is cool enough to hold in your hand, you can make the rice balls.

Wet your hands and place a large spoonful of rice into one hand. Press one umeboshi plum into the centre of that rice and then place another large spoonful of rice over it. Mould the rice into a large ball, like a snowball, pressing firmly as you shape it. Place the ball on a plate and wet your hands again, ready to make the next ball. Repeat this procedure to make 8 balls.

Dry your hands and hold one sheet of nori over a low flame. Turn it slowly so that the whole sheet gets roasted. You will notice that the colour and texture of the nori changes somewhat as it roasts. Place the sheet on a separate plate and continue roasting all 8 sheets. (Note: you can sometimes buy the nori already roasted.) Rest a sheet of nori on your palm and place a rice ball in the centre of it. Now carefully fold the nori round the ball, moulding it in the snowball fashion as you do so. The nori will crack a bit, but continue, pressing the seaweed onto the moist rice. When the ball appears covered in the nori, simply mould it for another minute or two, again pressing quite firmly. Repeat this procedure for all 8 balls.

Tightly wrap each rice ball in plastic film and refrigerate or leave in a cool place. These will keep for 3 days and are excellent for lunch, snack or picnic. The whole point of them is their portability, so put one in your briefcase and go.

Oats In the past few years oats have shot from the obscurity of being considered a 'peasant food' to being the trendiest food around. The reason for this is their much-publicised ability to reduce the amount of circulating cholesterol in the human bloodstream. In fact, this effect was first observed several decades ago, but it was only in recent years that, as part of the quest for the answer to coronary heart disease, scientists once again scrutinized this humble and inexpensive food. Today, there is absolutely no question that the special type of soluble fibre found in oats can profoundly lower cholesterol levels, for example:

- A group of twenty men with high cholesterol were admitted to hospital so their diets could be accurately measured for twenty-one days. Some were fed a 'control' diet (with no oat bran) and others were fed exactly the same diet, but with added oat bran. After just three weeks, the men receiving oat bran supplementation had reduced their cholesterol levels by nearly 20 per cent.[12]

This is just one of many similar experiments. In fact, people eating a low-fat diet supplemented with oats usually average a reduction in cholesterol of between ten and 25 per cent. A diet which includes about 100g of oat bran daily and lasts for at least three weeks (the longer the better) should show a useful improvement in cholesterol levels. Occasionally, side effects are encountered, such as:

- A softening of the stools, which shouldn't be objectionable (it might be a welcome change!)
- Intestinal gas. Where more than 50g of oat bran are consumed a day, some bloating or abdominal pain might occur, in which case the intake should be reduced and medical advice obtained.

NUTRIENT ANALYSIS
1 CUP OATS (156g)

KCalories	606.84
Total Fat (g)	10.76
Monounsaturated Fat (g)	3.40
Polyunsaturated Fat (g)	3.95
Saturated Fat (g)	1.90
Carbohydrate (g)	103.38
Protein (g)	26.35
Crude Fibre (g)	1.72
Vitamin A (RE)	0.00
Ascorbic Acid (mg)	0.00
Thiamin (mg)	1.19
Riboflavin (mg)	0.22
Niacin (mg)	1.50
Pantothenic Acid (mg)	2.10
Vitamin B6 (mg)	0.19
Folacin (mcg)	87.36
Vitamin B12 (mcg)	0.00
Calcium (mg)	84.24
Iron (mg)	7.36
Zinc (mg)	6.19

Creamy Porridge

Serves 1
Preparation time 15 minutes

50g (2oz) rolled or porridge oats
285ml (½ pint) soya milk
140ml (¼ pint) water or fruit juice

Measure the ingredients into a saucepan and stir well (preferably with a spurtle, that wonderful wooden utensil specially designed for cooking porridge). Place the saucepan over a medium heat and bring to a low boil. Reduce the heat and simmer for 10–12 minutes, stirring often. The porridge will thicken considerably; be prepared to add more liquid if you want a more gloopy porridge. Pour into a breakfast bowl and top with sliced banana, raisins, chopped apple, a teaspoon of brown sugar, barley malt syrup, a dab of margarine and a sprinkling of salt or (to be historically authentic) a jigger of whiskey! Some people pour a little milk over the top of the porridge to stop it developing a skin. Serve at once and eat it steaming hot to set you up for several hours.

Sweet and Speedy High-Fibre Bread

Makes 1 large loaf
Preparation time 50 minutes

100g (4oz) whole wheat flour
100g (4oz) rolled oats
50g (2oz) oat bran
3 tbsp sugar
1 tbsp baking powder
60ml (2fl oz) oil
420ml (¾ pint) apple juice

Preheat the oven to 180°C/350°F/Gas Mark 4 and lightly oil a large loaf tin. Stir the dry ingredients together in a large mixing bowl, then add the oil and work to an even consistency. Add the apple juice, stir well and leave to stand for 3 minutes. Stir again, quite vigorously, then turn into the loaf tin. Bake for 35 minutes. Leave it to cool in the pan for 10 minutes before turning it out onto a wire rack. Slice and serve.

Hot Berry Muffins

Makes 24 muffins
Preparation time 45 minutes

170g (6oz) plain flour
50g (2oz) oat bran
2 tsp baking powder
1 tsp bicarbonate of soda
1 tsp ground allspice
1 tsp ground cinnamon
90ml (3fl oz) oil
225g (8oz) (approximately 285ml (½ pint)) fresh or
    frozen berries (i.e. blackberries, raspberries,
    blueberries, bilberries, blackcurrants)
1 tbsp plain flour
285ml (½ pint) apple juice

Preheat the oven to 180°C/350°F/Gas Mark 4 and line 24 muffin tins with paper baking cases. Mix the dry ingredients together in a large mixing bowl. Work in the oil to a fine, crumbly consistency. Measure the berries into a small bowl and sprinkle a little flour over them. Shake the berries until they are coated with the flour. Discard any excess flour and add the berries to the dry mix. Stir gently, add the apple juice and stir briefly until the ingredients are just moist. Spoon the batter into the baking cases (about two-thirds full) and bake for 20-25 minutes. Lift the muffins onto a wire rack to cool. Serve warm or cold.

Health Note

Apart from being a good source of soluble fibre, oats also provide useful amounts of thiamin and iron: one cup of cooked oats yields about one-fifth of the adult daily requirement for both these essential nutrients, often in short supply in the modern diet.

Okra Native to Africa, and also found in the indigenous cuisine of India, the Middle East, Spain and the Balkans, okra was brought to Western attention with the transportation of slaves to the southern United States and the West Indies. There are three principal varieties; tall green, dwarf green, and ladies' fingers. One of the original names for this plant was 'gumbo' although this has now been transferred to the thick stew made from it. It is a particularly interesting vegetable, partly for its unique shape, which lends immediate interest to any dish in which it is included; but mainly for the mucilaginous, thickening quality it imparts to all dishes.

Okra has a very delicate, slightly musty flavour by itself, and so combines with almost any other foodstuff or flavouring; the thick, juicy sauce it naturally produces greatly enhances the sensory allure of any dish. Although tinned okra is available, it should really be bought fresh for maximum thickening quality. Here you have to be careful; being an imported vegetable, it is often rather old by the time it is offered for sale, and older okra pods are definitely unattractive, being thick, woody and stringy – virtually inedible. Therefore, avoid dull, dry looking pods and choose young ones which are green, not grey, and snap to the touch. Avoid cooking okra in iron, copper or brass because this will discolour the okra and make it look black; use glass or enamel pots instead.

See also: Okra Uganda (p322); Fungi (p335); Malangwa Stew (p342)

NUTRIENT ANALYSIS
1 CUP OKRA, BOILED (160g)

KCalories	51.20
Total Fat (g)	0.27
Monounsaturated Fat (g)	0.04
Polyunsaturated Fat (g)	0.07
Saturated Fat (g)	0.07
Carbohydrate (g)	11.54
Protein (g)	2.99
Crude Fibre (g)	1.44
Vitamin A (RE)	92.80
Ascorbic Acid (mg)	26.08
Thiamin (mg)	0.21
Riboflavin (mg)	0.09
Niacin (mg)	1.39
Pantothenic Acid (mg)	0.34
Vitamin B6 (mg)	0.30
Folacin (mcg)	73.12
Vitamin B12 (mcg)	0.00
Calcium (mg)	100.80
Iron (mg)	0.72
Zinc (mg)	0.88

Bhindi Bhaji (Fried Ladies' Fingers)

Serves 4
Preparation time 40 minutes

450g (1lb) okra, washed and trimmed
4 tbsp oil
5 cloves garlic, finely chopped
2 medium onions, thinly sliced
2 teaspoons paprika
1 teaspoon mustard seeds
1 teaspoon turmeric
¼ tsp chilli powder
1 fresh chilli, thinly sliced (optional)
1 small sweet green or red pepper, thinly sliced

Prepare the okra by trimming off the top cap. Heat the oil in a saucepan and sauté the garlic and most of the onion (save out about a quarter of the slices) until clear and tender. Add the paprika, mustard seeds, turmeric and chilli and stir for 2 minutes. Add the okra, stir well and cook over a low heat for 20-25 minutes, stirring occasionally. Sprinkle the sweet pepper and remaining onion slices over the okra and cook a further 5–7 minutes. Stir well and serve with rice and other vegetable dishes.

Health Note

Okra is an excellent source of glutathione – a compound formed from the three amino acids glutamic acid, cysteine, and glucine – and one of the most important antioxidants (substances which can protect the body from heart disease, cancer and many inflammatory ailments). It has been used in natural medicine to treat stomach ulcers, sore throats and colitis. One cup of cooked okra will provide half of the adult vitamin C requirement, a third of the folic acid requirement, and about a fifth of the potassium, thiamin, vitamin B6 and calcium requirements.

Olives A fruit of vast economic importance in the ancient world (there are sixty-one mentions of it in the Bible alone) the olive is worthy of a far more central position in modern cuisine than the role of appetizer or *hors d'oeuvre* to which it is all too frequently relegated. In the ancient world, it was said that a single olive tree could supply a family with all the fruit it needed to eat, and all the oil it needed for cooking, lighting and anointing.

Two basic types of olives are available – green (unripe) and black (ripe). Since olive oil is mostly developed by the fruit in the final stages of maturation, black olives yield more calories than green olives. The vast majority of oil contained in olives is in the healthy monounsaturated form, consumption of which has been shown, by many scientific studies, to be one of the chief reasons for the good health of many Mediterranean peoples.

The best olives, whether green or black, are never to be found in small packs or jars – instead, try to locate a good Middle Eastern grocery store, or delicatessen, which sells olives loose from large vats. The staff of such establishments are generally very knowledgeable about their produce, and will often let you sample an olive or two before you decide which to buy. The precise variety and method of preservation you choose is, of course, a question of personal taste; but as far as black olives are concerned, some of the finest flavours are to be found in the kalamata olive (named after that region in Greece) – they make excellent appetizers and cook extremely well, yielding a deep and memorable flavour.

NUTRIENT ANALYSIS
10 OLIVES, CANNED (32g)

KCalories	36.80
Total Fat (g)	3.42
Monounsaturated Fat (g)	2.52
Polyunsaturated Fat (g)	0.29
Saturated Fat (g)	0.45
Carbohydrate (g)	2.00
Protein (g)	0.27
Crude Fibre (g)	0.45
Vitamin A (RE)	12.80
Ascorbic Acid (mg)	0.29
Thiamin (mg)	0.00
Riboflavin (mg)	0.00
Niacin (mg)	0.01
Pantothenic Acid (mg)	0.00
Vitamin B6 (mg)	0.00
Folacin (mcg)	0.00

Vitamin B12 (mcg)	0.00
Calcium (mg)	28.16
Iron (mg)	1.06
Zinc (mg)	0.07

Very Olive Pizza

Serves 4
Preparation time 1 hour (less if two people work together)

450g (1lb) kalamata olives in their juice
1 tbsp oil
1 medium onion, very finely chopped
200g (7oz) tomato paste
1x400g (14oz) tin chopped tomatoes
140–285ml (¼–½ pint) water
2 tbsp fresh basil or 2 tsp dried
1 tsp brown sugar

For the pizza base:
(Note: for another pizza base recipe, see p252)
450g (1lb) plain flour
2 tsp baking powder
1 tsp bicarbonate of soda
340–420ml (12–15fl oz) water

Preheat the oven to 180°C/350°F/Gas Mark 4. Drain the olives but save the juice. Remove the pits from the olives and slice each olive in half. Put to one side. Heat the oil in a saucepan or large frying pan and sauté the onion over a low heat until clear and tender, about 15 minutes. Add the tomato paste and chopped tomatoes and stir well. Add the water and basil, stir well and increase the heat. Bring to a simmer then reduce the heat slightly. Add the sugar and the reserved olive juice, stir well and leave to simmer very gently for 5–10 minutes, or until you are ready to use it. Meanwhile, measure the dry ingredients into a mixing bowl and stir well. Add the water, stir well and divide the dough into parts – depending on how many pizzas you will be making. (This recipe will feed 4; it's up to you how many pizzas you make, I usually make 3–4 medium-sized ones using flan dishes or baking trays.) Lightly oil the pizza dishes and spread the dough to the edges of the dish using the tips of your fingers; patch up any holes that appear in the dough. Spoon the tomato sauce over the pizza base, spreading it nearly to the edges. Cover, and I mean cover, the sauce with the olive halves and bake for 12–15 minutes. Slice and serve immediately, though this is excellent cold – if there is any left.

Olive and Pimento Spread

Makes approximately 200ml (7fl oz)
Preparation time 30 minutes

225g (8oz) kalamata olives, pitted and chopped
3 tbsp good olive oil
1 tbsp fresh basil, chopped
3 cloves garlic, chopped
50g (2oz) pimento, very finely chopped
50g (2oz) ground almonds (optional)

Blend the olives, oil, basil and garlic together in a food processor or chop these ingredients very finely before running them through a mouli. Turn the olive mixture into a bowl and stir in the chopped pimento. If you are using the almonds, add them at this stage (for a very different spread). Spoon the mixture into a pretty jar or serving bowl and garnish with a fresh basil leaf. Serve immediately or chill, covered, until you need it.

Health Note

Not many people consider olives to be 'health' foods – but they are! Apart from the healthy monounsaturated oils they contain, they also supply dietary iron – 10 large olives contains about one fifth of the adult daily requirement of iron. The calorie yield is surprisingly low – the same quantity provides about 50 calories.

Onions An essential flavouring ingredient in many of the world's finest vegetarian recipes, the many varieties of onion combine with a broad range of cooking techniques to produce a taste that can either be sweet or sour, acrid or bland. The main varieties of onion have their own specific uses:

• Pearl Onions. Generally used for pickling. Home made pickled onions are so much better than store bought ones. To make your own take 1kg (2lb) of onions, peel, sprinkle with salt and leave to stand for 12 hours, then rinse and dry them. Pour 1l (2 pints) of malt vinegar into a pan and add 4 tablespoons each of sugar and salt, and a packet (approximately 50g/2oz) of pickling spice. Boil together until the sugar and salt has dissolved, then add the onions and boil for 15–20 minutes. Bottle and, when cool, cover tightly.

• Spring Onions. Available from April to July, both the bulb and the stalks are used as an ingredient in salads or to garnish soups and sauces. They can also be used cut into thin lengths and included in a mixed vegetable stir-fry where their subtle onion flavour and deep green colour add tremendously to the final outcome of the dish.

- Yellow Onions. Available all the year, they tend towards the large size and medium mild flavour. They are highly versatile and are the mainstay of a great many soups, salads, tarts, pies, sauces and risottos. They can also be roughly quartered and speared on a kebab together with marinated tofu, red peppers, aubergines, baby sweet corn and marinated mushrooms. Larger onions can be stuffed and baked: top and tail some large onions, but leave the skins intact, push out the centre core and fill them with prepared Realeat VegeBurger mixture. Place in a hot oven for about 35 minutes, remove the skins and serve.
- Pink and Red Onions. Generally milder and sweeter than other types, and therefore good for slicing or dicing and including in salads and dressings such as onion raita (see below). Onions are notoriously challenging to peel or chop – peeling them underwater is one solution, although this also tends to remove some of the flavour. Another effective method is to put them in the freezer compartment of your refrigerator for 10 minutes immediately prior to preparation.

A number of classical onion based recipes are either entirely vegetarian or easily adapted; some of them follow.

NUTRIENT ANALYSIS
1 CUP ONIONS, RAW (160g)

KCalories	60.80
Total Fat (g)	0.26
Monounsaturated Fat (g)	0.04
Polyunsaturated Fat (g)	0.10
Saturated Fat (g)	0.04
Carbohydrate (g)	13.81
Protein (g)	1.86
Crude Fibre (g)	0.94
Vitamin A (RE)	0.00
Ascorbic Acid (mg)	10.24

Thiamin (mg)	0.07
Riboflavin (mg)	0.03
Niacin (mg)	0.24
Pantothenic Acid (mg)	0.17
Vitamin B6 (mg)	0.19
Folacin (mcg)	30.40
Vitamin B12 (mcg)	0.00
Calcium (mg)	32.00
Iron (mg)	0.35
Zinc (mg)	0.30

Onion Raita

Makes approximately 570ml (1 pint)
Preparation time 15 minutes, plus chilling time

2 × 285g (10oz) cartons soft tofu
2 medium onions, finely chopped
1 medium tomato, finely chopped
1–2 fresh chillies, finely chopped
1 tbsp fresh coriander, chopped
2 tsp fresh ginger, grated
1 tsp salt

Beat all the ingredients together in a mixing bowl. Adjust the spices to suit your taste then turn into the serving dish. Serve chilled as an accompaniment to spicy dishes, rice dishes, baked potatoes or salads.

Onion Soup

Serves 4
Preparation time 1 hour

2 tbsp margarine
1 tbsp oil
450g (1lb) onions, finely chopped
1 tbsp plain flour
2l (4 pints) vegetable stock
1 tsp salt
1 bay leaf
1 large onion, thinly sliced
1 tbsp miso (optional)
60ml (2fl oz) port (optional)

Heat the margarine and oil together in a large saucepan and sauté the onions over a medium heat. When the onions begin to soften, reduce the heat slightly and cook for about 15 minutes, stirring occasionally. Sprinkle the flour over the sauté and stir for 2–3 minutes. Add the stock and the salt and bring to the boil over a medium heat. Add the bay leaf and sliced onion and stir well. Reduce the heat and let the soup simmer gently for 30 minutes. Remove from the heat and stir in the miso and/or the port. Serve the soup hot in deep bowls. Some people toast a thick piece of French loaf and lay it in the bowl first; the soup is then ladled over the toast. Others float a piece of toasted bread or croutons on the soup. You might try these or simply serve with plenty of fresh or garlic bread (see page 217).

Just Onion Pizza

Serves 4
Preparation time 2 hours

For the pizza base:
(Note: for another pizza base recipe, see p250)
285ml (½ pint) tepid water
1 tbsp sugar
1 packet active dry yeast
450g (1lb) plain flour
60ml (2fl oz) oil

For the topping:
90ml (3fl oz) oil
6 cloves garlic, finely chopped
1.5k (3lbs) onions, finely chopped or sliced
1 tsp dried thyme
1 bay leaf
1 tsp freshly ground black pepper
½ tsp salt
2 tbsp fresh basil, chopped

Measure the water into a small jug or mixing bowl and dissolve the sugar and yeast in it. Stir gently, then leave for 10 minutes in a warm place. Measure the flour into a warmed mixing bowl. When the yeast is softened, add it to the flour along with the oil. Stir well then knead the dough, adding a little more flour if necessary to make a slightly firm dough that is not sticky. Knead for 5–10 minutes, then turn the dough into a lightly oiled bowl, cover with a tea towel and leave to rise for about 1 hour. Punch down the dough and divide into the number of pizzas you will make. Press the dough into the lightly oiled pizza dishes and spread the topping immediately or, for a lighter crust, let the dough sit for 30 minutes.

For the topping, heat the oil in a large frying pan and sauté the garlic for 2 minutes. Add the onions and continue to sauté for 5 minutes, stirring constantly.

Add the dried thyme and bay leaf, stir well and cook the onions over a low to medium heat, for about 45 minutes. Most of the moisture will evaporate and the onion will become very smooth and caramelized (your kitchen will smell wonderful!). Discard the bay leaf and sprinkle the onions with pepper and salt; stir well. Cover the pizza bases with the onion mixture and sprinkle the fresh basil over the top. Bake for 10–12 minutes, until the topping is golden brown.

Health Note

The nutrient content of onions is quite low, and this is likely to be further diminished by cooking. However, the sulphide compounds present in onions (which give them their characteristic pungency, and are quickly destroyed by cooking) may have useful antibiotic and anticarcinogenic properties. Onions also contain biologically active forms of flavonoids – antioxidant substances which play an important role in stopping arteries from clogging. In natural medicine, onions have been used to loosen phlegm and drain mucus, to assist in cases of asthma and bronchitis, and to stimulate the function of the liver.

Oranges Originally from China, the first orange variety to appear in the West was the Bigarade (bitter orange). The sweet orange is a comparative newcomer – some authorities consider that it was introduced as late as the 16th century by the Portuguese from India. Today, there are several different varieties, each with their own properties and characteristics:

- Seville. The closest relative of the original bitter orange. Almost all of the Spanish crop of Seville oranges is exported to England for marmalade production. The intensely sour flavour certainly renders this orange unsuitable for dessert use, but a creative cook will have no difficulty in incorporating their sharp flavour into a range of savoury dishes, such as curries, soups, sauces and pilafs. The Sevilles produce a far more intensely orange flavour than any of the sweeter varieties.
- Navel. Easily identified by the 'belly button' at the end of the orange where the flower stalk used to be, this variety is sweet, juicy, and seedless – best for eating raw or in fruit salads.

- Jaffa (or Shamouti). Usually possessing a rather sharper and more full-bodied taste than other varieties, they are probably the best to choose for juicing.
- Valencia. Very sharply flavoured, to the point of tartness, available both seeded and seedless, excellent for cooking.
- Blood oranges. Generally only available in the winter months, their striking appearance combines well with other fruit and, with the exception of the Maltese variety, these are generally the least acid of all oranges.

Orange juice should always be squeezed fresh from the fruit, because much of its nutrient value is destroyed by storage. There have been persistent reports of adulteration and contamination of commercially-prepared orange juices: for example, sugar and other sweetening substances – contradicting claims made on the label. The consumption of orange juice from aluminium-lined containers may also give rise to some concern; suggestions have been made that the citric acid contained in the juice can dissolve aluminium and therefore increase the amount of aluminium ingested.

The first oranges of any new crop into the shops are considered to be the most nutritious, possessing the greatest amount of minerals. Fruit which looks dull or which feels light for its size should be avoided, as should those with obvious skin imperfections. Under-ripe fruit bought at bargain prices will not ripen, and may well result in a stomach upset. If the peel or zest is to be used, then the fruit should ideally come from a known organic source.

NUTRIENT ANALYSIS
1 ORANGE, JUICED (86g)

KCalories	38.70
Total Fat (g)	0.17
Monounsaturated Fat (g)	0.03
Polyunsaturated Fat (g)	0.03
Saturated Fat (g)	0.02
Carbohydrate (g)	8.94
Protein (g)	0.60
Crude Fibre (g)	0.09
Vitamin A (RE)	17.20

Ascorbic Acid (mg)	43.00
Thiamin (mg)	0.08
Riboflavin (mg)	0.03
Niacin (mg)	0.34
Pantothenic Acid (mg)	0.16
Vitamin B6 (mg)	0.03
Folacin (mcg)	26.06
Vitamin B12 (mcg)	0.00
Calcium (mg)	9.46
Iron (mg)	0.17
Zinc (mg)	0.04

Oranges in Olive Oil
Preparation time 12 hours, plus 2 months

1kg (2lb) oranges
4 tbsp salt
pieces of cinnamon (optional)
split whole nutmegs (optional)
approximately 1l (2 pints) good olive oil

Purchase organic oranges if possible and slice each into approximately 8 thick slices. Remove most of the pips. Arrange the slices on a platter and sprinkle the salt over them. Leave for 12 hours or overnight. Drain the juice away and press the orange slices into a large, sterilized jar. If you wish, add the occasional piece of cinnamon and/or nutmeg as you layer the oranges. Also, you may enjoy creating a pleasing, alternating pattern of orange slices and orange rind lining the glass jar. Pour the olive oil over the oranges, leave it to stand for 5 minutes then jostle the jar. Add more oil if necessary to completely immerse the oranges. Seal the jar and place in a cool, dark place for 2–3 months. Lift out the slices as you need them, always ensuring you use clean utensils (preferably wooden or enamel) and that the oil covers the remaining orange slices. The oil is a rare and delicious addition to salad dressings or by itself over fresh toast (instead of butter). The orange slices are precious additions to stir-fries (chopped), sauces and some desserts.

Spicy Orange Relish
Makes approximately 570ml (1 pint)
Preparation time 1 hour plus 24 hours

2 medium oranges, finely chopped and deseeded
50g (2oz) currants

1 small sweet red pepper, finely diced
1 small onion, very finely chopped
3 cloves garlic, finely chopped
1 fresh chilli, very finely chopped
285ml (½ pint) wine vinegar
50g (2oz) sugar

Mix the oranges, currants, pepper, onion, garlic and chilli together in a mixing bowl. Press the mixture into sterilized jars. In a small, enamel saucepan, heat the vinegar and sugar together, stirring well to dissolve the sugar. When the liquid boils, remove it from the heat and immediately pour over the orange mixture in the jars. Ensure that the liquid covers the orange mix then seal the jars and leave to cool. You may use this after 24 hours, but it develops nicely if left for a week or more.

Orange Lentil Soup
Serves 4
Preparation time 1 hour

340g (12oz) red lentils, washed and drained
850ml–1l (1½–2 pints) vegetable stock or water
1 small acorn squash
1 tbsp oil
2 medium onions, finely chopped
1 tbsp fresh ginger, grated
2 tsp cumin
1 tsp ground coriander
1 tsp ground cinnamon
½–1 tsp chilli powder
salt to taste
285ml (½ pint) fresh orange juice
1 orange, sliced

Preheat the oven to 180°C/350°F/Gas Mark 4. Turn the cleaned lentils into a large saucepan and pour the stock over. Cover the pan and place on a medium heat; bring to the boil, skim any foam from the surface and reduce the heat. Cover the pan and leave to simmer gently for about 25 minutes, stirring occasionally. The lentils should lose their form completely. Add more stock or water to achieve the thickness you enjoy. Meanwhile, quarter the squash and remove the seed pulp. Place the squash quarters on a baking tray which has about 12mm (½ inch) of water in it. Bake for 20–25 minutes, until the squash is tender. When it is cooked, immediately remove it from the oven and scoop the flesh away from the skin. Also meanwhile, heat the oil in a large frying pan over a medium heat

and sauté the onions until clear and tender. Do not hurry this process: for this dish, the longer the onions sauté for, the better their flavour and texture. After about 15 minutes, add the ginger, cumin, coriander, cinnamon and chilli. Sauté a further 5 minutes, stirring often. Add the cooked squash to the sauté and stir with a slight mashing movement. Add the salt at this stage. Combine the onion and squash sauté to the cooked lentils and stir well. You may run the whole lot through a mouli if you like a really even consistency; I don't mind the occasional piece of squash. When the soup has come back to a simmer, add the orange juice, stir well and remove from the heat. Serve hot in pretty bowls that set off the yellow of this soup, and garnish with a slice of fresh orange. A meal in itself.

Orange Lollies
Makes 12 lollies
Preparation time 15 minutes, plus freezing time

3 ripe bananas, peeled
3 fresh oranges, peeled with pith and pips removed
570ml (1 pint) orange juice
570ml (1 pint) pineapple juice

Blend all ingredients together in a blender until smooth. Pour into lollie moulds, insert lollie sticks and place in the freezer.

Orange Sandies
Makes approximately 2 dozen biscuits
Preparation time 1 hour

340g (12oz) plain flour
100g (4oz) sugar
2 tsp baking powder
½ tsp bicarbonate of soda
140g (5oz) margarine
50–75g (2–3oz) dried or candied orange peel
1 tbsp grated orange rind
5 tbsp orange juice (1–2 oranges)
1 tsp vanilla essence

Preheat the oven to 180°C/350°F/Gas Mark 4. Mix the dry ingredients in a large bowl then work in the margarine to an even, crumbly consistency. Add the peel and the grated orange rind and mix well. Add the orange juice and vanilla to the dry ingredients. Mix very well, adding more juice if necessary to make a very firm dough, then shape the dough into a ball. Place the dough on a floured board and roll into a large circle about 12mm (½ inch) thick. Cut into biscuits with a round or shaped cutter, place on a baking tray and bake for 15 minutes. Lift immediately onto a wire cooling rack. Serve warm or cool.

Health Note

Oranges are best known for their high vitamin C content: one average sized orange will generally supply all of an adult's daily requirement for this vitamin. It also contains one fifth of the folic acid requirement, and useful amounts of calcium and thiamin. Oranges have been used for a variety of purposes in natural medicine, although their extreme acidity means that they should not be used in cases of stomach ulcers or other intestinal inflammation. Oranges have been used to assist with withdrawal from alcohol, to reduce mucus secretions, and to treat hypertension, arthritis, and pulmonary disorders. Grilled oranges have remarkable anti-infective properties, and are easily made: quarter several oranges and place them under the grill until they just begin to char. Several oranges prepared thus, and consumed frequently throughout the day, can help the body fight a wide variety of infections.

Papaya Sometimes called pawpaw (not to be confused with the North American papaw, or custard apple), papaya is an exotic fruit which is increasingly available at supermarkets and greengrocers. It looks like a pear shaped melon, and has pink flesh when ripe, with the melting texture of an avocado and a delicate aroma of freesias. The papaya is native to Central America, but the majority of the world's produce is now grown in Hawaii and South Africa. According to Christopher Columbus, the original Carib name for this fruit, Ababai, meant 'the fruit of the angels', and a perfectly ripe specimen may indeed be thus described.

Sadly, much of the fruit reaching Europe seems to have a watery, sometimes even musty, flavour and needs to be enlivened by sprinklings of lime juice or even a drizzling of rum. For this reason, do not buy a papaya that is anything other than obviously ripe. The aerogelatinous mess of black seeds should be discarded (they have a peppery taste, and are apparently sometimes dried and used as a mild spice). Less ripe

fruits can be used as an ingredient in fruit salads, completely ripe ones may be sliced in half and their cavities filled with a suitably complementary dressing.

NUTRIENT ANALYSIS
1 PAPAYA, FRESH (304g)

KCalories	118.56
Total Fat (g)	0.43
Monounsaturated Fat (g)	0.12
Polyunsaturated Fat (g)	0.09
Saturated Fat (g)	0.13
Carbohydrate (g)	29.82
Protein (g)	1.85
Crude Fibre (g)	2.34
Vitamin A (RE)	85.12
Ascorbic Acid (mg)	187.87
Thiamin (mg)	0.08
Riboflavin (mg)	0.10
Niacin (mg)	1.03
Pantothenic Acid (mg)	0.66
Vitamin B6 (mg)	0.06
Folacin (mcg)	115.52
Vitamin B12 (mcg)	0.00
Calcium (mg)	72.96
Iron (mg)	0.30
Zinc (mg)	0.21

Papaya Avocado Salad

Serves 4
Preparation time 20 minutes

3 tbsp cider vinegar
90ml (3fl oz) walnut oil
2 ripe papayas, seeded, peeled and sliced lengthwise
2 ripe avocados, seeded, peeled and sliced lengthwise
285g (10oz) firm plain tofu, cut into thin strips
a large handful of lambs' lettuce, washed and drained
½ tsp freshly ground black pepper
½ tsp ground cinnamon
50g (2oz) crushed walnuts

Measure the vinegar and oil into a small jug and stir

well. Arrange the papaya, avocado, tofu and lambs lettuce alternately in a circle on each plate. Sprinkle a little of the pepper and cinnamon over each arrangement and garnish with a little crushed walnut. Finally, drizzle the dressing over each salad and serve immediately. If you prefer a cold salad, simply chill the ingredients before you make it. If you are quick, it will be nicely chilled when it is served.

Health Note

> Natural medicine uses papayas to stimulate the digestive processes, to dissolve mucus, and in the treatment of stomach ulcers. Papayas are also famous for containing an enzyme, papain, which has the ability to break down the muscle structure of flesh. In their country of origin papaya leaves and the milky latex exuded by unripe fruits are used to make tough meat more palatable. Until the practice was banned, certain Western slaughterhouses would inject papain into live animals for the same purpose. Nutritionally, one average raw papaya contains over three times the adult daily recommended allowance of vitamin C, two-thirds the vitamin A requirement, and over a third of the potassium requirement.

Parsley The most widely used flavouring and garnish for many dishes, parsley comes in three varieties, although only two are commonly used:

- Curly Leaved. Used as a garnish, chopped and sprinkled over many cooked foods before serving. Can be included in salads, finely chopped as an ingredient in sauces and juiced with other vegetables.
- Common Parsley. Flat, serrated leaves, an essential ingredient in tabbouleh (see page 347). May be lightly steamed or stir-fried with other vegetables.

See also: Parsley Salad (p320); Kisir (p347)

NUTRIENT ANALYSIS
10 PARSLEY SPRIGS (10g)

KCalories	3.30
Total Fat (g)	0.03

Monounsaturated Fat (g)	0.00
Polyunsaturated Fat (g)	trace
Saturated Fat (g)	0.00
Carbohydrate (g)	0.69
Protein (g)	0.22
Crude Fibre (g)	0.12
Vitamin A (RE)	52.00
Ascorbic Acid (mg)	9.00
Thiamin (mg)	0.01
Riboflavin (mg)	0.01
Niacin (mg)	0.07
Pantothenic Acid (mg)	0.03
Vitamin B6 (mg)	0.02
Folacin (mcg)	18.31
Vitamin B12 (mcg)	0.00
Calcium (mg)	13.00
Iron (mg)	0.62
Zinc (mg)	0.07

Herb Paste
Makes approximately 570ml (1 pint)
Preparation time 15 minutes

285ml (½ pint) fresh parsley, chopped
140ml (¼ pint) fresh basil, chopped
140ml (¼ pint) fresh coriander, chopped
3 cloves garlic, finely chopped
1 tsp salt
140–200ml (5–7fl oz) olive oil
2 tbsp cider vinegar

This really is best made in a food processor, if you can. Combine all the ingredients and blend until finely minced. Add more oil if necessary to achieve the consistency you desire. Serve over freshly cooked pasta, baked potatoes or toasted French loaf. A sprinkling of freshly ground black pepper is a tasty garnish. If you prefer, press the mixture into a sterilized jar, top up with oil and seal. Leave for 1 week then use within the next.

Parsley Sauce
Serves 4
Preparation time 1 hour

1 tbsp oil
5 cloves garlic, finely chopped
2 medium onions, finely chopped
1–2 tsp freshly ground black pepper
1 fresh chilli, finely chopped
2 sweet red or green peppers, diced
285ml (½ pint) fresh parsley, chopped
1 tbsp fresh basil, chopped
1 tsp dried sage
1 tsp dried oregano
140ml (¼ pint) vegetable stock

Heat the oil in a large saucepan and sauté the garlic and onions over a medium heat until they are clear and tender. Add the black pepper and chilli and stir for 2 minutes. Add the remaining items, except the stock, and bring to a low boil. Stir well, cover the pan and reduce the heat. Simmer for 45 minutes, adding the stock if necessary to make a slightly thickened sauce. Serve hot over pasta, in lasagne, in a quiche or to top baked potatoes or fill vol-au-vents.

Parsley Baked Potatoes

Serves 4
Preparation time 1 hour

1k (2lb) new potatoes, scrubbed and halved
3 tbsp tomato paste
5 tbsp water
5 cloves garlic, very finely chopped
1 tsp salt
1 tsp paprika
90ml (3fl oz) olive oil
285ml (½ pint) fresh parsley, finely chopped

Preheat the oven to 180°C/350°F/Gas Mark 4. Turn the potatoes into a casserole dish. Blend the remaining ingredients and pour over the potatoes. Stir gently to coat the potatoes with the dressing. Cover the dish and bake for 45 minutes, until the potatoes are tender.

Health Note

Parsley's considerable health-promoting properties mean that we should all try to make something more of it than just a (generally uneaten) garnish. 90g (3oz) of fresh chopped parsley supplies twice the adult daily recommended requirement of vitamin C, half the requirement for folic acid, vitamin A and iron, and about a fifth of the requirement for potassium and calcium. Parsley is rich in chlorophyll, which makes it a very cleansing and deodorizing herb. It is often used after eating garlic to make the lingering odour disappear. Recently, it has been found to contain one of the highest levels of glutathione in foodstuffs – and glutathione is a vital ingredient of the body's antioxidant defence system. Lack of antioxidants almost certainly contributes to the cause and development of many of today's most formidable diseases. From the latest research, it also seems likely that low glutathione levels hasten the development of AIDS in HIV-positive people.

Parsnip A much underrated vegetable, the parsnip is capable of being transformed into a stunning range of culinary masterpieces; and as a bonus, makes a crisp white wine of extraordinary potency, too! Rightly appreciated by the Romans, yet almost entirely overlooked by the French, it has been left to the British to dazzle the modern world with their achievements on behalf of this humble and unassuming root vegetable. The parsnip presents itself in two forms, funnel shaped and round like a turnip. Their flavour is essentially identical, and your choice should be governed by availability and its ultimate use. Parsnips are truly a winter vegetable and it is pointless buying parsnips before the first frost of the year, since they will lack the essential sweetness that distinguishes this vegetable. Good specimens should be robust, intact, with juicy flesh and not obviously woody, dried or limp in appearance. Unless they have been organically grown, they should be peeled before use.

NUTRIENT ANALYSIS
1 CUP PARSNIPS, BOILED (156g)

KCalories	126.36
Total Fat (g)	0.47
Monounsaturated Fat (g)	0.17
Polyunsaturated Fat (g)	0.07
Saturated Fat (g)	0.08
Carbohydrate (g)	30.47
Protein (g)	2.06
Crude Fibre (g)	3.43

Vitamin A (RE)	0.00
Ascorbic Acid (mg)	20.28
Thiamin (mg)	0.13
Riboflavin (mg)	0.08
Niacin (mg)	1.13
Pantothenic Acid (mg)	0.92
Vitamin B6 (mg)	0.15
Folacin (mcg)	90.79
Vitamin B12 (mcg)	0.00
Calcium (mg)	57.72
Iron (mg)	0.90
Zinc (mg)	0.41

Parsnip Patties

Serves 4
Preparation time 45 minutes

2 large parsnips (or 4 small ones), peeled and
 quartered
1 tbsp margarine
50g (2oz) plain flour
oil

Steam the parsnips until tender then turn into a bowl
and mash. Add the margarine and enough flour to
thicken the mash, mix well. Form into small patties,
heat the oil in a frying pan and fry the patties on both
sides until crisp and golden brown. Serve with a
selection of lightly-steamed green vegetables.

Quick and Gorgeous Parsnip Soup

Serves 4
Preparation time 45 minutes

3 medium parsnips, peeled and chopped
1 large onion, chopped
3 stalks celery, chopped
2 tbsp oil
2 tbsp flour
1l (2 pints) soya milk
½ tsp freshly ground black pepper
¼ tsp salt
juice of ½ lemon
2 tbsp fresh parsley, chopped

Prepare the parsnips, onion and celery. Heat the oil in
a saucepan and add these vegetables to it. Stir well and
sauté for 15 minutes over a medium heat. When the

vegetables are tender and golden, sprinkle the flour
over them, stir and gradually add the soya milk. Cook
until the liquid is hot, but not boiling, then put the
soup through a mouli or food processor and liquidize
to a smooth consistency. Return to the saucepan and
add the pepper and salt. Bring to a simmer; add a little
lemon juice at this stage to provide some sharpness.
The consistency of the soup may be adjusted by
adding vegetable stock or water. Leave to simmer
for 10 minutes then serve hot with parsley to garnish.

Parsnip Chips

Preparation time 35 minutes

Parsnips make much better chips than potatoes. A
traditional way of making them is as follows: clean the
parsnips, cut them from top to tail to make four
quarters and continue cutting until pencil thin
wedges have been produced, which can then be cut
into lengths of about 4cms (2 inches). Put these chips
into cold water in a saucepan and bring to the boil; boil
them for 7–10 minutes. Drain, then dry the chips in a
clean tea towel and dredge them in a little plain flour.
Heat fresh oil in a frying pan and shallow-fry the
parsnips in hot oil until golden brown. 'Serve piled up
on a hot dish; they should be crisp golden fingers, and
with baked autumn tomatoes and dripping toast make
a country supper in themselves'.[13]

Health Note

Nutritionally, one cup of boiled parsnips
provides about half the adult daily requirement
for folic acid, and one third of the vitamin C and
potassium requirements. Parsnips are used in
natural medicine to improve the bowel action,
as a diuretic, to relieve gout, colitis, insomnia,
diarrhoea, and for a generally detoxifying effect.

Peaches In 1226 AD (some authorities suggest 1216)
on 19th October King John Mackland died after
consuming a surfeit of peaches, thus graphically
attesting to their lusciously seductive properties.
The good king was, however, all of 48 years old –
a rather extraordinary life-span for the times – which
perhaps bears witness to their remarkable health
giving properties, too.

Thought to have originated in China, the peach was
originally small, sour, and hairy. Through careful selective breeding, over several thousand years, the sweetness

and size of the fruit has been greatly augmented, although the hairy nap still remains on most varieties. When Alexander the Great discovered the fruit growing in Persia in the 4th century BC, he introduced it to Greece (and thence to Rome), in the process giving it its modern name *Prunus Persica:* Persian plum tree.

There are many varieties of peach, but for the consumer, there are two basic and distinctive categories: the colour of the flesh (white or yellow); and whether the pit adheres to the flesh (Clingstone) or easily separates from it (Freestone). It is the received wisdom amongst many gourmets that the ripe peach is so sublime a food that further cooking or enhancement of its flavour is simply gilding the lily. This would certainly be true if most Western countries had ready access to tree-ripened fruit. Sadly, northerly climates do not allow the peach tree to excel, with the result that fruit has to be imported and therefore picked well before it is ripe. Consequently, there is everything to be said for developing a range of recipes which brings out all the best characteristics of this sensual fruit.

Peaches are generally available, and at their prime, between the months of June to September. The fruit should be intact, unbruised, and heavy for their size (this indicates a high water content, sapless peaches are most unpleasant). Small, hard peaches or those tinged with green should be avoided; they simply will not ripen satisfactorily (although they could, at a pinch, be used for highly cooked and spiced foodstuffs such as chutneys and jams). Ideally, the skin of the peach should be left on it when served, since much of the nutrition and volatile oils are contained in this layer. If this is not desired, the skin can be easily removed by immersing the peaches in water which has previously been brought to a boil and then removed from the heat for about 30 seconds. This will allow the skin to slide away effortlessly.

NUTRIENT ANALYSIS
1 PEACH (87g)

KCalories	37.41
Total Fat (g)	0.08
Monounsaturated Fat (g)	0.03
Polyunsaturated Fat (g)	0.04
Saturated Fat (g)	0.01
Carbohydrate (g)	9.66
Protein (g)	0.61

Crude Fibre (g)	0.56
Vitamin A (RE)	46.98
Ascorbic Acid (mg)	5.74
Thiamin (mg)	0.01
Riboflavin (mg)	0.04
Niacin (mg)	0.86
Pantothenic Acid (mg)	0.15
Vitamin B6 (mg)	0.02
Folacin (mcg)	2.96
Vitamin B12 (mcg)	0.00
Calcium (mg)	4.35
Iron (mg)	0.10
Zinc (mg)	0.12

Peach Whizz

Serves 4
Preparation time 1 hour 30 minutes

4 ripe peaches
570ml (1 pint) apple juice
½ tsp ground allspice
285ml (½ pint) plain soya yoghurt

Heat 570ml–1l (1–2 pints) of water in a saucepan and bring to a rapid boil. Use a slatted spoon to lower a peach into the boiling water; leave it there for 30 seconds then lift it out and slip off the skin. Repeat this procedure with each peach. Slice the peaches in half and remove their pips. Turn the peach halves into a food processor with the apple juice and purée to an even consistency. Pour this mixture into 4 large tumblers and put them in the freezer part of your refrigerator. Leave them for at least 1 hour, until the juice is mushy. Remove the tumblers from the freezer and sprinkle a little of the allspice over each serving. Spoon one-quarter of the yoghurt over each serving and stir the peach and yoghurt vigourously. Serve at once.

Peach Sauce

Makes approximately 570ml (1 pint)
Preparation time 30 minutes

4 ripe peaches, peeled (see above for method)
285ml (½ pint) orange juice (4–5 oranges)
2 tbsp cornstarch
¼ tsp ground nutmeg
50g (2oz) flaked almonds

Slice the peaches in half and remove their pips. Coarsely chop them and place in a blender with the orange juice. Purée to a smooth consistency then pour into a saucepan and place over a medium heat. Add the cornstarch and nutmeg. Cook, stirring constantly, until the sauce thickens. Add the almonds and heat them through. Remove from the heat and serve this sauce warm over pastries, cakes, pancakes, crêpes or fruit salads.

Peach Crumble

Serves 4–6
Preparation time 45 minutes

6–8 ripe peaches, peeled (see above for method)
1 tbsp cornflour
140ml (¼ pint) orange juice
170g (6oz) rolled oats
170g (6oz) brown sugar
100g (4oz) plain flour
1 tsp ground cinnamon
1 tbsp margarine

Preheat the oven to 180°C/350°F/Gas Mark 4. Halve the peaches and remove their pips. Slice the peach halves into four strips and lay them on the bottom of a baking dish. Mix the cornflour and juice together in a cup and pour over the peaches. Mix the oats, sugar, flour and cinnamon together and then work in the margarine to make a crumbly topping. Spread this mixture over the peaches and press lightly into place. Bake for 30 minutes, until the crumble is golden brown. Serve warm with Soya Creem or soya ice cream.

Health Note

Fresh peaches contain modest amounts of nutrients: one raw peach provides about a tenth of the adult daily requirement for vitamin C and lesser amounts of niacin and vitamin A. When dried, however, they become a concentrated stockpile of important nutrients: one cup yields two thirds of the daily adult iron requirement, one third of the niacin and vitamin A requirements, and one fifth of the riboflavin requirement. Peach leaves have been used by natural therapists to make a tea which is used to cleanse the kidneys.

Peanuts For several decades earlier in the 20th century, peanuts (also called groundnuts, gooba nuts or monkey nuts) seemed to be the unshakeable keystone around which the vegetarian diet was constructed. At the time, it must have seemed logical enough; the peanut contains at least as much protein as most types of meat, it is freely and cheaply available, and it does not demand any great culinary accomplishments to produce dishes which, at least superficially, bear a resemblance to their flesh-based cousins. It was at this period in the development of modern vegetarianism that such notorious and now clichéd foodstuffs as the nut roast were first produced. The peanut had its first heyday in that era; subsequently, it went on to find fame and fortune as a mass-market snack food.

In the 1960s, growing Western interest in all things oriental brought the soya bean to many people's attention for the first time; its infinitely greater culinary adaptability, and yet more impressive nutritional profile, were more than sufficient to topple the peanut from its position as the number one meat replacement. Whereas the peanut was always essentially a peanut, and recognized as such in every recipe, the soya bean could be processed into a form that was indistinguishable from meat. Furthermore, the soya bean came to the West with a culinary pedigree extending over many millenia; as a traditional ingredient in classical oriental cooking, its many forms, flavours and varieties utterly outshone the humble peanut. Today, the peanut occupies something of a fringe position in the vegetarian repertoire; most people are perhaps familiar with it only as a roasted snack, or else in the form of peanut butter. It will never again be seen as a direct meat replacement (products such as Realeat Vegeburger and Vegemince and the like have seen to that) yet it still has rather more to offer than perhaps most people are aware of.

How they compare: the peanut vs the soya bean

Nutrients in 100g of:	Soyabean (boiled)	Peanut (raw)
Calories (Kcal)	173	567
Protein (g)	16.64	25.8
Total fat (g)	8.97	49.24
Saturated fat (g)	1.297	6.834
Calcium (mg)	102	92
Iron (mg)	5.14	4.58

Many non-Western societies use peanuts in far more imaginative ways than we do. The cuisine of numerous tropical and semi-tropical countries use peanuts as the basis for a deliciously creamy, and often spicy, sauce which makes a fantastically adaptable crowning glory to an infinite range of cooked foods (see below); peanut curries are particularly tempting. A handful of peanuts makes an excellent and nutritious ingredient in many types of salad, as well.

See also: Shiro Wot (p311); Peanut Sauce (p313); Taushe (p315); Peanut Brittle (p316); Matooke and Peanut Sauce (p322); Gado Gado (p346)

NUTRIENT ANALYSIS
1oz PEANUTS, RAW (28g)

KCalories	158.76
Total Fat (g)	13.79
Monounsaturated Fat (g)	6.84
Polyunsaturated Fat (g)	4.36
Saturated Fat (g)	1.91
Carbohydrate (g)	4.52
Protein (g)	7.22
Crude Fibre (g)	1.36
Vitamin A (RE)	0.00
Ascorbic Acid (mg)	0.00
Thiamin (mg)	0.18
Riboflavin (mg)	0.04
Niacin (mg)	3.38
Pantothenic Acid (mg)	0.49
Vitamin B6 (mg)	0.10
Folacin (mcg)	67.14
Vitamin B12 (mcg)	0.00
Calcium (mg)	25.76
Iron (mg)	1.28
Zinc (mg)	0.92

Spicy Peanut Sauce

Makes approximately 570ml (1 pint)
Preparation time 30 minutes

1 tbsp oil

5 cloves garlic, finely chopped
1 large onion, finely chopped
1 tbsp fresh ginger, grated
1–2 fresh chillies, finely chopped
100g (4oz) chopped peanuts
140ml (¼ pint) peanut butter
570ml–1l (1–2 pints) vegetable stock or water
1 tsp chilli powder
1 tbsp soy sauce
juice of 1 lemon

Heat the oil in a saucepan over a medium heat and slowly sauté the garlic and onion until clear and tender, about 15 minutes. Add the ginger and chillies and stir for 2 minutes. Add the chopped peanuts and stir for 5 minutes. Stir the peanut butter into the sauté and, when it has melted a little, add half of the stock. Keep stirring as you bring the sauce to a low boil. The sauce will thicken and, at this stage, add the chilli powder and soy sauce. Add more stock to make a smooth, pourable sauce but one that is not too runny. Add the lemon juice when the sauce is ready, but keep it over the heat for a further 2–3 minutes while you stir the juice in. Remove from the heat and serve hot over steamed vegetables, vegetable-nut roasts or loaves, or rice dishes.

Health Note

Aflatoxins are poisonous alkaloids produced by a fungus, *aspergillus flavus*, which thrives in the warm conditions in which peanuts are frequently grown and stored. Aflatoxins are capable of causing acute liver damage, liver cirrhosis and liver cancer. In recent years, legislation has been introduced to try to prevent aflatoxin-contaminated foodstuffs from reaching the consumer, and reputable food manufacturers undertake their own careful checks to ensure the safety of the products they sell. There is little real reason to worry about the dose of aflatoxins ingested by vegetarians; but to be safe, any products with visible mould or dampness should be scrupulously rejected. Peanut oil is generally of very high quality, widely used in cooking and food processing, and is often considered to be nutritionally second only to olive oil, in as much as it has a similar essential fatty acid profile and is high in monounsaturates. Peanut butter is generally much higher in fat than raw peanuts, as significant amounts of other oils are often added during processing – 2 tbsp yield approximately 200 calories, and contain about one-fifth of the suggested daily adult intake of fat.

Pears 'You must sit up all night to eat a pear' is an old saying, reflecting not so much the arduous nature of the task nor the requirement for absolute privacy, but rather the very narrow interval between the time at which a pear is fully ripe and the rapid onset of spoilage and rot. Today, many consumers are sold grossly underripe pears, which in all probability will never achieve the optimum degree of maturity. This is an immense pity, because the sensuous glory of a lusciously melting ripe pear is quite unparalleled. Pears have, in fact, been appreciated for several thousand years, probably originating in Asia Minor and being enthusiastically cultivated by both Greeks and Romans (who discovered the considerable potential of dried pears, still one of the most versatile and tasty of all dried fruits today). There are perhaps 5000 to 8000 varieties of pear in the world, of which only a few dozen are actively cultivated. The most commonly encountered varieties are likely to be:

- Comice. Large, fat, with a pale yellow/green skin and a deliciously melting texture when ripe, very sweet and eminently suitable for consuming raw or in fruit salads.
- Williams. Called Bartlett in America and Australia. An early pear, dull green with a reddish tinge when ripe, sweet with a musky flavour and firm consistency, good for eating when ripe and will withstand cooking, preserving, etc.
- Conference. With a tough brown/green skin this winter variety tends to be long and thin and sometimes with a rather stringy texture. A useful addition to the winter diet when ripe, the flesh tends to disintegrate if not carefully cooked.
- Chinese/Asian Pears. A different species to the Western pear, and markedly inferior. A decidedly firm flesh with an often watery, underdeveloped taste, sometimes called sand pears for the gritty texture which can be decidedly unpleasant. Little reason to use these if other varieties are available.

Pears should be bought as near to their point of perfect ripeness as possible. To tell whether a pear is ripe or not, feel around the stalk end for a softening of the flesh, if it surrenders easily to your touch, then it is ready to buy and will be ready to eat within the next 24 hours.

NUTRIENT ANALYSIS
1 PEAR, FRESH (166g)

KCalories	97.94
Total Fat (g)	0.66
Monounsaturated Fat (g)	0.14
Polyunsaturated Fat (g)	0.16
Saturated Fat (g)	0.04
Carbohydrate (g)	25.08
Protein (g)	0.65
Crude Fibre (g)	2.32
Vitamin A (RE)	3.32
Ascorbic Acid (mg)	6.64
Thiamin (mg)	0.03
Riboflavin (mg)	0.07
Niacin (mg)	0.17
Pantothenic Acid (mg)	0.12
Vitamin B6 (mg)	0.03
Folacin (mcg)	12.12
Vitamin B12 (mcg)	0.00
Calcium (mg)	18.26
Iron (mg)	0.42
Zinc (mg)	0.20

Pears and Vine Leaves
Preparation time 12–24 hours

This old English recipe was recorded in the 16th century, and is probably much older. Take some vine leaves and line a large stewpot or saucepan with them, then cover them with peeled and halved pears, scattering a few cloves and a little sliced fresh ginger on top. Continue layering with vine leaves and pears until the pot is three-quarters full, cover with still cider, then place a weight on top of the final layer to ensure that the pears do not move around. Place over a low heat and stew for several hours – one version of the recipe suggests you do this all night – then turn off the heat and allow to cool. The pears will be soft and golden brown, ready to be served with a little sugar and Soya Creem.

Pickled Pears

Since hard, unripe pears are easier to obtain than those at the peak of ripeness, it is a good idea to have one or two recipes which can turn unpromising material into a culinary triumph. This recipe actually requires the pears to be quite hard, so that they do not disintegrate during cooking.
Makes approximately 4kg (8lb)
Preparation time 1 hour

1.5kg (3lbs) brown sugar
juice and grated rind of 1 lemon
285ml (½ pint) wine vinegar
25g (1oz) fresh ginger, bruised
1 tsp whole allspice
4kg (8lbs) hard pears, peeled, halved and deseeded

Place all the ingredients, except the pears, in a large enamel saucepan and bring to a rapid boil over a high heat. Boil for two minutes. Add the pears, cover the pan, and boil for 7–10 minutes longer, until the pears are tender. Spoon the pears into sterilized jars and pour a little of the juice over them. Seal the jars and allow to cool. These are an excellent companion to cold meals, curries or as a special starter or light dessert.

Simple Pear Salad

Serves 4
Preparation time 20 minutes

4 ripe, medium pears, peeled, quartered and cored, then diced
juice of 1 orange
grated peel of 1 orange
¼ tsp ground cloves
¼ tsp freshly ground black pepper
radiccio leaves
seeds of 2 pomegranates
50g (2oz) flaked almonds
2 tbsp wine vinegar
1 tbsp walnut oil

Turn the diced pears into a large salad bowl with the orange juice, peel, cloves and pepper; stir gently. Place a leaf or two of radiccio on each serving plate and arrange the diced pear onto them. Sprinkle some of the pomegranate seeds and almond flakes over each salad,

drizzle with a mixture of vinegar and walnut oil and serve.

Pear Butter

Makes 4l (8 pints)
Preparation time 3 hours

4kg (9lbs) pears, washed and roughly chopped
285ml (½ pint) water
2kg (4lbs) sugar
25g (1oz) fresh ginger, bruised
1 tsp freshly ground black pepper
1 tsp ground cloves
1 tsp ground cinnamon
140ml (¼ pint) cider vinegar

Turn the pears into a jam-making (or other very large) pan with the water and place over a medium heat. The pears may be any sort, ripe, unripe or overripe, as well as bruised or windfalls. Cook the pears until they completely lose their shape, stirring often and adjusting the heat to ensure they do not stick or burn. Press the cooked pears through a seive or mouli to remove the peel and seeds and return the smooth purée to the pan. Add the sugar and spices and bring to a low boil. Simmer gently for about 1 hour, stirring often. Add the vinegar and continue to cook for 15 minutes. Ladle the butter into sterilized jars, seal and leave to cool. This butter is an excellent, versatile sauce or spread.

Pears Cooked in Wine

Serves 4
Preparation time 45 minutes

140ml (¼ pint) water
225g (8oz) sugar
1l (2 pints) white wine
1x 7.5cm (3 inch) stick cinnamon
6 whole cloves
3 allspice pods
4–6 ripe pears, peeled but left whole
2 tbsp raspberry or blackcurrant syrup

Heat the water in a deep saucepan over a medium heat. When it is boiling add about half of the sugar and stir to dissolve. Then add more sugar alternately with the wine, stirring constantly, until the sugar is dissolved and all the wine is heated. Add the spices and bring the liquid to a low boil. Adjust the heat and simmer for about 15 minutes, until the liquid thickens and reduces. Place the pears upright in the pan and continue cooking for 12–15 minutes. They should become tender but not disintegrating. Remove the pears and place on a plate to cool; stir the raspberry or blackcurrant syrup into the hot wine sauce and leave to cool also. When the pears are tepid, you may, if you wish, return them to the sauce so that they take on some of its colour and flavour. Serve the pears cool with a spoonful of sauce and a garnish of fresh mint or orange leaf.

Health Note

Fresh pears have been used in natural medicine to alleviate constipation, treat high blood pressure and combat obesity. Both fresh and stewed pears (using little or no sugar) are amongst the foodstuffs which are least likely to provoke reactions of allergy or intolerance, and are therefore used on elimination diets. They have also been found to be beneficial for skin complaints, colitis and kidney disorders. One average-sized fresh pear contains only 10 per cent of the daily requirement of vitamin C for an adult; but when it is dried, its nutritional profile rockets. One cup of dried pears contains one fifth of the daily vitamin C and riboflavin requirements, and over a third of the iron requirements.

Peas The old saying that 'familiarity breeds contempt' is certainly true for the humble garden pea, which from prehistoric times has been one of humanity's most important and most nutritious of vegetables. Today, only the French continue to do culinary justice to this cheap, adaptable and absolutely dependable leguminous plant – which is all too often served as an afterthought, a garnish, or an accompaniment to far more expensive, and infinitely less healthy food. This was not always so; the gluttonous King William III so monopolized fresh peas whenever they appeared on the royal table as to assure his place as a 'peahog' in the history books. At the French court, Madame de Maintenon enthused thus about the pea at the beginning of the 18th century: 'The anticipation of eating them, the pleasure of having eaten them, and the joy of eating them again are the three subjects that our princes have been discussing for four days . . . It has become a fashion – indeed, a passion.'

Fresh green peas were a luxury for the few until comparatively recently; dried peas were not quite such an elegant foodstuff, although certainly every bit as important in times of winter famine. Today, peas are one of the few foods which, when frozen, are perhaps even better than the commonly obtained fresh variety. This is because the sugar contained within the pea quickly turns to starch after picking, making most of the sweetness disappear to be replaced by an unpleasant bitterness. Canned or bottled peas are also widely available and very cheap, but should be considered a second choice to frozen peas because of the additional processing involved, and the likely addition of various colourings and flavourings.

The sweetest and most flavoursome peas are undoubtedly the French *petit pois*, which are picked unripe to ensure maximum sweetness. Another enticing French innovation is the mangetout (also called snow pea or sugar pea) a variety of pea which is eaten whole, pods and all. These must be chosen young, and on no account should be overcooked to interfere with their crisp, fresh taste. Mangetout are an excellent ingredient in Chinese meals and stir-fries. The dried pea has fallen so much out of fashion that it is unobtainable in some places. Nevertheless, it is as useful now as it was hundreds of years ago, and is the basis for several excellent hearty soups and stews.

See also: Rupiza (p324); Simple Rice and Peas (p335)

NUTRIENT ANALYSIS
1 CUP PEAS (144g)

KCalories	116.64
Total Fat (g)	0.58
Monounsaturated Fat (g)	0.05
Polyunsaturated Fat (g)	0.27
Saturated Fat (g)	0.10
Carbohydrate (g)	20.82
Protein (g)	7.80
Crude Fibre (g)	3.18
Vitamin A (RE)	92.16
Ascorbic Acid (mg)	57.60
Thiamin (mg)	0.38
Riboflavin (mg)	0.19
Niacin (mg)	3.01
Pantothenic Acid (mg)	0.15

Vitamin B6 (mg)	0.24
Folacin (mcg)	93.60
Vitamin B12 (mcg)	0.00
Calcium (mg)	36.00
Iron (mg)	2.12
Zinc (mg)	1.79

Peapod Broth

If you manage to find fresh peas which are young and very recently harvested, it is a shame to throw away over half the food you have paid for. Peapods can themselves make an extremely fine soup, although to do so, you must ensure that they are free of chemicals (in other words, buy from a known organic source). Wash the pods thoroughly, place them in a pan with just enough water to cover them, cover the pan and boil them for an hour. Drain off the liquid, pressing it out of the pods, which should then be discarded. You now have a beautifully fresh-tasting stock for an unusual and nutritious soup.

Boneless Pea Soup

Serves 4
Preparation time 1 hour

1 tbsp oil
3 cloves garlic, finely chopped
1 medium onion, chopped
1 tsp freshly ground black pepper
2 tsp yeast extract
225g (8oz) split green peas, washed and drained
1l (2 pints) vegetable stock
1 bunch fresh coriander, chopped
½ tsp freshly ground black pepper (optional)

Heat the oil in a large saucepan over a medium heat and sauté the garlic and onion until clear and tender. Add the pepper and stir for 1 minute. Add the yeast extract and stir to dissolve then add the peas and vegetable stock. Bring the soup to the boil, stir well and remove any froth. Cover the pan, reduce the heat and leave to simmer for about 45 minutes. The peas should lose their form entirely. Taste the soup then add the coriander and pepper, if desired, and cook for a further 5 minutes. Serve hot with a garnish of coriander leaf, soya bacon-bits or 2 or 3 fresh peas.

Easy Peasy Overnight Salad

Serves 4
Preparation time 35 minutes, plus overnight marinade

225g (8oz) fresh garden peas, washed and drained
5 stalks celery, thinly sliced
1 large sweet red or yellow pepper, sliced
3–5 spring onions, chopped
50g (2oz) pimento, finely chopped
285g (10oz) plain tofu, cubed
140ml (¼ pint) oil
140ml (¼ pint) cider vinegar
1 tbsp sugar
1 tsp freshly ground black pepper
1 tsp paprika

Mix the vegetables in a large bowl. Place the tofu chunks in a glass bowl or oven dish. Blend the oil, vinegar, sugar and spices in a small saucepan and bring to the boil. Remove from the heat and pour over the mixed vegetables. Stir well for 2–3 minutes then turn the whole mixture into the dish with the tofu. Spread the salad to the edges and leave to cool. Cover the dish and leave to marinate, in the refrigerator if possible, for several hours or overnight. Serve cool as a meal in itself or over baked potatoes.

Spiced Rice and Split Peas

Serves 4
Preparation time 1 hour

100g (4oz) dried green or yellow split peas
225g (8oz) brown rice
1 tbsp oil
1 tsp cumin seeds
3 cloves garlic, finely chopped
1 medium onion, chopped
1 tsp turmeric
½ tsp ground cumin
1 tsp ground coriander
½ tsp cayenne
1 tbsp fresh mint, chopped
2 tbsp fresh parsley, chopped
½–1 tsp salt

Wash and drain the peas; place them in a saucepan and just cover with fresh water. Cover the pan and place on a medium heat. When the peas boil, skim any froth from the surface, cover the pan again and reduce the heat. Simmer for 45 minutes, until the peas have lost their form. Wash and drain the rice; turn into a saucepan and cover with just under twice its volume of fresh water. Cover the pan, place on a medium heat and bring to the boil. Reduce the heat and leave to simmer for about 40 minutes, until the rice is tender and the liquid absorbed. Meanwhile, heat the oil in a frying pan and sauté the cumin seeds for 3 minutes, stirring constantly. Add the garlic and onion and continue to sauté, over a low heat, for 15 minutes. Stir occasionally. Add the remaining spices and stir for 1 minute. Remove the sauté from the heat and stir it into the simmering rice. Do this quickly, then cover the cooking rice again and leave it to finish. Stir the chopped mint, parsley and the salt into the cooking peas at this stage (they are nearly finished) and leave them to finish cooking. Serve the rice in a large soup bowl with a ladleful of peas poured over. Serve hot.

Peas and Potato Bhaji

Serves 4
Preparation time 55 minutes

3 tbsp oil
5 cloves garlic, chopped
1 large onion, chopped
5 whole cloves
1x7.5cm(3 inch) piece cinnamon
3 tbsp fresh ginger, grated
½ tsp ground coriander
½–1 tsp chilli powder
1 tsp turmeric
2 large potatoes, peeled and cubed
1 medium courgette, diced
450g (1lb) fresh or frozen peas
285ml (½ pint) vegetable stock or water
1 tbsp garam masala (see page 344)

Heat the oil in a large saucepan and sauté the garlic and onion over a medium heat 5–10 minutes until clear and tender. Add the cloves, cinnamon and ginger and stir for 2 minutes. Add the coriander, chilli and turmeric and stir for 1 minute. Add the potatoes and courgette, stir well and cover the pan. Leave the mixture to cook over a medium heat for 7–10 minutes, stirring once in that time. Add the peas and stock, stir well and bring the liquid to a boil. Cover the pan, reduce the heat and cook until the potatoes are tender and the stock thickened, about 15 minutes. When the potatoes are cooked, stir in the garam masala, cover the pan and remove from the heat. Leave it to stand 5 minutes before serving over steamed rice.

Tofu and Mangetout Stir-Fry

Serves 4
Preparation time 30 minutes

1 tbsp oil
3 cloves garlic, chopped

1 large onion, thinly sliced
1 bay leaf
1x7.5cm(3 inch) piece stick cinnamon
½ tsp freshly ground black pepper
1 tbsp fresh ginger, grated
3 medium carrots, scrubbed or peeled and chopped
4 tbsp soy sauce
1 tbsp kuzu (arrowroot)
4 tbsp cold water
285ml (½ pint) vegetable stock
285g (10oz) firm plain tofu, sliced
450g (1lb) mangetout, washed and trimmed

Heat the oil in a wok or large frying pan over a medium heat. sauté the garlic and onion for 5 minutes. Add the bay leaf, cinnamon, pepper and ginger and stir for 2–3 minutes. Add the carrots, stir well and cover the pan. After 2 minutes, reduce the heat and leave to cook for 5 minutes. Stir again and pour in the soy sauce and the kuzu dissolved in cold water. Stir well. Add the vegetable stock and bring the sauce to the boil. Arrange the tofu then the mangetout over the sauce, cover the pan and reduce the heat. Leave to cook for 5–7 minutes. Serve hot over rice.

Risotto

Serves 4
Preparation time 45 minutes

2l (4 pints) vegetable stock
100g (4oz) margarine
1 small onion, thinly sliced
225g (8oz) mushrooms, trimmed and quartered
450g (1lb) short grain white rice
½ tsp salt
1 tsp freshly ground black pepper
450g (1lb) fresh peas
1 tbsp fresh parsley, chopped
225g (8oz) cheddar-style soya cheese, grated
1 tbsp margarine

Bring the stock to a boil and keep it simmering. Melt the margarine in a large saucepan over medium heat and sauté the onion until clear and tender. Add the mushrooms and sauté for 5–7 minutes, stirring often. Add the rice to the sauté and stir until each grain is well coated. When the rice begins to glisten, start adding the hot stock a ladleful at a time. Allow the first ladleful to be absorbed before adding the next, but do not let the rice dry out. Ten minutes after the rice is added, sprinkle in the salt and pepper and add the peas; stir well. Continue adding the hot stock and continue stirring. When the rice is almost done (about 25 minutes), add the parsley and soya cheese. Leave the risotto to cook for a further 5 minutes then remove from the heat, dab the surface with the margarine and cover the pan while you get the serving dish. Turn onto warmed plates or serving dish and serve immediately.

Health Note

A cup of cooked peas provides half the adult daily requirement for folic acid, and approximately one-third the requirement for vitamin C, thiamin, and iron. They also contain useful amounts of riboflavin, niacin, vitamin B6, vitamin A, zinc and protein. One cup of cooked dried peas (split peas) provides the same amount of folic acid, and one-quarter of the daily adult requirement of protein, thiamin and iron. Fresh peas have a naturally diuretic action, and have been used, puréed, to give relief from stomach ulcers.

Pecans Widely popular in North America, and increasingly available elsewhere, the pecan nut is a close relative of the hickory nut, which in turn are related to walnuts. Everything about the pecan is smoother than a walnut – the shell has a polished, lustrous appearance, the nut itself is streamlined and uniform, even the flavour is less rugged. Most pecans are imported from the United States, and therefore tend to be more expensive than the more locally grown walnuts. Other than this, the main difference between the two nuts is one of taste and texture. The pecan generally seems more oily and bland, while the greater amount of tannin often present in the walnut gives it far greater astringency which can sometimes dry the mouth. Pecans are probably the nuts of choice for inclusion in salads, stuffings and cooked nut dishes; walnuts are preferable where an absolutely distinct flavour is required, for example, in sweets and desserts, patisserie, and for pickling.
See also: Shoo-Fly Pie (p327)

NUTRIENT ANALYSIS
1oz PECANS, DRIED (25g)

KCalories	189.43
Total Fat (g)	19.21
Monounsaturated Fat (g)	11.97
Polyunsaturated Fat (g)	4.76
Saturated Fat (g)	1.54
Carbohydrate (g)	5.18
Protein (g)	2.20
Crude Fibre (g)	0.45
Vitamin A (RE)	3.69
Ascorbic Acid (mg)	0.57
Thiamin (mg)	0.24
Riboflavin (mg)	0.04
Niacin (mg)	0.25
Pantothenic Acid (mg)	0.48
Vitamin B6 (mg)	0.05
Folacin (mcg)	11.13
Vitamin B12 (mcg)	0.00
Calcium (mg)	10.22
Iron (mg)	0.60
Zinc (mg)	1.55

Pecan Pie

Makes 1 large pie, approximately 30cm (12 inches)
Preparation time 45 minutes

For the crust:
170g (6oz) plain flour
100g (4oz) shredded vegetable suet
1 tbsp cold water

For the filling:
100g (4oz) sugar
170g (6oz) barley malt syrup
1 tbsp molasses
2 tbsp oil
1 tsp vanilla essense
1 ½ tsp baking powder
225g (8oz) shelled pecans, chopped
100g (4oz) dried dates, finely chopped

Preheat the oven to 200°C/400°F/Gas Mark 6. Mix

the flour and suet together in a bowl and quickly work in the cold water to make a crumbly texture. Turn the mixture into a large pie dish and press it into place, ensuring the pastry reaches right up the sides of the dish. Chill the pie base, if possible.

Use a hand blender or wire whisk to whisk the sugar, syrup, molasses, oil and vanilla, adding as much air as possible to the mixture. Add the baking powder and whisk again, briefly, then quickly stir in the pecans and dates. Turn this mixture into the pie shell and bake for 15 minutes in the hot oven. Reduce the heat to 180°C/ 350°F/Gas Mark 4 and bake for a further 20 minutes. Leave to cool on a wire rack and serve warm or cold with lashings of Soya Creem.

Pecan & Potato Roast

Serves 4
Preparation time 1 hour 30 minutes

2 large, white potatoes, grated (if organic, don't peel them)
2 medium onions, finely chopped
100g (4oz) dry breadcrumbs
100g (4oz) pecans, chopped
1 tsp dried thyme
½ tsp dried sage
½ tsp freshly ground black pepper
2 tbsp tahini
2 tbsp soy sauce

Preheat the oven to 180°C/350°F/Gas Mark 4 and lightly oil a large loaf tin. Mix the potatoes and onions together in a mixing bowl. Mix the breadcrumbs, pecans and herbs and stir into the potato-onion mixture. Blend the tahini and soy sauce in a small bowl and stir into the potato and pecan mixture. Ensure the mixture is well blended, press into the loaf tin and bake for 1 hour. Slice and serve hot with a selection of vegetable side dishes. Any left-overs can be sliced (this stays firm when cold) and served in sandwiches or to accompany salads.

Peppers The capsicum family provides us with two broad categories of peppers: sweet, used as a vegetable; and chilli, used as a fiery flavouring. Native to North America, peppers were introduced to Europe in the late 15th century by Christopher Columbus and are now firmly established as household vegetables. Sweet peppers are generally either green (unripe) or red (ripe); although other varieties are sometimes encountered, notably yellow, orange and near black.

Green peppers are sometimes referred to as bell peppers, red ones as pimentos. They are intensively cultivated and widely available all year round. Peppers which have anything other than a glossy, taut appearance to their skins are not fresh and should be rejected. The stalk end is usually cut off and the peppers deseeded before use.

One of the most common, but least imaginative, uses to which peppers are put in vegetarian cookery is to be stuffed with rice or other fillings and baked. This is, in fact, such an easy dish (with countless variations) that it has become a routine entry on the vegetarian menus of many airlines, and other institutional caterers. While generally acceptable, stuffed peppers are rarely a great food; their density makes it difficult for the cooking heat to be distributed uniformly, and the intimidating bulk of an entire pepper – often with the stalk replaced to serve as a lid – can be offputting to all but the most famished. There are, indeed, better uses for peppers of all colours. They can, for example, have their skins quickly charred and removed; the resulting vegetable has more flavour and is a most attractive ingredient when chopped into salads. They are excellent marinated, and are also essential ingredients in several classical Mediterranean dishes, such as Gazpacho and Ratatouille (see pages 356 and 179). Sliced into bite sized chunks, they are superlative in vegetarian kebabs, a magical secret ingredient in basic tomato sauce for pasta (see below), and are excellent when used in relishes or pickles.

See also: Mechouia (p320); Pickled Fiery Peppers (p332); Sweet Pepper Curry (p343); Peppered Aubergine (p348)

NUTRIENT ANALYSIS
1 PEPPER, FRESH (74g)

KCalories	19.98
Total Fat (g)	0.14
Monounsaturated Fat (g)	0.01
Polyunsaturated Fat (g)	0.08
Saturated Fat (g)	0.02
Carbohydrate (g)	4.76
Protein (g)	0.66
Crude Fibre (g)	0.33
Vitamin A (RE)	46.62

Ascorbic Acid (mg)	66.08
Thiamin (mg)	0.05
Riboflavin (mg)	0.02
Niacin (mg)	0.38
Pantothenic Acid (mg)	0.06
Vitamin B6 (mg)	0.18
Folacin (mcg)	16.28
Vitamin B12 (mcg)	0.00
Calcium (mg)	6.66
Iron (mg)	0.34
Zinc (mg)	0.09

Cold Pepper Pasta

Serves 4
Preparation time 30 minutes

450g (1lb) three-colour pasta (shells, bows or spirals)
2 large sweet red peppers, sliced
1 large sweet green pepper, sliced
1 large sweet yellow pepper, sliced
2 tbsp fresh parsley, chopped
1 tbsp fresh coriander, chopped
3 medium tomatoes, chopped
285g (10oz) firm, plain tofu, cubed
225g (8oz) olives, pitted and sliced

For the dressing:
5 tbsp cider vinegar
5 tbsp olive oil,
1 tbsp tahini
1 tsp prepared mustard
1 tsp salt
½ tsp freshly ground black pepper
½ tsp dried oregano

Cook the pasta in plenty of boiling water until tender. Drain, rinse in cold water and leave to drain. Mix the peppers, herbs, tomatoes, tofu and olives together in a bowl. Add the cooled pasta and stir into the salad ingredients. Blend the dressing ingredients together in a jug and pour over the salad. Serve immediately or chill and serve.

Hidden Pepper Tomato Sauce

Serves 4
Preparation time 45 minutes

2 medium sweet green peppers, deseeded and coarsely chopped
2x 400g (14oz) tins chopped tomatoes
1 tbsp oil
5 cloves garlic, finely chopped
1 large onion, finely chopped
1 tsp freshly ground black pepper
200g (7oz) tomato purée
140ml (¼ pint) vegetable stock
1 tbsp soy sauce
4 tbsp fresh parsley, chopped
2 tbsp fresh basil, chopped
1 tsp dried oregano
1 tsp brown sugar
1 tsp cider vinegar

Purée the chopped peppers and one tin of chopped tomatoes in a food processor so that the peppers are thoroughly blended. Heat the oil in a large saucepan over a medium heat and sauté the garlic and onion until clear and tender. Add the black pepper and stir for 1 minute. Add the blended mixture, the remaining tin of chopped tomatoes, the tomato purée, vegetable stock and soy sauce. Stir well and bring to a low boil. Stir in the herbs, cover the pan, reduce the heat and simmer gently for 20 minutes. Add the brown sugar and vinegar, stir well and leave a final 5 minutes. Serve hot over pasta. This sauce benefits from standing 1–4 hours. Leave it covered and then reheat.

Health Note

Peppers are a hugely rich natural source of vitamin C – a cup of chopped, raw green peppers provides about one and a half times the adult daily requirement! Beyond this, green peppers contain a substance – as yet unidentified – which can counteract the effect of nitrosamines, a group of potent cancer-causing chemicals formed in the saliva and gastrointestinal tract from the combinations of nitrates and amines found in certain foods.

Pineapple Originating in the lowlands of Brazil, this tropical plant quickly spread to the West Indies, where it was discovered by Columbus and, after arousing intense interest in Europe, was propagated in European hothouses in the 17th century. Several varieties are now available in Western markets:

● Sugar Loaf. Large and mild flavoured, with pale flesh.

- Queen. The smallest of the standard sized pineapples, with a mellow flavour and intensely yellow flesh.
- Cayenne. Medium sized, tastes both sweet and sharp, yellow flesh.
- Miniature. Baby pineapples make attractive table decorations and can be halved and the skins used to contain various pineapple/liqueur fruit salads, sorbets or other dessert creations.

Buying an absolutely ripe pineapple is not always easy. Unlike many other fruits, it does not continue to ripen after picking (most of the fruit sugar is stored in the stem and only enters the pineapple during the final ripening process). A ripe pineapple will generally have a distinctive dark orange/yellow colour, should be pleasantly fragrant, and will feel heavy in proportion to its size. Another indicator of ripeness is the ease by which the innermost spikes of the sharp-leafed tuft can be detached from the top of the fruit. Ripe pineapple should be used immediately, because it will deteriorate if stored in the refrigerator. A mistake is often made preparing a pineapple by slicing it into rings from top to bottom. This makes the preparation process unnecessarily difficult; both the outer skin and the inner woody core (both inedible) are thus rendered difficult to remove. Additionally, the sweetest part of the pineapple lies at its base, and those people being served from the top will therefore receive a far more acidic fruit than those eating lower down. Much better to cut the pineapple lengthways instead.

NUTRIENT ANALYSIS
1 SLICE PINEAPPLE, FRESH (84g)

KCalories	41.16
Total Fat (g)	0.36
Monounsaturated Fat (g)	0.04
Polyunsaturated Fat (g)	0.12
Saturated Fat (g)	0.03
Carbohydrate (g)	10.41
Protein (g)	0.33
Crude Fibre (g)	0.45
Vitamin A (RE)	1.68
Ascorbic Acid (mg)	12.94
Thiamin (mg)	0.08

Riboflavin (mg)	0.03
Niacin (mg)	0.35
Pantothenic Acid (mg)	0.13
Vitamin B6 (mg)	0.07
Folacin (mcg)	8.90
Vitamin B12 (mcg)	0.00
Calcium (mg)	5.88
Iron (mg)	0.31
Zinc (mg)	0.07

Creamy Pineapple Coleslaw
Serves 4
Preparation time 45 minutes, plus chilling time

285g (10oz) plain tofu
170ml (6 floz) soya milk
4 tbsp olive oil
3 tbsp prepared mustard
5–6 gherkins, very finely chopped
1 fresh chilli, finely chopped
2 tbsp lemon juice
½ tsp salt
1 medium white cabbage, finely shredded
½ large ripe pineapple, cored, peeled and cubed (about 600ml/1 pint)
3 spring onions, finely chopped (optional)

Blend the tofu, soya milk and oil with a whisk or in a food processor. Turn into a mixing bowl and add the mustard, gherkins, chilli, lemon juice, and salt. Stir well. Add the cabbage, pineapple and onions, if desired, and stir well. Chill the salad before serving.

Pineapple Relish
Makes approximately 570ml (1 pint)
Preparation time 2 hours

½ medium pineapple, peeled, cored and chopped
1 × 285g (10oz) tin sweetcorn, drained
1 small sweet red pepper, chopped
3 spring onions, finely sliced
1 fresh chilli, finely chopped
1 tbsp fresh ginger, grated
juice of 2 limes
⅛ teaspoon salt

Measure the pineapple and sweetcorn into a mouli and turn it through a coarse setting. Make sure all the juices are retained and mix them with the pineapple, corn and the remaining ingredients in a large bowl. Cover and let stand at least 1 hour before serving with a garnish of fresh, chopped coriander; or spoon into a sterilized jar and seal for keeping.

Health Note

Like the papaya, the pineapple contains a powerful enzyme (in this case, bromelain) – so destructive that plantation and cannery workers must wear protective clothing to avoid their skins being eaten away. The presence of this enzyme has given rise to a number of unsubstantiated claims concerning the slimming and reducing properties of this fruit, in the vain hope that it can make superfluous flesh 'melt away'. Bromelain does, however, have some medically-useful properties: it can retard tumour growth; decrease blood coagulation; act as an anti-inflammatory agent; cleanse third-degree burns; and enhance the absorption of drugs. It is destroyed by heating, and is therefore not present in processed pineapple juice or canned pineapple (although fresh pineapple may very infrequently cause an anaphylactoid reaction). Practitioners of natural medicine use the pineapple to regulate the glandular processes, to treat bronchitis and catarrh, and to relieve the pain of arthritis. One cup of raw pineapple chunks contains about half the adult requirement for vitamin C.

Pistachios This seed is frequently encountered as an ingredient in and a garnish for Middle Eastern sweets and other delicacies. The pistachio originated from this part of the world, before spreading to Asia, and most pistachios today come from Iran, Turkey, Greece, Syria and Italy. The greenish coloured seed is usually eaten roasted and salted. When buying pistachios, avoid nuts that are not sold in their shells – in all probability, they will be unpleasantly soft, lack their characteristic flavour, and may even be rather musty. Certainly, it is always best to purchase nuts or seeds while still in their shells as the fats they contain so quickly go rancid.
See also: Phyllo (p348); Baklava (p349); Jallabis (p342); Carrot Halva (p346); Sfihan (p348)

NUTRIENT ANALYSIS
1oz PISTACHIOS, DRIED (28g)

KCalories	163.87
Total Fat (g)	13.74
Monounsaturated Fat (g)	9.28
Polyunsaturated Fat (g)	2.08
Saturated Fat (g)	1.74
Carbohydrate (g)	7.05
Protein (g)	5.84
Crude Fibre (g)	0.53
Vitamin A (RE)	6.53
Ascorbic Acid (mg)	2.04
Thiamin (mg)	0.23
Riboflavin (mg)	0.05
Niacin (mg)	0.31
Pantothenic Acid (mg)	0.34
Vitamin B6 (mg)	0.07
Folacin (mcg)	16.47
Vitamin B12 (mcg)	0.00
Calcium (mg)	38.34
Iron (mg)	1.93
Zinc (mg)	0.38

Health Note

One ounce of pistachio nuts yields about 160 calories and provides approximately 15 per cent of the suggested adult daily fat intake; the same quantity supplies one fifth of the thiamin, iron and potassium recommended daily intakes.

Plaintain The *other* kind of banana, plantain is neither so sweet nor quite so visually appealing as its sweet, yellow relation: the skin of the plantain is green, its flesh rather pink. African, Caribbean and Creole cuisines all use the plantain and many regions rely upon it as a staple food. A quick dish, popular in the Caribbean, is Green Banana Chips. Peel the plantains and slice them in half and then into thin chips. Wash the chips and gently dry them with a clean tea towel. Heat some oil in a frying pan and shallow fry the plantain chips until tender and lightly browned. Drain on a paper kitchen towel and serve hot with salt and pepper or a favourite sauce.

See also: Tatali (p312); Fu Fu (p315); Matooke and Peanut Sauce (p322); La Daub (p321); Plantain Pudding (p335)

Plums The variety of plums available today are thought to have had their origin in Western Asia, in the region south of the Caucasus mountains to the Caspian Sea. Many societies and cultures have esteemed, cherished and developed these sumptuous fruits; indeed, judging by the evidence of our own culture's singular lack of appreciation for the *prunus* family, we are in an irrecoverable terminal decline. There is a variety of plum to suit almost every palate, ranging from the sour to the honey sweet, from the saffron blonde to the mystical mauve. Some of those more frequently available are:

- Bullace. The ancestor of many more modern varieties, archaeological evidence shows that the Bullace was enjoyed and appreciated by our prehistoric forebears. More often seen growing wild than in the greengrocer's, it is best gathered just after the first frosts have struck, thus reducing its acidity and somewhat increasing its sugar content. It generally has a greenish red colour, and is slightly smaller than a golf ball. Best used for jams, preserves, pies and puddings.
- Damson. One of the most flavoursome of all plums, although somewhat out of favour in today's fast food culture because its tartness requires that it should be cooked with a sweetening agent before consumption. It makes an exquisite jam, is excellent stewed with a dash of cinnamon, and works exceedingly well in fruit crumbles and pies. The doyenne of English country winemakers, Mary Aylett, provides us with the following time-honoured recipe for damson wine: 'Put 8lbs of damsons into a crock, bruise them with a mallet or wooden spoon, and pour onto them 1 gallon of boiling water. Let all stand together for 48 hours, then strain the liquor on to 2½ pounds of sugar. Put into a cask and stand it in a warm place until the spontaneous ferment ceases, then top up the cask with a little boiled damson juice and sugar, and bung down closely. Bottle in 10 months time and drink within the year. If a dry wine is wanted keep for another year.'[14]

- Greengage. A multi-purpose fruit, equally good for eating fresh, cooking or preserving. It is small, round, with a greenish-yellow hue which is often erroneously considered to be an indication of underripeness.
- Mirabelle. More common in France than Britain, it is small, golden-yellow and when ripe has a perfectly balanced combination of sweet and sharp flavours. It is more exquisitely perfumed than any other plant, and is occasionally turned into a very fine liqueur.
- Sloe. Far too bitter to eat raw, these smallest examples of the plum family are renowned for the flavouring they impart to gin, and also for making excellent jam.
- Victoria. Large, sweet and juicy it is probably the most widely available dessert plum. If additional sweetness is needed, they can be halved, the pits removed, sprinkled with brown sugar and left for a half hour or so until they have produced a naturally sweet juice, in which they can be served.
- Santa Rosa. An American dessert plum which lacks the depth of flavour of the greengage or victoria, but which nevertheless is finding increasing popularity in export markets. The flesh is pinkish-yellow and the taste veers towards the tart, although it is often not sold at the peak of its ripeness, resulting in a generally flabby texture.

Plums should be purchased as close to their optimum point of ripeness as possible, and consumed immediately; otherwise they will spoil very quickly.

NUTRIENT ANALYSIS
1 CUP PLUMS, FRESH (165g)

KCalories	90.75
Total Fat (g)	1.02
Monounsaturated Fat (g)	0.67
Polyunsaturated Fat (g)	0.22
Saturated Fat (g)	0.08
Carbohydrate (g)	21.47
Protein (g)	1.30
Crude Fibre (g)	0.99
Vitamin A (RE)	52.80
Ascorbic Acid (mg)	15.68
Thiamin (mg)	0.07

Riboflavin (mg)	0.16
Niacin (mg)	0.83
Pantothenic Acid (mg)	0.30
Vitamin B6 (mg)	0.13
Folacin (mcg)	3.63
Vitamin B12 (mcg)	0.00
Calcium (mg)	6.60
Iron (mg)	0.17
Zinc (mg)	0.17

Health Note

Dried plums (prunes) are a concentrated source of nutrition: one cup of cooked prunes provides about a quarter of the adult daily requirement for vitamin B6 and iron. Additionally, they are an abundant source of the trace mineral boron, which plays a key role in calcium absorption. Boron helps the body synthesize both oestrogen and vitamin D, and thus reduces the rate at which calcium and magnesium is lost – a vital function in the prevention of osteoporosis.

Chunky Plum and Chilli Casserole

Serves 4–6
Preparation time 1 hour 15 minute, plus time to marinate

225g (8oz) TVP chunks
420ml (¾ pint) apple juice
420ml (¾ pint) vinegar
140ml (¼ pint) oil
2 tbsp soy sauce
1 tsp freshly ground black pepper
1 tsp ground cloves
1 tsp chilli powder
100g (4oz) plain flour
450g (1lb) plum jam
200g (7oz) tomato paste

Empty the TVP chunks into a deep bowl. Mix the apple juice, vinegar, oil, soy sauce and spices together and pour over the TVP chunks. Leave them to marinate for 4–12 hours, or overnight. Preheat the oven to 170°C/325°F/Gas Mark 3. Drain the TVP chunks but save the marinade. Turn the TVP chunks into a large casserole dish and sprinkle the flour over them. Gently turn the chunks in the flour for 2–3 minutes, to coat them. Mix the marinade with the plum jam and tomato purée. Blend well, adding more apple juice or vinegar to make the thickness of sauce you desire. (It should be slightly thick, but pourable.) Pour over the TVP in the casserole and bake for 1 hour. Serve hot with roast or steamed potatoes and greens. Garnish the dish with 2 or 3 plum halves if you like.

Easy Plum Sauce

Makes approximately 1l (2 pints)
Preparation time 1 hour

1kg (2lbs) fresh, tart plums, washed
570ml (1 pint) wine vinegar
1 tsp ground allspice
3 tbsp sugar
1 tbsp fresh mint, finely chopped

Turn the plums into a large saucepan and pour the vinegar over. Place over a medium heat and bring the vinegar to a boil. Add the allspice. Reduce the heat and simmer for 30 minutes, mashing and stirring often. Push the cooked plums through a sieve or mouli to remove the pips and skins. Return the pulp to the pan, add the sugar and fresh mint and simmer a further 10 minutes. Pour into sterilized jars and seal, or serve some immediately with sautéed tempeh, Tofu Steaks (p275) or Risotto (p266).

Health Note

Pickled plums (*ume* – available in health food shops as umeboshi) have been recognized as a powerful medicine in Asia for thousands of years. Repeatedly pickled and exposed to the sun for over a year, the result is a deeply savoury plum which richly complements any rice dish. Therapeutically, umeboshi plums possess a broad spectrum of active constituents, most of which are only now beginning to be examined by Western medicine. Umeboshi can be used to treat and prevent nausea, to dispel fatigue, to neutralize excess acid and to regularize both diarrhoea and constipation. They also have antibiotic properties, and can be used to combat a great many infections – in Japan, they have been used against plague, cholera and typhus.

Pomegranates One of the most beautiful of all fruits, the pomegranate's visual splendour and unsurpassed flavour has been celebrated for thousands of years. For the Israelites, the much-bemoaned absence of 'figs, vines and pomegranates' in the desert was yet another burden poor Moses had to endure. In the 'Song of Solomon' the Bible's most erotic book, the sensuous quality of pomegranates is well expressed: 'Thy lips are like a thread of scarlet, and thy speech is comely: thy temples are like a piece of a pomegranate within thy locks.'[15]

The prophet Mohammed enjoined his followers to 'eat the pomegranate, for it purges the system of envy and hatred.' It is referred to in ancient Sanskrit writings, in Homer's *Odyssey*, and in the *Arabian Nights*. King Solomon kept an orchard exclusively consisting of pomegranate trees, and the ancient Egyptians revered the fruit as a fertility symbol – they also made an extremely alcoholic brew from it.

According to Greek mythology, the pomegranate's overwhelming allure is responsible for plunging the world into winter for 6 months; Persephone was kidnapped by Pluto, Lord of the Underworld, and carried off to that subterranean kingdom. Although vowing not to eat until her freedom had been regained, the pomegranate proved altogether too enticing, and Persephone consumed 6 luscious seeds. Her mother, Demeter, finally negotiated her release with Pluto, but only on the condition that Persephone should spend 6 months of the year – one for each fruit consumed – in the Underworld. It is lucky for us that Persephone, Goddess of Spring, restricted herself to no more than 6 seeds.

For all its time-honoured appeal, the pomegranate is a challenging fruit to consume. The majority of it is inedible, and it is only the luscious ruby sacs surrounding the seeds which yield their exquisite nectar. Consequently, the pomegranate has never penetrated the cuisine of countries lying outside its natural areas of cultivation. This is a shame, because both its taste and appearance naturally lend themselves to highly creative cooking. Where simply the flavour of pomegranates is required, and not the seeds themselves, grenadine syrup may be purchased, which is made from extract of pomegranate. The fruits themselves vary considerably in taste. Some varieties are extremely sweet, with a slightly acidic undertone, whereas others can be so astringent as to leave the mouth quite dry. The only way to tell which particular flavour you are purchasing is to try a sample first.

Preparing the pomegrante is easy; they are simply cut in half and the seeds can be scraped out with a teaspoon, taking care to separate them from the very bitter white pulp which retains them in their honeycomb position. They can then be used to adorn any number of dishes, or alternatively, may be pressed through a sieve to extract the juice. Conventional electric juicing machines are not usually effective in extracting pomegranate juice – they tend to crush the seeds too, which again releases an unpleasant amount of bitterness. One raw pomegranate contains about one-fifth of the adult daily requirements for vitamin C and potassium. In natural medicine, the juice has been used to treat various bladder disorders.

NUTRIENT ANALYSIS
1 POMEGRANATE, FRESH (154g)

KCalories	104.72
Total Fat (g)	0.46
Monounsaturated Fat (g)	trace
Polyunsaturated Fat (g)	trace
Saturated Fat (g)	trace
Carbohydrate (g)	26.44
Protein (g)	1.46
Crude Fibre (g)	0.31
Vitamin A (RE)	0.00
Ascorbic Acid (mg)	9.39
Thiamin (mg)	0.05
Riboflavin (mg)	0.05
Niacin (mg)	0.46
Pantothenic Acid (mg)	0.92
Vitamin B6 (mg)	0.16
Folacin (mcg)	?
Vitamin B12 (mcg)	0.00
Calcium (mg)	4.62
Iron (mg)	0.46
Zinc (mg)	?

Rose and Pomegranate Salad
Serves 4
Preparation time 20 minutes, plus chilling time

4 ripe bananas, peeled and sliced
4 large oranges, peeled and divided into segments
4 pomegranates, quartered and deseeded (retain seeds)
50g (2oz) flaked almonds
juice of 1 lemon
½ tsp sugar
2 tbsp rosewater
watercress

Arrange the banana slices and orange segments in a pattern on each serving plate or bowl. Drop the pomegranate seeds over the arrangements and top with a few flaked almonds. Mix the lemon juice, sugar and rosewater together and drizzle over each salad. Garnish with a sprig of fresh watercress. Serve immediately or chill for 1 hour before serving.

Tofu Steaks in Pomegranate and Walnut Sauce

Serves 4
Preparation time 1 hour

2 tbsp oil
1 large onion, finely chopped
340g (12oz) walnuts, crushed
1 tsp freshly ground black pepper
1 tsp ground cinnamon
1 tsp ground coriander
3 tbsp tomato purée
850ml (1½ pints) vegetable stock or water
juice of 2 lemons
4–6 tbsp grenadine (pomegranate syrup)
4 Tofu Steaks (see page 339)
1 fresh pomegranate, quartered and deseeded (retain the seeds)

Heat the oil in a large saucepan and sauté the onion over a medium heat, until clear and tender. Add the walnuts and sauté for a further 5 minutes, stirring constantly. Add the spices and stir for 1 minute. Stir in the tomato purée and stock and bring to the boil. Cover the pan, reduce the heat and leave to simmer for 20 minutes. Add the lemon juice and grenadine and more stock if necessary, stir well. Place the Tofu Steaks over the sauce and cover the pan. Simmer for a further 10 minutes. Serve the Tofu Steaks over rice, cover with the sauce and garnish with a few fresh pomegranate seeds.

Potatoes It is, surely, one of the most preposterously unlikely stories ever to be associated with a foodstuff: a rapacious conquistador travels to the ends of the earth where he murders, cheats, extorts and loots the fabulous wealth of the Inca civilization . . . amidst this wholesale slaughter and larceny, some of the more intelligent brigands notice the modest tuber upon which the native Americans exist, totally unlike anything in the West . . . some plants are taken to Spain from where – in less than two centuries – the potato rapidly establishes itself as one of the world's most important staple foodstuffs. There is, perhaps, some irony to the story; purblind Pizarro can never have known that the humble tuber which his men had chanced upon would become infinitely more valuable than all the Inca gold he lusted after – and eventually died for.

The history of the potato is inextricably intertwined with the history of human exploitation and stupidity. In the early 1840s, about 4 million people in Ireland subsisted almost entirely on potatoes. In October 1845, a serious potato blight set in, destroying about three-quarters of the country's crop. In the four years that followed, one million men, women and children died of starvation. Paradoxically, large quantities of grain were being exported from Ireland during this terrible time, although the peasants were in desperate need of this food themselves. The potato crop in Ireland consisted of a single genetic strain, which made every potato susceptible to the same bacterial infection. Even though the lesson of this and other overwhelming tragedies should be obvious to every politician, scientist and agriculturalist, it is a sobering thought to realize that the world is increasingly dependent upon genetically uniform crops. The disappearance of genetic diversity, as it affects all life forms, is one of the most serious, but unpublicized threats to the continuation of planetary life. 'The loss of crop varieties', reports the respected World Resources Institute, 'has severe implications for global food security. Fewer than 100 species currently provide most of the world's food supply, yet thousands of species and many more thousands of varieties (subspecies) have been grown since the development of agriculture 12,000 years ago.'[16] Three-quarters of the total Western potato production is, today, concentrated in just four genetic strains. Similarly, six varieties account for three-quarters of the corn crop. There is an urgent lesson waiting to be learnt here.

Potatoes can be broadly divided into two categories: floury types, which have a dry and fluffy texture, very good for mashing, chips and soups; and waxy types, which hold their shape more firmly and are preferable for salads and frying. Potatoes should always be stored in a cool, dry, dark and well-ventilated location. The absence of light is particularly important because this discourages the development of solanine, a toxic glycoalkaloid which was once used to treat bronchitis, epilepsy and asthma, and which is a very effective natural insecticide for the potato. The potato is one of the most forgiving, and indeed one of the tastiest, of all vegetables; the recipes that follow include some classic potato dishes as well as some of the more unusual ones. They are all quick, easy and nutritious.

See also: Coconut Potato Patties (p338); Tare-ko-Aloo (p341); Irish Stew (p354); Sweet Potato and Tomato Sauté (p322); Sweet Potato Biscuits (p324); Nhopi (p324); Lu Pulu (p338); Fu Fu (p315); La Daub (p321)

NUTRIENT ANALYSIS
1 POTATO WITH SKIN, BAKED (202g)

KCalories	220.18
Total Fat (g)	0.20
Monounsaturated Fat (g)	0.00
Polyunsaturated Fat (g)	0.09
Saturated Fat (g)	0.05
Carbohydrate (g)	50.96
Protein (g)	4.65
Crude Fibre (g)	1.33
Vitamin A (RE)	0.00
Ascorbic Acid (mg)	26.06
Thiamin (mg)	0.22
Riboflavin (mg)	0.07
Niacin (mg)	3.32
Pantothenic Acid (mg)	1.12
Vitamin B6 (mg)	0.70
Folacin (mcg)	22.22
Vitamin B12 (mcg)	0.00
Calcium (mg)	20.20
Iron (mg)	2.75
Zinc (mg)	0.65

Scalloped Potatoes
Serves 4
Preparation time 1 hour 30 minutes

2 tbsp oil
3 cloves garlic, finely chopped
1 medium onion, chopped
2 tbsp plain flour
1 tsp salt
1 tsp cayenne pepper
420ml (¾ pint) soya milk
1 tbsp prepared mustard
4 medium potatoes, peeled and thinly sliced

Preheat the oven to 180°C/350°F/Gas Mark 4. Heat the oil in a saucepan and sauté the garlic and onion until clear and tender. Mix the flour, salt and cayenne together and sprinkle over the sauté. Stir well to make a thick paste (roux). Add the soya milk, a little at a time, stirring after each addition to make a slightly thick sauce. Stir in the prepared mustard when all the soya milk has been added. Remove the sauce from the heat. Arrange one quarter of the potato slices in a casserole dish and pour one quarter of the sauce over. Continue layering the remaining potoates and sauce. Cover the casserole and bake for 1 hour. Serve hot with steamed greens and sautéed tempeh.

Sag Aloo (Spinach and Potato Curry)
Serves 4
Preparation time 45 minutes

1 tbsp oil
4–5 cloves garlic, finely chopped
1 medium onion, chopped
2 tsp fresh ginger, grated
½ tsp cumin seeds
½ tsp ground coriander
½ tsp chilli powder
½ tsp tumeric
1 fresh chilli, finely chopped
1–2 medium tomatoes, chopped
450g (1lb) potatoes, scrubbed and coarsely chopped
140ml (¼ pint) water
450g (1lb) spinach, washed, trimmed and thinly sliced
juice of ½ lemon
2 tbsp fresh coriander, chopped

Heat the oil in a large saucepan and sauté the garlic and onion until clear and tender, about 10 minutes over a low to medium heat. Add the spices and stir for

2 minutes. Add the tomatoes and potatoes and stir well. Cover the pan and leave them to cook for 5–7 minutes. Add the water and stir well. Cover the pan and cook for another 5 minutes over a medium heat. Add the spinach, stir and cover the pan. Cook for 5 minutes. Add the lemon juice and coriander but do not stir. Cover and cook a final 5 minutes, ensuring the potatoes are tender. Serve hot with rice, dhal (see page 344), and a variety of pickles, chutneys or relishes.

Potato Gnocchi

Serves 4
Preparation time 45 minutes

1kg (2lbs) potatoes, peeled and quartered
1 tbsp soya flour
1 tbsp tahini
1 tbsp soya milk
285g (10oz) plain flour

Optional additions:
2 tbsp fresh parsley, chopped
1 tsp freshly ground black pepper and ½ tsp ground allspice
100g (4oz) broccoli, steamed and mashed into potatoes
¼ small beetroot, steamed and mashed into potatoes
2 tbsp soya bacon-bits
1 medium onion, finely chopped and sautéed until slightly crisp
1 medium carrot, grated

Steam the potatoes until tender then mash them in a bowl. Blend the soya flour, tahini and soya milk together in a cup and add to the potato. Mix well, sprinkle the flour over the potato, a little at a time, mixing well after each addition. You want to end up with a smooth, elastic and slightly sticky dough. Flour a board and roll half of the mixture into a 2.5cm/(1-inch) thick roll. Cut off 2.5–5cm/(1–2 inch) pieces and drop them into a pot of boiling water or vegetable stock. Let them cook for 7 minutes – until they bob to the surface – then serve them in one of the sauces in this book. (See Peanut Sauce p313; Rich Tomato Sauce p353; Hidden Pepper Tomato Sauce p269)

If you want a gnocchi with a strong colour, spicy flavour or unusual texture, try one or more of the options suggested above. Simply add them to the potatoes as you mash them and proceed as usual. You may need to adjust the amount of flour required.

Potato Skins with Tofu and Broccoli Filling

Serves 4
Preparation time 1 hour 10 minutes

4 large baking potatoes, scrubbed and scored
225g (8oz) broccoli, trimmed and cut into florets
1 tbsp oil
2 medium onions, chopped
100g (4oz) mushrooms, chopped
1 tsp freshly ground black pepper
¼ tsp ground nutmeg
285g (10oz) firm tofu
3 tbsp fresh parsley, finely chopped
1 tbsp prepared mustard

Preheat the oven to 200°C/400°F/Gas Mark 6. Bake the potatoes for about 45 minutes, until tender. Steam the broccoli for 12–15 minutes, until just tender but still very bright green. Remove from the pan and leave to one side. Meanwhile, heat the oil in a large frying pan and sauté the onion for 5 minutes. Add the mushrooms and sauté over a low to medium heat, stirring often. Add the black pepper and nutmeg and remove from the heat.

Slice the baked potatoes in half lengthwise and scoop out their insides, leaving a thick shell of potato skin. Combine this potato with the steamed broccoli and the tofu, parsley and mustard in a mixing bowl. Mash these ingredients together to make a smooth mixture. Add the mushroom and onion sauté and stir well. Spoon this mixture back into the potato skins, letting the filling rise well above the potato shell. Sprinkle with a little salt and return these to the oven for 15 mintues. Serve hot as a meal in itself, as a starter or as part of a salad or vegetable platter, or try with 1 or 2 of your favourite sauces.

Picnic Potato Salad

Serves 4
Preparation time 30 minutes

1kg (2lbs) new potatoes, scrubbed and halved
2 stalks celery, finely chopped
1 small onion, finely chopped
5 spring onions, finely chopped
1 large carrot, grated
3 gherkins, finely chopped
2 tbsp fresh parsley, chopped
½ tsp freshly ground black pepper
½ tsp mustard seeds
¼ tsp salt

For the dressing:
140g (5oz) plain tofu
3–5 tbsp oil
90ml (3fl oz) soya milk
2 tsp prepared mustard
2 tbsp cider vinegar

Steam the new potatoes for about 15 minutes or until just tender, then lift out to cool. Mix the remaining salad ingredients together in a large salad bowl. Using a hand-held electric blender or a wire whisk, blend the dressing ingredients together until light and aerated. Add the cool potatoes to the salad, pour the dressing over and stir well. Chill and serve.

Potato Garlic Fans

Serves 4
Preparation time 1 hour 15 minutes

4 medium baking potatoes, scrubbed
4 tbsp olive oil
1 tsp salt
5 cloves garlic, very finely chopped
½ tsp freshly ground black pepper
2 tbsp fresh parsley, chopped
2 tbsp fresh chives, chopped (optional)

Preheat the oven to 200°C/400°F/Gas Mark 6. Cut the potatoes into thin slices, cutting only 7/8 of the way through the potato. Put the sliced potatoes into a baking dish and open the slices somewhat. Drizzle a table-spoon of olive oil over each potato, ensuring a little gets between each slice. Sprinkle a pinch of salt over each potato and then drop a few tiny pieces of garlic between each slice. Sprinkle a little black pepper over the top then bake the potatoes for 45–60 minutes, until tender. Sprinkle fresh parsley and/or chives over each potato and serve piping hot with a robust mixed salad.

Hash Browns

Serves 4
Preparation time 45 minutes

4 large potatoes, scrubbed if organic, peeled if not
2–4 tbsp oil for frying
2 tbsp chopped chives, parsley, onions, garlic, soya bacon-bits or similar additional ingredient to taste (optional)
140ml (¼ pint) soya milk (optional)

Grate the potatoes through a coarse blade and turn the gratings into cold water. Rinse the potato in the water,

swirling it with your hand. Drain, rinse under cold running water and drain again. Turn onto a clean tea towel and pat the gratings dry. Heat a very little oil in a large frying pan over a high heat. Add the grated potato and fry for about 15 minutes, stirring the potato at first to cook all the gratings, then allowing the gratings to mould together in a sort of cake. At this stage, leave the potatoes to brown on one side, then use a spatula to cut the cake into 4 and turn the wedges over to brown on the other side. You may need to add a little more oil but use as little as possible to avoid greasiness. Serve immediately on a warm plate with grilled mushrooms and tomatoes, Apple Butter (p172) and dry toast.

An alternative method is to cook as above for the first 5–10 minutes, then to mix an additional ingredient, such as fresh herbs, with the soya milk. Pour this mixture slowly over the cooking potatoes and proceed as usual.

Potato Kibbi Steaklet

Serves 4–6
Preparation time 1 hour

1kg (2lb) potatoes, peeled and quartered
170g (6oz) bulgur
2 tsp olive oil
3 cloves garlic, chopped
2 medium onions, chopped
1 bunch fresh coriander, chopped
100g (4oz) plain flour
1 tsp freshly ground black pepper
¼ tsp ground cumin
140ml (¼ pint) olive oil

Steam the potatoes until just tender. Measure the bulgur into a mixing bowl and pour 420ml (¾ pint) boiling water over it, stir and leave the bulgur to absorb the liquid. Heat a little oil in a saucepan and sauté garlic and onions until clear and tender. Add the coriander and stir for 1 minute. Mash the potatoes in a mixing bowl; mix in the bulgur. Stir the flour and spices together and add to the potatoes along with the sauté. Mix well. Form the mixture into small patties. Heat the oil in a frying pan over a medium heat and fry the kibbi for about 20 minutes, until they are golden brown on both sides. Serve hot with your favourite spicy sauce, relish or chutney.

Roasted Potatoes in Lemon Garlic Butter

Serves 4
Preparation time 1 hour

4 large potatoes, peeled and quartered
3 tbsp olive oil
75g (3oz) margarine
5 cloves garlic, finely chopped
rind of 1 lemon, grated
juice of 1 lemon
½ tsp salt
2 tbsp fresh parsley, chopped
1 tbsp fresh chives, chopped

Preheat the oven to 180°C/350°F/Gas Mark 4. Steam the potatoes for 15 minutes, until just tender. Remove from the heat. Melt the oil and margarine together in a saucepan over a low heat and sauté the garlic until just golden, about 3 minutes. Remove from the heat and add the lemon rind and juice; stir well. Gently toss each potato in the lemon garlic butter then lift it into a lightly oiled oven dish. Repeat until all the potatoes are coated. Pour any excess over the potatoes in the dish, sprinkle with a little salt and the fresh parsley. Roast for 20 minutes, basting the potatoes once in that time. Serve hot with a garnish of fresh chopped chives.

Health Note

A word of advice: greenish patches under the skin of the potato are indications that the potato has been exposed to the light and solanine may be present. Solanine is also present in considerable quantities in potato sprouts, which is why potatoes which have started to sprout should never be consumed (nor should their leaves). Solanine and other glycoalkaloids can have teratogenic effects (ie may cause birth defects) and pregnant women should therefore be particularly careful not to consume potato sprouts. Some people may be sensitive to the very minor amounts of glycoalkaloids contained within the potato itself; such sensitivity may manifest as headaches, nausea and diarrhoea. For the rest of us, though, the potato is a good source of nutrition: one medium-sized baked potato, with skin, provides about half of the adult daily recommended allowance for vitamin C, and one-third of the requirements for vitamin B6, iron and potassium.

Pumpkin Much appreciated in America, Australia, and in parts of Europe too, but generally overlooked in Britain and many other countries where indigenous vegetables such as the marrow take its place. The pumpkin (including squash) is a most versatile vegetable, being capable of producing either sweet or savoury dishes, but its occasionally earthy flavour, which disappears if properly cooked, sometimes serves to discourage new cooks from experimenting with it.

It owes its special position in American cuisine to the fact that it composed an important part of the first Thanksgiving dinner, a celebration by the founding fathers to mark their first successful harvest on the new continent. It is worth remembering that Thanksgiving was itself a custom borrowed from the native Iroquois Indians; who gave thanks every October for the successful harvesting and storing of their crops. As historian Ronald Wright points out: 'At White Thanksgivings, the thanks, if there are any, go to a White god who helped his faithful survive in a supposed wilderness. The diners then sit down to eat turkey, pumpkin, maize, beans, and potatoes, none of which was known to pre-Columbian Europe. It was the heathen savage, not the Christian god, who fed them.'[17] Halloween-type pumpkins are not, in general, the best 'eaters' – they can tend towards woodiness, although they can be used successfully in preserves, chutneys, pickles, and in dishes where they are essentially a vehicle for other flavours. The most flavoursome pumpkins are generally not the monster varieties. Good eating varieties include butternut, acorn squash, onion squash and buttercup squash. Spaghetti squash has a bland, white flesh made up of delightful spaghetti-like strands. Bake or boil this squash until tender, then slice in half and scrape out the 'spaghetti'; toss in olive oil, season and serve. Pumpkins purchased immediately after a sharp frost are particularly delicious; their sweetness and general flavour are greatly enhanced.

The finest of all savoury pumpkins is the Japanese hokkaido (sometimes referred to as the kabocha) pumpkin. Relatively small, about 15–20cm (6–8 inches) in diameter, they have a thin, mottled, dark green skin and are increasingly available in the West. In addition, they are the easiest of all pumpkins to cook: quarter the pumpkin and remove the seeds, place on a baking tray to which 1cm (½-inch) of water has been added, and bake on the top shelf of a hot oven for 20–30 minutes, until the edges of the pumpkin begin to brown. An excellent and highly nutritious accompaniment to rice dishes, the flavour of the hokkaido pumpkin is of gourmet standard – rich, smooth, buttery and wholesome. Sprinkle with a little soy sauce if required.

Pumpkin seeds are one of the most delicious, nutritious and easy of all vegetarian snack foods. Although it is possible to extract them from the pumpkin yourself, the cleaning and preparation processes are fiddly and time-consuming, so they are better bought from wholefood shops. A scattering of pumpkin seeds will improve the nutritional profile of almost any dish: they can be used in all rice-based recipes, in all manner of salads, either sprouted or *au naturel*, in mueslis, stir-fries, sandwiches and, of course, simply as they are. To make an instant tasty pumpkin seed snack, put a skillet over a hot flame, add a handful of pumpkin seeds and shake the pan while the seeds roast. They will brown nicely and begin to pop. Roast them another minute or two then remove the pan from the heat and sprinkle some soy sauce over them. Stir well, turn into a serving dish, cool and serve immediately. This snack is loved by people of all ages, and is not only far cheaper but also far more nutritious than commercially prepared snack foods.

See also: Ponkie (p312); Nhopi (p324); Taushe (p315); Pumpkin Caramel Mould (p326); Pumpkin Soup (this page); Pumpkin Coconut Pudding (p333)

NUTRIENT ANALYSIS
1 CUP PUMPKIN, BOILED (244g)

KCalories	48.80
Total Fat (g)	0.17
Monounsaturated Fat (g)	0.02
Polyunsaturated Fat (g)	0.01
Saturated Fat (g)	0.09
Carbohydrate (g)	11.93
Protein (g)	1.76
Crude Fibre (g)	2.03
Vitamin A (RE)	263.52
Ascorbic Acid (mg)	11.47
Thiamin (mg)	0.08
Riboflavin (mg)	0.19
Niacin (mg)	1.01
Pantothenic Acid (mg)	0.49

Vitamin B6 (mg)	0.11
Folacin (mcg)	20.74
Vitamin B12 (mcg)	0.00
Calcium (mg)	36.60
Iron (mg)	1.39
Zinc (mg)	0.56

Simple Pumpkin Soup
Serves 4–6
Preparation time 1 hour

570ml (1 pint) (600g (1¼lb)) cooked or tinned
    pumpkin
570ml (1 pint) vegetable stock
juice of 2 oranges
2 tbsp oil
3 cloves garlic, chopped
1 small onion, chopped
2 stalks celery, chopped
1 tsp ground cardamom
½ tsp ground cinnamon
½ tsp ground coriander
½ tsp ground cumin
rind of 1 orange, grated
pinch of ground nutmeg
140ml (¼ pint) plain soya yoghurt (optional)

Blend the pumpkin, vegetable stock and orange juice with a wire whisk and set aside. Heat the oil in a large saucepan over a medium heat. Sauté the garlic, onion and celery until clear and tender, about 15 minutes. Add the spices and stir for a further 5 minutes. Add the pumpkin mixture and simmer for 15 minutes, stirring often. Pour into soup bowls and sprinkle a little of the orange rind and nutmeg over each serving. Serve hot, with a dollop of yoghurt if desired.

Favourite Pumpkin Pie
Makes one 12 inch deep-dish pie
Preparation time 1 hour plus chilling time

36 large digestive biscuits, crushed
100g (4oz) margarine, melted
450g (1lb) cooked or tinned pumpkin
170ml (6fl oz) soya milk
100g (4oz) sugar
1 tsp ground cinnamon
½ tsp ground ginger
½ tsp ground cloves

¼ tsp ground nutmeg
1x3g sachet of agar powder
285g (10oz) plain tofu
140ml (¼ pint) oil
140ml (¼ pint) soya milk

Preheat the oven to 180°C/350°C/Gas Mark 4. Stir the crushed biscuits and melted margarine together in a mixing bowl then turn immediately into the pie dish. Press the biscuit base firmly into place, ensuring the crust rises well up the sides of the pan. Bake this base for 8–12 minutes. Remove from the oven and leave to cool. Turn the pumpkin, soya milk and sugar into a saucepan and place over a medium heat. Add the spices, stir well and bring to a simmer; cook for 10–15 minutes, stirring occasionally. Dissolve the agar in 2 tablespoons of boiling water in a cup; pour this mixture into the pumpkin and remove the pumpkin from the heat. Place the pan in a sink full of cold water to speed cooling; stir occasionally. Whisk the tofu, oil and milk together to add as much air as possible and to make a thick sauce consistency. Fold this into the cooled pumpkin mixture. Turn the blend into the pie case and chill in the refrigerator for 2–4 hours, until it sets firm. Slice and serve chilled with lashings of Soya Creem.

Health Note

The nutritional profile of pumpkin seeds is phenomenal: 50g (2oz) provides three-quarters of the daily adult requirement for iron, and one-quarter of the protein and zinc requirements. Since iron and zinc are often lacking in the modern diet, it is well worth getting to know these Herculean seeds. The pumpkin itself is rich in vitamins A and C, and iron and potassium – one cup of boiled, mashed pumpkin yields about a quarter of the adult daily requirements for these nutrients. Pumpkins have been used in natural medicine to treat all kinds of intestinal problems, stomach ulcers and haemorrhoids.

Radishes Most frequently encountered as a red, round, salad vegetable or an ingredient in *hors d'oeuvre*, there are in fact a great many members of the radish family, most of which are rather more interesting and appetizing than the billiard balls we are all most familiar with. The radish seems to have originated in China from where it gradually spread to become a significant ingredient in the diets of the ancient Egyptians, Greeks and Romans. It is supposed that Columbus introduced radishes to the New World; they were certainly amongst the first vegetables to be grown by the colonists. Apart from the small pink-red variety, large black ones are very popular in French country cooking, and are starting to appear as a speciality vegetable in some supermarkets and greengrocers in Britain. Lesser known varieties include golden yellow and mauve.

A delicious import from Japan is the daikon radish, a prominent ingredient in traditional Japanese and macrobiotic cooking. It is available in many wholefood shops in the West, either as a pickled condiment, or as sengiri daikon, a naturally sundried relish which should be soaked in water for five to ten minutes before cooking with vegetables such as carrots, burdock and lotus root. Radishes should always be bought while they are absolutely firm to the touch. The slightest degree of springiness indicates that they are past their peak, and suitable only for the compost heap – the essence of radish is its crisp texture and flavour.

Radish Flowers
Although pink radishes make an attractive counterpoint in any green salad, they can be made even more visually enticing by turning them into radish flowers in the following manner: wash, trim the leaves and stem, then make four incisions all round the radish from its tip to its stem. Do not cut through the base. Drop into a bowl of cold water, add ice cubes, soon the petals will open out like flowers.

Black Radish hors d'oeuvre
This is a traditional, and very simple, dish from Normandy, where thin slices of large black radishes are generally served with wedges of salted butter. A good substitute for this is any vegan margarine which remains solid at room temperature. Peel radish and thinly slice, then salt and leave for an hour or so to allow some of the bitterness to escape. Wash, pat dry, and serve with liberal helpings of butter or margarine, freshly-baked wholemeal bread, and, if you want to be really authentic – a glass of cider, too.

NUTRIENT ANALYSIS
10 RADISHES, RAW (45g)

KCalories	7.65
Total Fat (g)	0.24
Monounsaturated Fat (g)	0.01
Polyunsaturated Fat (g)	0.02
Saturated Fat (g)	0.01
Carbohydrate (g)	1.62
Protein (g)	0.27
Crude Fibre (g)	0.24
Vitamin A (RE)	0.45
Ascorbic Acid (mg)	10.26
Thiamin (mg)	0.00
Riboflavin (mg)	0.02
Niacin (mg)	0.14
Pantothenic Acid (mg)	0.04
Vitamin B6 (mg)	0.03
Folacin (mcg)	12.15
Vitamin B12 (mcg)	0.00
Calcium (mg)	9.45
Iron (mg)	0.13
Zinc (mg)	0.14

Health Note

Nutritionally, radishes contain very little of the major nutrients, although 10 raw pink radishes will provide about one-fifth of the adult daily recommended intake of vitamin C. There is, however, some suggestion that their organic silicon content may assist in bone composition and healing. In the Middle Ages, radishes were used to cure madness, detect witches, and to cause demons to leave a body currently in their possession. Today, they are only rarely used for these purposes; although practitioners of natural medicine do use them to stimulate the appetite and to relieve nervous exhaustion. A refreshing and nutritious cocktail can be made by juicing three radishes, half an onion and pineapple juice to taste (radish juice is too strong to consume by itself and should always be a minor ingredient in any juice cocktail).

Raspberries Surely one of the most delicious of all berry fruits, raspberries combine strength of flavour with an intense sweetness which is offset by a pleasing acidity. Widely distributed throughout the northern hemisphere, it takes its scientific name (*rubus idaeus*) from Mount Ida in Turkey where, according to the Ancient Greeks, the nymph Ida accidentally pricked her finger while gathering white berries. Blood was spilt, the berries turned crimson, and the world had raspberries.

Although a number of interesting, and sometimes extraordinarily flavourful, wild varieties are available, most of the raspberries sold in supermarkets and grocers shops are of one type. The raspberry cane is in fruit from July to October (hothouse-grown raspberries will be available at other times of the year, but are never as tasty). Look for plump, firm fruit with a deep colour; if the stalks are still attached then the fruit may well not be ripe. Raspberries are a delicate fruit and should be carefully washed and cleaned before use; pay especial attention for any small beasties for whom your next dessert may be a temporary home.

For raspberries, as for all subtly flavoured fruits, the simplest forms of preparation are invariably the best. Thus a bowl of raspberries and Soya Creem or similar topping cannot really be beaten; although for the adults, raspberries steeped in a sweet red wine for a few hours, then served with a light sprinkling of sugar, runs a close second.

NUTRIENT ANALYSIS
1 CUP RASPBERRIES, FRESH (123g)

KCalories	60.27
Total Fat (g)	0.68
Monounsaturated Fat (g)	0.07
Polyunsaturated Fat (g)	0.38
Saturated Fat (g)	0.02
Carbohydrate (g)	14.23
Protein (g)	1.12
Crude Fibre (g)	3.69
Vitamin A (RE)	15.99

Ascorbic Acid (mg)	30.75
Thiamin (mg)	0.04
Riboflavin (mg)	0.11
Niacin (mg)	1.11
Pantothenic Acid (mg)	0.30
Vitamin B6 (mg)	0.07
Folacin (mcg)	31.98
Vitamin B12 (mcg)	0.00
Calcium (mg)	27.06
Iron (mg)	0.70
Zinc (mg)	0.57

Raspberry Vinegar
Makes approximately 2l (4 pints)
Preparation time 1 hour, plus 2 weeks!

1kg (2lbs) fresh raspberries, picked over
850ml (1½ pints) wine vinegar
850ml (1½ pints) red wine

Clean the raspberries without washing them and turn into a large sterilized jar(s). Mix the vinegar and wine together and pour over the berries. Tightly close the jar and leave undisturbed for at least 2 weeks. Strain the vinegar from the berries, preferably through a piece of muslin. Do not squeeze the berries. Collect the vinegar and decant into sterilized bottles. Especially good in salad dressings.

Raspberry Coulis
Makes approximately 1kg (2 lbs)
Preparation time 20 minutes

1kg (2lbs) fresh raspberries
400g (14oz) sugar

Wash the berries and carefully dry them in a clean tea towel. Turn them into a mixing bowl or food processor with the sugar and purée to an even consistency. Chill the coulis and serve over soya ice cream, dish into a bowl with a couple plain biscuits to accompany, or save to spoon over pies or puddings.
For a coulis with a deeper flavour, use vanilla sugar instead of plain sugar. Place a whole vanilla pod in a large jar and pour 1kg (2lb) of plain sugar over it. After a week or two, the sugar will have taken on the aroma and flavour of vanilla.

Raspberrofu
Serves 4
Preparation time 15 minutes

285g (10oz) plain firm tofu
1 tbsp barley malt syrup
140ml (¼ pint) apple juice
285g (10oz) fresh raspberries

Measure all the ingredients into a mixing bowl or food processor and purée to a thick, even consistency. Pour into glass bowls or dessert dishes and serve immediately with a garnish of crushed nuts or a single plain biscuit.

Health Note

One cup of raw raspberries yields about half of the adult daily requirement for vitamin C. Natural therapists consider raspberries, and their juice (which should be uncontaminated by sugar), a good cleanser and detoxifier. Raspberry leaf tea is held to be effective in relieving diarrhoea, and the venerable herbalist Mrs Grieve states that an infusion of 25g (1 oz) of the dried leaves in 1 pint of boiling water may be 'employed as a gargle for sore mouths, canker of the throat, and as a wash for wounds and ulcers.'[18]

Rhubarb 'What rhubarb, cyne, or what purgative drug would scour these English hence?' says Shakespeare's Macbeth, revealing both the traditional use to which rhubarb has been put (a laxative) and Macbeth's opinion of the English. In fact, rhubarb was not considered to be an edible vegetable until about 1810, when James Myatt, an enterprising market gardener of Deptford, England, made a vigorous attempt to persuade the consumers of the day to purchase it and cook it (heavily flavoured with sugar). The rhubarb plant made a curious progress towards Britain. Originating in Tibet, various species of rhubarb became prized for their astringent, tonic and purgative properties. From Tibet, it was brought overland first to Russia, then to Turkey and thence to Europe. An alternative route came by way of Canton and Singapore. The Greeks are said to have given it its name: *rheo* ('to flow') being another reference to its purgative properties.

Several different strains of rhubarb are grown, distinguished by colouration (stalks may range from green to a darkish mauve) and flavour. It is normally in season from May to July, although 'forced' rhubarb is grown outside of this period – this tends to lack the robust flavour of the more naturally grown plant. Buying rhubarb is quite easy: unless there are grossly visible signs of degradation, there are no particular signs to watch out for. Because it is the aim of the cooking process to break down rhubarb's naturally sinewy structure, a moderate degree of overcooking will not impair the finished dish.

Most people now know that rhubarb contains oxalic acid, which can be poisonous. The highest concentrations of this seem to be within the rib structure of the leaves, and indeed there were several fatalities from eating rhubarb leaves quite early in its culinary history. To be on the safe side, the leaves should always be discarded.

Nutritionally, rhubarb is surprisingly high in calcium, one cup of cooked rhubarb yields about half of the adult daily requirement. The bad news, however, is that calcium absorption appears to be somewhat inhibited by rhubarb's oxalic acid content, although experts disagree as to how significant this may be. Therefore, it will be prudent not to reckon on obtaining regular dietary calcium requirements from rhubarb. It has been hypothesized that the overconsumption of rhubarb may increase the risk of kidney and gallstone formation. The presence of oxalic acid may also reduce the amount of iron which is absorbed into the body from natural foodstuffs. In general, rhubarb should be avoided by people suffering from rheumatism, arthritis or gout because it may exacerbate these health problems.

NUTRIENT ANALYSIS
1 CUP RHUBARB, COOKED WITH SUGAR (240g)

KCalories	278.40
Total Fat (g)	0.12
Monounsaturated Fat (g)	trace
Polyunsaturated Fat (g)	trace
Saturated Fat (g)	trace
Carbohydrate (g)	74.88
Protein (g)	0.94
Crude Fibre (g)	1.44

Vitamin A (RE)	16.80
Ascorbic Acid (mg)	7.92
Thiamin (mg)	0.04
Riboflavin (mg)	0.06
Niacin (mg)	0.48
Pantothenic Acid (mg)	0.12
Vitamin B6 (mg)	0.05
Folacin (mcg)	12.72
Vitamin B12 (mcg)	0.00
Calcium (mg)	348.00
Iron (mg)	0.50
Zinc (mg)	0.19

Rhubarb Crumble

Serves 4–6
Preparation time 55 minutes

1l (2 pints) (approximately 675g (1½lbs)) fresh
  rhubarb, washed and chopped
100g (4oz) plain flour
50g (2oz) sugar
225g (8oz) rolled oats
100g (4oz) brown sugar
1 tsp ground cinnamon
4 tbsp margarine

Preheat the oven to 180°C/350°F/Gas Mark 4. Mix the rhubarb, flour and sugar in a large bowl and turn into a 23 × 33cm (9 × 13 inch) baking dish. Leave the fruit to sit for 10–15 minutes then stir again and distribute evenly in the dish. Mix the oats, brown sugar and cinnamon together in a bowl and work in the margarine to make a crumbly texture. Spread this over the rhubarb mixture and lightly press into place. Bake for 20 minutes, until the topping is golden. Serve hot or warm with Soya Creem.

Stewed Rhubarb

Serves 4
Preparation time 30 minutes

1kg (2lbs) fresh rhubarb, washed and chopped
225g (8oz) raisins
100g (4oz) dried dates, chopped
140ml (¼ pint) water or fruit juice
50g (2oz) crushed hazelnuts

This dish is excellent in its simplicity. Turn the fruits into a large enamel saucepan with the water or fruit juice and place over a medium heat. When the liquid simmers, stir well, cover the pan and reduce the heat. Cook slowly, stirring occasionally to prevent sticking, while the rhubarb loses its form. Add a little more water if necessary; the dried fruits will add sweetness and texture. After about 20 minutes, the fruit should be well cooked. Pour immediately into dessert bowls and garnish with a sprinkling of hazelnuts. Serve hot (though it may be served chilled), as a dessert or even a breakfast dish.

Health Note

> A word of caution: don't cook rhubarb in an aluminium pan. The pan will be sparkling clean afterwards, but your food will have absorbed aluminium compounds.

Rice 'It should never be forgotten that the large and continued consumption of the white, polished rice of commerce is likely to be injurious to the health. The nations of which rice is the staple diet eat it unhusked as a rule, when it is brownish and less attractive to the eye, but much more nutritious as well as cheaper.' So says the peerless Mrs Grieve in her *Modern Herbal*, and who am I to argue? White rice is lacklustre, lifeless, tasteless and irritating to prepare; brown rice is flavoursome, wholesome, and easy. Is there really a contest? Rice is probably the world's single most important foodstuff, being the staple food for over two billion people. Rice cultivation probably originated many thousands of years ago in ancient India, where the weather patterns – flooding for the plant's growth phase, drying out for the plant's maturation – perfectly suit its requirements.

Its progress towards the West was surprisingly slow. The Moors brought it to Spain in the 8th century, and rice cultivation was established in Italy by the 10th century. It is little wonder that, amongst European nations, these two countries have the widest repertoire of rice dishes, and the healthiest respect for this prodigiously bountiful plant. Rice can be broadly divided into two types – long grain and short grain. Choose long grain rice when you want the grains to stay separate during cooking, short grain if you want a stickier, more viscous appearance.

All rice – even brown rice – is processed to some extent, because the tough outer husk which protects the rice while it is growing is inedible. Rice thus threshed is termed paddy rice and this, after cleaning, becomes the brown rice we are familiar with in supermarkets and healthfood shops. To produce white rice, further processing is necessary, here described by the founder of macrobiotic cookery, Georges Ohsawa: 'Some sixty years ago, after the invention of the German polishing machines which strip each grain of rice of its protective, transparent outer coating, so called refined, polished, white rice came into fashion. These machines not only did what some people had previously done in threshing by hand; they did something worse – they stripped each grain of rice of its intermediate and inner shells as well, all of which contained precious minerals and nutrients. This "processing" of our perfect natural food has been extended further through precooking and packaging, until little is left but the perishable hydrate of carbon core – stripped of its preservative hulls – which cannot be stored without the use of chemical additives.' Several other terms are used to describe different types of rice, as follows:

- Polished rice. White rice which has been still further processed, to remove any trace of flour still sticking to the grain.
- Patna rice. One of the most common kinds of rice available, with a neutral flavour and good cooking qualities.
- Basmati rice. Long grain Indian rice, with a highly individual aroma and taste, a good choice for all types of Indian cooking but not Japanese or Chinese.
- Rice bran. The discarded, and nutritionally most valuable, portion of brown rice after it is turned into white rice – formerly used as an animal feedstuff, latterly discovered to have extraordinary health benefits, including the ability to lower cholesterol.
- Puffed rice. Used in the manufacture of breakfast cereals and rice cakes, puffed rice is simply rice that has been heated in a sealed container which is then rapidly depressurised, making it expand. Pleasant tasting, with a reasonable nutritional profile and low in calories.
- Rice flour. An excellent substitute for wheat flour for those who are allergic to gluten, suitable for many uses, including cakes, pastries and puddings, but not for breadmaking.

- Wild rice. Not a rice but a grass, of an entirely different species, wild rice grows in the northern United States, where it is harvested by native peoples – the Ojibwa, Chippewa and Menominee – usually paddling their canoes from plant to plant, knocking the seed bearing plants so that the ripest grains fall into the canoe. It is, understandably, an expensive food item, but worth it: the unique taste is appreciated by gourmets all over the world, and it can be judiciously extended by mixing with freshly cooked brown rice. A good ratio is 3 parts of brown rice to 1 part of wild rice; the grains should be mixed together in the pan before cooking commences and the instructions given below for cooking brown rice should be followed. Wild rice is extremely high in protein – ounce for ounce it contains twice as much as brown rice and three times as much as iron. Wild rice is particularly delicious when tossed with sautéed mushrooms and slivered almonds.
- Organic rice. Any kind of rice can be grown organically, although in practice, the ethics and values of organic growers dictate that it is usually brown rice. Many people believe there is a clear and distinct improvement in taste, and the world's finest organic rice is grown in northern Italy and the west coast of America.

There are probably more rituals associated with the preparation of perfect rice than with almost any other food. Almost every cookery book seems to give different instructions, which are sometimes decidedly eccentric. The most cabalistic I have come across involves dropping individual grains of rice from a height of 60cm (2 feet) into a pan of boiling water on which a layer of olive oil has been floated. Exercises such as this may be mind expanding in a Zen sort of way, but they do little to stave off the pangs of hunger and they do rather give vegetarian cookery a bad name. In point of fact, making perfect cooked rice is something of an art, but only in the same way that riding a bicycle could be said to be an art. It is very easy to learn, and once having got the hang of it, you will always be able to do it. The instructions that follow are the very easiest you are ever likely to come across, and you really can't go far wrong.

- Put some rice into a pan. There is no need to measure anything, just be aware that it will more or less double in volume by the time it is cooked.

- Pour in lots of water. This is the most important stage – the rice must be very well cleaned, and this has to be done by hand, so, immersing both hands, give the rice a good scrub, passing it through your fingers and rubbing vigorously. You will see husks and other debris come to the surface, and the rice will make the water quite milky. Drain the dirty water, add fresh water and repeat the scrubbing movement. Do this for three changes of water, after the third change, the rice will no longer make the water milky.
- Drain all the water out. With your fingers roughly level the rice in the pan. Now pour in fresh, cold water, to twice the volume of the rice. Therefore, if the rice fills the pan to a depth of 2.5cm (1 inch), pour in enough water to fill the pan to 5cm (2 inches).
- There is no need to add anything else, such as salt, to the water. Good quality brown rice has enough natural flavour not to need any enhancements, and condiments such as soy sauce can be added at the time of serving if required.
- Cover the pan. Place it on a medium to high heat, and bring to a boil. When it starts to boil, reduce the heat as much as possible to maintain a fairly low simmer. Do not remove the cover.
- Cook the rice for about 45 minutes. This time will vary slightly according to the exact type of rice, your cooker, etc. At this time, take a peek at the rice and push it open with a wooden spoon, to see if there's any remaining water at the bottom of the pan. The rice is perfectly finished if the very bottom layer of grains turn slightly yellow, and start to adhere to the pan. This, incidentally, is considered by macrobiotic cooks (who know a thing or two about preparing rice) to be the very finest, most health-giving of all rice. If you are preparing the rice to coincide with the cooking of various other foods, you can turn the heat off completely and, keeping the pan covered, simply let the rice steam itself for the last 5 minutes or so of its cooking. This will keep it nice and warm and give you a few minutes extra time to attend to the other foods.

See also: Sushi (p350); Simple Rice and Peas (p335); Risotto (p266); Coconut Rice (p313); Creole Rice (p314)

NUTRIENT ANALYSIS
1 CUP BROWN RICE, COOKED (195g)

KCalories	216.45
Total Fat (g)	1.76
Monounsaturated Fat (g)	0.64
Polyunsaturated Fat (g)	0.63
Saturated Fat (g)	0.35
Carbohydrate (g)	44.77
Protein (g)	5.03
Crude Fibre (g)	0.66
Vitamin A (RE)	0.00
Ascorbic Acid (mg)	0.00
Thiamin (mg)	0.19
Riboflavin (mg)	0.05
Niacin (mg)	2.98
Pantothenic Acid (mg)	0.56
Vitamin B6 (mg)	0.28
Folacin (mcg)	7.80
Vitamin B12 (mcg)	0.00
Calcium (mg)	19.50
Iron (mg)	0.82
Zinc (mg)	1.23

Health Note

Brown, unpolished rice is a healthy food partly because it naturally provides us with rice bran. Rice bran has been investigated by scientists for its many health-promoting properties: it contains b-sitosterol, a naturally occurring substance which lowers blood cholesterol. It can reduce the risk of bowel cancer, while contributing to internal hygiene by increasing stool size and frequency of elimination. It can reduce urinary calcium excretion, while drastically diminishing the frequency of kidney and bladder stone formation in people who are prone to these uncomfortable complaints. It can help insulin-dependent diabetics to normalize their blood sugar levels. And it can stimulate the production of mucus which has been shown to fight common diarrhoeal infections. For all these reasons, and many more still being investigated, brown rice should be a staple food for all of us.

Sesame Seeds These tiny but miraculous seeds are regularly consumed in various forms throughout much of the world; with the exception of the West – where they are virtually unknown (except for the occasional miserly scattering atop a stodgy hamburger bun). The Japanese wouldn't consider sitting down to a meal without a ready supply of *gomashio* (sesame seeds ground with sea salt); in Africa, Asia, the Middle East and China both the seed and its oil are recognized as a valuable, nutritious and – above all – delectable part of the diet. We obviously have a lot to learn! When buying sesame seeds, always choose unroasted, whole seeds. These are by far and away the tastiest and most nutritious. Before using them, lightly toast them by placing them in a hot skillet (no oil) over a medium heat, agitating the pan constantly for several seconds until the seeds' colour starts to change. Some seeds will pop and a gorgeous nutty aroma will be exuded. They are then ready to use as an ingredient in a limitless range of dishes, including:

- All kinds of salads
- Home-made bread
- Breakfast cereals
- Pies, casseroles and savoury bakes
- Stir-fried vegetables
- On pasta dishes

Sesame seeds are also the prime ingredient in that most essential part of Middle Eastern cuisine, tahini. This thick paste is versatile and a key component of the world's best dip, hummus.

Gomashio

This Japanese condiment has a range of uses which are not restricted to Far Eastern cookery. It can be bought ready made, but is simplicity itself to make at home in the kitchen. Toast some sesame seeds, and – with a mortar and pestle or extremely clean coffee grinder – combine 1 part sea salt to 8 parts sesame seeds, and grind coarsely. This garnish should be used to replace table salt on savoury dishes, grains, vegetables etc. It is far more flavoursome than even the finest sea salt, and is, of course, much healthier.

See also: Falafel (p202); Tahini Dip (p347); Hummus (p203)

NUTRIENT ANALYSIS
1oz SESAME SEEDS, ROASTED (25g)

KCalories	160.46
Total Fat (g)	13.63
Monounsaturated Fat (g)	5.15
Polyunsaturated Fat (g)	5.98
Saturated Fat (g)	1.91
Carbohydrate (g)	7.31
Protein (g)	4.82
Crude Fibre (g)	2.41
Vitamin A (RE)	0.28
Ascorbic Acid (mg)	0.00
Thiamin (mg)	0.23
Riboflavin (mg)	0.07
Niacin (mg)	1.30
Pantothenic Acid (mg)	0.01
Vitamin B6 (mg)	0.23
Folacin (mcg)	27.86
Vitamin B12 (mcg)	0.00
Calcium (mg)	280.88
Iron (mg)	4.19
Zinc (mg)	2.03

Noodles in Spicy Sesame Sauce

Serves 4
Preparation time 2 hours

one 15cm (6 inch) strip kombu (optional)
450g (1lb) ramen noodles
140ml (¼ pint) sesame oil
7 cloves garlic, finely chopped
2 tbsp fresh ginger, grated
5 spring onions, finely chopped
2 tsp freshly ground black pepper
1 tsp chilli powder
140ml (¼ pint) tahini
2 tbsp soy sauce
3 tbsp rice vinegar
1 tbsp tomato paste
140ml (¼ pint) cold water
1–2 medium tomatoes, finely chopped

Bring a large pot of salted water to the boil and drop in the strip of kombu. Leave to simmer for 5 minutes then add the ramen and cook for about 12 minutes, until just tender. Meanwhile, heat the oil in a saucepan and sauté the garlic and ginger, stirring constantly for 3 minutes over a medium heat. Add the onions and stir a further 3 minutes. Add the pepper and chilli and stir for 1 minute. Blend the remaining ingredients, except the chopped tomato, together in a jug and add to the saute. Stir well and bring to a simmer; cover the pan and remove it from the heat. When the ramen is cooked, drain it and turn immediately into broad, warm bowls. Spoon the sauce over each serving, garnish with chopped tomato and serve.

Health Note

A small quantity of sesame seeds provides a monster degree of nutrition. Just 25g (1oz) of whole roasted sesame seeds provides a mere 160 calories (6 per cent of the adult allowance), but supplies nearly half the iron requirement (they contain more iron than beef liver) and one-fifth of the zinc requirement! They also contain more calcium than any other common food – but this is in the form of calcium oxalate, which the body cannot easily use. Sesame seeds have a surplus of the two amino acids, methionine and tryptophan, which are often lacking in popular vegetable protein foods – meaning that a small sprinkling of sesame seeds greatly increases the usable protein in other foods. Sesame seeds are high in vitamin E, which acts as a preservative, making them resistant to oxidization. When buying them, check to see how they've been processed. Mechanically hulled seeds are superior to the two other processing methods (salt brine or chemical bath). The salt-processed seeds are very high in sodium, and the chemically-treated seeds develop a soapy flavour and lose much of their nutrition. Seeds which have been mechanically hulled, on the other hand, will keep for several years and have a sweet taste. You can spot them because they have a dull, matt appearance – the others are pure, glossy white.

Soya Beans It is said that the soya bean was a gift to all generations of mankind from the sages and wise rulers of China. When the very first specimens of the soya bean reached the West, at the end of the 18th century, their arrival coincided with the dawning of the industrial revolution. Sadly, it was the industrial uses of the soya bean that captivated the entrepreneurial minds of those who came to inspect the first specimens grown in London's Royal Botanic Gardens. Consequently, the first commercial use for the soya bean was as a source of oil to be used in the manufacture of soap, and the remains of the bean, after the oil had been extracted, were fed to cattle. This pattern of usage, so different from that in Asia, is at last beginning to change.

Soya milk is familiar to most people today. It is low in calories, contains no cholesterol, and is the ideal substitute for dairy milk, if you are allergic to lactose or if you simply want to reap the health benefits of a diet free of animal products. The most extensive and best-tasting range is probably that made by Granose, whose varieties include organic, low fat, sweetened, and with added vitamins and calcium. The full-flavour variety has a natural creamy flavour which is indistinguishable from cow's milk – without containing, of course, any of the animal fat. Other products, such as Soya Dessert, Soya Ice Cream and Soya Creem are also available.

I believe that today's expanding soya food industry should be warmly encouraged. For one reason, it makes sheer good economic sense when compared to the ludicrously high costs involved in meat production. One acre of land cultivated by conventional Western agricultural practices will feed an average adult for 77 days if it is used to raise beef. This may seem impressive, until you learn that that same acre can feed an adult for 527 days when it is devoted to growing wheat. However, if soya beans are grown on the same land, then it will yield enough protein to feed a person for over 6 years! This phenomenal productivity is caused in part by the ability of the soya bean to utilize the nitrogen of the air through the action of bacteria on its roots. The protein content of the bean when harvested is about 40 per cent, which rises to 50 per cent after it has been processed.

At the moment, most of the world's soya bean production goes to feed animals, rather than humans. If we buy more soya products, we're eating lower down on the food chain – and supporting an industry which uses the world's resources in a more intelligent way.

NUTRIENT ANALYSIS
1 CUP SOYA BEANS, BOILED (172g)

KCalories	297.56
Total Fat (g)	15.43
Monounsaturated Fat (g)	3.41
Polyunsaturated Fat (g)	8.71
Saturated Fat (g)	2.23
Carbohydrate (g)	17.06
Protein (g)	28.62
Crude Fibre (g)	3.49
Vitamin A (RE)	1.72
Ascorbic Acid (mg)	2.92
Thiamin (mg)	0.27
Riboflavin (mg)	0.49
Niacin (mg)	0.69
Pantothenic Acid (mg)	0.31
Vitamin B6 (mg)	0.40
Folacin (mcg)	92.54
Vitamin B12 (mcg)	0.00
Calcium (mg)	175.44
Iron (mg)	8.84
Zinc (mg)	1.98

Health Note

A word of caution: soya beans, like some other beans, contain a substance known as trypsin inhibitor. Trypsin is an enzyme secreted by the pancreas which helps us to digest dietary protein. Trypsin inhibitor, if consumed, will bind this enzyme and prevent proper digestion; rarely, pancreatitis might occur. Since trypsin activity is less in infants than older children, this is more likely to be a problem for them. The good news is that heating destroys the trypsin inhibitor, and for this reason, all soya products should be heated before eating (most, such as soya milk, tofu, etc, are heated during manufacture). In reality, the only possibility of consuming raw soya beans would be as bean sprouts, and for this reason I recommend that all bean sprouts should be cooked before consumption (see pages 168–9).

Tofu has a higher percentage of protein than any other natural food in existence, is very low in saturated fats and is entirely cholesterol-free. It has been a staple food for millions of people in Asia for centuries. In their classical treatise on the subject, William Shurtleff and Akiko Aoyagi explain its revered position: 'Along with rice, wheat, barley, and millet, soya beans were included among China's venerated *nuku* or 5 sacred grains, as early as the beginning of the Christian era ... the sense of the sacredness of soya bean foods is still alive in Japan today; here the words tofu, miso, and shoyu are commonly preceded in everyday speech by the honorific prefix 'O'. Rather than saying tofu, most people say "O – tofu", meaning honourable tofu...Today, the soya bean has become the king of the Japanese kitchen. Indeed, the arrival of tofu, miso and shoyu in Japan initiated a revolution in the national cuisine. Now when Japanese connoisseurs speak of these foods, they use many of the same terms we employ when evaluating cheeses or wines; traditional tofu masters often say that the consummation of their art is but to evoke the fine flavours latent in the soya bean...And when the new crop of soya beans arrives at tofu shops late each autumn, ardent devotees sample the first tofu with the discrimination and relish of French vintners.'[19]

Tofu is not like other foods. Amongst those who know it, it inspires both a huge degree of respect and a large dose of fascination. Like breadmaking, the process of making tofu is utterly absorbing, and a source of never ending fascination. Also like breadmaking, it often has a particularly strong appeal for men; and in cultures which prize it as a food, there are many mystiques and secrets surrounding the process. In Japan, traditional tofu masters have a saying that there are two things they will not show another person: how to make babies and how to make tofu. 'For the true tofu master', say Shurtleff and Aoyagi, 'practice is a living reality, giving energy and an ungraspable, deep meaning to daily work. To watch such a master at work is a rare and beautiful experience. His every gesture seems to emerge from a deep, still centre. Grace and economy of movement give a feeling of dance to even the most mundane of his actions. A sense of rhythm, alertness, and precision shows the results of years of patient training and untiring striving for excellence.' Although the average tofu maker's apprenticeship lasts eight years, it is by no means difficult to make good palatable tofu upon your first attempt (tofu fit for an emperor, however, may take a lifetime to master!).

See also: Simmered Tofu (p339); Fried Tofu (p339); Marinated Tofu (p339); Tofu 'Steak' with Mushrooms and Celery (p340); Tofu in Rich Sauce (p340)

Health Note

Eating tofu appreciably reduces the risk of cancer. That's the firm conclusion of several decades of large-scale studies. In Japan, scientists have tracked the health and cause of death of participants in a study which started in 1974. The results clearly show that eating tofu cuts the risk of stomach cancer. Other studies confirm this – but fail to point to one specific nutrient in tofu which is having this effect. Today, there is a growing realization among scientists that substances in the soya bean and its products which have traditionally been viewed as 'antinutrients' (protease inhibitors and phytic acid, for example) may be the very substances which give these products their powerful anticarcinogenic properties.[20] We clearly have much to learn.

How to make soymilk and tofu

Making soya milk and tofu is like making bread. It's relaxing and therapeutic, and costs far less than a psychiatrist. Have a go!

- Rinse a cup of soya beans and leave them to soak in 3 cups of water overnight – about 8–10 hours. Or, if you're in a hurry, pour the same amount of boiling water over the soya beans and soak until the beans double in size and are free of wrinkles (usually 2–4 hours).

- When they've finished soaking, drain them and put them in a blender with 2½ cups of boiling water for every cup of beans. Grind them to a fine slurry then pour the mixture into a pot.

- Cook over a medium high flame in the biggest pot you have – about 7–9l (1½–2 gallons) – stirring occasionally. As soon as the mixture starts to boil, turn the heat right down and leave it on a slow simmer for 20 minutes. Keep an eye on it though – it can boil up and foam over very quickly.

- After 20 minutes, put a colander in the second biggest pot you've got and line it with cheese-cloth. Then, pour or ladle your mixture into the colander, catching the pulp in the cloth, and the milk in the pot. Twist the cheesecloth tightly closed, and press on the pulp to extract whatever milk is left. At this stage, you have the milk! You can cool it, bottle it (it keeps for about 3 days), perhaps flavour it with a drop of almond essence, apple juice or a little cane sugar, and then drink it! Or you can continue and make tofu . . .
- When you've extracted the milk, prepare a solidifier. You can use different ingredients, depending on what kind of tofu you want. For subtle, sweet tofu, use 2 tsp calcium chloride (which you can get from your chemist). If you want mild soft tofu, use 2 tsp epsom salts. And if you want tart or sour tofu use 4 tbsp lemon juice, or 3 tblsp cider vinegar.
- Stir half the solidifier into your milk with a wooden spoon, wait until it's stopped swirling then pour a little more over the top. Put the lid on your second biggest pot to retain the heat for curdling and leave for 5 minutes. The tofu should start to form big, white curds. If it still looks milky, then poke the top few inches to activate curdling, and gently stir in a little more solidifier. Cover the pot and leave it for a couple of minutes.
- After 2 minutes you should have large white curds, floating in clear, yellow whey.
- If you have milky liquid left, add a bit more solidifier and give it another slow stir. Always stir gently so as not to break up the developing curds, and only stir the top few inches of the pot.
- When all the soya milk is formed into curds and clear whey, the tofu is ready for pressing. If you find you have very few curds, then either you added the solidifier too fast or the soya beans weren't ground fine enough leaving you with a thin milk and low yield.
- Now you're ready to press the tofu, and you need a tofu press. You can buy one, or make one yourself. All you need is a small box, about the size of a bread tin, with holes in it to let the whey drain out. You can make one out of wood, or – you guessed – simply drill small holes in your bread tin.
- Line a colander with cheese cloth, and ladle the curds into it. Pack the cheesecloth and curds into your tofu press. Put in the 'follower' (a piece of

wood cut to fit the inside of the press, or a second bread tin, without holes) and a weight (a jar of water, a clean rock or a brick will do) on top of the cheese cloth to press down on the curds. After about 20 minutes, longer if you want really firm tofu, remove the weight. The cheesecloth should be firm to the touch; gently peel the cloth away from the curds. This is your tofu.

- It tastes best fresh, but it will last for up to a week if you store it under water in the refrigerator, making sure to change the water every day.
- When you strained the slurry through the cheese-cloth, you separated it into soya milk, and a soya bean pulp which looks a little like sawdust. The pulp is high in dietary fibre, and absorbs flavours well. It improves soups, sautés and stews – or you can add it to your breakfast cereal. The Japanese use it to cure diarrhoea and also to enrich and stimulate the flow of a mother's milk. Whey left over from making tofu makes a tasty base for a broth or can be used as a shampoo or washing-up liquid. Try using it to polish your furniture – nothing need be wasted.

Commercially, tofu is available in either silken form (suitable for making low fat, high protein dressings and sauces) and firm, which can be utilized in an infinite number of ways. It can be scrambled, marinated, smoked, barbecued, crumbled into salads, in burgers, sandwiches and soups, or even used in a dessert. Start to use it, and you'll be dazzled by its potential!

Scrambled Tofu

Although this recipe gives precise measurements for specific vegetables, you may use whatever raw or left-over vegetables you have to hand. Simply heat them together with the spices and tofu, taste and adjust the flavour before serving piping hot.

Serves 4

Preparation time 30 minutes

1 tbsp oil
1 small onion, finely chopped
½ tsp freshly ground black pepper
1 medium carrot, finely chopped
1 medium potato, diced
225g (8oz) peas
¼ head cabbage, chopped
2 × 285g (10oz) cartons plain tofu
1½ tsp turmeric

3 spring onions, chopped
2 tbsp fresh parsley, chopped

Heat the oil in a large frying pan or saucepan and sauté the onion until clear and tender. Add the carrot and potato and cook for 7-10 minutes, stirring often. Add the peas and cabbage, stir well and cover the pan. Leave to cook over a medium heat for 5 minutes. Stir in the tofu and turmeric, cover the pan again and cook for 5 minutes. Finally, sprinkle the onions and parsley over the top, cover the pan and leave over a low heat for 5 minutes, while you prepare the plates. Serve hot over toast, steamed rice or baked potatoes.

NUTRIENT ANALYSIS
1 CUP TOFU, FIRM (252g)

KCalories	365.40
Total Fat (g)	21.97
Monounsaturated Fat (g)	4.85
Polyunsaturated Fat (g)	12.40
Saturated Fat (g)	3.18
Carbohydrate (g)	10.79
Protein (g)	39.77
Crude Fibre (g)	0.38
Vitamin A (RE)	42.84
Ascorbic Acid (mg)	0.50
Thiamin (mg)	0.40
Riboflavin (mg)	0.26
Niacin (mg)	0.96
Pantothenic Acid (mg)	0.34
Vitamin B6 (mg)	0.23
Folacin (mcg)	73.84
Vitamin B12 (mcg)	0.00
Calcium (mg)	1721.16
Iron (mg)	26.38
Zinc (mg)	3.96

Tempeh Pronounced 'tem – pay', this is a fermented soya bean product, made in the traditional manner for centuries throughout Indonesia where it is a basic food for millions of people. Like cheese, yoghurt and ginger beer, it is made with a cultured 'starter'. It is highly digestible, smells like fresh mushrooms and tastes remarkably similar to chicken or veal cutlets. Although it is quite easy to make at home, it is probably more convenient to buy it from the freezer cabinet of health food shops. Since the protein in tempeh is partially broken down during fermentation (the mould is called rhizopusoligosporus) it is a particularly suitable food for young children and older people.

Tempeh is typically sold in 15cm (6 inch) squares which are approximately 2.5cm (1 inch) thick. The easiest way to serve it is to cut the square into half diagonally, and then cut each half into three thinner, wedge-shaped slices. These should be then pan fried until crisp and golden brown on both sides, and then served with rice and a selection of vegetables. Shoyu or tamari sprinkled over the top will give it a little extra flavouring. Alternatively, it makes a sensational marinade (see below).

See also: Thiebou Diene (p321); Ackee in Pepper Sauce (p334)

NUTRIENT ANALYSIS
1 CUP TEMPEH (166g)

KCalories	330.34
Total Fat (g)	12.75
Monounsaturated Fat (g)	2.81
Polyunsaturated Fat (g)	7.19
Saturated Fat (g)	1.84
Carbohydrate (g)	28.27
Protein (g)	31.46
Crude Fibre (g)	4.96
Vitamin A (RE)	114.54
Ascorbic Acid (mg)	0.00
Thiamin (mg)	0.22
Riboflavin (mg)	0.18
Niacin (mg)	7.69
Pantothenic Acid (mg)	0.59
Vitamin B6 (mg)	0.50
Folacin (mcg)	86.32
Vitamin B12 (mcg)	1.66 (?)

Calcium (mg)	154.38
Iron (mg)	3.75
Zinc (mg)	3.00

Marinated Tempeh

Serves 4

Preparation time 1 hour 30 minutes, plus 6-8 hours marinating

2 × 225g (8oz) blocks tempeh, defrosted
5 cloves garlic, finely chopped
2 medium onions, chopped
1 tart apple, quartered, cored and chopped
200ml (7fl oz) oil
200ml (7fl oz) cider vinegar
juice of 2 lemons
60ml (2fl oz) soy sauce
25g (1oz) fresh ginger, sliced
2 tsp black peppercorns, crushed but not ground
1 tsp mustard seed, slightly crushed
12 whole cloves
1 × 7.5cm (3-inch) piece of cinnamon

Cut the tempeh into 2.5cm (1-inch) cubes and arrange in an oven dish. Mix the remaining ingredients together in a large jug. Stir well then pour over the tempeh. Cover the dish and leave to marinate for 6–8 hours (ideal for making in the morning and cooking when you get home from work!). You may, if you choose, let the tempeh marinate for up to 24 hours. Preheat the oven to 190°C/375°F/Gas Mark 5 and bake the tempeh for 1 hour. Serve hot over rice with steamed greens and sautéed carrots to accompany.

Health Note

Does tempeh contain vitamin B12? The answer is both yes and no. Tempeh probably originated in Indonesia, and a recent scientific analysis of tempeh samples purchased from various markets in Jakarta reveals that a high amount of the vitamin was present.[22] However, analysis of commercially-prepared Western tempeh shows exactly the opposite. What seems to be happening is this: as we know, vitamin B12 is produced exclusively by bacteria. In the East, tempeh is produced in an environment which contains a great bacterial diversity which in the West would be considered 'unhygienic'. Here, our production processes are tightly controlled to prevent anything other than the tempeh spores from flourishing. The result is that we consume tempeh which has no appreciable vitamin B12 content. Says vegan expert Dr. Michael Klaper: 'It's the price we pay for our disconnection from soil and water. If we were getting buckets of water from the stream or pulling carrots from a garden where the raccoons and rabbits run, we'd be getting B12.' Dr John McDougall, another expert on the meat-free way of living, couldn't agree more. 'There are helpful bacteria and harmful ones,' he says, 'and we've eliminated all of them. It boils down to the fact that people are too darned clean.'

Miso Paste-like in appearance and texture, miso is a fermented mixture of soya beans, salt and usually another cereal grain, such as rice or barley. It has subtle, aromatic flavours and comes in many different colours including orange, brown and yellow. It is one of the staples of every Japanese and Chinese kitchen, it is made by inoculating the basic ingredients with a mould (*koji*) and leaving it to age in cedarwood kegs for at least one year. It is most commonly used as an ingredient in soups, sauces, dressings, spreads, casseroles and other vegetable dishes. The miso industry is amongst the largest food industries in Japan today, and synthetic misos, which include various colourings and additives, are quite widely available. Buy traditionally-made miso wherever possible, since it is not only free of additives, but the complex fermentation process produces a wealth of substances such as enzymes and beneficial bacteria which have a positive effect upon human health. In Japan, it is commonly respected as a food that is also a medicine. The various types of miso include:

- Hacho miso. Soya bean miso, the heartiest and thickest of all, having a rich almost chocolate-like flavour
- Mugi miso. Barley miso, made with a combination of soya beans and barley, a mellow tasting miso whose colour can range from almost white through yellow to red.
- Kome miso. Rice miso, made from a combination of soya beans, rice and sea salt, the most commonly consumed in Japan, with a light and almost sweet taste.

A simple miso soup can be made by lightly sautéeing a selection of sliced vegetables (onions, leeks, turnips, potatoes) in a small amount of oil. Water is then added, and the soup slowly simmered, with a strip of kombu or wakame seaweed, for about half an hour. Finally, turn off the heat, and add a good dollop of miso to flavour. On no account should the soup be boiled with the miso in it, because this will destroy many of the beneficial, health-giving substances which the miso contains.

NUTRIENT ANALYSIS
½ CUP MISO (138g)

KCalories	284.28
Total Fat (g)	8.38
Monounsaturated Fat (g)	1.85
Polyunsaturated Fat (g)	4.73
Saturated Fat (g)	1.21
Carbohydrate (g)	38.58
Protein (g)	16.30
Crude Fibre (g)	3.41
Vitamin A (RE)	12.42
Ascorbic Acid (mg)	0.00
Thiamin (mg)	0.13
Riboflavin (mg)	0.35
Niacin (mg)	1.19
Pantothenic Acid (mg)	0.36
Vitamin B6 (mg)	0.30
Folacin (mcg)	45.54
Vitamin B12 (mcg)	0.00
Calcium (mg)	91.08
Iron (mg)	3.78
Zinc (mg)	4.58

Health Note

Epidemiological studies have shown that consuming miso (usually as soup) can reduce deaths from stomach cancer. Miso is a complex substance, and a number of factors are likely to be responsible for this protective effect:

Researchers from Okayama University Medical School in Japan have established that miso has antioxidant properties – probably arising from the antioxidants, isoflavones, and saponins present in the soya bean itself. Substances produced during miso's fermentation may also play an important role. One caution: research also shows that extremely salty miso soup (2g of salt per bowl, or more) probably *reverses* this effect – so go for the low-salt varieties.

Soy Sauce This is an ancient and traditional Japanese seasoning which has achieved prominence and acceptance the world over. It is a dark, rich sauce with a savoury, salty taste as well as a deep, mellowing background flavour. Very little is required within a dish or serving. There are three types:

- The first is the commercial, accelerated-production type which is widely available and usually sold as soy sauce. It is made in a very short time by speeding the process of fermentation using chemical additives. It usually contains colourings and preservatives as well.
- The second is called shoyu and is made by fermenting wheat and soya beans together for at least 3 years. During this time, the flavour develops making it a delicious addition to most savoury meals; the amino acids present in the ferment aid digestion. It is easy to find in healthfood, macrobiotic or Japanese grocery shops
- The third is tamari and is made by fermenting just soya beans and salt over a long period of time, between two and three years. It is less widely available than shoyu as, traditionally, much less of it is made. It is not used so often in cooking or as a table condiment as shoyu as its flavour is much stronger.

Both shoyu and tamari are fermented with koji, a mould which grows at the temperature of the human body and which develops enzymes helpful in the digestion of proteins and starches, similar to those found in our saliva.

Soya Flour This flour is made of ground, dried soya beans and produces a very dense, rich flour. It may be mixed with wheat flour (a ratio of one part soya flour to eight parts wheat flour is common) to increase the protein content of your bread. It is useful for binding purposes in some recipes (see Egg Replacers, p212).

Texturized Vegetable Protein Also known as TVP, this product is made from soya beans processed into a high-protein, low-fat food. TVP is made to resemble the look and texture of some meat products: it is available in mince or chunk form and in plain or meaty flavours such as chicken, beef or bacon. TVP is very versatile and easy to cook with, readily absorbing the flavours of herbs, spices, gravies and other meal components. It may be added to meals at the sauté stage of cooking, or hydrated with stock, water or other liquid at a ratio of one part TVP to two parts liquid. All healthfood shops sell TVP products such as Protoveg.
See also: Chilli Without Carne (p325)

Natto Though less readily available than tempeh at the moment, natto can generally be found in Chinese or Japanese grocery stores. Like tempeh, it is made by fermenting soya beans, but in this case, for less than 24 hours. It has an intriguing gossamer-like quality, and is one of the most unusual foods you will ever eat. The fermentation process makes the high quality protein of the soya beans particularly easy to digest. Serve natto in a small bowl beside a serving of freshly steamed rice, stir-fried vegetables and your favourite dipping sauce.

NUTRIENT ANALYSIS
½ CUP NATTO (88g)

KCalories	186.56
Total Fat (g)	9.68
Monounsaturated Fat (g)	2.14
Polyunsaturated Fat (g)	5.46
Saturated Fat (g)	1.40
Carbohydrate (g)	12.63
Protein (g)	15.59
Crude Fibre (g)	1.41
Vitamin A (RE)	0.00
Ascorbic Acid (mg)	11.44
Thiamin (mg)	0.14
Riboflavin (mg)	0.17
Niacin (mg)	0.00
Pantothenic Acid (mg)	0.19
Vitamin B6 (mg)	0.11
Folacin (mcg)	7.04
Vitamin B12 (mcg)	0.00
Calcium (mg)	190.96
Iron (mg)	7.57
Zinc (mg)	2.67

Spinach One of the most adaptable and delectable of all vegetables, spinach's bad reputation has arisen solely through the most execrable cooking practices imaginable. It is a light and delicate vegetable, which deserves delicate handling and considerate cooking; instead, the ponderous hand and sterile mind of Victorian cookery has ruined this congenial plant for generations of hapless diners. The wretched Mrs Beeton, whose life must have been an eternal oscillation between the sugary and the blubbery, codified the sin thus: 'Put it [the spinach] into a saucepan with about a level tablespoonful of salt, and just sufficient water to cover the bottom of the pan. Boil uncovered from 15 to 25 minutes, occasionally pressing it down, and turning it over with a wooden spoon.' Such sadistic cruelty to vegetables is, sadly, absolutely typical of the Mrs Beeton school of cookery which, it is depressing to note, still has its adherents, even today. The French chef Paul Bocuse, himself no great advocate of *nouvelle cuisine*, suggests boiling spinach for no more than 8 minutes, but as you will see from the recipes below, even this may be too much.

Spinach is thought to have originated in Persia (Iran) from where it sped both East and West, reaching China via Nepal in 647 AD and Spain in 1100 AD. It was often cooked with sugar in the Middle Ages, and became a favourite food for Lent, since it ripened at just the right time.

There are essentially two types: the smooth seeded (lighter colour, ripens in the summer) and the prickly seeded (darker colour, ripens in the winter). The smooth seeded is generally accepted to have the finer taste. When buying spinach, you should always choose leaves which are firm and vigorous. Younger leaves are smaller and lighter in colour, and should be chosen in preference to darker, tougher ones for raw consumption or for use in dishes which would not benefit from the earthy flavourings of the older plants. Also, remember how dramatically spinach decreases during the cooking process. What may seem to be an extravagant overpurchase in the supermarket dematerializes quite alarmingly in the kitchen. As a rough guide, 1kg (2lbs) of fresh spinach is about the right quantity to buy to feed 2–4 people, when served with rice and one or two other vegetables. Spinach should be prepared sympathetically. Snip off the pink root tips and gently wash each leaf by hand under running water to dislodge the inevitable mud and grit (just one remaining grain of sand can ruin an entire meal). On no account should you leave the spinach to soak in water, as this will rapidly produce a flaccid and demineralized vegetable.

See also: Spanikopita (p349); Sag Aloo (p276); Mnkhwani (p314); Muriwo ne Dovi (p323); Lu Pulu (p338)

Health Note

Nutritionally, spinach is every bit as good as Popeye always believed. Just one cup of boiled spinach provides one-and-a-half times the adult recommended daily allowance for folic acid and vitamin A, two-thirds of the requirement for iron, and one-third of the requirement for vitamin C, riboflavin, vitamin B6, calcium and potassium. It also contains useful amounts of thiamin and zinc. Like rhubarb, spinach contains oxalic acid and the comments given under that vegetable apply. However, there is little doubt that spinach, consumed a couple of times a week, is a very useful and nutritious addition to the vegetarian diet. Natural therapists have used spinach to treat anaemia, constipation, arthritis and high blood pressure. Fresh spinach also contains varying amounts of glutathione, the antioxidant which can prevent heart disease, cancer and other inflammatory ailments. Spinach, together with carrots, has been found by many scientific studies to drastically reduce the risk of strokes and heart attacks.

NUTRIENT ANALYSIS
1 CUP SPINACH, BOILED (180g)

KCalories	41.40
Total Fat (g)	0.47
Monounsaturated Fat (g)	0.01
Polyunsaturated Fat (g)	0.19
Saturated Fat (g)	0.08
Carbohydrate (g)	6.75
Protein (g)	5.35
Crude Fibre (g)	1.58
Vitamin A (RE)	1474.20
Ascorbic Acid (mg)	17.64
Thiamin (mg)	0.17
Riboflavin (mg)	0.42
Niacin (mg)	0.88
Pantothenic Acid (mg)	0.26
Vitamin B6 (mg)	0.44
Folacin (mcg)	262.44
Vitamin B12 (mcg)	0.00
Calcium (mg)	244.80
Iron (mg)	6.43
Zinc (mg)	1.37

Spiced Spinach

Serves 4
Preparation time 40 minutes

1kg (2lbs) fresh spinach, washed, trimmed and chopped
1 tbsp oil
5–7 cloves garlic, chopped
1 tsp cumin seeds
3 spring onions, chopped
1 fresh chilli, finely chopped
5 cardamom pods, slightly crushed
5 whole cloves
several small pieces of cinnamon
½ tsp chilli powder
50g (2oz) pine nuts (optional)
2 medium tomatoes, chopped

Prepare the spinach, dry it in a clean tea towel and put to one side. Heat the oil in a large, deep saucepan over a medium to high heat and sauté the garlic and cumin seeds for 2–3 minutes, stirring constantly. Add the onions, chilli, cardamom, cloves, cinnamon and chilli powder and stir for 3 minutes, stirring constantly. Add the pine nuts at this time if using them. Turn the dry spinach into the saucepan and place the tomatoes on top. Cover the pan and leave to cook for 3–5 minutes. Stir well, cover the pan again and cook a further 3–5 minutes. Serve hot with steamed rice and your favourite dhal (see page 344).

Cream of Spinach Soup

Serves 4
Preparation time 1 hour

450g (1lb) fresh spinach, washed, trimmed and
    chopped
1 tbsp oil
3 cloves garlic, finely chopped
2 medium onions, chopped
1 tsp freshly ground black pepper
2 tsp yeast extract
570ml (1 pint) vegetable stock or water
1 tbsp oil
2 tsp caraway seeds
1 tbsp plain flour or cornflour
570ml (1 pint) soya milk
1 tsp ground coriander

Prepare the spinach and turn into a colander to drain. Heat the oil in a large, deep saucepan over a medium heat and sauté the garlic and onions until clear and tender. Add the pepper and stir for 1 minute. Stir in the yeast extract then add the vegetable stock and bring to a low boil. Add the spinach, cover the pan and reduce the heat. Leave to simmer gently for 3–5 minutes. Meanwhile, heat the other measure of oil in a saucepan and sauté the caraway seeds for 2 minutes. Sprinkle the flour over the oil and stir to make a thick paste (roux). Add the soya milk, a little at a time, stirring after each addition to make a sauce. Sprinkle the coriander over the sauce, stir well and remove from the heat. Pour this sauce into the soup, stirring constantly as you do so. Add a little more stock if necessary to create the thickness of soup you enjoy. Serve hot with garlic bread (see page 217) and a garnish of coriander leaf.

Spinach and Tomato Quiche

Serves 4
Preparation time 1 hour

For the pastry base:
170g (6oz) plain flour
100g (4oz) shredded vegetable suet
1 tbsp cold water

For the filling:
1 tbsp oil
3 cloves garlic, finely chopped
1 medium onion, thinly sliced
½ tsp freshly ground black pepper
¼ tsp ground nutmeg
450g (1lb) fresh spinach, washed, trimmed, chopped
    and dried
2 medium tomatoes, sliced
285g (10oz) plain tofu
6 tbsp oil
200ml (7fl oz) soya milk

Preheat the oven to 180°C/350°F/Gas Mark 4. Mix the flour and suet together in a mixing bowl and work in the water to make a crumbly texture. Press this mixture into a 30.5cm (12-inch) flan dish, ensuring it rises up the sides of the dish. Heat the oil in a frying pan and sauté the garlic and onion until clear and tender. Add the pepper and nutmeg and stir for 1 minute. Remove the sauté from the heat. Spoon this mixture into the flan case and spread to the edges. Arrange the spinach over the sauté and the sliced tomatoes over the spinach. Blend the remaining ingredients together in a food processor and pour over the flan. Bake for 35 minutes, until a golden crust forms on top of the quiche. Serve hot with a potato dish and steamed green beans, or cold with a salad.

Strawberries The saying 'good looks aren't everything' might have been devised specifically for the strawberry; for nowhere else in the plant kingdom does the promise so greatly overstate the reality. It was not always thus – the wild strawberry from which today's enfeebled specimens originate was indeed a fruit of distinction, as the expert on edible wild plants Richard Mabey points out: 'The tiny fruits of the wild strawberry are often no bigger than a child's beads. Yet each one holds more sweetness and flavour than any of the monsters grown for commerce. Most of these are freaks, so dogmatically bred to astonish by their colour and size that their insides taste like snow.'[23] Any fruit which needs to be doused in copious quantities of sugar before any flavour worth mentioning can be coaxed out of it is, surely, something of a national disgrace. And yet, the food writers and producers of cookery books are uniformly silent on this subject.

The history of the strawberry provides us with a vivid example of the perils of genetic engineering, a lesson which (I say it again, see under Potato, p275) we ignore at our peril. Wild strawberries were, originally, indigenous to both the old and the new worlds. The earliest settlers in North America observed the native Americans producing strawberry bread with fruit and cornmeal – a forerunner of today's strawberry shortcake. Specimen plants from both North America (*Fragaria virginiana*) and South America (*Fragaria chiloensis*) were taken back to France and hybridized, *et voila*, the ancestor of the modern strawberry was born.

In the 19th century, the British did much to 'improve' the quality of the strawberry, producing fruit of greater and greater size, and therefore, marketability. It is sad that the wild strawberry is now so rarely encountered in Western countries, because its intense flavour puts all of today's commercial varieties to shame, and reveals them to be, in fact, degenerate fruit. The most disturbing part of this story is that the process is being repeated with other fruit; the apple, for example, is increasingly being bred for its superficial good looks. In Shakespeare's *Henry V*, the Bishop of Ely says: 'The strawberry grows underneath the nettle and wholesome berries thrive and ripen best neighbour'd by fruit of baser quality.' Today, it would be the nettle that has more flavour. Given that you are unlikely to find a strawberry with a taste that is anything more than a ghost of its once-great self, the other points to look for when purchasing them are:

- Uniform ripening. It is a common salesman's trick to turn strawberries which have only ripened on one side so that the green colour is hidden, make sure you examine the top layer of strawberries in a punnet to check for this and also to ensure that the strawberries underneath are both ripe and free from mould.
- They should have a clear, shiny skin, be unbruised and firm to the touch. They deteriorate very quickly and cannot be stored. Freezing strawberries is a popular occupation in some households, but one has to question whether the end product – watery pink mush – really justifies the effort involved.
- Look for fruit which have their leaves and short stalks still attached, as they will be considerably fresher than those which do not.

The flesh of the strawberry is very delicate, and requires careful handling during the preparation process. Like most commercially produced fruit and vegetables, they are likely to have been exposed to the usual cocktail of agrochemicals, and must therefore be washed before consumption. Immersion for 15 to 20 minutes in a bowl of water into which 140ml (¼ pint) of vinegar has been stirred, will do much to remove grime and other contaminants.

Health Note

Strawberries are usually high in vitamin C, one cup of raw fruit will provide about one-and-a-half times the adult recommended daily allowance. Natural therapists hold that strawberries are effective in cleansing the skin, although as with many natural therapies, the initial reaction may be a worsening of the condition. They have also been used to treat gout, constipation, high blood pressure and syphilis. In times gone by, pale and interesting ladies would seek to render themselves even more death-like, and doubtless additionally fascinating, by the application of a cut strawberry rubbed over the face immediately after washing.

NUTRIENT ANALYSIS
1 CUP STRAWBERRIES, FRESH (149g)

KCalories	44.70
Total Fat (g)	0.55
Monounsaturated Fat (g)	0.08
Polyunsaturated Fat (g)	0.28
Saturated Fat (g)	0.03
Carbohydrate (g)	10.46
Protein (g)	0.91
Crude Fibre (g)	0.79

Vitamin A (RE)	4.47
Ascorbic Acid (mg)	84.48
Thiamin (mg)	0.03
Riboflavin (mg)	0.10
Niacin (mg)	0.34
Pantothenic Acid (mg)	0.51
Vitamin B6 (mg)	0.09
Folacin (mcg)	26.37
Vitamin B12 (mcg)	0.00
Calcium (mg)	20.86
Iron (mg)	0.57
Zinc (mg)	0.19

Strawberry Milkshake

Serves 1
Preparation time 10 minutes

225g (8oz) fresh strawberries, dehulled and washed
285ml (½ pint) soya milk, chilled
¼ tsp vanilla essence

Place these ingredients into a food processor and purée until smooth. Pour into a pretty glass, garnish with a leaf of fresh mint or a couple flaked almonds and serve. You can make the strawberries go further by adding 1 ripe banana and another 285ml (½ pint) soya milk to this recipe, in which case it serves two.

Strawberry Tart

Makes 1 30.5cm (12 inch) flan
Preparation time 2 hours

For the pastry base:
170g (6oz) plain flour
100g (4oz) shredded vegetable suet
1 tbsp cold water

For the filling:
1kg (2lbs) fresh strawberries, dehulled and washed
3 tbsp sugar
1x3g pkt agar powder
140ml (¼ pint) cold water
420ml (¾ pint) apple juice or water
2 tbsp grenadine (optional)

Preheat the oven to 180°C/350°F/Gas Mark 4. Mix

the flour and suet together in a mixing bowl and work in the water to make a crumbly texture. Turn this mixture into the flan dish and press into place, ensuring the pastry rises up the sides of the dish. Bake the pastry base for 15 minutes. Remove from the oven and leave to cool.

Take about one-quarter of the strawberries and purée, with the sugar, to a smooth paste. Spread this in the cooled flan case. Slice the remaining strawberries in half (if they are small, you may leave them whole) and arrange over the strawberry spread. Dissolve the agar in the cold water and bring to the boil over a medium heat. Stir well then remove from the heat and stir in the apple juice. Stir in the grenadine syrup at this stage, if you like. Let the agar mixture cool to blood temperature, then pour it slowly over the strawberries in the flan case ensuring an even coverage. Chill the flan in the refrigerator until the jelly has set. Serve chilled with Soya Creem or your favourite dessert sauce.

Sunflower Seeds The seeds of this beautiful and inspiring flower are a veritable power house of nutrition, so much so that they should really be a regular part of every vegetarian's diet. In common with pumpkin seeds, they provide a concentrated yet natural dose of those nutrients which are not easy to obtain in the modern diet, but unlike pumpkin seeds, sunflower seeds are milder, moister and more rounded, which is a consideration for older people and those who dislike the sharp points often found on pumpkin seeds.

Originating from Mexico and Peru, the sunflower reached Europe via North America, although the Spanish could do very little with it for the first couple of hundred years. It is curious to note that the modern world owes a debt of gratitude to Peter the Great for taking steps to popularize this seed. This innovative emperor scoured Western Europe, acquiring knowledge of Western technology which was then used to modernize Russia. One of Peter's discoveries was the sunflower, which arrived in Russia at the moment when the church had, for its own mysterious reasons, banned the eating of oily plants on fast days. The sunflower, being such a recent introduction, was not on the proscribed list, and therefore became immediately popular amongst the peasantry, who took to chewing it on fast days. Subsequently, Russia became, and still is, the largest producer of sunflowers.

Today, sunflower seeds are available in all health

food shops and many supermarkets, and they can be bought dehulled (this is a very finicky operation to perform at home) but unroasted or otherwise processed. Like pumpkin seeds, they make an excellent and highly nutritious snack when slightly roasted in a hot skillet (with no added oil) then lightly sprinkled with soya sauce for added seasoning, at the very end of the roasting. Like many other seeds, they can be successfully sprouted, and their sprouts make a very palatable ingredient in winter salads.

Sunflower seed spread is available in most health-food shops and is especially welcome to those who are allergic to peanut butter. Sunflower seed spread is somewhat like tahini, but rather thicker, and makes a good basic ingredient for packed lunch sandwiches.

Sunflower oil is famed for its health-giving properties, is high in polyunsaturated fat, contains a high proportion of essential fatty acids, and its neutral taste and flavour means that it can be used for both cooking and salad dressings. Bright light will cause this oil to deteriorate, so it should always be stored in a dark bottle or cupboard.

NUTRIENT ANALYSIS
1oz SUNFLOWER SEEDS (25g)

KCalories	161.88
Total Fat (g)	14.08
Monounsaturated Fat (g)	2.69
Polyunsaturated Fat (g)	9.30
Saturated Fat (g)	1.48
Carbohydrate (g)	5.33
Protein (g)	6.47
Crude Fibre (g)	1.18
Vitamin A (RE)	1.42
Ascorbic Acid (mg)	0.40
Thiamin (mg)	0.65
Riboflavin (mg)	0.07
Niacin (mg)	1.28
Pantothenic Acid (mg)	1.92
Vitamin B6 (mg)	0.22
Folacin (mcg)	64.58
Vitamin B12 (mcg)	0.00
Calcium (mg)	32.94
Iron (mg)	1.92
Zinc (mg)	1.44

Sunflower Flapjacks

Serves 4
Preparation time 1 hour

For the pastry:
170g (6oz) plain flour
100g (4oz) rolled oats
2 tsp baking powder
1 tsp bicarbonate of soda
1 tsp ground cinnamon
90ml (3 fl oz) oil
140ml (¼ pint) barley malt syrup

For the filling:
100g (4oz) sunflower seeds, crushed
100g (4oz) dried dates, chopped
140ml (¼ pint) apple juice

Preheat the oven to 180°C/350°F/Gas Mark 4 and lightly oil a 23x23cm (9x9 inch) baking tin. Mix the dry ingredients together in a bowl and stir in the oil and syrup, working to an even consistency. Turn just over half of this mixture into the baking tin and press firmly into place. Combine the ingredients for the filling and run through a mouli if possible (it is acceptable without this stage). Spread the filling over the base; turn the remaining flour and oat mixture over the filling and lightly press into place. Bake for 25 minutes. Cool in the tin on a wire rack, slice and serve.

Health Note

Just a couple of ounces of toasted sunflower seeds (350 Kcalories) provides 40 per cent of the adult daily recommended allowance for iron, and one-fifth of the protein and zinc requirements. In natural medicine, sunflower seeds are used as a general restorative and body builder, particularly for children, and sunflower seeds have been used to treat poor fingernails, tooth decay, arthritis and dryness of skin. Sunflower seed oil is one of the best possible sources of the essential fatty acids; do make sure, however, to buy cold pressed (not heat treated) oil and keep it in a cool dark place, with the top tightly secured to prevent oxidization. Use it for dressings, spreading on bread in place of butter, and other unheated purposes – but not for frying.

Tempeh see **Soya Beans**

Tofu see **Soya Beans**

Tomatoes Sadly, there is every indication that the tomato is going the way of the strawberry and the apple – a ravishingly beautiful fruit to look at, but wholly lacking in taste and flavour. Although the varieties of tomatoes commercially available are still some way from this bland oblivion, there really is no comparison between the taste of a commercial plant and the homegrown specimen. Tomatoes are not particularly difficult to grow, and if you have green fingers, you will enjoy it – and most certainly enjoy the fruits of your labour.

In the 400 years since the tomato's arrival in Spain from Peru, where it was discovered growing wild in the Andes, the ubiquitous tomato has been both vilified and revered. Largely regarded as a decorative, but poisonous, plant until the beginning of the 18th century, its culinary success was slow to ignite, there being few volunteers to risk their lives with this dangerous-looking berry. Once popularized in Spain, however, word of it quickly spread to the kingdom of Naples, which was at that time a Spanish possession. It rapidly gained acceptance throughout the whole of Italy; to the extent that it is now quite impossible to imagine Italian food without the tomato as a central ingredient.

By 1790, the Parisians were experimenting with tomatoes, and its international success was assured. Even so, many cultures still viewed it with deep suspicion. To this day, practitioners of macrobiotic cookery will have nothing to do with it, nor with other members of the deadly nightshade family. In America, the citizens of Newport, Rhode Island, were so impressed with the foolhardy bravery of one M. F. Corne, (being the first inhabitant to consume this crimson comestible) that they rather touchingly erected a statue to him. At the time, it was widely believed that the tomato plant caused cancer, and that its seeds would precipitate an attack of appendicitis.

Today, it is a highly processed food, sometimes ripened with the use of ethylene gas; and one of the first foodstuffs to be genetically engineered for an extended shelf life. Although there are countless varieties of tomato, most of these are only available to those who choose to grow their own. In the shops, only a handful of varieties are commonly available, amongst them:

- Cherry Tomato. Small, pretty, and sweet: they can be added whole or quartered to salads and used as garnish on other dishes, and for those who enjoy spending long hours on small, intricate tasks, the tops and insides can be carefully removed, and replaced with a savoury stuffing for use at *soigné* cocktail parties.
- Beef Tomato. An offputting name for vegetarians, these tomatoes are the very opposite of the cherry variety: extremely large, somewhat bland, and very dense. They may be stuffed, or sliced for use in sandwiches, burgers or salads.
- Plum Tomato. Not always available in greengrocer, but invariably available canned, they are the tomato of choice for all pasta dishes and have a beautifully intense and sweet flavour.

Tomatoes should be bought and used at maximum ripeness, which is not easy to judge purely from the colour. Tomatoes exhibiting patches of green are certainly not ripe, but even those with an all round redness may still not be ripe. The test is to cut one in half, and see whether the seeds are themselves green: if so, the tomato is not yet ready. The smell, too, will give a good indication of the tomato's quality and readiness. As one grower told me, with lamentable delicacy but absolute precision, 'A good tomato should smell of cat's piss.' Certain vegetables combine extremely well with tomatoes to produce classical flavours. The dried herb oregano massively improves the depth of flavour of even canned tomatoes, as does fresh basil (dried basil is often too intense).

See also: Hidden Pepper Tomato Sauce (p269); Rich Tomato Sauce (p353)

NUTRIENT ANALYSIS
1 CUP TOMATOES, FRESH (180g)

KCalories	37.80
Total Fat (g)	0.59
Monounsaturated Fat (g)	0.09

Polyunsaturated Fat (g)	0.24
Saturated Fat (g)	0.08
Carbohydrate (g)	8.35
Protein (g)	1.53
Crude Fibre (g)	1.17
Vitamin A (RE)	111.60
Ascorbic Acid (mg)	34.38
Thiamin (mg)	0.11
Riboflavin (mg)	0.09
Niacin (mg)	1.13
Pantothenic Acid (mg)	0.44
Vitamin B6 (mg)	0.14
Folacin (mcg)	27.00
Vitamin B12 (mcg)	0.00
Calcium (mg)	9.00
Iron (mg)	0.81
Zinc (mg)	0.16

Simple Tomato Salad

Serves 4
Preparation time 35 minutes

4 ripe 'beef' tomatoes
1 tbsp salt
1 tsp celery seed
¼ tsp freshly ground black pepper
1 tbsp fresh basil, chopped
1 tbsp fresh parsley, chopped
1 lemon, quartered

Wash and slice the tomatoes and arrange on a large platter. Sprinkle the salt over them and leave to one side for 30 minutes. Drain away the juices and sprinkle with the celery seed and pepper. Combine the basil and parsley and sprinkle over the seasonings. Serve at once with a wedge of lemon for each serving, to be squeezed over the salad. This salad is excellent with a serving of Marinated Tofu (p339).

Health Note

The genetically-engineered tomato is the first of many genetically-altered foodstuffs to hit the supermarket shelves over the next decades. By inactivating a gene that produces an enzyme which causes rotting, scientists have created a tomato that can be picked ripe and shipped without turning mushy. Genetic engineering poses many serious questions for vegetarians – particularly when animal genes are introduced into plants. Today, scientists are working on ways to insert an 'antifreeze' gene from the Arctic flounder into tomatoes intended for making tomato paste (it will freeze and thaw better) and to splice chicken genes into the potato to increase disease resistance.

Tomorrow, it's likely that human genes will be given to fish (to increase their size) and also to pigs (in order to create leaner pork). Such novel foods raise many ethical questions which we must address today if we wish to influence the food on tomorrow's menu.

Turnips Traditionally considered to be peasant food, because of their ability to flourish in poor soil, ripen quickly and store well, sophisticated Western cuisine has more or less turned its back on this humble member of the cabbage family, which is very much our loss. It is in fact a very adaptable vegetable, lending itself to a multitude of uses either raw or cooked, and its cheapness and nutritional profile (particularly when the leaves are consumed) make it overdue for a revival in its popularity.

There is no general agreement as to the origin of this vegetable; Russia, Siberia and Asia Minor have all been proposed. Certainly, it was well known to the Greeks and Romans, a staple food for many during the Middle Ages, and one of the first vegetables to be systematically improved by modern agricultural practices (by Viscount Townshend in the early 18th century, who after an unsuccessful political career retired to devote his life to the vegetable – thus earning the nickname Turnip Townshend for posterity).

Turnips vary considerably in size and colour – the largest is reported to have weighed 45.5kg (100lbs) and was grown in California in 1850, and the smallest can be no bigger than a billiard ball. The flesh is generally white, although yellow and pink varieties also exist. There are two main harvests. Spring turnips are mild in flavour and therefore good for grating into salads raw, but they will not keep and should be used soon after purchase. They should preferably be bought with their leaves intact as the leaves are both delicious and highly nutritious. Winter turnips are much stronger in flavour (blanching them for 10 minutes ameliorates this), are best included in a hearty winter casserole or soup, and will keep for some time in a cool place. They should be prepared according to the toughness of their skins. Winter turnips are likely to be particularly thick skinned and therefore should be peeled; spring ones should simply be cleaned thoroughly.

NUTRIENT ANALYSIS
1 CUP TURNIPS, FRESH (130g)

KCalories	35.10
Total Fat (g)	0.13
Monounsaturated Fat (g)	0.01
Polyunsaturated Fat (g)	0.07
Saturated Fat (g)	0.01
Carbohydrate (g)	8.10
Protein (g)	1.17
Crude Fibre (g)	1.17
Vitamin A (RE)	0.00
Ascorbic Acid (mg)	27.30
Thiamin (mg)	0.05
Riboflavin (mg)	0.04
Niacin (mg)	0.52
Pantothenic Acid (mg)	0.26
Vitamin B6 (mg)	0.12
Folacin (mcg)	18.85
Vitamin B12 (mcg)	0.00
Calcium (mg)	39.00
Iron (mg)	0.39
Zinc (mg)	0.35

Blushing Pickled Turnips

Makes approximately 1l (2 pints)
Preparation time 3 days, plus 1 week

3–5 medium turnips, scrubbed and sliced into 'chips'
3 tbsp salt
1 small onion, quartered
1 fresh chilli

285ml (½ pint) rice vinegar
2 tbsp barley malt syrup
1 very small beetroot, scrubbed, topped and tailed

Place a layer of the sliced turnips in a pickle press and sprinkle a little of the salt over them. Continue layering turnip and salt, close the press and leave for 3 days. Drain the liquid away and pack the turnips into a large, sterilized jar with the onion and chilli. Place the vinegar, syrup and beetroot in an enamel saucepan over a medium heat. Stir constantly to dissolve the syrup and bring the mixture to a low boil. When the vinegar is very hot and coloured by the beetroot, remove it from the heat, remove the beetroot and pour the liquid over the the turnip in the jar. Seal the jar and leave for at least 1 week. Serve with a selection of olives, crudités and dips.

Health Note

Fresh turnip, as used in salads, is rich in vitamin C: one cup yields about half the adult daily requirement. Turnip greens are equally rich in this nutrient – one cup of boiled greens provides two-thirds of the adult daily requirement. Additionally, turnip greens yield three-quarters of the daily requirement for folic acid and vitamin A, and a quarter of the adult daily requirement for calcium. It is interesting to note that, measure for measure, turnip greens are as rich in calcium as milk is. In common with other members of the cabbage family, such as brussels sprouts, collard and kale, turnip greens contain a group of chemicals known as indoles, which can stop or delay the lethal effects of certain carcinogenic chemicals.

Walnuts 'A woman, a dog and a walnut tree, the more you beat them, the better they be.' So runs the obnoxious old English rhyme, which is – at least – true in one respect: administering a good thrashing to a walnut tree will often persuade it to bear fruit – I have seen it with my own eyes. This custom was so widespread, that older walnut trees – and they can live for 200 years or more – sometimes still bear the visible scars of beatings administered a century or more ago. Although commonly referred to as the English walnut, the tree in fact originated in Persia (Iran) and was highly regarded by both Greeks and Romans, the latter dedicating it to Jupiter from which its Latin taxonomy *juglans*, is derived. There is no significant difference in the varieties or species of walnut commonly available; instead, they are distinguished by the degree of ripeness of the nut when harvested, and by the way it is subsequently processed. Fresh nuts are occasionally encountered during the month of October; they are picked while still green and with a high moisture content, and consequently will not keep. These are the nuts that are made into pickled walnuts, a popular delicacy of considerable flavour when made properly (many commercially prepared pickled walnuts use substandard ingredients and taste either excessively sweet or acidic).

A little later in the season, the nuts are sold dried. The shells are particularly hard, and with the widespread availability of ready shelled nuts, it is tempting to forego all the hard work involved in cracking them yourself. Two warnings: first, like all nuts their flavour will rapidly deteriorate once removed from their protective shells; secondly, their essential oil is not stable (it is exquisite on salads, but will rapidly go rancid) so you must ensure that you are buying very recently shelled nuts. If possible, sample one or two before buying to ensure that they are not old – their flavour becomes harsh with time. Walnuts naturally lend themselves to both sweet and savoury uses, some of which are shown below.

See also: Shoo-Fly Pie (p327); Walnut, Date and Apple Strudel (p355)

NUTRIENT ANALYSIS
1oz WALNUTS, DRIED (25g)

KCalories	182.33
Total Fat (g)	17.57
Monounsaturated Fat (g)	4.03
Polyunsaturated Fat (g)	11.11
Saturated Fat (g)	1.59
Carbohydrate (g)	5.21
Protein (g)	4.06
Crude Fibre (g)	1.31
Vitamin A (RE)	3.41
Ascorbic Acid (mg)	0.91
Thiamin (mg)	0.11

Riboflavin (mg)	0.04
Niacin (mg)	0.30
Pantothenic Acid (mg)	0.18
Vitamin B6 (mg)	0.16
Folacin (mcg)	18.74
Vitamin B12 (mcg)	0.00
Calcium (mg)	26.70
Iron (mg)	0.69
Zinc (mg)	0.78

Classic Walnut and Red Cabbage Salad
Serves 4
Preparation time 30 minutes

100–170g (4–6oz) walnut halves
1 small red cabbage, shredded
2 tart eating apples, quartered, cored and chopped
1 small onion, thinly sliced
1 tbsp fresh parsley, chopped
3 cloves garlic, finely chopped
2 tbsp cider vinegar
3 tbsp olive oil
½ tsp dried marjoram
¼ tsp salt
½ tsp freshly ground black pepper

Mix the walnuts, cabbage, apple, onion, parsley and garlic together in a large salad bowl. Blend the remaining ingredients together in a jar or jug and pour over the salad. Serve immediately with a dollop of plain soya yoghurt if desired. This salad will keep 24 hours if stirred occasionally; its texture and flavour alter during this time. A variation involves finely chopping 2 slices of preserved oranges (see Oranges in Olive Oil, p253) and tossing these in with the salad ingredients. Replace the olive oil in the dressing with olive oil in which the oranges have been preserved.

Health Note

Walnuts are high energy foods – 50g (2oz) yield approximately 360 calories. The majority of this comes from polyunsaturated fats; unlike brazil nuts, walnuts contain very little saturated fat. The same quantity of walnuts will supply about one-fifth of the adult daily requirements for thiamin, vitamin B6, folic acid, iron and zinc.

They are a good source of linoleic acid, an omega-6 fatty acid which is thought to have a protective effect against many modern diseases. Furthermore, they are also a good source of glutathione, an important antioxidant. The evidence from several recent scientific studies shows that people who regularly consume walnuts can significantly reduce their risk of heart disease. Not only this, it has now been demonstrated that walnuts can lower blood cholesterol levels as well! Practitioners of natural medicine have known about the health benefits of walnuts for centuries. Its bark and leaves have been used both as a laxative and in the treatment of skin problems, such as eczema and ulcers. The nuts themselves have been used to treat constipation, as a general restorative, and to treat patients afflicted with liver ailments.

Protein (g)	1.19
Crude Fibre (g)	0.47
Vitamin A (RE)	5.68
Ascorbic Acid (mg)	10.22
Thiamin (mg)	0.05
Riboflavin (mg)	0.05
Niacin (mg)	0.23
Pantothenic Acid (mg)	0.16
Vitamin B6 (mg)	0.12
Folacin (mcg)	19.23
Vitamin B12 (mcg)	0.00
Calcium (mg)	5.11
Iron (mg)	0.40
Zinc (mg)	0.25

Water Chestnuts Generally available in the West only in cans, water chestnuts are, in fact, tubers and in China are considered to be a grain rather than a nut, sometimes consumed in the form of flour. Crisp and luscious, they are commonly used, accompanied by bamboo shoots and bean sprouts, in oriental stir-fries. They have good 'mouth feel' as the food technologists put it, and possess the ability of fooling the taste buds into thinking that the dish into which they are included is much higher in fat than it really is. (For instructions on creating low fat stir-fries, see Bamboo Shoots, p182.) Conventional nutritional analysis is not particularly revealing; most authorities consider that they contain virtually no nutrients at all. It is likely, however, that they may contain significant amounts of essential trace minerals, depending upon the location and composition of their growing medium.

NUTRIENT ANALYSIS
1oz WATER CHESTNUTS, CANNED (28g)

KCalories	63.62
Total Fat (g)	0.32
Monounsaturated Fat (g)	0.17
Polyunsaturated Fat (g)	0.08
Saturated Fat (g)	0.05
Carbohydrate (g)	13.94

Watercress A relative of the common garden nasturtium, watercress has a mustardy flavour which is at its peak during the summer months. It is grown in running water, and is best bought from a commercial grower rather than self-gathered – this eliminates any danger of confusion with the poisonous 'fool's cress'. Also, watercress is an effective absorber of heavy metals and industrial pollutants (and might, therefore, make a good detoxifier) so must be cultivated in clean and controlled conditions. It adds a wonderful zest and spice to salads, and is a savoury 'extra' in many kinds of soups – just add a handful of the plant to a soup after the other vegetables are cooked so as not to destroy its spicy taste.

NUTRIENT ANALYSIS
½ CUP WATERCRESS, FRESH (28g)

KCalories	1.87
Total Fat (g)	0.02
Monounsaturated Fat (g)	0.00
Polyunsaturated Fat (g)	0.01
Saturated Fat (g)	0.00
Carbohydrate (g)	0.22
Protein (g)	0.39
Crude Fibre (g)	0.12

Vitamin A (RE)	79.90
Ascorbic Acid (mg)	7.31
Thiamin (mg)	0.02
Riboflavin (mg)	0.02
Niacin (mg)	0.03
Pantothenic Acid (mg)	0.05
Vitamin B6 (mg)	0.02
Folacin (mcg)	1.56
Vitamin B12 (mcg)	0.00
Calcium (mg)	20.40
Iron (mg)	0.03
Zinc (mg)	0.02

Health Note

One cup of chopped watercress supplies about a quarter of the adult requirement for vitamin C, and a fifth of the vitamin A requirement. It is an appetite stimulant and gentle diuretic, used in natural medicine in the treatment of jaundice, liver and kidney disorders. According to the herbalist Nicholas Culpepper, its juice when applied to the face will free the skin from blotches, spots and blemishes.

Watermelons 'When one has tasted it, he knows what angels eat,' believed American author Mark Twain, as had many before him. Native to Africa, the watermelon was much regarded by the ancient Egyptians, who were most proficient at its cultivation. Although it is generally consumed raw as a satisfying and thirst quenching snack, various cultures have found other uses for it – in America the rind is pickled or fried, in some European countries the skin may be candied, and the seeds (which in my opinion greatly interfere with its enjoyability) are roasted and salted for a popular snack in Iran and China. Other than fresh consumption, perhaps the best use for this oversized fruit is Watermelon Provençale, as below. Watermelons are often rather disappointing when purchased in more northerly countries: being picked whilst still unripe and exported from their preferred subtropical climate does nothing to enhance their flavour. Watermelons with ripe, fully-coloured skins

are likely to be sweeter and more flavoursome; a firm tap on the side will detect any tell-tale sign of hollowness, meaning that the fruit should be avoided.

NUTRIENT ANALYSIS
1 CUP WATERMELON, FRESH (160g)

KCalories	51.20
Total Fat (g)	0.69
Monounsaturated Fat (g)	trace
Polyunsaturated Fat (g)	trace
Saturated Fat (g)	trace
Carbohydrate (g)	11.49
Protein (g)	0.99
Crude Fibre (g)	0.48
Vitamin A (RE)	59.20
Ascorbic Acid (mg)	15.36
Thiamin (mg)	0.13
Riboflavin (mg)	0.03
Niacin (mg)	0.32
Pantothenic Acid (mg)	0.34
Vitamin B6 (mg)	0.23
Folacin (mcg)	3.52
Vitamin B12 (mcg)	0.00
Calcium (mg)	12.80
Iron (mg)	0.27
Zinc (mg)	0.11

Watermelon Provençale

Serves 4-8
Preparation time 15 minutes, plus 2-4 hours chilling time

1 medium watermelon
1l (2 pints) rosé wine (Tavel is the classic variety used)

Slice off the stalk end of the watermelon to form a sort of cap to the melon. Remove some of the seeds by first shaking the melon upside down then by scraping away some – but not too much – of the seed pulp. Hold the melon upright and pour in the wine. Place the cap back on the melon: some people seal the cap with wax, others tape it into place. Keeping the melon upright, place it in the refrigerator for 2–4 hours until well chilled. When ready to serve, pour the wine from the melon through a sieve and serve slices of the melon – with or without a glass of wine.

Health Note

Nutritionally, one cup of raw, diced watermelon yields about one-quarter the adult daily requirement for vitamin C, and a useful amount of vitamin B6. Watermelons, and their seeds, have been used by natural therapists in the treatment of kidney ailments, and to lower high blood pressure.

Footnotes

1 G. W. Chase Jr., W. O. Landen Jr., A. G. Soliman, 'Hypoglycin A content in the aril, seeds, and husks of ackee fruit at various stages of ripeness', *J Assoc Off Anal Chem*, Mar-Apr 1990

2 *The Associated Press*, 3 March 1993

3 E. M. Scholar, K. Wolterman, D. F. Brit, E. Bresnick, 'The Effect Of Diets Enriched In Cabbage And Collards On Murine Pulmonary Metastasis', *Nutr Cancer*, 12(2), pp121–6

4 *The Associated Press*, 18 March 1993

5 *Cancer Weekly*, 6 Jan 1992, p6 (2)

6 Acknowledgement to Lance Sanders, creator of ChemTao, for his work summarizing the therapeutic effects of garlic.

7 T. Abdullah, D. V. Kirkpatrick, L. Williams, L. Carter, 'Garlic as an antimicrobial and immune modulator in AIDS', Akbar Research Foundation, Panama City, Florida, USA, *Int Conf AIDS*, Jun 4-9 1989, 5, p466

8 *United Press International*, September 16, 1988

9 Amanda Rofe, 'The Honey Bee', *The Vegan*, Summer 1992

10 Numbers, Book 4

11 Ezekiel 4:9

12 J. W. Anderson, L. Story, B. Sieling, W. J. Chen, M. S. Petro, 'Hypocholesterolemic effects of oat-bran or bean intake for hypercholesterolemic men', *J American Journal Of Clinical Nutrition*, December 1984

13 Dorothy Hartley, *Food in England*, (Macdonald & Jane's Publishers, 1954)

14 Mary Aylett, *Encyclopaedia of Home Made Wines*, (Odhams Press Limited, 1957)

15 Song of Solomon, 4:3

16 World Resources Institute, *World Resources 1992-93*, (OUP, 1992)

17 Ronald Wright, *Stolen Continents, the Indian Story*, (John Murray Publishers Ltd, 1992)

18 Mrs M. Grieve, *A Modern Herbal*, (Jonathan Cape Limited, 1931)

19 William Shurtleff and Akiko Aoyagi, *The Book of Tofu*, (Autumn Press Inc, 1975)

20 M. Nagai, T. Hashimoto, H. Yanagawa, H. Yokoyamam, M. Minowa, 'Relationship of diet to the incidence of esophageal and stomach cancer in Japan', *Nutr Cancer*, 1982, 3 (4), p257–68

21 M. Messina and V. Messina, 'Increasing use of soyfoods and their potential role in cancer prevention', *J Am Diet Assoc*, Jul 1991, 91 (7), p836–40

22 S. Areekul, S. Pattanamatum, C. Cheeramakara, K. Churdchue, S. Nitayapabskoon, M. Chongsanguan, 'The source and content of vitamin B12 in the tempehs', *J Med Assoc Thai*, Mar 1990, 73 (3), p152–6

23 Richard Mabey, *Food for Free*, (William Collins Sons & Co. Ltd., 1972)

PART SIX:
THE WORLD'S BEST VEGETARIAN RECIPES

A unique collection of sensational recipes gathered from the four corners of the earth, using ingredients you can obtain almost anywhere

AFRICA

This huge continent holds extraordinary culinary treasures and surprises for the vegetarian cook. Like many other cuisines of the world, African cooking is broadly based on a grain - such as millet, rice or wheat – served with a topping of stew or ragout which is comprised of local roots, leaves and spices. Traditional African cuisine is simple, one- or two-pot cooking at its most colourful and flavourful. Most regions make use of a variety of meat and fish in their cooking. The recipes included here are either authentic non-meat dishes or have been successfully amended to provide you the flavour and feel of the original dish, but without the meat. Most of these recipes probably originated in the outdoors with the cooker being an open fire, but that is not to imply that they are without sophistication: the flavours, textures and presentation of foods achieved in some African cuisines, particularly Ethiopian and Moroccan, are unrivalled throughout the world.

CAMEROUN

Banana Bread

Who hasn't tried to make this classic tea-time treat? Everyone seems to have their favourite aunt's or lost uncle's recipe. This one is simple and reliable.

Makes 1 large loaf
Preparation time 1 hour

6 ripe bananas
100g (4oz) margarine
100g (4oz) sugar
2 tbsp water or soya milk
450g (1lb) plain flour
2 tsp baking powder
1 tsp bicarbonate of soda

Preheat the oven to180°C/350°F/ Gas Mark 4 and lightly grease a large bread tin. Peel the bananas and break them into a mixing bowl. Add the margarine, sugar and soya milk and beat to a smooth, creamy consistency. Mix the dry ingredients in a separate bowl then add to the creamed mixture. Blend together and turn immediately into the loaf tin. Bake for approximately 50 minutes, until a toothpick inserted in the centre of the loaf comes out clean. Cool on a wire rack for 10 minutes before removing the loaf from the tin. Leave on the cooling rack until completely cool. Serve in slices with your favourite spread and a refreshing drink.

EGYPT

Almond Semolina Cake

Serves 4
Preparation time 1 hour

For the syrup:
285ml (½ pint) water
450g (1 lb) sugar
juice of 1 lemon

For the cake:
140g (5oz) sugar
100g (4oz) margarine
1 tsp vanilla or almond essence
340g (12oz) semolina (fine or coarse)
1 tsp bicarbonate of soda
1 tsp baking powder
285ml (10fl oz) plain soya yoghurt
100g (4oz) flaked almonds

Heat the water in a saucepan and dissolve the sugar in it. Add the lemon juice and boil for 10–15 minutes to make a syrup, then remove from the heat and leave to cool.

Preheat the oven to 180°C/350°F/ Gas Mark 4 and lightly grease a 23cm(9 inch) cake tin. Blend the sugar, margarine and vanilla together in a mixing bowl. Stir in the semolina, soda and baking powder then add the yoghurt. Stir well, spread the mixture in the cake tin and sprinkle the almonds over. Bake for 30 minutes. Remove from the oven and leave to cool for 5–10 minutes. Turn out onto a serving tray and spoon syrup over the cake while it is still hot.

Khosnal (Dried Fruit Salad)

Serves 4
Preparation time 24 hours

225g (8oz) dried apricots
225g (8oz) dried figs
100g (4oz) dried apples
100g (4oz) dried bananas
100g (4oz) walnuts or hazelnuts, chopped

500ml (1 pint) orange juice
Chop the dried apricots, figs and apples and thinly slice the dried bananas. Mix together with the chopped nuts in a serving bowl and pour the juice over all. Stir well, adding a little more juice or water if necessary to cover the fruit. Cover the bowl and leave to chill in the refrigerator for 24 hours. Stir again and serve with a dollop of soya yoghurt or a dowsing of Soya Creem®.[1]

ETHIOPIA

Tikur Keman (Spice Blend)

This mixture is used to flavour stews (wots) and other dishes; adjust it to suit your taste. This amount is usually used for one dish.

Makes 3–4 tbsp
Preparation time 10 minutes

1 tbsp caraway seeds
3 cloves garlic, crushed
2 tsp fresh ginger, grated
1 tsp freshly ground black pepper
1 tsp ground coriander
½ tsp salt
¼ tsp ground allspice

Grind all the ingredients in a mortar and pestle until the caraway seeds are slightly crushed. Stir into the dish, either during the sauté or shortly before serving, and adjust to taste.

Berebere (Spice and Herb Blend)

This is another, more robust, blend which may be used alone or in combination with the above recipe in stews (wots) or other savoury dishes. The ingredients may be adjusted to suit your taste.

Makes 140g (5 oz)
Preparation time 15 minutes

5 spring onions, finely chopped
3 cloves garlic, finely chopped
1 tbsp fresh ginger, grated
1–2 fresh hot chillies, finely chopped
2 tbsp fresh basil, chopped

1 Soya Creem (contains no animal ingredients) is available in all health food shops, many supermarkets, and is a trademark of Granose Foods Ltd.

1 tsp freshly ground cardamom
1 tsp freshly ground black pepper
¼ tsp ground nutmeg

Blend all the ingredients and add to the dish during the sauté.

Shiro Wot (Peanut Stew)

It seems that wherever you travel in Africa you will find a local version of peanut stew. Here we have offered you two options as a substitute for the mutton or chicken which is added in some regions. The peanuts are the strongest element, so use your own preferences to create a stew of the texture and robustness you desire.

Serves 4
Preparation time 45 minutes

225g (8oz) raw peanuts
2 tbsp oil
1 medium onion, finely chopped
1–2 tsp mixed spices, to taste (see previous recipes)
salt to taste
1 tsp freshly ground black pepper
1 tbsp tomato pureé
570ml (1 pint) water
450g (1lb) carrots, diced (or other root vegetable)
100g (4oz) TVP chunks and an extra 285ml (½ pint)
    water (optional)
285g (10oz) plain, firm tofu, cubed (optional)

Grind the peanuts to a fine, even consistency. Heat the oil in a saucepan and sauté the onion for 5 minutes, stirring often. Add the spices, salt and pepper and sauté for a further 1 minute. Add the tomato pureé, water, carrots and the ground peanuts (if using TVP chunks, add them and the extra water at this stage also) and simmer for 25 minutes, stirring occasionally. Add the tofu if you like and simmer for a further 5 minutes before serving over rice, millet or Njera (see following).

Njera (Teff Bread)

This is a leavened bread made from teff, a very fine, dark brown grass seed which grows in Ethiopia. The word teff means 'lost' because the seeds are so very tiny they are impossible to recover if dropped or spilled. Teff is low-fat, high-fibre and its amino acids profile makes it easy to digest. It is especially recom-

mended for children, pregnant women, the elderly and those with protein deficiencies. This is not a foodstuff you are likely to find in your local supermarket but it is getting easier to find in small, 'ethnic' food stores or healthfood shops. Do seek it out, not only to experience a real staple of this African country, but also as a taste of a vitamin-rich, gluten-free alternative to wheat bread.

Makes 12 rolls
Preparation time 2 hours

285ml (½ pint) tepid water
1 tbsp sugar
25g (1oz) active dry yeast
450g (1lb) teff flour

Pour the water into a jug or bowl and dissolve the sugar and the yeast in it. Leave in a warm place for 20 minutes, until it begins to froth. Measure the teff into a mixing bowl and pour the yeast water over. Mix and then knead to a stiff dough. Form the dough into a ball and place in the bowl, covered with a clean cloth, for about 30 minutes while the dough rises.
Warm the oven to 200°C/400°F/ Gas Mark 6 and lightly grease a baking tray. Shape the dough into small rolls and place on the tray. Cover with the clean cloth and leave to rise in a warm place for another 30 minutes. Bake in the hot oven for 30–40 minutes. Cool and store in an airtight container or serve hot with your favourite sauce or stew.

Steamed Teff

The same grain, but simply steamed and eaten instead of rice or millet.

Serves 4
Preparation time 30 minutes

285g (10oz) teff
850ml (1½ pints) boiling stock or water
¼ tsp salt

Pour the teff into a large frying pan and roast over a high heat for 3–5 minutes, shaking the pan constantly. Turn into a saucepan, pour the boiling stock or water over and place over a medium heat. Stir well, cover the pan and simmer for 20 minutes, until the water has been absorbed. The teff will look like a chocolate pudding! However, use a fork to fluff the teff and at the same time turn it into a serving bowl. Serve as you would rice, with a sauce or stew ladled over.

GHANA

Tatali (Plantain and Cornmeal Fritters)

Serves 4
Preparation time 45 minutes

1kg (2lb) very ripe plantains
450g (1lb) cornmeal
1 medium onion, finely chopped
2 tsp grated fresh ginger
1 hot chilli pepper, finely chopped
pinch of salt
oil for frying

Mash the plantains then stir in the remaining ingredients and mix well. Heat some oil in a frying pan. Shape the mixture into 12–16 patties and place into the hot oil. Fry for about 5 minutes then turn using a spatula and cook a further 5 minutes, until the tatali are crisp and golden. Serve hot with a topping of stew, beans or your favourite spicy sauce.

Ponkie (Pumpkin Stew)

The title omits to mention the other ingredients! For instance aubergines, which in some parts of Africa are known as 'garden eggs'. In fact, this stew is slightly reminiscent of ratatouille, though you may wish to argue the point. A perfect meal for autumn and winter, when pumpkins grasp the limelight and get sweeter after every frost.

Serves 4
Preparation time 1 hour

1 medium aubergine, diced
2–3 tbsp salt
1kg (2lb) pumpkin or squash
285ml (½ pint) vegetable stock
225g (8oz) TVP mince
1 tbsp oil
1 large onion, chopped
1 tsp ground coriander
1 tsp chilli powder
1 large, sweet green pepper, coarsely chopped
2 large tomatoes, chopped

Place the diced aubergine on a broad dish, sprinkle

with salt and put to one side. Slice or quarter the pumpkin, clean away seeds and steam the flesh until just tender. Pour the stock over the TVP, stir well and leave to one side. Remove the flesh from the pumpkin shell and dice.

Heat the oil in a deep saucepan and sauté the onion until clear and tender. Add the TVP and any remaining stock, the coriander and chilli and continue to sauté over a medium heat, stirring often, for about 10 minutes. Add the chopped pepper, tomatoes and the diced pumpkin. Drain the aubergines and add to the pan. Stir well, reduce the heat, cover the pan and leave to simmer for about 25 minutes. Stir occasionally. Serve hot over rice, millet or boiled yam.

IVORY COAST

Atieke (Stew)

Often made with beef or mutton but authentic as a vegetable stew, this dish vies with those stews used to grace the couscous served in northern Africa.

Serves 4
Preparation time 1 hour 15 minutes

2 tbsp oil
6 cloves garlic, finely chopped
2 medium onions, finely chopped
1 tsp cayenne pepper
225g (8oz) TVP chunks
450g (1lb) tomatoes, finely chopped
140g (5oz) tomato purée
285ml (½ pint) water
5 medium carrots, cut into chunks
2 medium turnips, diced
1 medium swede, diced
1 aubergine, diced
½ cauliflower, chopped
½ cabbage, coarsely shredded
450g (1lb) green beans, sliced
2–3 sprigs fresh parsley, chopped

Heat the oil in a deep saucepan and sauté the garlic for 2 minutes. Add the onions and saute a further 3–5 minutes. Stir in the cayenne then the TVP chunks and continue to sauté until the oil is absorbed. Add the chopped tomato, tomato pureé and the water and stir well. Leave the pan over a medium heat while you add the carrots, turnips, swede and aubergine. Stir well, cover the pan and leave to cook for 10–15 minutes. Add the remaining ingredients except the parsley, stir well and add more water if necessary to make a sauce. Cover the pan and leave to simmer a further 30–40 minutes over a low heat. When the TVP chunks are tender and the sauce is thick, add the parsley, cover and leave to cook a further 5 minutes. Serve over rice or millet.

KENYA

Peanut Sauce

Make this sauce your own by adjusting the spices to suit. Peanut sauces are found all over Africa and in many other regions of the world, including Indonesia and the southern states of North America.

Serves 4
Preparation time 30 minutes

1 tbsp oil
3 cloves garlic, finely chopped
1 medium onion, finely chopped
½ tsp cumin, ground
½ tsp chilli powder
1 tsp freshly ground black pepper
2 large tomatoes, chopped
570ml (1 pint) soya milk or ½ milk and ½ water
225g (8oz) crunchy peanut butter

Heat the oil in a saucepan and sauté the garlic and onion until clear and tender. Add the spices and sauté a further 2 minutes. Stir in the tomatoes, milk and peanut butter and simmer gently for 10 minutes. This should be a rich and spicy sauce, so adjust the seasoning to taste. Serve over vegetables, rice, millet or as a dip for bread or raw vegetables.

Irio (Mashed Red Beans and Vegetables)

Serves 4
Preparation time, 1 hour plus soaking overnight

225g (8oz) dried kidney beans, washed and drained
285g (10oz) sweetcorn kernels
225g (8oz) potatoes, diced
225g (8oz) peas
100g (4oz) spinach, chopped
pinch of salt
1 tsp freshly ground black pepper
1 tbsp oil or margarine
2 tbsp soya milk
1 tbsp fresh parsley or coriander, chopped (optional)

Soak the beans in fresh water overnight then drain and rinse them. Cover with fresh water and cook in a pressure cooker for 25 minutes. Meanwhile, steam the sweetcorn, potatoes and peas for about 15 minutes. Drain the cooked beans and mix with the corn, potatoes, peas and spinach in a saucepan. Add the salt and pepper and cook for about 10 minutes, until the spinach is tender; add a tiny bit of water if necessary to prevent sticking. Mash the whole lot together with a little margarine and soya milk. Serve hot or cold, with bread or soup. Add fresh chopped herbs to the mash, if desired, just before you serve it.

Sweet Potatoes in Orange and Coconut Sauce

Serves 4
Preparation time 1 hour

900g (2lb) sweet potatoes, peeled
1 large orange, peeled and sliced
2 tbsp sugar
285ml (½ pint) coconut milk
50g (2oz) desiccated coconut
25g (1oz) margarine

Preheat the oven to 180°C/350°F/ Gas Mark 4. Steam the sweet potatoes until tender, about 20 minutes. When the potatoes are tender, slice them and arrange in a baking dish. Place the orange slices over the potato. Dissolve the sugar in the coconut milk and pour over the oranges. Sprinkle the desiccated coconut over this and dot tiny pieces of margarine over all. Bake in a moderate oven for about 35 minutes. Serve hot or cold.

Coconut Rice

Serves 4
Preparation time 30 minutes

1 tbsp oil
1 large onion, finely chopped
450g (1lb) long grain rice
1 tsp turmeric
1l (2 pints) hot coconut milk
9 whole cloves
6–7 small pieces (3cm/1 inch) stick cinnamon
pinch of salt
2 bay leaves, to garnish
sliced pimento or sweet red pepper, to garnish

Heat the oil in a large saucepan and sauté the onion until tender and clear. Add the rice and stir over a medium heat for about 5 minutes. Stir in the turmeric then add the hot coconut milk, cloves, cinnamon and salt. Stir well, cover the pan and simmer over a low heat for about 15 minutes. When the rice is tender and all of the milk has been absorbed, turn the rice into a hot serving dish, removing the pieces of spice if you wish. Garnish with bay leaf and pimento and serve hot.

Chai (Spiced Tea)

A similar drink of the same name, but sweetened, is served all over India.

Serves 4
Preparation time 10 minutes

285ml (½ pint) soya milk
285ml (½ pint) water
2 tsp strong tea leaves
½ tsp ground ginger
½ tsp ground cinnamon
3–4 cardamom pods, slightly broken

Mix the milk and water together in a saucepan and bring to a low boil. Add the tea and spices, stir well and reduce the heat. Simmer gently for 3–4 minutes. Strain and serve hot or cold.

MALAWI

Mnkhwani (Spicy Chopped Greens)

Serves 4
Preparation time 30 minutes

1 tbsp oil
5–7 cloves garlic, finely chopped
3 medium onions, chopped
5 medium tomatoes, chopped
100g (4oz) roasted peanuts, finely chopped or ground
pinch of salt
1 tsp freshly ground black pepper
450g (1lb) spinach or kale, washed, trimmed and
  chopped
juice of ½ lemon

Heat the oil in a large saucepan and sauté the garlic and onions until clear and tender. Add the chopped tomatoes, stir well then add the peanuts, salt and pepper. Simmer over a medium heat for 3 minutes then add the spinach and the lemon juice. Reduce the heat, cover the pan and cook over a low heat for about

15 minutes, until the spinach is tender. Serve as a spicy side dish or spoon over rice, millet or steamed sweet potatoes.

MAURITIUS

Creole Rice

Creole is not a place so much as an edible map of culinary and cultural journeys. Creole food is a seamless blend of African, Indian and Caribbean cuisines created by the transport of people and goods between these countries and their colonies. Hotbeds of Creole cooking are found in Africa, India, South America (especially the east coast), the southern United States and the West Indies. The main focus is use of local ingredients – a great many in any one dish – to make a stew or ragout that is highly spiced and aromatic. Banana and pineapple are popular, as are red beans and salads.

Serves 4
Preparaton time 40 minutes

1kg (2lb) Basmati rice
1.25l (2½ pints) water
2x 2.5cm/(1-inch) sticks of cinnamon
2 cardamom pods, slightly crushed
7 whole cloves
50g (2oz) saffron
1 tbsp oil
1 large onion, finely chopped
100g (4oz) mushrooms, sliced
2 green peppers, finely sliced
2 red peppers (pimentos), finely sliced
6 medium tomatoes, chopped
100g (4oz) garden peas
25g (1oz) fresh parsley, chopped

Wash and drain the rice. Place in a saucepan with the water, cinnamon, cardamom and cloves. Cover the pan and bring to the boil over a medium heat. Reduce the heat and cook until the rice is tender and the water is absorbed; about 30 minutes. Fold the saffron into the rice and leave to one side, on a warm hob if possible.

Meanwhile, heat the oil in a frying pan and sauté the onion until clear and tender. Add the remaining ingredients to the sauté in the order in which they are listed and cook for a further 7–10 minutes, stirring constantly. Fold the sautéed vegetables into the rice and turn the mixture into a hot serving dish. Serve immediately with a variety of relishes and other vegetable dishes.

NIGERIA

Wake-ewa (Black-Eyed Beans in Chilli Pepper Sauce)

Serves 4
Preparation time 40 minutes plus soaking overnight

450g (1lb) black-eyed beans, washed and drained
2 tbsp oil
1 large onion, coarsely chopped
2 tsp chilli powder
½ tsp ground coriander
½ tsp dried thyme
pinch of salt
3 large tomatoes, chopped

Soak the beans in fresh water overnight. Drain, rinse and turn into the pressure cooker. Cover with fresh water and cook at pressure for 25 minutes, until tender.

In a separate saucepan, heat the oil and sauté the onion in it. Add the spices when the onion is clear and tender, then add the thyme, salt and tomatoes. Cook over a low heat, stirring frequently, for about 15 minutes. When the beans are tender, stir them into the sauce. Serve immediately in a bowl on its own or in a generous helping over rice or millet.

Taushe (or Birabisko Da Taushe, Beef and Vegetable Stew over Millet)

Serves 4
Preparation time 45 minutes

450g (1lb) millet, washed and drained
1l (2 pints) water
2 tbsp oil
1 large onion, chopped
1 tsp freshly ground black pepper
1 tsp chilli powder
pinch of salt
225g (8oz) TVP chunks
8–10 medium tomatoes, chopped or 2 × 400g (14oz) tins chopped tomatoes
570ml (1 pint) water
675g (1 ½lb) pumpkin, peeled and cubed
225g (8oz) peanut butter

450g (1lb) kale or spring greens, washed, trimmed and chopped

Measure the clean millet and water into a deep saucepan, cover and bring to the boil then reduce the heat and leave to simmer until the millet is tender and all the water has been absorbed, about 30 minutes.

Heat the oil in a large saucepan and sauté the onion until clear and tender. Add the pepper, chilli, salt and TVP chunks and sauté for a further 3 minutes. Add the tomatoes, water and the pumpkin and cook over a medium heat for about 15 minutes, stirring occasionally. Add the peanut butter and the greens. Stir well and leave cooking over a low heat for a further 10 minutes. When the TVP and pumpkin are very tender, ladle the stew over the millet and serve. Rice may be substituted for millet, if preferred.

Funkaso (Sweet Millet Pancakes)

Millet flour is available at many healthfood shops or at Indian or Caribbean food stores.

Serves 4
Preparation time 30 minutes, plus 4 hours standing time

570ml (1 pint) hot water
50g (2oz) margarine
450g (1lb) millet flour (jero)
oil
caster sugar

Pour the hot water into a mixing bowl and melt the margarine in it. Add the flour, stirring quickly to make a runny batter. Leave to stand, covered with a cloth, for 2–4 hours. When ready to use, stir well. Heat a little oil in a frying pan and ladle some batter into it: the batter should be runny enough to spread easily in the pan. Cook for 3–5 minutes, until the underside is slightly browned, then turn to brown the other side. Lift the pancake onto a hot serving plate. Sprinkle with the sugar and serve.

Fu Fu (Mash)

This simple dish, a staple in the whole of west Africa, is often made with cassava. Yam, sweet potato and plantain are authentic substitutions.

Serves 4
Preparation time 45 minutes

450g (1lb) sweet potato or yam, peeled and cubed
225g (8oz) plantain, peeled
50g (2oz) margarine (optional)

140ml (¼ pint) soya milk (optional)
salt and freshly ground black pepper, to taste

Steam the sweet potato and plantain until tender, about 30 minutes. Place in a mixing bowl and mash, with a little margarine and soya milk if desired. Serve hot with a dash of salt and pepper. Fu Fu is usually served topped with a ladleful of stew, spiced beans or peanut sauce.

Akara Kosai (Bean Burgers)

Serves 4
Preparation time 1 hour, plus soaking overnight

100g (4oz) dried beans (ie butter, black-eyed, haricot)
3 cloves garlic, crushed
1 medium onion, finely chopped
2 tomatoes, finely chopped
1 tsp freshly ground black pepper
½ tsp chilli powder
pinch of salt
oil for frying

Wash and drain the beans and soak them overnight in fresh water. Drain, rinse and rub the soaked beans through your hands to loosen the skins. Rinse again. Cover with fresh water and cook over a medium heat for about 1 hour; or cook at pressure for 20 minutes. Drain the beans and turn into a mixing bowl. Stir in the remaining ingredients and mash the beans to make a thick paste. Heat some oil in a large frying pan and place rough patties of the bean paste into it. Press down and fry for 5 minutes, turn to the other side and cook for a further 5–7 minutes. Serve hot as a snack or with a sauce and a variety of other dishes.

Alala (Vegetable Bean Burgers)

Serves 4
Preparation time 30 minutes, plus soaking overnight

1 preparation of Akara Kosai (above)
100g (4oz) cabbage, spring greens or kale, washed and finely sliced and chopped
50g (2oz) peanut butter
oil

Mix the sliced vegetables and peanut butter into the bean mixture. Heat a little oil in a large frying pan and place rough patties of the mixture into it. Cook for 5 minutes, then turn and cook on the other side for a further 5–7 minutes. Serve these burgers beside a variety of vegetable dishes or on top of rice or millet

with a hot sauce over all.

Peanut Brittle

Makes 340g (12oz)
Preparation time 30 minutes

340g (12oz) sugar
140ml (¼ pint) water
225g (8oz) peanuts, roasted and skinned
1–2 tsp lemon juice
dab of margarine

Boil the sugar and water together for about 15 minutes to make a syrup. Meanwhile, roast the peanuts in a frying pan or a hot oven until the skins loosen. Rub the nuts to remove the skins then add the peanuts to the syrup. Add the lemon juice and keep boiling and stirring until the mixture thickens and darkens. Spread the margarine onto a baking tray. Pour the hot mixture onto the tray and leave to cool. Break into pieces and serve.

NORTH AFRICA

This region of Africa is normally considered to be made up of three countries: Algeria, Morocco and Tunisia, each having their own unique cuisine but together presenting a definite and sophisticated style of cooking that is famous and popular the world over. The dishes of this region are colourful, spiced and aromatic; because hospitality is so important to the people of this region, their meals are prepared as abundant offerings to friends and family with many and varied dishes arranged over the table. Food is often eaten with the fingers and many of the dishes require you to eat with a delicateness to which you may not be accustomed. As couscous is perhaps the most well-known dish of this region, I shall begin with that, giving you a recipe from the town of Fez, in Morocco.

Couscous

To be truly authentic, this dish should be prepared for 20–30 persons. You may wish to try this, of course, but I suspect the usual 4–6 persons might be the preferred option! Allow 3–4 hours for the preparation of this meal, though other activities are also possible during this time. The semolina grains are correctly prepared in a steamer called a Kskas: I found that a traditional steamer of the sort that fits exactly over the pan of water, served just as well after it was lined it with butter muslin. Alternatively, there is a kitchen utensil called a *couscoussier*, made specially for this dish. The main thing is to make a fairly airtight seal between the pan of broth and the cooking couscous.

Serves 4–6
Preparation time 4 hours

450g (1lb) dry couscous
1 tbsp oil
1 large onion, chopped
1 tsp freshly ground black pepper
1l (2 pints) water
400g (14oz) cooked chickpeas
4–6 medium carrots, scrubbed and chopped
a good pinch of salt
1 tbsp olive oil
2 turnips, peeled and cubed
100g (4oz) vegetable marrow, chopped
100g (4oz) fresh broad beans
100g (4oz) white cabbage, shredded
2 medium tomatoes, chopped
3–4 tbsp fresh coriander leaves, chopped
2 tbsp fresh parsley, finely chopped
50g (2oz) raisins

Moisten the couscous in a bowl by sprinkling it with a little (about 140ml /¼ pint) salty water. Use a pair of spoons to lift and fluff the couscous, allowing it to fully absorb the water. Pour the couscous into the top portion of a steamer.

Heat the oil in the bottom of the steamer and sauté the onion until clear and tender. Add the pepper and stir for 1 minute longer. Now add the water, chickpeas, carrots, salt and olive oil and place over a medium heat. Bring to the boil then reduce the heat and simmer, with the couscous in the upper portion of the steamer placed over the broth, for about 20 minutes. Gently agitate the couscous again, lifting it and ensuring that there are no lumps. Prepare the remaining vegetables, herbs and raisins and add to the broth. Stir well and place the couscous over the broth once again. Cover and cook over a medium heat for 30–40 minutes. Serve the couscous on a hot plate in a pyramidal mound. Top with the vegetable stew and serve immediately. Some people enjoy a very hot, peppery sauce in addition and you may wish to prepare this from a ladleful of the broth, adding chilli pepper to taste and serving it in a small gravy boat. The couscous need not be steamed over the broth: if you prefer, steam it over water in a separate pan, ensuring that you agitate the grains once or twice while it is steaming, to keep it free of lumps.

Vegetable Stew

Another delicious stew which you may serve over a mound of steaming couscous.

Serves 4–6
Preparation time 1 hour 30 minutes, plus soaking overnight

100g (4oz) dried chickpeas
2 tbsp oil
3 cloves garlic, finely chopped
2 medium onions, chopped
1 green pepper, deseeded and chopped
3 large carrots, diced
2 courgettes, thickly sliced
3 medium tomatoes, chopped
1 tsp ground cumin
1 tsp ground coriander
1 tsp freshly ground black pepper
pinch of salt
570ml (1 pint) vegetable stock or water
75g (3oz) raisins
1 tbsp fresh parsley, chopped
juice of 1 lemon

Wash and drain the chickpeas then soak them in fresh water overnight. Rinse and drain, cover with fresh water then cook in a pressure cooker for 25 minutes. Drain.

Heat the oil in a large saucepan and sauté first the garlic then the onions in it. Add the pepper, carrots and courgettes and sauté a further 10 minutes. Add the tomatoes, spices and salt, then the chickpeas, stock and raisins. Stir well and bring to the boil. Reduce the heat and simmer, covered, for about 30 minutes, until the vegetables are tender. Stir in the parsley and lemon juice just before serving over freshly steamed couscous.

Sweet Couscous

Serves 4
Preparation time 1 hour 30 minutes

225g (8oz) couscous
2 tbsp margarine or olive oil
100g (4oz) raisins
2 tbsp sugar

285ml (½ pint) soya milk, brought to scalding (not quite a simmer)
¼ tsp ground cinnamon

First moisten the couscous by sprinkling with a little water then pour the couscous into the steamer top and steam for 15 minutes. Turn the couscous into a bowl and gently lift and agitate the grains with a spoon to separate them. Sprinkle with water once again, then return to the steamer for another 15 minutes. Repeat this procedure if necessary until the couscous is tender. Add dabs of margarine, the raisins and the sugar to the couscous, stir and steam for a further 10 minutes. Serve hot in bowls with a bit of hot soya milk poured over and a tiny sprinkling of cinnamon on top.

Dafina

This meal is made in a single pot by the Jewish people of northern Africa. As starting fires is not allowed during the Sabbath, Dafina is prepared before sundown on Friday (when the Sabbath begins) and left to cook overnight on a low heat. It is served at midday on Saturday and, as with the next recipe, there are as many variations of Dafina as there are homes, so feel free to adjust this to suit your taste and your wallet. It is usually made with a piece of beef but, of course, I have substituted a mixture of TVP and mushrooms. Cooking the whole meal in one pot like this is a cookery method found elsewhere in the world and throughout history as well. We don't tend to use it much these days, but do try it: not only for the flavours but also as a satisfying and historically nostalgic experience.

Serves 4–6
Preparation time 30 minutes, plus 12 hours soaking and 12 hours cooking

225g (8oz) dried chickpeas
3 tbsp oil
1 large onion, chopped
225g (8oz) TVP chunks
450g (1lb) button mushrooms, cleaned and trimmed
2 tsp turmeric
1 tsp freshly ground black pepper
225g (8oz) long-grain brown rice
½ tsp turmeric
1 tbsp fresh parsley, chopped
5 cloves garlic, crushed
2 tsp olive oil
285g (10oz) firm tofu, cubed
4–6 small, whole turnips, topped and tailed and scored

4–6 small potatoes, peeled and thickly sliced
4–6 small sweet potatoes, peeled and thickly sliced or
    3 large parsnips, peeled and quartered
2 tsp freshly ground black pepper
1 tsp turmeric
1 tsp ground cinnamon
salt to taste

Wash and drain the chickpeas and soak in fresh water overnight. Heat the oil in a large stewpot and sauté the onion until clear and tender. Add the TVP and continue to sauté for about 5 minutes. Add the mushrooms, turmeric and pepper and stir for 2 minutes. Spread the mixture evenly along the bottom of the stewpot and reduce the heat.

Drain and rinse the chickpeas and arrange them in a layer over the TVP and mushrooms. Measure the rice into a bowl and pour boiling water over it. Stir well and leave to sit for 5 minutes. Drain and stir the turmeric, parsley, garlic and olive oil into the rice. Turn this mixture into a large square of butter muslin. Fold the muslin over and tie it so the rice will not leak out, yet has room to swell and expand. Place the rice 'parcel' over the layer of chickpeas in the stewpot.

Arrange the cubes of tofu over the rice along with the whole turnips. Now place a layer each of potato and sweet potato (or parsnip) and sprinkle the spices over all. Pour in enough water to cover the top layer by about 2.5cm (1/inch). Cover the pan and leave to cook over a very low heat for at least 12 hours! This is perhaps most economical if you have an Aga or similar cooker.

To serve, either serve each layer in its own separate dish, or serve them mixed together in a large tureen with just the rice turned out onto its own serving platter.

Harira

This is a versatile dish served in the homes and restaurants of Morocco throughout the holy month of Ramadan. It is usual during this month for Muslims to curtail all daytime activities and to abstain entirely from food and drink between sunrise and sundown. This soup is made during the dark, active hours and kept for serving as 'breakfast', at the next sundown. Also served at this meal is a bowlful of dates and milky, mint-flavoured coffee. Harira is made in as many varieties as there are homes and each family cherishes their version, though the basic idea remains a thick soup. Harira is often prepared for 20–30 persons; here it is prepared for a mere 4–6 people.

Serves 4–6
Preparation time 2 hours 30 minutes, plus soaking overnight

450g (1lb) standard commercial soup mixture or 140g (5oz) each of barley, split peas or lentils and chickpeas, haricot beans or other dried beans
450g (1lb) tomatoes, fresh or tinned, liquidized
1 bunch fresh parsley, chopped
1 bunch fresh coriander, chopped
3 stalks celery, finely diced
2 tbsp oil
1 large onion, chopped
225g (8oz) TVP chunks
2 tsp turmeric
1l (2 pints) vegetable stock or water
1 × 15cm(6/inch) strip of kombu
1 tsp freshly ground black pepper
salt to taste
rice or thin noodles, to taste (optional)
2 tsp kuzu (arrowroot)
juice of 1 lemon

Soak the soup mixture overnight. Pour the liquidized tomatoes into a bowl with the parsley, coriander and celery and leave to one side. Heat the oil in a large saucepan and sauté the onion until clear and tender. Add the TVP chunks and continue to sauté for a further 3–5 minutes. Now add the turmeric, stir well and then pour in the vegetable stock with the strip of kombu which will help deepen the flavour of the soup. Bring the stock to the boil, drain the soup mixture that has been soaking all night and add it to the stock. Cover the pan, reduce the heat and simmer for at least 2 hours, adding more stock if necessary. When the beans and barley have cooked, add the pepper, salt and, if you like, some thin noodles. Add the tomato and herb mixture and stir the soup very well. If it is still a bit thin, pour a ladleful of the soup over some arrowroot in a cup, stir to a paste then return it to the soup and stir well: it will thicken the soup nicely. Add the lemon juice just before serving and encourage each person to season their serving to taste. This soup keeps very well – indeed its flavour is thought to improve with keeping an extra day.

Lentil Soup

Serves 4
Preparation time 45 minutes

1 tbsp oil
3 cloves garlic, crushed
1 medium onion, chopped
225g (8oz) split red lentils
1l (2 pints) vegetable stock
1 large tomato, chopped
2 tsp oil
1 tsp cumin, lightly crushed
1 tsp freshly ground black pepper
salt to taste
1 lemon, sliced

Heat the oil in a saucepan and lightly sauté the garlic and onion. Wash and drain the lentils and add to the sauté with the vegetable stock. Bring to the boil over a medium heat then stir in the chopped tomato. Reduce the heat, cover the pan and simmer for about 30 minutes, until the lentils are very tender. Pour through a hand mouli on a coarse fitting then return to the saucepan and place over a low heat. Heat the second measure of oil in a small pan and sauté the cumin and pepper for about 1 minute. Stir immediately into the hot soup; salt to taste. Ladle into soup bowls and garnish with a thick slice of lemon.

Samsa

This delicacy is normally made with a thin pastry, called *malsouqua*, made from semolina. Here we list phyllo (filo) pastry which is easier to find and works quite well. You can get the geranium water from a good Indian grocers; use rose or orange water if you are really stuck.

Serves 4
Preparation time 1 hour

16 sheets phyllo pastry (see page 348)
1–2 tbsp olive oil
225ml (8fl oz) water
100g (4oz) sugar
1 tbsp lemon juice
1 tbsp geranium water
450g (1lb) almonds, blanched and ground
1 tbsp grated orange peel
25g (1oz) sesame seeds, roasted

Preheat the oven to 180°C/350°F/Gas Mark 4. Place a sheet of the pastry on a board and brush the surface with a little olive oil. Fold the sheet in half and oil that surface; fold once more (the sheet is now folded into quarters) and oil that surface. Repeat with the remaining 15 sheets, and put to one side. Boil the water with just under half of the sugar in a small saucepan. Add the lemon juice and stir constantly to make a syrup. When it has thickened, about 15 minutes, remove from the heat, add the geranium water, stir well and leave to cool.

Mix the almonds, orange peel and the rest of the sugar. Drop spoonsful of this mixture onto the centre of each phyllo then fold and roll the pastry round the filling. Bake the pastries until crisp and golden, about 15 minutes. Lift from the baking tray and lower each pastry into a bowlful of the syrup. Leave for about 5 minutes, then lift onto a plate and sprinkle with the roasted sesame seeds. Serve cool.

Baba Ganoush (Roasted Aubergine Dip)

Serves 4
Preparation time 1 hour

3 medium aubergines
3 tbsp olive oil
3 tbsp fresh parsley, chopped
1 tbsp tomato purée
5 cloves garlic, crushed
juice of 1–2 lemons
1 tsp freshly ground black pepper, or to taste
pinch of salt

Roast the aubergines in a hot oven or under a grill until the skins begin to blister and char. If the aubergines are squeezed they should feel soft and juicy. Remove them from the heat and peel away the skins. Chop the aubergines and squeeze as much juice from them as possible: wrap the aubergines in butter muslin or a clean tea towel and place on a plate or wire cooling rack and press. (Alternatively, you may find your own way of pressing juice from hot aubergine!) Blend the aubergines, oil, parsley and tomato purée together in a mouli or food processor. Add the remaining ingredients, adjusting each to suit your taste. Serve in individual serving bowls with plenty of fresh pitta bread.

Cucumber and Yoghurt Salad

Serves 4–6
Preparation time 1 hour 45 minutes

1 large cucumber, diced
2 tsp salt
425ml (¾ pint) plain soya yoghurt
5 cloves garlic, finely chopped or crushed

3–5 sprigs fresh mint, finely chopped
freshly ground black pepper to taste

Place the diced cucumber on a platter and sprinkle with the salt. Leave for about 1 hour. Mix the remaining ingredients together and put to one side also. Drain the cucumber and add to the yoghurt mixture. Turn into a serving dish and serve, though you may find the flavours blend rather better if it is allowed to chill for about 30 minutes before serving.

Mechouia (Chopped Salad)

Serves 4
Preparation time 1 hour 15 minutes

2 large tomatoes, chopped
2 green peppers, deseeded and chopped
2 red peppers, deseeded and chopped
1 medium onion, finely chopped
3 cloves garlic, crushed
6 tbsp olive oil
juice of 1 large lemon
2 tbsp fresh parsley, chopped
1 tbsp fresh mint, chopped
½ tsp freshly ground black pepper
pinch of salt
1 large cucumber, diced
2 tsp salt
1 lemon, sliced and quartered

Mix the chopped tomatoes, peppers and onion together in a large bowl. Measure the garlic, oil, lemon juice, herbs, pepper and salt into a jug and whisk into a dressing. Pour the dressing over the salad and leave for 1 hour. At the same time, arrange the diced cucumber on a broad dish and sprinkle with the salt. Leave for 1 hour also. At the end of this time, drain the cucumber and add to the salad. Stir well and serve garnished with the sliced lemon.

Parsley Salad

Serves 4
Preparation time 10 minutes

1 large bunch fresh parsley, chopped
1 medium onion, very finely chopped
1 lemon, peeled and finely chopped
juice of 1 further lemon

Simply mix the ingredients together, with a pinch of salt if you like, in a broad and colourful serving dish. Serve immediately.

Salatat Aswad (Aubergine Salad)

Serves 4
Preparation time 20 minutes, plus time to cool

2 medium aubergines
1 medium onion, finely chopped
2 tbsp tomato purée
¼ tsp chilli powder
pinch of salt
140ml (¼ pint) plain soya yoghurt

Drop the aubergines into a pot of boiling water for about 5 minutes then remove them, peel away the skins and chop the aubergine flesh. Place the chopped aubergine, onion, tomato purée, chilli and salt in a saucepan and cook for 10–15 minutes over a medium heat. Turn into a serving dish and leave to cool before stirring in the yoghurt. Serve with crudités or fresh pitta bread.

SENEGAL

Thiebou Diene (Fish and Vegetables Over Flavoured Rice)

This is something like a pilaf but more substantial and spicy. Of course, the fish becomes tempeh (a very fine substitute, I must say) but the rest of the dish remains authentic and deliciously aromatic and flavourful.

Serves 4–6
Preparation time 1 hour

450g (1lb) tempeh, defrosted
2–3 tbsp oil
25g (1oz) fresh parsley, chopped
4 spring onions, thinly sliced
3 cloves garlic, crushed
1 tsp freshly ground black pepper
1 tsp cayenne
½ tsp salt
juice of 1 lime
2 tbsp oil
2 medium onions, chopped
1 medium aubergine, cubed
2 small turnips, cubed
½ cauliflower, chopped
½ white cabbage, shredded
900g (2lb) tomatoes, chopped
140ml (5oz) tomato purée
570ml (1 pint) vegetable stock or water

450g (1lb) Basmati rice, washed and drained

Slice the defrosted tempeh into triangles, approximately 6 to each brick. Heat the oil in a frying pan and sauté the tempeh until slightly crisp and golden. Mix the parsley, onion, garlic, pepper, cayenne and salt together in a small bowl, pour over the lime juice and stir well. Arrange the tempeh on a platter and sprinkle the lime and herb mixture over it. Cover and put to one side.

Heat the oil in a large saucepan and sauté the onion until clear and tender. Add the aubergine and turnips and continue to sauté for a further 5 minutes. Now add the cauliflower and cabbage; after 5 more minutes add the tomatoes and tomato purée. Stir well, pour in the stock and bring to the boil over a medium heat. Cover the pan, reduce the heat and simmer for about 20–30 minutes, until the vegetables are very tender. Strain the vegetables from the stock and turn into a serving dish: cover them and put in a warm oven, with the tempeh if you like. Bring the broth back to the boil and add the rice to it, adding more water if necessary to ensure a ratio of 2 parts liquid to 1 part rice. Cover the pan, reduce the heat and leave to simmer for about 25 minutes, until the rice is tender and all the liquid is absorbed. Serve the rice onto hot plates with a wedge or two of tempeh in herb relish topped by a mound of vegetables.

SEYCHELLES

La Daub (Banana, Yam and Coconut Pudding)

Serves 4
Preparation time 45 minutes

450g (1lb) sweet potato, peeled and cubed
450g (1lb) yam, peeled and cubed
2 bananas or plantains, peeled
25g (1oz) sugar
425ml (¾ pint) coconut milk
1 tsp ground cinnamon
½ tsp vanilla essence

Mix all the ingredients together in a saucepan and place over a low heat. Cover the pan and simmer for about 40 minutes, until the roots are tender. Blend to a smooth consistency and serve hot or cold in pretty bowls. Try this with a garnish of desiccated coconut or a spoonful of soya ice cream.

Note: you may use another 450g (1lb) sweet potato instead of the yam if you prefer.

Pakoras (Vegetable Fritters)

Fritters similar to these are also popular in India.

Serves 4–6
Preparation time 45 minutes

225g (8oz) gram flour (ground chickpeas)
1 tsp ground cumin
½ tsp paprika
½ tsp cayenne
½ tsp ground cardamom
¼ tsp salt
3 cloves garlic, crushed
1 tbsp chives, chopped
1 tsp fresh ginger, grated
60ml (2fl oz) plain soya yoghurt
a little water
oil for shallow frying

Suggested vegetable fillings:
thinly sliced courgette
sliced potatoes or sweet potatoes
thickly sliced tofu
sliced onion

Mix the dry ingredients together in a mixing bowl then stir in the garlic, chives, ginger and yoghurt. Stir well, adding enough water to make a thick batter. Put to one side for 30 minutes. Meanwhile, prepare the vegetables you wish to use. Stir the batter once again then dip the vegetables in the batter and drop into hot oil (shallow fry). Turn, drain onto kitchen towel and serve hot as a starter or snack.

UGANDA

Matooke (Plantain) and Peanut Sauce

Serves 4
Preparation time 1 hour

2kg (4lb) plantain (matooke), peeled and washed
1 tbsp oil
1 large onion, chopped
2 spring onions, thinly sliced
1 tbsp curry powder
3 large tomatoes, chopped
225g (8oz) peanuts, ground
570ml (1 pint) water

Preheat the oven to 180°C/350°F/Gas Mark 4. Steam the plantain for 25–30 minutes, until tender. Meanwhile, heat the oil in a saucepan and sauté the onion and spring onions until clear and tender. Add the curry powder and stir for 1 minute. Now add the tomatoes, ground peanuts and half the water, stir and bring to the boil. Add the remaining water, stir and return to the boil. Reduce the heat and simmer gently for about 30 minutes, stirring occasionally. Add a little more water if necessary: aim for a thick sauce rather than a thick paste.

When the plantain are tender, turn them into a greased oven dish and mash them. Cover the dish and place in a moderate oven for about 20 minutes. Serve the mashed plantain hot with the peanut sauce poured over; accompany this dish with your favourite greens and perhaps some fresh sweetcorn.

Okra Uganda (Seasoned Ladies' Fingers)

Serves 4
Preparation time 30 minutes

450g (1lb) okra (ladies' fingers), washed
1 tsp curry powder
1 tsp freshly ground black pepper
1 tsp turmeric
¼ tsp salt
¼ tsp chilli powder
5 cloves garlic, finely chopped
1 tbsp oil
1 large onion, chopped
juice of 1 lime

Trim the thick caps off the okra and discard, then slice the okra into thin rings and place on a platter. Mix the dry ingredients and the garlic together in a small bowl then sprinkle over the okra rings. Heat the oil in a large frying pan and sauté the onion until clear and tender. Add the okra to the onions, stir once or twice then cover the pan and cook for 5–6 minutes. Stir the mixture again, cover and cook for a further 10 minutes, until the okra are just tender. Remove from the heat, sprinkle with the lime juice and serve hot over rice, millet or even hot toast

Sweet Potato and Tomato Sauté

Serves 4
Preparation time 45 minutes

2 large sweet potatoes, peeled, washed and quartered
3 large tomatoes

50g (2oz) margarine
1 tsp brown sugar
½ tsp freshly ground black pepper
¼ tsp chilli powder
pinch of salt

Steam the sweet potatoes for about 25 minutes then put to one side to cool slightly. Meanwhile, push a fork into the stalk end of each tomato and hold the tomato over a flame. Turn slowly, ensuring the heat reaches all parts of the tomato, until the skin bursts. Peel the skin away and put the tomato to one side. Repeat this procedure for each tomato.

Melt the margarine in a frying pan. Slice the steamed sweet potatoes and sauté them for about 5 minutes, until golden. Sprinkle the sugar, pepper, chilli and salt over the potatoes then arrange the tomato slices over all. Cover the pan and cook for 5 minutes, then gently stir and cook a further 5 minutes, uncovered. Serve hot over rice with tempeh and greens to accompany.

ZAMBIA

Polenta Pie

Serves 4–6
Preparation time 1 hour 30 minutes

450g (1lb) cornmeal
850ml (1½ pints) soya milk
50g (2oz) margarine

For the filling:
100g (4oz) TVP mince and 450g (1lb) mixed
    vegetables; or
285g (10oz) firm tofu, cubed and 340g (12oz) mixed
    vegetables;
or any combination of the above ingredients
and
1 tsp freshly ground black pepper
½ tsp ground coriander
½ tsp dried thyme
285ml (½ pint) vegetable stock

Preheat the oven to 180°C/350°F/Gas Mark 4 and grease a medium sized oven dish. Measure the cornmeal into a mixing bowl with 285ml (½ pint) of the milk; stir to make a smooth paste. Heat the rest of the milk in a saucepan and, when it has begun to boil, add the margarine and the cornmeal paste. Stir often over the next 5–10 minutes while the mixture thickens to make a slightly stiff dough. Remove from the heat and press about 2/3 of the cornmeal dough into the greased oven dish. A wet wooden spoon will enable you to press the hot dough without burning your hands. Keep the spoon wet to prevent it sticking too much.

Meanwhile, prepare the filling for the pie. As you can see, just about any combination of ingredients will do, provided you spice them nicely. Mix the TVP, tofu and/or vegetables with the spices, herb and vegetable stock and turn into the polenta-lined oven dish. Roll out the remaining cornmeal dough on a lightly floured board and place over the pie. Press and trim the edges and use any spare bits of dough to decorate the pie; brush the top of the pie with a little oil if you like a slightly crisp texture. Bake for about 1 hour. Serve hot beside greens, rice and other vegetable dishes.

ZIMBABWE

Muriwo ne Dovi (Greens in Peanut Sauce)

Serves 4
Preparation time 20 minutes

2 tsp oil
1 large onion, finely chopped
½–1 tsp freshly ground black pepper
pinch of salt
450g (1lb) spinach, spring greens or kale, washed,
    trimmed and finely chopped
2 medium tomatoes, chopped
3 tbsp peanut butter
140ml (¼ pint) water

Heat the oil in a saucepan and sauté the onion until clear and tender. Stir in the pepper and salt and sauté for a further 1 minute. Turn the chopped greens then the chopped tomatoes into the saucepan. Cover the pan and cook for 3–5 minutes over a medium heat. Stir the contents of the pan and cook, covered, for another 2 minutes. Mix the peanut butter and water together in a small bowl then turn into the saucepan. Stir well, cover and cook for 5 minutes over a low heat. Serve hot as an accompaniment to other dishes.

Sadza (Cornmeal Porridge)

This is a polenta-like staple of the southern region of

Africa, eaten once or twice a day by many Africans. As it stands, sadza is quite bland, so use your imagination as it can become a delicious and colourfully pleasant dish.

Serves 4
Preparation time 20 minutes

450g (1lb) fine cornmeal
850ml (1½ pints) water, boiling

Some suggested toppings per serving:
1 tsp brown sugar
50g (2oz) chopped apple and raisins combined
1 tsp margarine
140ml (¼ pint) soya milk
1 tbsp Soya Creem
Okra Uganda (see page 322)
Greens in Peanut Sauce (see page 323)
Rupiza (see page 324)

Turn the cornmeal into a saucepan and add two-thirds of the boiling water, a little at a time, stirring constantly to prevent lumps. Place the saucepan over a low heat and cook, covered, for about 7 minutes. Add more boiling water if necessary (aim to make a soft paste that will hold a peak shape when the stirring spoon is lifted from it) to achieve the desired texture. Serve hot with one or more of the suggested toppings, or a garnish of your own choosing.

Sweet Potato Biscuits

Serves 4–6
Preparation time 30 minutes

450g (1lb) raw sweet potato, grated
100ml (4fl oz) barley malt syrup
2–3 tsp grated lemon rind
1 tbsp soya milk
100g (4oz) margarine
100g (4oz) sugar
340g (12oz) plain flour
1½ tsp baking powder
pinch of salt

Preheat the oven to 180°C/350°F/Gas Mark 4 and lightly grease a baking tray. Grate the sweet potato into a large mixing bowl and add the syrup, lemon rind, milk, margarine and sugar. Blend to a smooth, creamy consistency. In a separate bowl, mix the flour, baking powder and salt. Add this dry mixture to the creamed mixture and blend well. Drop spoonsful of the mixture onto the baking tray and press down twice with a

floured fork to make a criss-cross pattern. Bake for about 20 minutes, until golden. Cool on the baking tray for 2 minutes, then lift onto a wire rack to cool completely.

Rupiza (Puréed Yellow Peas)

This marks an African version of a simple dish found in some form in most other areas of the world as well. Mashed peas, dhal, pease pudding – all are based on this simple idea. Adjust the seasonings to suit your own tastes. I found that roasting the peas before boiling them lent a pleasing and surprisingly nutty flavour to the finished dish.

Serves 4
Preparation time 1 hour, plus soaking overnight

225g (8oz) dried split yellow peas
½l (1¼ pints) water
1 tsp salt
2 tsp oil
3 cloves garlic, finely chopped
1 tsp freshly ground black pepper
½ tsp chilli powder

Pour the peas into a large frying pan and place over a medium heat. Roast the peas, stirring constantly, to a golden colour. Do not let them brown. Turn them into a bowl, cover with water and leave to soak overnight. Drain and rinse the peas and place them in a saucepan with the fresh water and the salt. Bring to the boil, reduce the heat, cover the pan and simmer for about 30 minutes, until the peas become tender. Heat the oil in a small frying pan and sauté the garlic until just golden. Add the spices, stir for a further 1 minute then add the sauté to the peas. Simmer the peas for a further 10 minutes until they are mushy and have lost their form. Serve hot over rice, polenta, millet or steamed root vegetables.

Nhopi (Mashed Pumpkin and Sweet Potato)

Similar to the Fu Fu of west Africa, but this dish has a little more zing!

Serves 4
Preparation time 45 minutes

450g (1lb) pumpkin, peeled and cubed
450g (1lb) sweet potato, peeled and cubed
pinch of salt
50g (2oz) margarine
1 tbsp soya milk

pinch of ground cinnamon
freshly ground black pepper, to taste

Steam the pumpkin and sweet potato for about 30 minutes, until tender. Turn into a mixing bowl and mash together with the remaining ingredients. Aim for a slightly fluffy, whipped smooth consistency. Serve hot with gravy, peanut sauce, spiced beans or vegetable stew.

THE AMERICAS

Considered two continents, this land mass stretches between the two poles with only a tiny break in the middle. Its cuisine is based on maize (corn), beans, potatoes, rice and a rich variety of locally grown fruits. Methods of cooking these staples vary from south to north with a few dishes – especially those of Creole origin – appearing several times on the journey.

MEXICO

See also: Guacamole (p181)

Frijoles (Spicy Black Beans)

Serves 4
Preparation time 1 hour, plus soaking overnight

340g (12oz) black turtle beans or red kidney beans
2 whole dried chillies, thinly sliced or ½ tsp chilli powder
75g (3oz) margarine
3–6 cloves garlic, finely chopped
3 medium onions, chopped
1x400g (14oz) tin tomatoes

Wash and drain the beans and soak them in fresh water overnight. Drain, rinse and just cover with fresh water in a pressure cooker or large saucepan. Add the chilli (sliced or powdered), and one-third each of the margarine, garlic and onion to the beans. Stir well and cook at pressure for 25 minutes, in a saucepan for 1 hour 30 minutes, until the beans are tender.

Melt the remaining margarine in a frying pan and sauté the rest of the garlic and onion until clear and tender. Add the tomatoes and stir well; cook for 5 minutes. Stir the beans and tomato mixture together, mashing the beans somewhat as you do so. Cook together for a final 10 minutes then serve hot with tortillas or rice.

Tortillas

Serves 4
Preparation time 30 minutes

340g (12oz) cornmeal
¾ tsp salt
340ml (12 fl oz) warm water
a little flour

Stir the cornmeal and salt together in a mixing bowl. Gradually add the warm water, first stirring then kneading to make a soft dough. Place the dough on a floured board and divide into 12 portions. Work the pieces into thin, flat circles: traditionally this is done entirely with the hands in a sort of patting, throwing movement. You may, of course, prefer to try a floured rolling pin.

Heat a large, ungreased frying pan or griddle over a medium heat and cook the tortillas for 1–2 minutes on each side. Serve immediately (though they will keep) with the frijoles, above.

Chilli Without Carne

This dish was originally made with meat that was heavily spiced with chilli peppers. The flavour, texture and aroma of this meatless version is authentic and irresistible. Aim for a level of spiciness at the borders of your tolerance and cook until this sauce has the consistency of ragout: thick and gloopy. Red beans are included here as an option; they are often included in the Americanized version of this dish.

Serves 4
Preparation time 45 minutes

1 tbsp oil
5 cloves garlic, finely chopped
2 medium onions, thinly sliced
½-1 tsp chilli powder
100g (4oz) TVP mince
570ml (1 pint) water
140g (5oz) tomato purée
1 × 400g (14oz) tin tomatoes or 6 medium tomatoes, chopped
1 whole chilli (optional)
450g (1lb) cooked red kidney beans (optional)
2 tsp soy sauce
1 tbsp vinegar

Heat the oil in a saucepan and sauté the garlic and onions until clear and tender. Add the chilli powder and sauté for a further 1 minute. Stir the TVP into the sauté to absorb all the oil and juices then add the water, tomato purée and chopped tomatoes. Stir well and leave over a medium heat. Add the whole chilli and/or red beans at this point and add a little more water if necessary to ensure the right consistency. Cover the pan, reduce the heat and leave to simmer for about 20 minutes. Add the soy sauce and vinegar about 5 minutes before serving. Serve hot in small bowls with a plate of fresh tortillas nearby and, if you're really keen, a small dish of fresh hot chillies!

Pumpkin Caramel Mould

Serves 4
Preparation time 45 minutes, plus 2 hours cooling time

450g (1lb) pumpkin, peeled and cut into chunks
720ml (1¼ pints) soya milk
140g (5oz) cornflour
peel and juice of 1 lemon
peel and juice of 4 oranges
285g (10oz) sugar
2 tsp tahini or peanut butter
½ tsp ground cinnamon
¼ tsp ground nutmeg
1 tbsp water
50g (2oz) coarsely ground nuts (optional)

Place the chunks of pumpkin in a steamer and steam until tender, about 15 minutes. Mix the milk and cornflour together in a saucepan and heat slowly and gently until it thickens. Add the steamed pumpkin, mashing it as you add it to the sauce. Stir well, then add the peel of the lemon and the peel and juice of the oranges, all but 75g (3oz) of the sugar, the tahini and the spices. Stir constantly over a low heat.

In a separate pan, heat the juice of the lemon, the water and the remaining 75g (3oz) sugar. Making caramel is done more by tilting the pan than by stirring, though it's not the end of the world if you do give the mixture the odd stir with a wooden spoon. When it has turned a lovely dark golden colour, pour this mixture into the ramekin or mould you are using and quickly roll and turn the mould so the caramel covers all of the bottom and much of the sides. As it cools it will stick to the sides. If you wish, sprinkle the ground nuts onto the base of the mould at this point.

Now pour the hot pumpkin mixture into the mould, let it cool then chill in the fridge until set. Allow a couple hours. Turn the mould over onto a serving plate and serve as it is or garnished with nuts, Soya Creem or your favourite hot sauce.

UNITED STATES OF AMERICA

The USA shows its history in its varied and developing cuisines. It is truly a culinary melting pot: every dish ever made anywhere else in the world will have its American version. Chances are the flavours and textures will have changed to accommodate availability of ingredients, but the mystique and romance of 'the old world' will make every American cook try a little harder with dishes which they perceive to be authentically from somewhere else. So you can see, it is a difficult task to find truly American dishes! These are a few that have been hoisted onto the pedestal: they are now either considered all-American or considered to represent a style of cookery and a way of eating that is genuine modern American.

Apple Pie

It was probably first made in Rome, was marched to certain areas of France, then endured the experimentations and alterations of several generations of immigrants before being elected a symbol of all that is the American. Every American mother has her own 'secret' recipe; this is one you can adopt as yours. The pastry is pressed rather than rolled, thereby greatly reducing the time and level of expertise required.

Serves 4–6
Preparation time 1 hour 30 minutes

For the crust:
340g (12oz) plain flour
½ tsp salt
½ tsp ground cinnamon
¼ tsp ground nutmeg
225g (8oz) shredded vegetable suet
2 tbsp cold water

For the filling:
1.5kg (3lb) cooking apples, peeled and sliced
140g (5oz) sugar, brown if possible
1 tbsp plain flour
½ tsp ground cinnamon
¼ tsp ground nutmeg
2 tbsp margarine

Preheat the oven to 220°C/425°F/Gas Mark 7. Mix the flour, salt and spices together in a mixing bowl.

Add the vegetable suet and stir well with a fork or spatula. Sprinkle the water over the mixture and use the fork or your fingers to work to an even, crumbly consistency. Spoon just over half of this mixture into a 30cm (12 inch) pie dish and press firmly to line the dish with pastry. Put the remaining pastry mixture to one side.

Prepare the apples and place in a large mixing bowl. Mix the sugar, flour and spices together in a small bowl and sprinkle over the apples. Stir gently to distribute the dry mix evenly, coating the apple slices to some extent. Turn the apples into the lined pie dish and spread evenly. Drop dabs of the margarine onto the apples then turn the remaining pastry mix over all. Spread this across the whole of the pie then press firmly into place, making the pastry edges meet if possible.

Bake in the hot oven for 10 minutes then reduce the heat to 180°C/350°F/Gas Mark 4 and bake for a further 40 minutes. Allow to partially cool before serving just warm with Soya Creem or soya ice cream.

Buckwheat Pancakes

Traditionally served as a robust breakfast in many American homes – particularly those with teenage boys growing rapidly into 6-footers. To further adhere to tradition, the cook stays cooking while everyone else eats! Plate after plate of pancakes are served (a griddle is often large enough to cover 2 hot-plates on the cooker and can therefore cook 3 or 4 pancakes at once) to clamouring family or friends until everyone is full. Then the cook prepares his own plate – hopefully enjoying the praise while he eats.

Serves 4–6
Preparation time 30 minutes, plus proving overnight

570ml (1 pint) soya milk
570ml (1 pint) water, boiled
25g (1oz) yeast, fresh or 1 packet dry yeast
675g (1½lb) buckwheat flour
1 tbsp molasses
285ml (½ pint) hot water
1 tsp bicarbonate of soda

Measure the milk and hot water into a large mixing bowl and leave to cool to tepid. Add yeast, stir well and leave to one side for 10 minutes. Now stir in the flour to make a thin, smooth batter: you may not need all of the flour. Cover the bowl with a clean cloth and a plate and leave in a warm place overnight. In the morning, dissolve the molasses in the hot water, then dissolve the bicarbonate of soda in it as well. Add this mixture to the batter. Stir well and drop large spoonsful onto a hot griddle. Each pancake should be at least 15cm (6 inches) in diameter. When the top is bubbly, lift the edge of the pancake with a spatula. When the underside is brown, turn the pancake over to brown the other side. Lift onto a hot plate and serve in a stack of 3 or 4 with margarine and maple syrup between each pancake. You might try apple sauce instead of syrup, or any sauce, syrup or spread that takes your fancy.

Shoo-Fly Pie

This is an early American dish that is sweet, sticky and very attractive to flies – so keep it under a net as it cools. Excellent served hot or cold.

Makes 2x25cm (9 inch) pies
Preparation time 45 minutes

For the crust:
340g (12oz) plain flour
½ tsp salt
225g (8oz) shredded vegetable suet
2 tbsp cold water

For the filling:
100g (4oz) plain flour
225g (8oz) brown sugar
225g (8oz) margarine
8 tbsp molasses or treacle
8 tbsp hot water
1 tsp bicarbonate of soda
100g (4oz) pecans, walnuts or hazelnuts, ground
   (optional)

Preheat the oven to 180°C/350°F/Gas Mark 4. Mix the flour and salt together in a mixing bowl. Add the vegetable suet and stir well with a fork or spatula. Sprinkle the water over the mixture and use the fork or your fingers to work to an even, crumbly consistency. Spoon half of this mixture into each of two 25cm (9 inch) pie dishes and press firmly to line the dishes with pastry. (There is no upper crust in this recipe.)

Mix the flour and sugar together in a mixing bowl then cut the margarine into it. Work in to make an even, crumbly texture. Dissolve the molasses in the hot water, then stir in the soda until it fizzes. Pour half of this mixture into each pie dish and sprinkle with nuts, half in each pie. Sprinkle half of the crumbly mixture over the nuts and molasses in each pie and bake for 25–30 minutes, until the crumble topping is firm. Serve hot or cold – on a fairly empty stomach!

White Bean Soup with Pepper-Squash Tortellini

This unique recipe from Chicagoan Bill Maddex combines the best of the Midwest's home-grown produce with that city's great sense of flair and style. It takes as much time to prepare as it would take you to stroll from Chicago's Jackson Park to Lincoln Park and back again, but what the heck? Great food is worth waiting for, isn't it? It will impress your friends as much as it impressed me on my first acquaintance and I've no doubt you'll want to hear more from Bill.

Serves 6
Preparation time 6 hours, plus soaking overnight

Red Pepper-Squash Tortellini

This is a beautiful dish in itself, but Bill combines it with the White Bean Soup (to follow) with a deft stroke of inspiration. This half of the recipe takes a bit longer to prepare, so we'll start here.

For the pasta:
250g (9oz) semolina flour
250g (9oz) unbleached flour
1 tsp extra virgin olive oil
½ tsp salt
140ml (¼ pint) warm water

For the filling:
2 large butternut squash, halved, destemmed and deseeded
3 large sweet red peppers, roasted, peeled and deseeded
1 tbsp shallot, minced
1 tbsp extra virgin olive oil
salt and nutmeg, to taste

Combine the flours then form into a mound on a clean work surface and make a well in the top. Put the oil and salt into the well and combine with the flours. Form a well in the top again and add a little of the water, working the sides into the water to combine. Mix in the remaining water, a little at a time until the dough is resilient, then knead it until somewhat dry and springy, about 10 minutes. Cover the dough and let it rest at least 30 minutes.

Preheat the oven to 200°C/400°F/Gas Mark 6. Place the squash, cut side down, on a lightly oiled baking sheet and bake until soft, about 1 hour. Remove the squash and let it cool until you can handle it. Peel and cut into cubes. Thinly slice the peppers. Heat the oil in a large pan over a medium heat. Add the shallot and sauté 1–2 minutes, until soft. Add the squash and peppers and cook until very soft. Season to taste with the salt and nutmeg, purée and strain.

Roll out the pasta dough until translucent. Cut into strips 20cm (8 inches) wide. Using a biscuit cutter or glass jar, cut 10cm (4 inch) diameter circles. Place 1-2 tsp of the filling in the centre of each circle. Barely moisten one finger tip in a bowl of fresh water and dampen the edge of each pasta circle. Fold dough over to form half circles. Pick up a half circle and roll it around your finger so that the pointed ends meet. Pinch the ends together and set onto a floured baking sheet. Repeat with the remaining dough and filling. Freeze the tortellini for 1 hour, transfer to a refrigerator and chill at least 1 further hour.

(Note: when the White Bean Soup is almost ready to serve, perform the final stage of this recipe. Meanwhile, make the White Bean Soup!) Bring salted water (to a depth of 15cm/(6 inches) to a boil in a very large saucepan over maximum heat. Add the tortellini, cover for 30 seconds. Uncover and watch carefully. When the pasta floats to the surface, cook 30 seconds longer, then drain and serve.

White Bean Soup

Again, worthy of praise all by itself but superlative with the tortellini. You can begin preparations while making the tortellini.

340g (12oz) cannelini beans, cleaned and soaked overnight
2 small bay leaves
7 cloves garlic (5 whole but bruised, 2 minced)
1 small head cauliflower, separated into florettes
1 tbsp extra virgin olive oil
1 small yellow onion, finely diced
1 small leek, white and light green parts, finely diced
1 small carrot, finely diced
1 small stalk celery, minced
1 15cm (6 inch) sprig fresh rosemary or 2 tsp dried rosemary
1 10cm (4 inch) sprig fresh thyme or 1 tsp dried thyme
1 tsp fresh oregano, minced or a large pinch dried oregano
salt and freshly ground black pepper to taste

170ml (6 fl oz) dry white wine
1.5l (3 pints) light vegetable stock
2 large tomatoes, peeled, deseeded and diced
12 large leaves fresh basil, julienned
Red Pepper-Squash Tortellini (above)

Drain beans and cover with 3l of water. Add one of the bay leaves and the bruised garlic, cover the pan and bring to a boil. Reduce the heat and simmer until tender but firm, about 45 minutes. Drain. Bring 3–4 litres of water to a rapid boil in a large soup pot with 2 tbsp of salt. Add the cauliflower, cover the pot for 30 seconds, uncover and cook 1 more minute. Drain the cauliflower and plunge immediately into ice water for 1 minute; drain again.

In a separate soup pot, heat the olive oil over a medium heat and add the onion and leek. Sauté for 2 minutes; add the remaining garlic, the carrot and celery and sauté a further 3 minutes. Add herbs and cook another 3 minutes. Season to taste with the salt and pepper and add the wine. Bring to a boil then immediately reduce to a simmer and cook until most of the liquid has evaporated. Add the vegetable stock, bring to a boil and add the beans. Reduce the heat and simmer, partially covered, until the beans are tender. Add the cauliflower and cook for 10 minutes more.

Serve the soup in large bowls, garnished with the tomatoes and basil, and topped with the Red Pepper-Squash Tortellini.

Mocha Fudge Torte

This is another impossibly wonderful gourmet dish created by Bill Maddex and I think something should be done about it, or him . . . Perhaps he should open a restaurant. Any backers out there?

Serves 8–10
Preparation time 1 hour 15 minutes, plus cooling time

250g (9oz) bittersweet chocolate
5 tbsp vegan margarine
1 tbsp liquid lecithin
5 tbsp warm water
3 tbsp Ener-G Egg Replacer
1 tbsp coffee liqueur
1 tsp vanilla extract
pinch of salt
3 tbsp warm (not hot) espresso coffee
225ml (8fl oz) warm water
4 tbsp Ener-G Egg Replacer

Preheat oven to 180°C/350°F/Gas Mark 4 and grease and flour a 25cm (9–10 inch) springform tin. Melt the chocolate with the margarine over a low heat in the top of a double boiler. Beat lecithin, the first measure of water and the first measure of Egg Replacer together until the powder is completely dissolved and the resulting paste is a pale yellow. Whisk the liqueur and vanilla into this mix then thoroughly whisk the whole lot into the chocolate; add salt and fold in the coffee. Beat the second measures of water and Egg Replacer until stiff, about 10 minutes, and fold carefully, a little at a time into the chocolate. It is vital that the resulting mousse be very well aerated. Turn gently into the prepared pan and bake until set, about 30 minutes.

Let cool in the pan, remove the collar from the pan, slice and serve – with vegan piping cream if possible (note: there are many commercial brands). This cake will deflate when cooling, but will stabilize before becoming too dense. The result will be a wonderful, light, smooth fudge cake.

SOUTH AMERICA

Two wonderfully nutritious and time-honoured seeds from South America are gradually being included in the European and North American diet. Until recently shrugged off as Third World foodstuffs, quinoa and amaranth are being welcomed by those who suffer digestive disorders, allergy to gluten or who simply wish to expand their culinary repertoire. Both seeds contain high amounts of fibre and very little fat. They also have the correct balance of amino acids for the body, which makes them particularly easy to digest. They are especially recommended for children, the elderly, pregnant women and people with protein deficiencies. Such individuals may have problems eating the large amounts of food normally needed to achieve their required nutritional intake. Quinoa and amaranth, with their highly concentrated protein and vitamin content, are therefore ideal.

Quinoa

Pronounced 'keen-wah', this seed has been cultivated since 3000 BC. The Incas called it 'The Mother Grain' and it is now grown by the Indians of the Andes. It contains an extraordinarily high 20 per cent protein, twice the amount normally found in wheat grains, and more amino acids too. Quinoa is a tiny, golden coloured grain with a delicate, slightly nutty flavour. It can look very attractive as part of a meal because, during cooking, the germ separates from the seed somewhat and extends outward in a spiral.

Cooked Quinoa

Serves 4
Preparation time 30 minutes

225g (8oz) quinoa, washed and drained
850ml (1½ pints) boiling water

Turn the quinoa into a saucepan, pour the boiling water over and simmer, covered, over a medium to low heat for 25 minutes. Serve instead of rice or potatoes with a topping of stew or sauce. Alternatively, serve with warm milk as a hot breakfast cereal. Some additional serving ideas include: Add quinoa to soups and cook for a further 15 minutes for an extra thick, nourishing food. Cook, then cool the quinoa and toss it with a mixture of chopped vegetables to make a salad. Dress the salad as usual. Use quinoa instead of rice to stuff peppers, marrow and squashes.

Quinoa Pudding

Serves 4
Preparation time 1 hour

100g (4oz) quinoa, washed and drained
570ml (1 pint) soya milk
50g (2oz) sugar
1 tbsp margarine
½ tsp ground cinnamon
¼ tsp ground nutmeg

Preheat the oven to 180°C/350°F/Gas Mark 4 and lightly oil a ramekin or oven dish. Turn the grain into a saucepan and add the milk. Bring to the boil, then simmer over a medium heat for five minutes. Remove from the heat and stir in the sugar, margarine and spices. Pour the mixture into the oven dish and bake for 45 minutes, or until a golden-coloured skin appears. Serve hot or cold, with a dressing of jam, apple sauce or Soya Creem.

Amaranth

Amaranth is a stunningly attractive plant with purple, red or gold flowers, grown by the Aztecs in South America and, more recently, by enterprising farmers in California. Amaranth is an especially valuable food because of its excellent nutritional profile: it is high in

phosphorus, iron, potassium, zinc, vitamin E, calcium and vitamin B complex. It also contains about 16 per cent protein, compared to the 10 per cent normally found in corn and other major cereals. The red variety is sometimes used to make a red, non-toxic food colouring.

The seeds, leaves and even the flowers of this versatile food can be eaten. The leaves taste a little like artichoke, and can be cooked in the same way as spinach, or stir-fried in a little soy sauce. The chewy seeds can be eaten as a breakfast cereal, a snack or as an addition to flour when making bread. And, of course, the cooked grain can be sprinkled on salads, mixed with vegetables to make casseroles, or even lightly roasted for use as a seasoning.

Amaranth 'Polenta'

Serves 4
Preparation time 40 minutes

570ml (1 pint) water or fruit juice
285g (10oz) amaranth seed

Bring the liquid to the boil over a medium heat and gradually add the amaranth seed. Reduce the heat, stir well and simmer the mixture for about 30 minutes. Serve with a sprinkling of nuts, fruit or honey. Or, for a savoury dish, top with your favourite sauce and garnish. This is excellent with a little soy sauce and freshly grated ginger.

Sprouted Amaranth Seeds

Preparation time 2–3 days

1 Buy organically grown seeds and remove any damaged or mouldy ones.
2 Wash approximately 4 tbsp of the seeds in a strainer, turn into a jam jar, cover with cold water and leave overnight.
3 The next day, drain off the water and put a piece of butter muslin over the top of the jar, held in place with a rubber band.
4 Lay the jar on its side in a warm dark place. Rinse it with fresh water 2 or 3 times during day (make sure you turn the jar upside down when you're finished rinsing, to drain out all the water).
5 After one day the sprout should have grown to the same length as the seed and is then ready for cooking.
6 If you want to eat the sprouts raw, let them sprout another day before using. In this case, make certain you rinse them 2–3 times during the day, as described.

GUYANA

Black Cake

The amount of rum called for in this cake is extraordinary: I suggest you either love it or leave it out, using fruit juice instead.

Serves 4–6
Preparation time 1 hour 30 minutes, plus overnight soaking

675g (1½lb) mixed dried fruit
50g (2oz) mixed peel
½ bottle (37.5cl/13.2 fl oz) dark rum
100g (4oz) peanuts or hazelnuts, chopped
1 tsp ground cinnamon
½ tsp ground ginger
¼ tsp ground nutmeg or allspice
225g (8oz) margarine
225g (8oz) brown sugar
1 tbsp molasses
285g (10oz) plain soya yoghurt
225g (8oz) plain flour
1 tsp baking powder

Measure the fruit and peel into a mixing bowl, stir well and pour in enough rum to cover. Cover the bowl and leave at least overnight, but preferably for 24–36 hours!

Preheat the oven to 150°C/300°F/Gas Mark 2 and grease a square, deep cake tin. Mix the chopped nuts with the spices and add to the soaked fruit. In a separate bowl, cream the margarine and brown sugar together to a smooth consistency. Blend in the molasses, then the yoghurt. Turn the fruit and nut mixture into this and stir the whole lot together. Stir the flour and baking powder together in a small bowl then fold into the creamed mixture, adding more rum to make a soft, spoonable mixture. Turn into the greased tin and bake for 1 hour. Insert a toothpick to test the cake is done as it may, on occasion, need to cook a little longer. Let the cake cool in the tin for 10 minutes, then turn it out onto a platter and slowly pour more rum, or fruit juice, over it – how much, precisely, is up to you!

Popcorn

This quick, nutritious snack has been popular for centuries. Its preparation is easy and theatrical and you can choose from so many different garnishes to finish the popped corn that you can be certain everyone will enjoy this treat.

Serves 4
Preparation time 10 minutes

1 tbsp oil
3 tbsp popcorn kernels

Suggested garnishes:
1 tsp salt
1 tbsp roasted sesame seeds
1 tbsp sugar mixed with ¼ tsp ground cinnamon
75g (3oz) hard soya cheese, grated
1 tsp paprika

Heat the oil in a deep, heavy-bottomed pan. Add the kernels and shake the pan to spread them evenly along the pan bottom. Cover the pan and leave over a fairly high heat, shaking the pan regularly, while the kernels pop. When the popping has ceased, turn the popped corn into a large bowl and sprinkle with your favourite garnish. Stir with a large spoon and scoop small bowlsful for each person. Serve immediately. Some people pour melted margarine over their servings, but this is a bit excessive as far as fat consumption is concerned.

Cornbread

The popularity of this bread extends north from South America, right through central America and into the southern states of north America. It is called Johnny Cake, Journey Cake and sometimes Spoon Bread. Indeed, it is something of a cross between cake and bread with the consistency of cake and the use of bread. It is served with the spicy ragouts of the Americas – such as Chilli or Frijoles – but also warm from the oven with lashings of maple syrup or apple sauce. It is best eaten the same day it is prepared.

Serves 4–6
Preparation time 45 minutes

450g (1lb) cornmeal
100g (4oz) plain flour
1 tsp salt
1 tsp bicarbonate of soda
2 tsp baking powder
1 tbsp tahini or peanut butter
285ml (½ pint) plain soya yoghurt
285ml (½ pint) soya milk
juice of 1 lemon

Preheat the oven to 180°C/350°F/Gas Mark 4 and grease a 23x23cm (9x9-inch) cake tin. Mix the dry ingredients together in a mixing bowl. In a separate bowl, blend the remaining ingredients to an even consistency. Add this mixture to the dry mixture, stir well and pour into the greased tin. Bake for 25–30 minutes. Cool in the pan then slice into squares, lift out of the tin and serve.

CARIBBEAN

Pickled Fiery Peppers

For this dish, it pays to learn a little about peppers, for there are a great many varieties (see page 268). You should either mix 2 or 3 varieties or seek out 1 type of fresh, hot pepper and turn it into this hot preserve. Unless you feel really cautious, you should not include the standard green and red sweet peppers sold in every greengrocers.

Makes 2x450g (1lb) jars
Preparation time 30 minutes

570ml (1 pint) white vinegar
6 cloves garlic, chopped
1 small onion, thinly sliced
1 tsp whole peppercorns
1 tbsp salt
25g (1oz) sugar, preferably white
225g (8oz) hot peppers (your choice)
140ml (¼ pint) rum

Mix the vinegar, garlic, onion, peppercorns, salt and sugar together in a saucepan and bring to the boil. Simmer for 5 minutes then remove from the heat and allow to cool while you prepare the peppers. Wash the peppers and decide how coarse or fine you want your pickle to be. You may leave the small peppers whole, for instance, or you may chop all the peppers into rings or fine pieces. Prepare the peppers and pack them into sterilized jars. Add the rum to the cooled vinegar brew and pour over the peppers. Seal the jars and leave for a week before using.

Hot Mango Chutney

Makes 4–6 × 450g (1lb) jars
Preparation time 1 hour 30 minutes, plus 24 hours soaking time

225g (8oz) raisins
225g (8oz) dates, chopped
2–3 hot peppers, chopped
1l (2 pints) malt vinegar
4–6 underripe mangoes, diced

100g (4oz) fresh ginger, grated
5 cloves garlic, crushed
2 large onions, finely chopped
1 tsp crushed mustard seed
5 whole cloves
50g (2oz) salt
1kg (2lb) brown sugar

Place the raisins, dates and chopped peppers in a mixing bowl and cover with the vinegar. Leave for 24 hours or overnight.

Measure the remaining ingredients into an enamel saucepan and stir in the fruit, pepper and vinegar mixture. Bring the mixture to a boil over a medium heat and simmer until the mixture is thick and dark, about 1 hour. Pour into sterilized jars, seal and put aside for 1–4 weeks.

Peppered Cabbage

Serves 4
Preparation time 25 minutes

½ head white cabbage, washed and coarsely shredded
2 medium onions, thinly sliced
1 teaspoon freshly ground black pepper
½ tsp salt
1 tbsp oil

Prepare the cabbage and onions and put in a large mixing bowl. Sprinkle the pepper and salt over and use your hands to rub the mixture until it is slightly softened and the seasoning well blended; about 5 minutes. Heat the oil in a saucepan and add the cabbage and onion mixture to it, cover the pan and cook over a low heat for 5 minutes. Stir the ingredients and cook a further 10 minutes, stirring once or twice more. Serve hot with rice, tempeh, Scrambled Tofu (see p291) or spiced beans.

Salad Creme

Makes approximately 140ml (¼ pint)
Preparation time 10 minutes

140ml (¼ pint) Soya Creem
1 tsp prepared mustard
1 tsp chives, chopped
¼ tsp salt
¼ tsp sugar
1 tbsp vinegar or lemon juice

Mix all the ingredients except the vinegar then add the vinegar a tiny bit at a time, shaking or stirring it after each addition to make a smooth, thick sauce.

Stuffed Cucumber Appetizer

Serves 4
Preparation time 20 minutes

225g (8oz) mixed vegetables (any sort), cooked and cooled
1 tbsp fresh parsley, chopped
140ml (¼ pint) salad creme (see previous recipe)
1 large cucumber
2 large tomatoes
8 wedges of dry toast
2 sprigs of watercress

Mix the cooled vegetables with the parsley and salad creme and put to one side. Slice the cucumber into eight thick rounds and scoop out the seed pulp. Slice the tomatoes into four rounds each and place each slice on a slice of dry toast. Place a cucumber round on each slice of tomato and fill with the vegetable and salad creme mixture. Garnish each with a piece of watercress and serve, 2 per person, as a starter or appetizer.

Vegetable Salad Jelly

This is a versatile and very pretty dish, colourful and interesting to look at, which is both refreshing and robust.

Serves 4–6
Preparation time 2-4 hours, including chilling

2 sachets (approximately 3g each) agar powder
2 tbsp sugar
420ml (¾ pint) boiling water
140ml (¼ pint) vinegar
juice of 1 lemon
420ml (¾ pint) cold water
2 spring onions, thinly sliced
1 large carrot, grated
2 stalks celery, very thinly sliced
1 sweet pepper, any colour, diced
100g (4oz) stuffed green olives, sliced
100g (4oz) baby sweetcorn or sweetcorn kernels
1 eating apple, finely diced (optional)

Mix the agar and sugar together in a saucepan; add the boiling water and stir until they have dissolved. Mix the vinegar, lemon juice and cold water and add to the hot mixture. Stir well and chill until it is partially set. Mix the vegetables together or plan how you wish to

arrange them in the jelly mould. You could arrange the baby sweetcorn and/or olive slices on the bottom of the mould, for example, so that when it is turned out they will appear uppermost. For this method, simply create layers of vegetables and jelly by spooning them into the mould. Alternatively, add the mixed vegetables to the partially-set jelly, stir well and turn the whole lot into the mould. Chill until very firm then turn onto a platter lined with crisp lettuce leaves, endive and radiccio. Serve with other salads and a selection of sauces and dressings.

Coconut Bread

Makes 2 loaves
Preparation time 1 hour 30 minutes

450g (1lb) plain flour
2 tsp baking powder
½ tsp bicarbonate of soda
170g (6oz) sugar
170g (6oz) raisins
100g (4oz) desiccated coconut
100g (4oz) margarine
1 tsp vanilla essence
4 tbsp soya milk or coconut milk

Preheat the oven to 180°C/350°F/Gas Mark 4 and grease 2 large loaf tins. Mix the first 5 ingredients together in a mixing bowl and put to one side. Blend the coconut, margarine and vanilla together in a separate bowl. When blended, gradually add the dry mixture: stirring after each addition and adding milk as necessary to make a firm dough. Divide the dough in two and work on a floured board; shape into loaves and place in the greased tins. Bake for 1 hour. Cool 10 minutes in the tins before turning out onto a wire rack. Serve with jam.

HONDURAS

Pumpkin Coconut Pudding

Serves 4
Preparation time 1 hour 15 minutes

900g (2lb) pumpkin, quartered and deseeded
340g (12oz) plain flour
450g (1lb) sugar
100g (4oz) margarine
140g (5oz) plain soya yoghurt
420ml (¾ pint) coconut milk

juice of 1 lime
1 tsp vanilla essence
2 tbsp rum

Preheat the oven to 180°C/350°F/Gas Mark 4 and grease a large oven dish or ramekin. Steam the pumpkin for about 20 minutes, until tender. Scrape the steamed pumpkin from its shell and turn into a large mixing bowl. Mix the flour and sugar and mash into the pumpkin; add the margarine and blend this mixture till smooth. Add the remaining ingredients, one at a time, stirring well after each addition. Turn the mixture into the oven dish and bake for 50 minutes. Serve with Soya Creem or a favourite hot sauce.

Journey Cakes

Similar to North American Baking Powder Biscuits, except for the coconut, and with the same name as another journey cake (see Cornbread, p331) popular in the Americas, but made from cornmeal. These are best eaten the same day they are prepared.

Serves 4
Preparation time 40 minutes

225g (8oz) plain flour
2 tsp baking powder
¼ tsp salt
100g (4oz) margarine
4 tbsp desiccated coconut
140ml (¼ pint) coconut milk

Preheat the oven to 180°C/350°F/Gas Mark 4. Mix the flour, baking powder and salt together in a mixing bowl. Work in the margarine to make an even, crumbly texture. Stir the coconut and coconut milk together in a jug and pour into a well in the dry mixture. Slowly stir the liquid in to make a firm dough. Roll the dough into golf-ball sized balls and flatten onto a baking tray. Bake for 20 minutes. Serve hot with your favourite spread, sauce or spiced beans.

JAMAICA

Ackee in Pepper Sauce

This dish is traditionally made with salt fish, so expect an amendment or two here. Really, the special and most luscious part of the dish is the ackee itself, a flower bud from a tropical tree. The dish is served in layers: ackees over fish, sauce over ackees. This version still has the layers but you'll find sautéed tempeh at the bottom, instead of fish. Tinned ackees are available from Afro-Caribbean food shops. Finally, make certain to use a good, tasty oil for this dish as it will really enhance the final outcome.

Serves 4
Preparation time 45-60 minutes

2 blocks tempeh, defrosted
2x450g (1lb) tins ackees, drained
1-3 tbsp oil
1 medium onion, thinly sliced
½ tsp freshly ground black pepper
1 fresh chilli, thinly sliced
1 stalk celery, thinly sliced
1 small sweet green pepper, thinly sliced
50g (2oz) creamed coconut, grated (optional)
a few spears of chives, finely chopped

If you are using tempeh, cut each block into six wedges and sauté them until golden brown. Arrange them on hot plates. Drain the ackees and steam for about 10 minutes, until hot and tender. Meanwhile, make the hot sauce. Heat the oil in a frying pan and sauté the onion until clear and tender. Add the pepper, chilli and celery, cover the pan and cook for a further 5–7 minutes over a low heat. Add the sweet pepper, cover the pan again and cook 3–5 minutes. If you are using coconut, add with the sweet pepper and cook, an extra 2–3 minutes.

Lift some hot ackees onto each serving of tempeh, then spoon some of the hot sauce over the ackees and sprinkle a little chopped chives over each serving. Serve immediately on its own or with rice, cornbread or other vegetable side dishes that please you.

Rice and Beans

This dish is generally prepared by cooking the beans slowly in a large saucepan, rather than in a pressure cooker, which, though it would greatly reduce the cooking time, might not produce such a mellow flavour.

Serves 4
Preparation time 2 hours, plus soaking overnight

170g (6oz) dried red kidney beans
3-5 cloves garlic, finely chopped
1 medium onion, chopped
½ tsp thyme
100g (4oz) coconut cream
340g (12oz) long grain brown rice

Wash and drain the beans and soak them overnight in fresh water. Drain and rinse the beans then place them in a large pot with fresh water to just cover. Bring to the boil, cover the pan, reduce the heat and simmer briskly for about 1 hour. Add the remaining ingredients except the rice, stir well and simmer a further 10 minutes. Now add the rice, ensuring there is liquid rising just above the surface of the rice and beans. Cover the pan and simmer gently for about 30 minutes. All the liquid should be absorbed and the rice should be tender. Serve hot with greens or a peanut sauce.

Simple Rice and Peas

This is a bit quicker to cook than the recipe above, and very tasty and attractive.

Serves 4
Preparation time 45 minutes, plus soaking overnight

100g (4oz) split yellow or green peas
225g (8oz) long grain white rice
25g (1oz) margarine
2–3 spring onions, thinly sliced (optional)
50g (2oz) crushed peanuts or slivered almonds (optional)

Wash and drain the peas and soak them overnight in fresh water. Drain and rinse and turn into a saucepan; cover with fresh cold water. Bring the water to the boil then reduce the heat and simmer, covered, for 15 minutes. Stir in the rice and add more water to cover the rice and peas by about half their depth again (ie if there is rice and peas to a depth of 5cm (2 inches), the water should rise 2.5cm (1 inch) above their surface). Cover the pan and simmer for a further 15-20 minutes. The rice and peas should be tender and the liquid absorbed. Stir in the margarine and the onions and peanuts, if desired. Cover the pan again and leave to one side, off the heat, for a further 5 minutes. Serve hot or cold. This dish is substantial enough to make a meal in itself, but it is so pretty that a selection of side dishes, chutneys and salads will be nicely set off by it.

Plantain Pudding

Serves 4
Preparation time 1 hour

6 plantain, peeled and grated
25g (1oz) margarine
285ml (½ pint) coconut milk

285g (10oz) brown sugar
1 tsp vanilla
2 tbsp raisins
1 tbsp tahini or peanut butter
1 tbsp soya flour
2 tbsp plain flour
½ tsp ground nutmeg
3 tbsp desiccated coconut
1 tbsp soya milk or water

Preheat the oven to 180°C/350°F/Gas Mark 4 and grease a soufflé or oven dish. Grate the plantain into a mixing bowl and rub in the margarine. Blend in the coconut milk, sugar and vanilla and stir in the raisins. Mix the tahini in a separate bowl with the flours, nutmeg and 2 tbsp of the desiccated coconut. Add 1 tbsp liquid to this mixture if necessary to make a thick paste. Blend this mixture into the plantian mixture and turn into the greased oven dish. Bake for 40 minutes. Serve cold with Soya Creem, soya ice cream or a favourite sauce and sprinkle each serving with a teaspoon of the remaining coconut.

LEEWARD ISLANDS

Fungi

No, not mushrooms! In Barbados a virtually identical dish is called Cou-cou. This recipe incorporates polenta, that marvellous cornmeal dish which pops up again and again, with fascinating variations such as this, in virtually every region of the globe.

Serves 4
Preparation time 30 minutes

450g (1lb) okra (ladies' fingers), trimmed and sliced
1.25l (2½ pints) boiling water
¼ tsp salt
450g (1lb) cornmeal
50g (2oz) margarine

Prepare the okra by slicing the caps off and cutting each into rounds or quarters. Boil the water in a large saucepan with the salt then drop in the okra and boil for about 5 minutes. Gradually add the cornmeal, stirring constantly to make an even consistency. Stir in the margarine, reduce the heat, cover the pan and leave for 10–20 minutes undisturbed. Check that the water has been fully absorbed and that the cornmeal is tender. Remove from the heat. Serve hot with salt and freshly ground black pepper, your favourite tomato sauce, vegetable stew or a tablespoon of grated soya cheese.

Sweet Fungi

We're not finished yet: still nothing to do with mushrooms!

Serves 4
Preparation time 30 minutes

1.25l (2½ pints) boiling water
100g (4oz) raisins
100g (4oz) sugar
¼ tsp ground nutmeg
450g (1lb) cornmeal
50g (2oz) margarine

Boil the water in a large saucepan then stir in the raisins, sugar and nutmeg and boil for about 5 minutes. Gradually add the cornmeal, stirring constantly to make an even consistency. Stir in the margarine, reduce the heat, cover the pan and leave for 10–20 minutes undisturbed. Remove from the heat. Serve hot with a teaspoon of barley malt syrup.

Boija

This is a delicious, nutritious and versatile bread that gets easier to make the more often you try it.

Makes 2 loaves
Preparation time 2 hours 30 minutes

75ml (3fl oz) tepid water
1 tsp sugar
25g (1oz) yeast, dry or fresh
675g (1½lb) plain flour
675g (1½lb) cornmeal
170g (6oz) desiccated coconut
3-4 ripe bananas, peeled and mashed
140g (5oz) sugar
1 tsp vanilla essence
285ml (½ pint) oil

Preheat the oven to 180°C/350°F/Gas Mark 4 and grease two large loaf tins. Stir the water and sugar together then add the yeast and stir well. Leave to one side for about 15 minutes to become frothy. Meanwhile, mix the flour, cornmeal and coconut together in a bowl. In a separate bowl, blend the bananas, sugar, vanilla and oil to an even, creamy consistency. Add the yeast mixture and stir well. Finally, work in the dry mix, adding a little more tepid water if necessary to make a stiff dough. Divide in two and turn into the greased tins. Cover with a clean cloth and place in a warm, draught-free place to rise until doubled in bulk, about 1 hour. Bake for 45–60 minutes. Cool in the tins for 10 minutes then turn onto wire racks to cool completely.

GRENADA

Cool Cucumber Soup

Serves 4
Preparation time 1 hour

1 tbsp oil
1 tbsp plain flour
¼ tsp salt
1 tsp freshly ground black pepper
675ml (1 ½ pints) soya milk
285ml (½ pint) vegetable stock
1 medium onion, finely chopped
1 large cucumber, grated
juice of 1 lemon
1 tbsp sherry
2 sprigs watercress or parsley

Heat the oil in the top of a double boiler. Mix the flour, salt and pepper together and sprinkle over the oil. Stir well to make a roux. Blend the soya milk and stock and add to the roux, a little at a time, stirring well after each addition. When the soup is creamy and smooth, add the onion and cucumber and cook, covered, for 15 minutes, stirring occasionally. Remove the soup from the heat and allow it to cool slowly for 15 minutes. Stir in the lemon juice and sherry, pour the soup into a tureen and chill in the refrigerator for at least 30 minutes. Stir and serve cold with a garnish of watercress.

Orange Banana Pudding

Serves 4–6
Preparation time 40 minutes

4–6 large bananas, peeled
juice of 1 large orange
2 tbsp brown sugar
½ tsp ground nutmeg
¼ tsp ground allspice
75g (3oz) desiccated coconut

Preheat the oven to 180°C/350°F/Gas Mark 4 and lightly grease an oven dish. Slice the bananas in halves or quarters along their length and arrange in the bottom of the dish. Mix the orange juice, sugar and spices together and spoon over the bananas. Finally, sprinkle the coconut over all and bake for about 25 minutes, until the bananas are soft and hot and the coconut is brown. Serve immediately.

PUERTO RICO

Frijoles Negros (Black Beans Ragout)

Serves 4
Preparation time 1 hour 15 minutes, plus overnight soaking

225g (8oz) dried black beans
2 tbsp oil
7 cloves garlic, finely chopped
2 medium onions, chopped
2 sweet peppers, deseeded and diced
1 fresh chilli pepper, thinly sliced
1 tsp salt
1 tsp freshly ground black pepper
1 tsp sugar
1 tsp dried oregano
3 bay leaves
½ tsp ground cumin
2 tbsp sherry or white wine
1 tbsp vinegar
3–4 spring onions, thinly sliced

Wash and drain the beans, cover them in fresh water and soak them overnight. Drain and rinse them and cover with fresh water in a pressure cooker. Cook at pressure for 20 minutes.

In a large saucepan, heat the oil and gently sauté the garlic and onions until clear and tender. Add the sweet peppers and the chilli pepper and continue the sauté for a further 5 minutes. Turn the cooked beans and their liquor into the large saucepan with the sauté and stir well over a medium heat. Add the remaining ingredients except the spring onions and keep stirring as the mixture cooks. Add a little water if necessary to make a thick but sloppy ragout. Cook over a medium heat for about 45 minutes, until the beans are very tender and the flavours well blended. This dish may be served immediately, or allowed to cool before serving cold, or reheated. The flavour often improves from this practice. Serve in bowls with a garnish of chopped spring onion. A serving of steaming rice is a simple, excellent accompaniment.

OCEANIA

That area of the globe that includes Australia, New Zealand, and many, many groups of islands. I was delighted with the recipes gathered from this region as it is not usually thought of in connection with food adventures.

AUSTRALIA AND NEW ZEALAND

Frozen Christmas Pudding

Serves 4–6
Preparation time 24 hours

170g (6oz) prunes, chopped
170g (6oz) glacé cherries, chopped
170g (6oz) raisins
170g (6oz) sultanas
170g (6oz) currants
50g (2oz) mixed peel
285ml (½ pint) rum
2l (4 pints) vanilla flavoured soya ice cream
225ml (8fl oz) Soya Creem
75g (3oz) slivered almonds
50g (2oz) plain dark chocolate, grated
50g (2oz) chopped walnuts

Mix the dried fruits together in a bowl and pour the rum over. Leave to stand, covered, for 6–12 hours. Turn the ice cream into a large mixing bowl and stir in the Creem, almonds, chocolate and walnuts. Add the dried fruits and rum and stir well. Turn the mixture into a very large (3l/5½ pints) mould and press it well down. Freeze overnight or until required.

FIJI

Banana Rum Bake

Serves 4
Preparation time 30 minutes

4 large bananas, peeled
2 tbsp margarine
2 tbsp brown sugar
140ml (¼ pint) dark rum

Preheat the oven to 180°C/350°F/Gas Mark 4 and lightly grease a baking dish. Slice the bananas in half along their length and arrange in the baking dish. Drop dabs of margarine along each half then sprinkle the sugar and rum over all. Bake for 15 minutes, covered, until bananas are hot and tender and the margarine, sugar and rum have blended into a luscious sauce. Serve hot, alone or with soya ice cream or Soya Creem.

TONGA

Lu Pulu With Vegetables

This recipe has been amended slightly to make use of an oven rather than a barbeque fire.

Serves 4
Preparation time 1 hour

1 tbsp oil
2 medium onions, thinly sliced
225g (8oz) TVP chunks
1 tsp freshly ground black pepper
570ml (1 pint) vegetable stock
3 large sweet potatoes, peeled and sliced
900g (2lb) spinach, washed and trimmed
200g (7oz) creamed coconut
2 tbsp hot water
450g (1lb) mixed vegetables (ie diced carrots, peas, sweetcorn, French beans)

Preheat the oven to 180°C/350°F/Gas Mark 4 and lightly grease an oven dish. Heat the oil in a saucepan and sauté the onions until clear and tender. Add the TVP chunks and the ground pepper and continue the sauté for a further 3 minutes. Add the vegetable stock, stir well and leave the mixture to simmer over a medium heat for 10–15 minutes; stir often.

Meanwhile, steam the sweet potatoes for about 10 minutes. Prepare the spinach but do not slice the leaves. Place the creamed coconut in a small saucepan with the hot water and melt over a low heat. Pour a little of the melted coconut onto the bottom of the oven dish and arrange half the potato slices over it. Use half of the spinach and place in a thick layer over the sweet potato, spoon all of the TVP sauté over these leaves. Press the remaining spinach leaves over the TVP layer and top the leaves with the remaining sweet potato slices. Spread the mixed vegetables over the sweet potato, pour the remaining melted coconut over all and cover the dish. Bake covered for 30 minutes then remove the cover and bake a further 10 minutes. Slice and serve hot.

PAPUA NEW GUINEA

Coconut Potato Patties

Serves 4
Preparation time 40 minutes

450g (1lb) potatoes, peeled and diced
100g (4oz) desiccated coconut
2–4 tbsp coconut or soya milk
1 tsp freshly ground black pepper
¼ tsp salt
1 tbsp margarine
oil

Steam the potatoes for about 20 minutes, until tender. Meanwhile, measure the desiccated coconut into a bowl and just cover with hot water. When the potatoes are cooked, drain the coconut (you may use some of this liquid in a moment) and mash into the potatoes. Add a little of the liquid or milk, the salt, pepper and margarine and mash to a creamy consistency.

Shape the mixture into patties. Heat a little oil in a frying pan or griddle and brown the patties on each side, about 10 minutes in total. Serve as a snack beside chutneys and salads or serve hot to accompany other vegetable dishes.

ASIA

This huge region of the world is almost a frame of mind more than a collection of lines on a map. For who can say precisely where the eastern reaches of Europe become the western reaches of Asia? Is Greek, Cypriot and Turkish food European because of the recent political stance of those countries, or is food from these countries Asian because of its history and cultural connection with the East? All I know is that, however the lines have been drawn in the past, food from Asia has a maturity and refined quality which only comes from having evolved over generations. What better recommendation.

CHINA

Grilled Aubergine

From deep within the boundaries of China, a dish that resembles the Middle-Eastern Baba Ganoush. The secret to a tasty dish is the roasting: the smokey flavour imparted by roasting over an open fire is best, but if you haven't one of those then a standard grill will do.

Serves 4
Preparation time 1 hour 30 minutes

3 medium aubergines
5 cloves garlic, finely chopped
1 fresh red chilli pepper, very thinly sliced
salt to taste
juice of 2–3 limes, to taste or juice of 2 lemons, to taste

Cook the aubergines over an open or charcoal fire, or under a grill – the skin will char slightly. Cook them slowly, turning them often, until they feel tender if pierced with a thin skewer. Allow to cool so that you can handle them, then slice them open and scoop out the pulp and place in a mixing bowl. Use a small mortar and pestle or a garlic press to crush together the garlic and chilli. Add to the aubergine pulp and work together to a thick, smooth paste. Add salt and lime to taste, stir well and serve cold with rice and a collection of other sauces and condiments.

Simmered Tofu

Serves 4
Preparation time 30 minutes

570ml (1 pint) vegetable stock
1 tsp freshly ground black pepper
1x5cm(2/inch) piece kombu (seaweed)
1 tbsp fresh ginger, thinly sliced

For the dipping sauce:
½ tsp Tabasco sauce
2 cloves garlic, crushed
1 tbsp fresh ginger, grated
4 tbsp soy sauce (tamari or shoyu)
2 spring onions, finely sliced
2x285g (10oz) blocks plain, firm tofu

Pour the stock into a saucepan and add the pepper, kombu and ginger slices. Place over a medium heat and bring to the boil. Reduce the heat and simmer gently while you prepare the dipping sauce. Mix the tabasco, garlic, ginger and soy sauce together in a jug and pour into four tiny sauce bowls. Slice the spring onions and sprinkle over each of the servings of dipping sauce.

Carefully cut each block of tofu into four thick slices and lower the slices carefully into the simmering broth. (You may cut the blocks into smaller pieces

if you like, in which case reduce the simmering time to 3–5 minutes.) Simmer for 5–7 minutes then lift out with a slotted spoon and serve onto individual small plates (two slices per person). Each person then dips pieces of the tofu into their bowl of Dipping Sauce before eating. Serve with steamed rice and a selection of other vegetable dishes.

Fried Tofu

Serves 4
Preparation time 20 minutes

2x285g (10oz) blocks plain, firm tofu
4 tbsp cornflour
4 tbsp oil
2 spring onions, finely sliced

Cut the tofu into 4–8 chunks per block and carefully coat in cornflour, trying not to break the chunks. Heat the oil in a frying pan and fry the tofu for about 5 minutes, turning over once in that time, until golden brown. Drain and serve immediately with a garnish of spring onion. Use the dipping sauce from the recipe above if desired, and serve with steamed rice and other vegetable dishes.

Marinated Tofu

Serves 4
Preparation time 16 hours

4x285g (10oz) blocks plain, firm tofu
1 small onion, very finely chopped
1 tbsp cloves
12 peppercorns
1 tbsp fennel seed
1 tbsp cinnamon stick pieces
1 tbsp freshly grated orange peel
2 whole dried chillies
2l (4 pints) vegetable stock or water

Wrap each block of tofu in its own piece of butter muslin. The wrap should be firm and thorough so that it will not slip or come undone, yet there is no need to tie it. Press the blocks of tofu overnight: use a tofu press or place several layers of clean tea towel on a wire cooling rack, place the wrapped tofu on top and cover with a chopping board. Place kitchen weights, books or jars full of rice onto the chopping board and leave the tofu to press and drain over a sink, bowl or draining board. If not using a tofu press, chances are your pressing creation will be worthy of a photograph!

Combine the remaining ingredients in an enamel

saucepan and leave overnight. Bring to a boil in the morning and simmer over a medium heat for 1–2 hours, in order to reduce the stock. Remove from the heat. Unwrap the beancurd and soak in the stock for 2-4 hours: it will change colour. Remove from the stock when you are ready to use the tofu. Slice and serve in sandwiches or salads or serve as a tofu 'steak' in a cooked meal (see following recipe).

Tofu 'Steak' with Mushrooms and Celery

Serves 4
Preparation time 25 minutes

450g (1lb) celery, cleaned and trimmed
450g (1lb) button mushrooms, trimmed and halved
2–3 tbsp oil
freshly ground black pepper, to taste
4 spring onions, sliced lengthwise and quartered
60ml (2fl oz) rice wine or sherry
4 blocks of Marinated Tofu (see above), already
  pressed
1 tbsp sesame oil

Chop the celery into thick chunks about 2.5cm (1 inch) long and drop them into boiling water for 1 minute. Drain and prepare the mushrooms. Heat the oil in a deep frying pan and sauté the celery and mushrooms over a medium heat for about 7 minutes, stirring often. Add black pepper if desired. Arrange the spring onions over the sauté, pour in the rice wine, place the tofu 'steaks' over the onion and cover the pan. Reduce the heat and cook for 5 minutes. Lift the cover long enough to sprinkle the sesame oil over the tofu 'steaks', cover again and cook for a further 5 minutes. Serve hot over rice.

Tofu in Rich Sauce

Serves 4
Preparation time 25 minutes

2–3 tbsp oil
5 cloves garlic, finely chopped
1 tbsp fresh ginger, grated
1 tbsp dark miso, cut into tiny lumps
4–5 spring onions, finely chopped
1 tsp tabasco sauce or 1 tbsp hot relish sauce
2 tbsp soy sauce
170ml (6fl oz) vegetable stock or water
2x285g (10oz) blocks plain, firm tofu, cubed
2 tsp kuzu (arrowroot)
140ml (¼ pint) water

2 tbsp chives or spring onion, chopped

Heat the oil in a large frying pan and sauté the garlic and ginger for 3 minutes. Add the miso and the spring onions and stir for 1 minute. Next add the tabasco, soy sauce and stock, stir well and bring to a simmer. Add the cubed tofu, cover the pan and simmer for 5 minutes. Meanwhile, blend the kuzu and water to a paste then add to the simmering sauce. Stir well for 2–3 minutes and serve hot over rice with a sprinkling of chives or spring onion to garnish.

Quickly Seitan

Seitan is made from wheat gluten and has a long and interesting history as a meat-replacement foodstuff. Buddhist monks in some parts of China developed a form of cookery called Zhai cookery which makes impressive use of seitan in dishes designed to resemble all forms of flesh. Whether or not you appreciate meat-mimics, seitan increases the protein content of meals and adds an interesting texture to them. It is a marvellous venue for spice and herb flavours and adds visual interest to a dish. Buy it frozen from healthfood shops.

Serves 4
Preparation time 20 minutes

450g (1lb) seitan (gluten), defrosted
2 tbsp oil
1 tbsp fresh ginger, grated
½ tsp freshly ground black pepper
4 spring onions, sliced lengthwise and quartered
450g (1lb) mushrooms, trimmed and halved
2 × 285g (10oz) tins bamboo shoots, drained and
  sliced into matchsticks
570ml (1 pint) vegetable stock
2 tbsp soy sauce
pinch brown sugar
1 tbsp sesame oil

Slice the seitan into thin strips and put to one side. Heat the oil in a wok or large frying pan and sauté the ginger and black pepper for 1 minute. Add the spring onions and stir for 1 minute. Add the mushrooms, bamboo shoots and the sliced seitan and sauté for a further 2–3 minutes, stirring constantly. Add the vegetable stock, soy sauce and brown sugar, stir well and cover the pan. Simmer over a medium heat for 5 minutes. Uncover the pan, stir and sprinkle with the sesame oil. Cover for 1 minute longer. Serve hot over steamed rice by lifting the mixture out of the gravy with a slatted spoon. Serve the remaining gravy according to taste, over the vegetables or by itself over rice.

Spicy Steamed Aubergine

Serves 4
Preparation time 2 hours

2 medium aubergines, peeled and quartered along their length
2–4 tbsp salt

For the sauce:
2 tbsp sesame oil
2 tbsp soy sauce
1 tbsp rice vinegar
3 cloves garlic, crushed
3 tbsp coriander leaves, finely chopped
1 fresh chilli, thinly sliced

Prepare the aubergine and place on a large platter. Sprinkle the salt over the aubergine and put to one side for 1 hour. Meanwhile, prepare the sauce: blend the remaining ingredients together in a jug or bowl and leave to stand.

After 1 hour, drain, rinse and drain the aubergines. Cut the slices into chunks then steam them for 30–40 minutes. Stir the chunks of aubergine into the sauce and serve hot with plenty of rice. Alternatively, you may mash the aubergine and sauce together to make a paste. Serve with a variety of other vegetable dishes.

Quick Sweet and Sour Mushrooms

Serves 4
Preparation time 15 minutes

450g (1lb) button mushrooms (or other available type)
3 tbsp oil
5 cloves garlic, finely chopped
1 fresh chilli, finely chopped
3 tbsp wine vinegar
1 tbsp brown sugar
1 tbsp soy sauce

Trim the mushrooms. You may halve them or leave them whole, according to the texture you prefer. Heat the oil in a large frying pan or wok and sauté the garlic and chilli for 2 minutes. Add the mushrooms and continue to sauté over a medium heat for 3–5 minutes. Add the remaining ingredients to make a sauce. Stir well, cover the pan and continue cooking for 5

minutes, until the mushrooms are tender. Serve at once over rice, with a selection of other dishes including tofu and greens.

Broccoli and Mushroom Stir-fry

Serves 4
Preparation time 25 minutes

1 tbsp oil
1 large onion, thinly sliced
1 tsp freshly ground black pepper
450g (1lb) button mushrooms, trimmed and halved
420ml (¾ pint) vegetable stock
450g (1lb) broccoli, cut into florets
1 tbsp sesame oil
1 tbsp rice wine
2 tsp kuzu (arrowroot)

Heat the oil in a wok or large frying pan over a medium heat and sauté the onion until clear and tender. Add the black pepper and stir for 1 minute, then add the mushrooms and sauté for 5 minutes, stirring often. Meanwhile, bring the vegetable stock to the boil and lower the broccoli florets into it for 2 minutes. Lift them out and put to one side. Add the sesame oil and rice wine to the stock and keep at a simmer. Remove 1–2 tbsp of the stock and stir into the kuzu to make a paste. Return this paste to the stock and stir constantly while the stock thickens.

Pour the thickened stock into the mushroom sauté and add the broccoli. Stir over a medium to high heat for 3 minutes. Serve hot with steamed rice.

NEPAL

Tare-ko-aloo (Fried Potatoes With Spices)

Serves 4
Preparation time 40 minutes

2 tbsp oil
3 cloves garlic, finely chopped
4 medium onions, finely chopped
1–2 tbsp fresh ginger, grated
2-4 green chillies, sliced in quarters lengthwise
1 tsp turmeric
2 tsp ground cumin
900g (2lb) potatoes, peeled and sliced
juice of 1 lemon
juice of 1 lime

Heat the oil in a large frying pan and sauté the garlic

until just golden. Add the onions and sauté until clear and tender. Next add the ginger and chillies and continue to sauté until some of the onion begins to brown. Add the turmeric and cumin and stir well for 1 minute. Add the potato slices and gently stir them into the saute. Cover the pan and leave them cooking for 5–7 minutes. Stir the sauté again to turn the potatoes, add all or some of the lemon juice and cover the pan. Leave to cook a further 5-7 minutes. Stir again and test the potatoes. When they are tender, serve immediately, alone or over rice, with a sprinkling of lime juice.

Malangwa Stew

Serves 4
Preparation time 1 hour

225g (8oz) TVP chunks
1l (2 pints) vegetable stock
2 tbsp tomato purée
2 tbsp oil
3 medium onions, chopped
1 tsp freshly ground black pepper
1 tsp chilli powder
450g (1lb) okra (ladies' fingers), trimmed
3 medium tomatoes, chopped
225g (8oz) melon (optional), mashed

For the topping:
100g (4oz) pumpkin seeds, finely ground
1 tbsp tahini (sesame paste)
140–285ml (¼–½ pint) water

Measure the TVP into a bowl. Stir the stock and tomato purée together and pour over the TVP. Leave to one side. Heat the oil in a large saucepan or stewpot and sauté the onions until clear and tender. Add the black pepper and chilli and stir for 1 minute. Add the okra and the chopped tomato to the sauté and cook over a medium heat for about 5 minutes. Add the TVP and stock mixture to the saute, stir well and leave to simmer, covered, for about 20 minutes. Stir the stew again, adding more stock if necessary to make a thick stew with tender chunks. Stir in the mashed melon and leave over a low heat for a further 10 minutes.

Mix the pumpkin seed and tahini together in a small saucepan over a low heat. Add water, a little at a time, stirring well after each addition to make a sauce. Serve the stew hot, over freshly steamed rice if you prefer, and spoon a little of the sauce over each serving.

SRI LANKA

Carrots in Coconut Sauce

Serves 4
Preparation time 45 minutes

2 tbsp oil
3 cloves garlic, finely chopped
1 large onion, finely chopped
2 tsp fresh ginger, grated
1 tsp mustard seeds
½ tsp turmeric
½ tsp ground cumin
¼ tsp ground coriander
¼–½ tsp chilli powder
450g (1lb) carrots, scrubbed and sliced into rounds
140ml (¼ pint) coconut milk
3 tbsp desiccated coconut

Heat the oil in a large frying pan and sauté the garlic, onion, ginger and mustard seeds until the onion is clear and tender. Add the remaining spices and stir for one minute before adding the carrots. Stir over a medium heat for 5 minutes. Add the coconut milk and desiccated coconut, stir well, cover the pan and leave to simmer for 15 minutes on a low heat. At the end of this time, stir well, adding more milk if necessary to give a rich sauce. Ensure the carrots are tender. Serve hot over rice with greens.

Jallabis (Fritters in Syrup With Pistachio Nuts)

Serves 4
Preparation time 30 minutes, plus standing overnight

420g (15oz) sugar
15g (½oz) (1 packet) dry yeast
720ml (1¼ pint) warm water
225g (8oz) plain flour
6 drops rose water
oil
100g (4oz) pistachios, crushed

Mix 1 tbsp of the sugar with the yeast in a small bowl. Stir in 140ml (¼ pint) warm water and leave to one side for 15 minutes while the yeast softens. Measure the flour into a mixing bowl and, when the yeast has begun to froth, stir in the yeast and a further 285ml (½ pint) warm water to make a creamy batter. Cover the bowl and place in a warm, draught-free place overnight.

Heat the remaining 285ml (½ pint) water with the

remaining 400g (14oz) sugar in a saucepan to make a syrup. Boil for 10–12 minutes then remove the pan from the heat and add the rose water. Meanwhile, heat some oil in a frying pan and drop spoonsful of the batter into the hot oil. Fry (shallow fry) until golden, turning once, then remove from the pan and drain well. Now place the cooked fritters in the syrup for 5 minutes, drain them again and arrange on a serving platter. Sprinkle the fritters with crushed pistachios and serve.

Sweet Pepper Curry

Serves 4
Preparation time 30 minutes

2 tbsp oil
2 medium onions, thinly sliced
1–2 tsp freshly ground black pepper
1 tsp dill seed
1 tsp turmeric
¼ tsp salt
1 medium potato, peeled and finely diced
570ml (1 pint) soya milk
285ml (½ pint) vegetable stock or water
1x5cm(2/inch) piece of cinnamon
2 bay leaves
2–3 medium sweet peppers, red, green or yellow (or 1 of each), quartered and sliced

Heat the oil in a large saucepan and sauté the onions until clear and tender. Add the pepper and dill and stir for 1 minute. Now add the turmeric and stir well. Add the salt and diced potato and leave to cook over a medium heat. Mix the soya milk and stock together and add to the sauté, a little at a time, stirring after each addition. Add the cinnamon and bay leaves, stir well, cover the pan and leave to simmer gently over a medium heat for 10–15 minutes. Prepare the peppers and add to the sauce. Bring back to the boil then simmer gently for 5–7 minutes, adding more liquid if necessary to make a creamy sauce. Serve hot over steamed rice.

Brinjal Bhaji (Fried Aubergine)

Serves 4
Preparation time 45 minutes

50g (2oz) tamarind
170ml (6fl oz) warm water
2 medium aubergines, halved along length and sliced into very thin strips

2 tbsp salt
oil
1 tbsp oil
5 cloves garlic, finely chopped
2 medium onions, finely chopped
1 tsp chilli powder
1 tsp dry mustard
1 tsp turmeric
2 bay leaves
2 medium tomatoes, chopped
140ml (¼ pint) soya milk (optional)

Soak the tamarind in the warm water and put to one side. Prepare the aubergines, arrange on a platter, sprinkle them with the salt and leave to one side for 30 minutes. At the end of this time, drain and rinse the slices of aubergine and quickly fry them in oil. Drain the fried slices on kitchen roll, pressing out as much oil as possible.

Heat 1 tbsp of fresh oil in a clean frying pan and sauté the garlic and onion until clear and tender. Add the chilli, mustard and turmeric and stir for 1 minute. Strain the liquid from the tamarind and add to the sauté with the bay leaves and chopped tomato. Stir well and simmer gently for 5 minutes. You may add a little soya milk at this point, if you wish, to make a slightly creamier sauce. Finally, add the fried aubergine, cover the pan and cook for 5 minutes. Serve hot over rice, accompanied by other vegetable dishes.

INDIA

Chapatis

These little unleavened breads are served folded in quarters and are used to collect and lift the food to the mouth, instead of spoons and forks. The trick is to then use your thumb to push the food from the chapati into your mouth, instead of trying to shove and gulp, as Westerners tend to at first effort. Gradually, this discreet little movement of the thumb will become second nature and you will enjoy the tidiness that is so impressive in people of that region. You can easily buy very flat pans or griddles in this country, usually from wholefood centres, that will suit chapati-making perfectly.

Serves 4 (3 for each person)
Preparation time 1 hour 30 minutes

225g (8oz) wholewheat flour

1 tsp salt
140ml (¼ pint) cold water (this volume is approximate and may have to be adjusted according to the flour you use)
a little melted margarine or oil (optional)

Measure the flour into a mixing bowl and stir in the salt. Make a well in the centre and add the water. First stir and then knead to make a firm dough. Turn the dough out onto a floured board and knead for a further 5 minutes. Cover the dough with a clean cloth and leave for 1 hour.

Divide the dough into 12 pieces and roll each into a little ball. Roll or press each ball into a circle, about 17–20cm (7–8 inches) in diameter. This makes a very thin bread. Heat the griddle or frying pan (no oil or grease, please) and lay the chapati on it. Keep over a high heat for 2–3 minutes, until the underside is speckled brown, then turn the chapati and cook the other side. Place the cooked chapati on a warm plate and brush with a tiny amount of oil or margarine or fold into quarters. Cover with a cloth to keep it warm, adding chapatis as you cook them. Cooked chapatis that have been left unfolded may be placed under a hot grill just before serving, if desired, to make them puff up slightly. Serve with rice and a variety of vegetable dishes.

Garam Masala for vegetable dishes

Making up your own spice mixtures is one of the most satisfying and creative aspects of cooking. After you have prepared this very simple mixture once, I hope you will be so smitten that you will begin to experiment with combinations of spices for all styles of cookery. This one is tried and tested but go ahead and change it to suit your tastes.

In the recipes of some eastern countries there is, written into the recipes, the term 'head of the household spice mixture' to allow for the creative input expected of each cook. As you learn about the characteristics of each spice available you will gain confidence, and combining them to achieve superlative flavours and distinct aromas will become a natural and sensuous aspect of every dish you prepare.

There are several books on the market specifically about spices and one or two of these might help you understand the nature of spices. However, there is really nothing like rolling up your sleeves and gaining practical experience. Use a mortar and pestle (for the muscular amongst you), a hand-turned peppermill, or an electric grinder, such as a coffee grinder, to grind your spices. It is best, and noticably different in flavour and aroma, to use whole spices – grinding them only when you need them. We all have need for little shortcuts now and again, however, so simply store any surplus ground spices in a labelled, air-tight jar in a dark cupboard. Over to you!

Makes 2-3 tbsp, enough for 1 dish
Preparation time 5 minutes

2 tsp freshly ground coriander
1 tsp freshly ground black pepper
1 tsp freshly ground cumin
½ tsp freshly crushed cardamom
½ tsp freshly ground cloves
½ tsp freshly ground cinnamon

If you can, grind these spices individually, measure them, then mix them. Alternatively, if you know that you will cook with garam masala again within the next 7–10 days, prepare a double or triple recipe, blend the spices and simply use half or one-third of it today.

Dhal

This word means 'lentils' and that is essentially what you get when you make this thick sauce or soup. Variations occur in two ways: what lentil you are cooking with and what spices you stir into them. I recommend you begin with the simple Red Lentil Dhal (see below) and then experiment with other lentils you might discover – first in your local supermarket, then in your local Asian grocers. As for spices, as well as experimenting with your own mixtures, begin to notice *when* in the cookery process the spices are added. You can greatly vary the strength and blend of flavours in the finished dhal by changing at what stage of cooking spices are added to the dish.

Dhal is a staple food, along with rice, of India; but you will find it under other names in most areas of the world (see Rupiza, page 324). Its nutritious simplicity and versatility ensures its continued popularity.

Red Lentil Dhal

Serves 4
Preparation time 45 minutes

450g (1lb) red lentils, washed and drained
1l (2 pints) water
1 tsp salt
2 tbsp oil
5 cloves garlic, finely chopped

1 medium onion, finely chopped
1 tbsp cumin
1 tsp turmeric
¼–½ tsp chilli powder (optional)
2 tbsp (see above, p344) garam masala
50g (2oz) fresh coriander, chopped

Turn the washed lentils into a deep saucepan and add the water and salt. Place over a medium heat, bring to the boil and remove some of the froth with a large spoon. Cover the pan, reduce the heat and leave to simmer for about 25 minutes, stirring occasionally. The lentils should lose their shape entirely.

Heat the oil in a frying pan and sauté the garlic and onion until clear and tender, about 10 minutes. Add the cumin and stir over a medium heat for 1–2 minutes, until it has turned golden. Add the chilli powder if desired and stir for a further 1 minute. Turn the sauté into the cooked lentils and stir well. Allow to simmer a further 5 minutes. Remove the lentils from the heat, stir in the garam masala and chopped coriander and serve immediately over steamed rice. For a more expansive meal, serve with a selection of vegetable dishes.

Channa Dhal (Brown Chickpea Dhal)

This lentil is slightly different from the chickpea used to make hummus and is often sold split. It takes a bit longer to cook and makes a richer, usually spicier dhal. If you cannot find channa in a shop near to you, chickpeas may be used instead with great success.

Serves 4
Preparation time 1 hour 15 minutes, plus soaking over-night

450g (1lb) channa lentils (Indian brown chickpeas or
    garbanzoes), washed and drained
1l (2 pints) water
1 tsp salt
1 × 15cm (6in) strip kombu seaweed (optional)
1 large onion, chopped
1x400g (14oz) tin chopped tomatoes or 2–3 large,
    fresh tomatoes, chopped
2 tbsp oil
5 cloves garlic, finely chopped
1 tbsp fresh ginger, grated
1 tsp chilli powder or to taste
50g (2oz) fresh parsley, chopped
2 tbsp (see recipe page 344) garam masala
1 lime, cut into wedges (optional)

Turn the drained channa into a mixing bowl and soak in fresh water overnight. This step is not crucial if the lentils are split. Drain and rinse the lentils and turn into a deep saucepan with the water, salt and kombu (this seaweed will help to soften the lentils). Bring to the boil over a medium heat, skim off any foam, then add the onion, cover the pan, reduce the heat and leave to simmer for 55 minutes. Remove the kombu at this stage. The channa should become very tender and will begin to lose their shape. Add the chopped tomatoes, stir well and continue to simmer the dhal.

Heat the oil in a frying pan and sauté the garlic for 3 minutes over a low to medium heat. The garlic should turn golden but not brown. Add the ginger and chilli and continue stirring for 1 minute. Turn the sauté into the dhal and stir well. Add the parsley and garam masala, stir and serve immediately over rice. Allow 1 wedge of lime for each person to squeeze over their serving, according to taste.

Moong Dhal (Mung Bean Dhal)

Mung beans are usually thought of in connection with bean sprouts, and excellent bean sprouts they make, too! Cooked mung are rich with a strong flavour. Mung beans can be purchased split, in which case they do not need soaking overnight, nor such a lengthy period of cooking.

Serves 4
Preparation time 1 hour 30 minutes, plus soaking over-night

450g (1lb) mung beans, washed and drained
1l (2 pints) water
1 tsp turmeric
1 tsp salt
2 tbsp oil
5 cloves garlic, finely chopped
1 medium onion, finely chopped
1 tbsp fresh ginger, grated
½–1 tsp chilli powder
½–1 tsp freshly ground black pepper
50g (2oz) fresh coriander, chopped
2 tbsp (see recipe p344) garam masala

Turn the washed beans into a mixing bowl and cover with fresh water. Leave soaking for 4–8 hours or overnight. If using split mung beans, this stage may be omitted. Drain and rinse the soaked beans and turn into a deep saucepan with the water, turmeric and salt. Bring to the boil over a medium heat, cover the pan and simmer for 45–50 minutes. Alternatively, cook in a pressure cooker for 25 minutes before turning into a saucepan.

Heat the oil in a frying pan and sauté the garlic and onion until clear and tender. Add the ginger, chilli and black pepper and stir for 1 minute. Add the sauté to the mung beans and continue cooking over a medium heat for 10–15 minutes. The mung beans should be very tender and losing their shape. Add the chopped coriander and garam masala, stir well and remove from the heat. Serve hot over steamed rice with a range of pickles or chutneys.

Carrot Halva

Serves 4–8
Preparation time 1 hour 30 minutes

570ml (1 pint) (approximately 900g/2lb) carrots, scrubbed and finely grated
1l (2 pints) soya milk
170ml (6fl oz) barley malt syrup
2 tbsp margarine
50g (2oz) slivered almonds
25g (1oz) crushed pistachios
5 cardamom pods, shelled and the seeds ground

Prepare the carrots and have ready. Heat the milk in a deep enamel saucepan over a medium heat. At the moment when it begins to boil, add the grated carrots and stir well. Keep cooking over a medium heat for about 1 hour, stirring often, until the mixture begins to thicken. Add the syrup and margarine and stir well for another 15 minutes. The mixture should be a deep carrot-colour and rather thick.

Lightly grease an oven dish and pour the carrot mixture into it, spreading evenly to the edges. Mix the nuts and cardamom together and sprinkle this mixture over the hot halva. Score with a knife into a 3cm (1 inch) square pattern. Allow to cool then cut into pieces along the score marks and serve as a dessert. Alternatively, wrap each piece carefully in greaseproof paper and a tiny piece of cloth, tie with ribbon, arrange several in a gift box and give!

INDONESIA

Gado Gado (Cold Vegetables in Spicy Peanut Sauce)

This dish is a classic Indonesian creation which is served the world over. Use whichever vegetables you find to hand if those listed are unavailable to you. Hard-boiled eggs usually feature in this dish, so I have substituted firm tofu chunks. Dig out your largest, most attractive serving platter and have fun with this delicious meal.

Serves 4
Preparation time 1 hour 20 minutes

For the vegetable arrangement:
2 medium potatoes, scrubbed and halved
2 medium carrots, peeled and cut into chunks
225g (8oz) green beans, trimmed and sliced
½ head of cauliflower, cut into florets
450g (1lb) spinach leaves, washed, drained, trimmed and sliced
100g (4oz) beansprouts, washed and drained (see p168–9)
¼ head of firm, white cabbage, coarsely shredded
¼ head iceberg lettuce, coarsely chopped
1 cucumber, washed and sliced
285g (10oz) plain, firm tofu, drained and cubed

For the sauce:
2 tbsp oil
3 cloves garlic, finely chopped
1 large onion, finely chopped
4 fresh chillies, finely chopped (adjust to taste)
1 tbsp fresh ginger, grated
570ml (1 pint) coconut milk
285g (10oz) crunchy peanut butter
1 tbsp brown sugar
juice of ½ lemon
2 tsp soy sauce

Steam the potatoes until tender, about 15 minutes. Steam the carrots, green beans and cauliflower until just tender, about 8 minutes. Mix the sliced spinach and beansprouts together and steam for 1–2 minutes. Allow all of these vegetables to cool. Slice the potatoes into thick rounds. Arrange all of the vegetables on a serving platter in a colourful and pleasing formation.

Heat the oil in a large frying pan and sauté the garlic, onion, chillies and ginger until the onions are clear and tender, for about 10 minutes, over a low to medium heat. Stir often. Blend the milk, peanut butter, sugar, lemon juice and soy sauce together in a jug then gradually add to the sauté, stirring after each addition. Keep the sauce simmering over a low heat for 10 minutes while the sauce thickens, stir frequently. Allow the sauce to cool then pour over the arrangement of vegetables on the platter and serve.

TURKEY

Kisir

This dish is similar to tabbouleh (see next column) but with some important differences. It is served hot or warm, for instance, and it originally used the juice of pomegranate rather than of lemon, as is listed here. Kisir is eaten either in a cool lettuce leaf or rolled into tiny balls just before being popped into the mouth. It traditionally accompanies the liquorice-flavoured alcoholic drink, arrack.

Serves 4
Preparation time 45 minutes

100ml (4 fl oz) olive oil
3 cloves garlic, finely chopped
1 bunch spring onions, trimmed and finely chopped
450g (1lb) bulgur (cracked wheat)
1l (2 pints) water, boiling
1 tbsp tomato purée and ½ tsp cayenne; or
3 tbsp hot tomato-chilli sauce (ie from Mexican, American or Indian cuisines)
freshly ground black pepper, to taste (I suggest ¼ tsp to start with)
¼ tsp cayenne
225g (8oz) fresh parsley, washed, trimmed and finely chopped
170ml (6 fl oz) lemon juice (approximately 3 lemons)
1 large cos lettuce, washed, drained and leaves separated
1 lemon, cut into wedges

Heat the oil over a very low heat in a large saucepan. Add the garlic and onions and sauté for 5–10 minutes, until they are tender. Add the bulgur to the sauté and stir until all the oil has been absorbed. Pour the boiling water over the bulgur and add the tomato and cayenne mixture or the spicy tomato sauce. Stir the bulgur well, bring to the boil then cover the pan and reduce the heat. Leave to cook for 12–15 minutes, until the bulgur is soft and fluffy, but not mushy. Remove from the heat and stir in the pepper, cayenne, parsley and lemon juice. Adjust the seasonings to suit your taste then cover the pan until ready to serve. Of course, you can eat this cold, but it is traditionally eaten hot, or at least

warm, on a leaf of cos lettuce. Serve with a small plate of lemon wedges to hand so that each person can adjust the flavour of their own serving.

LEBANON

Tabbouleh

Serves 4
Preparation time 45 minutes

225g (8oz) cracked wheat (bulgur)
570ml (1 pint) water, boiling
5–7 spring onions, trimmed and finely sliced
4 medium tomatoes, chopped
1 bunch (approximately 100g/4oz) fresh mint, finely chopped
225g (8oz) fresh parsley, finely chopped
140ml (¼ pint) good olive oil
juice of 3 large lemons
freshly ground black pepper, to taste (try ¼ tsp to start with)

Measure the bulgur into a mixing bowl and pour the boiling water over. Cover and leave to soak until all the liquid has been absorbed. Stir well and leave a further 10 minutes, uncovered. Meanwhile, prepare the onions, tomatoes and herbs and turn into a large mixing bowl. Pour over the oil and lemon juice and season to taste. Spoon the bulgur into this mixture, breaking up any lumps as you do so, and gently stir the tabbouleh. Leave to cool completely, stirring occasionally. Serve at once or leave to mature in a cool place for up to 8 hours. The flavour alters, some say 'improves', from standing. Serve as a salad or side-dish to a main meal.

ISRAEL

Tahini Dip

I cannot praise this dish enough: it is an exceptionally nutritious and substantial food, excellent for pregnant and lactating women. Children love this food as well, as it is easy to digest and very flavourful. Good teeth, strong bones and steady growth come naturally when this food is included in a child's diet.

Serves 4
Preparation time 20 minutes

1 × 340g (12oz) jar sesame paste (the darker it is, the more nutritious it is)
5 cloves garlic, crushed
140ml (¼ pint) water
140ml (¼ pint) lemon juice
¼ tsp freshly ground black pepper or paprika
pinch of salt
chopped fresh parsley to garnish

Mix all the ingredients except the parsley in a mixing bowl and whisk or purée them together. If you use a food processor, expect a smoother, creamier dip. Adjust the water and lemon juice to create the flavour and consistency you desire. Spoon into individual serving bowls and garnish with chopped parsley. Serve with plenty of hot, fresh pitta. Children love it in sandwiches, on crackers and with crudités.

Peppered Aubergine

Serves 4
Preparation time 3 hours, plus three days to mature

3 medium aubergines, sliced 2.5cm(1 inch) thick
3–4 tbsp salt
140ml (¼ pint) oil
2 sweet red peppers, diced
2 sweet green peppers, diced
3–4 pickled cucumbers, diced
570ml (1 pint) cider or wine vinegar
2–3 tsp freshly ground black pepper, increasing to taste
a little water

Arrange the slices of aubergine on a platter and sprinkle with the salt. Leave to one side for 1 hour 30 minutes. Drain and dry the slices with a clean towel. Heat the oil in a frying pan and fry the aubergines until tender. Lift out and drain, gently pressing out any excess oil. Fry the peppers and pickled cucumbers in the oil until just soft. Lift out and drain well. Measure the vinegar and pepper into a saucepan, dilute with water according to your taste. Bring to the boil and simmer 7–10 minutes.

Select a deep dish and arrange a layer of aubergine on the bottom. Spoon a little of the diced pepper mixture then another layer of aubergine, and so on. Aim to create a deep dish of at least four layers each of aubergine and pepper mixture. Pour the vinegar brew over the layers, cover the dish and place in the refrigerator for 2-3 days. Serve cold with salads or breads.

MIDDLE EAST

Phyllo Pastry

Makes 36 sheets
Preparation time 5 hours

500g (1lb 2oz) wholewheat flour
500g (1lb 2oz) plain flour
1 tsp salt
570ml (1 pint) water
3 tbsp very good quality olive, sesame or safflower oil
greaseproof paper
140g (5oz) powdered kuzu (arrowroot)

Mix the flours and salt together in a large mixing bowl and make a mound in the centre. Add the water to the flour so that it pours round the edge of the bowl (ie do not make a well in the centre of the flour). Stir well and, as it thickens, begin to knead the dough. Keep kneading for quarter of an hour until the gluten becomes quite stretchy. At this stage the dough should be soft and rather moist. Now slowly add the oil to the dough and continue kneading for a further quarter-hour – a total of half-an-hour! Cover the bowl containing the dough and leave to stand for 2–3 hours.

Turn the dough out onto a piece of marble or cool, seam-free counter and knead it vigorously for 5 minutes to work out any bubbles of air. Leave it to sit for a further 30 minutes. Now divide into 36 pieces. Place each piece between two sheets of greaseproof paper and roll very thin to the size of a baking tray, about 23cmx33cm (9x13 inches). Remove the top sheet of paper, dust the pastry with a little powdered kuzu and put to one side for at least 30 minutes. This will dry the pastry somewhat so that it is easier to handle and easier to freeze.

Repeat this procedure with each of the 36 lumps of dough. To freeze, ensure that greaseproof paper separates each sheet of phyllo, place them in a stack and roll the stack. Wrap tightly in foil or clingfilm and freeze. Use this pastry in one of the recipes that follow.

Sfihan (Phyllo and VegeMince Casserole)

Serves 4
Preparation time 5 hours, including time to chill

2 tbsp olive oil
2 medium onions, finely chopped
1 tsp ground cinnamon

½ tsp ground allspice
½ tsp freshly ground black pepper
¼ tsp salt
1x300g (10½oz) packet VegeMince
100g (4oz) pistachios (or pine nuts, flaked almonds or cashews)
140ml (¼ pint) soya milk
4 tbsp lemon juice
100g (4oz) margarine or olive oil
16–20 sheets phyllo pastry

Heat the oil in a large frying pan and sauté the onion until clear and tender. Add the spices and stir into the sauté for a further 1 minute. Add the VegeMince and stir over a low heat. In a separate frying pan, gently roast the nuts over a medium heat for 2–3 minutes, shaking the pan constantly. Remove both pans from the heat and stir the nuts into the VegeMince mixture. Add the soya milk and stir well before stirring in the lemon juice. Leave to one side, adding one or two tablespoons of soya milk if necessary to make a very slightly sloppy consistency.

Melt the margarine over a low heat. Spread a little in a 23cmx33cm (9x13 inch) oven dish. Place a sheet of phyllo pastry in the pan and brush a little of the melted margarine onto the sheet. Add another sheet of phyllo, brush with melted margarine and repeat in this way until there are 8–10 sheets of phyllo in a layer. Turn the nut and VegMince mixture onto the phyllo and spread evenly to the edges. Place a sheet of phyllo over this mixture and brush with margarine. Continue layering the sheets of phyllo, as before, brushing each with margarine, until there are another 8-10 sheets on top of the filling. Brush the top sheet of phyllo with double the quantity of margarine. Cover the dish and refrigerate for 4 hours, if possible.

Preheat the oven to 180°C/350°F/Gas Mark 4. Prick the surface of the sfihan with a fork along the lines you will cut it once baked. Bake the sfihan for 40 minutes, until golden. Cut into squares or triangles. Serve hot or cold.

Spanikopita

Serves 4
Preparation time 1 hour 15 minutes

170ml (6fl oz) olive oil
14–16 sheets phyllo pastry (see recipe above, p348)
900g (2lb) fresh spinach, washed and thinly sliced
3 cloves garlic, *very* finely chopped, not crushed

1 medium onion, *very* finely chopped
100g (4oz) hard soya cheese, grated
140g (5oz) firm tofu, roughly mashed
1 tsp freshly ground black pepper, or to taste
¼ tsp salt
¼ tsp ground nutmeg

Lightly oil a 23cmx33cm (9x13 inch) oven dish and place in it a sheet of phyllo pastry. Brush the pastry with a little of the olive oil and place another sheet on top. Brush this sheet with oil also and continue in this way until the layer of phyllo is 7–8 sheets thick. (Of course, you may alter the thickness of the phyllo layer to suit your taste; adjust the quantity of olive oil accordingly.)

Place the strips of spinach in a large mixing bowl. Mix the garlic, onion, soya cheese, tofu, pepper, salt and nutmeg in a small bowl. Add this mixture to the spinach and turn them gently together. Turn this mixture onto the phyllo and spread evenly to the edges. Alternatively, divide the spinach in half and place one half onto the phyllo layer, sprinkle the garlic and tofu over it, then spread the other half of the spinach over all.

Place a sheet of phyllo over the spinach mixture and brush with olive oil. Continue layering the sheets of phyllo as before, brushing a little olive oil onto each sheet, until there are 7–8 sheets. Brush the top sheet with double the quantity of olive oil. Cover the dish and refrigerate for 2–4 hours, if possible.

Preheat the oven to 180°C/350°F/Gas Mark 4. Prick the surface of the spanikopita with a fork along the lines you will cut it once baked. Bake for 45 minutes, until golden. Cut into squares or triangles. Serve hot or cold.

Baklava

Makes approximately 18
Preparation time 1 hour

24 sheets of phyllo pastry (see p348)
100g (4oz) margarine, melted

For the filling:
450g (1lb) blanched almonds
170g (6oz) sugar
1 tsp ground cardamom

For the syrup:
340g (12oz) sugar
285ml (½ pint) water
140ml (¼ pint) rosewater

Preheat the oven to 180°C/350°F/Gas Mark 4. Defrost the phyllo if you have frozen it and have it ready to hand with the melted margarine and a basting brush. Grind the nuts with the sugar and cardamom. Spread a little of the margarine in the bottom of a 23x33cm (9x13 inch) baking dish and place a sheet of phyllo over it. Brush the surface of the pastry with margarine and place another sheet over that. Continue in this way until you have a layer of pastry 6 sheets thick. Spread a layer of the nut mixture over the pastry and lay another 3–4 sheets of phyllo over that. Add another layer of nuts, a layer of phyllo and so on until the nut mixture has been used. Top with a thick layer (5–6 sheets) of phyllo. Slice the baklava into squares or wedges stopping just short of the bottom layer of phyllo. Bake in the hot oven for 30 minutes. Meanwhile, heat the sugar and water together in a saucepan. Bring to the boil and boil for 15–20 minutes to make a syrup. Remove from the heat and stir in the rosewater. When the Baklava has finished baking, pour the syrup over and leave to cool before lifting from the pan.

Mussakka (Aubergine and Chickpea Casserole)

Serves 4
Preparation time 2 hours, plus soaking overnight

225g (8oz) dried chickpeas, washed and drained
90ml (3fl oz) oil
2 medium aubergine, thickly sliced and each slice quartered
2 large onions, chopped
2x400g (14oz) tins chopped tomatoes or 8 medium tomatoes, chopped
2 sweet green peppers, coarsely chopped
4–5 tbsp tomato purée
285ml (½ pint) water
1 tsp freshly ground black pepper
½ tsp salt
½ tsp each of ground ginger, allspice and cinnamon
¼ tsp ground nutmeg
¼ tsp chilli powder

Cover the washed chickpeas with fresh water and soak overnight. Drain, rinse and turn into a pressure cooker. Cover with fresh water and cook at pressure for 25 minutes. Drain, rinse under cold water and leave to cool.

Preheat the oven to 180°C/350°F/Gas Mark 4. Heat the oil in a frying pan over a high heat. Add the aubergine slices, cover the pan and fry for 5 minutes.

Turn the slices over, cover the pan again and fry a further 3 minutes. Lift the slices into a large casserole. Repeat until all the slices are cooked. Add the onion to the hot oil and sauté until tender and golden. Spread the onion over the aubergine slices in the casserole and turn the cooked chickpeas over the onions. Spread the ingredients to the edges of the dish.

Measure the remaining ingredients together into a food processor and purée to a fairly smooth sauce. Pour the sauce over the casserole, cover and bake for 1–1¼ hours. All the liquid should have been absorbed. Serve hot immediately or, for a more mature flavour, leave for 24 hours and reheat. Serve with a rice dish and an array of condiments and pickles.

JAPAN

Sushi

This classic dish is really a special way of preparing rice, which is then topped by a vegetable mixture and the whole thing rolled in a sheet of nori. Sushi is a very portable food, useful as a snack, lunch or appetizer, which keeps for several days if left unsliced. Experiment with different fillings and use leftover rice on occasion, if that is more convenient.

Serves 4–8 (Makes 8 sushi rolls)
Preparation time 1 hour 30 minutes

570ml (1 pint) water
1 strip kombu (seaweed)
400g (14oz) brown rice, preferably short grain
100ml (4fl oz) rice or wine vinegar
1 tbsp barley malt syrup
1 tsp salt
2 tbsp soy sauce
1 tbsp barley malt syrup
5 peppercorns, crushed
100–170g (4–6oz) mushrooms, cleaned, trimmed and chopped
8 spring onions, thinly sliced lengthwise
100g (4oz) fresh parsley or coriander, finely chopped
8 sheets nori

Heat the water and kombu in a saucepan over a medium heat. Bring to the boil and boil for 5 minutes. Remove the kombu and add the rice to the boiling water. Cover the pan, bring to the boil again and immediately reduce the heat. Leave the rice covered and simmering gently for about 45 minutes, until the rice is tender and the water absorbed. Remove from the heat and leave 5–10 minutes in the pan.

Heat the vinegar, syrup and salt in a small saucepan until well mixed and hot. Do not boil this mixture. Remove from the heat and cool until you can comfortably touch the liquid. Turn the rice out onto a large platter and spread it out to cool. Sprinkle the vinegar and syrup mixture over it, stirring the rice as you do so with a fork or table knife. Ideally, you should cool the rice quickly and some cooks even recommend using an electric fan, blowing over the rice, to speed this process. The quick cooling, combined with the coating of vinegar and syrup mixture that each grain of rice acquires, helps the rice stay sweet and moist for several days – perfect for the sushi process.

In a small saucepan, mix the soy sauce, syrup and peppercorns. Place over a medium heat, stir well and add the mushrooms just before the sauce begins to boil. Simmer for 5–10 minutes over a low heat, stirring often.

Prepare the spring onions and parsley and have ready on separate plates. If the nori is untoasted, you must toast each sheet over a flame until it alters colour and becomes slightly brittle. Put to one side. It is time to make the sushi rolls and for this you must keep the nori dry, but it helps to keep your hands wet so the rice does not stick to them.

Place a sheet of toasted nori on a dry board or bamboo mat (su). Spoon rice onto the nori, spreading to the side edges but leaving 3–4cms (¾ inch) clear at the front and back edges. Arrange the strips of spring onion on the rice, sprinkle the parsley and spoon some of the mushroom mixture over all. Begin to roll the nori, keeping one hand dry for the nori and the other wet so that you can keep tucking the rice and vegetables into place. When the roll is finished, dry both hands and roll the sushi backwards and forwards to make a firm, tight roll. Rest the sushi on a platter with the end of the nori pressing onto the platter. Repeat for the remaining 7 sheets of nori. Chill for 2–4 hours then slice into thin (1cm) rounds with a cold, wet knife. Arrange on individual serving plates and serve with freshly ground ginger blended with a little vinegar or with a tiny bowl of soy sauce for dipping. Sushi may be kept, wrapped in clingfilm, in the refrigerator for 3–4 days provided you keep the roll intact. This is a very portable food, perfect for picnics, parties and packed lunches.

Tofu Sukiyaki

Serves 4
Preparation time 45 minutes

100g (4oz) ramen noodles
570ml (1 pint) water
2 medium carrots, cut diagonally into thin slices
1 tsp miso
1 × 285g (10oz) tin bamboo shoots, drained and sliced into matchsticks
2 stalks celery, with leafy tops, cut diagonally into thin slices
100g (4oz) mushrooms, thinly sliced
4 spring onions, trimmed and thinly sliced lengthwise
100–170g (4–6oz) beansprouts
225g (8oz) fresh spinach, washed and sliced
25g (1oz) fresh parsley, finely chopped
2 × 285g (10oz) blocks tofu, cut into cubes or strips

For the sauce:
200ml (7fl oz) vegetable stock
60ml (2fl oz) soy sauce
2 tbsp sake or sherry or rice vinegar
1 tbsp barley malt syrup

Break the ramen into a mixing bowl. Measure the water into a saucepan and place over a medium heat. Place the carrots in a steamer over the water. Bring the water to the boil and steam the carrots for 3 minutes. Remove the pan from the heat: arrange the carrot slices in the bottom of a deep frying pan and dissolve the miso in the water. Pour this water over the ramen in the bowl and leave for 10-15 minutes.

Carefully arrange, in the order in which they are given, the remaining vegetables in layers over the carrots. Drain the ramen and place over the vegetables; arrange the tofu on top. Place the frying pan over a high heat and, at the same time, combine the sauce ingredients in a small saucepan and heat to simmering point. Immediately pour the sauce over the ingredients in the frying pan, bring to the boil, cover the pan and reduce the heat from high to medium. Simmer for 5–7 minutes. Serve hot with steamed rice.

EUROPE

A little closer to home now but no less fascinating. The movement of peoples has been relentless over the centuries, yet some dishes are still held up as national dishes and are preserved and venerated by home-cooks and restaurateurs alike. Collecting these has made me want to take a short holiday abroad . . .

AUSTRIA

Chestnut Creme

Serves 4
Preparation time 45 minutes, plus soaking dried chestnuts overnight

450g (1lb) chestnuts in their shells or 340g (12oz) dried, peeled chestnuts
1 vanilla pod (optional)
170g (6oz) sifted icing sugar
1x225g (8oz) carton Soya Creem

If using chestnuts in their shells, place them on a baking tray in a very hot oven for 10 minutes. Remove them and peel immediately. If using dried chestnuts, soak them in cold water overnight. Whichever of these you use, the next step is the same.

Boil the chestnuts in water for 20–30 minutes, until they are very soft. Add the vanilla pod to the boiling water if you like; discard the pod once the chestnuts are cooked. Drain the liquid away and work the chestnuts through a mouli, seive or blender. Stir the icing sugar into the purée and stir or whisk until very smooth. Spoon into individual serving bowls or, as is sometimes done in Austria, press the purée through the coarse grate of a hand-held grater held over each bowl. This gives the servings a very unusual, worm-like texture.

Pour a little Soya Creem round the edge of each serving, to create a ring of creem, and top with Chocolate Sauce (see below), either hot or cold. That will do, although you may wish to place a glacé cherry or some such accessory on top of the chocolate sauce.

Chocolate Sauce

Serves 4
Preparation time 30 minutes

50g (2oz) sugar
55ml (2fl oz) water
100g (4oz) strong, plain solid cooking chocolate

Add the sugar to the water in a small saucepan and bring to the boil. Boil until the syrup begins to candy: a little dropped onto a cold saucer will form a thread between the saucer and your finger or a spoon touched to it. Meanwhile, melt the chocolate in the top of a double boiler and keep warm until the syrup is ready. Add the syrup to the chocolate and stir until smooth and creamy. The sauce should be kept over the heat in the double boiler throughout this stage. Add a few drops of water if the sauce seems too thick, stirring well after each addition. Pour the sauce over the dish, Chestnut Creme (see left) for instance, while it is still hot.

FRANCE

Leeks Vinaigrette

Serves 4
Preparation time 35 minutes, plus time to cool

900g (2lb) leeks, trimmed
2 tbsp salt

For the dressing:
¼ tsp salt
55ml (2fl oz) cider vinegar
1 tbsp Dijon mustard
170ml (6fl oz) olive oil
2 sprigs watercress, washed and finely chopped

Leave the leeks whole, though well trimmed and tidy. Dissolve the salt in about 1(1¾ pints) of cold water and immerse the leeks in this solution. Agitate them and gently open the leafy tops so that any soil lodged there will be loosened. Take your time over this cleaning stage. Rinse the leeks under cold water and place in a steamer. Steam until just tender, ensuring the leeks keep their colour, especially the dark tops. Lift from the steamer and arrange in a shallow serving dish. Prepare the dressing by combining all the dressing ingredients in a jar and shaking to make an emulsion. Pour the dressing over the warm leeks, cover the dish and leave to cool. You may chill the dish in the refrigerator if you prefer, although it is delicious at room temperature. Garnish with a sprig of water-cress. Serve as a starter or as part of a main course salad platter.

Mushrooms in Garlic and Fresh Tarragon

I have prepared this recipe for use as a starter, if you wish to use it as a main course, then double the quantities. As a starter, I like to serve it on a single piece of dry, crisp toast so that the wonderful juices are not wasted. You could also serve it on a warmed plate by itself or with a small cluster of steamed broccoli or celery – both of these should be only just tender. As a main course, you could serve it over rice or as a filling to vol-au-vents, either dish accompanied by a green salad or steamed yellow vegetable such as squash. In any event, make certain you serve the mushrooms piping hot.

Serves 4
Preparation time 30 minutes

450g (1lb) mushrooms, cleaned and trimmed
2 tbsp olive oil
5 cloves garlic, very finely chopped
½ tsp freshly ground black pepper
juice of ½ lemon
3 spring onions, diced
1 sprig fresh tarragon, finely chopped
4 slices dry, crisp toast

Rub the mushrooms clean and trim the stalks of any woody parts. Depending on the size of the mushrooms, leave them whole or halve or quarter them. Heat the oil in a large frying pan and sauté the garlic for 2–3 minutes, until tender and just golden. Add the black pepper and stir for 1 minute. Now spread the mushrooms over the saute, stir once and cover the pan. Cook over a low heat for 7-10 minutes, stir again, cover the pan and cook for a further 3 minutes. Add the lemon juice, onions and tarragon, cover the pan and cook a final 3 minutes. Serve at once over the crisp toast ensuring that you serve all the juice as well.

ITALY

Polenta

This is simply cornmeal boiled in liquid to make a thick porridge which is used alone or as a basis for more complex dishes. It is usually associated with Italy, although cornmeal (maize) did not arrive in Italy until the early 1500s. Maize had for centuries been a staple of North and South American peoples – think of tortillas (p325), tacos and cornbread or Johnny Cake (p331) – and it is likely that explorers and traders simply brought it to Europe where it became popular in northern Italy, parts of France and indeed many of the Mediterranean countries. Polenta, or very similar

dishes, is found in Creole, African and European cooking as well as versions from both Americas. Once you become comfortable with the basic method, you can go on to create your own sauces and combinations. Children usually love polenta if for no other reason than its beautiful yellow colour.

Serves 4
Preparation time 1 hour

1l (2 pints) liquid (ie water, stock, soya milk, wine or combinations of these)
225g (8oz) coarse cornmeal
oil

Bring the liquid to boil in a large saucepan and gradually add the cornmeal, pouring it slowly and stirring constantly as you do so to prevent lumps. Reduce the heat and leave over a very low heat for 10–30 minutes, stirring often and adding more liquid, if you wish. When all the liquid is absorbed and the polenta is thick and creamy, pour into warm bowls and serve with a sauce or garnish (see following recipe).

Do make sure that you enjoy the colour of polenta when you serve it: pour a wreath of red or white sauce round the edges of the bowl and garnish the centre with chopped herbs or spring onion; or pour the sauce in the middle and make a wreath out of green herbs or steamed green vegetables or pour the sauce in the middle and make delicate 'spokes' of garnish coming out from the centre towards the edge of the bowl. This dish cries out for your artistic expression! Even the colour of serving bowl will affect your presentation.

Alternatively, to create another traditional polenta dish, pour the polenta into a lightly oiled pie dish and spread to the edges. Allow the polenta to cool then slice into wedges, heat a little oil in a frying pan and brown the wedges on both sides. Serve hot as you would potato croquettes, with Scrambled Tofu (see page 291) or with chutney, ketchup, syrup or your favourite sauce.

Rich Tomato Sauce

The Italians seem to have made a specialty of converting individual foods into meals of delicacy and elegance with unsurpassed flavour and irresistable aromas. After all, pasta (of which there is several dozen varieties) is simply a paste made of flour and water! How better to dress such simple and versatile food than with a sauce made of tomatoes, simply and subtly flavoured with fresh herbs and spices.

Makes 1 litre (2 pints)
Preparation time 1 hour

2 tbsp oil
5 cloves garlic, finely chopped
2 medium onions, finely chopped
½ tsp freshly ground black pepper
¼ tsp ground cinnamon
1.5kg (3lb) fresh tomatoes, chopped or 3 × 200g
    (14oz) tins chopped tomatoes
200g (14oz) tomato purée
285ml (½ pint) water
1 tsp dried marjoram or oregano
1 tsp brown sugar
1 tsp soy sauce
1 tbsp fresh basil, chopped
1 tbsp fresh parsley, chopped

Heat the oil in a large iron saucepan and sauté the garlic and onion, over a medium heat, until clear and tender. Add the black pepper and cinnamon and stir for 1 minute. Add the chopped tomato and tomato purée and stir well. Cook, covered, over a medium heat for 10–15 minutes. Add the water and marjoram or oregano, stir well and continue cooking over a low heat for 20–30 minutes, stirring occasionally. (This sauce improves when allowed to cook slowly, or even from being left for a few hours and then reheating.) Add the remaining ingredients, stir well and leave to simmer for 5 minutes. Serve immediately or allow to mature and reheat later. Serve hot over polenta, pasta or steamed rice.

IRELAND

Irish Stew

This stew is the essence of versatility. It was originally made in layers of onions, potatoes and mutton, yet was considered a meal for 'hard times'. This version is much more flavourful and healthy yet continues to be inexpensive and versatile. It loves a long, slow cooking time, if you can manage it – an Aga, slow-cooker or similar is ideal.

Serves 4–6
Preparation time 2–6 hours

450g (1lb) TVP chunks
140ml (¼ pint) oil

55ml (2fl oz) soy sauce
55ml (2fl oz) vinegar
water
1.5kg (3lb) potatoes, scrubbed and thickly sliced
1kg (2lb) onions, peeled and thinly sliced
2-4 tsp freshly ground black pepper
1 tsp dried thyme
3 tbsp fresh parsley, chopped or 2 tsp dried parsley
1.5l (3 pints) vegetable stock or water

Measure the TVP into a mixing bowl. Stir together the oil, soy sauce and vinegar and pour over the TVP. Stir well then cover the mixture with water and leave for 30 minutes.

Spoon a little of the soaked TVP mixture onto the bottom of a stewpot. Place a layer of potato then a layer of onion slices over the TVP and sprinkle a little of the pepper and herbs over all. Repeat the layers – TVP, potato, onion, pepper and herb – until all the ingredients have been used. Aim to place a few potatoes on the top then pour over the vegetable stock and cover the stewpot. Place in or on the cooker and cook as slowly as possible (1–5 hours) until all the ingredients are tender and the stock is thickened. Serve hot, in huge bowls, with fresh bread.

Versatility is easy with this dish: simply use whatever you have to hand to fill the stewpot! As stews are usually considered a winter meal, it is most likely that you will have root vegetables to hand. Swedes, turnips, parsnips and carrots are all ideal and easy components of this stew and really enhance the flavour of it. Combine about 1.5kg(3lb) of roots or use less TVP and more root, to suit your taste and the size of your stewpot.

Pickled Red Cabbage

Another traditional, rustic dish which could be easily altered to include any surplus from the garden. The technique remains the same, just add sliced onions, green cabbage, diced turnip or shredded carrot.

Serves 4
Preparation time 2 days

2 red cabbages, shredded
225g (8oz) salt
1 tbsp peppercorns
1 head garlic, peeled and finely chopped
2 bay leaves, crumbled
1-2 tbsp fresh basil, chopped

1l (2 pints) wine vinegar or cider vinegar

Place the shredded cabbage in a crock or large container and sprinkle with half of the salt. Stir and sprinkle the remaining salt, stir again. Cover the container and leave for 24 hours. Drain.

Place a layer of the cabbage in a large, deep jar. Sprinkle a few peppercorns over the cabbage then add a layer of chopped garlic. Repeat the layers of cabbage, peppercorn and garlic until all the ingredients have been used. Sprinkle the bayleaves and basil on top. Pour the vinegar to cover, seal the container and leave at least 24 hours in a cool place. Lift out servings of the pickle by reaching through the layers so that some of each layer is included. Keep the remainder chilled; it will keep for 3–7 days. To serve the pickle as a salad, add broken walnuts or slivered almonds and pieces of orange or satsuma. Serve with or on fresh bread, with soup or stew, in a baked potato or on its own in a pretty bowl.

Irish Soda Bread

This bread is made without yeast, as the title implies, and is best eaten very fresh – the same day it is cooked if possible. Homemade jams and cups of tea are at their best with this bread.

Makes 2 loaves
Preparation time 45 minutes

340g (12oz) wholewheat flour
340g (12oz) plain flour
3 tsp baking powder
1 ½ tsp bicarbonate of soda
1 tsp salt
3 tbsp oil
570ml (1 pint) soya milk
140ml (¼ pint) plain soya yoghurt

Preheat the oven to 190°C/375°F/Gas Mark 5 and lightly oil a baking tray. Mix the dry ingredients together in a large bowl. Whisk the oil, milk and yoghurt together in a jug and pour into the dry mix. Stir well then turn the dough onto a floured surface and knead for 5–7 minutes. Divide into two pieces and shape into a slightly flattened round loaf. Score the surface in an X to a depth of about 2.5cm (1 inch). Place the loaves on the baking tray and bake for 25-30 minutes. Leave to cool slightly on a wire rack then slice and serve warm.

GERMANY

Walnut, Date and Apple Strudel

Strudel is usually made with a different sort of pastry, one that is very eggy. I find this version very agreeable, not least because the pastry can be taken from the freezer – thereby reducing preparation time. Strudel is a classic coffee house dish, served warm.

Serves 4–8
Preparation time 45 minutes

4 sheets phyllo pastry (see p348)
1 tbsp olive oil
1 tsp lemon juice
3 digestive biscuits, finely crushed
grated peel of 1 lemon
450g (1lb) cooking apples, peeled and diced
225g (8oz) dried dates, finely chopped
100g (4oz) walnuts, chopped
1 tsp ground cinnamon
100g (4oz) sugar
1 tbsp lemon juice
1 tbsp icing sugar

Preheat the oven to 200°C/400°F/Gas Mark 6 and lightly oil a baking tray. Place a sheet of phyllo pastry on a cool working surface and lightly brush the pastry with olive oil. Place another sheet of phyllo on top, brush with oil and repeat in this way for all four sheets. Brush the top with oil. Mix the crushed digestives with the lemon peel and sprinkle over the phyllo. Mix the diced apples, dates and walnuts and sprinkle over the crushed digestives. Sprinkle first the cinnamon, then the sugar then the lemon juice over the fruit and nut mixture. Ensure the filling is spread evenly, quite close to all the edges of the pastry. Carefully roll the pastry, keeping the filling in place, and gently lift the strudel onto the baking tray. Bake for 35–40 minutes until the pastry is golden. Allow to cool 10 minutes then sprinkle with the icing sugar. Lift onto on a serving platter and serve in slices while slightly warm.

Pumpernickel Bread

Makes 2 loaves
Preparation time 4–5 hours

1 pkt active dry yeast
1 tsp sugar
140ml (¼ pint) warm water
75g (3oz) currants

2 tbsp oil
2 tbsp molasses
2 tbsp lemon peel, grated
1 tbsp caraway seeds
2 tsp salt
570ml (1 pint) soya milk, brought to scalding (not quite a simmer)
340g (12oz) rye flour
170g (6oz) wholewheat flour
100g (4oz) rolled oats
50g (2oz) fine cornmeal
50g (2oz) soya flour
170g (6oz) wholewheat flour

Dissolve the yeast and sugar in a cup with the warm water. Put to one side for about 15 minutes while the yeast softens. Mix the currants, oil, molasses, lemon peel, caraway seeds and salt in a mixing bowl and pour the hot milk over. Stir well and leave to cool to blood heat. Stir in the yeast then gradually add the dry ingredients, except the last measure of whole-wheat flour. Stir well then sprinkle a little of the last measure of wholewheat flour onto a board and begin to knead the dough. Knead for about 10 minutes, gradually working in all the remaining flour. The dough should be very firm. Turn into a greased bowl, cover with a clean tea towel and leave to rise for about 2 hours in a warm place. Punch down the dough and shape into 2 large loaves. Shape them into broad ovals and place on a lightly oiled baking tray which has been lightly sprinkled with fine cornmeal. Cover with the tea towels and leave to rise again, for about 1 hour. Preheat the oven to 190°C/375°F/Gas Mark 5. When the loaves have risen, brush them with 1 tbsp soya milk diluted with 1 tsp water. Bake for 45 minutes. Cool on the tray for 10 minutes, then lift onto wire racks to cool completely.

GREAT BRITAIN

Shepherd's Pie

Serves 4
Preparation time 1 hour 15 minutes

50g (2oz) red lentils, washed and drained
50g (2oz) TVP mince
2 tsp freshly ground black pepper
1 tbsp mixed sweet herbs

710ml (1¼ pints) vegetable stock or water
1 tbsp yeast extract
450g (1lb) potatoes, peeled and quartered
1 tbsp oil
3 cloves garlic, finely chopped
2 medium onions, finely chopped
3 medium carrots, peeled and sliced
225g (8oz) brussels sprouts, trimmed and halved
170ml (6fl oz) soya milk
1 tbsp margarine

Preheat the oven to 180°C/350°F/Gas Mark 4. Stir the lentils, TVP, pepper and herbs together in a mixing bowl. Measure the stock and dissolve the yeast extract in it. Pour the liquid over the TVP mixture and stir well. Put aside. Meanwhile, steam the potatoes until tender, about 15 minutes. Heat the oil in a frying pan and sauté the garlic and onions until clear and tender. Add the carrots and sprouts and stir a further 3–5 minutes. Turn the sauté into the lentil mixture and stir well. Spoon this mixture into an oven dish and spread to the edges. Mash the steamed potatoes with the milk and margarine and spoon the mash onto the vegetable filling. Run a fork across the top of the mash to give it texture. Bake the Shepherd's Pie, covered, for 25 minutes. Remove the cover and bake a further 10 minutes. Serve hot with other vegetables to accompany.

SPAIN

Gazpacho

Serves 4
Preparation time 2 hours

900g (2lbs) fresh tomatoes
5 cloves garlic, finely chopped
140ml (¼ pint) olive oil
1 medium onion, preferably red, thinly sliced
1 whole cucumber, peeled and finely chopped
1 sweet red pepper, deseeded and diced
140ml (¼ pint) red wine
285ml (½ pint) water
juice of 1 lemon
½ tsp salt
1 tsp freshly ground black pepper
1 sprig fresh dill weed, finely chopped
100g (4oz) croûtons or coarse breadcrumbs

Peel 450g (1lb) of the tomatoes by immersing them

for 30 seconds in boiling water. The skins will easily slip off. Purée these tomatoes with the garlic and oil and turn into a large bowl. Add the remaining ingredients and stir well. Chill the soup for at least 2 hours (it should be ice-cold) then ladle into serving bowls and serve.

Paella

Serves 4
Preparation time 1 hour 15 minutes

5 tbsp olive oil
5 cloves garlic, finely chopped
1 tsp cayenne
1 tsp freshly ground black pepper
1 bay leaf
1 medium onion, chopped
½ tsp saffron
450g (1lb) long grain rice
1l (2 pints) vegetable stock
1 sweet red pepper, finely chopped
225g (8oz) fresh peas
3 spring onions, finely chopped
1 medium carrot, grated
2 tbsp olive oil

Heat the oil in a large saucepan and sauté the garlic for 3 minutes. Add the cayenne, pepper, bay leaf and onion and stir for 3 minutes. Add the saffron and stir for 3 minutes longer. Add the rice to the sauté and stir well until the oil is absorbed. Meanwhile, bring the stock to a boil and, when the oil has been absorbed, add the stock to the rice. Stir and bring back to the boil. Cover the pan, reduce the heat and simmer for 30–40 minutes, until the rice has absorbed nearly all the stock. Arrange the red pepper, peas, onions and carrot over the rice and cover the pan again. Leave to cook for a further 10 minutes, until all the liquid is absorbed. Drizzle the remaining 2tbsp olive oil over the vegetables and fluff and fold the mixture with a fork. Serve hot.

THE LAST WORD

One day, sooner than you might suppose, we will all be vegetarian. Not that we will call ourselves that – the name will be redundant. The logic of vegetarianism is inexorable and inescapable; economically, nutritionally, environmentally, morally.

What kind of world will it be? It depends. Certainly, there will be more rational use of our world food resources, although starvation will still exist. It will be a greener and more pleasant place to live in, although the environment will still be too regularly polluted and defiled. We will all be considerably healthier too, although not necessarily any happier.

Wait a moment. This makes a peculiar finale to a book which advocates the vegetarian lifestyle so insistently. What's gone wrong?

Simply this. Diets do not by themseves change minds. There is no magic vitamin, no wondrous moral constituent in our food whch will generate compassion, consideration, and respect. Eating a vegetarian diet will not of itself make you a better person. Only you can do that.

What I am saying is this: go vegetarian for selfish reasons, and only you will benefit. Do it for love, and you will change the world.

I would like to thank everyone who has contributed to the realization of this project, and in particular: the editorial, production, publicity, marketing, sales and management personnel at Bloomsbury Publishing for their support, good humour, enthusiasm and professionalism; Dr. Ted Altar for his valued comments and contributions to the nutritional information; Dr. Neal Barnard of the Physicians Committee for Responsible Medicine, Colin and Lis Howlett, Barry Kew, Bill Maddex, Dr. David Ryde, Sarah Starkey, Michael Traub, Andrew Tyler, all my generous interviewees, Peggy for her many services, and Louis for all the dinosaurs.

APPENDIX ONE: RECIPE GUIDE

Simple Rice and Peas 335
Spanikopita 349
Spiced Rice & Split Peas 265
Spiced Spinach 296
Spicy Steamed Aubergine 341
Spinach & Tomato Quiche 297
Stew (Atieke) 312
Stuffed Tempeh 'Goose' with Raspberry
& Asparagus 178
Sweet Pepper Curry 343
Sweet Potato & Tomato Sauté 322
Tare-ko-aloo (Fried Potatoes with Spices) 341
Taushe (aka Birabisko Da Taushe,
Beef & Vegetable Stew over Millet) 315
Tempeh, Marinated 293
Thiebou Diene (Fish & Vegetables
over Flavoured Rice) 321
Tofu & Mangetout Stir Fry 266
Tofu in Rich Sauce 340
Tofu, Marinated 339
Tofu 'Steak' with Mushrooms & Celery 340
Tofu Steaks in Pomegranate & Walnut Sauce 275
Tofu Sukiyaki 351
Vegetable Stew 317
Very Olive Pizza 250
Wake-ewa (Black-Eyed Beans in Chilli
Pepper Sauce) 315
White Bean Soup with Pepper-Squash Tortellini 328
Yellow Peas, puréed (Rupiza) 324

Desserts
Almond Semolina Cake 310
Apple Chestnut Upside-Down Cake 173
Apple Pie 326
Apricot Delight 174
Avocado Nectarine Delight 246
Baklava 349
Banana Almond Cheesecake 184
Banana Rum Bake 337
Banana, Yam & Coconut Pudding (La Daub) 321
Black Cake 331
Carob Sauce 193
Carob Walnut Cake 193
Carrot Halva 346
Cherry Sauce, Thick 200
Chestnut Creme 352
Chocolate Sauce 352
Currant & Apricot Paste 209
Dried Fruit Salad (Khosnal) 310
Easy Lemon Syrup 232

Elderflower Fritters 213
Favourite Pumpkin Pie 280
Figgy Pudding 215
Frozen Christmas Puddiing 337
Funkaso (Sweet Millet Pancakes) 315
Hot & Spicy Fruit Compote 174
Jallabis (Fritters in Syrup with Pistachio Nuts) 342
Khosnal (Dried Fruit Salad) 310
Kiwi Fruit Flan 227
La Daub (Banana, Yam & Coconut Pudding) 321
Lemon Syrup 232
Mocha Fudge Torte 329
My Own Carrot Cake 194
Orange Banana Pudding 336
Orange Lollies 254
Peach Crumble 260
Peach Sauce 259
Peach Whizz 259
Peanut Brittle 316
Pears and Vine Leaves 262
Pears Cooked in Wine 263
Pecan Pie 267
Persian Fruit Salad 214
Phyllo Pastry 348
Plantain Pudding 335
Pretty Party Jelly 220
Pumpkin Caramel Mould 326
Pumpkin Coconut Pudding 333
Pumpkin Pie 280
Quinoa Pudding 330
Raspberrofu 283
Raspberry Coulis 283
Rhubarb Crumble 284
Samsa 319
Shoo-Fly Pie 329
Special Icing 195
Stewed Rhubarb 284
Strawberry Tart 299
Stuffed Dates 211
Sweet Couscous 317
Sweet Fungi 336
Thick Cherry Sauce 200
Vanilla Sugar 283
Versatile Carob Sauce 193
Walnut, Date & Apple Strudel 355
Watermelon Provençale 306

Pickles, Relishes & Preserves
Berebere (Spice and Herb Blend) 310
Blackberry Jam 187

APPENDIX TWO:
RESOURCE GUIDE

Vegetarian & Vegan Groups Around the World

The following national groups and organizations will be able to provide you with a range of resources and information about the meat-free way of living. Many of them organize regular meetings and other events to which you will be welcome. And many of them can suggest good restaurants for you to try when travelling to a foreign city or country. Only national organizations have been included in this listing – there will almost certainly be smaller regional groups or societies which can offer the traveller useful tips and advice – ask the national societies to help you to make contact with them. Most of these groups are voluntary organizations, so please make a donation, or consider joining them, when using their facilities. Plese note that addresses and phone numbers can change quite quickly.

AUSTRALIA

Vegan Society of Australia
P.O. Box 85, Seaford
VIC 3198
Tel. (03) 786 6192

Australian Vegetarian Society
P.O. Box 65, Paddington
NSW 2021
Tel. (02) 698 4339

BELGIUM

International Society of French Speaking Vegetarians
25 Avenue Chazal
B 1030
Brussels

Vegans International – Belgium
Fr Rooseveltlaan 223
9000 Ghent

Vegetariersbond Vzw
Koewacht 16a
9190 Stekene
Oost-Vlaanderen

BRAZIL

Sociedade Vegetariana Do Brasil – Brasilian Vegetarian Society
Rua: Riachuelo No 220 apt. 406
Centro
Rio de Janeiro
Cep 20230

CANADA

Toronto Vegetarian Association
736 Bathurst Street
Toronto
Ontario
M5S 2R4

Vancouver Island Vegetarian Association
9675 Fifth Street
Sidney
British Columbia
V8L 2W9

Vegetarian Lifestyle International
1500–1176 West Georgia Street
Vancouver
British Columbia
V6E 4A2

CZECH REPUBLIC

Vegetarian And World
03601 Martin
Fucikova 11

ESTONIA

Estonian Vegetarian Society
Kauba T.
30 a
Tallin
200013

FRANCE

Alliance Vegetarienne
Alvignac
46500
Gramat
Tel. (85) 33 63 33

French Vegan Society
c/o Godiwalla, 75 rue Mouffetard, 75005 Paris
Tel. (1) 43 31 82 41

Societe Veganiste De France
12 Allee jacques Becker
Aubervilliers 93300
Tel. (1) 48 33 63 41

GERMANY

Vegetarier-Bund Deutschlands EV
Blumenenstrasse 3
D-3000
Hanover
Tel. (511) 42 46 47

HONG KONG

Environmental Protection Vegetarian & Vegan (H.K.)
   Society
GPO Box 11634
Hong Kong
Tel. (775) 2798
Fax. (775) 2756

Hong Kong Vegetarian Society
c/o 34 Belcher's Street
4/F Block 11
Kennedy Town

Vegetarians And Vegans In Hong Kong
Flat 1 11/F
3 Ede Road
Kowloon Tong
Tel. (338) 8902

INDIA

Indian Vegetarian Congress
2nd Floor 17 Damodaran Street
Gopalapuram
Madras 600 086
Tel. (44) 473648

ITALY

Associazione Culturale Vegetariana
Via Aristolele 67
(MM Precotto)
20128 Milano

Associazione Vegetariana Italiana
Via XXV Aprile 41
20026
Novate Milanese

JAMAICA

Vegetarian Society of Jamaica Ltd
c/o 36 Calypso Crescent
Caribbean Terrace
Kingston 17

JAPAN

Japanese Midori Vegetarian Society
6-34-24 Higashioizumi
Nerima-ku
Tokyo
Tel. (3) 3922 0724
Fax. (3) 3922 7400

Japanese Vegetarian Union
c/o Japan Medical Centre of Health Care
718 Dalsen
410-21 Nirayama
Tel. (559) 785849

LATVIA

Vegetarian Society of Latvia
Stabu Street 18 dz 14
Riga
226001

LITHUANIA

Vegetarian and Vegan Society of Lithuania
Antakalnio 67-17
Vilnus
232040

MAURITIUS

Vegetarian Society of Mauritius
c/o Hare Krishna Land
Pont Fer Pheonix PO Box 108
Quatre-Bornes
Tel. (2220 6965804

NETHERLANDS

De Nederlandse Vegetariersbond
Larensweg 26
1221 CM
Hilversum
Tel. (35) 834796

European Vegetarian Union
Larensweg 26
1221 CM
Hilversum
Tel. (35) 834796

Veganisten Organistatie Vereniging (Dutch Vegan Society)
Postbus 1087
6801 BB Arnhem
Tel. (85) 420746

NEW ZEALAND

New Zealand Vegetarian Society
P.O. Box 77034
Auckland 3

NIGERIA

Nigerian Vegetarian Education Network
PO Box 489
Orlu
Imo State

Nigerian Vegetarian Society
PO Box 3893
Oshodi
Lagos

PORTUGAL

Vegetarian Club of Lisbon
Sakoni Centro Comercial Mouraria
Loja 230.A.236 largo Martim Moniz
1100 Lisbon
Tel. (1) 875652

REPUBLIC OF IRELAND

Vegetarian Guide to Ireland
East Clare Community Co-op
Main Street
Scariff
County Clare

Vegetarian Society of Ireland
P.O. Box 3010
Dublin 4

RUSSIA

St Petersburg Vegetarian Society
Post Box 161
193315
St Petersburg
Tel. (812) 266 1449

Tolstoyan Moscow Society
Molostovykh Street Building 11
Korpus 2 Appartment 160
Moscow
111555

Vegetarian Society of Russia
39-3-23 Volsky Bulvar
109462 Moscow

SOUTH AFRICA

Vegans in South Africa
Box 36242
Glosderry
7702
South Africa

SWEDEN

Svenska Vegetariska Foreningen
Radmansgatan 88
11329
Stockholm
Tel. (8) 32 49 29

Swedish Vegan And Vegetarian Society
Klovervagen 6
S-64700
Mariefred
Tel. (159) 12467

Swedish Vegan Society
c/o Troeng
Klovervagen 6
S–150 30
Mariefred

TANZANIA

Vegetarian Association
P.O. Box 71439
Dar Es Salaam

UNITED KINGDOM

The Vegetarian Society of the United Kingdom
Parkdale
Dunham Road
Altringham
Cheshire
WA14 4QG
Tel. (061) 928 0793

The Vegan Society
7 Battle Road
St Leonards-on-Sea
East Sussex TN37 7AA
Tel. (0424) 427393

Jewish Vegetarian Society
855 Finchley Rd
London NW11 8LX
Tel. (081) 458 2441 or (081) 455 0692

Young Indian Vegetarians
226 London Road
West Croydon
Surrey
CRO 2TF
Tel. (081) 681 8884

Vegetarian Society of Ulster
66 Ravenhill Gardens
Belfast
BT6 8GQ
Tel. (0232) 457888

UNITED STATES

American Vegan Society (AVS)
P.O. Box H, Malaga
NJ 08328
Tel. (609) 694 2887

North American Vegetarian Society (NAVS)
P.O. Box 72, Dolgeville
NY 13329
Tel. (518) 568 7970

Vegetarian Resource Group (VRG)
P.O. Box 1463, Baltimore
MD 21203
Tel. (301) 366 8343

Vegetarian Awareness Network in Nashville, TN
Tel. (615) 558 8343

EarthSave
706 Frederick Street
Santa Cruz
CA 96062
Tel. (408) 423 4069

Vegan Action
P.O. Box 2701
Madison
WI 53701

Vegetarian Education Network (VE Net)
P.O. Box 3347
West Chester
PA 19381
Tel. (717) 529 8638

Vegetarian Life, Special Interest Group of MENSA
P.O. Box 3425
Shell Beach
CA 93448

Vegetarian Society, Inc.
P.O. Box 34427
Los Angeles
CA 90034
Tel. (619) 492 8803/(714) 647 5590

Afro-American Vegetarian Society
P.O. Box 46
Colonial Park Station
New York
NY 10039

Friends Vegetarian Society of North America
P.O. Box 6956
Louisville
KY 40206

Jewish Vegetarians of North America
P.O. Box 1463
Baltimore
MD 21203
or 6938 Reliance Road
Federalsburg
MD 21632
Tel. (410) 754 5550

Physicians Committee for Responsible Medicine
P.O. Box 6322
Washington
DC 20015
Tel. (202) 686 2210
Fax. (202) 686 2216

Association of Vegetarian Dieticians & Nutrition Educators
(VEGEDINE)
3674 Cronk Road
Montour Falls
NY 14865
Tel. (607) 535 6089

Suppliers of Non-Leather Shoes, Clothing & Accessories

Cotton On (*catalogue of cotton clothes*)
29 Clifton Street
Lytham
Lancashire
FY8 5HW

UNITED KINGDOM

Wild Things
7 Upper Goat Lane
Norwich
NR2 1EW
Tel. (0603) 765595)

The Green Catalogue
Freepost SN 20091
Chippenham
Wilts
SN13 6QZ
Tel. (0934) 732469

Campaign Against Leather and Fur (CALF)
Box 17
198 Blackstock Road
London
N5 1EN

Vegetarian Shoes
12 Gardner St
Brighton
BN1 1UP
Tel. (0273) 691913

Veggie Jacks (*non-leather jackets, belts, bags*)
32 Gloucester Road
Brighton
BN1 4AQ
Tel. (0273) 626498

Coisas Portugeusas (*non-leather wallets*)
Greenstone Byre
Charlton
Shaftesbury
Dorset
SP7 0EN
Tel. (0747) 828840

Beauty Without Cruelty
57 King Henry's Walk
London
N1 4NH
Tel. (071) 254 2929
(*Publishes* Compassion *which lists many non-animal products*)

Animus (*badges, diaries and accessories*)
34 Marshall Street
London
W1V 1LL

UNITED STATES OF AMERICA

Heartland Products Ltd.
Box 218
Dakota City
IA 50529
Tel. (515) 332 3087

Aesop Unlimited
P.O. Box 315, N.
Cambridge
MA 02140
Tel. (617) 628 8030

Beauty Without Cruelty
175 W. 12th St.
No. 16G
New York
NY 10011-8275

CANADA

The Animal Rights Catalog (*shoes, jackets, accessories, gifts*)
No. 205
1857 W 4th Avenue
Vancouver
British Columbia
V6J 1M4
Tel. (604) 328 4747

AUSTRALIA

Beauty Without Cruelty Australia
GPO Box 1787
Brisbane
Queensland 4001

SOUTH AFRICA

Beauty Without Cruelty
PO Box/Postbus 23321
Claremont 7735

Beauty Without Cruelty South Africa
Head Office
PO Box 97
Newlands 7725
Cape Town

Suppliers of Dog and Cat Foods

UNITED KINGDOM

Happidog Petfoods (*dog food*)
Bridgend
Brownhill Lane
Longton
Preston
PR4 4SJ

Wafcol (*dog food*)
The Nutrition Bakery
Haigh Avenue
Stockport
SK4 1NU

Green Ark Co. (*dog food and supplements*)
Low Flatt
Alston
Cumbria
CA9 3DE

The Watermill (*dog food*)
Little Salkeld
Penrith
CA10 1NN

Denes (*herbal supplements for dogs and cats*)
PO Box 691
2 Osmond Road
Hove
East Sussex
BN3 3SD

Katz Go Vegan (*cat food*)
P.O. Box 161
7 Battle Road
St. Leonards-on-Sea
East Sussex
TN37 7AA
('Vegekit' for kittens; 'Vegecat' for cats over 10 months old)

UNITED STATES OF AMERICA

Nature's Recipe (*dog food*)
341 Bonnie Circle
Corona
CA 91720
Tel. (800) 843 4008 or (714) 278 4280

Pet Guard (*dog food*)
P.O. Box 728
Orange Park
FL 32067-0728
Tel. (800) 874 3221

Famous Fido's Doggie Deli Inc. (*cookies, croissants and bagels for dogs*)
1533 W. Devon Ave.
Chicago
IL 60660
Tel. (312) 761 6028

Natural Life Pet Products, Inc. (*dog food*)
P.O. Box 943
Frontenac
Kansas 66762
Tel. (800) 367 2391 or (316) 7711

Evolution (*dog and cat food*)
815 S. Robert St.
St. Paul
MN 55107
Tel. (800) 524 9697 or (612) 228 1819

Wow-Bow Distributors (*dog and cat food and vitamins*)
309 Burr Rd.
East Northport
NY 11731
Tel. (800) 326 0230 or (516) 449 8572

Wysong Corporation (*dog and cat food*)
Dept. CF
1880 N. Eastman Ave.
Midland
MI 48640
Tel. (800) 748 0188 or (517) 631 0009
For cats with food allergies, Wysong has developed a hypoallergenic diet: Canine/Feline Anergen III, is a vegetarian diet for food sensitive cats, containing special high-protein vegetables.

Sojourner Farms (*organic dog and cat food*)
410 W. Washington
Ann Arbor
Michigan 48104
Tel. (313) 994 3974

Harbingers of a New Age (*cat food and supplement*)
717 E. Missoula Ave
Troy
MT 59935-9609
Tel. (406) 295 4944

CANADA

The Animal Rights Catalog (*pet food*)
No. 205
1857 W 4th Avenue
Vancouver
British Columbia
V6J 1M4
Tel. (604) 328 4747

Hill's Science Diet (*dog food*)
Box 990
Streetsville PO
Mississauga
Ontario
L5M 2C5
Tel. (800) 668 4626

Animal Rights, Welfare & Anti-Vivisection Organisations

UNITED KINGDOM

Animal Aid
The Old Chapel
Bradford St
Tonbridge
TN9 1AW
Tel. (0732) 364546
Animal Aid Youth Group is the junior branch of this organization

Teachers for Animal Rights
29 Lynwood Road
London
SW17 8SB

British Union for the Abolition of Vivisection
16A Crane Grove
Islington
London
N7 8LB
Tel. (071) 700 4888 or (071) 607 9533

Respect For Animals
PO Box 500
Nottingham
NG1 3AS

Dr Hadwen Trust For Humane Research
6c Brand St
Hitchin
Hertfordshire
SG5 1HX

National Anti-Vivisection Society
Ravenside
261 Goldhawk Road
London
W12 9PE
Tel. (081) 846 9777
Animals' Defenders is the junior branch of this organization

Disabled Against Animal Research and Exploitation
(DAARE)
PO Box 8
Daventry
Northamptonshire
NN11 4RQ

International League Of Doctors For Abolition Of Vivisection
Lynmouth
Devon
EX35 6EE

Doctors in Britain Against Animal Experiments (DBAE)
PO Box 302
London
N8 9HD

Nurses Anti-Vivisection Movement
Hillcrest Cottages
2 Hillcrest
Uppertown
Bonsall
Derbyshire
DE4 1AW

Compassion in World Farming
20 Lavant Street
Petersfield
Hampshire
GU32 3EW
Tel. (0730) 64208 or (0730) 68863
Farm Animal Rangers is the junior branch of this organization

World Society for the Protection of Animals (WSPA)
Park Place
10 Lawn Lane
London
SW8 1UD
Tel. (071) 793 0540

Royal Society for the Prevention of Cruelty to Animals
(RSPCA)
The Causeway
Horsham
West Sussex
RH12 1HG
Tel. (0403) 64181

Animal Protection Foundation
PO Box 168
Cardiff
CF5 5YH
Tel. (0222) 569914

Christian Consultative Council for the Welfare of Animals
(CCCWA)
269 Belstead Road
Ipswich
Suffolk
IP2 9DY

Quaker Concern for Animal Welfare
Webb's Cottage
Woolpits Road
Saling
Braintree
Essex
CM7 5DZ

National Animal Rescue Association
21 Highlands Avenue
Spinney Hill
Northampton
NN3 1BG
Tel. (0604) 647552
*This 24-hour number will give help or advice when possible
about any animal in any emergency*

Zoo Check
Cherry Tree Cottage
Coldharbour
Dorking
Surrey
RH5 6HA
Tel. (0306) 712091
This organization incorporates Elefriend and Junior Elefriends

Captive Animals Protection Society *(circuses, zoos, wildlife
  parks)*
36 Braemore Court
Kingsway
Hove
East Sussex
BN3 4FG
Tel. (0273) 737756

Swan Song *(formerly Swan Rescue Service)*
PO Box 3
Beccles
Suffolk
NR34 0DF

Advocates for Animals
10 Queensferry St
Edinburgh
EH2 4PG
Scotland

Animal Concern *(formerly Scottish Anti-Vivisection Society)*
62 Old Dumbarton Road
Glasgow
G3 8RE
Scotland
Tel. (041) 334 6014

Scottish Society for the Prevention of Cruelty to Animals
19 Melville Street
Edinburgh
EH3 7PL
Scotland
Tel. (031) 225 6418

Ulster Society for the Prevention of Cruelty to Animals
  (USPCA)
11 Drumview Road
Lisburn
County Antrim
BT27 6YF
Northern Ireland
Tel. (0232) 813126

REPUBLIC OF IRELAND

Irish Society for the Prevention of Cruelty to Animals
1 Grand Canal Quay
Dubin 2
Eire
Tel. (1) 775922

Irish Anti-Vivisection Society
Crosshaven
C. Cork
Eire
Tel. (21) 831146

UNITED STATES OF AMERICA

The American Anti-Vivisection Society
801 Old York Road
Suite 204
Jenkintown
PA 19046-1685

In Defense of Animals
815 West Francisco Blvd
San Rafael
CA 94901

Unitarian Universalists for Ethical Treatment of Animals
  (UFETA)
230 w. 78th Street
New York
NY 10024

CANADA

Animal Alliance of Canada
1640 Bayview Avenue
Suite 1918
Toronto
Ontario M4G 4E9

AUSTRALIA

Animal Guardians
PO Box 59
Pascoe Vale South
Victoria 3044

Association Against Painful Experiments on Animals
GPO Box 1435M
Melbourne
Victoria 3001

Australia and New Zealand Federation of Animal Societies
PO Box 1023
Collingwood
Victoria 3066

Australian Association for Humane Research
PO Box 779
Darlinghurst
New South Wales 2010

Australian Wildlife Protection Council
37 Waterport Road
Port Elliot
S. A. 5212

Western Australia Group Against Vivisection
GPO Box T1798
Perth 6001

Australian Fund For Animals
Box C 616
Clarence Street Post Office
Sydney 2000

World Society for the Protection of Animals (Australia)
PO Box 365
Canterbury
Victoria 3126

NEW ZEALAND

Anti-Cruelty Society
447 Albert Street
Palmerston North

New Zealand Anti-Vivisection Society Inc.
PO Box 2065
Wellington

Save Animals From Experiments
2/10 The Promenade
Takapuna
Auckland 9

Society for the Prevention of Cruelty to Animals (SPCA)
PO Box 43221
Mangere
Auckland

World Society for the Protection of Animals (South Pacific)
3 Totara Avenue
New Lynn
Auckland 1232

SOUTH AFRICA

South Africans for the Abolition of Vivisection
PO Box 3018
Honeydew
2040

Concern for Environment and Wildlife

UNITED KINGDOM

London Wildlife Trust
Central Office
80 York Way
London
N1 9AG
Tel. (071) 278 6612

Royal Society for Nature Conservation (RSNC)
The Green
Nettleham
Lincoln
LN2 2NR
Tel. (0522) 752326
Watch is the junior branch of this organization

British Hedgehog Preservation Society
Knowbury House
Knowbury
Ludlow
Shropshire
SY8 3LQ

Soil Association
86 Colston Street
Bristol
BS1 5BB
Tel. (0272) 290661

Sustainable Agriculture, Food and Environment
 Alliance (SAFE)
21 Tower Street
London
WC2H 9NS
Tel. (071) 240 1811

Friends of the Earth (FOE)
26-28 Underwood Street
London
N1 7JQ
Tel. (071) 490 1555
Earth Action is the junior branch of this organization

Environmental Investigation Agency (EIA)
2 Pear Tree Court
London
EC1R 0DS
Tel. (071) 490 7040

Fauna and Flora Preservation Society
1 Kensington Gore
London
SW7 2AT
Tel. (071) 823 8899

Greenpeace UK
London Office
Canonbury Villas
London
N1
Tel. (071) 354 5100

Protection and Conservation of Animals and Plant Life
   International
29 Broughton Drive
Grassendale
Liverpool
L19 0PB
Tel. (051) 494 0470

The Ethical Investment Fund
10 Queen Street
London
W1X 7PD
Tel. (071) 491 0558

Ethical Investment Research Service
71 Bondway
London
SW8
Tel. (071) 735 1351

UNITED STATES OF AMERICA

Environmental Protection Agency (EPA)
401 M Street SW
Washington, D.C.
20460
Tel. (202) 382 2090

AUSTRALIA

Australian Wildlife Protection Council
37 Waterport Road
Port Elliot
S.A. 5212

Greenpeace Australia
1/787 George Street
Sydney
New South Wales 2000

Greenpeace South Australia
310 Angus Street
Adelaide 5000

NEW ZEALAND

Greenpeace New Zealand
Private Bag
Wellesley Street
Auckland

Ethics, Philosophy and Education

UNITED KINGDOM

Earthkind
Humane Education Centre
Bounds Green Road
London
N22 4EU
Tel. (081) 889 1595

Teachers for Animal Rights
29 Lynwood Road
London
SW17 8SB

Athene Trust
3a Charles Street
Petersfield
Hampshire
GU32 3EH
Tel. (0730) 68070

Universities' Federation for Animal Welfare (UFAW)
8 Hamilton Close
South Mimms
Potters Bar
Herts
EN6 3QD
Tel. (0707) 58202

Network of Individuals and Campaigns for Humane
   Education (NICHE)
c/o Department of Psychology
University of Stirling
Stirling
FK5 4LA
Scotland
Tel. (0786) 67677

AUSTRALIA

The Great Ape Project
PO Box 1023
Collingwood
Melbourne
Victoria 3066

INDEX

*Details of and page numbers for all the recipes in this book can be found in
Appendix One: Recipe Guide, page 359.*